THE INSIDERS' GUIDE® TO

Atlanta

THE INSIDERS' GUIDE®

TO

Atlanta

by
H.M. Cauley
and
Karen E. Wantuck

Insiders' Publishing Inc.

Published by:
Insiders' Publishing Inc.
105 Budleigh St.
P.O. Box 2057
Manteo, NC 27954
(919) 473-6100
www.insiders.com

Sales and Marketing:
Falcon Distribution Services
P.O. Box 1718
Helena, MT 59624
(800) 582-2665
www.falconguide.com
•

THIRD EDITION
1st printing
•

Publications from The Insiders' Guide®
series are available at special discounts
for bulk purchases for sales promotions,
premiums or fundraisings. Special
editions, including personalized covers,
can be created in large quantities for
special needs. For more information,
please write to Insiders' Publishing Inc.,
P.O. Box 2057, Manteo, NC 27954, or
call (919) 473-6100 Ext. 241.

ISBN 1-57380-026-0

Insiders' Publishing Inc.

Publisher/Editor-in-Chief
Beth P. Storie

President/General Manager
Michael McOwen

Creative Services Director
Giles MacMillan

Art Director
David Haynes

Managing Editor
Dave McCarter

Project Editor
Amy Baynard

Project Artist
Bart Smith

Regional Advertising Sales
Greg Swanson

Local Advertising Sales
Jan Clemmons

Preface

Welcome to Atlanta!

Over the years, new ideas and new people — people like you — have made Atlanta the social, cultural and economic capital of the American South. From its earliest days as Terminus, Atlanta's soundtrack has been the music of motion: Unceasing change has been its one constant. Its chief product has always been a service — transportation and distribution — that, by its nature, provokes endless renewal.

From the day in 1835 when the Whitehall Tavern opened at a wagon crossroads in what is today the West End neighborhood, Atlantans have looked toward the future, excited about the arrival of the next stagecoach, train, automobile or jet plane. Atlanta was created from the wilderness; it grew into a major railroad center; it found itself a prime military target in the Civil War; and it was deliberately and utterly destroyed — all before the 17th anniversary of its incorporation as a city!

With nearly its entire population displaced, 90 percent of its buildings in cinders and its rail system in ruins, that might have been the end of the story — but for what we call the Atlanta spirit. Somehow, though humbled and broken by the Civil War, Atlanta rose from its ashes like the mythical Phoenix whose image graces the city's seal.

In the days and decades following the Civil War, ongoing upheaval and continuous infusions of new people, money and ideas created an outlook unique among Southern cities. Here the focus is the future, not the past. Here what is old may be respected, but what is new is adored. Here is a city that seems to reinvent itself every year: Streets get new names; office complexes, residential communities and strip malls pop up seemingly overnight.

It is here that bold innovations have flourished. An Atlanta pharmacist invented the world's most popular soft drink. An Atlanta journalist wrote the world's most popular novel. It was here, too, that an Atlanta minister would lead the South and the United States from the cruel vestiges of segregation toward the true realization of the ideals of the Declaration of Independence: "that all men are created equal."

Atlanta from its earliest days was a crossroads and it still is that today, sitting solidly in the center of a network of roads, rails and air routes. But it has also become a new kind of crossroads, this time on the information superhighway. Twenty-four hours a day, every day of the year, satellites beam news, weather, sports and entertainment programming from Atlanta to the rest of the world. Atlanta is home base for the mega services offered by media mogul Ted Turner through his company's merger with Time Warner: Cable News Network (CNN), CNN International, CNN en Espanol, CNNSI (Sports International), CNNFN (Financial News), CNN Airport Network; Headline News, Cartoon Network, Cartoon Network in Latin America, Cartoon Network in Europe, Cartoon Network in Japan, Turner Network Television (TNT), TNT in Latin America, TNT in Europe, TNT & Cartoon Network in Asia Pacific and SuperStation TBS. The 24-hour Weather Channel beams up-to-the-minute worldwide weather forecasts from Atlanta.

Modern Atlanta is composed of many parts. There's downtown, with its soaring skyscrapers and big-city pace. Southwest Atlanta is home to Atlanta University Center, the nation's largest consortium of historically African-American colleges. Along the tree-lined streets of Midtown, Virginia-Highland and Inman Park, renovators have breathed new life into fine old homes. In the shops and clubs of eclectic Little Five Points and high-style Buckhead, trendsetters are ever on the prowl for the new and different.

And Atlanta just keeps right on growing,

with new residential areas popping up farther and farther from the city proper. Tens of thousands of Atlantans commute from homes once so remote they would have been a long day's buggy ride away.

Atlanta's a party town with an all-encompassing variety of nightclubs, from booming discos to intimate jazz clubs to cozy neighborhood pubs. When it's chow time, your choices include the world's largest drive-in, classic Southern restaurants and barbecue joints, exquisite five-star dining rooms and everything in between. And with attractions such as Six Flags Over Georgia, White Water, the Atlanta Cyclorama, Zoo Atlanta, Fernbank Science Center, SciTrek and The World of Coca-Cola, there's plenty of excitement for younger visitors, too.

Almost everything about Atlanta has changed in the 160 years since the first drink was poured in the old Whitehall Tavern. Little Terminus went from the end of the line to the center of the South; from a smoldering, war-ravaged ruin to the premier Southern city of the United States; from complete obscurity to the host of the 1996 Olympics.

How'd we do it? Through the one constant that remained through all of our changes — the adventurous spirit of that spunky little rail crossroads. This is no place to sit still or to dwell endlessly on days gone by. Of course Atlantans are proud of the city's past, and we jealously guard our old landmarks. In fact, because so much of our history was swept away during the Civil War, we try to hold onto even our recent past as an outcry over the 1997 demolition of the Omni and Atlanta Fulton County Stadium demonstrated. But once we've voiced our objections, without riots or demonstrations, we're quite pragmatic people. There's no room here for empty, ritualized traditionalism: What's of no use is simply swept away.

That adventurous spirit — and the ability to attract people who share it — remains Atlanta's abiding strength. Whether you're a longtime resident, a new Atlantan, a first-time visitor or a frequent guest in town, we're glad to see you. And just like our 19th-century predecessors watching the trains pull in, we're eager to hear your news and ideas, for they help us keep our city fresh and exciting and ready for the future.

Thank you for coming — and welcome to Atlanta!

About the Authors

H.M. Cauley

Helen Cauley grew up in Philadelphia. Her mother claims she began writing seriously in the 2nd grade, when she won recognition for a treatise of Mother's Day, and was soon banging out short stories on a portable typewriter. After one misguided semester as a sociology major, she switched to the journalism program at Temple University and was a writer and editor at the daily student paper. She went on to work in public relations for two small Philadelphia colleges before getting out of the business for a stint as a personnel manager for Macy's and John Wanamaker.

Just before moving to the South in 1990, Helen got back into writing as a correspondent for the *Pottstown Mercury* in suburban Philadelphia. Her arrival in Atlanta corresponded with the birth of *The Atlanta Journal-Constitution's Homefinder*, a Sunday section devoted to residential real estate, neighborhoods and lifestyles. As a regular contributor, Helen has had the chance to combine her love of old and new houses with the opportunity to meet people around the greater Atlanta area and to wear out several county maps in the process. She has toured some of the city's most exquisite and exclusive properties and has gotten hundreds of Atlantans to talk about where they live.

Exploring new communities and meeting the people who call them home has provided Helen with plenty of stories, which have found their way into the newspaper's Travel, Business and suburban editions. Three years ago, she took over the weekly people and events column, *Around Town*, for the Buckhead CityLife section. Her features have appeared in various local magazines, including *Atlanta Magazine, Southern Flair*, *Peachtree*, *Atlanta Singles* and *Atlanta Now*. National credits have included *Women's World* and *Automotive News*. Freelancing has also provided her with the flexibility to raise her two teenagers, Ellen and Tommy.

Helen is still fond of old houses and enjoys traveling around discovering them in charming small towns. Although her own house is only 10 years old, she's glad it's close to Marietta, with its town square, community theater and historic districts.

Karen E. Wantuck

Karen E. Wantuck was born in New York City and has been trying to lose her city accent ever since. Four years at SUNY Buffalo, where she received her undergraduate degree in arts education, didn't help. But a semester abroad in Italy did: She found she was a gifted mimic who picked up foreign languages easily.

Upon her return to the States, Karen was hired to teach fine arts, as well as Italian, to students at Commack High School on Long Island, New York. A sabbatical allowed her time to complete a Masters in Arts Education from Hunter College in New York City, and after teaching her seventh year, Karen forfeited tenure for a teaching job at Morehead State University in Kentucky. The position allowed her to set up the college's printmaking department and pursue her own career as a printmaker. In the two years she spent in Kentucky, her etchings, lithographs and seriographs were shown nationwide in museums and galleries.

After resigning from Morehead State, Karen received a printmaking scholarship at the University of Georgia. Two years and another master's degree later, she moved from Athens to Atlanta. One week after settling in, Karen became art critic for *Creative Loafing*. That same year, she was also hired as cultural arts director at the Atlanta Jewish Community Center to administrate a visual arts program, music school and theatrical production ensemble.

Karen's writing has appeared in *American Photographer*, *Savvy* and *Glamour* magazines, *Advertising News of New York*, *Craft Horizons* and *Goldsmith's Journal*. Locally she has written for *Atlanta Magazine*, *Business Atlanta Magazine*, *The Atlanta Journal-Constitution*, *Atlanta Jewish Times* and *Style Magazine*.

In 1980 Karen left her job and began freelancing full time as a writer/designer/desktop publisher. Her clients have included associations, entrepreneurs, doctors, lawyers and a few giants such as Kinko Copies, US West, and Canon USA.

Acknowledgments

Helen ...

There are literally hundreds of people who helped put this book together. To those who promptly returned phone calls and faxes, gave tours, answered endless questions and were gracious through it all, my thanks.

It certainly would also not have happened without the guidance and patience of editor extraordinaire, Amy Baynard, at Insiders' Publishing, who also has my sympathy for living somewhere so far out that even Overnight Express Mail takes two days. I'm also grateful for the years of expertise that have been shared with me by such excellent editors as Sandy John, Arthur Brice, Karl Ritzler, Cindy Gorley, Laura Wisniewski, Valerie Hill Morgan, Jennifer French Parker and Alice Murray, just to name a few.

I'm fortunate to have had the support of the people I live with through this project. Thanks, Ellen and Tommy, for letting your phone calls get interrupted and for spending summer hours trekking around the city. Thanks to their vastly improved proofreading skills, I think you'll find this Atlanta edition typo-free. And though they won't admit it, they've learned an incredible amount of Atlanta trivia (Alex Trebeck, we're ready!).

Appreciation is also in order to my friends, who put up with my not being available to do anything but work for several months. A special word of thanks to Carol, Ron, Margaret and Louise, who cheered me on when the going got rough.

Most of all, the biggest thanks go to my mother, Evelyn Cauley, who encouraged me from a very young age to keep writing and who has been longing for the day when my name would appear on a publication that doesn't get recycled. Here it is, Mother; the first signed copy is yours.

Karen ...

Many thanks to the Atlanta Public Library Info Line, a call-in service that has never let me down. Although the men and women who staff the service are only supposed to spend no longer than five minutes looking facts up for a caller, they have found data for me and called me back when answers weren't that readily available.

To all the overworked and under-appreciated PR people who were gracious enough to provide current information about the hospitals, sports venues, entertainment complexes and media for whom they work , I offer a heartfelt "Thanks." They were agreeable and speedy with their assistance and without them, my job would have been immeasurably more difficult. In particular, I thank Philip Evans Jr. of Turner Broadcasting, Amy Moudy of The Atlanta Opera and Hilda Lockhart of The Japan America Society of Georgia.

Special thanks to my husband, Eric Taylor, who always believes in me and agreeably produces those much-needed backrubs when the computer makes my shoulders ache. Of course, he reaps the benefits of my compulsion to work: He gets to go skiing three times a year without me and is perfecting his golf skills on those weekends when the writing calls me away from him.

Thanks to little Elliot for brightening up my life with his pixie smile and quick wit and providing a respite from the sourness of adults, tedium of mundane chores, and the now-and-then pettiness of my own soul. And to Denny and Andre who allowed me to share in his life, I can only say "Bless you."

And lastly, thanks to Roz and Ralph Wantuck, my parents, who think I can do no wrong and who are with me every day of my life. Whatever I am I owe to them, and I am grateful. I wish them ever longer life.

The Margaret Mitchell House was slated for destruction before
a board of Atlantans rallied support to preserve it.

Table of Contents

Directory of Maps

Atlanta

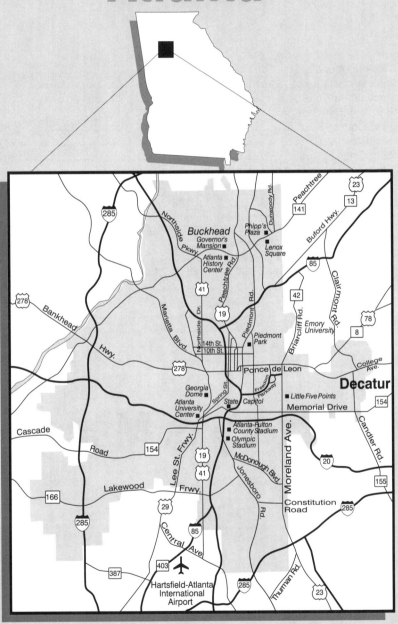

Greater Atlanta

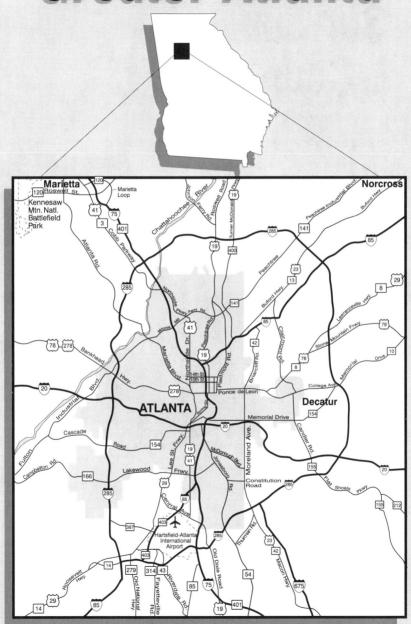

Atlanta's Surrounding Counties

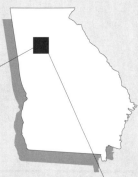

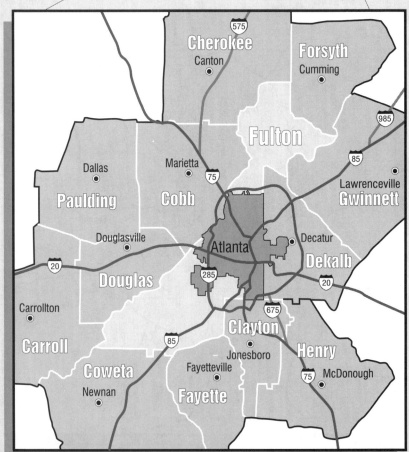

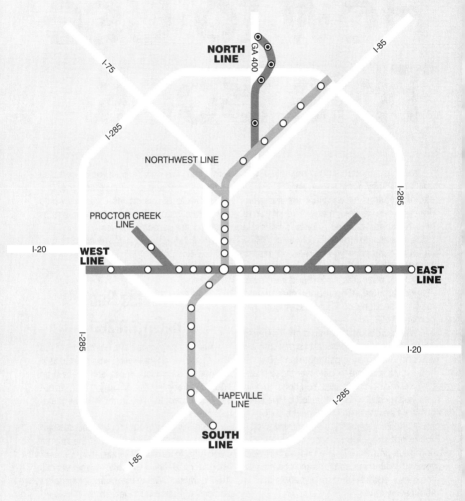

NORTH LINE

GA 400

NORTHWEST LINE

PROCTOR CREEK LINE

WEST LINE

EAST LINE

HAPEVILLE LINE

SOUTH LINE

I-75

I-85

I-285

I-20

I-285

I-20

I-285

I-85

■ East-West Line
■ North-South Line
□ Interstate Highways
◉ Under Construction

marta.®

How to Use This Book

We've planned this book so it gives you quick and easy access to everyday, practical information. All chapters are independent and can be read in any order: If you're famished and your first priority is finding a place to eat, turn immediately to our Restaurants chapter. If you're reading this on an Atlanta-bound flight and need to know how to get out of the airport and into town, flip right to our Getting Around chapter and read the sections on Hartsfield Atlanta Airport and MARTA.

We've organized our information to make it easy for you to explore areas that interest you and breeze by those that don't. But we hope you'll find time to look over those chapters you might initially skip. You don't have to be a history buff to be enthralled by the story of Atlanta's birth, destruction and rebirth, which you'll find in our History chapter. And even if you're not shopping for a home, our Neighborhoods and Real Estate chapter will help you understand the locations and characteristics of city districts you'll hear people talking about every day.

This is no coffee-table book: It's designed to be used. Don't leave it in your hotel room! Keep it in your glove compartment, briefcase or backpack; make notes in it. No matter where you travel in the Atlanta area, take this book with you to find the best food, entertainment, lodging, attractions and things to do.

While we have made every effort to ensure accuracy and to include all the best of Atlanta, we're only human. Atlanta is a city characterized by ceaseless change, and no one can keep up with every single aspect of life here. If you find mistakes in our book, if you disagree with something we've said, if you'd like to see additions or changes in future editions, or if you'd like to pat us on the back, we would appreciate your taking the time to write to us in care of our corporate offices:

The Insiders' Guide® to Atlanta
P.O. Box 2057
Manteo, North Carolina 27954

How This Book Is Organized

Atlanta's city limits have not been revised since 1952, when they were expanded to take in another 92 square miles and more than 100,000 people. As of July 1997 about 396,052+ people lived in the 131.8-square-mile city.

Several city and county governments share authority over the central part of the Atlanta metro area. In a practical sense, Atlanta's "real" boundary is defined by I-285 — what we call "the Perimeter." Within the Perimeter are large portions of Fulton and DeKalb counties and small slices of Cobb and Clayton counties. This can get confusing: One person may live in Atlanta city and DeKalb County, another in Decatur city in DeKalb County and another in College Park in Fulton County (and pay taxes to both!). But to avoid confusion, all three people would probably give the short answer "Atlanta" when asked where they're from because there is some panache to being from a big city. And Atlanta is a big city, more than doubling in population during the last 20 years. The term "metro Atlanta" refers to Atlanta, the city, as well as the 16 counties in closest prox-

imity. The entire metro area boasts a population of almost 3 million souls.

So, to help keep life simple, we've organized our book along the following lines: We've used "Atlanta" and "Beyond Atlanta" to geographically arrange many chapters and categories within chapters. Any restaurant, shop, theater, etc. that falls under "Atlanta" lies within the I-285 Perimeter. Anything under "Beyond Atlanta" lies outside the I-285 Perimeter, and we've often organized those attractions and businesses by county. Within the entries, we've often indicated in which neighborhood or area you'll find the eatery, nightspot or attraction since most folks in town can at least point you in the direction of Buckhead, Morningside or Inman Park, even if a particular address is not familiar to them.

Two small portions of the city of Atlanta are actually outside the Perimeter: The Ben Hill section in the southwest and the Adamsville section in the west. Consistent with our use of the Perimeter as Atlanta's practical boundary, we will consider these areas to be "Beyond Atlanta."

Know the New Code

For years, Atlanta has enjoyed the nation's largest toll-free calling zone. In 1995 that zone was greatly expanded: Now many outlying areas that had previously been pricey long-distance calls from Atlanta are free calls.

In the process, however, driven by the demand for new phone numbers for fax machines, cellular phones and pagers, the Atlanta calling zone required two more area codes: 770 and 678. This may seem a little confusing, but we'll try to make it simple.

The center of the Atlanta region — an area that corresponds approximately (but not exactly) to the inside of I-285 — is primarily the area code 404. For the most part, the area surrounding Atlanta is the 770 area code. But all new phone numbers be they inside or outside of the Perimeter get the 678 area code. You'll find no 678 area code numbers listed in this guide because we went to press prior to January 1998 when new numbers got that designation.

It is not necessary to dial 1 before local area codes; just dial the area code and the number. Calls between the 404, 770 and 678 area codes are toll-free local calls.

And here's a bit of trivia: Because small portions of two Alabama counties (with the area code 205) are now part of the local Atlanta calling zone, our zone can truthfully be said to contain parts of four area codes, two states and two time zones. Happy calling!

From the very beginning, Atlanta promoted itself as a modern city, different from the tradition-bound South.

History

Insightful Beginnings

It was, indeed, a curious spot to build a town.

Deep in the northwest Georgia woods, more than 1,000 feet above sea level, near no commercially navigable waterway, on land of marginal agricultural value in an area only recently held by the Cherokee and Creek — the wilderness that was to become Atlanta had little to recommend it.

But in the early 1800s, Georgia, the largest state east of the Mississippi River, badly needed a better transportation corridor to the prosperous North. Acting on the results of a forward-looking land survey, the state Legislature voted to build the Western & Atlantic railroad from the Tennessee state line southward, ending at a point where three tall granite ridges converged. Here, the new line was to link with extensions of railroads from other parts of the state.

The tiny railroad settlement had a humble beginning: Even its name — Terminus — said this was the end of the line. "The terminus," declared W&A engineer Stephen Long in 1837, "will be a good location for one tavern, a blacksmith shop, a grocery store and nothing else."

In fact, as unbelievable as it would have seemed at the time, little Terminus (briefly called Marthasville, then Atlanta) was already on its way to becoming the economic and cultural center of the southern United States. Just 20 years after regular train service began, Atlanta was linked by rail to Chattanooga, Tennessee; Augusta, Georgia; Macon, Georgia; Mobile, Alabama; and many points beyond.

Because the tracks made it a crossroads in the quickly booming overland transportation industry, Atlanta evolved from the start as a new kind of town: an inland port. People, goods, money and news were always moving through. The constant flow of travelers and rough-and-ready railroad men gave the town a bawdy flavor. The first tavern opened in 1835; the first church-and-schoolhouse had to wait until 1845. In the first mayoral election in 1848, the temperance candidate was defeated by a Decatur Street tinsmith and still-maker backed by the Free and Rowdy Party.

From the very beginning, Atlanta promoted itself as a modern city, different from the tradition-bound South. Atlanta's bustling, forward-looking spirit is well-evidenced in the following two items quoted by Norman Shavin and Bruce Galphin in their excellent illustrated history, *Atlanta: Triumph of a People*. An educator who arrived in 1847 found the citizens quite welcoming, noting that they "bow and shake hands with everybody they meet, as there are so many coming in all the time that they cannot remember with whom they are acquainted." And an 1859 city directory boasted, "Our people show their democratic impulses by each allowing his neighbor to attend to his own business, and our ladies are even allowed to attend to their domestic and household affairs without being ruled out of respectable society." Between 1850 and 1860, Atlanta's population swelled from 2,500 to nearly 10,000.

The Civil War

But proud Atlanta's shining rails were about to be twisted into its noose. The U.S. Civil War was the first war in history in which railroads played a major role, and Atlanta beat as the iron heart of the Confederacy, pumping soldiers and supplies to battlefronts across the South. In the unsentimental eyes of U.S. Gen. William Tecumseh Sherman, the railroad hub was a key military target — even though it sat at the center of a city of, by then, more than 20,000.

In the spring of 1864, Atlantans knew Sherman was on the march from the Tennessee border and that he had set his sights on their city, but most were confident that Confederate troops would halt the advance. Besides, they believed that the city, ringed by 10 miles of sharpened stakes, rifle pits and forts with cannon, would never fall. In fact, the fortifications did hold: Not a single Union soldier fought his way across them. (Ironically, a Yankee designed them: Col. Lemuel P. Grant was a brilliant civil engineer who moved South in the railroad-building prewar years. Today Grant Park, home to Zoo Atlanta and the Cyclorama, bears his name.)

By summer, the city's bravado was replaced by dread as the booming battles, now within earshot of the city, grew louder daily. After suffering ghastly casualties on July 22 in what became known as the Battle of Atlanta, the Confederate troops were forced to take refuge inside the city's fortifications.

Once their big guns were within range, Union troops mercilessly shelled the city. From July 20, when the shells claimed their first civilian victim (a little girl playing with her dog), until the bombardment ceased on August 25, hell rained down on Atlanta, and terrified residents cowered in makeshift bomb shelters. When Union troops seized the railroad south of the city on September 1, the Confederates realized their hopeless plight and abandoned Atlanta to avoid capture. The Rebels blew up 81 freight cars full of ammunition and seven locomotives to prevent their use by enemy forces. The enormous fire destroyed two-thirds of the city, including the Atlanta rolling mill — one of only two factories in the South that could turn out badly needed iron rails.

After the mayor's formal surrender on September 2, Atlanta became a Union camp. Sherman ordered the remaining civilians evacuated: A total of 1,644 people were forced out to face more hardships farther south. On the night of November 14, as his 62,000 men pulled out to march to Savannah, Sherman ordered most of the town's remaining structures set afire. Of the 4,000 buildings in the city at the war's beginning, only 400 survived the conflagration. One month shy of the 17th anniversary of its incorporation as a city, Atlanta lay in ruins.

Rising from the Ashes

Throughout the South for fifty years there would be bitter-eyed women who looked backward, to dead times, to dead men, evoking memories that hurt and were futile, bearing poverty with bitter pride because they had those memories. But Scarlett was never to look back.
— Chapter 25, *Gone With the Wind*

The numbers tell the tragic tale: The Civil War claimed more than 618,000 American lives, more than the combined U.S. losses of every other war from the Revolution to the Korean War. That bloody spring and summer of 1864, 31,687 Union troops and 34,979 Confederates lost their lives in the Atlanta Campaign, which accounted for more fatalities than the number of Americans killed in battle during all the years of the Vietnam War.

After Confederate Gen. Robert E. Lee's surrender on April 9, 1865, a pall of misery and destitution hung heavy over once-haughty Dixie. But Atlanta, like the spitfire heroine who would symbolize the city in Margaret Mitchell's novel 70 years later, got on with life. The South was split into five military governorships and, as the headquarters of the third Military District under U.S. Gen. John Pope, Atlanta was again at the center of things. Federal troops continued to occupy the city for the better part of 10 years.

The railroads had been wrecked in the war, as Union soldiers ripped up the rails, roasted them over fires and twisted them into what were called "Sherman's neckties." But with help from the Army, newly liberated black work-

---

INSIDERS' TIP

For Atlanta history buffs, the ultimate resource is *Atlanta and Environs* by Franklin M. Garrett. The 91-year-old Garrett, who is the historian of the Atlanta History Center, published his two-volume, 1,070-page work in 1954. Harold M. Martin wrote the tome's 620-page third volume, which was published in 1987 and tells the city's history through the 1970s.

ers and Northern investors, the four rail lines were restored in just two years, and a new line was working its way to Charlotte, North Carolina, by 1869.

Life was tough in the harsh winter of 1864-65, and a smallpox epidemic swept through in 1866. Even so, the town was struggling its way back to civilization. Theatrical performances resumed in 1865, and by 1866 the reborn city boasted two opera houses. That October, a 75-member touring company presented Italian grand opera on three consecutive nights, although the steep ticket price ($2) kept many Atlantans away.

In 1868, the Georgia capital was relocated to Atlanta from Milledgeville, a decision that was ratified in a popular referendum in 1877. By 1867, 250 stores were open in the city. Atlanta was home to 21,000 people in 1870 and to 37,000 in 1880.

Everywhere there were signs of progress: In 1871, the first horse-drawn streetcar began to service a 2-mile route. In the 1870s, the city inaugurated free mail delivery and a downtown garbage collection service.

In 1886, Atlanta produced what remains its most famous export. John Pemberton, a Marietta Street pharmacist, blended a "brain tonic" with a secret recipe of extracts from the coca plant and kola nuts. When a customer happened to order his Coca-Cola syrup with soda instead of plain water, the world's favorite soft drink was born. Dr. Pemberton sold ownership of his product for $2,300 to entrepreneur Asa Candler in 1887. Available only in Atlanta at first, Coca-Cola soon spread across the South and the nation. By 1899, the company was shipping 300,000 gallons of syrup a year and beginning to sell the premixed drink in bottles.

In 1890, the city had 65,000 residents, only 12 percent of whom had called the "first" Atlanta home. In the South, only Richmond, Virginia; Nashville, Tennessee; and New Orleans, Louisiana; were larger than Atlanta. By 1894, electricity, not mules, powered the streetcars on their routes.

Foreshadowing the importance of the modern-day convention business, Atlanta hosted large expositions in 1881, 1887 and 1895, attracting international attention and investment. Gen. Sherman himself came to the 1881 ex-

position; President Grover Cleveland attended the 1887 fair. The Liberty Bell was displayed at the 1895 Cotton States and International Exposition, which attracted nearly a million visitors in its three-month run and boldly included pavilions celebrating the progress and accomplishments of blacks and women. The latter two fairs were held on the site of the present Piedmont Park, which was purchased by the city for $93,000.

The Dawning of a New Century

As the 20th century dawned, Atlanta's population stood at 90,000; by 1910, it had jumped to 155,000.

Atlanta's African-American population grew rapidly during the war years as slaves were ordered in to aid the Confederacy, and many of these new citizens returned to make their homes in the city after the war. By 1870, the black community was five times larger than it had been in 1860. By 1890, blacks made up 43 percent of the population and 50 percent of the workforce.

Northern missionaries and other reformers started Freedmen's Schools to educate ex-slaves and their children. (One such school operated in a box car divided into classrooms.) This early movement planted the seeds that made Atlanta a center of black higher education, and today the Atlanta University Center is the largest consortium of historically African-American colleges in the nation.

Even in the days of enforced racial separation, Atlanta prided itself on being a town with the good sense to put business before prejudice — although it was not always successful. On September 22, 1906, a white mob, enraged by inflammatory newspaper reports of numerous "outrages" against white women, attacked and murdered blacks and burned black homes. Order was not fully restored until September 27, and the rioting left a dozen blacks and several whites dead. The white rampage, reported throughout the nation and in Europe, badly damaged Atlanta's emerging reputation.

In the wake of the riot, much of Atlanta's African-American business community with-

Headstrong Heroine

She was small, but it's said she enjoyed corn liquor, cigarettes and a good dirty joke. Peggy Mitchell was a popular features writer when she left *The Atlanta Journal* in 1926 to nurse an injured ankle and make a life with her new husband. In response to his persistent suggestions, she began a novel.

Born in 1900 in a house that had been spared Sherman's torch, Mitchell was fascinated by the Civil War and spent many childhood hours listening to the harrowing tales of its elderly survivors. So vivid were their recollections that Mitchell thought the war had ended just before she was born, and she was utterly astonished at age 10 when some black farm workers broke the news to her that the South had actually lost the war.

Close-up

Typing at the table she used as a desk, dressed in her husband's baggy clothes and wearing a writer's green eyeshade, Margaret Mitchell spent the next 10 years writing a novel (originally called *Another Day*, then *Tomorrow is Another Day*) about a strong-willed Southern girl of Irish descent (originally named Pansy O'Hara) who came of age in the last days before the war, survived the destruction of Atlanta and grew rich during Reconstruction.

Mitchell began by writing the novel's last chapter. When visitors came calling, she hid the growing stacks of manuscripts under a large towel, for she jealously guarded her privacy and shuddered to think that anyone would find the novel autobiographical. (In fact, the twice-married, headstrong Mitchell had much in common with her plucky heroine.)

Most reluctantly, Mitchell gave the ragtag manuscript to a Macmillian agent scouting the South for new writers in 1935; she then immediately panicked and wired him: "Send the manuscript back. I've changed my mind." But it was too late. The agent, like the millions and millions of readers who followed him, was instantly hooked.

Gone With the Wind sold 50,000 copies on the first day it was offered. In the years

— continued on next page

Photo: Atlanta Historical Society

It took Margaret Mitchell 10 years to complete *Gone With the Wind.*

since, it has sold more than 28 million copies around the world and remains the bestselling novel of all time. David O. Selznick paid $50,000 for the movie rights; the December 15, 1939, world premiere in Atlanta was a spectacular event reported around the globe; the movie won 10 Academy Awards and, by its 50th anniversary, had grossed more than $840 million.

Mitchell's modern outlook and ideas caused minor scandals more than once, so it's easy to understand the bewilderment she expressed in a 1936 letter. "Being a product of the Jazz Age, being one of those short-haired, short-skirted, hard-boiled women who preachers said would go to hell or be hanged before they were thirty, I am naturally a little embarrassed at finding myself the incarnate spirit of the old South!"

In a letter written the year before GWTW's 1936 publication, Mitchell confided, "In a weak moment, I have written a book . . . ." It was a book that catapulted its author to international celebrity and forever affected the way the world thought of her hometown.

drew to Auburn Avenue (then called Wheat Street). Auburn became Atlanta's other main street, offering a full range of retail, service and entertainment concerns as well as religious and social organizations. Among its most successful businesses was Atlanta Life Insurance Co., founded by Alonzo Herndon, an ex-slave and sharecropper who built a lucrative barber business and became Atlanta's first African-American millionaire. In 1956, *Fortune* magazine called Auburn "the richest Negro street in the world."

Civil Rights

It was only natural that Atlanta, long a center of black culture and education, would become a center of civil rights activities in the tumultuous 1960s. And although integration was certainly a contentious issue, forward-thinking black and white leaders helped Atlanta avoid the eruptions of violence that tore apart so many U.S. cities in those years. It was tough, but Atlanta lived up to Mayor William Hartsfield's boast in a 1959 *Newsweek* article: "Atlanta is a city too busy to hate."

At the center of the civil rights movement throughout its most dramatic years was Dr. Martin Luther King Jr. He was born in a modest frame house on Auburn Avenue on January 15, 1929. A gifted student, he was admitted to Morehouse College at age 15 and earned his doctorate from Boston University in 1955. After leading the successful drive to desegregate buses in Montgomery, Alabama, King returned to Atlanta in 1960 as president

and co-founder of the Southern Christian Leadership Conference and co-pastor (with his father) of Ebenezer Baptist Church.

In October of 1960, King and 51 others were arrested when they staged a sit-in to protest segregation at Rich's department store; in all, some 180 people went to jail. Most refused to post bail in order to attract attention to their demands. King's arrest was especially problematic because he was on probation for driving without a Georgia license (his license was from Alabama). His probation was revoked, and he was sentenced to six months in the state penitentiary. Presidential candidate John F. Kennedy is said to have intervened personally to secure King's early release.

In Atlanta, as in most Southern communities, the desegregation of public schools was hotly debated. But here integration proceeded far more smoothly than in many cities. On August 30, 1961, nine black students made history by enrolling in formerly all-white high schools. That afternoon, President Kennedy publicly congratulated the city, urging other communities "to look closely at what Atlanta has done and to meet their responsibility, as the officials of Atlanta and Georgia have done, with courage, tolerance and, above all, respect for the law."

To the chagrin of many conservatives, King was awarded the Nobel Prize for Peace in Sweden in 1964. Although still a very controversial figure in his hometown, King was honored with a banquet staged by city leaders, Coca-Cola magnate Robert W. Woodruff chief among them.

On April 4, 1968, an assassin's bullet stilled King's voice for peace and progress. Gripped by grief and rage, more than 100 U.S. cities exploded in violence, but Atlanta, again, was spared. The eyes of the world focused on the city on April 9, when hundreds of thousands watched King's cortege make its way slowly from Ebenezer Baptist Church to Morehouse College, where president emeritus Dr. Benjamin E. Mays said, "To be honored by being requested to give the eulogy at the funeral of Dr. Martin Luther King is like asking one to eulogize his deceased son, so close and so precious was he to me."

Today King's body rests in an elevated marble tomb at the Martin Luther King, Jr. Center for Nonviolent Social Change on Auburn Avenue, near his boyhood home and beside his church. The Center lies within the boundaries of the 42-acre Martin Luther King Jr. National Historic Site and annually welcomes about a million visitors each year, making it one of the city's leading tourist attractions.

After King's death, Atlanta continued to make important strides toward social justice for all. In 1974, 35-year-old Maynard Jackson became the youngest mayor in Atlanta's history and the first African American to become mayor of a major Southern city. Jackson's aunt, Metropolitan Opera soprano Mattiwilda Dobbs, performed at his inauguration; she had refused to sing in Atlanta when audiences here were segregated.

The atmosphere fostered by the coalition of civil rights leaders and white liberals made the city a progressive oasis in conservative Georgia. Even as some affluent whites fled the city for the suburbs in the 1960s and '70s, many more people took their places. Flower children, gays and lesbians, peace activists and a variety of intellectuals and nonconformists made their homes here, eager to live in a harmonious and evolving integrated urban environment.

While the city is hardly the "People's Republic of Atlanta" that its detractors sometimes portray, its politics remain decidedly left-leaning. In the '70s, Atlanta was a center of anti-war activity: Presidential candidate Senator George McGovern once led a peace march down Auburn Avenue with Mayor Sam Massell. In the '80s, Atlanta was deeply involved in the fight to free South Africa. Recently released political prisoner Nelson Mandela was wildly received by an enormous throng at Georgia Tech's Bobby Dodd Stadium when he came here to thank the city in 1990. And each June, the mayor proclaims Lesbian and Gay Pride Week in recognition of that community's contributions to the city's life.

And then there's the matter of the Georgia state flag. The Georgia Legislature modified the flag in 1956, in a defiant anti-integration gesture, to include the Confederate battle emblem. After a movement to remove the Stars and Bars failed in the state Legislature, Atlanta City Council acted on its own, banishing the banner from City Hall and replacing it (on February 4, 1993) with the pre-1956 flag.

Ushering in the Jet Age

If Atlanta was born in 1837 on the day the Western & Atlantic surveyors drove in the "zero milepost" that marked the end of the rail line, modern Atlanta was born in 1925 on the day the city took a five-year, rent-free lease on an abandoned auto racetrack in Hapeville, 10 miles south of town, promising to develop the overgrown 287-acre site as an airfield.

Interest in flying built slowly at first. Atlanta was already at the center of a web of tracks and roads; aviation was more of an expensive curiosity than a major factor in transportation. But when young William Hartsfield looked at planes, he saw the future. First as an alderman, then, for 22 years as Atlanta's mayor, Hartsfield pushed for improvements in aviation. By the early 1930s, Atlanta had the second-largest number of air routes in the country.

From the beginning, the demand for aviation services far outstripped Candler Field's capacity. More land was acquired, runways added and better facilities built, but the booming aviation business quickly outgrew each improvement. In 1955, 2 million passengers passed through the airport, making it the busiest in the nation. A $21 million ultramodern facility (the largest single terminal building in the country) opened in 1961. It, too, was quickly too small. "Whether you're bound for heaven or hell," said the old joke, "you'll have to change planes in Atlanta."

In January 1977, work began on the world's largest terminal building at the airport (now renamed Hartsfield Atlanta International Airport to honor the mayor whose vision had readied Atlanta for the jet age). The project cost a half-billion dollars and took 3½ years to complete. Throughout construction, normal operations continued at the world's second-busiest airport. The new Hartsfield, built around a space-age, automated people-moving system 40 feet underground, opened to much fanfare on September 21, 1980. Hartsfield is home to Delta Air Lines, one of the world's leading carriers. Delta offers more than 600 domestic and international flights a day out of the airport. In 1996, the airline carried more than 97 million passengers worldwide, and averaged about 2 million out of Atlanta each month.

Even huge Hartsfield had its limitations, and in September 1994, the city unveiled the new Concourse E for international travel. It is, predictably, the largest concourse in the nation. A dramatic new central atrium connecting the north and south terminals opened in late 1995. It was one of some 60 airport improvement projects under way to make Hartsfield a more welcoming first stop for Atlanta's Olympic visitors.

Accommodating Atlantans and the World

Throughout recent decades, Atlanta has continued to acquire the high-visibility accessories of a world-class city and to host events of international interest.

The city built an arts center with the largest regional theater in the Southeast and a symphony hall; a 4,591-seat civic center that hosted the Metropolitan Opera; a 16,000-seat coliseum; a baseball/football stadium; a 2.5-million-square-foot convention center; and the world's largest cable-supported domed stadium. Atlantans even pulled together to prevent the destruction of the lavish, 4,678-seat Fox Theatre, built in 1929, and now one of the nation's few surviving grand movie palaces.

In 1966, Atlanta became the first city ever to acquire professional baseball and football teams in the same year. Professional basketball followed in 1968. Atlanta's Omni complex was the site of the 1988 National Democratic Convention, which was watched worldwide. The city's new Georgia Dome hosted Super Bowl XXVIII in 1994, attracting sports fans and media from around the world.

Then the unbelievable happened: In 1990, Atlanta shocked the world when it overcame stiff competition and was awarded the 1996 Olympics, the 100th anniversary of the modern Olympic Games. At first, all seemed to be theory and planning. But in 1994, the Olympics began to change Atlanta's silhouette.

Atlantans watched the Olympic Village rise on the west side of the Downtown Connector, and we saw the mammoth Olympic stadium take shape right beside Atlanta-Fulton County Stadium, then the home of the Braves. The number of international visitors, which was always significant, seemed to skyrocket as people from around the world showed up for an advance look at the Olympic city.

Preparing to welcome the world was quite a tall order, but Atlanta had plenty of practice. The still-rebuilding city hosted a major exposition just 17 years after it was burned to the ground. Atlantans and Georgians from across the state responded to the challenges of the Olympics with energy and enthusiasm. Though it only lasted for two weeks in that summer of 1996, the Olympics remain a milestone event for many who eagerly share their remembrances of the excitement and pride that spilled into every street. The lasting legacy of the Games can be found in various locations around town: where kids still splash in the fountains at Centennial Park; where the Braves now play at Turner Field, the former Olympic stadium; where outdoor sculptures, murals and other artworks anchor parks and street corners.

Now that you understand a bit about Atlanta's past, it's time to begin exploring the modern city. So drop this book in your bag, grab your sunglasses and/or your umbrella (more about the weather later), and let's have some fun in Atlanta!

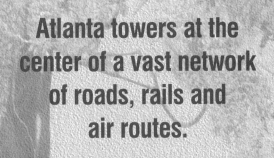

Atlanta towers at the
center of a vast network
of roads, rails and
air routes.

Getting Around

By now you probably know that transportation — in the form of railroads, highways and airports — built Atlanta. But it might surprise you to learn that our area was a transportation center long before the advent of modern travel.

Atlanta stands at the convergence of three giant granite ridges, and these were used by Native Americans as land bridges between the coastal, piedmont and mountain regions of southeastern North America. As European settlers drove out the native population, wagon roads, railroads and finally highways followed the same routes as those old trails.

Modern Atlanta towers at the center of a vast network of roads, rails and air routes. With so many people and packages arriving, leaving and passing through, a certain amount of chaos is unavoidable, and most Atlantans are good-humored about it. But as the city has grown to accommodate thousands of new residents and businesses each year, getting around Atlanta has become more challenging — and a lot less convenient. Atlantans voted in 1994 to fund a massive infrastructure repair program whose effects have been felt all over town. The disruptions accompanying this work closed bridges, opened potholes, widened sidewalks, narrowed lanes and generally had Atlantans covering their ears, holding their noses and reaching for aspirin tablets. Of course, it was all done for the goal of a better Atlanta.

This chapter is planned to help you understand the basics of finding your way into, around and back out of Atlanta. Read it; spend a little time studying the maps we've included; and soon you'll be buzzing around town like a native. (OK, you'll be sitting in traffic jams like a native.)

First, let's talk about Atlanta's highways and streets.

Roadways

Interstates and Highways

Atlanta is served by three interstate highways. On radio traffic reports, these are frequently identified by their location relative to downtown instead of by number.

Interstate 85 N. (the **Northeast Expressway**) connects Atlanta with Greenville, South Carolina, and Charlotte, North Carolina, before merging with I-95 near Richmond, Virginia. South of the city, **I-85 S.** (the **Southwest Expressway**) continues on to Montgomery, Alabama.

Interstate 75 N. (the **Northwest Expressway**) extends from Atlanta to Chattanooga and Knoxville in Tennessee; Cincinnati, Ohio; Detroit, Michigan; and the Canadian border. Below Atlanta, **I-75 S.** (the **Southeast Expressway**) is the route to Florida via the Georgia cities of Macon and Valdosta.

Interstate 20 W. (the **West Expressway**) goes from Atlanta to Birmingham, Alabama; Jackson, Mississippi; Dallas, Texas; and beyond. **I-20 E.** (the **East Expressway**) continues to Augusta, Georgia; and Columbia, South Carolina; connecting with I-95 in Florence, South Carolina.

There are two connecting interstate highways that are important to understand:

Interstate 285 (the **Perimeter**) is the 62.77-mile ring road encircling Atlanta.

I-75 and **I-85** merge just north of Georgia Tech and become the same road, curving around the downtown business district. This section is called the **Downtown Connector** and is marked on maps as 75/85. The interchange connecting the combined 75/85 with I-20 is near Turner Field, the former Olympic Stadium and home of the Atlanta Braves. Interstates 75 and 85 go their separate ways just north of Hartsfield Atlanta Airport; I-85 goes to the airport and on to Montgomery, and I-75 continues south to Macon and Florida.

Another bit of shorthand you're likely to hear on radio reports is **Spaghetti Junction**. This is not a favorite spot for pasta, but rather the looping, futuristic interchange that connects the Northeast Expressway with I-285.

Interstate 675 is a short stretch that connects the southeast side of I-285 with I-75 about 10 miles south of town. It's hard to find — some maps cover it up with ads or a street index — but it's a real time saver. If you're heading south from the east side of town, take Moreland Avenue south until it crosses I-285; I-675 is on your left. It's handy for hooking up with I-75 S. during rush hour, since it lets you steer clear of the Downtown Connector and the congested section of I-285 between the interchanges for I-75 and I-85.

On the northwest side of town, **Interstate 575** branches off from I-75 above Marietta, cuts through rapidly-growing Cherokee County and heads into the North Georgia Mountains. A heavily-travelled commuter route, I-575 is regularly snarled during rush hours as it feeds into and exits from I-75.

North of the city, **Georgia Highway 400** travels toward Lake Lanier. Southbound Ga. 400 connects to the Northeast Expressway near Lindbergh Plaza. Ga. 400's extension inside I-285 to I-85 is a toll road (50¢). The toll plaza is just north of the Buckhead/Lenox Road Exit.

On the toll portion of Ga. 400, have your 50¢ ready. As you drive north, the booths on the right have attendants to make change; the center lanes take exact change only; the left lanes are for "cruise card" holders only. (A cruise card is an electronic device attached to your sun visor; it automatically debits your account each time you pass through the toll

FYI

Three area codes serve the metro Atlanta area: 404, 770 and 678. Whether you live on Peachtree Street or in New York City, you must dial the code to reach any number in the area. The difference? Outside the area, you must dial "1," then the area code and phone number; inside the area, you need only dial the area code followed by the phone number.

plaza. A camera photographs the license plate of anyone who zips through the cruise lanes without a card; freeway freeloaders will shortly receive a ticket and a fine by mail.)

The Freedom Parkway is one of Atlanta's newest roads. Opened in the fall of 1994, the 3.1-mile parkway begins at the Downtown Connector at International Boulevard and leads north to Ponce de Leon (just east of Midtown) and east to Moreland Avenue (just south of North Avenue) after dividing at the Carter Presidential Center. For years, the road was at the center of a legal battle between the Georgia Department of Transportation and area residents, who did not like the initially proposed larger highway's potential impact on their neighborhoods. In the end, the neighbors won significant changes in the parkway. It has jogging trails, bike paths and a 35 mph speed limit.

HOV Lanes

With a series of truly scary newspaper ads ("Misery. Suffering. Anger. Frustration. Brought to you by your friends at Georgia DOT"), the state Department of Transportation kicked off a massive, $41-million project to add express lanes (also known as carpool or HOV, high-occupancy vehicles, lanes) to the interstates inside Atlanta's Perimeter. Atlanta drivers shuddered and hoped the DOT was overstating the project's disruption, but it turns out the DOT wasn't. It was especially vexing that the project began in 1994, only months after the widening and redesign of the freeways — underway since the 1970s — was pronounced complete. "Here we go again," Atlanta drivers moaned in unison.

Why add express lanes? The DOT estimated that freeway traffic increased 20 to 40 percent in Atlanta from 1994 to 1995. The En-

Photo: MARTA

On weekdays, MARTA trains run every four to eight minutes.

vironmental Protection Agency rates Atlanta as a "serious" nonattainment area for ozone smog pollution. Carpool lanes encourage folks to ride together and help reduce the city's output of auto exhausts. And during rush hour, they're less congested and move more smoothly than other bumper-to-bumper lanes.

Most importantly, the DOT had made a commitment to build the lanes as part of the deal that secured federal funds to improve Atlanta's freeways in the 1970s and '80s. So it simply had to be done. Three hundred and thirty lane miles of existing roadway were resurfaced and restriped; 60 lane miles of new express lanes were added.

Even with that project out of the way, it seems there's always some section of roadway under construction. The speed limit in the vicinity of all DOT work sites is 45 mph, and Georgia Highway Patrol officers have been out in abundance to enforce it. Speeding in construction sites has caused numerous deadly accidents; slow down and take it easy.

Express lanes were added to I-75, I-85, the Downtown Connector (75/85), and I-20 east of the city. An express lane will not be added to the less congested stretch of I-20 west of the city. Express lanes are marked with a dia-

mond symbol and a sign reading "Left Lane — Buses and car pools only." Only buses and vehicles with two or more persons can use the express lanes during their hours of operation. The express lanes on I-75, I-85 and the Downtown Connector operate at all times, 24 hours a day, seven days a week. On I-20 east of the city, the inbound express lane operates during morning rush hour, from 6:30 to 9:30 AM; the outbound express lane operates from 4 to 7 PM.

For information on the latest lane and ramp openings and closings, the locations of construction crews each day, and road conditions, call the DOT at (404) 656-5267.

Interstate Tips

Now that we've given you the run down of the various interstates and their aliases, here are a few tips to bear in mind as you're merging into traffic.

• In 1995, after a series of horrible multi-car collisions on Atlanta's interstates, the Georgia Highway Patrol began putting the brakes on speeders. In a get-tough operation called Operation Hardnose, troopers prowled the freeways vowing to ticket drivers going even one mile over the speed limit. Hundreds of tickets were written day after day; some Atlantans got the message, but many others speed on. The effort continues at random on highways around town.

• Be aware that the posted speed limits on Atlanta's freeways are enforced, including the 45 mph limit in the vicinity of construction sites. Troopers are cheerfully shattering the commonly held false perception that you won't get a ticket unless you're more than 10 miles over the limit. Be aware also that troopers patrol more heavily on big travel holidays and when large numbers of people are expected to drive into the city from out of state.

• Driving north on the Downtown Connector, I-75 and I-85 split just after you pass downtown: You must take one or the other. The division comes up only 1.25 miles after the first sign announcing it, so you have to be prepared to act fast. This seemingly straightforward stretch of interstate has confused many a driver, and it's easy to see why. The three lanes for I-85 (the Northeast Expressway) are on the left; the three lanes for I-75 (the Northwest Expressway) are on the right — exactly backwards from what you'd instinctively expect. Begin to move into the appropriate lanes as soon as you safely can after seeing the first signs for the upcoming split, or you may get caught on the wrong side. And, even if you've paid attention and found your lane early, be alert for other drivers frantically switching sides at the last minute.

• As you approach Atlanta by interstate, be particularly cautious around I-285, as its interchanges with the expressways are frequently the sites of accidents. All 18-wheel vehicles traveling the interstates are required by law to take the Perimeter, unless their destination is inside Atlanta. Many a trucker has jackknifed on I-285's ramps after failing to slow down. And even seasoned Atlanta drivers find themselves braking or changing lanes at the last minute because they're baffled by the signage, which is particularly confusing on the west side of town. There, as they try to enter I-285 from I-75, the left lanes head east; the right lanes head west.

• Traffic on the north side of I-285 has gone way beyond the road's capacity. Morning and afternoon rush hours on this highway are when Atlanta most resembles Los Angeles. East of I-75 across the top of the Perimeter, past I-85, through Spaghetti Junction and sometimes all the way over to I-20 E., the northside Perimeter at rush hour can be totally maddening. It often seems there are only two speeds on this highway: 65 mph and stopped. The top end Perimeter is undergoing improvements, but it's likely to remain one of Atlanta's most crowded roads. If you must travel to or from the north/northeast Perimeter area on a daily basis, it's worth your while to investigate alternate routes or travel times.

• The Ga. 400 extension has won raves from those commuting from Roswell, Alpharetta and Lake Lanier. It's also very popular with Atlantans who can travel the fast lanes to new shopping malls and sites on the northside. The reason has to do with the location of the toll plaza: It's just north of the exit for Lenox Road/Buckhead. This is a real break for in-towners: It means you can ride for free from the beginning of Ga. 400 directly up to mega-malls Lenox Square and Phipps Plaza. From downtown, take I-85 N. to the Ga. 400-Cumming-Buckhead toll road Exit 29; get off at Exit 2 "Lenox Road-Buckhead, last exit before toll." Turn right at the "To Peachtree Road" sign: Phipps Plaza will be on your left; the Ritz-Carlton Buckhead will be on your right; Lenox Square is just across Peachtree.

Surface Streets

Something like 55 streets in Atlanta have the word "Peachtree" in their names. How did this mania begin?

The first Peachtree was a Creek Indian village on the Chattahoochee River called Standing Peachtree. An army outpost built nearby took the name Fort Peachtree. The road that linked it to Fort Daniel in Gwinnett County was the first Peachtree Road. (The Old Peachtree Road Exit on the Northeast Expressway has confused many a traveler heading into Atlanta, since it's more than 30 minutes outside town.)

www.insiders.com

See this and many other **Insiders' Guide®** destinations online — in their entirety.

Visit us today!

From this has come a forest of Peachtrees. But even if you could keep this jumble straight, there are more hazards ahead.

It's not uncommon for the same street to have two, three or even more names in different locations. You're driving on Juniper Street and suddenly it's Courtland; you head east on Decatur Street, and it turns into DeKalb Avenue.

This is sometimes the result of the way the city developed, block by block. In other places, it dates from the days of racial segregation, when it was meant to convey an unsubtle message of divided territory. This was the case at Ponce de Leon Avenue, once a racial dividing line. South of Ponce, Monroe becomes Boulevard; Briarcliff becomes Moreland. In many suburban counties, the streets frequently change names depending on the direction you're headed: For instance, in Cobb County, the road west from Marietta to Powder Springs is Powder Springs Road. The same street in Powder Springs is called Marietta Street. Sometimes its handy to think about where you want to go, and take the appropriately named road!

A favorite Atlanta city hall activity is renaming streets, or sections of streets, to honor civic leaders or to recognize social changes. Although a noble gesture in itself, this too causes confusion. Take Irwin that at Peachtree becomes John Wesley Dobbs Avenue. Before it was renamed in 1994 for the distinguished businessman and activist, the final stretch was called Houston (pronounced "house-ton" in Atlanta-speak). Such changes typically take years to show up on most maps, however.

Furthermore, terms such as "street" and "avenue" and "boulevard" are often used without apparent rhyme or reason. Peachtree Street runs north and south, but 10th Street runs east and west. North Avenue runs east and west, but Piedmont Avenue runs north and south. Ralph McGill Boulevard runs east and west, but Boulevard (south Monroe Drive) runs north and south. (Before it was renamed as a tribute to the progressive newspaper editor, Ralph McGill Boulevard was called Forrest Avenue, honoring a Confederate general and father of the Ku Klux Klan.)

In driving around Atlanta, you'll find you have more options when traveling north and south than when traveling east and west. In the afternoon rush hour, you may move south along Peachtree at a brisk clip, then turn left onto Ponce de Leon to find traffic crawling east toward Decatur. Commuters trying to avoid crosstown traffic often work out curious diagonal routes through neighborhoods, keeping off the clogged main streets. This may not save time, but some folks prefer it to sitting still. But beware: To cut down on the number of commuters buzzing along the residential streets, many in-town neighborhoods have succeeded at restricting the times drivers may turn into their area. In some cases, they've made streets one-way to keep commuters out. Particularly in the Buckhead area, pay close attention to signs posted at neighborhood entrances that spell out the restrictions.

There's no overnight way to learn your way around Atlanta's streets, but here are a few suggestions that should help:

• Concentrate on learning the main roads first. About Peachtree's various forms: It is first street, then road and eventually boulevard. It is Peachtree Street from downtown to a point just north of the Midtown district where it becomes Peachtree Road. We're told that decades ago, this is where the paved road ended and a country dirt road began.

• Atlanta is a hilly town, and Peachtree Street runs along its highest ridge. Peachtree begins downtown (its short, southernmost stretch is called Whitehall, after Atlanta's first store and bar) then passes through the hotel district, Midtown, Peachtree Battle and Buckhead. In Buckhead the street forks: To the right, Peachtree Road continues on past Lenox Square, Phipps Plaza, Oglethorpe University and on to I-285, which it crosses as Peachtree Industrial Boulevard. The left fork in Buckhead becomes Roswell Road: It travels north to Sandy Springs, Roswell and Alpharetta. Peachtree is Atlanta's main street and though often crowded is always a dependable north/south route.

• Piedmont Avenue can be a good alternative to Peachtree for traveling between downtown, Midtown and Buckhead.

• Ponce de Leon Avenue is an easy route to Decatur and to Stone Mountain. Eastbound, Ponce forks just after the stone railroad overpass: To the left, Scott Boulevard continues out to the Lawrenceville Highway; to the right, East Ponce de Leon goes to downtown

Decatur (where the speed limit is strictly enforced) and Stone Mountain.

• Martin Luther King Jr. Drive is the direct route between downtown and the Atlanta University Center area. Within the AU district, James P. Brawley Drive runs north and south between M. L. King Jr. Drive and Spelman College, near I-20.

• U.S. Highway 41 (also known at different locations as Northside Drive, Northside Parkway and Cobb Parkway) is a noninterstate route out to the Cumberland Mall/Galleria area and on to Dobbins Air Force Base and Marietta.

• Five Points is the center of downtown Atlanta. It's formed by the intersection of Peachtree, Decatur/Marietta streets and Edgewood Avenue.

• Little Five Points is 2.5 miles east of downtown at the convergence of Moreland, McLendon and Euclid avenues. It's one of Atlanta's most eclectic shopping areas and a multicultural mecca, a scaled-down version of New York's East Village.

• Downtown is the area around Five Points. Midtown is the area around Piedmont Park; it's the first neighborhood bordering Peachtree north of downtown. Uptown is Buckhead, filled with lots of upscale clubs, restaurants and boutiques; it's populated with shoppers by day and bar-hoppers by night. The heart of Buckhead is about 6 miles up Peachtree Street from Five Points.

Here are a few general pointers for getting your bearings on Atlanta's streets:

• Start by studying the maps we've included in our book. Spend a little time getting to know the major streets and highways. Once you understand a few of the main north/south and crosstown routes, you'll feel more confident and find your knowledge of Atlanta's roads increasing rapidly. Then graduate to a good, larger street map. They're inexpensive, widely available and always come in handy.

• Take MARTA. Riding MARTA's buses and trains (whose tracks are usually above-ground) is a great way to get your bearings and study the lay of the city without having to fight traffic.

• When you're riding with friends (or a knowledgeable cabby), ask the driver what route he or she is taking. You'll find you're on the same streets again and again, though you may not always recognize them at first.

• Ask veteran Atlantans for their favorite shortcuts. Most newcomers understandably stick to the busy main roads. Friends or co-workers may be able to give you tips about routes that bypass the worst jams.

• For goodness sake, don't be shy about asking directions. You'll frequently hear long-time Atlantans having involved conversations about main routes and alternates, street openings and closings. Many a conversation begins with "What's the best way to get from ___ to ___ now?" There's definitely no stigma attached to asking for directions; it may even make you seem more like a native.

• When you're going somewhere new, always call ahead for directions. Simply locating the street on a map may not be good enough. Sometimes two streets share the same name and even the same directional indicator (such as N.E.), but they're miles apart in completely different parts of town. Many times, addresses apply to an entire shopping center, not just the particular establishment you're trying to locate, so it helps to know if your destination is part of a complex. Also, even the newest maps seldom reflect all the intricacies of Atlanta's often-changed street names.

• In Atlanta, it's always hard to say today what route will be best tomorrow. This city's rebuilding began in 1865 and shows no sign of letting up, so road construction and utility work are always a part of life. Back in the 1980s, the popular Wit's End Players comedy troupe even had a song about it in their act: "They're Tearing Up Peachtree Street Again."

INSIDERS' TIP

If you're picking up arriving friends at Hartsfield, ask them to wait on the covered center median that runs the length of the baggage claim/ticketing area. It's much easier to stop and collect your friends and their bags there than in the crowded lanes closest to the terminal building.

Photo: Bureau of Cultural Affairs

Travel-themed artwork is everywhere at Hartsfield International Airport.

Rules of the Road

Because traffic laws differ from state to state, take a moment to look over the following rules. You may obtain a free copy of *Georgia Driver*, the official state handbook, at any driver's license renewal location. Call (404) 657-9300 for more information.

• The driver and all front-seat passengers of every car must wear a seat belt. Persons between 4 and 18 must wear a seat belt in the car at all times.

• Children younger than 4 must ride in an approved child safety seat. (This law has exceptions: A seat belt is sufficient for kids between 3 and 4, and the law does not apply to nonresidents of Georgia.)

• After coming to a complete stop at an intersection, you may make a right turn on red, traffic permitting. Some intersections, however, are posted as no turn on red.

• A left turn on red is permissible only when turning from the left lane of a one-way street on to another one-way street on which traffic is moving to the driver's left.

• Your headlights must be on (day or night) when you are driving through rain, fog, snow or smoke.

• You must stop when approaching (from either direction) a school bus with its stop sign out and its lights flashing. On a highway divided by a median, you are required to stop when you are behind a stopped bus but not when you're coming from the opposite direction.

• You must pull to the right and stop to yield to official vehicles answering an emergency call. Police cars have blue emergency lights; ambulances and fire trucks have red lights.

• You must yield to pedestrians at marked and unmarked crosswalks without traffic signals, in intersections, at stop signs, when turning and when entering the street from a driveway. You must yield to a blind person with a white cane or guide dog.

• The maximum speed limit in Georgia typically is 55 mph. On rural interstates, where posted, the speed limit is 65 mph. In all business and residential districts, the speed limit is 30 mph unless otherwise posted.

• If you can steer it, clear it. Drivers involved in a minor accident are required to remove the accident vehicles from the roadway immediately; then you can call for assistance.

• Drivers are considered drunk in Georgia when they register 0.08gm percent or more. Penalties are severe; don't get caught driving drunk in Georgia. Drivers younger than the legal drinking age (21) are considered drunk if tests show they have consumed any amount of alcohol.

• Motorcycle drivers and passengers must wear a helmet.

• Bicycle riders younger than 16 must wear a bicycle helmet.

• If you are moving to the state, you are required to get a Georgia license and to register your car in your county within 30 days.

It's Customary

From the moment you notice the interstate traffic speeding up (although the speed limit decreases) as you motor into Atlanta, you may find driving here intimidating. Rush hour never seems to end on some of our main roads. And the 55 streets named Peachtree don't exactly help you get your bearings either.

But for most people, driving around Atlanta gets easier fast. The best drivers seem to develop an alert yet laid-back attitude. The alert part is essential, since traffic here is often quick and close and the streets are curvy and hilly. But the laid-back part, though harder to develop, is essential too. (It explains why some people never get speeding tickets and others get them over and over.) The worst thing is to take the traffic personally. Confrontational people are miserable driving in Atlanta.

Given that many of our thoroughfares are carrying far more cars than they were built to handle, Atlanta traffic would be an ongoing disaster were it not for our secret weapon: Most Atlanta drivers are actually quite courteous.

We're not suggesting for a moment that there are no hot-head speed demons on the streets of Atlanta. There are some, but fortunately they're the exception, outnumbered by drivers who realize that a little neighborliness and cooperation can help get everybody home on time.

Here are a couple of other pointers along these lines:

• Blowing your horn when you're stuck in traffic is not a custom here — and it won't help you make friends either. During a recent visit to Manhattan, we heard more horns in one hour than we hear in a month in Atlanta. Here we consider excessive horn blowing downright rude.

• Use your turn signals. Most drivers will be happy to let you maneuver through traffic if you give them a clue as to what you're trying to do.

• Don't tailgate. Rear-ending someone is a terrible way to meet.

• Don't run red lights, and don't speed. Going almost anywhere in Atlanta involves traveling through residential areas filled with kids, dogs, bicyclists and people backing out of driveways. Zooming around neighborhoods at 55 mph can lead to a ticket or a tragedy.

• MARTA buses make their way through many streets that are not really wide enough for them; this is especially a problem at sharp turns. When a bus is trying to turn a corner and its way is blocked by cars waiting at the light, all the cars must back up to make way for the bus. This is less likely to happen if you observe the stop-line at intersections.

• Having cautioned you against excessive horn-blowing, we should note that judicious use of your horn can definitely help prevent accidents. Keep one hand close to your horn, especially when you're driving in tight, fast-moving traffic. If your reaction time is quick, you can "beep" weaving drivers back into their lane before they bump into you.

Cruising

We freely admit Atlanta's worst shortcoming: no beaches. Deprived of an oceanside main drag, lots of young people take to cruising Peachtree between downtown and Midtown on warm weekend nights. The resulting traffic tie-ups can be annoying but concentrated on and around Peachtree. The situation has improved greatly since no cruising signs have been well-posted and enforced. But if you find yourself in a jam, just get off Peachtree and pick up one of the other north/south streets, such as Piedmont, Courtland, West Peachtree, Spring or Techwood.

MARTA

Atlanta's mass transit system is called MARTA (Metropolitan Atlanta Rapid Transit Authority). MARTA is one of the most advanced rapid transit systems in the United States.

Though approved by referendum in 1965,

MARTA lacked money until 1971, when voters agreed to fund the system with a sales tax. To win approval of the tax, an arrangement was made to cut bus fares from 40¢ to 15¢ and to hold them there for seven years. The tax passed; the promise was kept; MARTA was on its way.

Today MARTA serves the 800-square-mile district at the heart of the metro area. The first MARTA rail stations opened in June 1979. When the Airport station opened in June 1988, Atlanta became one of the few U.S. cities to offer direct rail service from the airport to downtown. 1996 was another big year for MARTA. The new north line extension opened in June, along with the Buckhead, Medical Center and Dunwoody rail stations. Two more north line stations are under construction and set to open in 2000.

MARTA operates 240 electric rail cars on 46 miles of track with regular service to 36 rapid rail stations. In addition, 785 buses traverse 150 routes covering 1,500 miles. On an average weekday, the system records 500,000 passenger boardings.

Weekdays, trains run every 4 to 8 minutes between 5 AM and 7 PM; from 7 PM until 1 AM, they run every 10 minutes. On Saturday, trains run every 10 minutes between 5 AM and 7 PM; from 7 PM until 1 AM, they run every 15 minutes. On Sunday and holidays, trains run every 15 minutes from 5:30 to 12:30 AM. Extra trains are typically called into service during big downtown events.

Bus schedules vary, but there's a printed timetable for every route. You can get free schedules at Five Points station and at MARTA information kiosks. Each bus usually has a supply of its own schedule; ask your driver.

A single MARTA fare (required for each passenger older than 3) is currently $1.50, including two free transfers. (This means you can take a bus to the train, change at Five Points to a train on the other line, ride to another station, then take a bus from the station to your destination — all for a single fare. You can't, however, use a transfer as your return fare in a round trip.)

All buses and train stations accept the MARTA TransCard. For a flat fee ($12 for the Monday-through-Sunday weekly card, $45 for the monthly card) patrons get unlim- ited use of the entire system. TransCard us- ers do not need transfers. Token packs (10 for $15 or the 20 for $25 pack) and TransCards are sold at RideStore locations (at Five Points, Airport and Lenox stations, at MARTA headquarters, beside Lindbergh station and in many grocery and conve- nience stores throughout the service area).

The weekly TransCard is good for a calen- dar week (not for unlimited travel on any seven days); the monthly card is good for a calendar month. Weekly and monthly cards are both available before the date they take effect, so you can buy your next week's card before you start your weekend.

MARTA route and schedule information is available by phone from 6 AM to 10 PM Mon- day through Friday and from 8 AM to 4 PM Saturdays, Sundays and holidays; call (404) 848-4711. Tell the operator your location and destination; she or he will tell you which bus to take, where to catch it, whether you need to transfer and when the bus runs.

(Please note: Every effort has been made to ensure accuracy, but MARTA's services, schedules and fares are subject to change.)

Riding the Train

MARTA's rapid rail system is easy and fun to use.

Each MARTA station is different, with its own architectural style and works of art. Most spectacular is Peachtree Center station, which was blasted out of the solid-granite ridge under Peachtree Street. Getting here is half the fun! Access is by incredibly steep, 192-foot escalators- some of the longest in the Southeast. (Of course, you may take the elevator if you prefer.) Exposed rock forms a natural cave around the platforms, where you'll wait for your train some 12 stories be- low Peachtree Street!

MARTA's rail lines intersect at the huge Five Points station, where you can transfer between east/west and north/south lines. You can also pick up the north line to Dunwoody at the Lindbergh station. You don't need a transfer to go from one train line to the other, as they're both inside the station. Five Points station has its own entrance to Underground Atlanta via a tunnel under Peachtree Street;

it's on your right just before you exit the station on the Peachtree side.

Rail station turnstiles accept exact change in coin (but not pennies, half-dollars or dollar bills) and MARTA tokens, which are sold in vending machines at all stations. Token machines take $1, $5, $10 and $20 bills; and, although generally reliable, these machines can sometimes be excessively picky about wrinkled money. If this happens, try another machine. If no machine will cooperate (or if one eats your money) don't panic. Pick up the nearby white courtesy phone and tell your troubles to the MARTA employee who answers. She or he will give you permission to enter through the "Handicapped" gate (just ignore that loud alarm).

Take the appropriate escalator to the train boarding area. In stations where the platform is between the tracks, the escalator is marked, "To All Trains." Other stations have two platforms with the tracks in-between. In these, you must use the escalator marked with the direction in which you're traveling.

Signs on the front and side of each train indicate its final stop. The opening of the new north line created some confusion, since every northbound train could no longer be counted on to go to Lenox Square. Here's how to tell where a train is headed:

An "Airport" train is southbound and will take you all the way to Hartsfield at the end of the south line. An "Indian Creek" train is eastbound and will take you through Decatur out to the end of the east line. The westbound "Hamilton E. Holmes" trains go to the end of the west line, while "Bankhead" trains (also westbound) branch off on the northwest Proctor Creek line. A "Doraville" train goes on to the end of the northeast line (this is also the train to Lenox station). "Dunwoody" trains service the new Buckhead, Medical Center and Dunwoody (near Perimeter Mall) stations on the north line. "Doraville" and "Dunwoody" trains alternate in their service along the central portion of the north line. The northernmost station at which to transfer between these two trains is Lindbergh Center.

In the MARTA station, wait well behind the white strip at the edge of the platform until the arriving train has come to a complete stop. When the doors open, allow departing passengers the opportunity to exit the train before you board. MARTA's electric trains are speedy: As soon as you board, sit down or grab the nearest handrail to avoid losing your balance as the train whisks away.

When the train begins slowing down for your stop, gather up your belongings and your group and prepare to disembark. Atlanta is not Tokyo, but the trains are fast-paced. If you're in the middle of a crowded rail car and take your time getting to the exit, the doors may close before you have a chance to get off.

Signs inside all MARTA stations indicate bus stops, surrounding streets and major buildings. If you need directions, pick up a white courtesy phone and ask the operator for assistance.

Riding the Bus

To board a MARTA bus, wait at a bus stop (indicated by either a white concrete obelisk or a tricolor pole-mounted MARTA sign). The front of each bus is marked with the route number and the route name. Different bus routes use the same bus stops — make sure to board the right bus. (Express bus routes include stretches along which passengers are neither picked up nor discharged. Before boarding a bus marked "express," ask the driver whether you'll be able to disembark at your desired stop.) When you see your bus approaching, raise your hand to signal to the driver that you wish to board.

Enter through the front door. Drop your fare into the fare box, hand your transfer to the driver, or pass your TransCard through the card reader. Fare boxes accept cash (including dollar bills and any combination of coins) and MARTA tokens, but drivers do not make change. If you'd like a transfer, you must request it when you pay your fare. Using the local shorthand, just

INSIDERS' TIP

For recorded information on MARTA's rapid rail service to Hartsfield Atlanta Airport, call (404) 848-3450.

say "train" if you'd like a rail transfer or "bus" if you're changing buses. Some bus routes terminate inside stations, where you won't need a transfer to board the train. Your driver will let you know if this is the case.

If you're unsure about directions, tell the driver your destination as you board; sit up front and you'll be let off at the closest stop. Pressing the yellow stop request strip or pulling the cord will signal the driver that you want off at the next scheduled stop. Use the rear door when exiting.

Special Events

Shuttle service from the Five Points station to Turner Field, home of the Braves, begins 90 minutes before the start of games and runs continuously until an hour after the game. You'll need a transfer to board the shuttle, so remember to get one when you pay your fare as you enter the MARTA system.

Especially if the weather is nice, lots of Braves fans take the train to the Georgia State station and walk to the stadium; it's less than three-quarters of a mile. The extra effort really pays off after the game: If you take the train from Georgia State, you'll be back in your car and on your way home long before traffic clears out around the stadium.

During the summer concert season, shuttle service from the Lakewood/Ft. McPherson station to the Lakewood Amphitheater begins 90 minutes before showtime and continues after the show until the venue is empty.

Special Services

For MARTA schedule information, call (404) 848-4711. Call anytime for recorded information on rail and airport service, (404) 848-3450; stadium shuttle, (404) 848-3457; and elderly and handicapped services, (404) 848-3452.

To make a suggestion or report a problem, or for any other information, call MARTA's customer service center at (404) 848-4800.

All MARTA buses and trains have seats designated as "reserved" for any elderly or handicapped persons on board. Disabled persons and those 65 and older are eligible for a special reduced 75¢ fare. The required half-fare card may be obtained free of charge at

Photo: Georgia's Stone Mountain Park

Ride the rails aboard a Civil War-era steam train at Georgia's Stone Mountain Park.

any RideStore. All MARTA stations have at least one entrance that is fully accessible to the elderly and those with disabilities.

Almost all of MARTA's buses are handicapped accessible and have lifts. However, MARTA also operates L-VANS, which provide door-to-door service. A single fare on these buses is $3. For more information, call (404) 848-4800. Handicapped patrons who make use of buses along MARTA's regular routes are not charged extra.

Deaf persons may use MARTA's TTY schedule information line, (404) 848-5665.

Parking

MARTA has thousands of parking spaces for use by system passengers, including more than 22,000 spaces at rail stations and 2,800 spaces at park and ride lots. Parking is free at all times in all MARTA lots except the following.

There is a $1 charge to park in the covered decks at the Lenox and Lindbergh stations. Deposit $1 in the appropriate numbered slot in the parking fee box; you pay in advance. For airport patrons, the Brookhaven and Medical Center stations offer fenced parking lots with 24-hour security. Parking is $3 per day, payable upon exiting the lot.

MARTA to the Airport

Hartsfield Atlanta Airport is the last stop on the south rail line; board the train marked "Airport." North/south train cars have a designated space where you may stow your luggage; of course, you should keep an eye on it at all times. The ride from Five Points station to the airport is about 15 minutes. As you exit Airport station, follow the signs to your airline's ticketing area. South terminal is to your right; north terminal is to your left. There is no extra charge for the trip to the airport; the fare is $1.50. Taking MARTA back to the city after your trip is a breeze: The station is adjacent to baggage claim.

Recent Improvements

With the June 1996 opening of the north line extension came the debut of three new MARTA stations. Here's a look at these new rail facilities.

The Buckhead station is 7.4 miles north of Five Points on a 1.35-acre site. It's on the median of Ga. 400 at Capital City Plaza on Peachtree Street in Buckhead. The subway station is near the Atlanta Financial Center complex; an underground tunnel lets patrons enter from either side of Peachtree. Built at a cost of $12 million, Buckhead station has a passenger drop-off area but no parking facility.

Twelve miles north of Five Points, Medical Center station sits on a 9.6-acre site. A pedestrian walkway over Peachtree-Dunwoody Road provides access to Northside Hospital. Other major facilities served by this station include St. Joseph's Hospital and Scottish Rite Children's Hospital. It has no parking facility but provides for handicapped parking, bicycles and taxis. Medical Center station, built at a cost of almost $23 million, is a 21-minute train ride from Five Points; getting to the airport from here will take about 36 minutes.

Dunwoody station is the end of the north line (for now — two more stations will open in 2000). It's at the corner of Hammond Drive and Perimeter Center Parkway and serves workers and shoppers in the Perimeter Center area. Dunwoody station is an above-ground facility, 13.1 miles north of Five Points. The

$21.6 million station includes a four-level, 572-car parking deck, as well as additional spaces that opened in late 1997.

Also new in 1996, to welcome the city's international visitors, MARTA installed kiosks at 11 rail stations offering recorded assistance in five languages: Japanese, German, French, Spanish and English. You'll find these helpful kiosks inside the MARTA stations at Five Points, Peachtree Center and elsewhere.

Security

MARTA maintains its own 290-member police force. Armed uniformed and plain-clothes officers heavily patrol the system. Surveillance cameras are also used to deter vandals, gate-jumpers and other criminals.

All stations include white-colored passenger-assistance telephones, which connect riders with helpful MARTA operators, and blue police emergency telephones, which connect callers to the MARTA police. Both are located near the fare gates and on the platforms. Every rail car has an intercom that connects passengers with the train conductor.

One word of caution: In spite of the vigilance of the MARTA police, crime does occur in the system. Especially when traveling alone or at night, keep your guard up. Access to many stations is by long stairways and pedestrian overpasses, which can be scary. If you feel you're being followed, avoid walking alone into these areas. If you're frightened, stay in the main part of the station, in plain view of the security cameras, and use the blue telephone to request assistance from the MARTA police. Avoid strangers in the parking lot; have your keys ready and walk briskly to your car.

Rules

Be sure to observe the following rules:

• On all buses and in all trains and rail stations, it is illegal to smoke, eat, drink, litter or play radios or stereos without earphones.

• Moving between train cars, unless directed to do so by MARTA personnel in an emergency, is forbidden.

• MARTA's high-voltage tracks are extremely dangerous. Passengers must never climb onto the tracks or attempt to cross them.

Cobb Community Transit

Atlanta's northwest neighbor Cobb County operates its own bus system on local and express routes around Cobb and to Atlanta. CCT buses access MARTA regularly at the Arts Center station; weekday express buses connect at the Dunwoody station. The system operates both local (adult fare $1.25) and express (adult fare $3 one-way, $4 round trip) routes. Kids less than 42 inches tall ride free; youth through high school fare is 80¢; senior citizen and handicapped fare is 60¢. Although holiday schedules apply on most special days, CCT does not run on Thanksgiving, Christmas, New Year's Day, 4th of July and Labor Day. For information on schedules and monthly passes, call (770) 427-4444.

Hartsfield Atlanta International Airport

Hartsfield Atlanta International Airport is 10 miles south of downtown on I-85. It compares in size and population to a small city. Including airline, City of Atlanta, Federal Aviation Administration Airport and concession tenants and employees, some 35,000 people earn a payroll totaling $1.5 billion at 3,750-acre Hartsfield. The airport's direct and indirect impact on the Georgia economy is more than $15 billion per year, making it the largest employment center in the state.

Hartsfield handled more than 63 million passengers in 1996 and is expecting volume to jump to 121 million annually by 2015. Hartsfield has 24 international gates and 158 domestic gates. Its four parallel runways are laid out east to west; the longest is 11,889 feet (more than 2.25 miles) long.

In 70 years, Hartsfield went from a lonesome landing field to one of the world's major airports. Rail travel was king, and airplanes were little more than extravagant oddities in 1925 when the city leased an abandoned, 287-acre racetrack as Atlanta's first airport. But the popularity of flying grew quickly, and so did traffic at Candler Field. The airport began to grow, acquiring surrounding properties and increasing its aviation capacity.

In 1961, the airport boasted the largest single terminal in the country, but it wasn't big enough for long — booming Atlanta's huge demand for aviation services required a huge airport, and a massive new building project was undertaken.

For 3½ years in the late 1970s, the Atlanta airport was the biggest construction project in the South. When the new Hartsfield (the name honors the Atlanta Mayor William B. Hartsfield, who was a tireless booster of aviation) opened in 1980, it was the largest airport in the world. But before long, Atlanta's growth again began to test its capacity.

In 1991, the city broke ground on the airport's sixth concourse, E, which opened in September 1994. Dedicated exclusively to international travel, the 1.3-million-square foot, five-story addition is the largest international concourse in the nation. It has 24 gates (expandable to 34) and can handle 18 of those humongous 747-400s simultaneously, processing 6,000 arriving passengers an hour through Immigration and Customs.

Because of all the essential security, international concourses can sometimes look more like detention facilities than airports: Hartsfield's Concourse E is a stunning exception; its design is appropriate to the exciting and romantic idea of international travel. Light is beautifully used throughout, beaming from the broad skylights and the streamlined lighting fixtures. Since 1996, corridor walls, display cases and gate areas at this concourse showcase a collection of more than 32 pieces of art put together by the Bureau of Cultural Affairs as part of its Public Art Program at Hartsfield Atlanta International Airport.

In October 1995, Hartsfield unveiled its latest addition: a 225,000-square-foot, four-story atrium (referred to as The Atrium). Topped with a 60-foot-wide skylight and encompassing some 40 restaurants, shops and services, the $24 million atrium provides an aesthetic focus for the airport as it connects the north and south terminals. A two-story glass clock tower at the atrium's center can be programmed to play more than 1,000 songs. The Atrium was envisioned as a place for people to rendezvous at the airport. Spaced throughout it are planters and comfortable living room-style seating for approximately 100 people.

The Atrium's many amenities include a

20,000-square-foot conference center (with the capability to run 15 simultaneous meetings), the offices of the United Service Organization and Travelers' Aid, a 9,000-square-foot Houlihan's restaurant and piano bar, a 2,100-square-foot Buckhead Bread Co. cafe, as well as Paschal's (famous local soul food), Wendy's, Domino's Pizza, Edy's Ice Cream and more shops included in what is now known as The Shops at Hartsfield (a name picked from a public contest).

Throughout the airport, generic food concessions are being replaced with name-brand restaurants, such as Chick-fil-A, Burger King, Ben and Jerry's and Starbuck's Coffee. It's all part of the Hartsfield Improvement Project, a $170 million list of 60 different upgrade projects brought about by the 1996 Olympic Games presence in Atlanta.

After the international gates were switched to Concourse E, their former concourse was moved to domestic use. The new Concourse T is quite convenient: It's the only concourse you access directly from the terminal without using the 1.75-mile-long transportation mall connecting the terminal to the concourses.

A fifth runway will be added, probably by spring 2002, and $440 million has been set aside for this endeavor.

Here's a brief walk-through of Hartsfield for arriving and departing domestic and international passengers.

Domestic Arrivals

Your domestic flight will taxi in to concourse A, B, C, D or T. In welcoming you to Atlanta, your flight attendant will likely tell you the number of the carousel where the flight's checked baggage will be delivered. A flashing sign at your arrival gate in the concourse will also show the carousel number.

Follow the signs for Terminal/Baggage Claim. You'll go down an escalator or elevator to the transportation mall, Hartsfield's 1.75-mile-long backbone that connects the concourses to the terminal. Computer-operated

trains (free of charge) run about every two minutes, traveling between all concourses and the terminal. Automated announcements will direct you onboard.

If you like, you may walk through the transportation mall or take the moving sidewalk, but we don't recommend this unless you are going only between near concourses. If your plane comes in at the last domestic gate on Concourse D and you take the train, you'll be at baggage claim in less than 15 minutes. The moving sidewalk route, which also involves long stretches of nonmoving sidewalk, will take closer to 30 minutes.

At the last stop, "Terminal/Baggage Claim," you'll be directed up the escalator or elevator to baggage claim and all ground transportation. Here you'll also find the rental car counters. Signs will direct you to the appropriate baggage area for your airline: North terminal baggage claim is to your right; south terminal baggage claim is to your left. Flight numbers flash over the various baggage carousels as the bags roll up the conveyor belt. Passengers are required to present their half of the baggage check ticket for each checked bag before leaving baggage claim; uniformed employees near the exits will ask for your check tickets. If you don't have the check tickets, you'll be asked to show identification.

If you're being picked up by a friend, exit through the glass doors to the curbside area. Since there are two baggage claim areas (one on either side of the terminal), it's important to let your friend know what airline you're flying.

For all other transportation — taxi, limo, shuttle bus or MARTA train — follow the signs to ground transportation at the west curb.

Special note for arriving American Airlines passengers: American Airlines flights use Concourse T. You won't need to ride the train to the terminal; you're already there. From your arriving gate, follow the signs downstairs to American baggage claim. Directly outside, American has its own curb where you can get a cab. If friends are picking you up, tell them to take the lanes for the north terminal, then follow the signs to American baggage claim. This curb is much less crowded than the main ones upstairs, so getting out of the airport is a snap. If you're taking MARTA or catching a shuttle bus, you'll need to go back upstairs to the main baggage claim and follow the signs to ground transportation.

Domestic Departures

As you approach Hartsfield from I-85, large signs will direct you to either the north or south terminal, depending on your airline. (All Delta flights use the south terminal.)

Most airlines have curbside check-in for ticketed passengers, and all have ticket agents inside the terminal. If you have your boarding pass and no luggage to check, you may be able to learn your concourse and gate from one of the TV monitors near the ticket counters and in the transportation mall. However, not all airlines are listed on the monitors, so you may need to ask your airline's agent.

Everyone going from the terminal to any concourse must pass through the central security screening checkpoint. From security, take the train or moving sidewalk to your concourse; follow the signs to your gate.

International Departures

International ticketing for Delta, Sabena, Varig and ALM Antillean is in the south terminal; ticketing for all other international flights is in the north terminal. Check your bags at your airline's counter and proceed through security and the transportation mall to Concourse E, where signs will direct you to your gate.

Should your flight be delayed, you won't have to console yourself with an overcooked hot dog and yesterday's paper. Concourse E's food court includes Burger King, Starbuck's and Mo' Better Chicken. Browse the excellent selection of U.S. and international publications at W.H. Smith, or pick up a new tape or CD for that long flight at The Wall.

Thomas Cook Currency Services Inc. has three locations inside Hartsfield Airport, all on Concourse E. A fee of $4.50 or 1 percent of the foreign exchange if it's more than $450 is charged. Call (800) 287-7362 for specific information. Travelex, located in a stand in the atrium at Hartsfield, also exchanges currency from about 75 countries. Travelex charges $4 or 1 percent of the total amount of the trade, whichever will net Travelex more. Call (404) 766-2700.

International Arrivals

As your international flight arrives at Concourse E, you'll first be directed to Immigration. From there you'll go downstairs to claim your bags and pass through Customs.

Once you've cleared Customs, you must recheck your bags at your airline's counter. If you're continuing to another city, they will be checked through to your final destination. But, even if Atlanta is your final destination, you are still required to recheck your bags — they will then be delivered to the terminal, where you can pick them up at baggage claim. This FAA-mandated policy is designed to alleviate overcrowding on the underground trains but caused lots of confusion when it was implemented.

To cut down on hassles and congestion for arriving international passengers, the airport added four baggage claim carousels (for a total of 12 international carousels). Multilingual announcements describe the customs and baggage recheck procedures. In addition, most airlines now show an inflight video that orients arriving passengers to the airport. Also, in the Immigration and Naturalization Service area, 18 translators, whose badges indicate the languages they speak, assist non-English-speaking arriving passengers. Multilingual signs in the transportation mall tell passengers how to get around the airport.

Smoking

Smoking lounges are located throughout the airport; these are open to persons 18 and older. Feel free to smoke in the following lounges:

- Concourse A near gates 14 and 23
- Concourse B near gates 7 and 24
- Concourse C near gates 17 and 26
- Concourse T near gates 3 and 13
- Concourse E near gates 33 and 34

Security

Security alerts have become routine at U.S. airports. When a security alert is in force, getting into the airport and onto your plane is certain to take longer, so allow yourself plenty of time. Exactly what's involved in a security alert is top-secret, of course, but during a security alert, expect the following:

• Each passenger will likely be required to show a photo ID with a name matching the name on the ticket before being allowed to board.

• Agents will ask if you packed your own bag, whether you left it unattended at any time and whether anyone asked you to transport a package for them.

• Security checkpoint inspections may become more thorough; to avoid delay, drop your keys and any metal pens or accessories in your purse or briefcase before passing through the metal detector.

• During an alert, only vehicles that can drive under a 5-foot 5-inch metal bar are allowed to park in the short-term lots near the terminal. Vans and large vehicles may park in the airport's other lots.

• Your car may be towed away if you leave it unattended in the drop-off/pickup lanes for even one minute.

Airport Parking

Hartsfield has more than 26,000 parking spaces. Lots near the terminal are for short-term parking ($1 an hour for the first and second hours; $2 per hour for each additional hour; maximum $24 per 24 hours). The economy lots are for long-term parking ($1 per hour; maximum $5 per 24 hours). Long-term deck parking is $1 per hour; maximum $9 per 24 hours. The park-and-ride lots at Hartsfield are $1 per hour; maximum $6 per 24 hours. You may access all these lots from either side (north or south) of the terminal. You may pay with cash, a credit card or a check. If you have to lug your luggage very far, you may wish to rent a cart, but they are hard to come by, for $1.50 from the stands in baggage claim.

In addition, satellite lots around the airport have thousands more parking spaces. These lots run vans or buses to the airline curbsides and pick up returning passengers at ground transportation — eliminating that long walk back to the car when you're dead-tired from your trip.

Hartsfield's lots can fill up at peak travel times such as holidays, some weekends and whenever the airlines slash fares to whip up business. If all the airport lots are filled, you'll have to backtrack and park at one of the satellites. To avoid this delay, call the airport parking office, (404) 530-6725, before you leave and ask whether parking is adequate.

Satellite lots provide an additional 10,000 spaces. Here are some companies; call for directions. Ask about return procedures: Some companies note your returning flight and meet you outside ground transportation; others require you to call when you arrive.

Airport Valet Parking, $8 per day, (404) 761-4133.

Park Air Express, $6.75 per day, $5.75 per day with AAA membership or a business card; seventh day free, (404) 762-0966.

Park N Fly, $8.75 per day, (404) 763-3185.

Park N Fly Plus, daily rates: valet, covered: $13; valet, uncovered: $11; self-park: $7.75; (404) 761-0364, (404) 761-6220.

Park N Go, daily rates: covered: $8.75; uncovered: $7.50; (404) 669-9300.

Park N Ticket, $8.00 per day, (404) 669-3800.

Prestige Parking, $8 per day, (404) 559-4475.

Value Rent-a-Car, $7.50 per day, (404) 763-0220.

Rental Cars

Rental car counters are in the corridor

INSIDERS' TIP

Say what? The "L" in DeKalb (a county, an airport, an avenue and then some) is silent: Say "de-CAB." The Georgia towns of Vienna and Cairo are pronounced respectively "VHY-Anna" and "KAY-ro."

between north and south baggage claim. The numbers given are for the airport offices unless otherwise noted. From left to right, you'll find **Value**, (404) 763-0220, in College Park; **Alamo**, (404) 768-4161; **Dollar**, (404) 766-0244, in College Park; **Budget**, (404) 530-3000; **Hertz**, (404) 530-2925; **Avis**, (404) 530-2725; and **National**, (404) 530-2800. Check with individual companies for car rental policies and procedures.

Ground Transportation Directory

A lighted directory listing ground transportation alternatives is at the west curb, just before you exit the terminal. As you exit at west curb and walk away from the terminal, you'll encounter the following types of vehicles in this order: taxis, rental car shuttles, downtown and metro area buses, non-metro area buses, courtesy vehicles and prearranged limousines.

MARTA

The easiest, fastest and cheapest transportation into the city is the MARTA train. The station entrance is near baggage claim at the west curb, just before you reach the outside doors. You can enter the MARTA station from either the north or the south terminal. MARTA trains run from early in the morning until past midnight. The fare is $1.50, and an attendant is on hand to answer your questions. Stairs, escalators and elevators are available for getting from the airport entrance up to the platform. (For detailed information, please see the previous MARTA section in this chapter.)

Taxis

Taxis line up in the first lane at the west curb at Hartsfield. Follow the ground transportation signs. If you like, an agent outside will arrange for you to share a cab into the city.

Atlanta's approximately 2,000 cabs operate under a limited flat rate structure. From the airport to the downtown business and con-

vention district, the fare is $18 for one passenger; $10 each for two; and $8 each for three or more passengers all plus tax of 7 percent. The rate is not to exceed $24.

From the airport to the Buckhead business district, the fare is $28 for one passenger; $15 each for two; and $10 per person for three or more. The fare is not to exceed $30; add $1 to the fare for each additional Buckhead destination.

A flat fare is also used for travel within downtown and Buckhead districts. The flat rate is $5 for one person; $1 for each additional person. At these rates, the fare adds up fast. If four people take a taxi from the Westin Peachtree Plaza to the Omni hotel, the fare will be $8, even though they only traveled about five blocks.

The downtown business and convention district is bounded by Boulevard, 14th Street, Northside Drive and Memorial Drive (extended to Turner Field during Braves games). The Buckhead business district is harder to explain, but it's basically the heart of Buckhead, from Pharr Road up to Wieuca Road (that's just north of Lenox Square and Phipps Plaza).

For all other destinations, rates are $1.60 for the first seventh of a mile, 21¢ for each additional seventh of a mile and $1 per each extra passenger all of which include the tax. Per-hour waiting time is $15; use of additional space for luggage is $5. Add 7 percent sales tax to all fares. Disabled persons and senior citizens with ID who are residents of the City of Atlanta are eligible for a 20 percent discount off the total fare, and they must purchase a $5 card that is renewed on their birthday.

For more information on Atlanta's taxis or to report a problem, call (404) 658-7600. Some cab company numbers are **Atlanta Yellow Cab**, (404) 521-0200; **Buckhead Safety Cab**, (404) 233-1152; **Checker Cab**, (404) 351-1111; and **Style Taxi**, (404) 522-8294.

Hotel Courtesy Vehicles

Some 30 Atlanta hotels provide airport transportation for their guests. These hotels and their phone numbers are listed on the ground transportation directory.

Limousines and Hired Cars

If you'd prefer to arrive at your Atlanta destination in high style, you may wish to hire a limousine or sedan; some 127 limo companies serve Hartsfield Airport. Although it's best to reserve your car a day before your arrival, companies can often accommodate you with less notice.

Rates vary by company and by destination. Rates for a sedan to downtown are in the $55-to-$75 range; for a stretch limo, expect to pay about $65 to $90. Rates do not include tax and gratuity.

When you make your reservation, ask about pickup arrangements. Most drivers meet their arriving passengers outside in the ground transportation area. There's typically an additional charge of around $10 to be met at your arrival gate; international gate service may add $20 to $30.

Following are some Atlanta hired car companies: **Atlanta Limousine**, (404) 351-LIMO; **Carey Limousine**, (404) 223-2000; **First Corporate Limo**, (770) 933-9000; **Limousines Service**, (770) 414-8999; **London Livery Ltd.**, (404) 351-1996, (800) 351-1997 (rate includes gate service); and **Superior Limousine Inc.**, (770) 532-3115, (800) 932-3115 (specializing in service to north Georgia). All accept major credit cards. Check the Yellow Pages for a more complete listing.

Metro Area Shuttles

Here's a partial listing of airport shuttle services. Reservations may be required; call for complete information. When two rates are shown, the second is for a round trip.

AAA Airport Express offers scheduled service to Northlake-Airport, $17 one-way, $30 round-trip; Norcross, Gwinnett, Suwanee and Lawrenceville, $19, $35; Lake Lanier, Gainesville, Château Élan, Braselton and Athens, $25, $45. Call for departure times and reservations, (800) 354-7874; local (404) 767-2000. Shuttles run from 6 AM to 11:30 PM.

Airport Connection offers scheduled service: from the airport (6 AM to 11:30 PM); to the airport (6 AM to 5 PM; later by reservation). Rates are $19 one-way, $32 round-trip, to Galleria, Norcross and Perimeter Center.

Reservations are not required, and tickets may be purchased from the driver. Service departs on the half-hour to most locations. An add-on fee of $1 each way is required of credit card payees. Call (770) 457-5757, (800) 457-5756 for more information.

Atlanta Airport Shuttle offers scheduled service to all downtown hotels for $10 one-way, $17 round-trip; Buckhead, $15, $24; and Emory, $15, $24. Hours are 7 AM to 11 PM. Call for departure times and reservations, (404) 524-3400, (800) 842-2770.

Interstate Airport Jitney departs 54 times a day from Hartsfield between 8:15 AM and 11:15 PM to Perimeter Center, Windy Hill and Delk Road ($19 one-way, $32 round-trip). Call for special arrangements to Lake Lanier and other destinations. A 24-passenger minibus, limos and hired sedans are also available. Call (770) 932-6757.

Non-Metro Shuttles

These firms transport passengers out of town or out of state. When two rates are shown, the second is for a round trip.

Alabama Limousine departs for Anniston, Alabama, and Ft. McClellan weekdays at 11 AM and 9:30 PM, Saturday at 5 PM and Sunday at 8:30 PM. One-way fare is $25. Reservations are required, (800) 824-6463.

Groome Transportation offers service to Macon, $24, $42; Warner Robins, $27, $50; and Fort Valley, $45, $80. On weekdays shuttles depart on the hour from 9 AM to 9 PM. On Saturdays they depart every two hours between 9 AM and 9 PM. On Sunday shuttles depart every two hours between 9 AM and 3 PM and every hour from 3 to 9 PM. Reservations are not accepted. Shuttles depart from the second island ground transportation. Call (800) 537-7903 or (912) 741-3636.

Other Area Airports

DeKalb-Peachtree Airport
3915 Clairmont Rd. • (770) 936-5440

DeKalb Peachtree is a general aviation airport near I-85 in DeKalb County. Known by the initials PDK, the airport, built on the site of a World War I training base, is the second busiest in Georgia and the 50th busiest of its kind in the United States. The airport has no commercial or scheduled flights; most users are corporate aircraft. More than 1,000 people work at PDK, which contributes some $113 million annually to the local economy.

Private individuals can land at PDK; the tower telefrequency is 120.9. There is no landing fee, but ramp fees, if fuel is not purchased, and overnight fees, which vary by size of craft, are charged. Seven flight schools based at the airport provide lessons. For flight school numbers as well as the fixed base operator (FBO) numbers at PDK, call the number above.

Fulton County Airport — Brown Field
3952 Aviation Cir. • (404) 699-4200

This 600-acre general aviation facility, known locally as Charlie Brown, is owned by Fulton County. It has three active runways and is used by many domestic and international corporate aircraft and also by state and federal government planes. Like DeKalb-Peachtree Airport, Brown Field is available to private aircraft and charges no landing fees. Ramp fees, if fuel is not purchased, and overnight fees apply. The Charlie Brown Flying School, (404) 696-2233, gives lessons. The tower telefrequency is 118.5. The airport's location is convenient to I-20, Martin Luther King Jr. Drive and Fulton Industrial Boulevard.

Railways and Trailways

Amtrak
Brookwood Station, 1688 Peachtree St. N.W. • (404) 881-3060

Amtrak's long, silver trains stop at Brookwood Station. The station is at the corner of Deering Road, just north of the Peachtree overpass across the Downtown Connector. Famous Atlanta architect Neel Reid designed the building, which was the smaller of Atlanta's two passenger rail terminals and was once considered in the suburbs. In 1925, 142 passenger trains rolled through Brookwood each day.

Today Amtrak's Crescent line stops here. Atlanta enjoys daily service to and from New

York's Penn Station and daily service to and from New Orleans.

Here's the schedule for Amtrak's Atlanta service:

Atlanta to New York — Train leaves every day at 7:46 PM, arriving at New York's Penn Station the following day at 2:10 PM.

New York to Atlanta — Train leaves Penn Station every day at 2:45 PM, arriving in Atlanta the following day at 9:05 AM.

Atlanta to New Orleans — Train leaves at 9:25 AM, arriving in New Orleans at 8 PM.

New Orleans to Atlanta — Train leaves at 7:00 AM, arriving in Atlanta at 7:07 PM.

Arriving passengers should note that the Amtrak station is at a very busy corner — take care crossing the streets, especially if you're lugging lots of over packed bags. When you walk out of the Amtrak station and face Peachtree Street, downtown will be to your right; Buckhead will be to your left. If you're not being met and your destination is not nearby, you can take a cab (which you can easily get at the station) or take MARTA.

To take MARTA downtown from Brookwood Station, wait at the bus stop on the same side of the street and take the 23 Lenox/Arts Center MARTA bus southbound ($1.50 exact change; it runs frequently throughout the day and evening) to the Arts Center MARTA station. No transfer is necessary to board the train (southbound to downtown; northbound to Buckhead). You'll find more information about Marta detailed previously in the chapter.

Greyhound Bus Lines
232 Forsyth St. S.W. • (404) 584-1728, (800) 231-2222

Greyhound runs some 90 buses a day out of Atlanta. In addition to the main terminal which is downtown near the Garnett Street MARTA station, the company operates four other bus stations in the metro area.

Tickets may be purchased by phone with a credit card; however, you must allow two weeks to receive them by mail. To travel on shorter notice, you must make your reservations at a Greyhound terminal: For the nearest location, check the business pages of the phone book.

As the number of
international Atlantans
has grown, so has the
marketplace for
international products
and services.

International Atlanta

For the past 20 years, Atlanta has been billing itself as an International City, yet up until five years ago one would have been hard-pressed to find other than English-speaking shops anywhere in the city. Today, Atlanta truly is international with entire sections of town that can be claimed as Korean, Chinese or Hispanic. In fact, we've become so diverse that an ordinance was passed requiring signage in English as well as the clientele's language so that police officers and the fire department would be able to figure out just where they were supposed to show up when there was a problem.

Our city's excellent location as a transportation hub, its role as the economic capital of the South and its welcoming climate have made it a magnet for tourists and new residents alike, not only from the United States but also from all over the globe. As people from other nations have taken advantage of Atlanta's welcome, the city's demographic makeup has become increasingly international.

The Centennial Olympics in 1996 is thought to have encouraged folks from near and far to take up residence in our fair city and to bring their businesses with them — but we have no firm statistics on that as of yet. What we do know is that since the 1970s Atlanta has experienced a 425 percent increase in its foreign-born population and one in 10 people in metro Atlanta are foreign born, representing about 70 countries and speaking about 90 different languages. The Asian population is growing the fastest, and according to 1997 calculations from the Georgia State University Center for Applied Research in Anthropology, we have approximately 193,200 people of Asian descent, who, along with the Hispanic population, live mostly in DeKalb County. Gwinnett County is the second most populated county for foreign-born residents.

As the number of international Atlantans has grown to approximately 266,000 individuals, so has the marketplace for international products and services. The number and variety of businesses and social organizations each community supports is empirical evidence of its own particular tastes as well as a graphic demonstration of its buying power.

This chapter has been compiled with three groups of readers in mind: international visitors to our city, new Atlantans who have moved here from other countries and everyone who enjoys the excitement of learning about other cultures (without having to cross borders to do it). You'll find international shopping opportunities in Atlanta, currency exchange information and a sampling of some of the city's many multicultural social and educational groups. Atlanta area consulates of foreign governments are listed for the benefit of visitors who need to speak with a diplomatic representative of their home nation during their visit. International dining can be found in the various ethnic categories of our Restaurants chapter. There are about 10 foreign language papers published in our city, some of which are noted in our Media section. Many of these publications are available at the shops that attract a foreign-born clientele. Newspapers from all over the globe are distributed at some area newsstands.

Currency Exchange

If you're staying at a major hotel, ask the concierge to direct you to the nearest supplier of currency exchange services. Many banks offering same-day, on-site currency exchange are in the downtown area. Some branches that don't offer full-service currency exchange do sell dollars on demand. Call the numbers shown below for each bank's policies.

Thomas Cook Currency Services Inc. has three locations inside Hartsfield Airport, all on the international Concourse E. Call toll-free, (800) 287-7362 for specific information.

Two of the **American Express Travel Service** offices in Atlanta exchange currency: the Buckhead office in the Lenox Plaza Building, 184 Peachtree Road, (404) 262-7561 and at Perimeter Mall, 4400 Ashford Dunwoody Road, (770) 395-1305. For current rates, call (800) 525-7623.

First Union offers on-site currency exchange at its Midtown office, 999 Peachtree Street and also at downtown at 241 Peachtree Center. Call (800) 275-3862.

NationsBank offers on-site currency exchange at the NationsBank Plaza, 600 Peachtree Street. Call (404) 607-4850.

SouthTrust Bank sells dollars at all of its approximately 100 Atlanta area offices. Customers selling dollars may pick up their foreign currency the next day. Call (404) 853-5485.

SunTrust Bank offers on-site currency exchange at 10 offices, including its Five Points location at One Park Place. Call (404) 588-7226.

Wachovia offers on-site currency exchange at its Five Points location, 2 Peachtree Street, and at approximately 12 branch offices. Call (404) 332-5066.

FYI

Three area codes serve the metro Atlanta area: 404, 770 and 678. Whether you live on Peachtree Street or in New York City, you must dial the code to reach any number in the area. The difference? Outside the area, you must dial "1," then the area code and phone number; inside the area, you need only dial the area code followed by the phone number.

Consulates

The following is a list of nations with foreign offices in Atlanta. Some of these representatives are part-time foreign service officers who perform their duties from their residence or place of employment; others work from permanently staffed, full-time diplomatic offices. Call each office for more details.

Consulate General of Argentina, 245 Peachtree Ctr. Ave., Ste. 2101 • (404) 880-0805

Consulate General of Australia, 303 Peachtree St., Ste. 2920 • (404) 880-1700

Consulate of Austria, 10 N. Parkway Square, 4200 Northside Pkwy. N.W. • (404) 264-9858

Consulate of Belgium, 235 Peachtree St. N.E., Ste. 850 North Tower • (404) 659-2150

Consulate of Brazil, 229 Peachtree St. N.E. • (404) 521-0061

Consulate General of Canada, 1175 Peachtree St. N.E., 100 Colony Sq., Ste. 1700 • (404) 532-2000

China Council, 4160 Ancroft Cir., Norcross • (770) 449-6226

Consulate of Columbia, 3379 Peachtree Rd. N.E. • (404) 237-1045

Consulate of Costa Rica, 1870 The Exchange, Ste. 100 • (770) 951-7025

Honorary Consulate of Denmark, 1100 Spring St., Ste. 550 • (404) 876-5511

Honorary Consulate of Dominican Republic, 191 Peachtree St. • (404) 572-4814

Honorary Consulate of Finland, 9240 Huntcliff Tr. N.E. • (770) 993-6696

Consulate General of France, 285

Peachtree Ctr. Ave., Ste. 2800, Marquis II • (404) 522-4226

Consulate General of Germany, 285 Peachtree Ctr. Ave., Ste. 901 • (404) 659-4760

Consulate General of Great Britain, 245 Peachtree Center Ave., Ste. 2700, Marquis One • (404) 524-5856

Consulate of Greece, 3340 Peachtree Rd. N.E., Ste. 1670 • (404) 261-3313

Honorary Consulate of Guatemala, 4772 E. Conway Dr. N.W. • (404) 255-7019

Honorary Consulate of the Republic of Honduras, 3091 Chaparral Pl., Lithonia • (770) 482-1332

Hong Kong Association, 3390 Peachtree Rd. Ste. 1000 • (404) 238-0875

Consulate General of Iceland, 1677 Tullie Cir. N.E., Ste. 118 • (404) 321-0777

Indo-American Chamber of Commerce, P.O. Box 467333, Atlanta GA 30346 • (770) 395-6838

Consulate General of Israel, 1100 Spring St. N.W., Ste. 440 • (404) 875-7851

Honorary Consulate of Ireland, 191 Peachtree St. N.E., 21st Fl. • (404) 816-7977

Honorary Consulate of Italy, 755 Mt. Vernon Hwy., Ste. 270 • (404) 303-0503

Consulate General of Japan, 100 Colony Sq., Ste. 2000 • (404) 892-2700

Consulate General of Korea, 229 Peachtree St. N.E., Ste. 500 • (404) 522-1611

Consulate General of Liberia, 2265 Cascade Rd. S.W. • (404) 755-8539

Honorary Consulate of Luxembourg, 3343 Peachtree Rd. N.E. Ste. 1800 • (404) 264-2662

General Consulate of Mexico, 3220 Peachtree Rd. N.E. • (404) 266-2233

Consulate of The Netherlands, The Randstad Bldg., 2015 S. Park Pl. • (770) 937-7123

Honorary Consulate of Norway, 300 Northcreek, Bldg. 300, Ste. 650, 3715 Northside Pkwy. • (404) 239-0885

Consulate of Panama, 229 Peachtree Street N.E., Ste. 1209 • (404) 522-4114

Honorary Consulate of the Philippines, 950 E. Paces Ferry Rd., N.E. Ste. 3380 • (404) 239-5740

Consulate of the Republic of Sierra Leone West Africa, P.O. Box 831981, Stone Mountain GA 30083 • (404) 292-2009

Honorary Consulate of Spain, 1010 Huntcliff Tr., Ste. 3215 • (770) 518-2440

Consulate of Sweden, 1100 Peachtree St., Ste. 2000 • (404) 817-7797

Consulate General of Switzerland, 1275 Peachtree St. N.E., Ste. 425 • (404) 870-2000

Royal Thai Consulate, 3333 Cumberland Cir., Ste. 400 • (770) 988-3304

Taipei Economic & Cultural Office, 1349 W. Peachtree St., Ste. 1290 • (404) 872-0123

Honorary Consulate of the Republic of Turkey, 7155 Brandon Mill Rd. • (770) 913-0900

International Malls

Until fairly recently, Atlanta did not have geographically compact districts populated largely by a single immigrant community. Now, however, you can drive to specific parts of town and find apartment housing with resident managers who speak your language as well as locate shops that vend just the herb, vegetable or fabric popular in a specific country.

Buford Highway, for example, beginning at the crossroads of N. Druid Hills Road, is populated by people from Central and South America. From the Clairmont Road crossing on towards Interstate 285, the population changes to Asian peoples, first Vietnamese, then Korean and Chinese. You'll see billboards and shop signage in three or more languages at some locations. Mexican restaurants, Vietnamese videos, Chinese herbs, Spanish greeting cards and Asian foods of every variety bombard the senses. What a shopper's delight!

Asian

99 Ranch Market
5150 Buford Hwy. • (770) 458-8899

With a dazzling variety of fresh and packaged food and a sweets aisle (try a bag of White Rabbit creamy candy), this Asian market is small in comparison to others in the community but convenient.

Asian Square
5150 Buford Hwy. • no phone

You'll find 99 Ranch market (a full-size Asian supermarket detailed above), a bakery, jewelry store and a Vietnamese video store in this square.

Dido

2390 Chamblee-Tucker Rd., Chamblee
• (770) 455-3846
Dido's sells Japanese groceries, magazines and medicines in the heart of Atlanta's Asian community.

www.insiders.com

See this and many other **Insiders' Guide®** destinations online — in their entirety.

Visit us today!

Iwase Books

Around Lenox Center (next to Lenox Square/Rich's side)
• (404) 814-0462
Iwase Books offers thousands of Japanese books and magazines, plus videos, stationery and gifts.

Korea Town Mall

5302 Buford Hwy. • no phone
Korea Town Mall is home to a Korean video shop, gifts shops, a Sushi bar and a Chinese restaurant.

Momotaro Hair Salon

3209 Paces Ferry Rd. • (404) 261-7163
Momotaro's has Japanese-speaking stylists and clientele. Haircuts are $38 for women and $32 for men.

Northwoods Plaza

Buford Hwy. and Shallowford Rd.
• no phone
There are many international tenants at this strip mall including an herb store, an Asian fashion shop and an Oriental food market.

Oriental Mall

4166 Buford Hwy. just beyond Clairmont Rd. • (404) 982-0509
Formerly Outlet Square, this mall was purchased by Asians in 1997 and now almost all of the shops and restaurants primarily serve the Vietnamese shopper. An enormous Asian su-permarket (see the Hong Kong Super Market under "International" in this chapter), hair and nail salons, a furniture shop as well as legal and medical services are the major attractions. There is also an electronics store selling a vast array of Vietnamese videos and a shop with an extensive collection of fabrics for Vietnamese-style dresses.

Pinetree Plaza

5269 Buford Hwy.
• no phone
Another center with multinational shopping, Pinetree Plaza includes many Asian restaurants and a furniture store. Around the back is unassuming Kim's Pharmacy and Herb Store, which serves as the office from which Kim, a California-licensed acupuncturist, conducts his practice.

Tomato

2086 Cobb Pkwy., Smyrna
• (770) 933-0108
This Japanese grocery store sells canned goods, sake, fresh vegetables and fresh fish. The staff does not speak English.

Vietnamese Town Mall

4646 Buford Hwy. • no phone
Vietnamese restaurants, a nail supply boutique, a fashion store and other shops catering to the Vietnamese community can be found here.

British Isles

Irish Country Pine

511 E. Paces Ferry Rd. • (404) 261-7924
Irish Country Pine imports fine furniture, decorative items and more.

Irish Crystal Co.

3168 Peachtree Rd. N.E. • (404) 266-3783
Irish Crystal Co. imports Irish crystal and fine bed and table linens.

INSIDERS' TIP

The international publications listed in our Media chapter are a good way to learn more about the many facets of multicultural Atlanta.

Photo: The World of Coca-Cola Atlanta

More than 200 countries sell Coca-Cola.

Taste of Britain
73 S. Peachtree St., Norcross
• (770) 242 8585
This shop specializes in British groceries and gifts as well as Scottish tartans.

Caribbean

Carnival Grocery
5616-D Redan Rd., Stone Mountain
• (770) 469-3119
In addition to selling groceries, this Caribbean grocery store offers Jamaican foods for take-out. Jerk chicken, ox-tail curried goat, fresh produce and salted meats are popular items.

Royal Caribbean Bakery
4859 Memorial Dr. • (404) 299-7714
Royal Caribbean Bakery sells breads and

main dishes (including jerk chicken and brown fish stew) to go; it also sells groceries and spices.

Hispanic

Fiesta Food
2581 Piedmont Rd. N.E. • (404) 237-7308
Specializing in packaged, canned and fresh produce for the Hispanic community, Fiesta Food is also close to Coco Loco (see our Restaurants chapter).

Roland Center
3640-54 Shallowford Rd. • no phone
Just north of its intersection with Buford Highway, Roland Center has several Latin American businesses including a bakery, grocery and music shop that offers CDs, tapes, videos and greeting cards in Spanish.

Indian

Sona Imports
1707 Church St., Decatur • (404) 292-7979
Baked goods, bulk foods, health and beauty aids and Indian videos are available at this shop in downtown Decatur.

Taj Mahal Imports
1612 Woodcliff Dr. (behind the Chick-fil-A)
• (404) 321-5940
Taj Mahal Imports retails thousands of products from India, including religious statues, cookware, books, magazines, newspapers, videos, incense, spices and much more.

Texas Sari Sapne
1594 Woodcliff Dr. • (404) 633-7274
At the intersection of Briarcliff and N. Druid Hills roads (entrance on both roads), Texas Sari Sapne features Indian apparel, kitchen appliances and more.

International

DeKalb Farmers Market
3000 E. Ponce de Leon Ave., Decatur
• (404) 377-6400
DeKalb Farmers Market, the oldest of the truly international food markets, attracts busloads of folks from Alabama, Tennessee — even Florida. All mingle with the locals searching for exotic spices, canned goods, fresh fish, breads and pastries made on the premises, as well as regional and imported vegetables and fruit. Employees come from every corner of the globe and wear badges listing the languages they speak.

Harry's Farmers Markets
2025 Satellite Pt., Duluth • (770) 416-6900
1180 Upper Hembree Rd., Roswell
• (770) 664-6300
70 Powers Ferry Rd., Marietta
• (770) 578-4400
Harry's Farmers Markets are a gourmet's dream-come-true, filled with delicacies from around the world. From the commonplace to the exotic, including fish, cheese, wine, flowers, coffee and gourmet meals to go, at Harry's you can eat well and grow large. Also see our Shopping chapter for more farmers markets and Harry's take-out shops, Harry's In A Hurry.

Hong Kong Super Market
Buford Hwy. at Oriental Mall
• (404) 325-3999
The Hong Kong Super Market is as large as a Kroger or Publix. Japanese dried mushrooms, Vietnamese fish paste, Chinese noodles, fresh veggies, raw fish, flip- flop slippers, pots and pans, ginseng — you name it, Hong Kong Market has it. The market is well-staffed by folks who speak all manner of Asian dialects as well as English.

International Super Markets Buford Highway Farmer's Market
5660 Buford Hwy., Doraville
• (770) 458-2296
This market stocks a variety of fresh produce, meats and fish. You'll find exotic items from all over, gourmet coffee and traditional grocery store fare.

Las Palmeras
368 Fifth Street N.E. • (404) 872-0846
For six years, Las Palmeras has specialized in selling packaged, canned and fresh Cuban food.

Nayarit Mexican American Food Store
558 Boulevard S.E. (in Grant Park)
• (404) 622-2187
Aside from fresh produce and canned foods, Nayarit sells ready-to-eat tacos and Cuban sandwiches. The staff does not speak English.

Educational and Business Organizations

Alliance Francaise d'Atlanta Inc.
1360 Peachtree St. N.E., Ste. 200
• (404) 875-1211
Founded in Paris in 1883, Alliance Francaise has more than 1,200 chapters in 120 nations. The Atlanta chapter, one of 150 in the United

Photo: The Japan America Society

The Japan America Society of Georgia hosts many events
to educate Georgians about Japanese customs.

States, was founded in 1912 to encourage the study of the French language and culture and to promote friendly relations between French-speaking people and Americans.

In addition to a full range of French language courses, the Alliance has a library of 3,500 volumes and sponsors many special activities, which include art exhibits, recitals, annual trips to French-speaking countries and a big bash to celebrate Bastille Day, July 14.

American-Israel Chamber of Commerce
1100 Spring St., Ste. 410 • (404) 874-6970

Like most other chambers of commerce this one is dedicated primarily to enhancing business. In this case the Chamber facilitates the development of business between the Southeastern United States and Israel. Many members, however, join so that they might network among themselves. There is a social as well as educational element to all Chamber of Commerce gatherings since most include a speaker and refreshments. The American-Israel Chamber also sponsors trade trips to Israel.

Atlanta Hispanic Chamber of Commerce
2964 Peachtree Rd. N.W., Ste. 350
• (404) 264-0879

In 1997 this Chamber of Commerce sponsored its ninth annual awards honoring Hispanic business people making a mark in Atlanta. With Hispanic buying power in Georgia of approximately $2.7 billion in '97, it's not difficult to understand why this group has approximately 400 members.

Atlanta Virtuosi Foundation, Inc.
P.O. Box 77047, Atlanta GA 30357
• (770) 938-8611

The objective of this group is to preserve the musical traditions of the Hispanic world.

INSIDERS' TIP

Atlanta may not have a San Francisco-style Chinatown or anything like New York's Little Italy, but you can drive Buford Highway for miles and see only shops that cater to the Asian community.

See our Festivals and Events chapter for details on presentations and festivals sponsored by the Foundation including the Annual Hispanic Festival of the Arts.

Berlitz Language Center
Lenox Tower, 3400 Peachtree Rd. N.E.
• (404) 261-5062

The Atlanta office of the worldwide Berlitz Language Centers offers beginning and intermediate courses in Spanish, French, German, Italian, Japanese, Portuguese and English. Taught by native speakers possessing a college education (or the foreign equivalent), the center's educational opportunities range from classes with no more than 10 students, semiprivate instruction for two persons or individual instruction. The Total Immersion method is designed to instill conversational fluency in a new language in two to six weeks.

The Berlitz method teaches vocabulary and grammar as they occur in context while the student hears and speaks only the new language.

British American Business Group
1199 Euclid Ave. • (404) 681-2224

British American Business Group (BABG) strives to open lines of communication (business and social) between British companies doing business in Georgia and U.S. companies transacting business in Great Britain. The Canadian American Society and the Australian American Chamber of Commerce are also handled out of these offices. These groups serve as affinity gatherings for folks who just want to have fun with like-minded individuals. Social get-togethers from formal balls to pub crawls are scheduled throughout the year for each group.

Georgia Council for International Visitors
3340 Peachtree Rd. N.E. • (404) 240-0042

The Georgia Council for International Visitors arranges professional and cultural exchanges among international visitors and U.S. citizens. The group's services include arranging host families for international visitors, conducting an eight-week discussion group on world affairs and holding monthly meetings of the International Businesswomen's Network.

German American Chamber of Commerce
3340 Peachtree Rd. • (404) 239-9494

The exclusive purpose of this Chamber is to facilitate business between the United States and Germany. The Chamber has 450 members who attend luncheons, galas and make alliances through the Chamber with delegations from the German business sector.

Goethe-Institut Atlanta
Colony Square, Plaza Level, 1197
Peachtree St. N.E. • (404) 892-2388

The Atlanta institute is one of 11 U.S. locations of the Munich-based Goethe-Institut that was created in 1951 to promote the German language and intercultural exchanges. It is supported by the German government.

Goethe-Institut Atlanta offers German language courses at levels from beginning through advanced. Its library, containing more than 10,000 volumes, is free and open to the public. The Institut's programs include art exhibits, films, lectures and performances. Many special events are free, and visitors enjoy free parking in the Colony Square garage. The Institut also organizes language courses in Germany. Call the Institut for a calendar of events and more information.

Irish Social and Information Club
2769 Meadow Dr., Marietta
• (404) 264-3444

This group helps newcomers from Ireland settle into life in Atlanta. It holds regular monthly meetings and pointedly notes that "social" comes before "information" in its name; the party's the thing. Call for more information.

The Japan-America Society of Georgia
225 Peachtree St. South Tower, Ste. 710
• (404) 524-7399

In 1980 a group of business and academic leaders formed The Japan-America Society of Georgia to increase knowledge among Georgians about Japanese culture; today it has more than 1,000 members. The society sponsors many programs throughout the year to enhance Georgians' understanding of Japan's customs and people and to provide Japanese visitors with an opportunity to make friends with Georgians. JapanFest, held each autumn, is a series of entertainment and educational events. Classes in Japanese arts, such as flower arranging and lantern making, are scheduled throughout the year. In 1990 the society hosted a dinner for Toshiki Kaifu on the occasion of the first-ever visit to the South by a Japanese Prime Minister.

Korean Association of Greater Atlanta
5775 Buford Hwy. • (770) 458-7798

This is where the Korean community goes for information and help. The association organized the Korean Community Center (at the same address) for medical, social and senior citizens assistance, transportation, court interpreters and other aid to the Korean community, which is believed to encompass approximately 40,000 in metro Atlanta.

League of United Latin American Citizens (LULAC)
Concilio 950 de Atlanta, P.O. Box 12104, Atlanta GA 30355 • (770) 924-3440

If you're looking for information about social services and existing laws concerning the Hispanic community, this would be a good place to start.

Foreign Language/Music Radio Programs

Friday Night Live with Ken Rye & Ken Batie
WCLK 91.9 FM • (404) 880-WCLK

Ken Rye and Ken Batie talk and play Latin music and jazz on Fridays from 9 PM until 1 AM.

Radio Free Georgia
WRFG 89.3 FM • (404) 523-3471

WRFG is Atlanta's only community-operated station. It has extensive international programming. Call the station to have a one-page program guide faxed to you. Here are a few of the highlights, all of which are subject to change without notice. Many of the DJs work for gratis — if they leave, so goes the program.

Music from India: 4 to 8 PM, Saturday
Serenata Latina: 8 to 11 PM, Saturday
The Reggae Mix: 11 PM to 1 AM, Saturday
The Celtic Show: 1 to 3 PM, Sunday

Accommodations

The big cotton expositions of 1881, 1887 and 1895 laid the foundations for the modern-day convention business that has helped make Atlanta's hotel trade a vital part of the city's economic fabric. Today, the hospitality industry employs approximately 115,000 workers in Fulton County and accounts for $215 million in local taxes alone.

A building boom in the 1980s resulted in many new hotels, and the 1996 Olympics encouraged even more construction. And although hotels fill up during major conventions such as the Bobbin Show, there are plenty of slow times when hotels are more than willing to cut their rates dramatically.

Subsequently, the cost of an average night's lodging and food here is surprisingly economical compared to other major U.S. cities. In a 1997 report from Hendersonville, Tennessee-based Smith Travel Research ranking the cost of a night's lodging in the top-25 U.S. markets, Atlanta's average rate was below that of 21 other cities. It's rate was slightly more than half the cost of a room in New York City, the most expensive market. On the other hand, it's easy to spend a bundle for a deluxe stay in Atlanta's best hotels.

In the listing that follows, hotels and motels are arranged by area: Downtown; Midtown; Buckhead; Northeast Expressway/Emory; Northwest Expressway; Airport and the areas beyond Atlanta, including Barrow County, Cobb County, DeKalb County, Douglas County, Fulton County, Gwinnett County and Hall County. When a hotel has a toll-free reservations number, it is included in the listing along with its local number.

All Atlanta hotel accommodations (at least the ones we list) provide guests with a choice of smoking or nonsmoking rooms. They are also all handicapped-accessible since that is the law of the land these days. Thinking about bringing along your pets? Even The Ritz-Carlton Buckhead says there is a no-pet policy. If Elizabeth Taylor, however, wanted her pet lap dog to keep her company, we think exceptions would be made. For the rest of us, though, it's best to leave the kitty at home and board the bulldog.

Price Code

Each hotel's listing includes a symbol indicating a price range for a one-night stay, mid-week, double-occupancy excluding tax. All hotels accept major credit cards unless otherwise noted.

$	Less than $50
$$	$50 to $100
$$$	$100 to $150
$$$$	$150 and more

Note: Pricing information was provided by the hotels and is presented as a guide to help you approximate likely costs. Rates are often higher during major conventions or other peak travel times. On weekends and whenever business travel slows down, even the best hotels may cut their rates dramatically — it pays to shop around. Look for the lowest rates during the winter months on weeks when no major convention is in town. Off-peak specials can easily take the rate into the next lower price category.

In the city of Atlanta and in Fulton County, hotels charge a 7 percent room tax that is in addition to the usual 6 percent sales tax, for a total tax of 13 percent on the cost of lodging. If that seems like a lot to you, please remember that some of that tax goes to attracting people like you to our city through advertising campaigns, entertaining the press and sending boosters around the world with hopes of stimulating businesses to move here. Such activities are partially responsible for keeping Atlanta's economy booming. It also helps educate the children that may one day serve you in the hospitality industry.

Our goal is to present a good cross-section of the various types of hospitality properties available around Atlanta. Due to space limitations, we cannot list every Atlanta location for each national chain. If you prefer to lodge with a particular chain but don't see a hotel listed that's convenient for you, ask the company's central 800-number operator about other Atlanta locations. Unlike other chapters in this guide, we're breaking this one chapter into more specific geographic locations for your convenience.

For more accommodations options, be sure to see our Bed and Breakfasts chapter.

Hotels

Atlanta

Downtown

Interstates 85, 75 and 20 all come together where you see the gold dome of the Capitol Building. From here north to 5th and Peachtree streets and fanning out east to Boulevard Drive and west to Northside Drive is referred to as downtown Atlanta.

Atlanta Downtown Travelodge
$$ • 311 Courtland St. N.E.
• (404) 659-4545, (800) 578-7878

Two blocks off Peachtree Street, this family-owned and -operated 71-room hotel is near the Marriott Marquis and Atlanta Hilton. Its amenities include a free continental breakfast and daily newspaper; cable TV with HBO; in-room coffee maker; free covered parking; and a heated outdoor pool. The hotel is just off the Downtown Connector at the Courtland Street Exit and within walking distance of Macy's.

Atlanta Hilton and Towers
$$$$ • 255 Courtland St. N.E.
• (404) 659-2000, (800) HILTONS

The 30-story downtown Hilton has 1,224 rooms (including 40 suites), a health club with an outdoor pool and four outdoor tennis courts. The top three guest floors comprise the private Hilton Towers, whose lounge offers complimentary continental breakfast in the morning and

hot hors d'oeuvres in the evening. Atop the hotel are the nightclub Another World and the renowned fine dining restaurant Nikolai's Roof (see our Restaurants chapter); downstairs is the South Pacific cuisine of Trader Vic's.

Atlanta Marriott Marquis
$$$$ • 265 Peachtree Center Ave. N.E.
• (404) 521-0000, (800) 228-9290

This is the hotel we take our houseguests to see. Just park the car in the circular entry (ask permission of the staff before you leave the vehicle: Tell them you want to go and gawk), take the escalator up one level and just look up and gasp. Suspended as far up as the eye can see is a Japanese-kite style work of art that seems to float for miles above within the 500-foot open atrium. Throughout the hotel are 25,000 plants, which lend a softening touch to this otherwise high-tech environment. The John Portman-designed 47-story Marquis offers 32 elevators, two of which travel at 1,000 feet per minute, and a few of them are glass enclosed for those of us who enjoy what feels like a near death experience to some. Instead of being aligned, the floors are offset producing an effect rather like a fan unfolding. Each floor has windows in the corridors offering great views of the city.

The 1,674-room Marquis is Atlanta's largest hotel and has received AAA's Four-Diamond Award. It has 150,000 square feet of function space, five restaurants and 10 bars. There is also a health club (complimentary for guests) with an indoor/outdoor heated swimming pool. The hotel is connected directly to MARTA via Peachtree Center.

Atlanta Renaissance Hotel Downtown
$$$$ • 590 W. Peachtree St. N.W.
• (404) 881-6000, (800) 468-3571

The 25-story Renaissance is just east of the I-75/85 connector in the northern part of the downtown district; it's actually closer to Midtown. The hotel has 504 rooms, two restaurants and an outdoor pool. Guests on the Renaissance Club floors receive deluxe accommodations and amenities, including a complimentary continental breakfast and nightly hors d'oeuvres. The North Avenue MARTA station is just up the street.

Comfort Inn Hotel Downtown Atlanta

$$ • 101 International Blvd. N.E.
• (404) 524-5555, (800) 535-0707

This 260-room property is convenient to the Apparel, Merchandise and Inforum marts, and it's adjacent to Centennial Olympic Park where the Arts Festival of Atlanta is held (see our Festivals and Events chapter). On-site parking, a restaurant, a lounge and an outdoor pool are among the hotel's amenities.

Courtyard Downtown Atlanta

$$ • 175 Piedmont Ave. N.E.
• (404) 659-2727

On Piedmont Avenue just off the Downtown Connector (the merged I-75/85), this Courtyard has 211 rooms and suites, an outdoor pool and a fitness center. The hotel offers limited convention and banquet services for up to 25 people. This is an enclosed building primarily attracting more of a business clientele than its sister hotel, the

Marriott Fairfield. It has more upscale furnishings, a coffee maker, an iron and voice mail in each room .

Days Inn Atlanta/Downtown

$$$ • 300 Spring St. N.W. • (404) 523-1144

Across from the Apparel, Inforum and Merchandise marts, this 263-room hotel offers remote-control cable TV with HBO and an outdoor pool. Kids 17 and younger stay free.

Hampton Inn Atlanta

$$ • 759 Washington St. • (404) 658-1961, (800) HAMPTON

You can't get much closer to big-league action than this 87-room hotel just up the street from the home of the Braves. The hotel has an outdoor pool and a weight room and is convenient to downtown, the Georgia Capitol, City Hall, Zoo Atlanta and the Georgia State MARTA station. It is just off Interstate 20. Guests enjoy complimentary continental breakfasts and free local phone calls.

Hyatt Regency Atlanta

$$$$ • 265 Peachtree St. N.E.
• (404) 577-1234, (800) 233-1234

If you had moved to Atlanta in the '60s, the bold blue dome of the Hyatt Regency would have been the most dominant structure of Atlanta's skyline. It symbolized the brash city's enchantment with the future. Even now, though it's overshadowed by taller buildings, the John Portman-designed Hyatt Regency and its glowing UFO-shaped top remain among the city's best-known landmarks.

The 23-story open atrium, a stunning architectural first when the hotel opened in 1967, is still beautiful today with its space-age glass elevators gracefully zipping up and down, a concept that has been copied throughout the world. In the Avanzare restaurant you can savor Italian cuisine while you gaze at exotic fish in the 1,800-gallon salt water aquarium. Beneath the blue dome is the revolving Polaris restaurant and cocktail lounge. Nearby buildings on three sides now limit the view from the Polaris, but it's still a great meeting place and a lot of fun when you get a glimpse of Stone Mountain as the bar swings past an adjacent structure. The hotel has 1,264 guest rooms and 285,000 square feet of function space; it's served by the Peachtree Center MARTA station.

In an adjoining building a 30,000-square-foot ballroom, a 40,000-square-foot exhibit hall and a 19,750-square-foot conference center help make up the complex .

Marriott Fairfield Inn

$$ • 175 Piedmont Ave. N.E.
• (404) 659-7777

Run by the same folks as the Courtyard Downtown Atlanta (mentioned previously), the Marriott Fairfield Inn shares the same address, parking lot, outdoor pool and fitness center with its sister facility. An exterior corridor hotel, the Fairfield Inn has 242 rooms and suites and banquet services for 35.

FYI

Three area codes serve the metro Atlanta area: 404, 770 and 678. Whether you live on Peachtree Street or in New York City, you must dial the code to reach any number in the area. The difference? Outside the area, you must dial "1," then the area code and phone number; inside the area, you need only dial the area code followed by the phone number.

Omni Hotel at CNN Center

$$$$ • Marietta St. at Techwood Dr.
• (404) 659-0000, (800) THE OMNI

The Omni Hotel is inside CNN Center and adjacent to Georgia World Congress Center, the Georgia Dome, MARTA and within walking distance of the headquarters of *The Atlanta Journal-Constitution*. It has 465 deluxe rooms and suites and 40,000 square feet of meeting space. Bugatti is a fine dining restaurant serving northern Italian cuisine (see our Restaurants chapter). Within CNN Center are restaurants, shops, a six-screen movie theater and the always-bustling CNN newsrooms. Stay at the Omni and you'll have celebrity neighbors: Media tycoon Ted Turner and his wife Jane Fonda keep a luxury apartment in CNN Center when they're not spending time at their Buffalo ranch in Wyoming or whisking up to New York to confer with the folks at Time Warner, Ted's partners in the communications business.

Paschal's Motor Hotel

$$ • 830 Martin Luther King Jr. Dr. S.W.
• (404) 577-3150

Five minutes west of downtown near the Georgia Dome and Atlanta University Center, Paschal's is an important part of Atlanta's history. Begun as a modest restaurant opened by brothers James and Robert Paschal, it eventually became a large restaurant and a 120-room hotel (see our Restaurants chapter). Today it caters mainly to Clark Atlanta University students who rent on a monthly basis. Only two floors are available to guests other than the students. Paschal's is a nerve center of Atlanta's African-American community; it's said that much political history has taken place over the restaurant's famous fried chicken. Many R&B legends have played its Le Carousel Lounge.

Radisson Hotel Atlanta

$$ • 165 Courtland St. • (404) 659-6500, (800) 333-3333

One block from Peachtree Center, the 754-

room Radisson features an indoor pool, a business center and a fully equipped health club. The hotel has 60,000 square feet of meeting space and offers two-level hospitality suites for entertaining.

The Ritz-Carlton Atlanta
$$$$ • 181 Peachtree St. N.E.
• (404) 659-0400, (800) 241-3333

Luxury is always the order of the day at the highly rated Ritz. Oil paintings and Persian rugs adorn the lobby; each of the 447 rooms and suites has a bay window. This elegant hotel (and its mate, The Ritz-Carlton Buckhead) are favorites of visiting celebrities. Tea is served each afternoon in The Lobby Lounge and The Bar; The Restaurant serves award-winning French cuisine. (See our Restaurants chapter.)

The Suite Hotel at Underground
$$$ • 54 Peachtree St. N.E.
• (404) 223-5555, (800) 477-5549

On the Peachtree Street level at the west end of Underground Atlanta, this is downtown's only all-suite hotel. The building dates from 1916. Each one of the 157 suites includes a marble bath, two cable TVs with movies and three telephones; some suites feature whirlpool tubs. You can't beat the location for convenience: It's adjacent to all the shopping and fun at Underground, directly across Peachtree Street from the Five Points MARTA station and close to the Capitol and state, county and city office buildings.

The Westin Peachtree Plaza
$$$ • 210 Peachtree St. N.W.
• (404) 659-1400, (800) 228-3000

The amazing John Portman-designed Peachtree Plaza opened in 1976 and for years was the tallest hotel in the world (it's still the tallest hotel in the United States). Within the 73-story glass cylinder are 1,068 rooms including six bilevel super-suites suitable for entertaining up to 150 guests. The hotel includes three restaurants and an indoor/outdoor pool with health club facilities.

Even if you don't stay here, you owe yourself a drink in the rotating Sun Dial Lounge (see our Restaurants and Nightlife chapters). The ride up — nonstop to the 71st floor in-

side a glass elevator on the outside of the building — is the closest most people ever come to being fired from a cannon. The drinks are pricey, but the view is priceless. There's a $3 charge per person to visit the lounge/observation tower. The Peachtree Plaza is served by the Peachtree Center MARTA station.

Midtown

When the landscape changes from mainly tall office buildings to apartments and lovely renovated homes, you'll know you are in Midtown. Unofficially it begins around 5th and Peachtree streets and continues north past the High Museum to Peachtree Road, meeting West Peachtree Street at a fork just opposite The Temple. Eastwards Midtown crosses Piedmont Road and continues over until Ponce de Leon Avenue. It's bounded on the west by I-85.

Atlanta Marriott Suites Midtown
$$$ • 35 14th St. N.W. • (404) 876-8888, (800) 228-9290

Each of the 254 suites in this 18-story Marriott has a living room, a king-size bed and a marble bath with separate tub and shower, two remote-controlled TVs, two dual-line telephones, a refrigerator and a wet bar. Complimentary coffee is served each morning. The health club has a whirlpool and an indoor/outdoor pool. The hotel is convenient to Colony Square, Woodruff Arts Center, One Atlantic Center, the AT&T building and numerous restaurants and nightclubs.

Cheshire Motor Inn
$ • Cheshire Bridge Rd. • (404) 872-9628, (800) 827-9628

At the edge of Midtown, the Cheshire Motor Inn is inexpensive and no frills but right in the heart of things if you have to go downtown, uptown or out-of-town and are on a tight budget. Located just off I-85 (and almost at the junction of Ga. 400), Cheshire Motor Inn, a family-run operation for all of its 35 years, has seen the neighborhood through all its ups and downs. At the moment, Cheshire Bridge Road is both funky and nice: funky because numerous strip clubs and gay bars are found scattered amongst some of Atlanta's nicest and most popular restaurants including San Gennaro, Nino's and Nakato (see our Restaurants chapter). Cheshire Bridge also has more than its fair share of Thai restaurants. At this inn, you can drive your car right to your room and if you pick one toward the back end of the complex, when you go out your door you'll have a view of towering pines, kudzu (see our close-up in the Neighborhoods and Real Estate chapter), and the handsomely landscaped backyards of a few snazzy Morningside homes.

Courtyard by Marriott Midtown
$$ • 1132 Techwood Dr. N.W.
• (404) 607-1112, (800) 321-2211

The Midtown Courtyard is off 14th Street on the Georgia Tech side of the Downtown Connector. The hotel has an outdoor pool and cable TV with HBO; it also offers a complimentary shuttle service to the Midtown MARTA station, Georgia Tech and the downtown marts.

Days Inn — Midtown Peachtree Street
$$ • 683 Peachtree St. N.E.
• (404) 874-9200, (800) 329-7466

Frankly, my dear, this 12-story, 138-room Days Inn is right beside the Georgian Terrace where the stars of *Gone With the Wind* stayed during its gala 1939 world premiere. It was built in 1925, and its location — directly across Peachtree from the Fox — is especially convenient for those in town to attend performances at the great theater. Numerous restaurants and bars are close-by; for spicy Caribbean food, try Bridgetown Grill, 689 Peachtree (see our Restaurants chapter). A complimentary continental breakfast is offered; guest parking is $6 per day with unlimited in/out privileges for guests who give a deposit and receive a parking card.

Four Seasons
$$$ • 75 14th St. N.E. • (404) 881-9898, (800) 952-0702

Formerly the Continental Grand, this Four Seasons hotel has retained all that was grand: In the three-story lobby, light from the 10-foot-high Baccarat chandelier plays across the rose-colored Spanish marble walls around the broad grand staircase. A lounge on the mezzanine serves cocktails and afternoon high tea. The Cafe is a sit-down, white tablecloth restaurant that serves breakfast, lunch and dinner from early morning till 11 PM every day. It also has a Japanese breakfast of rice and fish. The menu is "international with a Southern flair." The Ballroom showcases a skyline view from its 6,000-square-foot open terrace. The health club boasts the latest exercise equipment, and its gorgeous indoor lap pool suggests a Roman bath.

The hotel occupies the first 20 floors of The Grand, a striking, 51-story skyscraper designed by the Atlanta firm Rabun Hatch & Associates. Above the hotel are offices and luxury condos.

The Granada Suite Hotel
$$$ • 1302 W. Peachtree St.
• (404) 876-6100, (800) 548-5631

Built in 1924, the Granada has a charming Spanish Colonial style not often seen in Atlanta. Originally designed as a garden apartment building, it underwent an award-winning renovation in 1986 and is now an all-suite hotel. Suites feature a full-size kitchen with a wet bar, refrigerator, microwave and coffee maker. Enjoy a daily complimentary continental breakfast and complimentary cocktails on weekday evenings. An evening courtesy shuttle ferries guests to Midtown and downtown restaurants and clubs; the Arts Center MARTA station is right across the street.

The Highland Inn
$$ • 644 N. Highland Ave.
• (404) 874-5756

Tucked away in the heart of the Virginia-Highland nightlife and shopping district, this three-story, 105-room inn has the flavor of a European hostel. Each room is furnished differently, with a variety of paintings and accents. Guests are invited to help themselves to a continental breakfast of pastries and croissants, served each morning in the lobby. Rooms include cable TV, air-conditioning units, radiators and private bathrooms.

Accommodations around Atlanta range from intimate
bed and breakfasts to grand resorts.

Holiday Inn Atlanta Central
**$$ • 418 Armour Dr. • (404) 873-4661,
(800) 282-8222**

Formerly the Lanier Plaza Hotel, this Holiday Inn is just 5 miles from the hustle and bustle of downtown. More like a rural hacienda than a major metropolitan hotel, there are more than 34,000 square feet of meeting and banquet spaces as well as 346 rooms spread out around a large patio pool area with adjacent reflecting pool, fountain and lush garden. Fifteen suites have fireplaces, whirlpools and wet bars. The 120-seat Chantilly Goodtime Grill and the Reflections Lounge, a 40-seat facility, handle a mostly business crowd who arrive by airport shuttle or car. Parking is abundant right on the grounds.

Residence Inn by Marriott — Midtown
**$$$ • 1041 W. Peachtree St. N.W.
• (404) 872-8885, (800) 331-3131**

Here's a convenient location: on West Peachtree (one way, northbound) between the Downtown Connector and the Midtown MARTA station. West Peachtree and the parallel Spring Street (one way, southbound) are nearly always quick routes between downtown and Midtown. Each of the 66 suites has a fully equipped kitchen and cable TV with HBO. A complimentary continental breakfast is served daily.

The hotel has a terrific landmark: It's right behind the giant broadcast tower that beams out the signal for WTBS Channel 17, the original cable SuperStation.

Regency Suites Hotel
**$$$ • 975 W. Peachtree St. at 10th St.
• (404) 876-5003, (800) 642-3629**

Each of the Regency's 96 suites includes a microwave-equipped kitchen, cable TV with HBO and a living room with a queen-size sleeper sofa. In addition to a free continental breakfast daily, the hotel serves a complimentary "lite fare" dinner Monday through Thursday evenings. The location is superb: Downtown and

The Georgia Lottery

We think you hit it lucky just by being in Atlanta where it's easy to find a job and even easier to start a business. But if getting rich quickly is your dream, spend a buck or two on any of the eight games in the state lottery and your number could come in.

In Georgia where churches outnumber billboards (well, maybe not), getting legalized gambling past the Legislature, where the subject of a lottery had been kicked

 Close-up

around for years, was no easy matter. Finally, in 1992 after a tough campaign by pro- and anti-lottery forces, voters proved at the polls in a statewide referendum that they supported a lottery. The first "scratch-off" game tickets went on sale on June 29, 1993 and first-day sales

topped out at $13 million. The first-week sales brought in $52 million.

In August 1993, the "Ca$h 3" daily numbers game debuted and continues today along with Fantasy 5, The Big Game, Quick Cash, Cash 4 and Powerball.

In its first year, Lotto Georgia had 30 jackpot winners who claimed more than $135 million in prizes. Another 5.4 million players won a share of $57.5 million.

Georgia Lottery's proceeds are invested in education. In the first 18 months of play, the lottery's contribution to education was $221 million ahead of the General Assembly's projections. By the end of its second fiscal year, the Georgia Lottery Corp. had contributed $863 million to education. By July of 1997 the lottery had sold $5.9 billion in tickets of which $2 billion has been spent on HOPE college scholarships, prekindergarten programs for 4-year-olds and for computers in the schools. It is anticipated that a negotiated agreement in mid-1997 with two of the Lottery's vendors will save $93 million, profits earmarked for educational programs.

The following is presented only as an informal introduction to the games of the Georgia Lottery. New games are added periodically, and old ones are abandoned.

For the official rules and claims procedures, see the back of your playslip or game card. A few instant games cost $2 per ticket; otherwise, tickets for all Georgia Lottery games are $1 each (there is no sales tax on lottery tickets). Only persons 18 or older may buy Georgia Lottery tickets.

There are two basic types of Georgia Lottery games: instant games and on-line games.

Instant Games

These "scratch-off" tickets are sold under a variety of names and the place where you buy your tickets will have a display explaining each game and how it works. Just pick your game and tell the lottery retailer how many tickets you want. Instructions right on the ticket will explain how to win; scratch off the covering from the gray area and see if this is your lucky day. Instant games are sold wherever you see the "Georgia Lottery" sign.

— continued on next page

On-line Games

These are "the numbers" games. You can choose your own numbers or let the computer choose them for you: Just mark the QP box on the playslip, or ask for a Quik Pik and tell the retailer which game you're playing (if you don't specify, he or she will likely assume you're playing "big lotto," as the weekly game is sometimes called). Only retailers with the "Lotto Georgia" sign have the computer that prints tickets for these four games:

Lotto Georgia: Following the instructions on the back of the playslip, pick six numbers between 1 and 46 by placing a heavy vertical mark over each number you select. You may use pencil or pen but not red ink. You can play up to five different number combinations on a single playslip; if you'd like to play the same numbers for several weeks in a row, mark the "multi-draw" option on the playslip. If you make a mistake, mark the "void" box at the bottom of the panel; do not erase. Give your playslip to the retailer, whose computer will then print your ticket.

The Lotto Georgia jackpot for picking all six numbers is always at least $2 million; lesser pay-outs go to winners who pick three, four or five of the six numbers. Jackpot winners receive their money in the form of a check each year for 20 years.

The Lotto Georgia drawing is held every Saturday night at 11:01 PM and is broadcast live from Atlanta on WSB TV Channel 2.

Georgia Powerball: In 1995, the multi-state, super-jackpot game Powerball hit town. Powerball is similar to Lotto, but you pick five numbers from 1 through 45 and one additional number — the Powerball — also from 1 to 45. You may choose all your own numbers, let the computer choose them (mark QP for Quik Pik), or choose some yourself and let the computer choose the rest. (This partial Quik Pik is an option on Powerball only.) Payouts range from $1 for picking the Powerball only to jackpots of a few million to more than $100 million. You can watch Powerball drawings live on WSB TV Channel 2 every Wednesday and Saturday night at 11 PM.

Fantasy 5: This game is also similar to Lotto Georgia. You pick five numbers (instead of six) from 1 through 35 (instead of 46). You win by picking three or more numbers correctly. The prize for picking all five is tens of thousands of dollars to $100,000 or more, depending on how many players win, and it's paid in a single jaw-dropping check. The Fantasy 5 drawing is held every Monday, Tuesday, Thursday and Friday night at 11 PM and is broadcast live from Atlanta on WSB TV Channel 2.

Ca$h 3: In this game, you pick three numbers from 0 to 9. Bets are placed according to whether you think your numbers will fall in the exact order (a "straight" bet) or in another order (a "box" bet). You may fill out a Ca$h 3 playslip, write your numbers on a piece of paper or tell the retailer the numbers you want to play. The Georgia Lottery's brochure on Ca$h 3 explains the different bets and pay-outs. The maximum payout is $500. The Ca$h 3 drawing is held every night at 6:59 PM and broadcast live from Atlanta on WSB TV Channel 2.

In all on-line games, your playslip is of no value; only your computer-printed ticket is valid; if you lose a winning ticket, anyone who finds it can legally claim the prize unless you've signed the back. Prizes of up to $599 may be claimed at any on-line lottery retailer; see the back of the playslip for how to claim prizes of $600 and more.

Good luck, and remember: If you don't play, you can't win!

Buckhead are just minutes away, and the Midtown MARTA station is right next door.

Sheraton Colony Square
$$$ • 188 14th St. N.E. • (404) 892-6000, (800) 422-7895

The 461-room Sheraton is part of Colony Square, which opened in 1969 as the South's first multiuse complex; its other features are offices, luxury residences and 160,000 square feet of retail space and restaurants, including a food court and the popular Country Place restaurant (see our Restaurants chapter). The Sheraton's 18th- and 19th-floor

Colony Club rooms have extra amenities; guests here receive complimentary continental breakfast and evening cocktails. Piedmont Park and the Woodruff Arts Center are just one block away; there are numerous good restaurants within a couple of blocks.

Wyndham Midtown

$$$ • 125 10th St. N.E. • (404) 873-4800, (800) 996-3426

Renovations in 1997 have freshened this centrally located 11-story hotel. Being on the busy corner of Peachtree and 10th in the heart of Midtown, you'll have an easy walk to the Fox Theatre, Woodruff Arts Center, Piedmont Park and numerous Midtown restaurants and clubs. The 191-room Wyndham's 7,000-square-foot Midtown Athletic Club features an indoor lap pool. Hotel amenities include in-room coffee makers and cable TV. The deluxe band buses frequently parked outside attest to the well-located Wyndham's popularity with touring rock and country music stars. (The hotel is across 10th Street from the Margaret Mitchell Museum, which is housed in the apartment building where Mitchell wrote *Gone With the Wind*. See Attractions.) A van is available to take groups to local restaurants and shops. The Juniper Street Cafe offers three meals, and the Butler's Pub is open evenings for drinks and snacks.

Buckhead

Beginning at about Pharr and Peachtree roads and continuing north for a few miles, Buckhead, the poshest section of Atlanta, fans out east until Piedmont Road and west to Northside Drive. Here you'll find the Governor's Mansion and million-dollar homes as well as restaurants, galleries and the finest shopping centers.

AmeriSuites Atlanta/Buckhead

$$ • 3242 Peachtree Rd. N.E.
• (404) 869-6160, (800) 833-1516

Set well back from Peachtree Road just off Piedmont Road at Tower Place, AmeriSuites is within walking distance of Lenox Square and Phipps Plaza as well as the Buckhead MARTA Station. The hotel lobby has comfy sofas, a coffee bar and cafe. An outdoor pool, accessible from the parking lot, looks inviting in the summer, even though its unsecured without out a lifeguard. There are 140 suites within this eight-floor hotel that are equipped with refrigerator, microwave, wet bar, coffee maker and coffee. Guests may partake of a continental breakfast buffet, complimentary parking, free local phone calls, voice mail, TV and video cassette player and Manager's reception. A business center with 1,600 square feet of meeting space is also available as is a small exercise room.

Courtyard Marriott Buckhead

$$ • 3332 Peachtree Rd. • (404) 869-0818, (800) 321-2211

Within waving distance of the Grand Hyatt Atlanta, AmeriSuites and Wyndham Garden Hotel, competition must be stiff at this busy spot just off Piedmont Road at Tower Place. This Courtyard Marriott has real street appeal with a nicely landscaped corner and a charming bronze sculpture of three frolicking kids and their dog trying to fly kites. The marble lobby is also inviting with a centrally located fireplace that is an ideal meeting place in the winter. A full wall of glass overlooks a small but green sunning garden just off the indoor pool and exercise room. Nine floors with 181 rooms — of which one on each floor has a Jacuzzi in the living area — include coffee maker, iron, hair dryers available upon request and cable TV with HBO. A shuttle will deliver you to any destination within a 1-mile radius of the hotel (meaning you can get to malls and restaurants without having to do the short walk yourself, a blessing during Atlanta's withering heat in the summer and frequent downpours in the winter).

Embassy Suites Atlanta/Buckhead

$$$ • 3285 Peachtree Rd. N.E.
• (404) 261-7733, (800) EMBASSY

On Peachtree Road in Buckhead, each of the Embassy hotel's suites has two remote-control TVs, two telephone lines with voice mail, a refrigerator, a microwave and a coffee maker. There are indoor and outdoor pools, whirlpool and sauna facilities and the fine amenities package includes a free cooked-to-order breakfast every morning in the atrium. Complimentary cocktails are served nightly from 5:30 to 7:30 PM. There is also free transportation within a mile radius, which includes Phipps Plaza, Lenox Square, Lenox MARTA Station and many restaurants and bars. Arriving guests may telephone from Lenox and Buckhead MARTA stations for free pickup. Secured parking for hotel guests is available.

Grand Hyatt Atlanta
$$$$ • 3300 Peachtree Rd. N.E.
• (404) 365-8100, (800) 233-1234

Atlanta's luxury hotels compete fiercely for the many prestigious charity balls that fill the social calendar during the year. This hotel opened in 1990 as the Nikko and immediately attracted high-profile affairs. The dramatic, 440-room hotel's lavish lobby overlooks a three-story waterfall topped by a garden. You can stroll the Japanese garden via the second floor where the Serenity Garden is true to its name. A pebble path leads you past native azaleas and other flora and gently flowing fountains. Along the way there are plank benches for sitting a spell and contemplating the day. The garden terminates at an American-style bar surrounding a very large swimming pool and sunning deck. The Library Bar serves cocktails in a cozy club-like atmosphere. Two separate fine dining restaurants offer Continental (Cassis Restaurant) and Japanese (Kamogawa) cuisine (see our Restaurants chapter). Guests on the top five floors have access to a private lounge with a view of the city. Excellent service is a hallmark of this hotel.

Hampton Inn/Atlanta Buckhead
$$ • 3398 Piedmont Rd. N.E.
• (404) 233-5656, (800) HAMPTON

Here's a moderately priced hotel in the heart of Buckhead. The 154-room Hampton is centrally located between Buckhead's major dining/entertainment area and megamalls Lenox Square and Phipps Plaza, near the Grand Hyatt and the Tower Place office complex. A free continental breakfast is served daily; there's no charge for local calls; and the hotel has an outdoor pool.

Holiday Inn at Lenox
$$ • 3377 Peachtree Rd. N.E.
• (404) 264-1111, (800) 526-0247

It's a shopper's dream come true: The 11-floor, 297-room Holiday Inn at Lenox is beside Lenox Square and just south of Phipps Plaza. Rooms include cable TV with HBO, voice mail, modem hookups and coffee makers. There's an outdoor pool, and the Lenox MARTA station is a short walk away.

J.W. Marriott Hotel at Lenox
$$$$ • 3300 Lenox Rd. N.E.
• (404) 262-3344, (800) 228-9290

This mirrored building was built literally in the back parking lot of Lenox Square and is directly across from the Lenox MARTA station entrance. There are 361 guest rooms including four suites and six executive parlors equipped with Murphy beds that, when raised, allow for a business meeting space. Special features include a health club with an indoor pool. All rooms are equipped with cable TV (with movies), dedicated modem jacks, two telephones, robes, hair dryers and designer toiletries. An enclosed walkway, lined with the work of local and regional artists, leads to the 1.5 million-square-foot Lenox Square.

Residence Inn by Marriott Buckhead
$$$ • 2960 Piedmont Rd. N.E.
• (404) 239-0677, (800) 331-3131

Just south of the intersection of Piedmont and Pharr roads and landscaped with pretty crape myrtle trees in fuchsia and white, this Residence Inn has a great location — close to the Buckhead Diner and The Buckhead Life Group's other restaurants including Pricci (see our Restaurants chapter). Amenities appeal especially to long-term travelers: fully equipped kitchens, a complimentary grocery shopping service, complimentary executive breakfast and hospitality hours, newspapers and health club privileges. There's also a pool, where guests are invited to a Wednesday evening barbecue. Most suites have curbside parking and a private entrance.

The Ritz-Carlton Buckhead
$$$$ • 3434 Peachtree Rd. N.E.
• (404) 237-2700, (800) 241-3333

Directly across from Lenox Square and

Phipps Plaza stands the flagship hotel in the Ritz-Carlton chain. Lavishly appointed with art and antiques, the 553-room Ritz is a favorite of celebrities (everyone from touring rock superstars to visiting royalty stays here). The Dining Room is one of the city's best-known fine dining restaurants (see our Restaurants chapter). The fitness center has an indoor pool. Guests on the Club level enjoy greater privacy, an exclusive lounge and five complimentary meal presentations daily. On weekends guests dance to a three-piece band with a singer.

Summerfield Suites Hotel Atlanta Buckhead
$$$ • 505 Pharr Rd. • (404) 262-7880, (800) 833-4353

Suites at this hotel include two or three color TVs and a VCR; the larger suites have three beds and two baths. There's a complimentary grocery shopping service Monday through Friday. The hotel hosts a complimentary beer and wine happy hour Monday through Thursday and offers a continental breakfast every morning. On weekdays, the hotel's shuttle provides free transportation within a 3-mile radius, which covers all of Buckhead. The exercise facility has a heated pool and whirlpool.

Swissôtel Atlanta
$$$ • 3391 Peachtree Rd. N.E.
• (404) 365-0065, (800) 253-1397

The Swissôtel is patterned after the elegant fashion of modern Europe: sleek and smooth with curving lines and sweeping expanses of glass. It was designed by the Atlanta firm Rabun Hatch and Associates. The interior art is spectacular and belies the rather uninteresting exterior. The hotel is the site of numerous charity balls during the year. Each of the 365 guest rooms in the 22-floor property features three phones and a modem hookup, voice mail, cable TV with HBO, bath-robes and a hair dryer. The hotel's health club has an indoor pool. A special benefit is a complimentary shuttle service to destinations within 3 miles of the hotel, which includes all of Buckhead. Lenox Square is next door; the Lenox MARTA station is only a half-mile from the hotel. Celebrity visitors to the Swissôtel have included Whitney Houston and The Judds.

The Terrace Garden Buckhead
$$$ • 3405 Lenox Rd. N.E.
• (404) 261-9250, (800) 241-8260

Lenox Square, Phipps Plaza and the Lenox MARTA station are just steps away from the Terrace Garden where the 360 rooms and suites feature cable TV, voice mail and computer ports. Club level guests get deluxe accommodations and complimentary continental breakfasts.

Wyndham Garden Hotel Atlanta Buckhead
$$$ • 3340 Peachtree Rd. N.E.
• (404) 231-1234, (800) WYNDHAM

Just beyond the Grand Hyatt and facing the Courtyard Marriott and Tower Place is the Wyndham Garden Hotel with 221 rooms on five floors. Formerly called the Tower Place hotel, the dark, masculine library-style paneling throughout the lobby and Beauregard Lounge are a holdover from the early days. The Savannah Restaurant on the first floor is where you can have all your meals if you opt not to partake of the fabulous restaurants at Lenox Square or Phipps Plaza nearby. Anthonys is also an easy walk down Piedmont Road as is Bone's (see our Restaurants chapter). And Soto's for sushi is just across Piedmont Road. Amenities at Wyndham Garden include coffee makers with complimentary coffee, hair dryers and remote-controlled cable TV. A real plus is complimentary privileges at Sports Life Fitness Center right there at Tower Walk. The

INSIDERS' TIP

Look for deeply discounted hotel rates on weekends and holidays at major hotels, but not on July 4th when Atlanta is booked up for the Peachtree Road Race (see our Spectator Sports chapter).

hotel has 7,290 square feet of meeting space that is available for rental to guests as well as nonguests.

Northeast Expressway/ Emory

On both sides of I-85 are former service roads that were used during the construction of the expressway. These roads are now lined with warehouses, discount shops, hotels and motels attracting people on the move.

Emory University has spawned its own host of motels and hotels around and about the campus for visiting parents and business folk. Take I-85 east at Clairmont Road and proceed to N. Decatur Road where you'll turn right. You can't miss the campus and surrounding accommodations.

Atlanta Marriott Central
$$$ • 2000 Century Center Blvd. N.E. • (404) 325-0000, (800) 325-3535

Alongside I-85, 8 miles northeast of downtown Atlanta, Century Center is a major corporate development that includes the Marriott hotel. Its 287 rooms surround a 15-story atrium. Guest rooms include in-room movies and a dual-line phone system. With easy access to both the Northeast Expressway and the Perimeter, the hotel is well-situated for those doing business on the north side and in the counties northeast of Atlanta.

Emory Conference Center Hotel
$$$ • 1615 Clifton Rd. N.E. • (404) 712-6000, (800) 933-6679

On five floors available for groups or individuals, this hotel has 198 rooms with amenities including exercise facilities with an indoor pool, sauna, spa with a massage therapist available by appointment, iron and board in every room and coffee maker. A lobby lounge with pool tables and a large screen TV, a dining room with full kitchen service providing food service during off hours, a tennis court and a basketball court are on the premises. A nature trail for less strenuous exercise is also part of the grounds. Nearby is Fernbank Museum (see our Attractions chapter), Emory Hospital and University and

Centers for Disease Control (see our Healthcare chapter), and it's an easy cab ride to Virginia-Highland and all the nightlife and restaurants that have made the neighborhood a hub for in-town folks.

Emory Inn
$$ • 1641 Clifton Rd. N.E. • (404) 712-6700, (800) 933-6679

Emory Inn is near the center of the Emory University and Hospital area, directly across the street from the Centers for Disease Control and Prevention. The inn has 105 guest rooms, a lounge and cafe; a pool and a hydrotherapy pool are outside. The inn also manages the nearby D. Abbott Turner Center, an architecturally award-winning, 7,000-square-foot facility that can accommodate groups of up to 250 people. Amenities are identical to those listed for the Emory Conference Center Hotel (detailed previously), which this group also manages.

Hampton Inn North Druid Hills
$$ • 1975 N. Druid Hills Rd. N.E. • (404) 320-6600, (800) HAMPTON

With 111 rooms, this Hampton Inn is conveniently situated between the Emory area and Buckhead at Exit 31 off I-85. There's a complimentary continental breakfast daily, and the hotel has a pool and an exercise room. The immediate area offers a range of moderately priced dining choices.

Holiday Inn Atlanta — Northlake
$$$ • 4156 LaVista Rd. • (770) 938-1026, (800) HOLIDAY

Just inside the Perimeter in the busy Northlake area, this Holiday Inn's amenities include cable TV with movies, an exercise facility and an outdoor pool with a hot tub on deck. Club-level guests enjoy continental breakfast and evening cocktails Monday through Friday. The Candler suite features a wet bar, fireplace and formal dining area. In the hotel's restaurant, you may order from the menu or choose from the breakfast or lunch buffet (weekdays). Hot and cold hors d'oeuvres are presented each weekday evening in the lounge. For large functions, the Capitol ballroom seats 350; it has its own entrance lobby and a deck overlooking the pool and patio.

Holiday Inn Select Decatur

$$ • 130 Clairemont Ave. • (404) 371-0204, (800) 225-6079

In downtown Decatur, this 185-room hotel pampers its guests with an amenities package that includes in-room hair dryers, irons and ironing boards and coffee makers, plus free local phone calls, editions of *USA Today* and transportation within a 5-mile radius. On the Executive Level, enjoy complimentary continental breakfast and the Sunday-through-Thursday nightly cocktail reception. The nearby Decatur MARTA station makes getting around the metro area a snap.

Holiday Inn Select Perimeter Dunwoody

$$$ • 4386 Chamblee Dunwoody Rd. • (770) 457-6363, (800) HOLIDAY

This hotel is southwest of the intersection of Chamblee Dunwoody Road and I-285 (Exit 22), convenient to the Perimeter Mall area. Each of the 250 guest rooms has two telephones and cable TV with HBO. The fitness center has an outdoor pool. The hotel has a New Orleans look with wrought-iron detailing.

Radisson Inn

$$ • 2061 N. Druid Hills Rd. N.E. • (404) 321-4174, (800) 333-3333

Emory University and Buckhead are five-minute drives from the 208-room Radisson Inn, a nine-story full-service hotel. Amenities include cable TV with HBO and free parking. Guests receive in-room coffee service and complimentary continental breakfast.

Red Roof Inn Druid Hills

$$ • 1960 N. Druid Hills Rd., I-85 at Exit 31 • (404) 321-1653, (800) THE ROOF

This 115-room budget property is convenient to both the Emory area and the attractions of Buckhead. Unlimited free local calls are a bonus, and children 18 and younger stay for free in their parents' room.

Wyndham Garden Northlake

$$ • 2158 Ranchwood Dr. • (770) 934-6000, (800) WYNDHAM

The Northlake area is a big retail destination (thanks not only to Northlake Mall but also to the retail developments that have sprung up around it). This 131-room Wyndham is just a minute from the mall and close to Kaiser Permanente's Crescent Center. Guests enjoy cable TV with HBO. The Northlake area enjoys easy access to I-285.

Northwest Expressway

Up and down the corridors surrounding I-75 are hotels and motels for business people visiting or traveling through Georgia.

Courtyard by Marriott Cumberland Center

$$ • 3000 Cumberland Cir. • (770) 952-2555, (800) 321-2211

This 182-room hotel across from Cumberland Mall has a full-service health club with an indoor pool, sauna and spa. Covered parking and in-room coffee are complimentary; rooms include cable TV with HBO.

Embassy Suites Galleria

$$$ • 2815 Akers Mill Rd. • (770) 984-9300, (800) EMBASSY

Walking to Cumberland Mall, the Galleria and the Cobb Convention Center is just a stroll, really, through the various parking lots around these shopping and meeting facilities. With the pedestrian walkway over Cobb Parkway now complete, it's a breeze to get to the only Sears inside the Perimeter in this part of town. With 261 rooms on nine stories, this Embassy Suites has an interesting lobby with palm trees surrounding a pyramid restaurant. Although there is no exercise room in the building, a shuttle good for a 3-mile radius will drive to SportsLife, which offers guest privileges. Two-room suites, full American breakfast in the lobby and free, cocktail receptions daily are part of the amenities.

INSIDERS' TIP

The Sunday edition of *The Atlanta Journal-Constitution* lists the winning numbers for Powerball and the Georgia Lotto on the inside cover of section A.

Hampton Inn Atlanta Cumberland
$$ • 2775 Cumberland Pkwy.
• (770) 333-6006, (800) HAMPTON

One block from Cumberland Mall, Cobb Galleria Centre and the Galleria Specialty Mall, this 128-room inn offers guests free continental breakfasts, free local calls and cable TV with HBO. Rates here are on the lower end of the $50-to-$100 range.

Harvey Hotel Powers Ferry
$$ • 6345 Powers Ferry Rd. N.W.
• (770) 955-1700, (800) 922-9222

Harvey Hotel has 299 sleeping rooms and four parlor suites. All rooms have an AM/FM clock radio. At the fitness center you'll find an indoor/outdoor heated pool. A courtesy van provides free transportation within a 3-mile radius.

Homewood Suites Atlanta — Cumberland
$$ • 3200 Cobb Pkwy. S.W.
• (770) 988-9449, (800) CALL HOME

Each of the Homewood's 124 luxury suites designed for extended stay include two color TVs, a VCR and a kitchen with a refrigerator, stove, microwave and coffee maker; 28 suites even have fireplaces. Guests receive a free *USA Today* and continental breakfast served in the lobby, plus there's a complimentary evening social hour. Free transportation is provided within a 5-mile radius.

Renaissance Waverly
$$$ • 2450 Galleria Pkwy.
• (770) 953-4500, (800) HOTELS1

Connected to the new $50 million Cobb Galleria Centre trade show complex, this luxury hotel has 521 rooms arranged around a sunlit, 14-story atrium. Guest rooms have two telephones and cable TV. Coffee and a copy of *USA Today* are delivered free of charge with a guest's wake-up call. The Club Floor offers complimentary continental breakfast and evening hors d'oeuvres and nonalcoholic beverages, plus deluxe accommodations and amenities. Through the Galleria and across the street is the 150-store Cumberland Mall. The hotel provides free transportation within a 1-mile radius.

Sheraton Galleria
$$$ • 2844 Cobb Pkwy. S.E.
• (770) 955-3900

The 17-story, all-suite Sheraton is next to the 1.2 million-square-foot Cumberland Mall and across the street from Cobb Galleria Centre convention facility and the Galleria Specialty Mall. Each suite includes two phones with voice mail, two remote-control TVs, a VCR (movies may be rented), a refrigerator with an honor bar, a microwave and a coffee maker with free coffee and tea. A complimentary full breakfast buffet is served daily until 10:30 AM. The fitness center has indoor and outdoor pools, and a courtesy van provides free transportation within a 3-mile radius. The business center is available around the clock.

Wyndham Garden Hotel — Vinings
$$$ • 2857 Paces Ferry Rd.
• (770) 432-5555, (800) 996-3426

The Vinings Wyndham is inside I-285 south of its intersection with U.S. 41. Each of the 159 guest rooms includes remote-control cable TV, a hair dryer and a coffee maker. There is an adjacent athletic center with a heated outdoor pool and two lighted tennis courts that hotel guests may use. At the center of the property is a landscaped, tree-shaded garden. The Garden Cafe serves breakfast, lunch and dinner daily. Cumberland Mall and Cobb Galleria Centre are 5 minutes away; downtown Atlanta is 15 minutes southeast.

Airport

Atlanta Airport Hilton and Towers
$$$ • 1031 Virginia Ave., Hapeville
• (404) 767-9000, (800) HILTONS

North of Hartsfield Airport, this 503-room hotel has in-room coffee makers and a sports bar with a 100-inch TV. Monitors in the lobby display updated flight information for all the major airlines. Children, regardless of age, stay for free in their parents' room.

Club Hotel by Doubletree
$$ • 5010 Old National Hwy.
• (404) 761-4000, (800) 334-3364

This 232-room hotel is just outside the

Perimeter and south of Hartsfield Airport. Amenities include airport pickup and complimentary morning coffee and *USA Today*. Two hospitality suites are ideal for entertaining; the conference center has nine function rooms and a ballroom for 350. The hotel has an indoor/outdoor heated pool and a health club.

Courtyard by Marriott Atlanta Airport North
$$ • 3399 International Blvd., Hapeville
• (404) 559-1043, (800) 321-2211

The world headquarters of Delta Airlines is only a quarter-mile from this Courtyard, which operates a complimentary airport shuttle. The hotel has an exercise room and an outdoor pool; guest rooms include coffee and tea service and remote-control cable TV with HBO.

Courtyard by Marriott Atlanta Airport South
$$ • 2050 Sullivan Rd., College Park
• (770) 997-2220, (800) 321-2211

This Courtyard is inside the Perimeter just south of Hartsfield Airport. It has an indoor pool and operates a free airport shuttle service for guests. You'll find HBO, CNN and movies in each room, accessible through the remote control at your bedside. There are computer and fax hookups in each room. Weekday copies of *USA Today* are delivered to your door. All rooms feature coffee and tea service.

Embassy Suites Atlanta Airport
$$$ • 4700 Southport Rd. at Embassy Dr.
• (404) 767-1988, (800) EMBASSY

This 234-suite hotel has coffee makers, hair dryers, irons and boards, microwaves and refrigerators in its two-room suites. Like all of the other Embassy Suites, there are two TVs with cable and HBO in each room. Kids younger than 18 stay free in their parents' room. A complimentary full breakfast is cooked to order daily, and evening hors d'oeuvres with alcoholic and nonalcoholic drinks can be found at happy hour every night.

Hampton Inn Atlanta Airport
$$ • 1888 Sullivan Rd., College Park
• (770) 996-2220, (800) HAMPTON

Rates at this 130-room inn south of Hartsfield Airport are typically on the lower end of the $50-to-$100 range. The hotel has a pool and operates a free airport shuttle for guests.

Holiday Inn Atlanta Airport North
$$ • 1380 Virginia Ave., East Point
• (404) 762-8411

Hartsfield Airport is just a mile away from this 500-room Holiday Inn, and there's a complimentary 24-hour airport shuttle service for guests; you can also use the shuttle to access the Airport MARTA station for quick transportation into town. Fitness buffs will enjoy outdoor pool, exercise room and lighted tennis courts. The hotel has a coffee shop, restaurant and lounge.

Renaissance Atlanta Hotel
$$$ • One Hartsfield Centre Pkwy.
• (404) 209-9999, (800) HOTELS1

Just seven minutes from the airport, Renaissance Atlanta Hotel has 387 rooms and 17 suites. Call from the airport and receive direct pickup services when you arrive. When departing, the free shuttle takes you to MARTA from the hotel so you may catch the train direct to the airport. Each room has a coffee maker, cable TV and a minibar. The hotel's health club has a swimming pool, sauna and whirlpool open to all guests. There's a restaurant serving breakfast, lunch and dinner, a bar and a lobby gift shop.

INSIDERS' TIP

Hungry conventioneers attending events at the Georgia World Congress Center on Marietta Street will find a valuable service at the Atlanta Convention and Visitors' Bureau (ACVB) booth there. The staff will make reservations at restaurants around town that also happen to be members of the ACVB. In the first two months the service was offered, the ACVB booked 1,000 reservations.

Beyond Atlanta

Barrow County

Château Élan

$$$$ • 100 Tour de France, Braselton
• (770) 932-0900, (800) 233-WINE

Set on 3,100 acres 45 minutes northeast of Atlanta off I-85 (Exit 48), this unusual resort mixes business with pleasure. The complex includes a French-inspired chateau, a 25,000-square-foot conference center, 306 rooms, a 170-acre golf course, a par 3 walking course, a Stan Smith-designed, seven-court tennis center, an equestrian show center, a European-style health spa, an art gallery, horseback and nature trails and more than 200 acres of vineyards producing a variety of fine wines.

Each of the resort's deluxe rooms and suites includes an oversize bath with separate garden tub and shower, three dual-line phones, a personal safe and a minibar. Golf, tennis and luxurious spa packages are offered. There are also several restaurants on the grounds that offer a range from fine dining to pub food. Since it opened in 1984, the Château Élan winery has received more than 210 medals of excellence. Today, it produces 15 varieties of wine; free tours with wine tastings take place every day except Christmas.

Clayton County

Holiday Inn Atlanta South

$$ • 6288 Old Dixie Hwy., Jonesboro
• (770) 968-4300

Seven miles south of Hartsfield Airport, this 180-room Holiday Inn offers free parking, an outdoor pool and sun deck, cable TV, pay-per-view movies and a self-service laundry. The restaurant serves three meals daily; the bar re-creates the feel of an old library, complete with books. Clayton State College, with its world-class recital facility Spivey Hall, is just 3 miles away.

Cobb County

Atlanta Marriott Northwest

$$$ • 200 Interstate N. Pkwy.
• (770) 952-7900, (800) 228-9290

This 400-room hotel was completely renovated in 1996. Each room includes cable TV with HBO, two direct dial phones with voice mail, an iron and an ironing board. At the fitness center are three lighted tennis courts, an indoor/outdoor pool and a whirlpool. This 16-floor hotel has three concierge levels. Airport shuttles take guests nonstop to the airport.

French Quarter Suites

$$$ • 2780 Whitley Rd. • (770) 980-1900, (800) 843-5858

A complete renovation of the French Quarter's 155 suites was finished in early spring 1998. Each guest room opens onto a glass-roofed courtyard with exotic plants and a fountain. There's a phone in every room of every suite, and each unit has a large whirlpool bath and cable TV with HBO and Showtime. Other amenities include business travelers' services, in-room coffee service, hair dryers and complimentary breakfast each morning in the courtyard. A specialty restaurant serves dinner; the Bourbon Street Cabaret maintains the jazzy theme. A big brunch is served in the courtyard on Sunday. Ask about the romantic package rates.

Hawthorn Suites Hotel Atlanta — Northwest

$$$ • 1500 Parkwood Cir.
• (770) 952-9595, (800) 338-7812

The 280-unit, all-suite Hawthorn is nestled on 13 landscaped acres northeast of the I-75/I-285 interchange. A complimentary breakfast buffet is served daily, and the outdoor picnic areas feature gas grills. Each

INSIDERS' TIP

On weekends and whenever business travel slows down, even the best hotels may cut their rates dramatically.

one- or two-bedroom suite includes cable TVs, a fully equipped kitchen plus a balcony or patio. Among the recreational amenities are an outdoor pool with waterfalls and a whirlpool, two lighted tennis courts and a basketball court.

Holiday Inn Hotel and Suites — Marietta
$$ • 2265 Kingston Ct., Marietta
• (770) 952-7581, (800) HOLIDAY

Near I-75 at Exit 111 (Delk Road), this 196-room hotel will be completely renovated by spring 1998. The face-lift includes a new tower with 46 suites; each two-room unit will have a wet bar, refrigerator, coffee service and microwave. Suite rates include a full breakfast. The grounds have a large outdoor pool, complimentary parking and a 10,000-square-foot conference center. It's convenient to the Lockheed factory, the Cumberland Mall area and White Water water park.

Marietta Conference Center and Resort
$$$$ • 500 Powder Springs St., Marietta
• (770) 427-2500, (888) 685-2500

Sitting on one of the highest spots in the city of Marietta, this hotel, resort and conference center offers spectacular views of the county's countryside. Located just a few blocks from the town square, the center has 199 rooms, all with desks, two phones with data lines and voice mail, minibars, hair dryers, coffee makers, irons and ironing boards. There's a 20,000-square-foot meeting area as well as a 6,500-square-foot ballroom, an outdoor pool with hot tub, health club, two lighted tennis courts and a golf course.

At the time of the Civil War, the center's grounds were home to the Georgia Military Institute. Union forces burned the school, but left behind the headmaster's home, Brumby Hall. The modest cottage, decorated in period furnishings, and its extensive formal gardens are popular for outdoor events and weddings.

The center has a pub with billiard tables, darts and televisions. The elegant Hamilton's restaurant has a main room overlooking the golf course, as well as an intimate private dining room (see our Restaurants chapter).

Northwest Atlanta Hilton
$$$ • 2055 S. Park Pl. • (770) 953-9300, (800) 234-9304

Near the Windy Hill exit off I-75 in Marietta, the Hilton has 222 deluxe guest rooms, an indoor/outdoor pool and a fitness room. You'll receive a complimentary paper daily. A van provides free transportation to attractions within a 5-mile radius, which include the Galleria Centre, Cumberland Mall and the wet, wild thrills of White Water amusement park. There is no charge for children, regardless of age, when they occupy the same room as their parents.

DeKalb County

Atlanta Marriott — Perimeter Center
$$$ • 246 Perimeter Center Pkwy. N.E.
• (770) 394-6500, (800) 228-9290

The 402-room Marriott is just outside I-285 at Exit 21 about halfway between I-75 and I-85 at the heart of the booming Perimeter Center area. It offers an indoor/outdoor pool, lighted tennis courts, an exercise center, a lounge and a full-service restaurant that provides room service. Guest rooms feature two phones and cable TV with HBO and The Disney Channel. Concierge-level guests receive a complimentary newspaper, a continental breakfast and hors d'oeuvres. Right across the street is the 1.2-million-square-foot Perimeter Mall and the Dunwoody MARTA station; the surrounding area is a booming retail mecca featuring everything from exclusive specialty shops to large electronics discounter Best Buy.

Crowne Plaza Ravinia
$$$$ • 4355 Ashford-Dunwoody Rd.
• (770) 395-7700, (800) 227-6963

In a park-like, wooded 10-acre setting near Perimeter Mall, the Crowne Plaza Ravinia has a two-story greenhouse lobby. Its 15 floors include 495 rooms, 29 deluxe suites and a club level with a private lounge, where guests enjoy a complimentary breakfast buffet and evening cocktail hour. The fitness center has an indoor pool, a lighted tennis court, a sauna and a whirlpool. Off the lobby is the Market, a cafe court where guests can pick up yogurt, pizza or French pastries.

Embassy Suites Perimeter Center

$$$ • 1030 Crowne Pointe Pkwy.
• (770) 394-5454, (800) EMBASSY

Each suite includes a living room with a queen-size sofa bed, a separate bedroom, plus two televisions, a coffee maker, microwave, wet bar and refrigerator. There's an indoor pool, and guests are invited for a free, cooked-to-order breakfast every morning as well as a two-hour reception nightly. A shuttle will drop you off at Perimeter Mall or the corporate offices within a 3-mile radius.

Hampton Inn Stone Mountain

$$ • 1737 Mountain Industrial Blvd., Stone Mountain • (770) 934-0004,
(800) HAMPTON

The 129-room Hampton Inn is 15 minutes east of downtown and just 3 miles from all the fun at Georgia's Stone Mountain Park. Amenities include an exercise room and a pool, free continental breakfast and free local calls.

The Marque of Atlanta — Perimeter Center

$$$ • 111 Perimeter Center W.
• (770) 396-6800, (800) 683-6100

The Marque is a luxury hotel with a restaurant and lounge in a park-like setting near Perimeter Mall. All rooms have a balcony and cable TV; suites have fully equipped kitchens.

The fitness center includes an exercise room and an outdoor pool.

Douglas County

Hampton Inn — Six Flags

$$ • 1100 N. Blairs Bridge Rd., Austell
• (770) 941-1499, (800) HAMPTON

The 74-room Hampton Inn has a pool and is only 3 miles from all the screams and excitement of Six Flags Over Georgia. It's about 15 minutes from downtown Atlanta on I-20.

Fulton County

Courtyard by Marriott Roswell

$$ • 1500 Market Blvd., Roswell
• (770) 992-7200, (800) 321-2211

This north metro hotel is 3 miles from historic Roswell and close by the Chattahoochee Nature Center. The 154 rooms include coffee and tea service and cable TV with HBO. There's an outdoor pool, an indoor whirlpool and a minigym. Ask about special rates for extended stays.

Doubletree Guest Suites

$$$ • 6120 Peachtree Dunwoody Rd.
• (770) 668-0808, (800) 222-TREE

Two blocks from Perimeter Mall, this 224-suite hotel features an indoor/outdoor pool, fully equipped health club, restaurant and room service. Each suite has two cable TVs, a coffee maker, wet bar, refrigerator and a patio or balcony.

Holiday Inn Atlanta Roswell
$$$$ • 1075 Holcomb Bridge Rd., Roswell • (770) 992-9600, (800) HOLIDAY

Billed as Roswell's only full-service hotel, this 172-room Holiday Inn is 3 miles from North Point Mall and Chattahoochee River Park. Amenities include remote satellite TV with Showtime and free morning coffee every day. Airport shuttle and secretarial services are available. The hotel also has a restaurant, bar, banquet and conference facilities for up to 400 people.

Masters Economy Inn Six Flags
$ • 4120 Fulton Industrial Blvd. • (404) 696-4690, (800) 633-3434

This 167-room motel is 7 miles west of downtown and just 3 miles from Six Flags Over Georgia. Local calls are free; rooms include cable TV with HBO. There's an outdoor pool.

Summerfield Suites
$$$ • 760 Mt. Vernon Hwy. • (404) 250-0110, (800) 833-4353

The Summerfield is in the Perimeter Mall area; the 122 suites have full kitchens, video cassette players and voice mail. A complimentary breakfast buffet is served each morning; a beer and wine social is offered Monday through Thursday evenings. An exercise room with a pool and whirlpool is available for guests.

Westin Atlanta North at Perimeter
$$$ • 7 Concourse Pkwy. • (770) 395-3900, (800) WESTIN-1

At The Concourse, a 64-acre wooded, corporate center near Perimeter Mall, the 370-room Westin rises 20 stories above a lake. Sixteen suites and junior suites are offered, along with 26 meeting rooms, a tiered conference room and a business center. Guests pay $10 per day to use the adjacent 85,000-square-foot Concourse Athletic Club, which has seven clay tennis courts, indoor and outdoor 25-meter pools, a full-size gym, a cushioned indoor running track and private tanning. The hotel's restaurant, Cafe Marmalade, serves breakfast, lunch and dinner (see our Restaurants chapter). From I-285,

take Exit 20 and go north on Peachtree Dunwoody Road; you can't miss the twin Concourse office towers on your left.

Wyndham Garden Hotel — Perimeter Center
$$$ • 800 Hammond Dr. N.E. • (404) 252-3344, (800) WYNDHAM

Five minutes from Perimeter Mall, the 143-room Wyndham features a landscaped garden, an indoor/outdoor pool and a fully equipped exercise room. Rooms include cable TV, two telephones and coffee makers. The hotel operates a complimentary shuttle to local offices and attractions.

Gwinnett County

Best Western — Falcon Inn & Conference Center
$$ • Two Falcon Pl., Suwanee • (770) 945-6751, (800) 528-1234

This 100-room hotel is home to the Atlanta Falcons football team, which moves in for six weeks each summer for training camp. Their practice field is located behind the hotel. Each room has cable TV with HBO and other premium channels, hair dryers and newspapers. The hotel's restaurant is closed on the weekends, when a free continental breakfast is served. There is also 15,000 square feet of conference center space, an outdoor pool and a jogging track around a pond.

Courtyard by Marriott
$$$ • Gwinnett Mall, 3550 Venture Pkwy., Duluth • (770) 476-4666, (800) 321-2211

The shopping excitement of the 1.2 million-square-foot Gwinnett Place Mall is just a quarter-mile from this 146-room Courtyard, which is 18 miles from downtown and 30 miles from Hartsfield Airport. Along with standard rooms, there are 12 suites, an outdoor pool, in-room coffee and tea service and cable TV with HBO.

StudioPLUS
$$ • 7065 Jimmy Carter Blvd., Norcross • (770) 582-9984

This extended-stay hotel features spacious studio suites with queen-size beds, fully equipped kitchens, cable TV, weekly housekeeping and personal phone lines. Mail, faxes and packages are delivered right to your room. A fitness center, laundry room and outdoor pool are on the property. Rates, which range from $59 to $79 per night for up to six nights, are lower the longer you stay.

Wyndham Garden Gwinnett
$$ • 1948 Day Dr., Duluth • (770) 476-1211, (800) 996-3426

Full breakfast buffet, outdoor pool and in-room movies are the amenities at this 131-room high-rise hotel across from Gwinnett Place Mall. There's also a free shuttle that will take you to the nearby SportsLife health club for complimentary visits during your stay.

Hall County

Comfort Inn
$$ • I-985 at Mundy Mill Rd., Exit 4, Oakwood • (770) 287-1000, (800) 221-2222

This 72-room hotel is 5 miles south of Gainesville and 4.5 miles from all the action at the Road Atlanta racetrack. There are five king suites, five whirlpool suites and an outdoor pool. A deluxe complimentary continental breakfast is served each morning.

Lake Lanier Islands Hilton Resort
$$$ • 7000 Holiday Rd., Lake Lanier Islands • (770) 945-8787, (800) 768-5253, (800) HILTONS

Lake Lanier Islands is a waterfront recreational complex 30 minutes northeast of Atlanta on Lake Sidney Lanier. It features a concert amphitheater, campgrounds and a water park with the largest wave pool in Georgia. The Hilton resort offers a par 72 golf course, tennis, water sports and fine dining. Some of the 224 guest rooms have a view of the lake. With 12,500 square feet of meeting space, the hotel can accommodate meetings of up to 350 people. Children, regardless of age, stay for free in their parents' room.

Renaissance Pinelsle Resort
$$$ • 9000 Holiday Rd., Lake Lanier Islands • (770) 945-8921, (800) HOTELS-1

Each of the Renaissance's 250 rooms includes cable TV, two robes, a stocked refreshment center and a safe. There's a hot tub on an enclosed patio outside each of the 28 spa rooms. Complimentary coffee and a newspaper are delivered with each guest's wake-up call. Guests can golf on the par 72 course, play tennis on one of the four outdoor lighted courts or three enclosed courts, swim in the indoor/outdoor pool or relax in the three-story elevated outdoor hot tub. In the style of European hotels, the hotel is "tip-free." Gratuities are already included in rates and prices. Rates are seasonal; they're lower between November and March.

Hostels

Atlanta Dream Hostel
$, no credit cards • 115 Church St., Decatur • (404) 370-0380

This rambling, art-filled hostel offers communal lodging for the young and young at heart. It's wonderfully eclectic: There's a big backyard with rabbits, peacocks and antique cars. Beneath a large awning, the patio is finished in a mosaic of marble fragments. Most lodging is dormitory-style, though there are also single and double rooms, some with a private bath. The daily rate (less than $50) is incredibly cheap, so be kind to the owner and act as your own maid. The hostel is convenient to the downtown Decatur MARTA station. The surrounding area offers several affordable dining choices.

Hosteling International — Atlanta
$ • 229 Ponce de Leon Ave. • (404) 875-2882

On the southern edge of Midtown, this 100-bed, dormitory-style hostel sleeps four to six guests in a room; some private baths are available. Common area amenities include TV, pinball and a pool table. Complimentary doughnuts are served daily. Nonmembers of Hosteling International pay an additional $3 fee. There is a two-night minimum stay for credit-card users. Piedmont Park and many Midtown attractions are nearby.

Owners of bed and
breakfasts treat guests
like members of
their family.

Bed and Breakfasts

Atlantans, best-noted for their devotion to Southern hospitality, are also known for the pride they take in their homes. The combination of the two is best discovered in the area's bed and breakfasts, where owners throw open their doors and treat guests like members of the family.

In historic homes, Victorian cottages and cozy bungalows, Atlanta's many bed and breakfast inns offer visitors a range of options, from homelike comfort to elegant pampering. The variety of bed and breakfast accommodations grew in the years leading up to the arrival of the Olympic Games in 1996, and while many have since ceased to operate, many very good inns have remained.

There are several general guidelines shared by the majority of Atlanta's bed and breakfast establishments. Of course, there are exceptions to every rule. We have tried to indicate where an inn may be different, but it's always a good idea to have the innkeeper answer any specific questions you may have about children, pets, smoking and payment.

On the whole, smoking is not allowed anywhere inside the building, but often guests may smoke outside in a designated area. There's usually no accommodation for pets or, in some cases, children. Other innkeepers only permit children older than 12. While old houses and cottages provide quaint guest rooms, they usually do not have handicapped facilities. Some innkeepers do not accept credit cards on site but will allow reservations to be charged through a central reservation service.

The metro area has two free reservation services to help visitors find an inn that best suits their style. **Bed &Breakfast Atlanta**, (404) 875-0525 or (800) 967-3224, specializes in 70 metro-area inns as well as private homes. **RSVP Grits** (Great Reservations in the South), (404) 843-3933 or (800) 823-7787, will put travelers in touch with more than 50 of the best inns around Atlanta and the north Georgia area. Inn rates are the same whether booked directly or through the innkeeper. Major credit cards can be used to book a room, even if the individual innkeepers do not accept them.

Price Code

Each inn's listing includes a symbol indicating a price range for a one-night double-occupancy stay (excluding tax) in the middle of the week.

$	$50 to $100
$$	$100 to $150
$$$	$150 and more

Note: Pricing information was provided by the inns and is presented as a guide to help you approximate costs. Rates may be higher during major conventions or other peak travel times, but generally, innkeepers say their prices are the same each evening.

Atlanta

Beverly Hills Inn
$$ • 65 Sheridan Dr. N.E.
• (404) 233-8520

Just three minutes from the Atlanta History Center and five minutes from Lenox Square and Phipps Plaza, this 1929, four-level inn is operated like an intimate European hotel. It was originally built as a chic apartment house, which explains why each of the 18 guest rooms has a kitchen. Other room amenities include a balcony; a private, tiled bath; and an ironing board and iron. The inn's common areas show off the original hardwood floors, decorated with Oriental rugs, and plaster walls. The library has a bottle of sherry for guests to share as well as a fax and modem hookup. The conservatory on the lower level opens to a cool patio where a complimentary breakfast is served daily. Arriving guests receive a welcoming bottle of wine and a hearty handshake from innkeeper Mit Amin. Check out his London cab parked at the curb.

The Bonaventure
$$ • 650 Bonaventure Ave. • (404) 817-7024

This inn, once one of the city's premier music schools, is listed on the National Register of Historic Places. Some of the best features of the yellow-brick, 1908 structure still remain: leaded-glass windows, heart-pine floors, pocket doors and fireplaces in every room. The original pony stables are behind the carriage house in the backyard. During the school's heyday, concerts were given on the front porch and in the parlor. Today's guests enjoy full breakfasts of quiche, stuffed French toast, egg casseroles and scones presented by innkeepers Mary Beth Wallace and Ruthie Zaleon in the dining room or on the verandah. There are three guest rooms to choose from, including one with a featherbed and another with a sun porch.

Buckhead Bed & Breakfast Inn
$$ • 70 Lenox Pointe • (404) 261-8284

For three years, this elegant Buckhead inn has provided romantic weekends and gracious accommodations to travelers. There are 19 rooms, many with their motifs in their titles (the Holly Room, the Oak Room). Each has a private bath, four-poster bed, writing desk, armoire and computer modem lines. Conference facilities can accommodate 50 people. Innkeeper Jerry Cates and his staff serve a light complimentary breakfast of pastries, fruit salads and beverages.

Fallin Gate
$ • 381 Cherokee Ave. • (404) 522-7371

Built in 1905, this late Victorian cottage in Grant Park is named for its original owner. Behind the white picket fence are two guest rooms: one with a queen-size bed, armoire and fireplace; another with a brass double bed, carved mantel over the fireplace and an oak dresser. Full breakfasts may include such treats as pear crepes, baked eggs, fresh breads and biscuits. Guests not from the South are required by owner Sandra Bemis to at least try the grits. (Don't worry — they come with cheese and other flavorings for novices.)

The Gaslight Inn
$$$ • 1001 St. Charles Ave. N.E. • (404) 875-1001

This 1913 Virginia-Highland inn was completely renovated by owner Jim Moss in 1990. The white and blue house is decorated with period furnishings; an old-time gaslight beside the front walk is a welcoming beacon. Three guest rooms are decorated with features such as stained-glass windows, four-poster beds and fireplaces; one has a private entrance to a small garden. There are also two suites: the English suite has a fireplace, steam shower, whirlpool tub and deck overlooking a walled garden; the St. Charles suite has a private balcony, fireplace, wet bar and whirlpool tub. Behind the main house is the Ivy Cottage, a tiny house whose entire second floor is a mini-apartment, with a fully equipped kitchen, living area and bedroom. All rooms have a private bath and TV and come with an elaborate continental breakfast of cereals, juices, fruit salads and homemade bagels, muffins and croissants. The grounds are particularly colorful in spring, when more than 2,000 bulbs burst into bloom.

FYI

Three area codes serve the metro Atlanta area: 404, 770 and 678. Whether you live on Peachtree Street or in New York City, you must dial the code to reach any number in the area. The difference? Outside the area, you must dial "1," then the area code and phone number; inside the area, you need only dial the area code followed by the phone number.

The Woodruff B&B Inn
223 Ponce de Leon Ave.
Atlanta, GA 30308
Phone: (404) 875-9449
Fax: (404) 870-0042
1-800-473-9449

Southern Hospitality awaits you at this three story Victorian inn. Rooms beautifully decorated with period antiques, hardwood floors, and oriental rugs take you back to a more romantic time. A full Southern breakfast is served each morning. We have already reserved a smile for you, may we reserve you a room?

Greycourt Bed and Breakfast
$ • 47 Delta Pl. • (404) 523-4239

This two-story Victorian was built in Inman Park in 1904 for a saloon keeper. Today, it is maintained by innkeepers John and Kris Dwyer. The ground-floor suite includes the home's original library, a private phone and a stocked kitchen. Two additional bedrooms are on the second floor. The entire home is decorated in Victorian antiques, but you may find it hard to leave the luxurious front porch, where antique wicker chairs and rockers beckon. A continental breakfast is served during the week, including breads, English muffins, bagels, fruit, pancakes, egg dishes and yogurt. On weekends, the Dwyers' go all out offering blueberry pancakes, egg dishes or any items requested by guests of the inn.

Heartfield Manor Bed and Breakfast
$$ • 182 Elizabeth St. • (404) 523-8633

For the last 12 years, this renovated apartment house in Inman Park has served as a bed and breakfast. Built in 1903, the Craftsman-style house now has three guest rooms, all with private baths, that overlook a small neighborhood park. The decor is English cottage, with beamed ceilings, wood fireplaces and period antiques. The rear deck doubles as a playscape for kids, who will find plenty of toys, courtesy of owner Sandra Heartfield's

grandchildren. Croissants, muffins and fresh fruits await hungry guests in the morning.

Inman Park Bed and Breakfast — Woodruff Cottage
$ • 100 Waverly Wy. • (404) 688-9498

Built in 1912 for Robert Woodruff, a Coca-Cola magnate, this red-brick Inman Park home has always been known as his "honeymoon cottage" — even though it boasts more than 4,500 square feet. There's a walled garden, a screened porch, 12-foot ceilings, elaborate crown moldings, four fireplaces and three guest rooms filled with antique oak bureaux and dressers. Each room has a private bath; two have claw-foot tubs. Innkeeper Eleanor Matthews decorated the inn with her own family antiques and Persian rugs to make the large house welcoming. Breakfast usually features items such as muffins, scones, cereals, fruits and yogurt.

King-Keith House Bed & Breakfast
$ • 889 Edgewood Ave. N.E.
• (404) 688-7330, (800) 728-3879

An 1890 Queen Anne-style home in a National Register of Historic Places neighborhood, this inn is one of the oldest homes in Inman Park and is named for its original owner, hardware magnate George King. It features a wraparound porch with an attached gazebo and delicate lace-work arches. The Inman

Park/Reynoldstown MARTA station is two blocks away, and it's a pleasant walk down the tree-shaded streets of Inman Park to the shops, restaurants and clubs of Little Five Points.

Five guest rooms have private baths and are furnished in period antiques. Guests have access to a private, up-stairs porch. The house has 12-foot ceilings, carved fireplaces and a baby grand piano. Inn-keepers Windell and Jan Keith serve a full breakfast every day that always includes different breads, cereals and fruits with either eggs, French toast or quiche.

www.insiders.com

See this and many other **Insiders' Guide®** destinations online — in their entirety.

Visit us today!

Lismore House
$, no credit cards • 855 Penn Ave.
• (404) 817-9640

Named for an Irish county and the glass-ware pattern on the dining room table, this house dates to 1917 and is one of the few Tudor-style homes in the Midtown area. The second owner was an international speaker who invited many famous people to his home, including Winston Churchill. The house was also an apartment building until it was restored as a family home three years ago. Co-owner Sam Rhodes bowed to the Irish heritage of his partner, Sean Hanratty, who named the three guest rooms for his favorite counties — Galway, Clare and Dublin. They're individu-ally decorated with period pieces and have private baths. Continental breakfasts are served daily and usually include an assort-ment of fruits, pastries, quiche and hot and cold cereals.

Shellmont Bed & Breakfast
$$ • 821 Piedmont Ave. N.E.
• (404) 872-9290

Built in 1891 and designed by noted archi-tect Walter T. Downing, the Shellmont is listed on the National Register of Historic Places and is a designated Atlanta city landmark. The ar-chitect broke with tradition and took his inspira-tion in Renaissance and Classical forms, rather than in the prevailing Queen Anne style. Stained-glass windows, original stenciling and three fish ponds in the gardens are some of the features.

It's in the wonderfully wooded Midtown neigh-borhood and is close to Piedmont Park and The Fox Theatre. All rooms have queen-size beds, private baths, TVs and data port phones. Lodging is offered in five rooms in the main house; each is decorated in different styles of the Victorian period. One has a carved Eastlake bed with matching dresser and armoire and walls that are decorated with repro-ductions of the original wallpaper border. Another room boasts a collection of Victorian oak pieces, in-cluding a settee and chair. Innkeepers Debbie and Ed McCord welcome children 12 and younger to stay in the carriage house, com-plete with living room, bath and equipped kitchen. A full breakfast is served every day; look for Belgian waffles and whipped cream, fresh and dried fruits, and three kinds of cere-als to jump-start your morning.

Springvale-East Bed & Breakfast
$, no credit cards • 960 Edgewood Ave.
N.E. • (404) 523-5804

Across the street from the historic Edgewood Trolley Barn in Inman Park, Springvale-East has two main-floor sleeping rooms, each with a double bed, that share a bath. Up the spiral stairs is a self-contained second-floor unit with a queen-size bed in a large living/sleeping area, a kitchen, a dining area, a laundry room and a bath with a shower. Off-street parking is available. Innkeeper Bob Eberwein says most of his guests don't want more than coffee in the morning, but he will-ingly whips up whatever they do get a hanker-ing for — be it eggs or cereal.

Sugar Magnolia
$ • 804 Edgewood Ave. N.E.
• (404) 222-0226

This charming Queen Anne Victorian home in Inman Park was built in 1892. It has a three-story turret, a grand staircase and six fire-places. Innkeepers Debi Starnes and Jim Emshoff serve a continental breakfast of fresh fruits, muffins, cereals and juices in the dining room. There are three guest rooms in the main house; there's also an efficiency apartment in a cottage. Each room has period furnishings,

Many innkeepers serve breakfast on outdoor patios or porches.

TV and a private bath. The guest rooms don't share adjoining walls, so it's nice and quiet.

Virginia Highland Inn
$$ • 630 Orme Cir. • (404) 892-2735

This 1920s bungalow has two suites, Albert and Victoria, with their own private entrances, sitting porches, TVs, desks and baths. Recently restored, the house is furnished with 20th-century antiques. The spacious cottage garden provides the seasonal bouquets throughout the house. There's also a pond and an outside cat who tries to charm guests into letting him in. Breakfast is served in either the sunny kitchen or near the fireplace in the formal dining room. Innkeeper Adele Northrup creates menus prepared to guests' requests.

The Woodruff Bed & Breakfast Inn
$$ • 223 Ponce de Leon Ave. N.E.
• (404) 875-9449

This three-story, turn-of-the-century Victorian home was rehabilitated into a bed and breakfast in 1989. For years, it was a house of ill repute; in fact, the home's title comes from the madam, Miss Bessie Woodruff. The inn is near The Fox Theatre and Midtown's restaurants and bars; it's a short stroll away from Piedmont Park. Choose from deluxe suites with private baths, single rooms with private baths or family suites. The special-occasion suite has a hot tub and comes with champagne and flowers. Enjoy a full Southern breakfast of fresh fruit and muffins, eggs, bacon and grits; French toast and pancakes are made to order by innkeepers Joan and Douglas Jones.

Beyond Atlanta

Blue and Gray Bed and Breakfast
$ • 2511 Kingswood Dr., Marietta
• (770) 425-0392

This bed and breakfast in the home of John and Connie Kone has been in operation for eight years. The owners welcome guests into their residence's two rooms: one has a double bed; the other has a double and a twin. Both have televisions and VCRs, and guests are invited to peruse the owners' extensive video collection. A full breakfast may include quiche, fresh fruit and orange, cinnamon or sausage rolls. In warm weather, guests may enjoy their meals on the back porch overlooking woods and a horse pasture.

Boxwood Heights Bed and Breakfast
$ • 511 Toombs St., Palmetto
• (770) 463-9966, (888) 463-0101

The boxwoods, camellias and roses around this old house on the south side of town date back to the turn of the century. Inside, there are 13-foot ceilings and nine fireplaces. Four guest rooms have king- or queen-size beds and claw-foot tubs. Innkeepers Steve Kopelman and Clay Rakestraw present a hot breakfast as part of your stay; plan to wake up hungry for the casseroles, fruit salads, homemade breads, biscuits and muffins, ham and cheese grits, and scrambled eggs. Elegant china, sterling silver and crystal make breakfast here a meal to remember.

Gould Haus
$ • 952 Heritage Hills, Decatur
• (404) 633-7373

Overlooking the south fork of Peachtree Creek, this three-story stucco house was designed by an Atlanta architect in 1985. Emory University and Emory Hospital are less than 2 miles away; the Decatur MARTA station is also nearby. The private, two-room suite with off-street parking and a small kitchen is perfect for a long-term stay. Guests are invited to feed the ducks in the creek or take a dip in the swimming pool. Complimentary wine and cheese are served as is a daily breakfast of French toast, omelettes, muffins, croissants and fruit from the kitchen of innkeeper Maggi Gould.

INSIDERS' TIP

Like some politics with your breakfast? Debi Starnes, the innkeeper at Inman Park's Sugar Magnolia, knows all about the latest goings-on at city hall. When she's not greeting guests, she's a member of the Atlanta City Council.

Old Garden Inn
$ • 51 Temple Ave., Newnan
• (770) 304-0594, (800) 731-5011

A turn-of-the-century Greek Revival house, this bed and breakfast boasts 132 beveled window panes in the entrance hall, a wide front porch and guest rooms with robes, hair dryers and refrigerators. Breakfast may include such delights as banana dumplings with raspberry sauce. The inn is within walking distance of Newnan's shopping and business district, as well as its historic neighborhoods.

Serenbe Bed and Breakfast
$$ • 10950 Hutcheson Ferry Rd.,
Palmetto • (770) 463-2610

"Elegance and wilderness" is the theme of this turn-of-the-century farm that is now home to a luxurious bed and breakfast. The property of innkeepers Steve and Marie Nygren includes 350 acres of rolling countryside south of the city and more than 100 farm animals. A stocked lake provides fishing and canoeing opportunities. There's a pool and hot tub and several flower and vegetable gardens to enjoy. Hayrides and marshmallow roasts will enthrall the youngsters. The inn has a three-bedroom, four-bath guesthouse and a two-bedroom cottage. Both are decorated with regional folk art and antiques and have fireplaces. There's also a conference facility that can handle meetings for up to 35 people.

Breakfast is a major affair that frequently features Southern favorites such as grits souffle with collards, scrambled eggs, homemade muffins, Canadian bacon and French toast with sauteed pears picked fresh from the owners' orchard.

Village Inn Bed and Breakfast
$$ • 992 Ridge Ave., Stone Mountain
• (770) 469-3459

In the heart of historic Stone Mountain Village, the inn's 1850s Federal farmhouse is one of the oldest houses in the area. During the Civil War, it functioned as a Confederate hospital. The three-story inn has six rooms, all with private baths. Five have two-person whirlpool tubs and antique country furnishings. Innkeepers Rob and Deandra Bailey serve guests a full breakfast that usually includes an egg dish, grits or hashbrowns and a selection of breads.

Whitlock Inn
$$ • 57 Whitlock Ave., Marietta
• (770) 428-1495

Whitlock Inn, built in the 1900s, sits in a National Historic Register district, a block from the Marietta courthouse square and across the street from the First Methodist Church, whose bells still mark the evensong with hymns. There are five guest rooms, each with private baths, cable TVs and phones. A rooftop garden and rocking chair porches offer quiet retreats. There's also a ballroom that seats 100 for special events or conferences. A continental breakfast includes fruits, muffins, breads and beverages; afternoon snacks are served in the parlor by innkeeper Alexis Edwards.

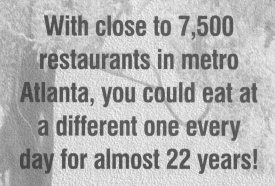

With close to 7,500 restaurants in metro Atlanta, you could eat at a different one every day for almost 22 years!

Restaurants

Eating out and eating well are one and the same in Atlanta, which has, according to The Georgia Hospitality and Travel Association, 7,500 restaurants in metro Atlanta! Quite something when you consider that the entire state of Georgia has approximately 15,000 restaurants in all.

But it's not so surprising when you consider that the Atlanta restaurant industry has several built-in advantages. The city's advanced transportation network and numerous farmers markets make fresh food accessible and affordable. And Atlanta is a magnet to people from many backgrounds, so ethnic cooking is readily accessible. Economic diversity also exerts a demand for good food at practically every price level. Subsequently, in Atlanta one may dine in sumptuous luxury at The Ritz-Carlton Buckhead or, just a few miles away, have possibly the world's best onion rings brought right to your car at the North Avenue Varsity Drive-In.

Such a vibrant marketplace naturally promotes change: For every Atlanta restaurant that succeeds, there are many more that don't. With so much competition for the public's dining dollar, customers and critics alike do not tolerate bad food or bad service for very long. Restaurants that don't make the grade are usually out of business within a year. In nearly every case, we've restricted our restaurant recommendations to places that have been open at least one year; some have been in business for decades.

With close to 7,500 restaurants in metro Atlanta, you could eat at a different one every day for almost 22 years! Clearly, our task — choosing a tiny fraction of those available to tell you about — is not easy. We've tried to let neither haute cuisine nor hot dog stands hog too much space; there is, as we've said, excellent food at nearly every price in Atlanta. Whether you're looking for an outdoor patio to lunch al fresco on a lovely spring day, a place to grab a veggie burger or somewhere to celebrate a special occasion, you'll find it among our selections.

National restaurant chains have locations everywhere you look in the metro area. Because you already know about most of them, and due to space limitations, we generally don't include chains in our chapter. If you're craving for a particular chain's food, the Yellow Pages in the telephone book is the place to look. You will find a few chain restaurants in this guide that either originated here, such as Mick's, or can only be found in a few other cities, such as the Hard Rock Cafe and the Zesto Drive-Ins.

Price Code

The price key symbol in each restaurant listing gives the range for the cost of dinner for two, excluding cocktails, beer or wine, appetizer, dessert, tax and tip. Obviously, your own bill at a given restaurant may be higher or lower, depending on what you order and fluctuating restaurant prices. These symbols provide only a general guide.

$	Less than $15
$$	$15 to $30
$$$	$30 to $50
$$$$	$50 and more

Most Atlanta restaurants take all major credit cards, but some take no plastic at all. We'll let you know when this is the case.

In general, the following is true of reservations: Some of Atlanta's fine dining establishments request (or even require) them; some mid-priced restaurants will accommodate a reservation for a larger-than-average-size party. A few places that get particularly busy will let you come in early, sign-up for a table, go to your movie and when you come back, you'll be seated before others who may have been waiting on a bench outside the door for an hour or so. It never hurts to ask just what the policy is.

Atlanta restaurants are required to offer non-smoking sections; some have banned smoking altogether. Whether or not you choose to smoke, most restaurants will have no problem accommodating your seating request.

We've divided this chapter into two major parts: Atlanta and Beyond Atlanta. Restaurants in the Atlanta section are within the I-285 Perimeter. Those in the Beyond Atlanta section are outside the Perimeter. Within these two major sections we've listed restaurants alphabetically by types of cuisine. The categories are American, Caribbean and African, Chinese, Continental and Fine Dining, Cross-cultural Favorites, Greek/Mediterranean, Indian, Italian and Pizza, Japanese, Korean, Latin, Seafood, Southern and Barbecue, Thai, Vegetarian and Vietnamese. We've divided some of these categories into subcategories. For example, you'll find Cajun restaurants in their own subcategory under Southern Food and Barbecue, and you'll find steakhouses as well as many other categories under American. So, take your time, browse through this chapter and visit some of our favorite dining spots. Bon appetit!

FYI

Three area codes serve the metro Atlanta area: 404, 770 and 678. Whether you live on Peachtree Street or in New York City, you must dial the code to reach any number in the area. The difference? Outside the area, you must dial "1," then the area code and phone number; inside the area, you need only dial the area code followed by the phone number.

Atlanta

American

Basic American

American Roadhouse
$$ • 842 N. Highland Ave. N.E.
• (404) 872-2822
Serving breakfast all day and blue plate specials, American Roadhouse is popular with neighbors in Virginia-Highland. Main dishes include meat loaf and pasta; the vegetables

are fresh. The Roadhouse has beer and wine and free parking; it's open until 11 PM nightly and until midnight on weekends.

Atkins Park
$$ • 794 N. Highland Ave. N.E.
• (404) 876-7249
With a liquor license first issued in 1927, Atkins Park has the distinction of being the oldest bar in Atlanta. It harkens back to the age of dark, wood-paneled, beery neighborhood bars. A perennial favorite in Virginia-Highland, Atkins Park offers a changing menu, including herbed grouper, rosemary ocean scallops, pasta and burgers. Atkins Park is open nightly until 3:30 AM and serves brunch on Saturday and Sunday until 3 PM; when available, there is free parking in the rear.

Blue Ribbon Grill
$$$ • 4006 LaVista Rd., Tucker • (770) 491-1570
The fare at Blue Ribbon ranges from meat loaf and other Southern favorites to hand-cut steaks, prime rib, chicken pot pie and fresh fish. There's a full bar; the restaurant seats about 156 diners. Large parties may call ahead for reservations or even fax in their order if they prefer. The restaurant is open for lunch on weekdays, for brunch on Saturday and for dinner Monday through Saturday.

The Cabin
$$ • 2678 Buford Hwy. • (404) 315-7676
In a log cabin setting with game animal heads mounted on all walls, this restaurant specializes in aged Midwestern beef, wild game and fresh seafood. There's a bar in the basement, and martinis are a specialty. Dress is casual; valet parking is available. The Cabin serves lunch weekdays, dinner nightly and is closed on Sunday.

Cheesecake Factory
$$ • 3024 Peachtree Rd. N.W.
• (404) 816-2555
Yes, you'll find plenty of cheesecake (some 50 varieties!) in this large Buckhead

NORCROSS STATION

Cafe

A Casual Restaurant in the Old Train Depot Historic Downtown Norcross

- Dine Outdoors on our Spacious Deck or Inside the Rustic Train Station
  - Carry-Out Available

Specialities Include

- Tender Baby-Back Ribs
- Fresh Seafood, Steaks, and Pasta
- Salads, Sandwiches and More

770-409-9889

Monday-Thursday 11am to 9:30 pm
Friday & Saturday 11am to 10pm
Closed Sundays

eatery, but there's also much more to enjoy. Casually elegant decor attracts families and singles alike for an eclectic American menu, featuring pasta, steaks and seafood. There is also a full bar. The Factory is open daily for lunch and dinner. You'll find the valet parking particularly useful in this busy Buckhead neighborhood.

Downwind Restaurant and Lounge

$$ • DeKalb-Peachtree Airport (entrance at Clairmont and Airport Rds.)
• (770) 452-0973

You can get a close-up view of the air traffic at DeKalb-Peachtree Airport (Georgia's second-busiest) while you dine at the Downwind. PDK (as it's called in aviation lingo) is a general aviation airport heavily used by private pilots; it has more than 1,000 employees. The Downwind has a full bar, serves lunch and offers dinner specials nightly: Steak, seafood and pasta are all featured. Entrees are priced from $6.95 to $12.95. Downwind is open for lunch and for dinner until 11 PM; it's closed Sunday and has free parking.

Einstein's

$$ • 1077 Juniper St. N.E.
• (404) 876-7925

You don't have to be a genius to see that Einstein's has caught on in a big way since opening in 1992. It has since consumed almost an entire block on Juniper Street, which is walking distance to the Woodruff Art Center. Popular munchables include Einstein's Reuben sandwich, the hummus dip appetizer and a variety of pastas. Dine indoors or on one of the two outside patios, where gas heat lamps chase away the chill in cooler months. The restaurant serves lunch and dinner daily; it's open late and is a fun place to grab a drink and a snack after the theater.

Euclid Avenue Yacht Club

$ • 1136 Euclid Ave. N.E.
• (404) 688-CLUB

Grab a local microbrew and some out-standing pub grub at this friendly eatery in Little Five Points. You'll find burgers, sandwiches, Philly cheesesteaks, hot dogs and more seven days a week. Feast on a daily blue plate special, which can be anything from chicken pot pie to a fancy pasta dish or a big slab of fish. Sip wine by the bottle or glass or choose from more than 60 different kinds of draft and bottled beer. Best of all, everything on the menu is $7 or less, often way less.

George's

$ • 1041 N. Highland Ave. N.E.
• (404) 892-3648

This friendly, family-owned neighborhood tavern serves tasty bar food, including burgers, hot dogs, chili, black bean soup and Reuben sandwiches. George's is open every day for lunch and dinner.

Hard Rock Cafe

$$ • 215 Peachtree St. N.E.
• (404) 688-7625

The neon-emblazoned Peachtree location of the famous London-based restaurant chain opened in 1992 and quickly became a tourist favorite. Inside is an array of rock 'n' roll memorabilia, from an Elton John outfit to an Elvis Presley guitar. Menu standouts include hamburgers and the pig sandwich, made from pork shoulder roast. The cafe rocks daily for lunch and dinner and stays open until 2 AM.

Houston's

$$ • 3321 Lenox Rd. N.E.
• (404) 237-7534
$$ • 2166 Peachtree Rd. N.W.
• (404) 351-2442
$$ • 1955 Powers Ferry Rd. S.E.
• (770) 563-1180

The Houston's on Lenox Road, Atlanta's first, opened in 1978; today the city is home to the corporate headquarters of the 36-location company. Houston's menu includes barbecued ribs, grilled fresh fish and prime rib. Lunch and dinner are served daily; Houston's is open until 11 PM daily.

Manuel's Tavern

$ • 602 N. Highland Ave. N.E.
• (404) 525-3447
$ • 4877 Memorial Dr., Stone Mountain
• (404) 296-6919

Manuel's Tavern has been an in-town gathering place since 1956 when Manny Maloof founded the N. Highland Avenue spot. Maloof was politically active his entire life (at one time he was CEO of DeKalb County), and today the walls of his tavern are covered with beer signs and pictures of sports heroes, Democratic Party leaders and icons who frequent the place. Through the years, the Atlanta Press Club has held meetings and debates here. Regulars roam from the main room to the "ballroom" (really the dining room), from bar to booth to table, catching up on all the latest while enjoying Manuel's wings, sandwiches, burgers and salads. It can get hectic on a busy night, but the atmosphere is friendly and inviting. Both locations are open daily for lunch and dinner.

Mick's

$$ • 557 Peachtree St. • (404) 875-6425
$$ • 2110 Peachtree Rd.
• (404) 351-6425
$$ • Lenox Square, 3393 Peachtree Rd.
N.E. • (404) 262-6425
$$ • 4540 Ashford Dunwoody Rd.
• (770)394-6425
$$ • 116 E. Ponce de Leon Ave., Decatur
• (404) 373-7797
$$ • Underground Atlanta, Peachtree and Alabama Sts. • (404) 525-2825

The first address is the original Mick's. It was started by two young men who have since retired after selling their string of popular eateries to a conglomerate (it has since been sold again). The second location is at the entrance to the Bennett Street antique and arts shopping district (see The Arts and Shopping chapters) and has a lovely outdoor patio on Peachtree Road. All Mick's are upbeat, welcoming restaurants noted for their tasty food and large portions. The big burgers are a favorite; other popular items include chicken with penne pasta, fried chicken salad, fried green tomatoes, corn and tomato linguine. For dessert, try the Oreo cheesecake or fresh cobbler of the day. The wide-ranging menu and good value make Mick's a hit with families and couples alike. All locations have a full bar. There are five other locations in the area — check the Yellow Pages.

Peachtree Cafe
$$ • 268 E. Paces Ferry Rd. N.E.
• (404) 233-4402

Peachtree Cafe has been on Atlanta's menu since 1978; its cuisine is American with Italian and other influences. Popular dishes include a salmon sandwich on flat focaccia bread with herbed goat cheese and oven-roasted tomatoes, roasted free-range chicken and Oriental salad with greens, marinated chicken and haricots verts. The cafe is open daily for lunch and dinner, reservations are accepted, and there's valet parking. Sunday brunch lasts from 11 AM to 4 PM. You can dine in true cafe style at a marble table on the small outdoor patio. Get your name and address on the mailing list and receive 2fers in the mail good at this cafe as well as three restaurants in the area owned by the same group.

Pittypat's Porch
$$$ • 25 International Blvd. N.W.
• (404) 525-8228

A favorite tourists stop, this restaurant takes its name from Scarlett O'Hara's aunt by marriage, Pittypat Hamilton. Pittypat's presents American Southern cuisine in a casual atmosphere reminiscent of Gone With the Wind, complete with rocking chairs and hand fans. Crab cakes, baby-back ribs, venison pie, fried chicken and fresh seafood are all on the menu, and your dinner includes vegetables and a salad bar with 10 Southern salads. Pitty's is right across from the Westin Peachtree Plaza Hotel. It's open daily for dinner only. Reservations are accepted.

Planet Hollywood
$$ • 218 Peachtree St. N.W.
• (404) 523-7300

Planet Hollywood opened in the summer of 1995 with great fanfare and lots of celebrities. The 21,000-square-foot, four-level, $6 million restaurant seats about 460 people and includes a handprint wall with palm impressions of some of Hollywood's finest. Planet Hollywood locations are open worldwide; each showcases movie and TV memorabilia, such as Judy Garland's dress from The Wizard of Oz and Macaulay Culkin's sled from Home Alone. Planet Hollywood's best-known shareholders are movie stars Arnold Schwarzenegger, Sylvester Stallone, Bruce Willis and Demi Moore, and they show up now and then promoting new movies. The restaurant offers classic California cuisine including unusual pastas, turkey burgers, gourmet pizzas and vegetarian items. Entrees are priced from $6 to $20. Movie montage films and coming attraction movie trailers entertain diners. Planet Hollywood is open daily for lunch and dinner.

R. Thomas Deluxe Grill
$$ • 1812 Peachtree Rd. N.W.
• (404) 872-2942

R. Thomas' year-round outdoor patio has, without a doubt, the best outdoor statuary and ornament collection of any Atlanta restaurant. But those attracted to the yard art end up staying for the eats, which include big burgers (both meaty and meatless), penne pasta, vegetarian tacos and plump wings. Beer and wine are served, and parking is free. This place sometimes attracts celebrities: Madonna, Jasmine Guy and Eric Clapton are all said to have munched here. A number of exotic birds reside in cages against the Grill's exterior wall, even during the winter when a heat lamp keeps them talking.

Roasters Rotisserie
$$ • 2770 Lenox Rd. • (404) 237-1122
$$ • 11585 Jonesbridge Rd., Alpharetta
• (770) 753-0055

Rotisserie-roasted chicken is the star at Roasters, which offers American and Southern food. Barbecue pork ribs are another specialty, and the menu generally offers 15 to 20 selections of fresh vegetables. For smaller appetites, there are sandwiches and salads. The Lenox location serves beer and wine only; the Alpharetta location has bottled beer only. Parking is free; both locations are open daily for lunch and dinner. You can eat outside on a lovely patio among the condo complexes and watch the cars whiz by on Lenox Road.

St. Charles Deli
$$ • 2970-43 Briarcliff Rd. at Loehman's Plaza • (404) 636-5201

Breakfast, lunch and dinner are served daily in this deli-style restaurant at Loehman's Plaza. The artichoke dip and toast-points appetizer is good, and the burgers, vegetable club and Reuben sandwiches are bestsellers. You can sit outside at a few small tables with a view of the parking lot. Beer and wine are available.

Taco Mac
$$ • 1006 N. Highland Ave. N.E.
• (404) 873-6529
$$ • 375 Pharr Rd. N.E. • (404) 239-0650
$$ • 771 Cherokee Ave. S.E.
• (404) 624-4641
$$ • 5830 Roswell Rd. N.W.
• (404) 257-0735

Taco Mac has been a laid-back Atlanta party spot since 1979, when it first opened on N. Highland Avenue. The fare is American bar food with a Mexican twang: Favorites include chicken salad, chicken wings, burritos, tacos and salads. Each location is a little different. North Highland Taco Mac features more than 300 beers. Most locations have a patio for warm weather fun outdoors. There are numerous other locations, reaching even into Birmingham, Alabama. Lunch and dinner are served daily.

Vortex Bar & Grill
$$ • 438 Moreland Ave. • (404) 688-1828
$$ • 878 Peachtree St. • (404) 875-1667

For burgers and beer and an outrageous ambiance, nothing beats the Vortex. The Peachtree location in Midtown is new and decorated with "flea market" stuff. Having moved from a former site on W. Peachtree Street, the new space is 4,500 square feet, which means never having to hear, "there's a wait." At the Vortex on Moreland Avenue in Little Five Points, you can't miss the shocking skull entrance. Though the decor is way out, the food is fairly traditional. Aside from great hamburgers, bar food such as nachos and chicken wings and strips are good bets. Lunch and dinner are served daily.

Vickery's Crescent Avenue Bar and Grill
$$ • 1106 Crescent Ave. N.E.
• (404) 881-1106

Crescent Avenue's charming homes long ago were converted into popular eateries. Vickery's opened in 1983 and serves American bar and grill food with a Cuban flair. The atmosphere is casual and friendly, and there's a full bar. In addition to daily specials, the hamburgers are hugely popular as are the Cuban-style roasted chicken and a variety of salads and sandwiches. Especially during the spring and fall, the tree-shaded brick patio on Crescent Avenue is a lovely place to relax for a few hours. Vickery's eclectic crowd makes for great people-watching. It's open daily for lunch, dinner and late-night snacks.

Zac's
$$$ • 308 W. Ponce de Leon Ave. N.E., Decatur • (404) 373-9468

This popular restaurant's fare ranges from standard American (meat loaf, chicken pot pie) to upscale trendy (black-and-white linguine with salmon and bay scallops in seafood sauce). Beer and wine are available. Zac's serves lunch Tuesday through Friday, dinner Tuesday through Saturday and brunch on Saturday and Sunday.

Fine Dining

Blue Ridge Grill
$$$ • 1261 W. Paces Ferry Rd. N.W.
• (404) 233-5030

With large booths, a welcoming porch, beamed ceilings and a large stone fireplace, this restaurant's decor evokes the charm of a lodge in the southern Appalachian Mountains. Its fare includes dishes such as horseradish-crusted grouper, swordfish, barbecued pork chops and Georgia game mixed grill. Entrees are priced from $14 to $24. Relax at the full bar. Blue Ridge Grill is open for lunch and dinner.

Living High on the Hog

Barbecue as a Southern tradition began well before the states even had names. North American Indians showed European explorers how to dry meat and fish on a framework of green saplings spread over a slowly smoldering fire. The explorers called this *barbacoa*, a term still used in Spanish. In the early 1700s, when North Carolina was

a colony, barbecuing was part of the celebration for the end of the tobacco harvest. When French settlers applied the technology, they preferred to slowly roast whole animals on an open fire, and this cooking method was known as *Barbe a queue.*

With this kind of ancient — by American standards — history, it is not surprising that passions run deep about barbecue. In the South, where everyone has an opinion about how a hog should be prepared, which cuts of meat to use, what variety of animal should be chosen and whether or not it should be pulled, sliced, or chopped, even how to spell the word (barbecue or barbeque), folks get pretty hot under the collar about what makes a particular recipe the best.

In Kentucky, according to author Calvin Trillin, mutton rather than pig is the barbecue meat of preference while in Oklahoma and Texas brisket and sausage gets the thumbs up. But the most controversial issue by far involves the sauce. "And that is a river of debate that burns smoky brown or clear red, depending on your geographic preference," states barbecue maven and Atlanta writer Jim Auchmutey, waxing poetically about his favorite topic. In most Southern states including Texas, the preference is for a thick, sweet, tomato-based sauce. But in the low lands of South Carolina, barbecue sauces are prepared with a cider vinegar and black-pepper base that proves to be a complex taste combination some folks either love or hate.

A plate of pulled pork, Brunswick stew and slaw makes for a tasty meal.

Pig Pickin', where an entire hog is cooked, is the popular method of barbecuing. Diehards use a homemade rig consisting of an old water tank or a pit in the ground upon which the meat is slow-cooked on a bed of wood. When the meat is ready, the crowds, hungry from their hours-long wait, pick the meat from the bone with their fingers.

In Atlanta, you can find the best of both sauce styles — the tangy South Carolina barbecue as well as the more popular tomato-based sauce. Both are slavered on pork or beef that is pulled, chopped or sliced, and tiny cups of extra sauce may be placed on your plate for dipping.

A profile of the barbecue tradition in the South exists in Bennett Brown III and his Atlanta catering company, LowCountry Barbeque. Started in 1986, the company specializes in Pig Pickin' parties, and Brown has introduced many bigwigs, including cookbook writer and TV star Julia Child, to the joys of the whole hog.

— continued on next page

Brown's childhood memories include long nights of watching his dad and cronies dig a pit and stay up through the night and into the following day keeping wood stoked under a slow-cooking hog for the next evening's party. The men would tell stories, drink beer and enjoy each other's company. At 11 years old, Brown was permitted to fix a pig in a pit by himself. It was a rite of passage, and so meaningful, he made a career out of barbecuing.

Great barbecue is available to all of us in Atlanta, at downright country prices, and we don't have to stay up all night roasting a pig for it either. Dozens of restaurants specialize in nothing but barbecue. It's easy to sample the local fare and join in the debate about where you get the best. And while you're at it, don't forget to order Brunswick stew, another Southern tradition. It'll be right there on the menu; it might even come with your platter of pulled pork, bun and pickles. What's Brunswick stew? It's a concoction of veggies and bits and pieces of meat. According to Christianne Lauterbach, food critic for *Atlanta Magazine*, the best stew should be "thick enough to spread on crackers, sweet with the goodness of pork and golden corn and most generous in its meat-to-vegetable ratio."

Hungry? Well, come and get it.

Buckhead Diner
$$$ • 3073 Piedmont Rd. N.E.
• (404) 262-3336

Definitely not what the word "diner" suggests, this eatery is more like a plush dining car from the *Orient Express* with an eclectic modern American cuisine. Part of the fabulous Buckhead Life Restaurant Group chain including Pricci and Pano's & Paul's, Buckhead Diner provides excellence from the first morsel to the last. You might want to start with the salt and pepper calamari, go on to a specialty, such as the veal and wild mushroom meat loaf or the grilled smoked pork chop and finish up with the white chocolate banana cream pie. Ever heard of an upscale restaurant serving cheese grits? Well, there's a first time for everything. A diner with valet parking? You bet! The diner is open daily for lunch and dinner.

Bugatti
$$$$ • 100 CNN Center at Marietta St.
• (404) 818-4450

Restaurants come and go quickly in Atlanta, but Bugatti has prospered in downtown's Omni Hotel since the '70s. The menu, once primarily Italian, has become more inclusive of continental offerings over the years. The restaurant's elegant decor with comfortable plush chairs and indirect lighting seats 120. Conventioneers to the Georgia World Congress Center and sports fans attending events at the nearby arenas may drop by for drinks before or after meetings or games, while tourists staying at other downtown hotels dine on basil wrapped ahi tuna spring rolls with ginger cream and pickled plums or a shrimp-and-scallop cocktail with fresh horseradish and chilled tomato fondue. A triple-header platter for lobster lovers includes lobster risotto, grilled lobster tail and a lobster cognac broth. Meat eaters will relish roasted rack of lamb with potato mixed with sun dried figs, roasted chestnuts and Brollo wine sauce, and a dessert favorite is a banana dome infused with semi-sweet chocolate, pineapple essence and a chocolate shortbread cookie. Lunch and dinner are served daily.

Canoe
$$$ • 4199 Paces Ferry Rd. N.W.
• (770) 43-CANOE

On the banks of the Chattahoochee River in northwest Atlanta, Canoe has revived the barrel-vaulted brick building once known as Robinson's Tropical Gardens: It's said many a young romance bloomed at this riverfront restaurant and nightspot in the golden post-WWII years. In accordance with its goal of offering delicious, healthy food for today's diner, Canoe's fare includes grilled farm-raised chicken with wild mushroom potato puree with port wine and cranberries, goat cheese and potato tortellini with artichokes, autumn greens, pine nuts and white truffle oil, and a wild mushroom soup with polenta croutons. You can call ahead for reservations, or take advantage of any waiting time to stroll riverside. Valet parking is available. Dinner is served nightly.

City Grill
$$$$ • 50 Hurt Plaza • (404) 524-2489

This restaurant, in the heart of downtown, is in a former Federal Reserve Bank built in 1913. Its decor conveys an appropriate sense of affluence. The cuisine is American regional with a Southern flair: Specialties include Southern-fried quail, barbecued shrimp and crab cakes. The atmosphere is fine dining on the relaxed side. Call for reservations. City Grill is closed on Sunday; it serves lunch on weekdays and dinner Monday through Saturday.

The Country Place
$$ • 1197 Peachtree St. N.E.
• (404) 881-0144

When it opened in 1978 in Colony square as part of The Peasant Restaurant chain, this was a favorite spot for after-theater dining. Although the Peasant chain has changed hands a few times, the food is still consistently good. The casually upscale Country Place still offers an American menu with generous portions at reasonable prices, which includes pan-sauteed swordfish, lump crab cakes and prime rib. The house salad is excellent and comes with the meal as does the signature bread balls, which are more doughnut than anything since they are fried and sweet. And the mile-high ice-cream pie is incredible and enough for at least two sweet seekers. It consists of three layers of ice cream and a bottom crust of chocolate graham crackers, all drizzled with butterscotch syrup and topped with whipped cream. A piano bar just prior to the dining room is also a draw. There's live entertainment beginning at 6 PM Thursday through Saturday. Reservations are accepted for lunch and dinner daily. You can park for free for up to three hours in the Colony Square garage; ask for validation.

Dailey's Restaurant and Bar
$$$ • 17 International Blvd. N.W.
• (404) 681-3303

Dailey's opened in 1981; it's a shadowy, noisy and altogether pleasant downtown eatery serving creative American fare. Just down the street from the Hark Rock Cafe, Dailey's attracts a more mature crowd. Big sellers are the swordfish au Poivre, strip steak and rice-paper salmon. For dessert, try Dailey's famous French fried ice cream. The big portions make Dailey's popular with sports celebrities, politicians and the downtown business and convention crowd. Dinner is served nightly; lunch is served daily, except Sunday.

Horseradish Grill
$$$ • 4320 Powers Ferry Rd. N.W.
• (404) 255-7277

This trendy, casual restaurant near Chastain Park opened in 1994 after a major remodeling of its space, the former Red Barn Inn, which was one of Atlanta's oldest restaurants. Its cuisine is in-season Southern fare, and all grilled items are cooked over a hickory fire. Specialty dishes include a peanut and cracker encrusted Georgia mountain trout with a port wine and onion confit, veal chops with wild mushrooms and sweet potato dumpling, and strip steaks. The full bar has a dazzling array of spirits, especially single-malt scotches. In spite of receiving accolades in *Esquire*, *Bon Appétit* and *Atlanta* magazines, management aspires to preserve the restaurant's reputation for catering to locals: Some 50 percent of patrons are repeat guests. The Horseradish Grill is open daily for lunch (except Saturday) and dinner; there's valet parking.

Kudzu Cafe
$$$ • 3215 Peachtree Rd. N.E.
• (404) 262-0661

The creeping and all-but-indestructible kudzu vine has been the bane of generations of Southern gardeners (see our close-up in the Neighborhoods and Real Estate chapter), but here it is pressed into use as the design motif for a pleasant upscale restaurant. The fare is heavily influenced by Southern favorites, but it's been updated with less fat and a more imaginative presentation. Specialties include fried green tomatoes, hickory-smoked pork chops, the vegetable plate and a diet-destroyer known as the Kudzu Moon Pie. The dining room has lots of booths and artwork by Southern photographers. In business since

1992, the Kudzu Cafe is open daily for lunch and dinner, offers valet parking and takes reservations.

Pano's & Paul's
$$$$ • 1232 W. Paces Ferry Rd. N.W.
• (404) 261-3662

Since 1979, Pano's & Paul's has been serving modern American/Continental cuisine in a luxurious environment of chandeliers and tuxedoed waiters. Well-heeled locals frequent the place for its superb aged meats, batter-fried lobster tails with honey mustard dressing and live Maine lobster stuffed with crabmeat. A venison and ostrich combo is also a meaty dish. Pano's & Paul's is the first of a very successful number of restaurants now known as the Buckhead Life Restaurant Group famous for the fantastic breads it makes for all its places. The restaurant has a full bar, requires reservations and recommends jackets for gentlemen. Like many of The Buckhead Group's places, the decor is unique. Some, such as 103 West and Pano's & Paul's, drip with fabric and darker colors, others, such as Pricci and The Buckhead Dinner are modern and airy. Pano's & Paul's serves dinner only Monday through Saturday.

The Peasant Restaurant and Bar
$$$ • 3402 Piedmont Rd. N.E.
• (404) 231-8740

The Peasant on Piedmont serves creative American cuisine with Southwestern and Cajun influences. With a greenhouse dining room and wicker furniture, the ambiance is casually elegant; the restaurant draws locals and conventioneers. Pepper-crusted tuna, lobster risotto, New York strip steak and cheese-filled tortellini are recommended dishes. Lunch is served daily except Saturday; dinner is served nightly. The restaurant has valet parking.

The Peasant Uptown
$$$ • Phipps Plaza, 3500 Peachtree Rd.
• (404) 261-6341

In 1974, the Peasant Uptown was the first restaurant to spin-off from the Pleasant Peasant downtown (see separate listing). The Peasant Uptown serves lunch and dinner daily in a casually elegant setting that suggests a greenhouse. The crowd includes Atlantans as well as many out-of-towners who come to shop at Phipps Plaza and Lenox Square. The garlic filet and the pan-seared sea bass are two specialties. There's valet parking; and reservations are accepted.

Pleasant Peasant
$$$ • 555 Peachtree St. N.E.
• (404) 874-3223

When the Pleasant Peasant opened in 1973 as the first of a group of restaurants owned and operated by Dick Daily and Steve Nygren, it immediately became an Atlanta dining favorite. The restaurant was the first in Atlanta to have handsome young waiters presenting themselves (as in, "I'm Tom, your waiter for the evening") and menus on chalkboards. All the Peasant restaurants have retained their lively, exciting mood even though Mick's and Daily's, which were also part of this group, have changed hands a number of times. Recommended entrees include steak au Poivre, herbed-marinated rack of lamb and plum pork tenderloin. The Peasant is open weekdays for lunch and nightly for dinner; valet parking is available at night. Reservations are accepted.

South City Kitchen
$$$ • 1144 Crescent Ave. N.E.
• (404) 873-7358

In an old Midtown house, South City cooks up a new Southern cuisine that would no doubt baffle the Southern cooks of a century ago, but the place is going gangbusters. The innovative menu includes a grilled center-cut pork chop on stir-fried mustard greens, sauteed shrimp and scallops over stone-ground grits with garlic gravy, roasted cinnamon chicken over corn-bread stuffing and a sour mash jus. Entrees range to $21.95. South City is open daily for lunch and dinner.

Steakhouses

Bone's
$$$$ • 3130 Piedmont Rd. N.E.
• (404) 237-2663

In business since 1979, Bone's serves steak and seafood in a fine dining atmosphere that's clubby yet lively. Menu favorites include live Maine lobster (flown in daily), rib-eye steaks and lamb chops. Bone's has a full bar and offers valet parking. The restaurant recommends reservations and that gentlemen wear a coat and tie. Bone's is open weekdays for lunch and every night for dinner.

Chops
$$$$ • 70 W. Paces Ferry Rd. N.W.
• (404) 262-2675

Chops steakhouse, open since 1989, has received national attention in *Esquire* and elsewhere. The atmosphere is casual chic, suggesting a 1930s-era men's club with dark wood, art deco light fixtures and oversized chairs. The menu includes steaks, lamb chops, fish and lobsters. The wine list is a connoisseur's dream, with more than 400 selections up to $3,000 a bottle. Reservations are strongly recommended; there's valet parking. Chops is open every night for dinner and for lunch on weekdays. The Lobster Bar on the lower level, (404) 231-7128, offers lobsters from one to eight pounds and steaks.

Coohill's Restaurant
$$$ • 1100 Peachtree St. N.E.
• (404) 724-0901

Formerly named Bistango and owned by the same folks who bring us Ciboulette, this fashionable Midtown spot draws a cross section of patrons to its elegant setting. Popular with theatergoers, the restaurant is just two blocks south of Woodruff Arts Center, where many cultural events are staged. Steaks and chops are the order of the day. The vegetable side orders, which you order as separate dishes, are enough for two. If you or your dining companion loves meat, this is the place. Or order a few appetizers for a terrific meal, such as steak tartar, lump crab cocktail and a variety of soups. Coohill's is open for lunch

Monday through Friday and for dinner Monday through Saturday. The restaurant accepts reservations.

Cowtippers
$$ • 1600 Piedmont Rd. • (404) 874-3469

A whimsical Western steakhouse theme welcomes you at this popular in-town eatery featuring hearty fare, a friendly staff and a lively crowd, who love to sit on the Cowtippers outside deck and enjoy the ribs and sweet potatoes. Steaks, prime rib, barbecue chicken, shrimp and veggie kebabs are also on the menu. And you can wash it all down with a selection from the full bar. Cowtippers serves lunch and dinner daily.

Highland Tap
$$$ • 1026 N. Highland Ave. N.E.
• (404) 875-3673

This popular in-town steakhouse is in a granite-walled cellar below the intersection of N. Highland and Virginia avenues. In a masculine room reminiscent of the 1940s, the restaurant's menu includes steaks, lamb chops and duck. Martini aficionados should try the Tap's four-ounce "world-class martini." The restaurant is open every day for lunch and dinner, except there's no lunch on Monday; brunch is served on weekends.

Morton's of Chicago
$$$$ • 303 Peachtree St.
• (404) 577-4366
$$$$ • 3379 Peachtree Rd. N.E.
• (404) 816-6535

In Peachtree Center, Morton's masculine, clubby decor suggests a Chicago speakeasy. You'll enjoy porterhouse, prime rib or live Maine lobster. Morton's is open nightly for dinner. Reservations are recommended, as are jackets for the gentlemen. There's valet parking.

INSIDERS' TIP

If you want to enjoy a great restaurant-cooked meal without leaving home, Takeout Taxi, (404) 728-8888, and Buckhead Gourmet Delivery, (404) 261-6325, bring the best to your door. Charges range from $3.99 to $5 with minimum order requirements from $10 to $15 depending on the meal and the provider. Both services pick up and deliver from dozens of restaurants we've mentioned in this chapter. Don't forget to tip the driver!

Photo: The World of Coca-Cola Atlanta

This replica of a 1930s soda fountain is just one of
the exhibits at The World of Coca-Cola Atlanta.

Pilgreen's Restaurant and Lounge
$$$ • 1081 Lee St. S.W. • (404) 758-4669
$$$ • 6335 Jonesboro Rd., Morrow
• (770) 961-1666

Pilgreen's steakhouse is an Atlanta tradition, still operated by the family that established it in 1932. The atmosphere is casual and friendly, and many customers are regulars. Specialties of the house include filets, T-bones and the steak for two. Each location has a full bar. The original Lee Street restaurant has free secured parking; it's closed on Sundays and after at 3 PM on Mondays. Lunch and dinner are served the rest of the week. The Morrow location is open for lunch and dinner Sunday through Friday and for dinner only on Saturday.

Sun Dial Restaurant and Lounge
$$$$ • Westin Peachtree Plaza Hotel,
210 Peachtree St. N.W. • (404) 589-7506

There's nothing like dining atop the world's second-tallest hotel to make your troubles seem oh-so-small. Seventy-one floors above Peachtree Street, Sun Dial is a room with a dazzling view; and, since the whole place rotates, you'll get to see it all. The three-course dinner begins with a shrimp appetizer, and the entrees include smoked prime rib, filet mignon, chicken, swordfish and salmon. The Sun Dial is open every day for lunch and dinner, including all holidays; reservations are accepted. Even if you only stop by for a cocktail in the upper-level lounge, the Sun Dial (especially the non-stop ride up in a glass-enclosed elevator outside the building!) is always a thrill. There's a $4-per-person charge to visit the lounge/observation level. The Mose Davis Trio plays Fridays and Saturdays, and Mose plays piano during the week.

Tasty, Quick and Cheap

EATS
$, no credit cards • 600 Ponce de Leon
Ave. N.E. • (404) 888-9149

EATS is a favorite with college kids and other Generation Xers who groove on the casual atmosphere, eclectic music and terrific, inexpensive food. There are separate counters and sometimes long lines: One serves pasta (the big seller is cheese tortellini with marinara sauce), and another serves jerk chicken and vegetables. EATS is open daily for lunch and dinner. Beer and wine are sold here.

Susie's Coffee Shop

$, no credit cards • 1660 McLendon Ave. N.E. • (404) 371-0889

Susie's is an old-fashioned coffee shop and grill that's a regular stop for residents in the Candler Park and Lake Claire neighborhoods. The friendly, cozy shop with a counter and a few tables serves breakfast and lunch daily. Breakfast and burgers are cooked to order by Susie herself in front of a large window on McLendon. The home-fried potatoes are terrific. Susie's does not serve alcohol.

Tasty Town Restaurant

$, no credit cards • 67 Forsyth St. N.W. • (404) 522-5865

This pleasant, nostalgic little restaurant near the Central Library is a great place to grab lunch downtown. A variety of sandwiches is offered, along with main courses such as fried trout. Nothing shakes off the midday blues like the chopped sirloin steak and a half-dozen cups of Tasty Town's rich coffee. It's open for breakfast and lunch Monday through Saturday. No alcohol is served.

The Varsity

$, no credit cards • 61 North Ave. N.W. • (404) 881-1706
$, no credit cards • 1085 Lindbergh Dr. N.E. • (404) 261-8843
$, no credit cards • 6045 Dawson Blvd. N.W., Norcross • (770) 840-8519

At the corner of Spring Street, the original Varsity is just across the North Avenue bridge from Georgia Tech. It opened in 1928 and claims the distinction of being the world's largest drive-in: Every day, this single restaurant serves up to 2 miles of hot dogs, a ton of onion rings and 5,000 pies. The city put The Varsity at North Avenue on its registry of historic buildings, which will keep it from changing forever after. Friendly carhops will bring your food to your car, or you can eat inside and watch TV in one of the several large dining rooms. The serving counters inside are a beehive of activity: The slogan here is, "Have your money in your hand and your order in your mind." The onion rings may just be the best on the planet. The Varsity does not serve alcohol.

Woody's Famous Philadelphia Cheesesteaks

$, no credit cards • 981 Monroe Dr. N.E. • (404) 876-1939

Woody's, just across from Grady High School on a spit of land between Monroe Drive and Virginia Avenue, has been providing students and Insiders with good cheesesteaks and submarine sandwiches since 1975. This tiny restaurant is nothing fancy, and its operating hours were recently trimmed to 11 AM until 5 PM. It's closed Sunday and Monday. Check out the extensive variety of Breyer's ice creams. No alcohol is served.

Zesto Drive-In

$ • 544 Ponce de Leon Ave. N.E. • (404) 607-1118
$ • 3165 Glenwood Rd., Decatur • (404) 289-9519
$ • 377 Moreland Ave. • (404) 523-1973
$ • 2469 Piedmont Rd. N.E. • (404) 237-8689

Since 1949, Atlanta has been stopping by Zesto's. The Illinois-based soft ice-cream chain was once in 46 states. Today, few restaurants remain, but, with seven locations, Atlanta is still a hotbed of them. Try a Chubby Decker hamburger and a side order of fried okra (if you're in the right Zesto's — each one's menu is quirkily different from the others) and top it off with a Nut Brown Crown. The satiny soft ice cream is the real thing. The Ponce restaurant, a recently built chrome-colored "classic" diner, is the best-looking Zesto's. Check the Yellow Pages for other locations.

Caribbean/African

Bridgetown Grill

$$ • 689 Peachtree St. N.E. • (404) 873-5361
$$ • 1156 Euclid Ave. • (404) 653-0110
$$ • 7285 Roswell Rd. • (404) 394-1575

Bridgetown Grill is just across from the Fox Theatre. Some people call it fusion, some call it Jamaican. Whatever you call it, the food is simply delicious — jerk chicken, guava-barbecued ribs, conch fritters and Jamaican burritos, two spicy chicken burritos topped with Habanero cheese sauce, guacamole and salsa served with black beans and rice and plantains. Service is friendly in this casual, relaxed setting. Brightly painted walls, banners and artwork create an upbeat atmosphere. You can get lunch and dinner seven days a week. The Peachtree and Roswell locations have full-service bars. The Grill on Euclid Avenue serves beer and wine only.

Imperial Fez
$$$ • 2285 Peachtree Rd. N.E.
• (404) 351-0870

Leave your worries (and your shoes) at the door and be swept into the sultan's palace for an evening of tinkling bells, pulsating drums and lovely ladies swaying in the old-fashioned (Eastern) way. This promises to be an exotic experience with sinuous veiled dancers and tantalizing aromas and flavors. Be prepared to sit on cushions (if you have a bad back, request extra cushions or be sure to pick a spot against a bolster). Feast on authentic Moroccan cuisine with no MSG, curry or lard in the dishes. It's not unusual for a guest (male more often than female) to spontaneously stand and dance with a performer, which adds to the evening's fun. There are special prices for children 12 and younger; otherwise, everyone else at a table must order his or her own entree; no separate checks. A fixed price of $35 per person gets you a five-course meal including soup, five different salads and appetizers, a choice of entrees including lamb, Cornish hen with apricots, seafood and vegetarian specialties and dessert of fresh fruits and pastries. (Drinks will up the ante.) Bring extra dollars to place in the dancer's garb when they dance at your table. Reservations are recommended.

Patti Hut
$ • 595 Piedmont Ave. N.E.
• (404) 892-5133

In the Rio Shopping Center, this small, squeaky clean casual place pleases the palate. Get ready for some tasty treats, such as big juicy chunks of the freshest jerk chicken, tender curry goat stew and oxtails seasoned with Jamaican spices. The rice and bean dishes are nutritiously filling. Peruse the steam table's bountiful vegetables and spike them with the house-made Scotch Bonnet pepper sauce. You may sop up the greens' juice with Patti Hut's special corn bread. Locals line up for the Monday special, which may be corned beef and cabbage. With your meal, have a Jamaican ginger beer or a fruit-based soda and spicy fries and fried plantains on the side. Low cost and large portions delight the regulars, who dine inside, at the few tables out on the sidewalk or take their goodies home. Patti Hut serves lunch and dinner, Monday through Saturday.

Chinese

Chin Chin
$$ • 3887 Peachtree Rd. N.E.
• (404) 816-2229

Enjoy mouth-watering Chinese cuisine in this restaurant's pleasant surroundings. Crowd-pleasing entrees include tangerine steak, golden crispy prawns, shredded pork in garlic sauce and sauteed vegetables. Open every day for lunch and dinner, Chin Chin offers a full bar and free delivery within a 3-mile radius. Chin Chin's chef's specials and a few other entrees will take you higher than the range we cited above, but you can grab a good bargain with the lunch special. Choose from 33 items priced from $4.95 to $5.75. On Sundays, it opens at 3 PM.

Chopstix
$$$ • 4279 Roswell Rd. N.E.
• (404) 255-4868

Don't let the name fool you. This is not standard Chinese food fare, nor are the prices. At Chopstix you eat by candlelight with fine china, linen-covered tables and gourmet Chinese food worthy of the prices. Most of the clientele are loyal followers who have discovered this excellent restaurant almost hidden in Chastain Square.

Hot and cold appetizers include stir-fried alligator and mango roasted duck salad. The extensive menu includes many shrimp and scallop dishes as well as seafood, shellfish, pork, chicken and beef entrees. Princess prawn, ginger duck in a crispy rice-bowl, and Satay seafood hot pot with eggplant, shrimp, scallops and lobster are among the favorites. Dress casually and relax with cocktails, beer or wine in the piano bar. Reservations are recommended. Chopstix serves lunch on weekdays and dinner every night.

Grand China

$$ • 2975 Peachtree Rd. N.E.
• (404) 231-8690

Order from a sizable menu for reliable food in this longtime Buckhead fixture. Szechuan, Cantonese and Taiwanese entrees join those originating in Singapore.

The bar, with its lattice motif bamboo shades, offers a pleasant setting. Try the General Tsao Chicken, small chunks of boneless chicken breast lightly fried, then covered with a hot-sour sauce and sesame seeds. Noodle dishes, both hot and cold, are favorites. An outdoor section is open in good weather. Grand China is open every day for lunch and dinner. No reservations are needed.

Hsu's Gourmet Chinese Restaurant

$$$ • 192 Peachtree Center Ave.
• (404) 659-2788

For fine dining in downtown Atlanta, visit this charming and picturesque restaurant. The food is new Cantonese cuisine in Hong Kong style and has won many fans among residents and visitors. Try the shrimp with fresh mango, grilled stuffed scallops or Peking duck served in two courses: crispy skin in a Chinese pancake and grilled duck meat with honey ginger sauce. Hsu's offers a full-service bar as well as wines by the glass or bottle.

Little Szechuan

$ • Northwoods Plaza, 5091-C Buford Hwy. • (770) 451-0192

Another of the good Asian restaurants clustered in strip centers on Buford Highway, Little Szechuan concentrates on food, not atmosphere. Mandarin Chinese cuisine with Szechuan spices dominates the menu. Creative and well-seasoned, the dishes here include stir-fried Szechuan string beans, shredded pork with garlic sauce, chicken in sherry with garlic sauce, steamed fish with black beans and spicy garlic shrimp. Look for sizable portions and fast service. You can buy beer and wine, and there's lots of free parking

outside. Little Szechuan serves lunch and dinner every day except Tuesday. The restaurant accepts reservations for parties of six or more and has a big party room for parties of up to 50.

New China

$$ • 2899-B N. Druid Hills Rd. N.E.
• (404) 325-0331

This restaurant in Toco Hills Shopping Center offers a large selection of seafood, beef, pork and poultry entrees. House specialties include sizzling triple treasure, a dish combining scallops, chicken, roast pork and Chinese vegetables; steak Kew with shrimp and Yu Shian seafood, which mixes lobster, crabmeat, scallops and shrimp with garlic, ginger and Chinese vegetables. New China serves dinner nightly.

The Orient at Vinings

$$$ • 4199 Paces Ferry Rd.
• (770) 438-8866

Cantonese cuisine with modern touches is the specialty here in a relaxed contemporary setting that includes a refurbished railroad car. Specialties include firecracker pork, rainbow shrimp and Szechuan cuttlefish. Ask about the weekly lunch special. Friendly service is a mainstay of this popular restaurant. Reservations are suggested. The Orient is open for dinner every night and for lunch Monday through Friday. It serves brunch on Sunday.

Pung Mie

$$$ • 5145 Buford Hwy., Doraville
• (770) 455-0435

Popular dishes in this well-recommended place include asparagus shrimp, noodle soups and braised sea cucumbers with pig leg. A range of Chinese-Korean specialties keeps customers of all nationalities coming back for more. You can drink beer or sake; fruit desserts are included in the meal. Pung Mie is open for lunch and dinner seven days a week.

INSIDERS' TIP

Call the Vegetarian Society of Georgia's 24-hour recording, (770) 662-4019, for updates on cooking classes, educational programs and a complimentary copy of the society's newsletter.

Uncle Tai's Restaurant

$$$ • Phipps Plaza, 3500 Peachtree Rd.
• (404) 816-8888

Upscale and sophisticated, this restaurant specializes in authentic Hunan cuisine. Gourmet specialties include jumbo shrimp in chili sauce and sliced lamb with scallions. You may also order salads, soups and light fare. You can order all dishes hot, medium or mild. The restaurant's Phipps Plaza setting (across from Lenox Square) makes it a natural for important business gatherings or social events. You can eat in or take out. It's open for lunch and dinner seven days a week.

Continental

57th Fighter Group Restaurant

$$$ • 3829 Clairmont Rd.
• (770) 457-7757

This theme restaurant, whose decor suggests a World War II French farmhouse, is near DeKalb-Peachtree Airport, which handles most of the small private plane traffic in Atlanta. You can relax at a table with a runway view while you enjoy the continental fare, which includes lemon veal, citrus salmon and prime rib. The dance floor swings to Big Band tunes performed by an eight-piece band on the first Sunday of each month. A DJ supplies the music on Fridays and Saturdays. The atmosphere is comfortably casual with dinner served nightly; lunch served on weekdays, brunch on Sunday. Expect to spend $40 to $50 per couple. Reservations are accepted, and there's a full bar.

103 West

$$$ • 103 W. Paces Ferry Rd. N.W.
• (404) 233-5993

In the heart of Buckhead, 103 West serves continental and French cuisine in an atmosphere of fine dining and interior decor that is heavy and just dripping with faux 17th-century opulence. It's owned by the same great folks who bring us Pricci, the Buckhead Diner, Pano's & Paul's and a few other fine dining establishments, so you can count on enjoying the most delicious breads (they make their own and are famous for them). Popular menu items include grilled cold-water lobster tail in

a thin, crisp batter with honey and Chinese mustard sauce, roasted double breast of chicken filled with wild mushrooms on sauteed baby spinach with rosemary garlic sauce, and parmesan-crusted medallions of veal with select vegetables and garganelli pasta in tarragon butter. There's valet parking; 103 West serves dinner only and is closed on Sunday; jackets are requested for the gentlemen. Noontime is reserved for the many associations that hold their monthly luncheons here: Atlanta Women's Network has been meeting at 103 for years.

The Abbey

$$$$ • 163 Ponce de Leon Ave.
• (404) 876-8532

Looking for a dinner that's almost a religious experience? Try The Abbey, a fine dining restaurant serving contemporary cuisine in a deconsecrated Methodist church that takes up a whole block between Ponce de Leon and North avenues. Mustard garlic crusted rack of lamb, prime veal strip steak with crabmeat compote and pan-seared breast of duck in cinnamon honey glaze are popular entrees. The restaurant has been in business since 1968 and has been at this location since 1978; it draws tourists as well as locals out celebrating that special occasion. It's open daily for dinner only; there's valet parking; reservations are suggested.

Anthonys

$$$$ • 3109 Piedmont Rd. N.E.
• (404) 262-7379

It's easy to miss Anthonys' signage on Piedmont because the restaurant itself is hidden way back in the woods on one of the largest undeveloped pieces of land on this otherwise busy road. In a beautiful 1797 plantation home with seven working fireplaces, Anthonys' house was originally built in Washington, Georgia, where it was spared by Gen. Sherman, supposedly because the family had an infant. An Atlanta restaurant landmark since 1967, Anthonys offers fine dining in a unique atmosphere. Each room is decorated with antique paintings, chandeliers, chairs and tables; seven fireplaces make the rooms even cozier in winter months. The second-floor sun porch is a popular spot for anniversaries, birthdays and other special occasions that require tête-à-tête dining. The management has been testing dining outdoors on a variety of patios under towering hardwood trees. Popular entrees include Veal Anthony (which is milk-fed veal loin stuffed with Maine lobster tail sauteed with wild mushrooms, garlic and Madeira wine served over crispy herbs, risotto cake and balsamic roasted onion). Another favorite is the pumpkin seed and coriander crusted grouper with chipotle maple sweet potatoes and three pepper salad with warm cranberry apple salsa. Anthonys is open seven nights a week for dinner; reservations are suggested; there's valet parking.

Babette's Cafe
$$$ • 471 N. Highland Ave.
• (404) 523-9121

On the outskirts of Little Five Points, Babette's presents European provincial fare that includes a fried oyster appetizer on dill biscuits with cucumber sauce, artichoke and olive ravioli, mussels with strawberries and serrano peppers and the seasonal French stew cassoulet. There's a full bar; dinner is served nightly Tuesday through Sunday; brunch is served on Sunday, and it may require a wait as this place is popular with locals.

Cassis
$$$$ • 3300 Peachtree Rd. in the Grand Hotel • (404) 365-8100

With sophisticated decor and a menu to match, Cassis resides in the snazzy Grand Hotel (formerly the Hotel Nikko) in Atlanta's Buckhead area. A spectacular view of the Hotel's Oriental garden and waterfall is definitely a plus here. The restaurant takes an innovative approach to Mediterranean cuisine. Look for yellowfin tuna sliced and seared with avocado rice noodles, Maine lobster and shrimp ravioli with cucumber and ginger, filet mignon and vegetable strudel. Cassis serves breakfast, lunch and dinner daily as well as Sunday brunch. Reservations are accepted; all diners enjoy complimentary valet parking.

The Dining Room
$$$$ • The Ritz-Carlton Buckhead, 3434 Peachtree Rd. N.E. • (404) 237-2700

One of the finest restaurants in Atlanta, The Dining Room, a small (by Atlanta standards) wood-paneled room, elegantly appointed with art and antiques, offers a prix fixe dinner nightly except Sunday, with or without special wines from the master sommelier. We highly recommend you take the sommelier's suggestions and experience the meal the way the chef intended. You may also order à la carte. Guenter Seeger, who was chef here for 11 years, put the place on the charts. Now under the direction of Frenchman Joel Antunes, the menu has become continental with a vivid touch of the Orient — not surprising since the young chef perfected his craft in Bangkok, Thailand, at the Oriental Hotel, a posh resort. Dishes change nightly. Appetizers might include foie gras and artichoke terrine, rare tuna with tarragon and chervil served with julienned beets, or shelled mussels with hot pepper and cumin seasoned tomatoes. Entrees for the evening might feature medallions of lamb in a brown sauce with sweet and sour eggplant confit and fava beans and chickpeas; veal with artichoke risotto, cherry tomatoes tarted up with lemon grass and chanterelles; or smoked salmon with parsley sauce. Best of all are the desserts, which come to the table looking more like sculptures than edible pastry, fruits, mousse and chocolates. Even if you are not much of a drinker, select the set meal of either three courses ($65) or five ($78) with wines chosen by the sommelier. The Dining Room strongly encourages reservations, provides valet parking and asks that gentlemen wear jackets.

The Mansion
$$ • 179 Ponce de Leon Ave. N.E.
• (404) 876-0727

A grand 1885 home on a hill is the setting for The Mansion, a continental restaurant that opened in 1976. The estate, which occupies an entire block, was the home of Edward Peters, whose father, Richard, was the original developer of Atlanta's Midtown neighborhood. In surroundings rich with period furnishings and antiques, The Mansion serves lunch and dinner daily and brunch on Sunday. You may wish to start with an appetizer, such as steamed lobster with wilted spinach and lobster bisque, then choose from entrees such as beef Wellington, potato-crusted snapper with roasted peppers and dual pepper sauce, or pan-seared breast of chicken with saffron rice. Entree prices range up to $24.95. The Mansion's elegant walled pool area is a popular spot for weddings. Dress is smart; reservations are accepted. The entrance to the parking area is on Piedmont (northbound) just above North Avenue. During the 1996 Olympics, the German delegation booked The Mansion and The Abbey (across Piedmont) for the duration of the Games.

Nikolai's Roof

$$$$ • The Atlanta Hilton and Towers, 255 Courtland St. N.E. • (404) 221-6362

When nothing less than total extravagance will do, there's Nikolai's Roof — if you planned ahead, that is. Advance reservations are nearly always necessary at this famous fine dining restaurant atop the Atlanta Hilton, which specializes in French and Russian cuisine. A six-course prix fixe dinner of $62.50 per person is served nightly, with seatings at 6:30 and 9:30; the menu changes with the availability of game and other specialty items. There's an extensive wine list and a number of flavored Russian vodkas. Coat and tie are requested for the gentlemen. Nikolai's, which provides stupendous views of Atlanta north of downtown, has been dazzling diners since 1976.

The Restaurant

$$$$ • The Ritz-Carlton Atlanta, 181 Peachtree St. N.E. • (404) 659-0400

Seating only 85 guests in an intimate, English hunt club atmosphere on the second level, The Restaurant offers Mediterranean-influenced French cuisine. Specialties include foie gras, souffles and a variety of game and fish. Reservations are recommended; jackets are required for gentlemen; there's valet parking. The Restaurant is open for dinner only and is closed on Sunday.

English

Reggie's British Pub and Restaurant

$$$ • CNN Center, Marietta St. at Techwood Dr. N.W. • (404) 525-1437

Cheerio, old chap! Even though the founder of Reggie's passed on in 1997 to the big banquet in the sky, this casual Victorian pub that began in 1976 remains as a testament to English ale. The menu spotlights American fare and British specialties, such as scotch eggs, bangers and mash, steak and kidney pie and vegetarian burgers. The full bar features more than 40 beers, with eight on draft. Reggie's hosts the Grand Losers Party every July 4th and is honored to be the Atlanta venue for Veterans of the Royal Air Force, who gather each September to commemorate the Battle of Britain. Lunch and dinner are served daily.

French

Anis

$$ • 2974 Grandview Ave. N.E. • (404) 233-9889

You know the food will be good when a French restaurant has a large French clientele. Anis has built a good reputation quickly since opening in 1994 and is quite popular. The fare is French Provencale and many of the wait staff speak French. Located in a brick house on a once-quiet Buckhead street that now boasts a number of restaurants, Anis has a large patio that is great for outdoor dining. It can get crowded, but the staff knows its business, and everyone is taken care of. Prices are reasonable. Beer and wine are available; there's live entertainment on Thursday night. Anis is open Monday through Saturday for lunch and dinner. The restaurant opens at 6 PM on Sundays for dinner. Parking on this formerly residential street now restaurant row is always challenging. There is underground parking available across the street at Colony Square and open air lots throughout the 14th and Peachtree streets area.

Brasserie Le Coze

$$$ • Lenox Square, 3393 Peachtree Rd. N.E. • (404) 266-1440

Designed as a reproduction of a turn-of-the-century Parisian brasserie with dark wood paneling, this restaurant serves French and other cuisines. Signature dishes include mussels with white wine and shallots; seared salmon with lentils, pearl onions and lardons; or roast skate wings served with spinach potato in a brown butter caper sauce. The signature coq au vin is served only on Saturdays. Le Coze has its own pastry chef. There's a full bar; an outdoor patio is open in warm weather. Lunch and dinner are served Monday through Saturday; reservations are accepted.

Ciboulette
$$$$ • 1529 Piedmont Rd. N.E.
• (404) 874-7600

This upscale restaurant can be easily overlooked in a strip mall across from Ansley Mall on Piedmont Road. But local folks know where to find it and frequent the place whenever they save up the moola. The modern French menu includes foie gras du jour and duet of brandade and crab cakes appetizers, plus hot smoked salmon with wild mushrooms, ginger and soy, and roast squab with cabbage au jus. Expect to spend $100 for dinner for two, more if you have wine. Reservations are accepted; there's a full bar and an extensive wine list. The open kitchen lets you watch the chef at work. Ciboulette is closed on Sundays.

Petite Auberge
$$ • Toco Hills Shopping Center, 2935 N. Druid Hills Rd. N.E. • (404) 634-6268

This French continental restaurant opened in 1974 and can easily be missed in the family-oriented mall in which it has been located from the beginning. Stand-out entrees include sea bass, bouillabaisse maison, filet mignon and beef Wellington. Entree prices range to $18.95. It's open Monday through Saturday for dinner and on weekdays only for lunch. Dinner reservations are accepted.

South of France
$$ • Cheshire Square, 2345 Cheshire Bridge Rd. • (404) 325-6963

Off the beaten track, South of France has been serving simple French cuisine in an intimate atmosphere since 1977. Specialties include quail with port wine, roast duckling with a brandied peach sauce and braised rabbit in red wine sauce. South of France serves dinner Monday through Saturday and lunch on weekdays. There's a full bar, and the restaurant accepts reservations. Keep an eye out for celebrities — we once saw Ted and Jane (Turner and Fonda) having dinner here.

Cross-Cultural Favorites

Cafe Tu Tu Tango
$$ • 220 Pharr Rd. • (404) 841-6222

This Buckhead restaurant evokes the air of an artist's loft with creative use of light and color and a profusion of regional artwork. The setting includes a painter at work before an easel. Called multiethnic in influence, the tapas-style menu consists of appetizer-size entrees intended for sharing. The choices are invariably delicious and highly original. Barcelona stir-fry, Cajun chicken egg rolls, seared tuna sashimi — see what we mean by multiethnic? The cafe's full-service bar is a popular meeting spot. The restaurant is open every day for lunch and dinner and until the wee hours on the weekend. We've put Cafe Tu Tu Tango in the $10-to-20 price range, because entrees generally cost between $4 and $8. Many people choose to order more than two, which can kick the check up to the next price range.

Chow
$$$ • 1026 N. Highland Ave.
• (404) 872-0869
$$$ • 303 Peachtree Center Ave.
• (404) 222-0210.

Chow, which opened in 1985, offers casual dining atmosphere that appeals to its neighbors in laid-back Virginia-Highland. Specialties include ginger tuna and lemon basil chicken. Lunch and dinner are served daily (except there's no lunch at the Peachtree Center location on Saturday and Sunday). The weekend brunches are festive affairs at the Highland branch only. The downtown location (Peachtree Center) has secured parking and a lovely exterior deck where you may also dine. Reservations are accepted.

Dante's Down the Hatch
$$$ • 3380 Peachtree Rd. N.E.
• (404) 266-1600
$$$ • Underground Atlanta, Peachtree and Atlanta Sts. • (404) 577-1800

How about a place that looks like a big ship tied to a wharf where you can hear live jazz, watch alligators swim past the bar and eat all your courses from a fondue pot? That's Dante's, an Atlanta original with two locations. The original Dante's was one of the best-known spots in the first Underground Atlanta. It closed downtown for a while and opened uptown in Buckhead. But when Underground was renovated, Dante's downtown location reopened. The design of both restaurants does indeed suggest a sailing ship at dock, and there's live jazz on the ship seven nights a week. The fare is fondue from meat to fruits, and your server will be happy to instruct you in the basics. The full bar boasts more than 300 wines. Both Dante's serve dinner nightly; reservations are recommended. See our Nightlife chapter for more details about Dante's.

Tom Tom
$$$ • Lenox Square, 3393 Peachtree Rd. N.E. • (404) 264-1163

Tom Tom's fusion menu showcases Asian, Mediterranean, Southwestern and French cuisines. The menu features salads, sandwiches, pizzas, quesadillas and bistro bites, appetizers that range from rice-paper spring rolls to ceviche of shrimp and scallops in lime juice. Entrees include spinach ravioli, barbecued salmon and a leg of lamb studded with rosemary and garlic. Tom Tom's serves lunch and dinner seven days a week and features a daily chef's special.

Greek/Mediterranean

Basil's Mediterranean Cafe
$$$ • 2985 Grandview Ave. N.E. • (404) 233-9755

In the heart of Buckhead, Basil's outdoor patio is a big hit. Favorites of patrons here include grilled lamb chop in wine sauce served with rosemary-scented mashed potatoes and beans, and grilled salmon on ratatouille with basil pesto and steamed potatoes. After dinner, unwind with a delightful coffee drink from the full bar. Appetizers are terrific including a Mideastern dish comprised of tabbouleh, hummus and baba ghanoush. Basil's serves lunch and dinner daily except Sunday; reservations are accepted.

Oasis Cafe
$$ • Sage Hill Shopping Center, 1799 Briarcliff Rd. • (404) 876-0003

This family-owned restaurant makes everything up fresh. Its Middle Eastern special-

ties include kebabs, stuffed grape leaves, mjadra (made with lentils, rice, onions, tomato, yogurt and cucumber). All entrees include soup and a salad; there are lunch and dinner specials daily. Beer and wine are served. Friday and Saturday night a violin and guitarist play classical music. The Oasis is closed on Sundays.

Parthenon Greek Restaurant
$$$ • 6125 Roswell Rd. N.E. • (404) 256-1686

Besides the lamb specials, look for the Parthenon Special, a combination of gyro, sausage and grilled onions with a special homemade sauce. Or try the chef's special, a type of Greek lasagna with stuffed grape leaves and vegetables. Entrees are priced from $9.25 to $14.95. All entrees come with a Greek salad; beer and Greek wines are available. Desserts include rice pudding and baklava. It's open for lunch and dinner every day but Sunday.

Shipfeifer on Peachtree
$$ • 1814 Peachtree Rd. • (404) 875-1106

Specializing in Mediterranean and vegetarian food since 1974 (when it was the only place in Atlanta where you could buy a gyro), this cozy place is popular with patrons from nearby office buildings and residents of the in-town area. You could eat for less than the price range shown by choosing from the menu's sandwich and sandwich wrap sections. The menu aims to please many tastes with a variety of dishes. Try the filling moussaka, a casserole of ground beef blended with herbs, spices and eggplant, topped with feta cheese and a creamy Bechamel sauce. A puff pastry filled with mushrooms, calamata olives, artichokes, peppers, onions, tomatoes and cheese will satisfy a craving for vegetables. The most expensive entree is $8.50. Children's meals are offered. Baklava, the famous Greek honey nut pastry, is the star dessert. For a beverage, you may choose from domestic or imported beers and specialty coffees. Free parking is provided behind the restaurant, which is open for lunch and dinner seven days a week. Half the menu is geared toward the vegetarian palate.

Indian

Calcutta
$$ • 1138 Euclid Ave. • (404) 681-1838

Set in the Little Five Points district, Calcutta is known for high-quality dishes and low prices. Chicken Tandoori is a favorite with many diners here. Lunch and dinner are served seven days a week. Wine and Indian beers are available.

Haveli Indian Cuisine
$$ • 225 Spring St. N.E. • (404) 522-4545
$$ • 2650 Cobb Pkwy., Smyrna
• (770) 955-4525

Haveli's menu includes seafood, vegetarian dishes, goat, lamb and chicken, with tandoori and curry specialties. Open for dinner seven nights a week, Haveli serves lunch every day except on Sunday and features an all-you-can-eat lunch buffet.

Indian Delights
$, no credit cards • 1707 Church St., Decatur • (404) 296-2965

High on food quality, this restaurant features dishes from the southern part of India. The spotlight is on creatively seasoned grains and vegetables at inexpensive prices. Masala dosa, a large crepe filled with curried potatoes, is a favorite. Spicy soups, homemade noodles and hot sauces will bring you back for more. Indian Delights doesn't serve alcohol. The restaurant is open for lunch and dinner every day but Monday.

Raja Indian Restaurant
$$ • 2955 Peachtree Rd. N.E.
• (404) 237-2661

This small restaurant has developed a following of residents by serving an assortment of fine entrees. Offerings include Tandoori specials, vegetarian dishes, hot curries and samosas. Rice entrees include the tasty shrimp biryani, pilau rice cooked with shrimp, raisins, nuts and peas. For your beverage, choose from American and Indian beers, plus Indian herbal teas. It's open for lunch and dinner seven nights a week.

Italian and Pizza

Abruzzi Ristorante
$$$$ • 2355 Peachtree Rd. N.E.
• (404) 261-8186

Tucked away in the upscale Peachtree Battle Shopping Center, Abruzzi has been a favorite of Buckhead area residents and their guests since 1989. Combining low-key elegance with superior service, this coat-and-tie restaurant offers many specialties, such as superb homemade pasta, seasonal game dishes, risotto with salmon, sea bass and vegetable ravioli. A daily selection of homemade gelato and other desserts tempts even the most steadfast dieter. The restaurant offers a full bar and ample parking in front. Abruzzi is open every day except Sunday for dinner and Monday through Friday for lunch. Reservations are required.

Azio Pizza and Pasta
$$ • 220 Pharr Rd. N.E. • (404) 233-7626

This popular pizza and pasta place is in the heart of the Buckhead entertainment district. A stylish, casual bistro, Azio specializes in thin-crust, brick-oven pizzas. Also on the menu you'll find antipasti and a variety of salads. Azio is open for lunch and dinner daily.

Bertolini's Authentic Trattoria
$$$ • 3500 Peachtree Rd. N.E.
• (404) 233-2333

Bertolini's opened in 1992 in Phipps Plaza. Offering authentic northern Italian food at affordable prices, the restaurant recommends reservations. You can eat here for less than $20, but most entrees fall into a slightly higher

---

INSIDERS' TIP

Atlanta addresses can be misleading, especially where restaurants are concerned. It's not unusual to find an upscale eatery tucked in a strip shopping center. To avoid hunger pangs while driving around lost, call ahead to get specific directions and the name of the shopping center, if any.

range for dinner for two. Bertolini's offers lunch and dinner seven days a week. Fresh home-made pastas, brick-oven pizzas and fabulous desserts are served in an upscale casual atmo-sphere. Try the tagliolini al fruiti di mare with lobster, shrimp, scallops, scallions, tomatoes and cream. Or perhaps the sausage with polenta and roasted peppers would be more to your liking. A full-service bar is offered.

California Pizza Kitchen

$$ • Lenox Square, 3393 Peachtree Rd. N.E. • (404) 262-9221
$$ • 4600 Ashford Dunwoody Rd. N.E. • (770) 393-0390
$$ • 6301 North Point Pkwy., Alpharetta • (770) 664-8246

You can feast on imaginative pizzas, pas-tas and salads for both lunch and dinner in this restaurant's casual contemporary atmo-sphere. Snazzy entrees from the impressive menu include a mind-boggling array of pizzas with nearly 30 gourmet toppings including bar-becued chicken, Peking duck and Southwest-ern burrito. Other entrees include chicken te-quila pasta, pasta primavera and focaccia-bread sandwiches. Hours and alcohol avail-ability vary by location.

Camille's

$$ • 1186 N. Highland Ave. N.E. • (404) 872-7203

This popular, casual Virginia-Highland res-taurant serves pizzas, pasta dishes and house specialties including seafood fra diavolo, a med-ley of fish and shellfish in a spicy sauce; and seafood primavera, which mixes clams, mus-sels, shrimp and calamari with squash, arti-chokes and mushrooms. Other popular dishes include veal picatta and chicken marsala. We've put Camille's in the $10-to-$20 price category because you can get pizza, lasagne and other dishes in that range, but be aware that many of the entrees will take you to the next price cat-egory. Camille's serves dinner nightly.

Fellini's Pizza

$, no credit cards • 2809 Peachtree Rd. N.E. • (404) 266-0082
$, no credit cards • 1991 Howell Mill Rd. N.W. • (404) 352-0799
$, no credit cards • 923 Ponce de Leon Ave. N.E. • (404) 873-3088
$, no credit cards • 4429 Roswell Rd. N.E. • (404) 303-8248
$, no credit cards • 422 Seminole Ave. N.E. • (404) 525-2530
$, no credit cards • 1634 McLendon Ave. N.E. • (404) 687-9190

Wacky decor, loud music and classic-style pizza in a casual, high-energy setting — that's Fellini's in all six locations. Don't expect finesse, just good eats. Made with the freshest ingredients, the pizzas are regu-lar or Sicilian. Besides the traditional top-pings, try the white pizza, which is espe-cially good here. Plump calzones stuffed with sausage and cheese will fill you with satis-faction, as will the salads. The large veg-etarian pizza is excellent. Fellini's serves beer and wine and is open seven days a week for lunch and dinner. Fellini's doesn't take credit cards.

La Grotta Buckhead

$$$$ • 2637 Peachtree Rd. N.E. • (404) 231-1368

La Grotta Ravinia

$$$$ • 4355 Ashford Dunwoody Rd. • (770) 395-9925

Fine Italian cuisine here includes pasta dishes and favorites such as roasted quail stuffed with Italian sausage, grilled polenta and balsamic vinegar sauce and fillet of swordfish on a bed of spinach and Roma tomato with red pepper and fresh thyme coulis.

Menu selections include meals approved by the American Heart Association; the pastry cart items, alas, are not among them. Dinner is served Monday through Saturday at the Peachtree Road location, and reservations

INSIDERS' TIP

The old Southern names for meals — "dinner" for the midday and "supper" for the evening — are seldom used anymore, but you may encounter them. You can clear up the question as to which meals a restaurant serves by asking for the hours of service.

are recommended. The Ravinia location is open for lunch and dinner, is more airy and modern than the Buckhead restaurant and offers a wonderful view of the hotel's gardens from huge glass windows. Favorite menu items include grilled veal chop with herbs, shallots and finocchio sauteed in butter, and beef tenderloin grilled with Barolo mustard with mushrooms, spinach and roasted garlic mashed potatoes.

Nino's

$$ • 1931 Cheshire Bridge Rd. N.E.
• (404) 874-6505

This cozy, dim Italian restaurant is more authentic than any you'll find in the city. Even the waiters speak the language. Nino's serves both northern and southern cuisine quite simply without dressing up the plates, or the prices for that matter. House specialties include a number of pasta dishes as well as a variety of veal, beef, chicken and seafood entrees. Nino's offers a full bar and serves dinner Monday through Sunday. Reservations are accepted and even recommended, especially for weekend dining.

Pricci

$$$ • 500 Pharr Rd. N.E.
• (404) 237-2941

Even amidst the Buckhead district's estimated 200-plus restaurants, Pricci's glamorous setting makes it stand out, just like so many of the Buckhead Life Restaurant Group's other eateries including 103 West, Pano & Paul's and The Buckhead Diner. Delicacies await you in a chic interior where upscale informality reigns. Among the house specialties are regional dishes, homemade pastas and pizzas from wood-burning ovens. But pizza is not what this Italian restaurant is really about. A favorite with diners is the cold-water lobster tails sauteed with garlic, lemon and Pinot Grigio with black-and-white linguine marinara. Or try the baby lamb shank in Barolo wine sauce with pastina, braised vegetables and roasted garlic. Specialty desserts include cappuccino creme brulee.

A full-service bar and extensive wine list will meet high expectations. Pricci's recommends reservations. Lunch is served Monday through Friday and dinner every night.

Rocky's Brick Oven Pizzeria

$$ • 1770 Peachtree St. N.E.
• (404) 876-1111
$$ • 1395-D N. Highland Ave. N.E.
• (404) 870-ROCK

This source of delectable pizzas, pasta and other authentic treats is a popular gathering place. In this homey, bustling restaurant, mouth-watering pizzas can be mixed and matched from an extensive selection of ingredients. Indulge in the Rudolph Valentino pizza, complete with sweet-onion sauce and rosemary-seasoned roasted new potatoes on thin crust or pick a more robust thick-bottomed pie. The restaurant is named for the owner's Dad, and the pizza at Rocky's is baked in hickory- and oakwood-burning ovens made in Milan. Pricing is slightly different for either Neapolitan (thin) or Sicilian (thick) crusts. Two could squeak by on pizza for less than $20, but pasta dishes are slightly more expensive. Rocky's serves beer and wine; dinner is served seven nights a week. Rocky's also serves lunch on weekdays.

San Gennaro

$$ • 2196 Cheshire Bridge Rd.
• (404) 636-9447

Under the same ownership as Camille's, San Gennaro is like a trattoria on some sun-drenched Italian hillside. The rafters are hung with a few grape vines, and murals color a wall. Portions are big and entries include a generous house salad and a side of pasta with your choice of sauce. Mussels are recommended as is the stuffed eggplant appetizer. A large deck for dining built around an enormous hardwood tree is extremely popular and is enclosed and heated during the cooler months. Ask about opera nights, which take place now and then in an events room and include dinner and song.

Veni Vidi Vici

$$$$ • 41 14th St. N.E. • (404) 875-8424

If authentic northern Italian cuisine in a cosmopolitan, elegant atmosphere suits you, this is your kind of restaurant. Smack in the middle of the Midtown scene, Veni Vidi Vici, another eatery in the Buckhead Life Restaurant Group cadre of fine restaurants, rarely disappoints. Peruse the extensive hot and cold antipasti piccoli, which are small appetizers well-designed to pique, not squash, your appetite. Among the restaurant's specialties are suckling pig, balsamic chicken with roasted peppers and new potatoes, buffalo milk ricotta filled tortellini with butter and Parmigiano Reggiano, a slice of whole roasted salmon on tomato risotto with crispy carrots and grilled endives. Visit the boccie ball court next to the patio. Lunch is served on weekdays, and dinner is served every night. There's a full-service bar on the premises. Reservations are recommended.

Japanese

Hashiguchi Jr.
$$ • 3400 Wooddale Dr. N.E.
• (404) 841-9229
$$ • 3000 Windy Hill Rd., Marietta
• (770) 955-2337

In the Around Lenox Shopping Center near Lenox Square, this Japanese restaurant is a popular spot with sushi fanatics. Good service is yours at the full sushi counter. The spicy tuna roll is sure to awaken your taste buds, as will the clams steamed over sake. Check out the traditional tempura dishes, one of which features bass. Tofu, crisply fried and dressed with shredded ginger, shows culinary imagination. For beverages, try Japanese beer or sake, and finish your meal with a dish of green tea ice cream. Closed on Monday, Hashiguchi serves lunch with sushi specials and dinner Tuesday through Sunday. Reservations are accepted.

Ru Sans
$$ • 1529 Piedmont Ave. N.E.
• (404) 875-7042
$$ • 2313 Windy Hill Rd., Marietta
• (770) 933 8315
$$ • 1530 Old Alabama Rd., Roswell
• (770) 643-6747
$$ • 3365 Piedmont Rd. • (404) 239-9557

California-style sushi and Japanese fusion entrees fill the menu of this restaurant, which opened in 1993. Ru Sans on Piedmont Avenue is frequented mostly by the collegiate set who enjoy the fast pace, lively

atmosphere and laid-back presentation. Ru Sans is open for dinner every night and for lunch every day but Sunday. Sushi, tempura and yakitori bargains for $1 each are wildly popular. The sushi slices are enormous in comparison to some of the other restaurants that feature this kind of food. Beer and wine are available. The Marietta location has tepan tables (food is cooked at the table), and reservations are taken at that location only. The Ru Sans at Piedmont Road boasts a 100-foot-long sushi bar and a quick-serve take-out counter.

Korean

Asiana Garden
$$ • 5150 Buford Hwy. No. A-220, Doraville • (770) 452-1677

In the same center as 99 Market (see our International Atlanta chapter), this restaurant is a combination of Korean and Japanese cuisine served to a mostly Asian clientele. The Korean-style barbecue is a favorite as are Japanese dishes, which include shrimp and vegetable tempura, unaki-don (traditional broiled eel with special eel sauce) and a variety of noodle and soup dishes. Seafood, pork, poultry and beef entrees in generous portions are described in English on your menu. Miso soup comes free with your sushi order, and if you purchase noodle soup, six or more little bowls of interesting food to add to the soup come to your table. These include tiny fish, kim chee cabbage, green veggies and other goodies. Asiana is open for lunch Monday through Friday and for dinner seven nights a week.

Mirror of Korea
$$ • 1047 Ponce de Leon Ave. N.E.
• (404) 874-6243

Two miles from downtown, this restaurant offers authentic Korean cuisine. You'll find Korean specialties such as kim chee, spicy marinated cabbage; bool go ghi, a barbecue beef dish; and gahl bee, a beef short rib entree. Mirror of Korea also serves sushi, Chinese dishes and vegetarian items. The restaurant serves beer and wine and opens for lunch and dinner Monday through Saturday.

Latin

Caramba Cafe
$$ • 1409-D N. Highland Ave.
• (404) 874-1343

The food at this family-owned Mexican restaurant is prepared using vegetable oil. In addition to burritos, tacos, quesadillas and chalupas, the menu features a number of meat-free and cheese-free dishes. Mia's Margaritas are crowd-pleasers, and so is the homemade flan. Dinner is served nightly; parties of six or more may call for reservations.

Coco Loco
$$ • 2625 Piedmont Rd. N.E.
• (404) 364-0212

This small restaurant in a shopping center has been preparing delicious Cuban and Caribbean dishes, such as jerk chicken, fried plantains, conch fritters, paella, arroz con pollo and Cuban sandwiches, since 1988. There's a full bar, and live entertainment is featured on Saturday night. Coco Loco, where the attitude is fun and tropical, is open for lunch and dinner every day.

Don Juan's
$$$ • 1927 Piedmont Cir. N.E.
• (404) 874-4285

This Spanish continental restaurant opened in 1977. Specialties of the house include tapas, paella, veal, a variety of fresh fish and black bean soup. Dinner is served Monday through Saturday; parking is free. Don Juan's has a full bar.

El Azteca
$$ • 3424 Piedmont Rd. N.E.
• (404) 266-3787
$$ • 939 Ponce de Leon Ave.
• (404) 881-6040
$$ • 5800 Buford Hwy. • (770) 452-7192

As you roam around Atlanta, you're often not far from a friendly, colorful El Azteca restaurant. The local chain has been serving spicy, reasonably priced Mexican food since 1981. All locations have a full bar and an outside patio. The menu offers inexpensive lunch specials, an array of combination plates and specialty entrees such as beef and chicken fajitas and quesadillas. Lunch and dinner are served daily. Check the Yellow Pages for other locations.

El Toro
$$ • 5899 Roswell Rd. N.E.
• (404) 257-9951
$$ • 1775 Lawrenceville Hwy., Decatur
• (404) 321-9881
$$ • 4300 Buford Hwy. • (404) 636-7090
$$ • 2973-B Cobb Pkwy.
• (770) 955-9873
$$ • 5288 Buford Hwy. • (770) 455-6884

El Toro prepares all your Mexican favorites; the food is deliciously flavored and served quickly. Choose from an almost endless variety of combination platters and specialties. All locations have a full bar and are open daily for lunch and dinner. Check the Yellow Pages for suburban locations.

Frijoleros
$, no credit cards • 1031 Peachtree St.
N.E. • (404) 892-8226

Big burritos and quesadillas made fresh to order are what's cooking at Frijoleros on Peachtree near the corner of 11th Street. You can eat in the dining room, which is decorated with countless band posters, or outside on Peachtree. The atmosphere is hip and collegiate, and the delicious food is served in whopping portions. Beer is sold; Frijoleros is open daily for lunch and dinner, except on Sundays.

La Bamba Restaurante Mexicano
$$ • 1139 W. Peachtree St. N.E.
• (404) 892-8888

In a brightly painted house in the shadow of the IBM building at W. Peachtree and 14th streets, La Bamba serves up big portions of traditional Mexican favorites, such as fajitas, quesadillas, pepper steak and more. Margaritas are a specialty, and the best place to enjoy them (weather permitting) is the large outdoor deck. La Bamba is open daily for lunch and dinner; parking is free. Parties of six or more may call for reservations. We hear this spot is popular with local TV news people.

La Fonda Latina

$$ • 1150 Euclid Ave. N.E.
• (404) 577-8317
$$ • 2813 Peachtree Rd. N.E.
• (404) 816-8311
$$ • 4427 Roswell Rd. N.E.
• (404) 303-8201
$$ • 639 McClendon Ave.
• (404) 378-5200

The ambiance here is in the style of a Mexican cantina, with floral murals, fountains, perky music and friendly service. The location at Euclid Avenue is the place in Little Five Points for spicy Latin-influenced food, including the highly recommended paella served in a sizzling iron skillet, either as a vegetarian dish or loaded with chicken, seafood and sausage. The quesadillas come with big portions of black beans and yellow rice. Beer, wine and a delicious homemade sangria are poured at La Fonda. It's open daily for lunch and dinner.

Mambo Restaurante Cubano

$$$ • 1402 N. Highland Ave. N.E.
• (404) 876-2626

Mambo, which features a 9-foot-tall mural of a stylized Carmen Miranda, serves Cuban cuisine nightly for dinner. Crowd-pleasers include paella, Chino-Latino (a Cuban-Chinese fish dish) and ropa vieja (a dish of shredded beef, garlic, tomatoes and peppers). Beer and wine are served; lively Latin music is featured on CDs; reservations are accepted. If you sit on the outdoor patio, you can watch the line grow outside Indigo Restaurant which is directly across the street. And if you have to wait to be seated, visit the art galleries and shops next door (see The Arts and Shopping chapters).

Mexico City Gourmet

$$ • 2134 N. Decatur Rd. N.E.
• (404) 634-1128
$$ • 5500 Chamblee Dunwoody Rd.,
Dunwoody • (770)396-1111

Upscale but friendly, this restaurant delivers what its name suggests: imaginatively prepared Mexican food. Fish dishes and other specials are offered with favorites such as shrimp fajitas and chile rellenos. Both locations have a full bar; try the Perfect Margarita, made with Grand Marnier instead of triple sec.

Whether you want something quick or an elegant five-course meal, you'll find it in Atlanta.

Mexico City Gourmet is open daily for lunch and dinner.

Rio Bravo Cantina

$$ • 3172 Roswell Rd. N.W.
• (404) 262-7431
$$ • 5565 New Northside Dr. N.W.
• (770) 952-3241
$$ • 440 Ernest W. Barrett Pkwy. N.W.,
Kennesaw • (770) 429-0602

Rio Bravo started serving its Tex-Mex fare in Buckhead in 1984 and since has expanded to the suburbs, Tennessee and Florida and Alabama. Crowd-pleasers include the fajitas, quesadillas and cheese dip. Free valet parking is offered on weekends, and there's a large patio. Rio Bravo is open every day for lunch and dinner. All locations have a full bar. Check the Yellow Pages for other locations.

Sundown Cafe

$$ • 2165 Cheshire Bridge Rd. N.E.
• (404) 321-1118

Creative Mexican and Southwestern food is the attraction at Sundown. The menu changes frequently to showcase various appetizers and entrees. Eddie's pork, grilled and served with jalapeno gravy, is popular. Try the spicy Mexican turnip greens. Entrees are priced from $7.95 to $13.95. There's a full bar. Lunch is served weekdays; dinner is served Monday through Saturday. Patio dining is available here, too.

Tortillas
$, no credit cards • 774 Ponce de Leon Ave. N.E. • (404) 892-0193

This fun, lively California-style burrito place is big with students and anyone who likes inexpensive spicy food. These fat burritos are bursting with beans and rice, and the sauces are bright and bold. The music is mixed including punk, reggae, blues and college rock. From the second floor outdoor porch you can soak up the ever-changing scene on Ponce. Beer is available. Tortillas is open daily for lunch and dinner.

Seafood

Atlanta Fish Market
$$$ • 265 Pharr Rd. N.E. • (404) 262-3165

A huge fish sculpture looms over this popular Buckhead restaurant, which is part of the Buckhead Life Restaurant Group. Unveiled in November 1995, "the great fish," a 50-ton solid copper and steel artwork, is either an eyesore or a great Atlanta landmark, depending on whom you ask. The sculpture stands on its tail and curves upward, dwarfing the building. Inside, a pleasing combination of casual atmosphere and superior food sets the tone of this restaurant.

The Savannah-style fish house is part of a 13,000-square-foot complex that includes a lounge, second-floor private dining room and boutique-style food shop. The menu changes daily based on the availability of fresh seafood in season. Local favorites include lobster and Dungeness crab. You can order the catch of the day charbroiled or steamed Hong Kong style with fresh ginger and scallions in a light sherry soy sauce. Reservations are suggested for dinner seven nights a week. Lunch is served every day except Sunday. The Fish Market offers cocktails, beer and wine. The Pano's Food Shop is the on-site take-out shop.

Jim White's Half Shell
$$$ • 2394 Peachtree Rd. N.E. • (404) 237-9924

Another Buckhead staple, this restaurant has long delighted diners with house specialties of stone crab claws and Maryland crab cakes. Other favorites include fresh fillet of trout Pontchartrain, sauteed and topped with fresh tomatoes and crabmeat. Among the extensive seafood standards is Shoreman's Delight, a winning combo of rock lobster tail, crab and shrimp. In the Peachtree Battle Shopping Center, this casual-dress restaurant with a full-service bar serves dinner every night but Sunday. It offers a children's menu. Reservations are recommended for parties of five or more.

Indigo Coastal Grill
$$$ • 1397 N. Highland Ave. N.E. • (404) 876-0676

Be prepared to wait for a seat in this highly popular place that draws crowds with its varieties of coastal cuisine including tastes from Cape Cod to the Caribbean. The rustic decor's relaxed ambiance has overtones of Key West and features a vintage jukebox and a 110-gallon fish tank. Brown butcher paper covers the tables, and paraphernalia abounds. Check out the conch fritters and Dan's key lime pie. The fresh catch of the day, wrapped in parchment, is a favorite. Sesame and panko crusted catfish served with Jicama, snow peas and red pepper slaw with an Asian vinaigrette is another mouth-watering option. Indigo is open for dinner seven nights a week and also serves Sunday brunch. Reservations are accepted.

McKinnon's Louisiane Restaurant and Seafood Grill
$$$ • 3209 Maple Dr. N.E. • (404) 237-1313

For more than 20 years, McKinnon's has provided superior Cajun seafood to appreciative diners in two settings: the upscale main dining room and the more casual Grill Room. There's nothing ordinary about the offerings, such as crawfish tails salad. Blackened amberjack, crunchy on the outside, moist and tender on the inside, is a favorite. Crawfish etouffe, served over rice, is another. Guests can sing along at the piano on Friday and Saturday. At the intersection of

Maple Drive and Peachtree Road, the restaurant accepts reservations for dinner every night except Sunday.

Ray's on the River
$$$ • 6700 Powers Ferry Rd., Marietta
• (770) 955-1187

Ray's has drawn a lively crowd to its huge, many-roomed setting on the Chattahoochee River since 1984. Seafood flown in daily and fresh pasta are favorites here. Grilled, blackened, broiled, sauteed, baked or fried — have your choice of how your entree is prepared. Among the popular choices are oysters on the half shell and blackened fish Alexander, which is topped with Mornay sauce, shrimp and scallops. Other entrees include prime rib, chicken, large salads, homemade soups and desserts. A full-service bar, extensive wine list and live jazz create an enjoyable atmosphere. A call for priority seating will move you to the head of the line if you arrive at your appointed time. Ray's serves lunch and dinner seven days a week, plus Sunday brunch. On Tuesday through Saturday evenings, Ray's features live jazz with popular Atlanta entertainer Elgin Wells and his combo.

Southern Food and Barbecue

Barbecue Kitchen
$$, no credit cards • 1437 Virginia Ave., College Park • (404) 766-9906

If you love Southern food and lots of it, you'll flip at the Barbecue Kitchen. The main dishes include country ham, fried chicken and the restaurant's own pork barbecue, which is smoked right out back. Your dinner comes with three vegetables, such as mashed potatoes, collards and fried okra, and you can get a free reorder of each — but since you can order the same vegetables or three different ones, you're really getting a meat and six. All this place lacks is someone to help happy diners waddle back to their cars. This totally nonsmoking restaurant is open daily from 7:30 AM to 10:00 PM. No alcohol is served.

The Beautiful Restaurant
$$, no credit cards • 2260 Cascade Rd. S.W. • (404) 752-5931
$$, no credit cards • 397 Auburn Ave. N.E. • (404) 223-0080

Fresh vegetables, baked chicken, beef ribs and banana pudding are all popular with diners at The Beautiful soul food restaurants. The Cascade Road location is open 24 hours Thursday, Friday and Saturday, and 7 AM until midnight the rest of the week; the Auburn Avenue restaurant, which is across from Ebenezer Baptist Church, operates from 7 AM till 8:30 PM seven days a week. No alcohol is served.

The Colonnade
$$, no credit cards • 1879 Cheshire Bridge Rd. N.E. • (404) 874-5642

This large Southern restaurant has been an Atlanta tradition since 1927 and is a favorite with the older set as well as young people and families. Turkey and dressing tops the list of entrees, and there are generally some 30 vegetables on the menu. After church on Sunday, things really get crowded here. The Colonnade is open daily for lunch and dinner and has a full bar.

INSIDERS' TIP

You can do your grocery shopping via the Internet. Kroger Super Market stores can be reached at www.shopx.com. There's no minimum order required, and coupons, if you have any, are deducted when the order is made; the delivery person collects them. You can pay by check or credit card. Bruno's, another grocery chain, has a site at www.peapod.com. It applies the coupon savings to your next order. Bruno's limits its service to suburban locations.

Dusty's Barbecue

$$ • 1815 Briarcliff Rd. N.E.
• (404) 320-6264

There's always country music playing in the background at Dusty's, a tiny place on a triangle of land near Sage Hill Shopping Center and just down the block from the Emory University campus. Dusty's is decorated entirely in a "pig" motif. The barbecue (pork, beef or chicken) is the main attraction, but the potato salad, fried okra and hush puppies are good too, and the sweet tea is excellent. Beer and wine are available. Dusty's opened in 1981 and serves lunch and dinner daily.

Evans Fine Foods

$, no credit cards • 2125 N. Decatur Rd.
N.E. • (404) 634-6294

Evans has been fixing Southern food since 1946. Specialties include smothered breast of chicken, country-fried steak, rib-eyes and blueberry and blackberry cobbler. About 15 vegetables are offered daily. Evans is closed on Sunday and open other days from 5:30 AM to 9 PM. No alcohol is served.

Fat Matt's Rib Shack

$$, no credit cards • 1811 Piedmont Ave.
• (404) 607-1622

It really does look like a shack. Fat Matt's exterior was created by Atlanta airbrush legend sign painter "J.J. of L.A.," whose murals of food embellish numerous stores and restaurants in the city. Matt's fixes ribs, chopped pork barbecue and barbecued chicken, plus side dishes. It's open every day for lunch and dinner, and there's live blues every night. You can pig out until 11:30 PM weeknights and until 12:30 AM on weekends. Beer is sold here.

The Flying Pig

$$, no credit cards • 856 Virginia Ave.,
Hapeville • (404) 559-1000

The management of this spot, which originally opened in the 1950s, has quickly won the respect of barbecue-lovers. Beef, pork and ribs are pit-cooked on site; smoked chicken wings are also a crowd-pleaser. All the food is prepared in the kitchen right in front of the customers. There's an outside deck for warm weather dining. The Pig is closed on Saturday and Sunday. No alcohol is served.

Mary Mac's Tea Room

$$, no credit cards • 224 Ponce de Leon
Ave. N.E. • (404) 876-1800

Mary Mac's has been in business for 50 years at this location, and, although the founding Lupo family is no longer involved in its management, the restaurant remains a famous landmark of traditional Southern food. Favorites at the Tea Room include baked chicken and dressing, fried chicken, sweet-potato souffle, fresh-baked yeast rolls and the rich "pot liquor" broth. Mary Mac's serves lunch and dinner daily and breakfast on Saturday and Sunday. There's a full bar, but smoking is not allowed.

Our Way Cafe

$, no credit cards • 303 E. College Ave.,
Decatur • (404) 373-6665

This friendly Decatur cafeteria offers a delightfully updated Southern menu. Yes, you can get meat loaf, but other entrees typically include dishes such as spicy chicken enchiladas, salmon loaf and lemon pepper chicken. More than 10 vegetable choices and several desserts are available. Our Way is open weekdays for lunch only. No alcohol is served.

Paschal's Restaurant

$ • 830 Martin Luther King Dr. S.W.
• (404) 577-3150

Much history in the civil rights movement is said to have taken place over Paschal's soul food (catfish, pork chops, short ribs, steaks, collard greens, macaroni and cheese, yams), and the restaurant remains a landmark in the African-American community. Brothers James and Robert Paschal founded the restaurant in a smaller building across the street in 1947; it was so successful that they eventually built the current restaurant and a 150-room motor hotel that is now used for students housing. There's a full bar; Paschal's is open daily for breakfast, lunch and dinner. There's free parking in the lot behind the motor hotel.

Silver Grill

$$, no credit cards • 900 Monroe Dr. N.E.
• (404) 876-8145

Now being run by the third generation of its founding family, the Silver Grill has been cooking Southern food at this location since

1945. Fried chicken, country-fried steak and grilled chicken breast are longtime menu standouts; about 10 vegetables are generally offered each day. The Grill is open weekdays for lunch and dinner; no alcohol is served.

Son's Place
$, no credit cards • 100 Hurt St.
• (404) 581-0530

Son's Place traces its lineage back to Burton's Grill, a soul food landmark in Atlanta, where the late Deacon Burton, regal in his tall chef's hat, presided over a small army of women (all of whom he called "mama"), who cooked up the best skillet-fried chicken in town. The vegetables, such as mashed potatoes, collard greens and creamed corn, are deliciously flavored and thoroughly cooked in the traditional Southern fashion. Son's is a favorite with everyone from media people to civil rights leaders. It's right beside the Inman Park/Reynoldstown MARTA station; breakfast and lunch are served Monday through Friday, but no alcohol.

Southern Star Restaurant
$, no credit cards • 231 W. Ponce de Leon Ave., Decatur • (404) 377-0799

Open for breakfast and lunch Monday through Saturday, Southern Star began fixing its regional fare in 1980. It's in downtown Decatur and attracts many local office workers and people with business at the courthouse. Popular dishes include turkey and dressing, meat loaf, beef tips and Greek-style baked chicken. Fourteen to 18 vegetables are generally available, but no alcohol is served.

Cajun

French Quarter Food Shop
$$ • 923 Peachtree St. N.E.
• (404) 875-2489
$$ • 2144 Johnson Ferry Rd.
• (770) 458-2148

Here's a little of the bayou right on Peachtree. This small restaurant swings to Louisiana music and serves up spicy dishes such as etouffe and jambalaya at bargain prices. The fried shrimp and fried oyster po' boys are also popular. The owner, who is from Lafayette, Louisiana, proudly says that some of the same conventioneers come in to eat year after year whenever their business brings them back to Atlanta. Both locations have beer and wine and are closed on Sunday.

Fuzzy's
2015 N. Druid Hills Rd. • (404) 321-6166

Atlantan Joe Dale made a name for himself as one of the city's leading Cajun cooks. For years he operated his own restaurant; now, his crawfish etouffee and Cajun chicken sandwiches are on the menu at Fuzzy's, where '70s music and live blues bands keep guests entertained. Lunch and dinner are served daily, and everything is available to go.

Thai

Bangkok
$$ • 1492 Piedmont Rd. N.E.
• (404) 874-2514

Bangkok, which opened in 1977, claims to be the oldest Thai restaurant in Atlanta. In the Ansley Square Shopping Center, just south of the intersection of Piedmont Road and Monroe Drive in Midtown, Bangkok serves an adventurous and delicious version of Thai cuisine. If you like it hot, start with the spicy, aromatic tom yum (lemon grass) soup, then go for the spicy catfish with red curry sauce or the chicken or shrimp stir-fry with green beans, carrots and bamboo shoots in red chili sauce. Afterward, cool off with the exquisite homemade coconut ice cream. Bangkok has beer and wine; it's open weekdays for lunch and nightly for dinner.

King & I
$$ • Ansley Square, 1510-F Piedmont Ave. N.E. • (404) 892-7743
$$ • 4058 Peachtree Road N.E.
• (404) 262-7985.

Delicious Thai food served by a friendly staff is the attraction at King & I, which joined the Atlanta restaurant scene in the early '80s. Recommended dishes include the spring roll appetizer, pad Thai noodles and shrimp with hot garlic sauce. King & I serves large portions at reasonable prices. Beer and wine are available; the restaurant serves lunch on weekdays and dinner nightly.

Pad Thai

$$$ • 1021 Virginia Ave.
• (404) 892-2070

Owned by the same folks as the King & I, Pad Thai is the more elegant of the two, although you don't have to be any more dressed for the occasion. This charming restaurant in the heart of the Virginia-Highland community is known for seafood dishes with squid, eggplant and hoisin sauce and basil rolls. If you are looking for a tête-à-tête to go with your Thai eggplant, choose Pad Thai for lunch or dinner.

Surin of Thailand

$$ • 810 N. Highland Ave. N.E.
• (404) 892-7789

Since opening in 1991, Surin continues to draw faithful followers with delicacies served in a delightful setting. Gleaming wooden floors, dark-blue tablecloths and Thai banners create a charming backdrop. Traditional dishes include chicken coconut soup and Thai noodles pan-fried with shrimp and egg and garnished with peanuts and bean sprouts. Or try Koa-Mok-Kai, a luncheon special of marinated chicken and rice. The array of appetizers tempts you to make a meal of them. Try the tender poached basil rolls filled with shrimp, shredded pork, basil lettuce and bean sprouts, or the Surin baskets, six edible baskets filled with a mixture of spiced chicken, shrimp and corn. Surin offers a full bar and parking behind the restaurant. Surin serves lunch and dinner seven days a week and doesn't take reservations.

Zab-E-Lee

$ • Service Merchandise Plaza, 4837 Old National Hwy., College Park
• (404) 768-2705

This relaxed, no-frills storefront place serves flavorful meat salads, curries, pad Thai and other delicious dishes. Restaurant critics rave about the food at Zab-E-Lee, which takes no reservations. Beer and wine are available.

Vegetarian

The Flying Biscuit

$$ • 1655 McLendon Ave. N.E.
• (404) 687-8888

Known to many as an all-day breakfast cafe, The Biscuit displays its unique personality for lunch and dinner as well. This cozy 30-seat-plus location has a welcoming ambiance with hand-painted tables and ceramic serving pieces. For breakfast, try Egg-ceptional Eggs, served yolk-up on black-bean cakes with a fresh tomatillo salsa. For a side order, how about fresh turkey sausage with sage and creamy rosemary potatoes? Or dig into fluffy stacks of organic oatmeal pancakes topped with warm maple syrup. Lunch and dinner choices include hearty burgers (grain, vegetable or turkey) and moist turkey meat loaf dressed with horseradish sauce. Service is friendly, and you can graze for little or spend more to feast. Closed on Mondays, The Flying Biscuit does not accept reservations.

Lettuce Souprise You

$ • Rio Shopping Center, 595 Piedmont Rd. N.E. • (404) 874-4998
$ • Loehman's Plaza, 2470 Briarcliff Rd. N.E. • (404) 636-8549
$ • 1109 Cumberland Mall N.W.
• (770) 438-2288
$ • 5975 Roswell Rd. N.E.
• (404) 250-0304

Fresh, satisfying choices to make from a variety of stations including salad, soup and a hot pasta, and the fabulous muffin counter await your at this eatery. The muffins are made on the spot and are impossible to refuse, especially since they're included in your salad bar price. You can return for seconds of anything. The salad bar always offers a choice of cold pasta salads as well as the usual salad fixings. All locations are open seven days a week for lunch and dinner.

Vietnamese

Dong Khanh Restaurant

$$ • 4646 Buford Hwy. N.E.
• (770) 457-4840

Open seven days a week for lunch and dinner, Dong Khanh offers many Vietnamese and Chinese specials at reasonable prices. Spicy chicken, sauteed chili and lemon root, salted fish hot pot, fried pig intestine and frog legs sauteed with curry sauce are just a few of the varied dishes on this restaurant's extensive menu. Dong Khanh serves beer.

Vietnamese Cuisine
$$ • 3375 Buford Hwy. N.E.
• (404) 321-1840

Bring your appetite to this storefront eatery that promises gourmet Vietnamese food and lots of choices. Popular dishes include stir-fried chicken with lemon grass, pepper rolls and a soup that mixes vegetables, shrimp and pork. The restaurant offers beer and wine and serves lunch and dinner seven days a week. Some entrees will take you into a higher price category. Vietnamese Cuisine, in the Northeast Plaza, has plenty of free parking.

Beyond Atlanta

American

American Pie
$$ • 5840 Roswell Rd. N.W.
• (404) 255-7571

American Pie is the restaurant that thinks it's on Ocean Boulevard in Myrtle Beach instead of on Roswell Road in Sandy Springs (just outside the Perimeter). The swinging atmosphere is that of a beach club bar and grill, and the gaudy decor carries the theme through. You want TV? The Pie has about 50 TVs. You want refreshment? The Pie has five full bars. You want food? Try the grilled chicken supreme sandwich with barbecue sauce. You want big events? The Pie frequently stages big radio station promotions and other happenings to amuse its guests, who tend to be sports-loving singles out for fun. It's open daily from 11 AM to 4 AM, but closes at 3 AM Saturday night.

The Beehive
$$ • 1090 Alpharetta St., Roswell
• (770) 594-8765

The amazing success of this American eatery has astonished even its owners, who call the eclectic decor "college dorm gone crazy." Under the Christmas lights and doorway beads are tables for 80 patrons who feast on homemade pastas, Reubens and daily blue plate specials. Dinner is served Wednesday through Sunday beginning at 5 PM and ends at 11 PM on weekdays, midnight on weekends. There are no children's menus or high chairs, but the little ones are welcome. There's also full bar service.

Good Ol' Days
$ • 5841 Roswell Rd. • (404) 257-9183

The unique thing about Good Ol' Days is that the menu's sandwiches are prepared and served out of flower pots (don't ask why, just enjoy). Chicken wings are another specialty. This Sandy Springs location has a full bar; it's open daily for dinner and weekends for lunch. There is an outdoor patio and big-screen TV. You can dance the night away seven days a week — Good Ol' Days is open until 4 AM.

Green Manor
$$$ • 6400 Westbrook St., Union City
• (770) 964-4343

Built in 1910, this two-story brick manor house has a wide, wraparound porch, rocking chairs, a full bar, a picturesque gazebo and a ghost, said to appear in the upstairs windows. Taste some of the menu's elegant dishes on the sampler platter with petite filet, chicken and jumbo shrimp. Fresh vegetables and corn-bread salad are specialties. Chess pie, banana pudding and peach cobbler are some of the homemade desserts. Lunch features a Southern country buffet with fried okra and crispy green tomatoes. Linen-covered tables are spread throughout the home's high-ceiling parlor, dining room and sun porch. Lunch is served Monday through Friday and Sunday; dinner is served Friday and Saturday.

Longhorn Steaks
$$$ • 6390 Roswell Rd. N.W.
• (404) 843-1215
$$$ • 900 Mansell Rd., Roswell
• (770) 642-8588
$$$ • 2700 Town Center Dr., Kennesaw
• (770) 421-1101
$$$ • 7882 Tara Blvd., Jonesboro
• (770) 477-5365
$$$ • 2120 Killian Rd., Snellville
• (770) 972-4188

Established in Buckhead in 1981, Longhorn now has 63 restaurants in Georgia and seven other states. The steaks, such as the seven- or nine-ounce filet and the 20-ounce Porterhouse, are cut fresh daily by hand; the salmon is farm-raised in Canada. The atmosphere is steakhouse-Western: The service is friendly, and the bar is well-stocked. Steaks are priced from $10.95 to $17.95. Most locations are open daily for lunch and dinner. Call as you're heading out to get your name on the waiting list. Check the Yellow Pages for more locations.

Magnolia Restaurant and Tea Room

$$$, no credit cards • 5459 E. Mountain St., Stone Mountain • (770) 498-6304

This 1854 gingerbread house sits on more than 2 acres in the heart of Stone Mountain Village. The classic Southern setting provides a relaxed atmosphere in which to enjoy the Magnolia's American and French cuisine. Specialties include chicken salad stuffed into a heart-shaped puff pastry, banana cheesecake with pralines and daily seafood specials. The Sunday buffet is loaded with everything from Eggs Benedict to carved roast beef. Lunch is served Tuesday through Sunday; dinner runs from 6 to 9:30 PM on Friday and Saturday. Reservations are encouraged; beer and wine are served.

McKendrick's Steak House

$$$ • 4505 Ashford Dunwoody Rd. • (770) 512-8888

Be hungry when you head to this '40s-style bistro where USDA prime Midwestern beef, tempura lobster and one-pound cold-water lobster tails are the specialties. Beer, wine and alcohol are served. McKendrick's offers lunch Monday through Friday and dinner nightly.

Norcross Station Cafe

$$ • 40 S. Peachtree St., Norcross • (770) 409-9889

Like a little shaking and rattling with your burger or barbecued chicken? The trains that rumble by Norcross Station, in the town's restored depot, frequently send vibrations through the floorboards and table legs right to the silverware. It's part of the charm of this restaurant, where lunch and dinner are served every day but Sunday. Pull up a chair inside the rustic, high-ceilinged main room, or enjoy the enclosed and heated year-round outdoor deck overlooking the town's restored business district. Soups, salads, quiches and sandwiches are big for lunch; dinner features chef's specials as well as Creole and Cajun dishes, steaks, ribs and pastas.

Shillings on the Square

$$ • 19 N. Park Sq., Marietta • (770) 428-9520

This casual restaurant and bar has anchored a corner of the Marietta square for 20 years. Its neighborhood pub style is a favorite of locals looking for oversized sandwiches and finger foods late into the night or during a short lunch break. The kitchen opens at 10:30 AM and serves until midnight during the week; 2 AM on weekends.

For those with more elegant tastes, Upstairs at Shillings is an 80-seat fine dining room, with white tablecloths, candles and soft piano tunes putting diners in a relaxed mood. Entrees of steaks, seafood, veal, lamb and chicken are priced from $12.95 to $18.95. Dinner is served from 5:30 to 10 PM on weekdays, midnight on weekends.

Stoney River Legendary Steaks

$$$ • 5800 States Bridge Rd., Duluth • (770) 476-0102

Don't let the name fool you: There's much more to this eatery and bar than just steak. Although certified Angus beef is a specialty, the menu includes coastal shrimp, salmon, trout, baby-back ribs, bourbon chicken and pasta. The atmosphere is rustic country, with lots of cedar, stacked stone, hardwood floors and an open-hearth fireplace. Dinner is served seven days a week; brunch is added on Sunday. Stoney River is one of the area's most popular places to eat but does not take reservations: Don't be surprised if there's a two-hour wait on the weekends.

The Tea Room

$$ • 925 Canton St., Roswell • (770) 594-8822

This old store in Roswell's historic district has been a tea room since 1987. A mix of antique tables and buffets are decorated with teapots, cups and an assortment of tea paraphernalia. Lunch is light, with a variety of salads, quiches and soups and a selection of wines and beers. And yes, tea-lovers, tea is served daily — and correctly, in a china pot. The Tea Room is seven days a week.

Continental and Fine Dining

1848 House
$$$$ • 780 S. Cobb Dr., Marietta
• (770) 428-1848

The setting for this restaurant and bar is an authentic 1848 Greek Revival plantation home on 13 acres of land. Six of the 10 dining rooms feature fireplaces. The fare is contemporary Southern and American; specialities are the Charleston she-crab soup, pan-roasted quail, roast saddle of venison and grilled salmon with spaghetti squash, bacon and lemon sauce. During the Civil War, the house was used as a Union hospital, which is why it wasn't reduced to rubble (wait until after dessert to ask which room was used for surgery). The owners recently restored the original stone kitchen behind the house; the rustic room with a huge fireplace and beamed ceiling seats 16 and can be reserved for a $100 fee. The house is listed on the National Register of Historic Places. Dinner is served Tuesday through Sunday; a jazz brunch is presented Sunday; reservations are accepted.

Araxi
$$$ • 4651 Woodstock Rd., Roswell
• (770) 587-2700

Tucked in the Sandy Plains Village Shopping Center, Araxi offers continental cuisine in a chic, art deco setting (lots of glass, mirrors and wood). Fried lobster is one the most popular menu items. Open for dinner Monday through Saturday and for lunch weekdays, the restaurant accepts reservations.

Cafe Renaissance
$$$ • 7050 Jimmy Carter Blvd., Norcross
• (770) 441-0291

Hidden in the Peachtree Corners shopping center, Cafe Renaissance is a touch of the city in the suburbs. This New York-style bistro features country French and continental specialties, along with fresh fish and meat specials every day. The emphasis is on service; enjoy your favorite beverages at the full bar. Reservations are accepted. Lunch is served Monday through Friday, dinner Monday through Saturday.

Dick and Harry's
$$$ • 1570 Holcomb Bridge Rd., Roswell
• (770) 641-8757

Stepping inside the contemporary design of this eatery, it's easy to think you're really in New York or Chicago instead of Roswell. The 20-foot ceilings, hardwood floors and wood columns add to the sophisticated look. Though the menu's heavy on fresh fish and seafood (wood-grilled barbecue salmon and luscious 100-percent crab cakes), the kitchen also does a good job on oversized salads, pastas and chicken. Check out the full sheet of daily specials, from appetizers to desserts, before ordering. There's no printed children's menu, but if you ask, the staff gladly serves chicken fingers and pastas to the tykes. Lunch and dinner are served Monday through Friday, dinner only on Saturday.

Ebbets Grill
$$$ • 875 Mansell Rd., Roswell
• (770) 645-1299

Even though the name does come from the owners' love of baseball, this is definitely not a sports bar! The cuisine is continental: sweet-and-sour calamari, pistachio grouper, baby-back ribs glazed with smoked tomato and molasses sauce are a few of the bestsellers. Side dishes include American favorites such as creamed corn and garlic mashed potatoes. Lunch is served Monday through Friday; dinner begins at 5:30 PM and lasts until 10 PM during the week, 11 PM on weekends.

Gasthaus Le Cafe
$$$ • 310 Atlanta Rd., Cumming
• (770) 844-7244

Gasthaus Le Cafe offers German cuisine in an atmosphere of Southern hospitality. The menu includes soups, salads and sandwiches as well as house specialties including beef, goulash, Chicken Cordon Bleu and Wiener schnitzel, a lightly breaded veal cutlet sauteed in a wine sauce. Le Cafe serves wine and beer. It's open for lunch Tuesday through Friday. Dinner is served Tuesday through Saturday.

Hamilton's
$$$ • 500 Powder Springs St., Marietta
• (770) 427-2500

This restaurant in the Marietta Conference Center and Resort has beautiful views of Cobb

County's Kennesaw Mountain. In warmer weather, dine on the outdoor terrace. The food is great, too: Lunch includes an all-you-can-eat buffet with an extensive salad bar, several grilled and baked entrees, soups and a luscious dessert bar. Breakfast and dinner are also served daily.

Joey D's
$$$ • 1015 Crown Pointe Pkwy., Dunwoody • (770) 512-7063

American cuisine takes center stage at this upscale casual restaurant. Recommended items include New Orleans spicy shrimp, grilled seafood, steaks and chops. Joey D's opened in 1990 and has a full bar and free parking. Reservations are accepted. Joey D's serves lunch and dinner daily.

Kurt's
$$$ • 4225 River Green Pkwy., Duluth • (770) 623-4128

There's a distinctly German twist to this longtime suburban restaurant, where the menu includes everything from oysters and crab to Wiener schnitzel, Sauerbraten and rack of lamb. There are also filet and pork tenderloins. The atmosphere is elegant; service is offered with a flourish. Roving chefs perform flaming feats tableside, and there's a full bar. Reservations are a must for dinner, served Monday through Saturday.

Le Clos
$$$$ • Château Élan Resort & Winery, 100 Tour de France Dr., Braselton • (770) 932-0900

Le Clos is the fine dining restaurant at the Château Élan Resort & Winery complex about 45 minutes northeast of Atlanta (Exit 48 off I-85). The prix fixe meal includes specially selected wines from the resort's own winery. Elegant Le Clos attracts diners from Atlanta, Athens, Gainesville and elsewhere. Dinner is served Wednesday through Saturday evenings; the first seating is at 6 PM. Jackets are requested for the gentlemen; call for reservations.

Lickskillet Farm Restaurant
$$$$ • 1380 Old Roswell Rd., Roswell • (770) 475-6484

Lickskillet Farm really was a farm at one

time. The house dates to 1846, and today, diners are seated in various rooms, from the parlor with a fireplace to the sun porch. Tables on the rear deck overlook the pond and the kitchen's herb garden. Fine dining in a casual setting is the offering here: The American continental gourmet menu features Cornish hen, rack of lamb, filet mignon, veal and seafood pasta. Dinner is served nightly; lunch is served Tuesday through Friday; brunch is served Sunday. Reservations are accepted.

Public House on Roswell Square
$$$$ • 605 Atlanta St., Roswell • (770) 992-4646

This restaurant on the historic Roswell square is in an 1854 brick warehouse that doubled as a Confederate hospital during the Civil War. Public House opened in 1976 and continues to offer its standout dishes, such as Appalachian trout, crab cakes, steak au Poivre and Southern Comfort pecan pork chops. Lunch is served from Monday through Friday and on Sunday. Dinner begins at 5:30 PM and lasts until 9 PM on Sunday, 10 PM Monday through Thursday and 11 PM on Friday and Saturday. The weekends also feature a piano bar.

Ruth's Chris Steakhouse
$$$ • 5788 Roswell Rd. • (404) 255-0035 $$$ • 950 E. Paces Ferry Rd. N.E. • (404) 365-0660

Ruth's offers fine dining in a clubby, casual atmosphere. The split-level building has four fireplaces and an overall attitude of contemporary luxury. Popular menu items include the stuffed mushroom appetizer, filet, lobster, bread pudding with whiskey sauce and chocolate mousse cheesecake. Dinner is served nightly at both locations. Ruth's Buckhead restaurant at E. Paces Ferry Road also serves lunch on weekdays.

Van Gogh's Restaurant
$$$$ • 70 W. Crossville Rd., Roswell • (770) 993-1156

Van Gogh's is like a bit of Buckhead out in Roswell: Fabulous food, impeccable service and a long wait on line. The five dining rooms are adorned with original art, which is for sale; there's a fireplace and a lovely antique bar. The ethnic-influenced American fare includes fresh lump meat crab cakes, grilled portobello mushrooms, fresh pastas and veal chops. Reservations are accepted for all meals except dinner Friday and Saturday nights. Lunch and dinner are served daily; dinner only is served on Sunday.

Winfield's
$$$ • 1 Galleria Pkwy. • (770) 955-5300

Winfield's serves creative American cuisine in a restaurant reminiscent of a European grand ballroom. Crab cakes, twice-smoked salmon with red-onion marmalade and corn relish, smoked chicken pasta with sun-dried tomato vinaigrette and herb-breaded lamb chops on red pepper sauce over whipped potatoes with grilled asparagus are all longtime favorites. The restaurant is popular with locals and with conventioneers from the Cobb Galleria Centre, where Winfield's is located. Dinner is served nightly; lunch is served daily except Saturday. Reservations are accepted.

Chinese

Mandarin House
$$ • 6263 Roswell Rd. N.E.
• (404) 255-5707
$$ • 1500 Pleasant Hill Rd., Duluth
• (770) 925-1050
$$ • 1750 Marietta Hwy., Canton
• (770) 479-7621

Opened in 1977, Mandarin House is Atlanta's longest-operating Chinese restaurant. Its extensive menu includes princess chicken; chicken and Chinese greens in an optional hot bean sauce; Szechuan-style kung pau beef, which mixes beef, peanuts and Chinese greens in a hot pepper sauce; and moo shu pork, a dish featuring pork and Chinese pancakes. Lunch and dinner are served daily.

Indian

Dawat Indian Cafe
$$ • 4025-K Satellite Blvd., Duluth
• (770) 623-6133

Tiny but tidy, Dawat offers a sumptuous vegetarian lunch buffet with curries, soup, rice pilau and more. Entrees include chicken tikka masala, a dish involving chicken, almonds and cream, and lamb vindaloo, a spicy lamb dish. Dawat offers plenty of parking and serves lunch daily, featuring a buffet on Saturday and Sunday, and dinner nightly.

Italian

Brooklyn Cafe
$$$ • 220 Sandy Springs Cir. N.W.
• (404) 843-8377

A mural of the Brooklyn bridge, floral-patterned tablecloths, an old-fashioned dark wood bar and attentive, friendly service contribute to the cozy, relaxed atmosphere of the Brooklyn Cafe. Founded by two Yankee transplants, the friendly Italian eatery offers "New York without the attitude" and an innovative menu with fresh takes on pasta, seafood, chicken and veal. Popular dishes include fried calamari with fra diavolo sauce; roast chicken with Italian sausage, roasted potatoes, black olives and pepperoncini; and veal sorrentino with roasted bell peppers, salami and provolone cheese in a marsala wine sauce. The restaurant features an extensive beer and wine list and daily dessert specials. Brooklyn Cafe serves lunch Monday through Friday. Dinner begins at 5:30 PM and goes until 10:30 PM on weeknights, 11:30 PM on weekends. The cafe doesn't take reservations, but if you call ahead and come at the time recommended, you'll step to the head of the line for a table.

Cafe Marmalade
$$$ • Westin Atlanta North at Perimeter,
7 Concourse Pkwy. • (770) 395-3900

The Westin's restaurant offers a traditional breakfast and lunch buffet, along with a range of menu items. But when it opens for dinner at 5 PM, the theme is distinctly Northern Italian. The casual but elegant atmosphere features tablecloths, oil lamps and servers who grate cheese at your table. The setting is intimate, with only 52 seats. Cafe Marmalade is open daily.

Dominick's
$$ • 95 S. Peachtree St., Norcross
• (770) 449-1611

In a historic building in old downtown Norcross, this family-style Italian restaurant serves its dishes on large platters meant to be shared. (The menu also lists prices for half-platters for those with skimpier appetites.) With both hearty, traditional Italian fare and lighter, health-conscious items, Dominick's menu includes pasta, chicken, veal and seafood dishes. Popular house specialties such as eggplant parmigiana and lasagna Bolognese delight diners and keep them coming back to this friendly, welcoming place. Lunch is served on weekdays; dinner is served nightly.

Ippolito's Family Style Italian Restaurant

$$ • 1525 Holcomb Bridge Rd., Roswell
• (770) 998-5683
$$ • Abernathy Square, 6623 Roswell Rd.
• (404) 256-3546
$$ • 11585 Jones Bridge Rd., Alpharetta
• (770) 663-0050
$$ • 425 Ernest Barrett Pkwy.
• (770) 514-8500

This friendly, mom and pop Italian restaurant is a favorite with locals. Ippolito's menu includes mussels marinara, pizzas, hoagies, calzones, salads, pasta, chicken, veal and seafood. The yeasty garlic rolls are served piping hot and swimming in butter. Dress is casual, and kids are welcome. Ippolito's serves lunch on weekdays and dinner seven nights a week.

Mi Spia

$$$ • 4505 Ashford Dunwoody Rd.
• (770) 393-1333

The sophisticated Mi Spia offers Italian food with a contemporary flair. This neighborhood bar and grill features a garden patio and a lively cocktail hour. Wood-trimmed French doors overlook a courtyard and enliven the airy dining room. The contemporary Italian menu includes oak-grilled veal chops, seafood, chicken, homemade breads and desserts keep the customers coming back. Mi Spia opens for dinner every night and serves lunch on weekdays. Smoking is allowed in the bar area only. Reservations are accepted.

New York Pizza Exchange

$$ • 2810 Paces Ferry Rd. N.E., Vinings
• (770) 434-9355

This upscale pizza house features pies, pasta dishes, calzones, strombolis and killer desserts such as Death by Chocolate cheesecake and raspberry white chocolate cheesecake. House specialties include the Spinach 'n' Stix appetizer, a fresh spinach and vegetable dip topped with mozzarella cheese; you dip Italian breadsticks into the luscious mixture. New York Pizza also serves salads, subs, beer and wine. The restaurant is open for lunch and dinner daily.

Japanese

Mt. Fiji Japanese Steak House and Sushi Bar

$$$ • 180 Cobb Pkwy., Marietta
• (770) 428-0955

Watching your food being sliced, diced, sauteed and flambeed right before your eyes is half the fun of eating at this cozy restaurant, hidden in a corner of the Marietta Trade shopping center. You'll be seated in a group around a large stainless-steel cooktop, where a chef will prepare the food to your exact specifications. And the chefs put on a show while doing it — flipping shrimp tails into their tall hats, tossing knives into the air and juggling soy sauce bottles behind their backs. Start with a sampling of sushi at the bar in the restaurant's lobby, but save room for dinner. There's usually more food than you can finish. Dinner is served nightly.

Shiki Japanese Restaurant

$$$ • 1492 Pleasant Hill Rd., Duluth
• (770) 279-0097

Shiki was voted best Japanese restaurant for the last few years by *Atlanta* magazine and *Creative Loafing*. It has a traditional dining room where, among many other entrees, you can order impeccably fresh fish presented artfully. At the sushi bar at the rear of the main room, a chef prepares a wide variety of tempting treats. On the hibachi side of the restaurant, you'll find quality steaks and seafood cooked on tableside grills. No matter which section you choose, you'll find exquisite presentation and thoughtful and gracious service. Shiki is open seven days a week and serves beer and wine. The restaurant recommends reservations.

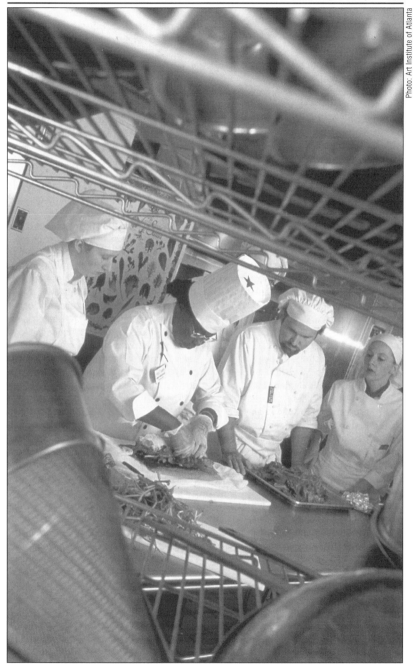

The School of Culinary Arts, a division of the Art Institute of Atlanta, is the largest provider of culinary arts education at the associate-degree level in Georgia.

Latin

Azteca Grill
$$ • 1140 Morrow Industrial Blvd.,
Morrow • (770) 968-0908

Spicy specialties at this Mexican and Southwestern restaurant include poblano corn chowder and a Mexican version of turnip greens. Enjoy your favorite beverages at the grill's full bar. There's outside dining in warm weather. The food comes continuously from 11 AM Monday through Saturday and from noon on Sunday.

Cozumel Mexican Restaurant
$$ • 2697 Spring Rd., Smyrna
• (770) 801-1487

This Mexican eatery northwest of Atlanta offers popular items such as steak ranchero, mixed fajitas and carne asada. Beer and wine are available. Cozumel is open every day for lunch and dinner.

Seafood

Chequers Seafood Grill
$$$ • 236 Perimeter Center Pkwy.
• (770) 391-9383
$$$ • Monarch Plaza, 3424 Peachtree
Rd. • (404) 842-9997

For 15 years, this clubby spot has been a favorite for seafood and steak lovers. And the oversized biscuits are pretty incredible, too. Lunch and dinner menus feature an array of fresh fish, as well as filet, crab cakes, soups and salads. Sunday brunch is an extensive affair, with made-to-order omelettes, shrimp and blintzes. Lunch is served Monday through Friday. Dinner is served nightly.

Embers Seafood Grill
$$$ • 234 Hildebrand Dr. N.W.
• (404) 256-0977

Excellent preparation, good service, sizable portions — what more could you ask for? The Embers' decor could be called a dressed-up seafood shack scheme. Good service and well-trained staff will gladly explain the details of entrees. There's a catch of the day as well as grilled Atlantic salmon,

swordfish, grouper and tuna. Scallops, shrimp, lobster, steaks and chicken round out an extensive menu that includes such favorites as blackened amberjack and the combo kebob combining swordfish, tuna, sea scallops, red onions and green peppers. A few pasta dishes and entree-size salads, made with fish, are also on the menu. For an appetizer, you might try the smoked barbecued shrimp or the delicious crab cakes. Dinner is served nightly; lunch is offered Monday through Friday.

Pappadeaux Seafood Kitchen
$$$ • 2830 Windy Hill Rd., Marietta
• (770) 984-8899

This Cajun seafood house always draws a crowd; even at lunch, the wait can be more than 45 minutes! But it's worth it: The portions are large, the selection vast and the tastes delectable. The wait passes quickly at the enormous bar. In addition to Cajun favorites, there are grilled, broiled and baked items, soups and salads. The setting is casual and noisy (no one will notice the kids' chatter in the large dining room). Lunch is served Monday through Friday; dinner begins at 3 PM on weekends. Pappadeaux does not take reservations.

Slocum's Tavern & Grill
$$ • 6025 Peachtree Pkwy., Norcross
• (770) 446-7725

Slocum's house specialty is yellowfin tuna marinated in teriyaki sauce, then grilled. There's a casual, neighborhood-pub atmosphere, complete with neon beer signs and TVs tuned to sports in the bar area. Slocum's draws anyone who loves juicy, fresh fish, great steaks, burgers and chicken wings, among other items. The restaurant serves lunch Monday through Saturday and dinner seven nights a week. Reservations are accepted for parties of six or more.

Squid Roe
$$$ • 2995 Johnson Ferry Rd. N.E.,
Marietta • (770) 587-FISH
Squid Roe Number Two
$$$ • 736 Johnson Ferry Rd.
• (770) 509-1996

This Key West-inspired East Cobb restaurant transports diners back to their favorite beach hangouts with its casual, nautical decor, starting with the sand outside the front door. Specializing in fresh seafood, Squid Roe offers a variety of daily specials as well as its signature she-crab soup and conch fritters. Although it only takes reservations for large parties, you can call ahead to get your name on a waiting list. Lunch and dinner are served at both locations.

Southern Food and Barbecue

Blue Willow Inn Restaurant
$$, no credit cards • 294 N. Cherokee Rd., Social Circle • (770) 464-2131

On five acres of land, the Blue Willow is housed in a 1907 Greek Revival mansion, where diners linger after dinner in the rocking chairs on the wide porch or in the gift shop. The fare, served buffet style, is authentic Southern cooking, including fried chicken, fried green tomatoes and bread pudding. Four to five meats and 10 to 12 vegetables are generally offered. In warm weather, you may choose to dine outside by the pool. Reservations are accepted. Due to local regulations, sweet tea and lemonade are the most potent drinks; however, patrons are welcome to bring their own wine or champagne. Social Circle is 45 minutes east of Atlanta; take I-20 to Exit 47.

Puckett's Restaurant
$, no credit cards • 4840 S. Lee St., Buford • (770) 945-6031

Puckett's fixes breakfast, lunch and dinner on weekdays only, from 7 AM to 7 PM. A typical day begins at 4:30 AM, when the homemade pies are baked. Other specialties include fried chicken and country-fried steak; seven or so vegetables are available. Friendly, down-home Puckett's has been in business since 1953. No alcohol is served.

Thai

Royal Thai Cuisine
$$ • 6365-A Spalding Dr., Norcross • (770) 449-7796
$$ • 3330 Piedmont Rd. • (404) 812-9110

Take your seat in the cozy upholstered booths surrounded by wood paneling and deep-green fabric panels, or dine on the outdoor deck of this small place known for good food. House specialties include soft-shelled crab with curry, boneless crispy duck in a basil sauce, and lamb with tea rose dumplings. Royal Thai serves Thai beer. You'll find efficient friendly service at lunch, Monday through Friday. Dinner is served nightly.

Vegetarian

Cafe Sunflower
$$ • 5975 Roswell Rd. N.E. • (404) 256-1675

Just a half-mile outside the Perimeter in Hammond Springs Shopping Center, Cafe Sunflower is a comfortable restaurant that specializes in imaginative and well-prepared wholesome food. The cuisine is a combo of Asian, Mediterranean and Southwestern influences. Try the fresh vegetables over fluffy brown rice or the wild mushroom fettucine. No alcohol is served, nor is smoking allowed. Cafe Sunflower welcomes reservations for lunch during the week and on Saturdays. Dinner reservations can be made seven days a week.

Unicorn Place Vegetarian Cuisine
$$ • 220 Sandy Springs Cir. N.W. • (404) 252-1165

Fresh and healthy food is the treat here, with lots of vegetables and salads to satisfy your hunger. An extensive menu of more than 40 items includes such novelties as veggie hot dogs and vegetarian sweet-and-sour pork. Unicorn serves lunch Monday through Saturday and dinner nightly.

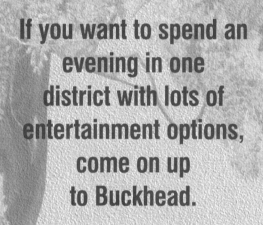

If you want to spend an evening in one district with lots of entertainment options, come on up to Buckhead.

Nightlife

*"I love the nightlife!
I've got to boogie!"*
— Atlanta's own Alicia Bridges

When the sun goes down, Atlanta gets a new attitude. Night brings an end to the day's problems, replacing them with more pleasant concerns. For a few happy hours, "Where are we going?" "Who's meeting us there?" and "What's everyone doing later?" become the most important issues.

Nightlife has always been a part of Atlanta. The first tavern, after all, opened 10 years before the first church. And Moses Formwalt, a tinsmith and still-maker backed by the Free and Rowdy Party, defeated the Morals Party's temperance candidate in the first mayoral election in 1848. (A small plaque at 6 Decatur Street N.E. marks the location of Formwalt's business.)

In the late 1960s and '70s, Atlanta's nightlife exploded. At legendary (now closed) nightclubs such as Richard's, the Electric Ballroom, the Agora Ballroom, Finnochio, the Great Southeast Music Hall and Rumors, Atlanta audiences rocked out up-close to stars such as the Allman Brothers, the Police, the Clash, Bonnie Raitt and the B-52's. Locals and tourists alike flocked to the original Underground Atlanta, a shadowy, boozy adult playground that was quite different from the present-day shopping and entertainment complex. Those were wild days in Atlanta: Midtown was a hippie zone, Piedmont Park was the site of frequent anti-war protests and drug raids, and X-rated bookstores and cinemas were as commonplace as today's coffeehouses.

Disco was king in the late '70s and early '80s, and Atlanta boasted Limelight, one of America's most elaborate disco palaces. Limelight (which reopened in 1997 as Atlanta Alive) occupied a cavernous space in the Kroger shopping center at the corner of Peachtree Road and Piedmont in Buckhead; to this day, locals still know that supermarket as Disco Kroger, its nickname from the nonstop party days. Limelight was a multilevel temple of decadence and delight, with an astounding light show and thumping speakers the size of small houses on the dance floor. No Atlanta club has again equaled the splendid excess of Sunday afternoons at Limelight, when thousands of twirling revelers would pack the disco at 3 PM for tea dance.

Today there's still something for everyone in Atlanta's nightlife lineup. You can relax with friends at an unpretentious neighborhood pub; sip pricey martinis at the latest see-and-be-seen trendy bar; gossip and giggle at a drag show; whoop and holler like a cowboy at an urban roadhouse; dance from dusk to dawn in a packed discotheque; groove to the latest, loudest live rock; mellow out to acoustic, folk or jazz performances; laugh yourself to tears at a comedy hotspot; or, if you prefer, sip cocktails while totally nude female and/or male dancers entertain.

The ever-changing nature of life in Atlanta is nowhere more evident than in the city's nightlife. Clubs, bars and coffeehouses open, close, remodel and disappear with amazing speed. We could tell you about the pricey seafood restaurant that's now a live music club showcasing the latest bands or the leather bar that became an upscale steakhouse, but take our word for it: Everything about Atlanta nightlife is subject to change, so call first or check the local press for up-to-date info.

Theme nights are a continuing trend in Atlanta nightspots. A club may have live rock bands one night, a gay dance party the next and attract a largely African-American singles crowd yet another evening. Even though a club's name remains the same, its nightly ambiance, music and entertainment may change with the wind.

Don't assume, just because you've been to a club before, that its entertainment and door policies will be the same when you return. It's always a good idea to call first if you're not sure. Many of the larger clubs now have sophisticated answering systems you can access with a touch-tone phone; these give travel directions and information about entertainment, nightly specials and cover charges.

A little about the history of prohibition in Atlanta is in order here. Imposed once by a county referendum, then later by the state and the federal governments, laws about drinking were not popular and were widely disregarded.

Atlanta first went dry on July 1, 1886, after a Fulton County referendum. But on November 26, 1887, the law was repealed — again, by referendum — and 40 liquor stores were operating in 1888.

A state prohibition law took effect in 1908, shutting down more than 100 Atlanta saloons and liquor stores and one brewery, but a loophole allowing alcohol sales in private clubs led to the proliferation of "locker clubs," typically upstairs in office buildings, which called themselves private clubs but were basically bars. Legally, at least, Atlanta had been dry for a dozen years when prohibition became law nationally.

Following the 1933 repeal of prohibition, Governor E.D. Rivers signed legislation in 1938 allowing local option alcohol sales. Fulton County went wet by a margin of better than three to one. A dozen liquor stores opened on April 25, 1938, and *The Atlanta Constitution* reported: "With their tongues 'hanging out', hundreds of Atlantans flocked to the legal liquor stores to make purchases of state-stamped legal whiskey, many of them buying legal liquor for the first time in their lives." For more historical information about prohibition, or Atlanta history in general, Franklin Garrett's book *Atlanta and Environs*, is the place to look.

These days, the sale of alcohol in supermarkets and liquor stores ends before midnight on Saturday night and does not resume until Monday morning.

Several local periodicals, which are detailed in our Media chapter, offer up-to-the-minute coverage for Atlanta's nightcrawlers: These are the best ways to find out what's happening on any given night or weekend in Atlanta. Look to *Creative Loafing* for an entertainment calendar with extensive information on the nightly action at dozens of clubs; *The University Reporter* for hot spots for college students and 20-somethings; and *The Hudspeth Report* for sports bars and casual restaurant reviews in Buckhead and north-side clubs. For information on some of the 30 bars and clubs that cater to gays and lesbians, pick up a copy of *Etcetera Magazine* or *Southern Voice*.

FYI

Three area codes serve the metro Atlanta area: 404, 770 and 678. Whether you live on Peachtree Street or in New York City, you must dial the code to reach any number in the area. The difference? Outside the area, you must dial "1," then the area code and phone number; inside the area, you need only dial the area code followed by the phone number.

Things to Keep in Your Mind and in Your Wallet

Bars in Atlanta may stay open as late as 4 AM, though not all do. On Saturday nights, all bars are required to close an hour earlier, at 3 AM, but a handful of clubs have special licenses that allow them to stay open and serve liquor around the clock. They are noted below.

Acceptance of credit cards varies. Some places that don't accept plastic at the door will

let you pay your tab with a card. Others don't accept credit cards but have an ATM on the premises. If your plan is "party now, pay later," call the club first and make sure your card will be accepted.

All persons entering a bar are required to have a picture ID. This is not about how old you look, and it's not about attendants who want to hassle you. It's about keeping within the law, and most clubs will refuse admittance to anyone, regardless of age, who does not have a picture ID. Avoid aggravation by making sure every person in your group has one.

Information on cover charges is given as a guide only and may not reflect the actual cost to enter a club on a given night; for example, many clubs hike the door charge on big nights such as New Year's Eve and Halloween or when there's special entertainment. In the listings that follow, a small cover charge means up to $5; a moderate cover charge means more than $5; and no mention of cover means there is none at this writing.

The drinking age for liquor, beer and wine in Georgia is 21. "Eighteen to party, 21 to drink" is the rule at some clubs, which usually issue a special bracelet authorizing your purchase of alcohol. Some clubs cater to a swank older crowd and have a higher minimum age (such as 23) for admittance. Call ahead to avoid disappointment. If you'll be partying downtown, please note: Many downtown streets are designated no parking, and the police issue parking tickets downtown at night. Avoid tickets, and keep your car safe by parking in an attended pay lot.

Finally, Georgia's drunk driving laws are very strict and getting stricter all the time. A driver who registers a blood-alcohol level of 0.08 gm or higher is considered drunk. A driver younger than 21 who registers any blood-alcohol level above 0 is considered intoxicated. The police use random roadblocks to apprehend drunk drivers; these are often on two-lane (as opposed to wider) streets in areas with a heavy concentration of nightclubs. Rather than taking a chance on getting busted or endangering yourself or others, take a cab, use a sober designated driver or ride MARTA. Unlike other major cities such as New York, Atlanta does not have cabs that cruise although you may find cabs around areas that have a preponderance of clubs. You can always ask club personnel to call a cab for you a few minutes before you're ready to leave.

To help you plan your nocturnal prowlings in Atlanta, this chapter describes some of the offerings in five major Atlanta entertainment districts: Buckhead, Downtown, Midtown, Little Five Points and Virginia-Highland. All bars listed within a geographic section may not necessarily be within walking distance — this is especially true in Buckhead. Bars of note outside these five zones are covered next, along with concert theaters, adult entertainment clubs and movie theaters.

Buckhead

Buckhead is not only the shopping center of the Southeast, with 1,400-plus retail units ringing up more than $1 billion in sales annually — it's also the nexus of Atlanta nightlife and dining, boasting more than 200 restaurants and clubs.

One of these entertainment complexes, Tower Place (Piedmont Road at Peachtree Street, just south of the Buckhead MARTA station), has been struggling with solvency, along with many of the clubs and restaurants that rushed into operation in 1996 hoping to cash in on Olympic visitors. Stocking up on beer and food for the hordes proved foolhardy since most visitors stayed downtown. Clubs that were undercapitalized folded. The Tower Place complex was decimated: Baja Beach Club, Dick's Last Resort and California Cafe bit the dust. At this writing, many spaces are still vacant. But the complex is beautiful to look at, and new clubs, restaurants and bars will no doubt fill in the complex because it's just too close to the action to stay empty long. When you go to Atlanta Live, which is just across Piedmont Avenue, check Tower Place out and see what's new.

The Buckhead district is spread out; the intersection of Peachtree Street and Pharr Road is near its center, with acres of party places nearby. If you want to spend an evening in one district with lots of entertainment options, come on up to Buckhead.

Atlanta Live
3330 Piedmont Rd. N.E. across from Tower Place • (404) 869-0003

When you put $700,000 into a club it better bring in the crowds. Generation Xers are finding their way here especially since The Artist Formerly Known As Prince put in an appearance. Atlanta Live is slightly out of the line of action of the Buckhead nightlife strip, but you can still expect to pay a steep cover (around $25) if someone great is playing. It will run you $10 on a live entertainment-free night. But for your dancing dollar you're getting plenty of room in which to hip-hop.

Bar
250 E. Paces Ferry Rd. • (404) 841-0033

"No theme, no attitude, just Bar" is the slogan at this bar without a story where patrons enjoy chugging "bobsled shooters," which are poured through an ice sculpture. Bar is open Wednesday through Saturday nights, and there's a small cover after 10 PM on weekends.

The Chameleon Club
3179 Peachtree Rd. • (404) 261-8004

The Chameleon Club showcases live rock bands; Wednesday is college night. There's a small cover after 10 PM.

The Chili Pepper
208 Pharr Rd. N.E. • (404) 812-9266

The Chili Pepper offers lots of dancing on three levels and a rooftop terrace in the heart of all the Buckhead club action. Neon-lit bars, cartoon decorated walls, velvet sofas and more fill this eclectic club where a DJ spins discs. Sorry, no food is served. After 10:30 PM, you'll pay a moderate cover charge.

www.insiders.com

See this and many other **Insiders' Guide®** destinations online — in their entirety.

Visit us today!

Photo: The World of Coca-Cola Atlanta

The city lights up at night and offers neighborhood pubs, trendy bars and dance clubs.

Jellyroll's
295 E. Paces Ferry Rd. N.E.
• (404) 261-6864

Jellyroll's is a dueling piano bar. Four piano players, in teams of two, take turns banging out the hits of yesterday and today. The audience participates, and the singing, dancing waitstaff has been known to leap onto the bar to demonstrate "The Time Warp" from *The Rocky Horror Picture Show*. Jellyroll's rocks Wednesday through Saturday nights; there's a small cover nightly.

Johnny's Hideaway
3771 Roswell Rd. • (404) 233-8026

This self-described "nightclub for big kids" showcases the music of the '40s, '50s and '60s. Dress is business casual, and the crowd tends to be 35 and older. Johnny's is open every night; there's a two-drink minimum but no cover.

Lulu's Bait Shack
3057 Peachtree St. (enter from Bolling Wy.) • (404) 262-5220

Lulu's Bait Shack is famous for its fishbowl size super-drinks; alligator tail, catfish and chicken are on the menu. Dance the night away to taped music from 10 PM to 4 AM.

Metropolitan Pizza Bar
3055 Bolling Way • (404) 264-0135

Metropolitan Pizza Bar serves pizza and salad, has live music on weekends and spins disco at the Wednesday night "Pizza a Go-Go" parties. Sometimes there's a small cover charge.

The Odyssey
210 Pharr Rd. • (404) 261-8476

The Odyssey is three bars in one. There's live acoustic music on the covered deck; a rock 'n' roll bar with more than 30 TVs; and a disco featuring hits from the '70s through to-day. The crowd is diverse, but most guests are in their 20s. Giant "bucket" drinks are a house specialty. The Odyssey is open every night.

Otto's
265 E. Paces Ferry Rd. N.E.
• (404) 233-1133

A sleek, upscale nightclub featuring nightly live music downstairs and a top-40 dance floor upstairs, Otto's is in the heart of Buckhead, so don't expect to find parking. On Friday, Saturday and Sunday after 9:30 PM, there's a moderate cover charge. Otto's casually elegant dress code is strictly enforced.

Tongue & Groove
3055 Peachtree Rd. N.E. • (404) 261-2325

When Tongue & Groove opened in Buckhead in 1994, it promised to "turn down the music and turn up the taste, letting people and their personalities take center stage in a stunningly designed space filled with subtle beauty." The club's interior is contemporary yet romantic and features custom furnishings and flattering lighting. Sushi and light fare are available. Expensive cigars and jumbo martinis are currently the rage at Tongue & Groove, which has a dance floor in the back room. Dress is upscale. Persons 23 and older are admitted; there's a moderate cover after 10 PM. On Thursday big band and swing are featured.

The World Bar
3071 Peachtree Rd. N.E. • (404) 266-0627

The World Bar has a dance floor and pool tables, and it's open Tuesday through Saturday nights. There's a small cover on Friday and Saturday nights only.

Underground Atlanta and Downtown

Underground Atlanta, within walking distance to many of the Olympic venues, fared a lot better than Tower Place. Nevertheless, the years have seen many bars come and go in Underground Atlanta. A persistent problem has been the lack of downtown housing, whose residents might be expected to patronize central city clubs. But with more apartment housing recently developed, nightlife entrepreneurs expect to see some action. At the moment, downtown's nightlife centers on the huge Underground Atlanta complex at Peachtree and Alabama streets. Most of Underground's bars and sit-down restaurants are arranged around the large open courtyard, Kenny's Alley. There's usually no cover charge at Underground's clubs, so bar-hopping is encouraged.

Underground Atlanta

Dante's Down the Hatch
• (404) 577-1800

Sip in jazzy sophisticated luxury at Dante's, which has been the big draw at the Underground since the '70s. Enter this dark environment, and you are on an ancient ship. Look over the railing and see pools of water in which alligators and turtles swim. The only food is fondue: Everything from meat to fruit gets dipped into something, be it oil or chocolate. There's great live jazz every night. You pay an entertainment charge for acoustical guitar ($2) or jazz ($6) on different sides of the restaurant.

Fat Tuesday
• (404) 523-7404

An array of frozen daiquiris is the club's "concept" offering, and you can snack on po' boys (a New Orleans-style sub sandwich with a variety of meats). Dance on the weekends to DJ spun music; during the week the music is pumped in via satellite.

Groundhog Tavern
• **(404) 659-2296**

Groundhog Tavern is a neighborhood-style bar and grill with some outdoor seating.

Hooter's
• **(404) 688-0062**

You can order chicken wings and other snacks at Hooter's, but the big attractions are the famed Hooter's girls, whose ample charms bring customers back again and again.

Downtown

Club Anytime
1055 Peachtree St. N.E. • (404) 607-8050

Special licensing (members only get around closing regulations) allows this dance club to stay open 24 hours, seven days a week. You'll pay a moderate cover charge to enjoy disco in the evenings; a jukebox, pool tables and billiards keep patrons entertained during the day.

Hyatt Regency Atlanta
265 Peachtree St. • (404) 577-1234

The revolving Polaris atop this first of John Portman's hotels looks like a flying saucer with shocking-blue glass from the outside. The Polaris room serves drinks and dinner. The Hyatt once towered over downtown; now taller buildings on three sides limit its view. But when your table slides by the northern windows, you'll enjoy a thrilling view of Midtown and north Atlanta.

Northside Tavern
1058 Howell Mill Rd. N.W. • (404) 874-8745

Truly off the beaten track, you'll find the Northside Tavern for music and dancing after you've had a great meal or seen some swell theater at King Plow. But know that you will definitely be overdressed 'cause this is a casual place. Try to get yourself on the mailing list so you can see the performers you prefer. There is no telling for taste, and this place offers a very diverse group of folks on any particular night. The back room has a couple of pool tables to occupy you 'til the jivin' begins. There's a small cover charge.

Tower II
735 Ralph McGill Blvd. • (404) 523-1535

This lesbian bar is the oldest women's bar in Atlanta and attracts a leather-jacket crowd. You'll find no frills here, inside or out.

The Westin Peachtree Plaza
Peachtree St. at International Blvd.
• (404) 659-1400

The Sun Dial lounge atop the Westin Peachtree Plaza, another of the many John Portman-designed structures in Atlanta, is the ultimate roof room. Dusk is an especially lovely time to visit when thousands of lights glitter to life. If the air is clear during daylight hours, you can see all the way to Stone Mountain. There is a $5 per person charge to visit the lounge. Hop on one of the outside, glassed-in elevators and fly up 72 floors. By the time you get there, you'll need a drink!

Midtown

Much of Midtown's nightlife is on or near Peachtree Street between 10th and 14th streets. Once known as The Strip, this was Atlanta's hippie mecca in the 1970s. It prospered as a lively nightclub and theater zone in the '80s, and although many club spaces were razed by developers, it's still a fun area that has room for continued growth.

Backstreet
845 Peachtree St. • (404) 873-1986

For almost a quarter-century, Backstreet has been Atlanta's biggest gay bar, open 24 hours a day through special licensing that requires membership. No big deal — you can become a member at the door ($10 for three months). This huge cha-cha palace is a three-level entertainment complex with a 2,500-square-foot high-energy dance floor disco and a separate room for live shows. Some of

Atlanta's best-known female impersonators perform upstairs in Charlie Brown's X-Rated Cabaret Wednesday through Sunday evenings; the weekend shows go until dawn. Although Backstreet is way-gay, fun-loving straights have a blast here as well, particularly if they're into dancing. Photo IDs are required no matter if you are 21 or 91.

Blake's
227 10th St. • (404) 892-5786

Blake's is a popular gay bar attracting area residents. A DJ entertains nightly, and finger foods are served.

The Cotton Club
1021 Peachtree St. N.E. • (404) 874-2516

The Cotton Club is a large performance club that showcases local and national alternative rock bands; the cover charge is small to moderate.

Dugan's
777 Ponce de Leon Ave. N.E.
• (404) 885-1217

Dugan's has tavern food and a large patio overlooking Ponce; on busy evenings, you may have to wait in line to get in.

Hoedown's
931 Monroe Dr. • (404) 876-0001

Formerly located on Cheshire Bridge, this place is hidden behind the Winn Dixie in the Midtown Promenade off Monroe Drive at Virginia Avenue. The gay and lesbian clientele pack the place, and there's a buffet on Sundays. Free dance lessons (can you guess what style? Why, country, of course!), are offered on Sundays, Tuesdays and Thursdays.

Jocks 'N Jills
112 10th St. • (404) 873-5405

If you want to root for the home teams, you'll have plenty of company at this sports bar with a multitude of TVs, plus food and a patio on Peachtree.

March
550 Amsterdam Ave. • (404) 872-6411

Off the beaten track on a dead-end street that by day is a shopper's paradise with discount warehouses, you'll find March, a lesbian bar. March has a DJ on Wednesdays. Girls Night Out, an events production company that puts together lesbian parties, holds its parties here. The techno design is futuristic with snazzy lights hanging from the ceiling. Doors open at 10 PM, and a moderate cover is charged.

Martini Club
140 Crescent Ave. • (404) 873-0794

Open 4 PM till 2 AM nightly, the Martini Club features 54 varieties of martinis including a Georgia Peach martini that is truly unique. Relax in the 1930s-style bar with chaise lounges and pictures of women in gowns from the period. You can also buy and smoke cigars here. Live piano music is featured nightly.

Masquerade
695 North Ave. • (404) 577-8178

Masquerade is the kind of place your mama must have warned you about: The average Masquerade patron probably has more body piercings and tattoos than the average business person has credit cards. But those into the gothic, punk and alternative rock scenes will have a blast here. In an antique factory that once turned out excelsior (wood shavings used as packing straw, much as foam "peanuts" are used today), Masquerade's monstrous space is divided into three theme areas: Hell, the throbbing downstairs dance room; Heaven, the big upstairs concert hall; and Purgatory, a more low-key performance art space that's — you guessed it — between the two. Masquerade showcases lots of local talent and books national acts for major concerts every week. It's open Wednesday through Sunday; the cover charge is moderate and varies significantly depending on who's playing.

The Metro
1080 Peachtree St. • (404) 874-9869

The Metro is a rowdy bar with go-go boys, dancing and drag shows seven days a week. Every night features another theme from wet jacket night to Latin night.

My Sister's Room
931 Monroe Dr. • (404) 875-6699

This lesbian bar has couches, a pool table, two air hockey tables and never charges a cover.

There's a jukebox in the game room, and occasionally My Sister's Room has live music.

The Otherside
1924 Piedmont Ave. • (404) 875-5238

Primarily a lesbian bar with live music and a small cover on the weekends, The Otherside is quiet during the week. The bar made national headlines in 1997 when a bomber (police believe it is the same person who set the bombs at an abortion clinic and at Centennial Olympic Park in 1996) placed two explosive devices at this site. Fortunately, no one was killed when they detonated.

Smith's Olde Bar
1578 Piedmont Ave. N.E. • (404) 875-1522

Smith's occupies the building that many old-timers will remember as Gene & Gabe's restaurant. Smith's features live entertainment seven nights a week. It opens daily for lunch and stays open until 4 AM weekdays and 3 AM on Saturday. There are four pool tables; the cover charge in the upstairs showroom varies from small to moderate, depending on who's playing. Recent shows have headlined acts such as Gracie Moon, Innocent Four, T-Model Ford and local favorites such as Atlanta recording artist Richard Bicknell.

Yin Yang Cafe
64 Third St. • (404) 607-0682

Yin Yang Cafe serves beer, wine and food. There's a small cover on nights with live jazz, usually Thursday through Sunday.

Little Five Points

About 2 miles east of Five Points, the heart of downtown Atlanta, lies Little Five Points. Its major intersection is the convergence of Moreland, Euclid and McLendon avenues. Little Five Points is Atlanta's most integrated, multicultural district, and the emphasis here is on the avant garde. The district's stores are filled with the most cutting-edge clubwear, and in its public areas you'll see lots of leather, body piercings, tattoos and exotic hair styles. When the weather's nice, Little Five is one of the best places in Atlanta to relax and soak up the scene.

Euclid Avenue Yacht Club
1136 Euclid Ave. N.E. • (404) 688-2582

The Yacht Club is a bar with a limited menu. Grab a front booth to take in the passing scene on the street in this Little Five Points neighborhood joint where pink hair and pierced bodies are more common than apple pie. The mahogany-paneled bar is decorated in a yacht-club theme with stuffed fish, an actual canoe and maritime photos from all over the world on the walls.

The Point
420 Moreland Ave. N.E. • (404) 659-3522

The Point is open every night in the heart of Little Five Points. Up-and-coming college rock bands play Tuesday through Saturday nights, when there's also a small to moderate cover charge. You can flashback at the Sunday contemporary disco party. The Point has a full bar and serves food.

Star Community Bar
437 Moreland Ave. N.E. • (404) 681-9018

Star Community Bar is open nightly and has a full bar. College, garage and rock-a-billy bands play here five or six nights a week; occasionally there's a show by a national act on the college circuit. The cover charge is small to moderate, depending on who's playing. The Star has an all-Elvis jukebox and an Elvis shrine housed in a former bank vault. In the basement is the Little Vinyl Lounge subterranean deco bar with a jukebox featuring 5,000 choices. You must enter through the top bar.

Virginia-Highland

The pleasant neighborhood around the intersection of Virginia and N. Highland avenues is the closest Atlanta gets to a New York City strolling strip where interesting, well-designed shops beckon with interesting window decor, sounds and aromas. It has also become something of a nightlife destination in its own right.

You'll find many Virginia-Highland restaurants in our Restaurants chapter and lots of shops in the area noted in the Shopping chapter.

Blind Willie's
828 N. Highland Ave. N.E. • (404) 873-2583

A neon alligator in the window welcomes you to Blind Willie's. Mose Allison and Jr. Wells have played this small blues joint that features live entertainment every night. Sundays are usually acoustic. There's a full bar with bar food; a moderate cover is charged nightly. Music starts at 10 PM.

Dark Horse Tavern
816 N. Highland Ave. N.E. • (404) 873-3607

Dark Horse Tavern has a rock performance space in the basement where local and national college bands play. If there is a cover for the showroom, it's usually small. The street-level room has a large bar and windows from which to observe the street life.

George's
**1041 N. Highland Ave. N.E.
• (404) 892-3648**

At the heart of Virginia-Highland, George's is a favorite hangout for neighborhood residents. Grab a burger and a beer and sit at an outside table any night except Sunday.

Highland Tap
**1026 N. Highland Ave. N.E.
• (404) 875-3673**

The Tap is covered in the Steakhouse section of our Restaurants chapter. Its jumbo 4-ounce martini is big with those who like their cocktails high and dry.

Limerick Junction
822 N. Highland Ave. • (404) 874-7147

Celebrate Celtic culture at Limerick Junction. There's an Irish sing-along nightly Wednesday through Saturday; on Sunday and Monday nights, there's live contemporary Irish

---

INSIDERS' TIP

Seating at The Fox Theatre is not staggered, so visibility from some locations may be difficult for the more diminutive in stature. If you get your tickets from the box office, you can ask to see where you'll be sitting.

or folk music. There's a small cover on Friday and Saturday nights.

Moe's and Joe's
1033 N. Highland Ave. N.E.
• (404) 873-6090

Moe's and Joe's serves hamburgers, fries and beer and has a few tables outside for people-watching.

Other Performance Clubs

Cafe 290
290 Hilderbrand Dr. N.E., Sandy Springs
• (404) 256-3942

Cafe 290, just north of I-285, is open nightly with live jazz or blues. A separate section houses a sports bar. A full menu is available; there's no cover if you dine in, otherwise on weekends you'll pay a cover.

Charades
105 N. Park Sq., Marietta • (770) 514-1999

A game room with pool tables and games adjoins a hall for dancing. A DJ plays Friday nights, and there are live bands on Wednesday evenings. Programming changes nightly, so if you want to go to dance, call to make sure the music will be to your liking.

Cowboy's Concert Hall
1750 N. Roberts Rd., Kennesaw
• (770) 426-5006

Cowboy's Concert Hall welcomes you and all your rowdy friends. This 4,800-square-foot country club has a 4,000-square-foot dance floor and holds about 3,700 cowboys and cowgirls. Wednesday is ladies' night. Most nights there's a small cover, which varies with the entertainment offered.

Dave and Buster's
2215 D&B Dr., Marietta • (770) 951-5554

This incredible amusement park for adults defies easy classification. Dave and Buster's is a 53,000-square-foot world of fun with some 300 employees. Here are 16 world-class mahogany and slate billiard tables, five shuffleboard courts, the Million-Dollar Midway with more than 100 video games and virtual reality simulators, a "for-fun" casino, a restaurant, full-service bars and a mystery dinner theater where the audience helps solve the crime. Dave & Buster's is open every day from before noon until midnight or later. Accompanied children are welcome but must remain with their parents at all times. Because Dave & Buster's serves alcohol, after 10 PM anyone younger than 21 must leave the premises.

Dottie's
307 Memorial Dr. S.E. • (404) 523-3444

Dottie's is a fun little honky-tonk near Grant Park. It has a full bar and is open every night. There's usually a live band of the alternative music genre on Wednesday, Friday, Saturday and Sunday. There might be a small cover on entertainment nights.

Eddie's Attic
515 McDonough St., Decatur
• (404) 377-4976

Eddie's Attic has a large gay and lesbian clientele depending on who's playing. The Indigo Girls, for example, had an opening party here in '97. Great sandwiches, salads and chicken fingers are served. There is also a tavern and a 225-person-capacity music hall with live original acoustic entertainment seven nights a week. There's no cover charged on the patio, which is open year round. A cover charge starts small and goes up for big-name acts for the music hall.

Freight Room
301 E. Howard Ave., Decatur
• (404) 378-5365

Freight Room spotlights a variety of music, including acoustic, bluegrass, jazz and zydeco. There's a small cover on Thursday, Friday and Saturday; the cover may be higher when national acts perform. There's a full-service restaurant, and the club is open nightly with live music. The Freight Room occupies a 110-year-old building that was once Decatur's railway station.

Mama's Country Showcase
3952 Covington Hwy., Decatur
• (404) 288-6262

Country music is featured at Mama's where a 3,000-square-foot dance floor holds about 2,000 boot-scooters. There are free dance lessons Wednesday and Thursday and a free buffet on Wednesday only. On Wednesdays, admission is free with a college ID or $5 without; on Thursdays, ladies are admitted free and men pay $5; and on Friday and Saturday, those 18 to 21 get in for $10, while those older than 21 pay $5. A DJ handles the music, and a restaurant is on the premises. If you're brave, you can hop on Tornado the mechanical bull. Mama's is closed Sunday through Tuesday.

The (Outer) Edge
585 Franklin Rd., Marietta • (770) 428-1393
The (Outer) Edge has live rock bands seven nights a week. There are 15 pool tables; the restaurant serves until 1 AM. A small nightly cover charge increases when national acts perform.

Comedy

Punch Line
280 Hilderbrand Dr. N.E. • (404) 252-5233
A list of comedians who have played the Punch Line reads like *TV Guide*: Jerry Seinfeld, Ellen Degeneres, Tim Allen and Brett Butler have all made audiences laugh, laugh, laugh here where they frequently try out their new material. Pam Stone of the TV series *Coach* got her start here as a waitress. The club is open Tuesday through Sunday; the cover charge is moderate to higher, depending upon who's performing. For weekends and special engagements, purchase tickets in advance. Seats go fast. A one-drink minimum is required in addition to the cover.

Uptown Comedy Corner
2140 Peachtree Rd. N.W. • (404) 350-6990
Uptown Comedy Corner showcases popular black comedians and draws a primarily African-American, upscale crowd. The club holds about 300 people. There are three shows Friday and Saturday and one show on Tuesday,

Wednesday and Thursday. Sunday and Tuesday are amateur nights. The cover charge is moderate during the week and higher on Friday and Saturday.

Adult Entertainment

Because they offer totally nude dancers, Atlanta's adult entertainment clubs are controversial — but they're also legendary. These establishments advertise heavily in print, on billboards and on the radio; even the city's official tourist magazine *Atlanta Now* includes a listing of some of them. You can find many adult clubs listed under "Nightclubs" in the Yellow Pages. Also check the *Adult Scene*, a free weekly published by *Creative Loafing*. Cover charges at these establishments range from small to moderate — and don't forget your tip and table-dance money!

The Gold Club, 2416 Piedmont Avenue N.E., (404) 233-1210, is within walking distance of the Lindbergh MARTA station. The Goldrush Showbar, 2608 Stewart Avenue S.W., (404) 766-2532, is located about 10 minutes north of Hartsfield Airport. The Diamond Club, 1400 Northside Drive N.W., (404) 352-0532, is near Interstate 75 and 14th street downtown. And the oldest of the strip clubs, The Cheetah at 887 Spring St. N.W., (404) 892-3037, is in the heart of downtown.

Two clubs feature male and female dancers: Guys and Dolls, 2788 E. Ponce de Leon Avenue, Decatur, (404) 377-2956; and The Coronet Club, 5275 Roswell Road N.E., (404) 250-1534.

Concert Theaters

Atlanta has several venues that offer the experience of seeing nationally known performers in fairly intimate surroundings. Ticket prices at these theaters vary with the acts appearing there.

INSIDERS' TIP

If you like to dance cheek-to-cheek in the old-fashioned way or do the Lindy Hop with the older set, The Ritz-Carlton Buckhead (3434 Peachtree Road across from Lenox Square and adjacent to Phipps Plaza) is the place to be on Friday and Saturday evenings after 9 PM. There's no cover.

Photo: Michael Portman/The Fox Theatre

Sing along with the Mighty Moeller organ at The Fox Theatre.

The Coca-Cola Roxy Theater
3110 Roswell Rd. • (404) 233-ROXY

In Buckhead, The Roxy holds 1,100 to 1,500 people in a space that was once a cinema and drafthouse. Recent shows have starred Elton John, World Party, Justin Hayward and Verve Pipe. The Roxy has a full bar. Tickets, which usually go for $13 to $20, are sold through TicketMaster, (404) 249-6400; the box office sells tickets for events only on the day of the show.

Variety Playhouse
1099 Euclid Avenue N.E. • (404) 521-1786

The Variety Playhouse seats 800 to 1,000 patrons in a former movie theater with a balcony and space for dancing in front of the stage. Grass Cactus, James Seaberry, Leo Kotke, Doc Watson and Grover Washington Jr. have all played the Variety. The theater features beer, wine and snacks at a concession stand. Tickets are available at the box office; payment is by cash, local check or credit cards with $1

added on for that service. To charge by phone, call TicketMaster, (404) 249-6400.

Amphitheaters

Chastain Park Amphitheater
Powers Ferry Rd. at Stella Dr.
• (404) 733-4800

Chastain Park offers world-class entertainment in an outdoor dining environment that makes for a truly enjoyable evening. The gently sloping amphitheater with 6,000 seats means good sight lines to the stage, where internationally known performers such as Manhattan Transfer, Gladys Knight, Patti LaBelle and Tricia Yearwood have recently performed.

Classical, country, jazz, rock 'n' roll — you name it, Chastain presents it. The Atlanta Symphony Orchestra calls Chastain home during the summer while backing the big showbiz names.

Peer around you at the repasts created by those attending. You'll see a few brown-baggers. But more often you'll see full-blown dinner parties, complete with linen cloths, candles, silver and champagne-filled crystal goblets, except for rock concerts when no tables are allowed and front-row center is for the stand-up-and-cheer crowd. For more on Chastain Park, see The Arts chapter.

Coca-Cola Lakewood Amphitheater
2002 Lakewood Way • (404) 627-9704

Beginning in 1916, Lakewood Fair Grounds was the site of the Southeastern Fair, which drew exhibitors and visitors from across the South. Today the Lakewood Amphitheater is the site of a concert series that runs from May to October. Headliners have included Bon Jovi, Jimmy Buffett, Crosby, Stills & Nash, Steely Dan, Harry Connick Jr. and the Allman Brothers Band. The two-day Lollapalooza festival (see our Festivals and Events chapter) draws thousands of tattooed and pierced devotees of punk and alternative rock.

Lakewood seats more than 18,000: Reserved seats are under the covered pavilion, while the broad lawn is general admission. Big-screen TVs suspended from the pavilion roof bring the action up-close for those on the lawn. Shows at Lakewood go on rain or shine. To charge tickets by phone, call TicketMaster, (404) 249-6400.

To reach Lakewood, take I-75/85 south from downtown to the Lakewood Freeway East Exit and follow the signs, or take the Lakewood Freeway West Exit to Stewart Avenue and follow the signs. Parking is included in the price of your ticket. Although the city is trying to clean up the neighborhoods around Lakewood, these are not areas in which to run out of gas or break down, so fill-up the tank and take your cellular phone along.

Note: For an outdoor facility, Lakewood has a lot of rules. You may bring in a blanket to sit on, but you may not bring in the following: coolers, containers, drinks or food prepared off-premises, lawn chairs, cameras and recording equipment. Avoid hassles by leaving prohibited items in your car. Alcohol and a full menu are available at all shows.

The Cinematic Theater

Even though most theaters begin screening early in the afternoon, we'll cover movies in our Nightlife chapter since that's when most people have time to attend the cinema.

A recent check of *The Atlanta Journal-Constitution's* "Leisure" guide is a good place to find what's showing on some of Atlanta's 400+ screens. A few first-run theaters accept credit cards and sell advance tickets by phone; their recorded messages let you know if this is the case. Most theaters have special matinee prices until 4 PM; some go as late as 6 PM.

A Movie and a Meal

Considering the speed with which new movies now move from first-run houses to bargain theaters, many people prefer to wait a few weeks and catch new flicks at lower prices. The typical price at bargain theaters is $1.75 to $5 for all seats. Here are some discount theaters within Atlanta's Perimeter highway as well as some older theaters that have become more tasteful, literally.

North Springs Cinema Grill
7270 Roswell Rd., Sandy Springs
• (770) 395-0724

Another renovated movie house showing second-run movies along with burgers, chicken wings, beer and pizza, the North Springs Cinema Grill serves a suburban crowd.

Admission is $3, food is extra, and you don't have to order meals to go.

Bargain Cinemas

Northeast Plaza Cinema 12
3365 Buford Hwy. • (404) 248-0624
All seats for these second-run movies cost just $1.75, and doors open at 12:30 PM. The theater is in a large discount mall just off N. Druid Hills Road on Buford Highway.

Toco Hills Theater
3003 N. Druid Hills Rd. • (404) 325-7090
Toco Hills shows first-run foreign movies for less than you'd pay at a big chain distributor. Matinees cost about $4, and evening shows are $5.75.

Alternative Cinema

Although we've lost several movie theaters that specialized in limited-run, revival and art films to commercial development, you can still catch art and foreign-language films at the following locations.

Cinefest
66 Courtland St., Ste. 211 • (404) 651-2463
In the University Center building at Georgia State University, this movie theater is sponsored in part by GSU's students. Many programs are double-features, including new popular movies, art films and cult classics. The program usually changes on Friday and again on Monday. The monthly schedule of coming attractions is available free in some in-town restaurants and bars. At the theater, you may sign the mailing list and receive the calendar free by mail. Public parking is available at the Underground.

The Fox Theatre
660 Peachtree St. N.E. • (404) 881-2100
On about a dozen nights between June and September, The Fox Theatre offers a summer film series that allows you to revel in the experience of seeing a movie in the lush, exotic environment of an authentic movie palace. The series shows a mix of current and classic films. Doors open at 6:45 PM; the sing-along with the Mighty Moeller organ begins at

7:20 PM; and a cartoon precedes the main feature that begins at 8 PM. Admission is $6 per person. Leaving the humidity and heat outside and luxuriating in The Fox's cool darkness is the perfect way to enjoy a sultry Atlanta night. (See our Attractions chapter for more on The Fox.)

Goethe-Institut Atlanta
Colony Square, 1197 Peachtree St. • (404) 892-2388
Goethe-Institut Atlanta has regular screenings of contemporary and historic German films. For more on the Goethe-Institut see our International Atlanta chapter.

The High Museum of Art
1280 Peachtree St. N.E. • (404) 733-4570
The High Museum of Art hosts screenings of various series of alternative and art movies at the Rich Auditorium. Become a member (various categories of membership are available) of the High, and you'll get a terrific program guide to pin up on the wall. (Turn to The Arts chapter for more information about the High.)

IMAGE Film/Video Center
75 Bennett St. (at the end of the block in Tula) N.W. • (404) 352-4225
In 1997 IMAGE sold 6,500 tickets for its Film & Video Festival, the best its done in 21 years (see our Festivals and Events chapter). IMAGE Film/Video Center annually has hundreds of public screenings of hard-to-find films and videos. In addition, the group offers more than 40 workshops each year. It also puts on filmmaker and video maker salons and produces Out On Film, a gay and lesbian film festival. Call for schedule information.

Lefont Screening Room
2581 Piedmont Rd. • (404) 231-1924
LeFont Garden Hills Theatre
2835 Peachtree Rd. • (404) 266-2202
George Lefont was a pioneer in Atlanta in bringing old flicks, foreign-language and recent Cannes award-winning films to the city. Although a few of his places have gone the way of penny candy, a few still fit the bill including the Screening Room and the Garden Hills Cinema. Admission is $4.50 for children and seniors, $6.50 for everyone else.

VININGS JUBILEE

IT'S A CHANGE OF PACE PLACE
THAT CELEBRATES GOOD FOOD, GOOD SHOPPING, GOOD TIMES

It's like nowhere else in Atlanta.

Filled with wonderful restaurants and specialty shops.

Nestled in the heart of historic Vinings Village.

Vinings Jubilee, 4200 Paces Ferry Road, Atlanta, Georgia 770~438~8080

Shopping

A transportation hub from its beginning, Atlanta naturally became a retail center as well. Just two years after the Civil War, more than 250 stores were wheeling and dealing in Atlanta. (Remember all the money Scarlett O'Hara and her second husband, Frank Kennedy, made with their store and lumberyard during Reconstruction?)

Atlanta is nothing if not a booming retail market with amazing extremes. Here you can shop Saks, Tiffany & Co., Gucci, Cartier and Neiman Marcus in megamalls that have become tourist attractions in themselves, while just a few rail stops away, you can shop the thrift stores to find designer jeans for less than $10. Every weekend with halfway decent weather, you'll find street after street of yard sales. Telephone poles are plastered with signs advertising upcoming yard sales, and the "Yard Sales" section in *Creative Loafing* and the "Garage Sales" section in *The Atlanta Journal-Constitution* offer the organized shopper who doesn't want to waste time aimlessly roaming the blocks a plan of attack.

Here's a glimpse of some of Atlanta's best-known retail centers and some lesser-known ones, too. We start at the city's malls and continue to outlets, shopping districts, antiques, thrift stores, consignment shops, farmers markets, bookstores, music stores and New Age shopping venues.

Look to our International Atlanta chapter for some intriguing shopping destinations that reflect our city's cultural diversity.

Malls

Atlanta

CNN Center
Marietta St. at Techwood Dr. N.W.
• (404) 827-2491
CNN Center includes the Omni Hotel and the studios and world headquarters of the Cable News Network. It offers fine dining (see the Restaurants chapter for our listing on Bugatti), fast food and a variety of Atlanta-themed gifts (The Atlanta Shop, Braves Clubhouse Store and The Turner Store).

You can take a 45-minute tour of the CNN headquarters. You can also reserve a seat in the audience of CNN's interactive show *TalkBack Live* Call (800) 410-4CNN. See our Attractions chapter for more information on these tours.

Cumberland Mall
Cobb Pkwy. N.W., south of I-285/75 in Cobb Co. • (770) 435-2206
The 1.2 million-square-foot Cumberland Mall was renovated in 1989; its anchors are Rich's, Macy's, Sears and JCPenney. Other stores include Ann Taylor, Bachrach, the Bombay Company, Abercrombie & Fitch and Gap Kids. The food court offers an array of choices, including Mick's, a restaurant that orginated in Atlanta and has become a national chain (see our Restaurants chapter).

Guest Services at Cumberland Mall provides shoppers with details of ongoing store and mall events, easy access to strollers and wheelchairs and gift certificates redeemable in all mall stores. A complimentary personal shopper service is available on request.

Galleria Specialty Mall
One Galleria Pkwy. N.W., Cobb Co.
• (770) 955-9100
The Cobb Galleria Centre complex includes a 108,000-square-foot exhibition hall, the Renaissance Waverly Hotel and the Galleria Specialty Mall. The Galleria Specialty Mall offers a number of boutiques owned and operated by local entrepreneurs, featuring men's, women's and children's apparel, gifts, jewelry and sports merchandise, including Peter Glenn for specialty sports such as in-

line skating and skiing and H. Stockton for men's fashion. In addition, the mall has a variety of restaurants including Mozzarella's Cafe, Jocks N' Jills sports bar, Ruby Tuesday and Winfield's. Service establishments include hair stylists, a newsstand, American Express Travel and a photography studio. Want to be entertained? The mall has an eight-screen theater and Cyberstation, a family entertainment center with state-of-the-art video games.

Galleria Specialty Mall is at the intersection of I-75, I-285 and Cobb Parkway.

Greenbriar Mall
2841 Greenbriar Pkwy. S.W.
• (404) 344-6611

Another one of Atlanta's first malls, Greenbriar opened in August 1965. Its 678,000 square feet include Rich's, Circuit City, Cub Foods, Magic Johnson Theatres with 12 screens and Burlington Coat Factory. Greenbriar features a large selection of stores carrying Afrocentric fashions and accessories for the home. If you're lost or confused, take heart: Greenbriar's Customer Service Booth can help you get oriented. You'll also find information about how to purchase a Greenbriar Mall Certificate, a gift certificate redeemable at any of the mall's retail merchants.

Follow I-285 to Lakewood Freeway; take Exit 4A off the freeway to get to the mall.

Lenox Square
3393 Peachtree Rd. N.E.
• (404) 233-6767

Atlanta's first large suburban shopping center opened in 1959 with 52 stores and 665,000 square feet. Buckhead was still on the fringes of Atlanta, and Atlantans were stunned at the $32 million cost of the new shopping center. The shopping center was enclosed and expanded in 1972 and expanded again in 1987; its food court grew in 1993.

Today, Lenox is the largest mall in Atlanta. It has 250 stores, attracts 14 million visitors annually, and its rate of sales per square foot is among the highest of all U.S. shopping cen-

ters. A $60 million expansion completed in 1995 increased its size to 1.5 million square feet.

Macy's, Neiman Marcus and Rich's anchor the 61-acre mall; other shops include Louis Vuitton, Cartier, Warner Bros., Disney and the Metropolitan Museum of Art Shop. There is also an expanded FAO Schwartz concept store that's triple the size of its previous Lenox location. Other merchants include Betsy Johnson, Bare Escentuals and The Franklin Mint Gallery. If you have questions, Lenox's concierges will be glad to help.

Lenox has acres of free parking and sections where valet parking is available, or you can take the train to the Lenox MARTA station. Opposite the station is the J.W. Marriott Hotel; adjacent to it, the Lenox Building has an enclosed passageway. Called Art Walk, it is decorated with intriguing art shows. The Art Walk leads directly to the mall.

The Mall at Peachtree Center
Peachtree St. N.E. at International Blvd.
• (404) 524-3787

This is the first retail complex in downtown and a component of the huge Peachtree Center development designed by famed Atlanta architect John Portman. The Mall is connected by pedestrian bridges to many downtown buildings, including the Marriott Marquis and Hyatt Regency. More than 75 mall businesses offer a variety of shopping and services.

Dine at fine restaurants such as Azio and Benihana, or grab a quick bite at a selection of food-court eateries including Jaffa Gate, American Lunch, Le Petit Bistro and Wall Street Deli. Shop for apparel and accessories at a variety of stores such as Brooks Brothers, Gallery Shoes and Chez Jackie. Buy sports merchandise at Stadium Stuff or collectibles at Atlanta International Museum Gift Shop.

Personal and travel service companies abound at this mall. Executive Shoe Shine, UPS Air Center and La Grande convenience

FYI
Three area codes serve the metro Atlanta area: 404, 770 and 678. Whether you live on Peachtree Street or in New York City, you must dial the code to reach any number in the area. The difference? Outside the area, you must dial "1," then the area code and phone number; inside the area, you need only dial the area code followed by the phone number.

Photo: Georgia Renaissance Festival

Shop in medieval castles, Tudor homes and enchanting cottages for arts and crafts created by village artisans at the Georgia Renaissance Festival.

store are among the variety of places dedicated to making your life simpler.

Architectural Book Center, owned by the American Institute of Architects (AIA), is a museum shop frequented by conventioneers and other city visitors. Peachtree Center is served by the Peachtree Center MARTA station.

North DeKalb Mall
Lawrenceville Hwy. at N. Druid Hills Rd.
• (404) 320-7960

One of Atlanta's first malls (it opened in 1965), North DeKalb Mall, formerly known as Market Square, was renovated in 1986. Its 650,657 square feet include Rich's and Stein Mart. The mall features a food court, a movie theater and a variety of retailers selling everything from sporting goods to jewelry.

To get to the mall from I-285, take the Lawrenceville Highway exit.

Northlake Mall
4800 Briarcliff Rd. • (770) 938-3564

Northlake has 125 specialty stores, along with Sears, Macy's, JCPenney and Parisian (an Alabama-based department store). At nearby Northlake Tower Festival, 3983 LaVista

Road, you'll find numerous superstores, such as PetSmart and Toys 'R' Us.

Take I-285 and exit at LaVista Road.

Phipps Plaza
3500 Peachtree Rd. N.E.
• (404) 262-0992

Diagonally across Peachtree from Lenox Square, Phipps Plaza is devoted strictly to upscale stores. When it opened in 1969, Phipps was the first two-story mall in the Southeast. A $140 million renovation in 1992 added a three-level wing and Parisian, which joined existing anchors Lord & Taylor and Saks Fifth Avenue. Other shops of note include the amazingly modernistic 24,000-square-foot Nike Town; the only Atlanta locations of Tiffany & Co., Ross-Simons, Gucci, Gianni Versace, A/X Armani Exchange, Kenneth Cole; Abercrombie & Fitch; and Lassiter's Bath & Boudoir. The mall also has a 14-screen movie theater, a food court and five white-tablecloth restaurants.

Phipps At Your Service offers shoppers a number of amenities including a full-service concierge center, gift wrapping and shipping, wheelchair and stroller availability and valet parking. You can also park in the mall's spacious lots and decks.

One amenity shoppers especially like is a mall-wide personal shopping service that's absolutely free. Phipps' personal shoppers save you time and stress by assembling merchandise for your review. Just dial (404) 262-0992 or (800) 810-7700 and tell them what you need.

Rio Shopping Center
Piedmont Rd. and North Ave. N.E.
• **(404) 874-6688**

Designed by the award-winning Miami-based firm Arquitectonica (which is working on the design for the new arena of the Atlanta Hawks and Thrashers slated to open in 1999), Rio was constructed about eight years ago. It is a small, two-story open-air mall that was ahead of its time in terms of design and in-town shopping needs (which means it struggled for years before it could hold tenants and attract clientele). A huge geodesic dome made of tubular metal that spewed water (in the beginning) was the centerpiece of the complex. It sat in the middle of a pool inhabited by giant gold-painted frog sculptures. But with little foot traffic, shops closed, frogs disappeared, and the mall was sold to new owners. However, the times they are a-changing, and Rio is experiencing a renaissance. Perhaps someday, the dome will spew again, and the amphibians will reappear en masse.

Tic-Tac-Toe, a popular place for men's and women's hats and unique T-shirts, and the Crab House are two of the original tenants who have withstood the test of time. Lettuce Souprise You, a buffet-style salad restaurant offers more than its name implies with pasta, potato and all-you-can-eat homemade muffins (see our Restaurants chapter).

Underground Atlanta
Peachtree at Alabama Sts. S.W.
• **(404) 523-2311**

Underground Atlanta evolved as a curious by-product of the city's growth. By 1890, more than 100 trains a day were passing through the downtown depot. Temporary iron bridges were built across the tracks to alleviate traffic congestion; then, in the 1920s, a permanent concrete viaduct was added, and the street was elevated. Businesses on old Alabama Street relocated upward to new Alabama Street, and the old storefronts sat abandoned below the street until they were rediscovered by a Georgia Tech graduate who developed the area as a retail and entertainment center in 1969.

Throughout most of the 1970s, Underground boomed as a rowdy party spot that was a favorite of locals and tourists. But after it lost about half its space to MARTA construction and the perception of crime became a problem, the old Underground closed in 1981.

Redeveloped as a public/private venture, the new Underground opened in 1989 and is almost three times the size of its predecessor. During the Centennial Olympics the Underground was a big success with locals and visitors who enjoyed the shops and vendor carts that lined both subterranean Lower Alabama Street and the above-ground pedestrian-only Upper Alabama Street. But in 1997 Underground began to decline once again. The shops we note here may, by publication date, have closed. But considering its history, Underground will most likely see another renaissance.

Shops of note include Just A Dollar, Doubleday Books, Gap, Victoria's Secret, Warner Bros. Studio Store, Sam Goody's, Stadium Stuff Super Store and The Nature Company. The food court has a good mix of ethnic

---

www.insiders.com

See this and many other **Insiders' Guide®** destinations online — in their entirety.

Visit us today!

INSIDERS' TIP

Yard-sale connoisseurs are also early risers. To get the best before everything gets picked over, hit the road early and head to Morningside, Ansley Park, Peachtree Hills and Virginia-Highland when pleasant weather brings everyone and everything to the curbs and carports.

and fast food. The open-air Kenny's Alley is a courtyard of bars and restaurants.

Some current discussions about what to do with the empty spaces at Underground have suggested converting the spaces into a downtown theater district to be used by several of the small theatrical troupes. The concept has city support. Now it's just a matter of raising enough funds for renovation and the construction of stages and auditorium seating.

The entrance to the Underground parking decks is on M.L. King Jr. Drive (one-way, westbound); there are other decks in the area as well. Or take MARTA to the Five Points station and enter through the pedestrian tunnel under Peachtree; it's on your right just before you exit the station.

Vinings Jubilee
4200 Paces Ferry Rd. N.W.
• **(770) 438-8080**

In historic Vinings Village, browse in Atlanta's only Victorian shopping center. More than 20 specialty boutiques, antique shops and eateries offer nourishment, apparel, decorative home accessories and antiques. Stores include Talbots, The Sandpiper and Pappagallo. If all that shopping leaves you famished, drop by the Atlanta Bread Company for a light lunch. If you need a quick jolt of caffeine, grab an espresso at Moon Bean & Co.

Beyond Atlanta

Gwinnett Place
I-85 at Exit 40, Gwinnett Co.
• **(770) 476-5160**

This 1.2 million-square-foot mall opened in 1984 and expanded in 1993. It has 220 shops and department stores including Macy's, JCPenney, Parisian, Rich's and Sears.

The surrounding streets are a favorite stop for car buyers: Most of the major car-makers have dealerships in this area, which is known as "Motor Mile."

North Point Mall
1000 N. Point Cir., Alpharetta
• **(770) 740-9273**

Opened in 1993, the 1.4 million-square-foot North Point features JCPenney, Lord & Taylor,

Dillard's, Mervyn's, Rich's and Sears. Nearly 200 specialty retailers, including The Body Shop, Ann Taylor, The Pet Stop, Ozone Hi-Tech Electronics and Littlewear, USA, offer a variety of goods to the mall's affluent clientele. North Point has a full-service customer service facility with an intercom/phone system attached to all freestanding mall directories, fax and photocopy services, and stroller and wheelchair availability. R.J. Reynolds Tobacco Co. has a smoking lounge inside this mall that is similar to one at the Northgate Mall in Chattanooga. This is the only place in the mall where you can smoke .

The Food Court has 15 restaurants and an outdoor patio. In a huge glass atrium beside the food court, a 30-foot-high carousel accommodates 38 riders; rides are $1 per person.

Take Ga. 400 to Exit 9 to get to North Point.

Perimeter Mall
4400 Ashford Dunwoody Rd. N.E.
• **(770) 394-4270**

Perimeter Mall opened in 1971, was expanded in 1982 and was renovated in 1993. Sitting just north of I-285, the 1.2 million-square-foot mall is the nerve center of the hyperdeveloped, always-busy northeast Perimeter sector in DeKalb County. Its anchors include JCPenney, Macy's, Rich's and Rich's main furniture showroom; the newest anchor is Atlanta's first Nordstrom's, which has a cafe that serves Starbuck's coffee with free refills and a 125,000-pair-strong shoe department. Perimeter Mall's Shopper Service Center offers strollers and wheelchairs; fax and photocopy services; emergency supplies such as aspirin, diapers and bandages; and gift wrapping and shipping. Greeters stationed at the three main mall entrances can help you find what you're looking for.

Just across Hammond Drive is Perimeter Expo, which includes Home Depot's upscale Expo Design Center, Best Buy, a large discounter of electronics, appliances and CDs, and Marshall's clothing discounter. Across Ashford Dunwoody Road you'll find Park Place, an upscale, open-air specialty center featuring two hair salons, men's and women's apparel shops including H. Stockton and Talbots, and restaurants such as Cafe Intermezzo, Mi Spia and Mick's (see our Restaurants chapter).

To get to the mall on I-285, take Exit 21. From Ga. 400, take Exit 5.

Shannon Southpark Mall
I-85 at Exit 13, Union City
• (770) 964-2200

Shannon opened in 1980 and expanded in 1986. More than 770,651 square feet house 110 stores including anchors JCPenney, Rich's and Sears. The mall has a customer service center and offers numerous health and personal services such as shoe repair, hair cutting, a vision center and a dental practice. Shannon Southpark also has a food court and various specialty shops selling home furnishings, athletic equipment, jewelry, books, electronics, gifts and apparel.

Southlake Mall
I-75 at Hwy. 54, Morrow • (770) 961-1050

On 88 acres south of town, the 1 million-square-foot Southlake Mall in Clayton County includes JCPenney, Macy's, Rich's, Sears and some 120 shops. Southlake, which opened in 1976, annually welcomes more than 11 million shoppers. This mall is convenient to Hartsfield International Airport.

Town Center at Cobb
I-75 at Exit 116, Kennesaw
• (770) 424-9486

Opened in 1986 and expanded in 1992, this 1.2 million-square-foot mall in Cobb County has 200 stores including Macy's, JCPenney, Parisian, Rich's and Sears. At the Town Center Courtesy Center, the staff can help you with gift ideas, point you toward the right store or sell you a mall gift certificate.

Bargain and Outlet Shopping

Metro Atlanta is hog-heaven for bargain hunters, offering malls, thrift stores and out-

let centers with pricing and quality that beats anyplace in the country. Dedicated shoppers can find deals on everything from earrings to armoires, designer duds to floor lamps. In this section we've listed a few individual stores and outlet centers where savings are a staple.

Atlanta

A.W.O.L.
3210 Roswell Rd. N.E. • (404) 231-3300

Go on, go A.W.O.L.! In the Buckhead shopping district, A.W.O.L. designer clothes outlet inspires shoppers with the motto, "Friends don't let friends pay retail." In this case, A.W.O.L. stands for "Always Wholesale or Less." Featuring men's and women's new and used designer clothing, A.W.O.L. stocks creations by name brand designers at 50 to 90 percent off suggested retail.

Hill Street Warehouse
1345 Collier Rd. N.E. • (404) 352-5001

This 50,000-square-foot warehouse holds a variety of home decorative accessories including antiques, Italian ceramics and terra cotta. It's all priced 70 percent below retail.

To get to the Warehouse, take I-75, exit at Howell Mill and go left on Collier Road.

Midtown Outlets
500 Amsterdam Ave. N.E.
• (770) 986-0340

Monroe Drive intersects with Amsterdam Avenue about a half-mile north of the corner of Monroe and Virginia Avenue. Turn left; at the end of this dead-end street you'll find an eclectic mix of off-price and specialty shops where you can find bargains on futons; designer rugs; feather and down comforters; jewelry; shoes; silk trees, plants and flowers; and men's and women's apparel. Stores include Shoemakers' Warehouse, Famous Garment Manufacturing Corporation and Oriental Designer Rugs.

Oriental Square Mall
4166 Buford Hwy. at Clairmont Rd.
• **no phone**

Previously called Outlet Square Mall, Oriental Square Mall is 303,000-square-foot that is anchored by Marshall's and Burlington Coat Factory. It house 40 additional shops, most catering to the Vietnamese shopper. Despite the mall's name, this is more of an off-price retail clearance mall than a traditional manufacturer's outlet center, although a J. Riggins outlet has been located here for about 10 years.

Beyond Atlanta

Calhoun Outlet Center
455 Bellwood Rd., Calhoun
• **(706) 602-1300**

This center is closer to Chattanooga than Atlanta, but its more than 60 shops include outlets for Anne Klein, Nike, London Fog, Jones New York, Springmaid/Wamsutta and Mikasa. To get to Calhoun Outlet Center, take I-75 to Exit 129. After exiting, go east on Ga. Highway 53, take a right on Outlet Center Drive then follow the signs.

Stone Mountain Handbag Outlet
963 Main St., Stone Mountain Village
• **(770) 498-1316**

Handbags, wallets, briefcases, totes, backpacks, string purses — this store carries a plethora of items you can use to haul your stuff. Choose from an array of leather and fabric items priced 20 to 50 percent below retail.

Tanger Factory Outlet Center
I-85 to Exit 53, U.S. Hwy. 441, Commerce
• **(706) 335-4537**

About an hour north of Atlanta, this center has 45 shops and promises savings of up to 65 percent off retail. Among others, you'll find

Geoffrey Beene, Bass, Liz Claiborne, Reebok and London Fog factory stores. Cross to the south side of I-85 and you'll find another Tanger's outlet center. This one is anchored by Vanity Fair and other shops including Adidas, Nautica and Rue 21.

Tanger Factory Outlet Center
I-75 to Exit 68, Locust Grove
• **(770) 957-0238**

Approximately 30 miles south of Atlanta and 50 miles north of Macon, this center features 36 designer and brand-name manufacturers' outlet stores. Toy Liquidators, Perfumania, Cape Isle Knitters, Leslie Fay and Russell/Jerzees are just a few of the popular outlets you'll find here.

Shopping Districts

Atlanta

Little Five Points
Moreland, Euclid and McLendon Aves.

This area is rather like Atlanta's answer to New York's East Village: Hip, funky and artistic shops with names such as **Throb**, **Wish** and **Boomerang**, all on Euclid Avenue, provide lingerie, hoisery, latex, leather and other hip-hop, shiny clubwear. The district's many old storefronts make it a favorite location site for movies and TV: Most memorably, this was where Morgan Freeman drove Jessica Tandy to the grocery store in *Driving Miss Daisy*. The part of the Piggly-Wiggly supermarket was portrayed by **Sevananda Natural Foods**, 1111 Euclid Avenue N.E.

Check the **Junkman's Daughter**, 464 Moreland Avenue N.E., for new and used clubwear and novelties. **Kolo**, 1144 Euclid Avenue N.E., and **Urban Tribe**, across the street, provide body piercing services. **Stefan's**, 1160 Euclid Avenue, sells used clothes with panache. **Crystal Blue**, 1168 Euclid Avenue, has incense, mood tapes and wonderful wooden pill boxes. Try a whole new look with makeup, wigs and accessories at **Fifi Mahony's**, 1152 Euclid Avenue. Need a pit stop or a beer in between shopping? Euclid Avenue Yacht Club, the Brewhouse, and La Fonda Mexican are great for that (see our Restaurants chapter).

Little Five Points is served by the Inman Park/Reynoldstown MARTA station. Be sure to exit on the north side of the tracks, especially at night. From the station walk north on Hurt Street, then right on Euclid (about six blocks); or take the 48 Lenox bus.

Buckhead
Pharr and Peachtree Rds.

Buckhead retailing is dominated by the huge malls Lenox Square and Phipps Plaza, but there are also plenty of small shops with unusual merchandise. The district covers a big area, some say all the way to Piedmont Road as well as up and down Peachtree Road.

Architectural Accents, 2711 Piedmont Road N.E., is full of fireplace surrounds, old tiles, antique frames, and more antique locks, handles and window hardware than you can imagine. **A.W.O.L.**, 3210 Roswell Road N.E., sells men's and women's clothing. **Seeing Is Believing**, 3167 Peachtree Road N.E., carries the most unusual eyewear. Staff at the **Beverly Bremer Silver Shop**, 3164 Peachtree Road N.E., can find damaged or missing pieces to complete heirloom silverware. **Beverly Hall Furniture Galleries**, 2789 Piedmont Road N.E., has handsome, new traditional pieces and carries contemporary items made by traditional manufacturers.

Highland Area
Virginia Ave. at N. Highland Ave.

You'll see plenty of street life in the Highland Area all the way from the Poncey-Highlands (which extends from North Avenue up to and somewhat beyond St. Charles Place) through to N. Highland Avenue and Lanier Boulevard. Beyond that, it's all residential until you come to Sage Shopping Center, which houses the only in-town Harris Teeter Market.

Affairs, 1401 N. Highland Avenue N.E., has small furniture, home accessories and lots of interesting knickknacks to investigate. **Bill Hallman Designs**, 1054 N. Highland Avenue N.E., sells hip clothes for men and women including very stacked heels, bikini undies (for men) and excellent leather goods. At **Back to Square One**, 1054 N. Highland Avenue N.E., you'll find handmade crafts by regional artists for the home and garden, planters, sculptures for the garden, bird houses and primitive antiques (contemporary American-made furniture with peeling paint). **The Common Pond**, 1402 N. Highland Avenue N.E., has environmentally friendly gifts for people and their pets. Earth Angel, 1196 N. Highland Ave. N.E., sells unusual undergarments, garters, beaded necklaces or other precious stuff for that special event. Women's clothes, jewelry and gift items are very reasonably priced at **Mooncake**, 1019 Virginia Ave. N.E. **20th Century Antiques**, 1044 N. Highland Avenue N.E., which is really two stores in one, has everything from jewelry to cutlery, handpainted end tables to chimes in one shop and mostly furniture, from '50s dinettes to '30s dressing tables, in the other. **Rapture**, 1039 N. Highland N.E., is the place for the slim man and woman who like beige and black and fine fabrics. Silver jewelry and funky art, including hand painted shower curtains, are sold at **Jules Jewels**, 1037 N. Highland N.E. And **Nature's Art Rock Shop**, 1021 Virginia Avenue N.E., has beautiful polished rocks, minerals, jewelry and fossils.

Chattahoochee Avenue Warehouse Shopping District
Take I-75 to Howell Mill, turn west, then right onto Chattahoochee Ave.

Bargains abound in the Chattahoochee Avenue warehouse shopping district. A no returns policy at any of these places means careful shopping is a must. And because these are warehouse showrooms, use the bathroom before you leave home. Also, it would be best to leave the kids with the nanny because this is strictly an adults-only kind of area. Most warehouses are open Friday, Saturday and Sunday only. Call to check days and hours of operation.

AJS Shoe Warehouse, 1788 Ellsworth Industrial Boulevard N.W. has real deals on women's shoes, handbags and accessories in a barn of a place. **Ballard's Backroom**, 1670 DeFoor Avenue N.W., features a unique, decorative household items at true discounts. **Freedman Men's Shoe Outlet**, 1240-A Old Chattahoochee Avenue N.W., has been known in Atlanta for years as a retailer of name brand, quality men's shoes. You'll find discounts on men's wear, including suits at **K&G Men's Center**, 1750-A Ellsworth Industrial Boulevard N.W. And **Salvage Etc.**, 975 Chattahoochee Avenue N.W., has all sorts of stuff including beat up, clawfoot tubs, old faucet handles, Formica counter tops minus an edging strip or two and piles and piles of junk (well, one person's junk is another's treasure).

Antiques, Decorator Items and Flea Markets

In addition to dozens of yard and estate sales nearly every weekend, Atlanta has several antique shopping districts and large flea markets. Prices at these establishments range from rock-bottom to sky-high. In many antique shops the price tag is just a starting point for negotiations; if you like to bargain hard, you may save big bucks. Use your common sense at the flea markets: We hope you're not too shocked to learn that those red vinyl bags on sale for $10 are not real Chanel — even though they are crudely stitched with the famous double-C logo.

Atlanta

Bennett Street
Three blocks north of Piedmont Hospital on the west side of Peachtree Rd.

Little Bennett Street is home to a large selection of antique and decorative art dealers. These are not junk shops; most of the merchandise here is of the "better" category, and the prices reflect this. If you're looking for fine antiques, you'll find them here. Near the end of Bennett Street is the TULA complex of showrooms and galleries (see TULA's listing under "Galleries" in The Arts chapter).

Buford Highway Flea Market
5000 Buford Hwy. • (770) 452-7140

A big rainbow on its billboard announces this flea market, and inside the merchandise is every bit as colorful. Inexpensive home decor items, jewelry, designer look-alikes, Atlanta souvenirs, perfumes and those cool velvety wall hangings with religious scenes are all in the mix here. The market is open Friday, Saturday and Sunday.

Chamblee's Antiques Row
Broad St. and Peachtree Rd., Chamblee • (770) 458-1614

More than 200 antique dealers offer a cornucopia of antiques and collectibles in this architecturally interesting shopping district. Many shops operate out of old homes, churches and stores, some dating from the mid-1800s. Antiques Row is within walking distance of the Chamblee MARTA station; you can also get there on the No. 25 Tilly Mill bus. Driving, turn off Peachtree Industrial Boulevard onto Broad Street; follow to the intersection of Broad Street and Peachtree Road. (We told you all the Peachtrees could get confusing!)

Cheshire Bridge Road N.E.
Between Piedmont and LaVista Rds.

On Cheshire Bridge Road between Piedmont and LaVista, numerous antique dealers are scattered among the restaurants, bars and "lingerie modeling" businesses. The larger antique shops rent out spaces to dealers, who always seem to be moving in or out. Competition for customers (and dealers) is keen. Expect to save at least 10 percent off the asking price unless an item is already marked down. Take time to stop in Cherub's Attic, 2179 Cheshire Bridge Road, and Milou's Market, 1927 Cheshire Bridge Road.

The Family Jewels
114 E. Ponce de Leon Ave., Decatur • (404) 377-3774

Shop here for a comprehensive collection of vintage jewelry, accessories, collectibles and antiques. This store on the square in Decatur has a wide selection of items such as Victorian collectibles, pottery, glassware, art deco and art nouveau pieces, paintings and prints. The Family Jewels is open Tuesday through Saturday or by appointment.

Georgia Lighting
530 14th St. N.W. • (404) 875-4754

Georgia Lighting's main store has a huge lighting showroom with an extensive collection of lighting products from all over the world, including landscape lighting and track lighting. A tent sale once a year always offers great bargains.

Great Gatsby's
5070 Peachtree Industrial Blvd., Chamblee • (770) 457-1905

This 100,000-square-foot "wholesale to the public" market is one of Atlanta's most fun stores. You can spend hours ogling everything including exquisite antiques, kitschy advertising memorabilia and huge architectural fragments. Gatsby's supplies hotels worldwide with unusual furnishings; a guitar that had belonged to John Lennon was once sold here at auction. Gatsby's is 2 miles inside I-285 on Peachtree Industrial Boulevard.

Lakewood Antiques Market
2000 Lakewood Ave. S.W.
• (404) 622-4488

This popular market is held on the second weekend of each month and features thousands of unusual antiques and collectibles. Parking is free; admission is $3 for adults and free for children 12 and younger. The market is held Friday, Saturday and Sunday, but there's a special early buyers' day on Thursday, when admission is $5. Take I-75/85 south from downtown; exit at Lakewood Freeway East and follow the signs.

Miami Circle N.E.

This short street is full of antique and decorator merchandise. As you drive north on Piedmont Road, Miami Circle is on your right; it's north of the Lindbergh MARTA station and just past the Cub Foods shopping center. Shops of note include Bobby Dobb Antiques & Kilims, Hilderbrand & Star Antiques and The Gables.

The Wrecking Bar
292 Moreland Ave. N.E. • (404) 525-0468

On Moreland just south of the Little Five Points intersection in a huge mansion is The Wrecking Bar, selling architectural art and antiques, from hardware and chandeliers to large mantles and statuary. The store occupies an 1895 mansion listed on the National Register for Historic Places.

Beyond Atlanta

A Flea An'Tique
Ga. Hwy. 20, Buford • (770) 932-6833

This upscale flea market, which bills itself as "North Atlanta's Best Kept Secret," features a variety of finds such as antiques, collectibles and quality used furniture. Going north on I-85, take Exit 45; if you're on I-985, take Exit 1. The market is behind Ace Hardware inside Buford Mall.

Antiques and Uniques
1727 Cleveland Hwy., Gainesville
• (770) 536-1651

This store sells top-quality upscale antiques and unusual items for discerning customers. Catering to a clientele of affluent homeowners, Antiques and Uniques features European antiques and well-made mahogany pieces as well as a variety of unusual lamps and other tasteful collectible items.

Antique Junction
939 Railroad St., Conyers
• (770) 922-5445

Near the Depot in Olde Town Conyers, this antique mall, in a 4,000-square-foot warehouse built in 1915, features dealers offering fine antiques, clocks, primitives, memorabilia and collectible items.

Collectors Choice
908 Commercial St., Conyers
• (770) 388-9434

This shop, in the picturesque Olde Town shopping district of Conyers, features a wide assortment of antique and period furniture. Browse the 6,500-square-foot showrooms for quality pieces of American and European furniture in styles ranging from Queen Anne to Victorian, Primitive American to Arts and Craft. The store also offers a unique array of collectible items and specialty gifts. Collectors Corner is closed on Sunday.

The Cotton House
21 Milton Ave., Alpharetta
- **(770) 475-3100**

In business for more than 40 years, this store has a large collection of furniture, gifts, home accessories and collectibles. It offers a variety of well-known name brands at competitive prices.

Crafts on the Square
165 Perry St., Lawrenceville
- **(770) 339-8532**

On the square in historic Lawrenceville, this store features a wide selection of handcrafted items from Georgia artists. The merchandise includes miniatures, wood crafts, cross-stitch and ceramics. In addition, Crafts on the Square will deliver Georgia gift baskets. These baskets, in the shape of the state, are filled with dogwood blossoms, cotton and gourmet foods that represent the tastes of Georgia. Customers can also design their own baskets or choose from a variety of specialty gift baskets including anniversary baskets, teacher baskets and Dr. Feelgood baskets, to name a few. The shop also has a Christmas room and craft supplies.

Dollar Rich
2931 Buford Hwy., Buford
- **(770) 271-3992**

Offering collectibles and "just about everything," Dollar Rich give shoppers a wide range of items through which to browse. What we locals call Buford Highway is also known as U.S. Highway 23.

Georgia Antique Center and International Market
6624 I-85 North Access Rd., Norcross
- **(770) 446-9292**

More than 200 shops offer antiques, collectibles (including baseball cards), Oriental rugs, pottery, rare coins and more. It's open every weekend.

The Gift Gallery & Accessories Ltd.
2231 Scenic Hwy., Snellville
- **(770) 979-7200**

This family-owned store features gift items for all ages and occasions as well as antiques and home accessories ranging from table tops to picture frames. If you don't see what you want, Gift Gallery will special order it for you.

Gwinnett Flea Market Center
5675 Jimmy Carter Blvd., Norcross
- **(770) 449-8189**

This big flea market is open Wednesdays, Thursdays and Sundays from 11 AM to 6 PM and Fridays and Saturdays from 11 AM to 8 PM. From Atlanta, take I-85 N. to Jimmy Carter Boulevard; exit and turn left; the market will be on your right.

Kudzu
48 South Park Sq., Marietta
- **(770) 425-8638**

On the square in Marietta, Kudzu carries a variety of Southern art and home accessories. Shop here for Georgia red-clay products, Celestial Scents designer fragrances, potpourris, Boyd's Bear and Angel and Noah collectibles, dried florals, garden statuary and Debbie Kingston D. Morgan prints.

Lamps N Things
1205 Johnson Ferry Rd. N.E., Marietta
- **(770) 971-0874**

In the Woodlawn Square Shopping Center, this 3,800-square-foot store offers thousands of lamp shades, plus lamps, mirrors, art, antiques and other home accessories. The store's personnel will also custom-make shades and lamps for individuals and decorators. Lamp repair services are offered.

Picket Fences
One S. Main St., Alpharetta
- **(770) 475-5758**

This shop sells handpainted furniture, home accessories and collectibles by Goebel, Spode and Beatrix Potter. It carries gourmet foods, such as syrups, jams and jellies, as well as a line of Georgia products, including trivets, refrigerator magnets, Christmas ornaments and other items made of Buckley's Georgia clay.

Pride of Dixie Antique Market
1700 Jeurgens Ct., Norcross
- **(770) 279-9853**

Held monthly on the fourth weekend, this market hosts some 800 booths. It's held in the

North Atlanta Trade Center in Norcross. Take I-85 to Exit 38; east on Indian Trail; right on Oakbrook Parkway; right on Jeurgens Court. Admission is $4; look for a $1-off coupon in the "Leisure" section of *The Atlanta Journal-Constitution* on Sundays prior to the these weekends. Parking is free.

Sharon's Lighting
10887 Alpharetta Hwy., Roswell
• (770) 587-4403
5544 Peachtree Industrial Blvd.,
Chamblee • (770) 455-0135

With a combined showroom space of 20,000 square feet, these two stores offer an extensive collection of lighting options. Sharon's illuminates your world (and boggles the mind of the decision-impaired) with 6,000 table lamps, wall lamps and floor lamps, and 10,000 shades from well-known manufacturers.

Scott Antique Market
Atlanta Expo Center, I-285 at Exit 40,
Jonesboro Rd. S.E. • (404) 366-0833

Open the second weekend of each month from 8 AM to 5 PM, this market offers everything from American antiques to English porcelain displayed by 1,500 dealers from across the country. Call for specific shows. To get there, take I-285 to Exit 40 (Jonesboro Road). Atlanta Expo Center is right off the exit. We've listed this in "Beyond Atlanta" although Atlanta Expo Center actually straddles I-285, with one building inside the highway and the other across the road.

Trade Winds
49 Park Sq., Roswell • (770) 587-4993

This shop in historic Roswell is packed with creative surprises. Browse here for gifts and collectibles.

Thrift Stores

Confirmed thrift store shoppers know that little islands of great value can sometimes be found amid the oceans of junk in Atlanta's thrift stores. If you're of an adventurous mind, you might discover an elegant outfit, or at least maybe your next Halloween getup. Large thrift stores typically don't have dressing rooms,

but you can still try before you buy if you dress appropriately. If you wear close-fitting shorts, a T-shirt and loafers you can easily kick off, you can try on your new outfit right in the store. Believe us, in these no-frills stores, no one will even notice. We've described some of the major thrifts; most of them have several locations, so see the Yellow Pages for the location nearest you. Insiders' Tip: Many thrifts only take cash, so hit the ATM or your piggy bank before you hit the stores.

Bargainata
791 Miami Cir. N.E. • (404) 262-7199

This gigantic warehouse sale comes only twice a year (once in the fall, once in spring). The fall sale lasts five days, the spring sale lasts four days; both sales always cause quite a stir. Bargainata, sponsored by the National Council of Jewish Women, marked its 28th year in 1997. Sort of a huge garage sale, Bargainata is a donated-item market that includes men's, women's, children's and babies' clothing and accessories as well as housewares. The sale starts with designer and other fine apparel priced low; by the last day, the remaining merchandise is sold at an additional 50 percent discount. You can drop off items here you no longer want and get a receipt noting your charitable contribution.

Goodwill Industries
2201 Glenwood Ave. S.E.
• (404) 373-5815

Goodwill Stores offer affordable prices on a variety of quality furniture, clothing and household items. Each store has a donation center, and other donation centers are scattered throughout the metro area. Check the Yellow Pages for Goodwill Industries nine other locations.

Salvation Army
746 Marietta St. N.W. • (404) 523-6214

The Salvation Army picks up more than 50 truckloads of donated furniture, clothing and household items every week. These donations provide merchandise for the Army's thrift stores, proceeds from which help support the Adult Rehabilitation Center. There are four other locations in the area.

The Arts Festival of Atlanta draws hundreds of
arts and crafts vendors each year.

St. Vincent de Paul
5748 Buford Hwy. • (770) 457-9648

This store (plus five others) stocks just
about everything: clothing, household items,
furniture, appliances, books, records, tapes,
jewelry and miscellaneous items. Ninety percent of the proceeds go to this charity, which
provides, among other things, emergency rent
checks to working folks in a bind.

Thrift House of the Cathedral of St. Philip
**Lindbergh Plaza Shopping Center, 2581
Piedmont Rd. • (404) 233-8652**

Books, clothes, shoes, draperies,
housewares, knickknacks and more are bar-
gain-priced at this thrift. The compact store is
chock-full of good deals on all kinds of items,
from silver trays to wicker baskets; you'll also
find the occasional piece of furniture.

Value Village
1320 Moreland Ave. • (770) 840-7283

Bargain hunters can find name-brand
clothes, some with price tags still attached,
among the used items at this, the largest thrift
store operation in the metro area. Donations
to the Kidney Foundation stock the shop, which
in addition to clothing include furniture, accessories and items for children. Priced to sell
every day, on Memorial Day and the Fourth of
July, everything goes for half the ticket price.
Value Village has five other locations.

Vintage/Consignment

Vintage wear is a step up from thrift-store
quality and price. Some clothing that starts
out in thrift stores winds up cleaned, pressed
and marked-up in the vintage shops. Still, because the thrifts can be downright grungy,

many people who can afford to prefer to shop the vintage stores, which are generally cleaner, take credit cards and have dressing rooms.

You can find great bargains at the many consignment shops throughout the metro area. These establishments are clothing recyclers; many carry current fashions and designer labels. Some also deal in vintage clothing. In this section we've listed a sampling of the consignment and vintage shops for men's and women's apparel.

Atlanta

Vintage

Junkman's Daughter
464 Moreland Ave. • (404) 577-3188

In Little Five Points, you can't miss this place with its fantastic, space age mural frontage in brilliant sky blue. Shop here along with pink-haired teens and hip grandmas for vintage and new clothing, housewares, tobacco, costumes and all sorts of accessories. You can rent outfits for Halloween, too. Think of Junkman's Daughter as an off-the-wall Target.

Stefan's
1160 Euclid Ave. N.E. • (404) 688-4929

Also in Little Five Points, Stefan's stocks a high-quality selection of vintage duds for men and women. The merchandise includes hats, scarves, jewelry and other accessories.

Consignment

ChickiBea
2130 N. Decatur Plaza • (404) 634-6995

The first consignment shop in Atlanta, ChickiBea's celebrated its 26th year in business in 1997. This is an upscale resale boutique for couture and designer women's clothes.

Clothes to the Edge
1052 St. Charles Ave. N.E.
• (404) 892-7340

Off N. Highland Avenue in the Virginia-Highlands neighborhood, Clothes to the Edge is an eclectic boutique where you can find pre-owned apparel and accessories ranging from classic to funky '70s disco glitz.

Consignment Boutique Upscale-Resale
1186-E N. Highland Ave. N.E.
• (404) 876-1554

Nestled behind Camille's restaurant in Virginia-Highland, this shop sells quality consignment apparel for men. It's closed on Mondays.

ConsignShop
Toco Hills Shopping Center, 2899-A N. Druid Hills Rd. N.E. • (404) 633-6257

ConsignShop offers something for both genders, featuring quality consignment clothing for men and women. It even has maternity and plus sizes.

Elegance Resale
3330 Piedmont Rd. N.E. • (404) 233-8996

In the Piedmont Peachtree Crossing shopping center, Elegance Resale has been in business for more than 15 years. The shop offers costume jewelry as well as women's designer fashions.

Fantastic Finds
220 Sandy Springs Cir. N.W.
• (404) 303-1313
4015 Holcomb Bridge Rd., Norcross
• (770) 446-5040

Shop here for high-quality previously owned women's clothing. Both shops are independently owned.

Play It Again
273 Buckhead Ave. N.E. • (404) 261-2135

Play It Again is one of the first consignment shops in Atlanta. It offers secondhand women's apparel in the heart of the city. Call and find out what day Play It Again will look at your goodies if you want to trade up.

Psycho Sisters
5152 Roswell Rd. N.W. • (404) 255-5578
1355 Roswell Rd., Marietta
• (770) 565-6310

Promising "cool clothes at cheap prices for cool people," these wacky siblings buy/sell/trade/consign a variety of garb. The name can be found on eight other locations some of which are franchise operations. The two locations noted above are owned by the two sisters who started it all.

Costumes

Whether you're impersonating a pope or a pirate, a belle or a baboon, you'll find just the right disguise at an Atlanta costume shop. These stores are busiest in October; don't wait until the day before Halloween to make your selection.

Atlanta

Atlanta Costume
2089 Monroe Dr. N.E. • (404) 874-7511

Need a Santa suit? Costumes for a play or promotion? Hats, wigs, makeup? This large costumer can help. Atlanta Costume also offers stage lighting supplies, mascots (big heads and bodies) and custom designing. The shop has extended hours in October.

Costumes Etc.
318 Pharr Rd. N.E. • (404) 239-9422

Costumes Etc. offers theatrical costumes, party disguises and much more. It builds mascots at the store, offers custom design and provides specialty costumes for photo and video shoots. Need puppets? Costumes Etc. has got them!

Beyond Atlanta

Eddie's Trick & Novelty
70 S. Park Sq., Marietta • (770) 428-4314
3665 Roswell Rd. N.E. • (404) 264-0527

This store has a large selection of masks and costumes for theater, clowns and masquerade. Check out the big supply of costumes for adults and children. Eddie's has everything from the Easter Bunny to Uncle Sam, the Old South to the Roaring '20s. Eddie's offers mascots and accessories, makeup and magic supplies as well.

Farmers Markets

Atlanta

DeKalb Farmers Market
3000 E. Ponce de Leon Ave., Decatur
• (404) 377-6400

DeKalb Farmers Market, the oldest of the truly international food markets, attracts busloads of folks from Alabama, Tennessee — even Florida. All mingle with the locals searching for exotic spices, canned goods, fresh fish and breads and pastries made on the premises as well as regional and imported vegetables and fruit. Employees come from every corner of the globe and wear badges listing the languages they speak. Register at the customer service desk to have your checks accepted at check-out or use the on-site teller machine to get cash.

Take a lunch (or dinner) break at the Market's cafeteria (same food both times of day): You pay by the ounce at bargain rates and can fill a plate with many of the foods found in the employees' native lands for $4 or less. Bottled beverages like Jamaican Ginger Beer and Mango nectar are available.

International Farmers Market
5193 Peachtree Industrial Blvd.
• (770) 455-1777

International Farmers Market offers fresh fruits and vegetables, seafood, meats and cheeses, and baked goods. Spices are sold in bulk. Beer and wine are available.

INSIDERS' TIP

Some of Atlanta's department stores offer complimentary personal shopping services, among them Neiman Marcus, (404) 266-8200 (Lenox Square); Parisian, (404) 814-3200 (Phipps Plaza, with other locations at Gwinnett Place and Town Center at Cobb); and Saks Fifth Avenue, (404) 261-7234 (Phipps Plaza). Banana Republic in Lenox Square, North Point Mall and Perimeter Mall offers a free in-home or in-office wardrobe consultation service by appointment, (770) 393-1130.

Morningside Farmers' Market
1325 N. Highland Ave. N.E. • no phone

This outdoor market in the parking lot beside Indigo Coastal Grill (see our Restaurants chapter) and in front of Eclectic Electric (see "Galleries" in The Arts chapter), is open only on Saturday mornings, but it's the place to go in town when you want organic fruits and vegetables. The scene also includes local chefs demonstrating favorite seasonal dishes, neighborhood celebs and a mingle-and-gab mood. Edible wildflowers, soybeans in the pod and other more recognizable foods are also for sale. You can shop from 8 AM until noon.

Beyond Atlanta

Atlanta State Farmers Market
16 Forest Pkwy., Forest Park
• (404) 366-6910

A 146-acre open-air retail and wholesale market, Atlanta State Farmers Market claims the distinction of being the largest in the Southeast and one of the largest in the world. It's open to the public round-the-clock every day except Christmas. More than 7,000 people visit the market each day. Inside the fenced compound, you drive your car around to visit vendors of everything from fresh produce to homemade preserves to Christmas trees during the holidays.

From I-75, take Exit 78.

Buford Highway Farmer's Market
5660 Buford Hwy., Doraville
• (770) 458-2296

This market stocks a variety of fresh produce, meats and fish. You'll find exotic items from all over, gourmet coffee and traditional grocery-store fare.

Harry's Farmers Markets
2025 Satellite Pkwy., Duluth
• (770) 416-6900
1180 Upper Hembree Rd., Alpharetta
• (770) 664-6300
70 Powers Ferry Rd., Marietta
• (770) 578-4400

Harry's Farmers Markets is a more upscale version of DeKalb Farmer's Market (which is owned by Harry's brother). All of these farmers markets are chock-full of delicacies from around the world as well as staples of life. The markets have it all, from the commonplace to the exotic including fish, cheese, wine, flowers, coffee and vegetables. Owner Harry Blazer took the skills he learned running these markets and opened Harry's In-A-Hurry, which features gourmet meals to go.

Books and Periodicals

Atlanta

Barnes & Noble
2900 Peachtree Rd. N.W.
• (404) 261-7747
7660 N. Point Pkwy., Ste. 200, Alpharetta
• (770) 993-8340
120 Perimeter Centre W., Dunwoody
• (770) 396-1200

At Barnes & Noble you'll find books, magazines, CDs and hot coffee in a roomy store that's easy to shop. Barnes & Noble stages about 30 events each month, including book signings and live musical performances. The store stocks more than 150,000 titles in every category and can special order from a data base of more than 160,000 publishers. The Peachtree location decor is wood-paneled and elegant.

Barnes & Noble also owns Doubleday Book Shop and B. Dalton Bookseller. Doubleday has locations at Phipps Plaza and Underground Atlanta; B. Daltons are scattered throughout the metro area.

Book Nook
3342 Clairmont Rd. N.E.
• (404) 633-1328
595 Roswell St., Marietta
• (770) 499-9914
6569 Church St., Riverdale
• (770) 994-3444
4664 Lawrenceville Hwy., Lilburn
• (770) 564-9462

Book Nook, in business for more than two decades, sells new and used books, records, comics, CDs and books on tape.

Book Warehouse of Georgia
1080 Bullsboro Dr. #13, Newnan
- **(770) 251 6594**

Book Warehouse offers an extensive selection of publishers' overstocks and remainders. The stock is equally divided between hard cover and paperback books. All categories including popular fiction, cookbooks, children's books, self-help, reference, coffeetable volumes are available at deeply discounted prices.

Borders Books & Music
3637 Peachtree Rd. N.E.
- **(404) 237-0707**

4745 Ashford-Dunwoody Rd., Dunwoody
- **(770) 396-0004**

3555 Gwinnett Place Dr., Duluth
- **(770) 495-4043**

Across the street from Phipps Plaza, the Peachtree Borders book shop is a bright and cheery place of roughly 35,000-square-feet with more than 83,000 titles and lots of newspapers and magazines. Borders, cater-corner (that's "catty-corner" in these parts) across Peachtree from Phipps Plaza, features an espresso bar/cafe and book signings with celebrity authors as well as local writers. The store carries an extensive collection of foreign language publications and lots of out-of-town newspapers.

Chapter 11, The Discount Bookstore
Ansley Mall, 1544 Piedmont Rd. N.E.
- **(404) 872-7986**

Peachtree Battle Shopping Center, 2345 Peachtree Rd. • (404) 237-7199

This Atlanta chain evolved from one store and has grown dramatically in the last few years to include, appropriately, 11 locations. All of the books sold are discounted by at least — you guessed it — 11 percent. The Peachtree store is in the old Oxford Bookstore location, which was gutted and redesigned to make room for more books and a brighter atmosphere. Chapter 11 sponsors many author book signings; be sure to ask which author is coming up on the calendar the next time you stop by one of the stores. (Check the Yellow Pages for other locations.)

Final Touch Gallery & Books
308 W. Ponce de Leon Ave., Decatur
- **(404) 378-1642**

The owners of this quaint shop started off just selling books but found they had to expand the inventory to stay in business. Fortunately, they kept the mix interesting, adding unusual items of furniture and gifts along with plenty of books. The store is particularly noted for its fabulous book signings, which are more like parties with catered food, wine and flowers. Check out the extensive selection of cookbooks.

Tall Tales
Toco Hills Shopping Center, 2999 N. Druid Hills Rd. N.E. • (404) 636-2498

Tall Tales is a full-service independent bookstore that's been in the same location for 18 years. It has extensive children's and fiction sections and a base of loyal customers. That's because service is the specialty here: Special-order books can often be delivered the very next day. The store will also search for out-of-print books. The highly literate staff will gladly help you make your selections.

Some special-interest book shops you may want to visit include:

Architectural Book Center
Peachtree Center Mall, 231 Peachtree St.
- **(404) 222-9920**

This bookstore shares a suite with AIA (American Institute of Architects, Georgia chapter). It sells retail books about architecture as well as gift items including statuary, frames,

---

INSIDERS' TIP

Shopping for lots of items or heavy clothes? Take along a wheeled luggage or grocery cart, and lug your purchases from department to department without straining back or elbows by carrying armloads of merchandise.

cards and puzzles oftentimes but not always related to architecture.

Brushstrokes
1510 Piedmont Ave. N.E.
• (404) 876-6567

In the Ansley Square Shopping Center just south of the intersection of Piedmont and Monroe, Brushstrokes is a popular stop for gay and lesbian magazines and gifts.

Cathedral of St. Philip
2744 Peachtree Rd. N.W.
• (404) 237-7582

Religious books and gifts are for sale at the bookstore in the Episcopal cathedral.

Charis Book
1189 Euclid Ave. • (404) 524-0304

This is a pleasant store in Little Five Points selling feminist books, gay and lesbian literature, music and children's books. It sponsors weekly community-oriented programs that often involve readings and book signings by noted authors.

The Civilized Traveller
Phipps Plaza, 3500 Peachtree Rd. N.E.
• (404) 264-1252

This store offers a big selection of travel books and tour guides, plus luggage, binoculars and other travel accessories.

Cokesbury Books and Church Supplies
2495 Lawrenceville Hwy., Decatur
• (404) 320-1034

Cokesbury sells religious books and other materials. It's affiliated with the United Methodist Church.

Eastern National Park & Monument Association Book Store
Inside the Cyclorama, 800 Cherokee Ave. S.E. • (404) 622-6264

This is a small shop with a fine collection of Civil War books and maps.

Georgia Book Store Inc.
124 Edgewood Ave. N.E.
• (404) 659-0959

Georgia Book Store Inc. gets a lot of walk-in traffic. On the corner of Edgewood Avenue and Courtland Street, across from Georgia State University, this bookstore is only a few blocks from some major downtown hotels and the Martin Luther King, Jr. National Historic Site. Although it's primarily a textbook store, carrying books offered for GSU courses as well as test-prep materials, Georgia Book Store also has sports-related items and local and regional souvenirs. The store still has some Olympic memorabilia for sale. Georgia Book Store has been in business since 1957. The original owner pioneered the idea of buying college students' books back when the courses were over; that's a staple of the business now.

Iwase
Around Lenox Shopping Center, 3400 Wooddale Dr. N.E. • (404) 814-0462

Iwase has thousands of Japanese-language books, periodicals and the ever popular Japanese comic books. Some of the staff speak English.

Presbyterian Book Store of Atlanta
1455 Tullie Rd. N.E., Ste. 111
• (404) 728-9985

Here you'll find Bibles, devotionals and other religious items as well as a smidgen of popular fiction.

Outwrite
991 Piedmont Rd. • (404) 607-0082

Outwrite is at the corner of Tenth Street and Piedmont Road in Midtown. Outwrite sells gay and lesbian books, magazines and cards and coffee.

Science Fiction & Mystery Book Shop
Cheshire Pointe Shopping Center, 2000-F Cheshire Bridge Rd. • (404) 634-3226

If you just have to find out whodunit — or you think you already know — sleuth on over to the Science Fiction & Mystery Book Shop. It also carries fantasy books.

Shrine of the Black Madonna
946 Ralph David Abernathy Blvd. S.W.
• (404) 752-6125

In West End, you'll find an excellent source of African-American books for both adults and children at the Shrine of the Black Madonna. The shrine also sponsors book signings.

Two Friends Bookstore
598 Cascade Rd. • (404) 758-7711
817 Ralph Abernathy Blvd. off I-20
• (404) 755-8105

These African American bookstores sell figurines, original, signed and numbered prints as well as books. Coffee is served to customers free-of-charge, and the stores hold book signings by national authors once or twice a month.

Beyond Atlanta

The Fayette Book Shop
692 Glynn St., Fayetteville
• (770) 461-5907

Tucked away in the back of an older shopping center, this independently owned bookstore has been providing great reading material and personalized customer service to readers on the south side of Atlanta for almost 20 years. There's also an extensive collection of teacher's materials — books, bulletin boards and stickers — as well as bestsellers, children's books and biographies.

Greater Atlanta Christian Bookstore
1575 Indian Tr.-Lilburn Rd., Norcross
• (770) 243-2370

This store has a big selection of Christian books, music, gifts and cards. It's on the campus of the Greater Atlanta Christian School.

Humpus Bumpus
703 Atlanta Rd., Cumming
• (770) 781-9705

Located in a 50-year-old brick house, each room of Humpus Bumpus contains a different category of books in an intimate environment with a cozy fireplace and hardwood floors. The name of the store, according to owner Paul Cossman, comes from *Mutiny on the Bounty*: Humpus Bumpus is what the South Pacific natives called a feast. Cossman's independent bookstore is heavy in books on Georgia his-

tory and Southern literature of both the new and used variety.

Take Ga. 400 to Exit 14.

Old New York Book Shop
660 Spindlewick Dr., Dunwoody
• (770) 393-2997

Old New York Book Shop specializes in out-of-print, rare and antiquarian books and collectibles. The owners offer some historical documents and autographs. Now based in the owners' home, the shop was once located in Midtown, where local authors came for book signings of their first novels. The shop is open by appointment only; be sure to call ahead for a specific date and time.

Music

Atlanta

Blockbuster Music
2099 Peachtree Rd. • (404) 605-7131

Formerly Turtles, this is the dominant music chain in Atlanta, with more than 60 metro locations. The largest store (address listed previously) is just opposite the entrance to Bennett Street.

Earwax Records
1052 Peachtree St. N.E. • (404) 875-5600

Earwax specializes in hip-hop, house and R&B with a little bit of reggae and jazz thrown in for good measure.

E D's Gourmet Records
Ansley Square Shopping Center, 1510-D Piedmont Ave. • (404) 876-1557

In a shopping center just south of Ansley Mall and with two Thai restaurants and a couple of gay bars, E D's has the dance hits. It's a favorite stop for club DJs. E D's sells both vinyl and CDs.

Full Moon Records
1653 McLendon Ave. N.E.
• (404) 377-1919

A mile east of Little Five Points in Candler Park, Full Moon Records buys, sells and trades records, tapes and CDs. Full Moon has a big selection of $1 records.

Tower Records
Around Lenox Shopping Center, 3400 Wooddale Dr. N.E. • (404) 264-1217

Next door to Lenox Square, Tower Records is a music superstore with a large separate classical room, thousands of books and magazines and sing-along tapes for karaoke. Pick up the slick, informative free magazines *Pulse!* and *Classical Pulse!*

Vibes
145-B Sycamore St., Decatur • (404) 373-5099

Great prices, great service and the phattest selection for old and new sounds on CD, cassette and 12-inch wax are what you'll find in this music store in downtown Decatur. Don't see what you want? Ask! The staff will special order it for you at no extra charge.

Wax 'n' Facts
432 Moreland Ave. N.E. • (404) 525-2275

Wax 'n' Facts sells new and used records, CDs and tapes and band T-shirts. A bit of trivia: Back in the '70s, the owner's independent record label released the first single by the B-52's.

Wuxtry
2096 N. Decatur Rd. • (404) 329-0020

Located a hop, skip and a jump from Emory University on the corner of Clairmont and N. Decatur roads, Wuxtry carries T-shirts for the college crowd, new and used records, tapes and CDs.

New Age Shops

We're using New Age as an umbrella term to denote shops catering to patrons interested in personal growth and awareness, metaphysical issues, holistic health and related concerns. The stores listed handle a variety of merchandise such as herbs, aromatherapy products, metaphysical books and tapes, incense, candles, oils, crystals and tarot cards.

Atlanta

Crystal Blue
1168 Euclid Ave. N.E. • (404) 522-4605

Crystal Blue in the Little Five Points shopping district carries a variety of products including minerals, crystals, wind chimes, figurines, crystal balls, incense, candles, tapes and books.

The Crystal Dolphin
780 N. Highland Ave. N.E., Ste. 6 • (404) 892-3880

In the popular Virginia Highlands shopping district, The Crystal Dolphin offers an array of gemstones, minerals, music, books and tapes. The store also carries incense, oils, Tibetan and Hindu artifacts and handcrafted jewelry.

Reader's Loft
1402 N. Highland Ave. N.E. • (404) 881-6511

Next to Mambo's restaurant, Reader's Loft features New Age books and gifts such as candles, fountains, ben-wa balls and tapes.

The Sphinx
1510 Piedmont Ave. N.E. • (404) 875-BOOK

The Sphinx, in the Ansley Square Shopping Center, is just south of the intersection of Piedmont Avenue and Monroe Drive. Shop here for merchandise that includes metaphysical books, incense, statues and music.

Unity Bookstore
4146 Chamblee Dunwoody Rd. N.E. • (770) 457-9888

This bookstore offers metaphysical books, music, greeting cards, candles, angels, gift items and recovery and 12-step materials. It's in the Atlanta Unity Church.

The Wish-Fulfilling Tree
2329 B. Cheshire Bridge Rd. N.E.
• **(404) 634-WISH**

This store is in the shopping center with the Tara Cinemas Theatre. Items on sale include books on Eastern philosophy, Western traditions, African religions, Egyptology as well as metaphysical videos, music, herbs, jewelry, gifts, incense, tapes, Tarot cards, candles, crystals and more. In the back is a great little heath food restaurant.

Beyond Atlanta

The Herb Shop
736 Ponce de Leon Ave. N.E.
• **(404) 881-9691**
3894 N. Druid Hills Rd., Decatur
• **(404) 634-6687**
3000 Windy Hill Rd., Ste. 7A, Marietta
• **(770) 956-7300**
10800 Alpharetta Hwy., Ste. 204, Roswell
• **(770) 518-7852**

These stores are independently owned, but they're all called The Herb Shop because they stock Nature's Sunshine products. There are about 19 shops in Atlanta and growing like, uh, herbs.

In addition to the previously listed locations, you'll find The Herb Shop at Cumberland Mall, North Point Mall and Perimeter Mall. Check the Yellow Pages for a complete list of locations in and around Atlanta.

Hoot Owl Attic
300 Hammond Dr., Sandy Springs
• **(404) 303 1030**

Hoot Owl Attic specializes in metaphysical items including books on the topic, gifts, incense, crystals, candles and jewelry featuring New Age concepts.

Krysalis
2785 Buford Hwy., Duluth
• **(770) 418-0903**

Krysalis offers a selection of metaphysical books, gifts, medallions, jewelry, crystals, candles and incense. You can also find self-help, self-discovery and 12-step program materials including books, cassettes, games and T-shirts.

Phoenix and Dragon
5531 Roswell Rd., Sandy Springs
• **(404) 255-5207**

This New Age bookstore promises "Miracles and Merriment!" It offers a wide selection of books on metaphysics, spirituality, holistic health, planetary healing, recovery and self-help as well as music, art, crystals, gemstones, scents and candles.

SunGlo
1028 Alpharetta St., Roswell
• **(770) 640-8184**

SunGlo accepts art consignments from talented local artists. Metaphysical goodies on sale include books, magazines, jewelry, candles, incense, crystals, music, and Native American items. SunGlo offers psychic readings every Saturday.

Attractions

Are you a history buff? An adventure junkie? A news hound? An animal lover? An armchair scientist? Whatever your interest, Atlanta has an attraction for you! In fact, there's so much to see and do in this city, your problem will be finding time to fit it all in.

It's been more than 150 years since Atlanta was first chartered as a city, but those years have been action-packed. Though still young compared to many other U.S. cities, Atlanta has seen a lot of history.

Though we Atlantans are always excited about the new and improved, we're also very curious about those places that speak to us about where our city and its people came from. All around the modern metropolis you'll find vivid reminders of other eras with their own triumphs, tragedies, heroes and villains. We've listed a number of places where bright glimpses of yesterday can still be seen today.

But proud as we are of our history, we live in the present and look toward the future. And while we're looking, we take time out for fun. This chapter highlights a variety of popular attractions that draw visitors year after year. You'll find more inviting destinations in The Arts, Parks and Recreation and Daytrips and Weekend Getaways chapters. Don't forget: Always call first to verify hours, dates of operation and admission prices. Funsters on a budget, please note our Fun Freebies section at the end of the chapter. Have a great time!

Atlanta

The APEX Museum
135 Auburn Ave. N.E. • (404) 521-APEX

The APEX, African-American Panoramic Experience, Museum is housed in a small building beside the Auburn Avenue Research Library on African-American Culture and History and across the street from the headquarters of the Atlanta Life Insurance Co. Eventu-

ally, plans call for the museum to have its own specially designed 97,000-square-foot facility on this site; its different sections will spotlight African-American achievement in various areas of endeavor, such as politics, entertainment and sports.

The present facility includes a replica of an Atlanta streetcar where visitors sit to watch a film, with narration by Julian Bond and a dramatic reading by Cicely Tyson that tells of Auburn Avenue's rich history as a center of black commerce and culture. Exhibits of African- and slavery-era artifacts occupy the museum's main room along with a replica of Yates & Milton, a black-owned drug store that originated on Auburn and eventually had four Atlanta locations. Among other items, the gift shop offers a reasonably priced and fascinating pictorial history book, *Sweet Auburn — Street of Pride*, published by the museum. Admission is $3 for adults and $2 for students and seniors. The museum is open 10 AM to 5 PM, Tuesday through Saturday.

Atlanta Botanical Garden
1345 Piedmont Ave. N.E., Piedmont Park at the Prado • (404) 876-5859, (404) 888-GROW plant hotline

Three miles from downtown stands a living museum to nature and gardening that is more passion than pastime for a great many Atlantans. Perched on 30 acres overlooking midtown's Piedmont Park, the Atlanta Botanical Garden (ABG) features 15 acres of outdoor display gardens and the 15-acre Storza Woods, one of the few remaining urban forests in Atlanta.

More than 3,000 ornamental plants flourish in the display gardens. Special sections devoted to roses, herbs, irises and summer bulbs crop up as you stroll through the innovatively landscaped grounds. Meditate a moment in the peaceful Japanese Garden, or delight your olfactory sense in the Fragrance

Garden. Stroll along sidewalks under vine-covered arbors, or relax near one of the cooling fountains. The ABG is full of pleasant, shaded seating areas, including the Alston Overlook, a covered structure nestled among the trees. Sculpture placed throughout the grounds enhances the natural beauty of the plants and flowers.

The Dorothy Chapman Fuqua Conservatory is a $5.5 million glass house that is home to an assortment of endangered and valuable plants. The Tropical Room's steamy, leafy environment makes you feel like you've left Atlanta for the Amazon. The Desert Room transports you through an arid spectacle of lush succulents. Adventurous types will love the special plants section with scary, dangling Ant Plants and a display of carnivores including the Venus Fly Trap. A sign dares you to stick a finger into one of the plants' hungry leaves. But you won't be invited to fondle the 12 varieties of poison dart frogs from Central and South America that live in three large terrariums filled with rainforest plants.

Dorothy and J.B. Fuqua traveled for two years to study 15 conservatories around the world before building the setting for this worldwide collection. Tiny, colorful birds flit among the trees and dart beneath a waterfall. The visual feast ranges from blooming orchids and unusual bromeliads to sprawling cacti and coffee plants. You can catch a spectacular view of part of the Atlanta skyline as you approach the conservatory from the ABG display gardens.

The ABG offers classes, lectures, symposia and demonstrations for ABG members and nonmembers. For information on ABG classes and tours, call the Education Department at (404) 876-5859, extension 226.

New in town and seeking fellow rose garden enthusiasts? ABG will refer you to an appropriate group. Many garden clubs and specialty societies meet regularly at ABG, with exhibits and competitions scheduled year round. The annual Southeast Flower Show

FYI

Three area codes serve the metro Atlanta area: 404, 770 and 678. Whether you live on Peachtree Street or in New York City, you must dial the code to reach any number in the area. The difference? Outside the area, you must dial "1," then the area code and phone number; inside the area, you need only dial the area code followed by the phone number.

presents an entire range of garden-related events such as artistic design displays, children's activities and more to benefit ABG (see our Festivals and Events chapter).

If you have questions about a particular plant or gardening method, call the Plant Hotline. A volunteer horticulturist or master gardener will be on hand, or return your call. The Sheffield Botanical Library stocks some 2,000 books and 80 periodicals for on-site library research only.

The ABG's Museum Shop is filled with unexpected finds for the gardeners on your gift list. Or what the heck, buy something for yourself! From April through October, you can lunch on sandwiches, salads and desserts on Lanier Terrace, overlooking the Rose Garden.

The Atlanta Botanical Garden is in the northwest corner of Piedmont Park. The entrance is on Piedmont Road between 14th Street and Monroe Drive, across from the intersection of Piedmont Avenue and The Prado. The garden allows child strollers everywhere but in the Conservatory. Limited parking is available. For public transportation, take MARTA to the Arts Center Station where you may transfer to the No. 36 North Decatur bus. On Sunday take the No. 31 Lindbergh bus from MARTA's Lindbergh or Five Points stations.

Atlanta Botanical Garden is open Tuesday through Sunday from 9 AM to 6 PM, November through March; from April through October, the Garden stays open from 9 AM to 7 PM. We recommend you allow at least an hour to tour the garden. The Fuqua Conservatory and the Museum Shop open at 10 AM. The garden is closed every Monday and on Thanksgiving, Christmas and New Year's Day.

Admission costs $6 for adults, $5 for seniors older than 65, $3 for children ages 6 to 12 and students with ID. Children younger than 6 and Atlanta Botanical Garden members get in free. Groups of 15 or more enjoy special admission rates if they schedule their visit in advance. After 3 PM every Thursday, everybody gets in free.

The Atlanta Cyclorama and Civil War Museum

800 Cherokee Ave. S.E. • (404) 624-1071

At the Atlanta Cyclorama, the scene never changes: It is forever the blistering afternoon of July 22, 1864, and out by the Georgia Railroad line 2 miles east of Five Points, thousands of men are locked in a desperate battle that will lead to the fall of Atlanta and the Confederacy's defeat.

Housed in a massive, custom-built structure in Grant Park, the Cyclorama is an amazingly vivid re-creation of the Battle of Atlanta. Taller than a five-story building and 358 feet in circumference, the 9,334-pound oil painting on canvas is considered the world's largest and has quite an interesting history.

Huge, round panorama paintings, most often depicting battle scenes, were once a popular form of entertainment. In 1885 the Milwaukee-based American Panorama Studio brought a team of expert European panorama artists to Atlanta. From a 40-foot observation tower constructed near the present-day intersection of DeKalb and Moreland avenues, the artists surveyed the battlefield, which had changed little in the two decades since the war. During their months of research in Atlanta, the artists sought the war recollections of numerous veterans and citizens.

The artists worked for 22 months in the studio to complete the painting, which was first exhibited in Minneapolis in 1887 and then brought to Atlanta in 1892 and exhibited in a drum-shaped wooden building on Edgewood Avenue. Patronage waned by the following year, and the painting was sold at a sheriff's auction for $1,100. It was eventually donated to the City of Atlanta in 1898 and displayed in a wooden building in Grant Park. Fear of fire led to the construction of an artificial stone structure, which was designed in the neoclassical style by John Francis Downing and dedicated in 1921. A huge central column was both the viewing platform and the roof's support. During the Depression, noted Atlanta historian and artist Wilbur Kurtz directed a restoration of the painting, and Work Projects Administration artists crafted the many foreground figures of soldiers, horses and wagons that make the Cyclorama a three-dimensional experience.

By 1979 the deteriorating Cyclorama was attracting more rats than tourists and badly needed extensive repairs. Noted conservator Gustav A. Berger's restoration team undertook the task. But the artists needed access to the fragile painting's back as well as its front, and it could not be removed from its specially designed building. Ingeniously, they removed a section of the structure's wall and hung the painting from an overhead track; this allowed them to rotate various sections into the work area as needed.

The project was not only tedious but downright dangerous, since the canvas had been coated with lead, arsenic and other toxins to repel insects. The diorama figures were restored under the direction of Joseph Hurt, a descendent of Troup Hurt, whose large brick house dominates the painting. The rather odd-looking modern space-frame system that spans the building's roof was necessitated when the load-bearing central column was replaced with a better viewing area. The $11 million restoration was completed in 1982.

Your visit to the Cyclorama begins with a 14-minute film narrated by James Earl Jones that features hundreds of costumed Civil War re-enactors. The film recounts Confederate generals Johnston and Hood's increasingly desperate efforts to protect Atlanta from Sherman's advancing troops. The guide then directs everyone upstairs to the Cyclorama. There, surrounded by the battle scene, the audience sits on a tiered viewing platform that slowly revolves as various parts of the painting come alive with computerized narration, light and sound effects.

For the most dramatic experience, skip the Cyclorama's front rows and head up to the back section. These high seats afford a wider view of the entire battle scene and better capture the original panoramic effect. It's fun to bring a pair of binoculars to spot small details in the painting and see where the artists attached the figures to the canvas.

During the gala events surrounding the 1939 world premiere of *Gone With the Wind* in Atlanta, Mayor William B. Hartsfield took the movie's stars to see the Cyclorama. Clark Gable is said to have remarked, "The only thing missing to make the Cyclorama perfect is Rhett Butler." In short order, the face of one figure — a fallen Union soldier in the foreground — was changed to a likeness of the famous actor.

The Cyclorama's museum has numerous informative displays about the Civil War and the painting itself. A half-hour video explains the tremendous restoration project. The museum also houses the locomotive *Texas* that was used in *The Great Locomotive Chase* (see the listing for Kennesaw Civil War Museum under Cobb County in this chapter). The gift shop has an extensive collection of Civil War books as well as souvenirs. It's worth mentioning that the Cyclorama does not espouse the Confederate point of view: It was restored during the tenure of Atlanta's first African-American mayor, Maynard Jackson, and its prevailing mood is anti-war, not pro-South.

The Atlanta Cyclorama is open daily 9:20 AM to 4:30 PM from Labor Day through May 31 and until 5:30 PM during the summer. It's closed Thanksgiving, Christmas, New Year's and Martin Luther King Jr.'s birthday. Presentations begin every 30 minutes throughout the day. Admission is $5 for adults, $4 for seniors 60 and older, $3 for children 6 to 12 and free for children younger than 6.

Atlanta History Center
130 W. Paces Ferry Rd. N.W.
• (404) 814-4000

Why was Atlanta of such strategic value in the Civil War? What was it like to live on a rural farm in the antebellum South or in an opulent Atlanta mansion in the 1930s? And what was a shotgun house, anyway?

You'll find the answers to these and many more questions at the Atlanta Historical Society's Atlanta History Center.

The society was formed in 1926; in 1966 it acquired the Edward Inman family's grand 25-acre estate, including the elegant Swan House mansion and most of the original furnishings. Many improvements were made over the years, culminating with the 1993 opening of the new 83,000-square-foot Atlanta History Museum. The history center is fun as well as educational. Here are a few of its highlights.

Start off at the permanent museum exhibit "Metropolitan Frontiers," a walk-through display where you can learn about the Native Americans who once called this region home, the arrival of the railroads, Atlanta's destruction and renaissance and the modern city's achievement of international status.

Behind the museum is the Tullie Smith Farm, an 1845 house that was moved to the center from its original site on an 800-acre tract near the present-day N. Druid Hills Road and I-85. A costumed guide takes guests through the house and describes the farm family's daily routine. Outside are a separate kitchen, a blacksmith shop and other outbuildings. Sturdy and unpretentious, this house is said to be a better example of a typical plantation home than the palatial, white-columned estates usually associated with the South.

Farther south is the Swan House, the 1928 mansion built by cotton broker and real estate magnate Edward Inman. Lavishly designed in a classic style, this grand home is one of the best-known examples of the work of famous Atlanta-based architect Philip Trammell Shutze. A guide shows visitors through the classically influenced yet personal home, whose futuristic residents insisted on having the recently invented shower instead of old-fashioned tubs in three of the four bathrooms. The Atlanta History Center's distinctive star emblem duplicates the pattern on the floor of the Swan House's foyer. A cascading fountain stretches from the home's front down across the terraced lawn facing the original entrance on Andrews Drive.

The center also includes a Victorian playhouse and 32 acres of botanically labeled gardens. The 3.5-million-item McElreath Hall research facility and archives is free and open to the public Tuesday through Saturday, 10 AM to 5 PM. Also on the grounds is the Swan Coach House Restaurant, 3130 Slaton Drive N.W. (see our Restaurants chapter), where delectables from chicken salad croissants to crab cakes are served Monday through Saturday in the mansion's former coach house. While there, check out the attached gift shop and art gallery, where jewelry, infant clothing and speciality items produced by local arti-

sans are featured at remarkably reasonable prices. You may shop or dine at the restaurant (on divine crab cakes!) without purchasing a ticket to the History Center.

Periodically, the Atlanta History Center mounts ambitious exhibitions in the galleries of the History Museum. Two of the permanent displays are not to be missed:

"Turning Point: The American Civil War" is a 9,000-square-foot exhibit that opened in June 1996. Detailing why Atlanta was such a strategic target in the Civil War and how the city's fall sealed the Confederacy's doom, this presentation is a hit with Civil War buffs as well as those curious about what the womenfolk were doing while their men were at the front.

"Shaping Traditions: Folk Arts in a Changing South" opened in May 1996. Crafts, textiles, pottery, music and more are examined as the means whereby communities build bridges between the past and present. Included in the 5,000-square-foot display are interactive videos and audio presentations of music and stories.

Thirsty sightseers will find refreshment in the museum's Coca-Cola Cafe, a recreation of a '50s diner, where the menu includes a sweet Coca-Cola cake. The Cafe is open from 10 AM to 4 PM.

The center's regular hours are Monday through Saturday, 10 AM to 5:30 PM, and Sunday, noon to 5:30 PM. Admission is $7 for adults, $5 for students older than 18 and seniors, $4 for youths 6 to 17, and free for kids 5 and younger. Add $1 for a guided tour of the two historic homes.

The Atlanta Preservation Center Walking Tours
156 Seventh St. N.E., Ste. 3
• (404) 876-2040

Progress has its price, and much of the architecture that once symbolized Atlanta has, for various reasons, disappeared. Even so, the visitor to the modern city can still encounter remarkably preserved places that afford insight into how Atlantans once lived. The Atlanta Preservation Center's walking tours through Atlanta's historic districts are a great way to experience different parts of the city's heritage.

APC's tour of the Fox Theatre, offered four times weekly throughout the year, is especially popular, since it's the only way to see the grand movie palace's interior without buying a ticket to a show. The Fox tour is given Mondays, Wednesdays and Thursdays at 10 AM and Saturdays at 10 AM and 11 AM; meet at the 660 Peachtree Street entrance.

APC's other tours, which are all conducted outdoors, are given from March through November. All tours (except the Fox Theatre) are canceled in the event of rain; no tours are given on legal holidays. Admission for each tour is $5 for adults; $3 for students; and $4 for persons 65 and older. Reservations are necessary only for groups of 10 or more. On-board guides for bus tours are also available. For recorded information call (404) 876-2040. Here's what's featured on the outdoor tours:

The Sweet Auburn/MLK District tour takes visitors through this center of African-American Atlanta's early commerce and social life. At the heart of the community is the Martin Luther King Jr. National Historic District, featuring Dr. King's birth home, church and tomb. The tour is given on Saturdays at 10:30 AM; meet in front of the APEX Museum, 135 Auburn Avenue, near Courtland Street.

West End, one of Atlanta's oldest neighborhoods, got its start in 1835 when railroad surveyors picked the spot that would become the center of Atlanta, and it was spared destruction in the Civil War. The West End/Hammonds House and Wren's Nest tour includes the 1857 Hammonds House (Georgia's only museum devoted to African-American fine art) and the 1867 Wren's Nest (the beautifully restored Victorian home of Joel Chandler Harris, creator of "Uncle Remus"). The tour is given on the third Sunday of each month at 2 PM; meet on the steps of the Wren's Nest, 1050 Ralph David Abernathy Boulevard.

The Historic Downtown tour spotlights the architecture at the core of Atlanta's first high-rise district and includes six historic building interiors. The tour is given Fridays at noon and Saturdays at 11 AM; meet at the Candler Building, 127 Peachtree Street.

What is Underground Atlanta, and how did it get down there? You can get the whole story on the Historic Underground/Birth of Atlanta tour that also features the Georgia State Capitol, several other government buildings and three prominent churches founded before the Civil War. The tour is given by request on Saturday or Sunday.

The Walking Miss Daisy's Druid Hills tour will take you through the elegant 1893 neighborhood laid out by Frederick Law Olmsted and featured in the Oscar-winning movie for best picture, *Driving Miss Daisy*. Here, along winding, tree-lined streets, are exquisite mansions designed by renowned Atlanta-based architects Neel Reid, W.T. Downing and Philip Shutze. For maximum impact, take this tour in the springtime when Druid Hills is splendidly arrayed with blooming dogwoods and azaleas. The tour is given Saturdays and Wednesdays at 11 AM; meet in front of St. John's Lutheran Church, 1410 Ponce de Leon Avenue, at the corner of Oakdale Road.

On the Ansley Park tour, you can enjoy the lovely lawns and elegant homes of another of Atlanta's original suburbs designed with automobile (not trolley car) commuters in mind. Ansley Park has many fine homes by such architects as Downing, Reid and Shutze and was the site of Georgia's Governor's mansion for more than 40 years. The tour is given Sundays at 1 PM and Thursdays at noon; meet in front of the First Church of Christ Scientist at the corner of Peachtree Road and 15th Street.

The Inman Park tour has visitors strolling through Atlanta's first planned suburb, which was developed by Joel Hurt in the 1880s. Not coincidentally, Hurt ran Atlanta's first electric streetcar line to his new suburb two miles east of downtown, which was then part of a separate town called Edgewood. Hurt's own home is still standing, as are the homes of Coca-Cola magnates Asa Candler and Ernest Woodruff. After many years of decline, Inman Park began to rouse itself in the late 1960s and is now a nationally recognized symbol of neighborhood preservation and revitalization. The tour is given Thursdays at 11 AM and Sundays at 2 PM; meet at the corner of Hurt and Edgewood Avenues.

Two other walking tours are offered on selected dates throughout the year. One wanders through the rolling hills of Atlanta's "front lawn" in Piedmont Park. Learn how the 1895 Cotton States and International Exhibition held here gave Atlanta a giant boost in business and how the Olmsted Brothers' crafted the landscape plan. The other focuses on the Atlanta University Center, the nation's largest concentration of historically black colleges. This tour reveals how AUC's colleges, several of which were founded very soon after the Civil War, have exerted a powerful influence on black intellectual life worldwide. The tour includes the lavish home of entrepreneur Alonzo Herndon, Atlanta's first African-American millionaire. Call to confirm the exact dates and times of these special tours.

Carter Presidential Center
1 Copenhill Ave. N.E. • (404) 331-0296

The Carter Presidential Center occupies a hilltop known as Copenhill. From the Augustus Hurt house that stood here, U.S. Gen. William Tecumseh Sherman watched the raging Battle of Atlanta in 1864.

This privately financed $25 million center was completed in 1986 after two year's construction. The Jimmy Carter Library and Museum are the center's public portions. This 70,000-square foot building contains some 27 million pages of original documents from the Carter White House, along with 1.5 million photographs and other materials.

The museum features a 30-minute film on the Presidency in general and on Carter's four-year term, a collection of miniature gowns that are replicas of those worn by First Ladies of the past and interactive displays focusing on the accomplishments (human rights) and the challenges (the Iran hostage crisis) of the Carter years. You can also visit a reproduction of the Oval Office and see some of the gifts presented to President and Mrs. Carter by other heads of state. Those with a special interest in Carter, his years in the White House and presidential trivia will thoroughly enjoy the museum. The gift shop sells Carter campaign memorabilia as well as Atlanta souvenirs and reproductions of various presidential china patterns.

The museum is open Monday through Saturday from 9 AM to 4:45 PM and Sunday from noon to 4:45 PM. Admission is $5 for adults

and $4 for senior citizens 55 and older; children 16 and younger are admitted free. The Carter Presidential Center can be accessed via the Freedom Parkway or N. Highland Avenue; there's plenty of free parking.

No admission is necessary to dine in the cafe (which has a lovely outdoor patio), visit the public rest rooms or stroll the landscaped grounds. The center's four interconnected buildings frame an elaborate Japanese garden and a pond; this area boasts a splendid view of the downtown skyline.

Centennial Olympic Park
Marietta St. and Techwood Dr. • no phone

For a few days during the summer of 1996, the focus of the world shifted from the Olympic Games to the fatal bombing at one of the city's newest attractions: Centennial Olympic Park. Although the association with that tragic event is surely to be on a visitors minds as they stroll past the victims' memorial, the Park remains a delightful open space in the heart of downtown. The hot summer days still draw crowds who come to frolic in the Fountain of Rings that shoots streams of water into the air from ground-level. At night the tall towers that line the park's walkways are dotted with lights. A major draw for many out-of-towners and locals alike is discovering the exact location of the Olympic brick they bought with their name on it. An information center with brick locators, cafe and shopping spots are also part of the Park.

CNN Center
1 CNN Center, Marietta St. at Techwood Dr. N.W. • (404) 827-2201

You'll find lots to see and do at CNN Center, headquarters of Ted Turner's mighty communications empire. Get a behind-the-scenes look at news in the making through the popular Cable News Network Studio Tour. You'll spend about 45 minutes touring three studios: CNN, Headline News and CNN International. Studio tours run from 9 AM to 6 PM daily. Call (404) 827-2300 for advanced reservations. For tours that haven't sold out, walk-up tickets go on sale on a first-come, first-served basis at 8:30 AM every day. Tours cost $7 for adults, $5 for seniors 65 and older and $4.50 for children. For groups of 35 or more, admission is $5. Public tours usually have 35 people. Those with deeper pockets might want to check out the VIP Tour, an up-close-and-personal excursion that costs $24.50. VIPs tour the studios in groups of eight or less and enjoy extended access to the newsroom floor. This tour also offers a small gift package, including pen, key chain and mug, and a snack at the commissary.

If you long to be on a talk show, reserve a seat in the audience of *Talk Back Live*, CNN's live interactive town meeting, broadcast daily from the center's atrium studio. For information and reservations, dial (800) 410-4CNN. You can pick up free tickets to *Talk Back Live* at the Turner Store's Lenox and CNN Center locations as well as from the concierge desks at major hotels throughout the city. But be aware: A ticket does not guarantee a seat in the show's audience. Only a reservation carries a guarantee of admission. Tickets are taken on a first-come, first-served basis.

Other fun things at CNN include such Atlanta-themed shops as the Braves Clubhouse Store, the Atlanta Shop and the Turner Store. You can snack in the food court, dine in full-service restaurants or take in a movie at the Cinema Six. You can even spend the night at the Omni hotel.

An apartment in CNN Center is the Atlanta residence of Ted Turner and Jane Fonda.

CNN Center, across the street from Centennial Park, is within walking distance of the Georgia Dome and the Georgia World Congress Center. It's just a stroll away from Underground Atlanta. You can get there on MARTA. CNN is also listed in our Shopping and Media chapters.

A Coca-Cola Excursion
Various sites around Atlanta • no phone

Make no mistake: When you're in Atlanta, you're in Coca-Cola country. The world's most popular soft drink was invented here, and it was all the rage in Atlanta before it was available anywhere else. Over the years the company's leaders, especially founder Asa G. Candler and longtime president Robert W. Woodruff, poured money into worthy Atlanta institutions (most notably Emory University), often through generous but anonymous gifts.

Coca-Cola was invented by Dr. John S. Pemberton in his home, which stood at 107 Marietta Street. It was first served to a thirsty world in May 1886 at Jacobs' Pharmacy, 2 Marietta Street. The recipe for Coke's top-secret essence, code-named "Merchandise 7X" is kept under lock and key in a vault in the SunTrust Bank building, Park Place at Auburn Avenue. The nearby 17-story Candler Building, Peachtree Street at Dobbs Avenue, was once home to Coke's executive offices. An architectural marvel when new, the Candler Building has recently been grandly restored.

Coca-Cola's world headquarters building towers over Midtown at 1 Coca-Cola Plaza on the corner of North Avenue and Luckie Street. Just down the street is The Varsity, North Avenue at Spring Street, the world's largest drive-in and predictably the world's largest retail user of Coca-Cola syrup. May Heaven protect you should you ask for that "other" cola drink here.

Inman Park, Atlanta's first suburb, was home to Coke's founder Asa Candler from 1903 to 1916. His red brick mansion, now a private residence, stands on the corner of Euclid Avenue and Elizabeth Street and was named Callan Castle after the family's ancestral home in Ireland. Near the Virginia-Highland area, Candler's eldest son Howard built the magnificent Gothic-Tudor mansion Callanwolde at 980 Briarcliff Road; today it's a fine arts center maintained by DeKalb County (see our related entry in The Arts chapter). Asa Griggs Candler Jr.'s home at 1260 Briarcliff Road is now part of the Georgia Mental Health Institute. Lullwater House, 1463 Clifton Road N.E., built in 1925 for Candler's son, Walter Turner Candler, has been the residence of Emory University's presidents since 1963. St. John's Melkite Catholic Church, 1428 Ponce de Leon Avenue N.E., is another former home of Asa Chandler.

Atlanta's loyalty to the Coca-Cola tradition is steadfast. Remember the backlash against that all-but-forgotten marketing disaster "New Coke"? When company executives rolled out the "new, improved taste" in a flashy downtown celebration at Woodruff Park on April 23, 1985, the crowd included lifelong Atlanta Coke consumers who — in front of the world's media — poured bottles of the new, sweeter drink onto the street. Less than three months later, with Coke drinkers around the country still clamoring for their old favorite, the corporation acquiesced and returned the original formula to

Photo: L.A. Middlesteadt, ABG

The Dorothy Chapman Fuqua Conservatory houses endangered
and valuable plants at the Atlanta Botanical Garden.

the market as "Coca-Cola Classic." By 1994 the overall soft drink market share of New Coke (renamed Coke II) had fallen to 0.1 percent.

If you'll settle for nothing less than being fully awash in a river of Coca-Cola history, images and lore, go directly to The World of Coca-Cola (see separate item in this chapter). And while you're in Atlanta, don't forget: Things go better with the pause that refreshes! It's the real thing! Refreshing! Delicious!

Fernbank Museum of Natural History
767 Clifton Rd. N.E. • (404) 378-0127

The very popular Fernbank Museum is the largest natural history museum in the Southeast. Since it opened in 1992, more than 2.5 million visitors have flocked to Fernbank.

Permanent exhibits include A Walk Through Time in Georgia, 17 galleries that explore landform regions of Georgia and the chronological development of life on Earth. Highlights include The Origin of the Universe, a high-definition video that projects the drama of Earth's formation. Dinosaur Hall features seven life-size dinosaurs and three massive murals of the Cretaceous, Jurassic and Triassic eras. The Okefenokee Swamp Gallery surrounds the visitor with the sights, sounds and exotic beauty of the swamp.

Fernbank boasts Georgia's first IMAX Theater, with a five-story screen to accommodate the largest film format in the world. IMAX's special curved screen and powerful digitally recorded sound system draw you right into the action.

Other permanent exhibits include the McClatchey Gallery, Cultures of the World, which houses a significant jewelry collection donated by Mrs. Dorothy McClatchey, a prominent resident of Atlanta. The World of Shells features shells from around the globe and a Caribbean coral reef saltwater aquarium.

Spectrum of the Senses presents 65 interactive exhibits that help visitors understand the scientific principles of light and sound. This gallery brims over with computers, colored lights, video projectors and lasers. For everyone from brainy science nerds to the scientifically impaired, this popular gallery features activities that can be experienced at several intellectual levels. Some are simple; others are high-tech.

The museum is open Monday through Saturday, 10 AM to 5 PM; Sunday, noon to 5 PM. Friday evenings (except in May and December) are reserved for Martinis and IMAX, where a full bar serves refreshments before special showings of the films at 7 PM.

Admission costs $8.95 for adults, $7.95 for students and seniors older than 62 and $6.95 for children 3 to 12. Fernbank members and children younger than 2 get in free. IMAX Theater admission only for adults is $6.95 for one, or two for $11.95; $5.95 for students and seniors, $9.95 for two; and $4.95 for children 3 to 12, $7.95 for two. Combination IMAX and museum tickets cost $13.95 for adults, $11.95 for students and seniors and $9.95 for children 3 to 12. Combination tickets for two IMAX films and the museum are $18.95 for adults; $15.95 for students and seniors; $12.95 for children. Group rates are available.

Fernbank Science Center
156 Heaton Park Dr. N.E. • (404) 378-4311

Fernbank Science Center is an intriguing attraction about a mile from the Fernbank Museum of Natural History. Home to one of the nation's largest planetariums, the Science Center also boasts an exhibit hall featuring an authentic moon rock, an original Apollo space capsule and much more.

If you're into stargazing, you've come to the right place. On clear Thursday and Friday nights, the Science Center's observatory lets you step up to its big telescope and view whatever celestial body — Venus, Mercury, the moon — is looking good that night. Questions about the heavens? Ask the astronomer on duty.

Nature lovers can explore the 1.5 miles of trails through the 65-acre Fernbank Forest. A relaxing respite from the hubbub of city life, this virgin forest is one of the largest remaining in any metropolitan area in the Southeast.

Staffers and visiting scientists conduct active research projects at the Science Center. Currently scientists are using a 132-foot-high meteorological tower to study low-level ozone and the effects of vegetation on mediating weather.

The center opens Monday, 8:30 AM to 5 PM; Tuesday through Friday, 8:30 AM to 10 PM; Saturday, 10 AM to 5 PM; and Sunday, 1 to 5 PM. The Science Center is owned and funded by the DeKalb County school system. That means it's closed on school system administrative holidays. Call to make sure you haven't hit one.

General admission is free. Planetarium shows cost $2 for adults, $1 for students and children 5 and older. Special children's programs cost 50¢ per person. To reach the Science Center from Ponce de Leon Avenue, turn on Artwood Road then follow the signs directing you to the Center on Heaton Park Drive.

The Fox Theatre
660 Peachtree St. N.E. • (404) 881-2100

To visit the Fox Theatre is to be swept into another world. In an age of minimalist architecture and 12-plex movies in minimalls, the Fox is the real deal: no mere theater but a complete environment, lush and ornate almost beyond belief. This dazzling movie palace is so closely associated with Atlanta today that it's inconceivable it was almost torn down just 20 years ago.

Planning for the structure began in 1916. It was to be the headquarters for the Yaarab Temple of the Ancient Arabic Order of the Nobles of the Mystic Shrine (the Shriners). In 1929 as it neared completion, financial difficulties forced the Shriners into a deal with movie magnate William Fox, and the temple's plans were altered to include a

---

INSIDERS' TIP

The escalator in the CNN Center is the longest freestanding escalator in the world, rising 160 feet or approximately eight stories in height.

spectacular movie theater and exterior street-level retail space.

Oozing with Middle Eastern opulence, the Fox opened on Christmas Day, 1929. One awed newspaper reporter wrote that the building possessed "an almost disturbing grandeur beyond imagination." But after a mere 125 weeks featuring talking pictures, the Fox, squeezed by the Great Depression, closed. After having been built at a cost of more than $2.75 million, it was sold at auction for $75,000. The theater reopened in 1935.

Then in 1947, when the Fox gained immeasurable prestige, it became the venue for the touring Metropolitan Opera's Atlanta performances. Beneath the great theater's twinkling starry ceiling, thousands thrilled to such vocal greats as Ezio Pinza, Robert Merrill, Richard Tucker, Renata Tebaldi, Roberta Peters, Anna Moffo, Teresa Stratas, Montserrat Caballe and others. The Met's stars often got lost inside the Fox's cavernous backstage areas until someone came up with an ingenious solution: the names of the New York streets around the Metropolitan Opera House were chalked on the Fox's walls to help the singers find their way.

The Met's annual springtime visits to the Fox were a high point in Atlanta's social year. Tickets were much-sought-after treasures, and music-lovers from around the South poured in for the week-long round of parties, performances and midnight suppers. Peachtree was closed to allow patrons easy access to the Georgian Terrace Hotel (and its bar) across the street from the theater.

A 1948 weather-related calamity made headlines around the world when it almost caused what would have been only the second canceled performance in the long history of the Met's spring tour. Torrential rains washed out the tracks between Richmond and Atlanta, delaying for hours the arrival of the train carrying the company's costumes. At last the decision was made to perform Carmen in street clothes. The performance began at 10 PM; the costumes arrived after the first act; and the curtain did not come down until 1 AM. The Met last performed at the Fox in 1968.

By 1975, unable to fill its nearly 5,000 seats as a first-run movie house, the Fox closed again; this time things looked grim indeed. Plans were to raze the theater to make way for the skyscraper headquarters of Southern Bell. Distraught by the looming loss of this architectural jewel, thousands of Atlantans joined in the work of Atlanta Landmarks Inc., a nonprofit organization. The necessary $1.8 million was raised six months in advance of the deadline, and the Fox was saved and reopened in time to celebrate its 50th birthday. Since then, the group has spent more than $6 million to fix the Fox.

Today the Fox is a favorite venue for concerts and touring Broadway shows; a summer film series still affords the unequaled experience of seeing a movie in a "real" movie theater.

The Fox is too amazing to describe briefly, but here are a few highlights and tips:

• With six motorized elevator lifts, the 140-foot-wide stage remains one of the largest ever built. Another elevator raises and lowers the 3,622-pipe, four-keyboard Mighty Möller organ, which is played for a sing-along before each movie during the summer film series, just as it was in the 1930s.

• The ceiling of the 64,000-square-foot auditorium suggests night under a Bedouin chieftain's tent beneath a clear desert sky. The tent is not canvas as might be expected but a reinforced plaster canopy that helps draw sound up to the rear of the balcony. The 96 stars twinkling in the blue sky are 11-watt bulbs fixed above two-inch crystals. Clouds, rain and other special effects are produced by projector. The pre-movie sing-along usually includes "Sunrise, Sunset," during which the theater's sky brightens from darkness to day before slipping back to dusk.

• The entire second level of the Fox (the loge, first and second dress circles and gallery) and the front of the orchestra section enjoy views of the sky. To the rear of row M in the orchestra section, the balcony overhang hides the sky. Especially for movies, the front rows of the loge are the best in the house.

• Don't miss the marble and velvet restrooms and lounges! Even these areas are fabulous in the Fox.

• Several full bars serve cocktails and other beverages during all events, including movies, and you're welcome to enjoy drinks and snacks inside the auditorium during most performances. Smoking is permitted only in the exterior entrance arcade and on the smoking porch facing Ponce de Leon Avenue.

For information on touring the Fox, see our entry on the Atlanta Preservation Center's walking tours.

Georgia Department of Archives and History
330 Capitol Ave. S.E. • (404) 656-2393

Although not set up as a tourist attraction, the Georgia Department of Archives and History is an invaluable resource for serious scholars and those researching genealogy. The department was created in 1918. From 1931 to 1965, the state's archives were maintained in Rhodes Hall (see separate listing later in this chapter).

The Ben W. Fortson Jr. State Archives and Records Building between the Capitol and Turner Field is often mistaken for a prison, but the tall, windowless structure provides a secure, controlled environment for some 85,000 cubic feet of official records and more than 65,000 reels of records on microfilm. Among these governmental and nongovernmental documents are family letters and papers, business account books, organizational and church records and photographs.

The facility is open to the public Monday through Friday, 8 AM to 4:45 PM, and Saturdays 9:30 AM to 3:15 PM. Visitors must show identification and complete an application for a research card to gain access to the Search Room. To protect the fragile records and documents that date back to the Revolutionary War, the department has strict rules regulating what materials may be brought inside. For more information, call the department's reference line, (404) 656-2350.

The Georgia Governor's Mansion
391 W. Paces Ferry Rd. N.E.
• (404) 261-1776

The Georgia Governor's Mansion was dedicated in 1968. Like the state's first Governor's mansion, built in Milledgeville in 1838, the modern mansion is in the Greek Revival style; it was designed by Georgia architect A. Thomas Bradbury. The 24,000-square-foot house is the property of Georgia's citizens and, by law, remains the same even when its primary resident changes.

Neoclassical paintings and furnishings from the 19th century complement the mansion's design. On the main floor are a library with

Backstage at The Fox

Since it opened in 1929, The Fox Theatre has hosted some remarkable performances under the twinkling starlike lights in its blue sky ceiling. Among the most famous were the traveling shows of the touring Metropolitan Opera that brought some of the great divas to the Atlanta stage.

Today, The Fox plays a variety of roles: moviehouse, concert hall, first-run theater, and a place for magician David Copperfield to disappear. Through the years it has survived problems of low-attendance, bankruptcy and near-destruction by fire; it continues to be one of the city's premier performing venues.

But some of the best acts The Fox has seen didn't take place on stage, in front of the audience. Stories of the antics and quirks of guest actors, singers and artists are handed down from crew to crew each year. Here are just a few of the backstage shows the public didn't see:

• In 1982, *The King and I's* Yul Brenner insisted on remodeling the main dressing room in a dark chocolate color scheme, which provoked severe candy attacks among crew members who visited his room.

• Stephanie Mills, of *The Wiz*, had her dressing room repainted a shocking shade of pink.

• Kenny Rogers insisted that his wardrobe be crisply pressed and laid out. He even asked the stage manager to iron his socks!

— continued on next page

• Bob Hope has been known to ask a stagehand to hold a Styrofoam cup to catch his putts during backstage golf practice.

You can't work with complicated, full-scale productions in a theater the size of the Fox without a few glitches now and then. And there have been some memorable ones:

• During a performance of *Sleeping Beauty* presented by the Atlanta Ballet, the lighting crew was furiously keeping up with the lighting cues. When the floodlights accidently came on too early, they exposed Prince and Beauty casually waiting at the rear of the stage, their arms folded. The two scrambled to the front of the stage, and Beauty leapt into bed. The performance was forever remembered as Leaping Beauty.

• Singer Johnny Mathis got his microphone cord stuck in the crack between the

Photo: Michael Portman/The Fox Theatre

The Fox Theatre was intended to be the headquarters for the Shriners.

elevator lifts on stage. While still singing, he tried to push it down into the crack to release it, but the cord kept getting shorter and shorter. Finally, Mathis finished on his knees as stagehands appeared with a replacement microphone.

• The Rolling Stones literally rolled in just minutes before a 1981 concert. Their flight from a sightseeing trip to Savannah was fogged-in for so long, it looked like the show wouldn't go on. Their plane finally was able to land in Macon, and the band was hurriedly driven to Atlanta, while the audience waited almost two hours after the opening act.

• There have only been four times in the Fox's recent history when the show was completely interrupted. *The Nutcracker's* Mouse King fell into the orchestra pit onto the horn and cello players. The giant turntable that rotated the stage got stuck during a 1989 performance of *Les Miz*. The fog machine malfunctioned during a 1990 run of *Starlight Express*, leaving an oil slick just as the skaters hit the stage. The performers fell in a heap, and the show was stopped to mop up the mess. The computerized soundtrack used during Lily Tomlin's performance was out of sync and had to be reprogrammed.

many books by Georgia authors and the state drawing and dining rooms. The second floor is the first family's private home and includes the large Presidential Suite for visiting dignitaries. The lower floor of the mansion boasts a ballroom that seats 150 for dinner.

The Governor's Mansion is open to the public each week on Tuesday, Wednesday and Thursday from 10 AM to 11:30 AM. The tour is self-guided, but hostesses in each room explain items of significance. The tour is free, but reservations are required for groups of 15

or more. Drive up to the main gate; there's parking on the 18-acre grounds. While you're at the mansion, you may wish to visit the Atlanta History Center, just down the road and mentioned previously in this chapter.

Georgia's Historical Markers
Various locations around Atlanta and the state, Georgia Parks and Historic Sites Division • (404) 656-7092

As you explore Atlanta and Georgia, you can gain a wealth of background from the state's historical markers. You can't miss them: the olive-green cast-aluminum signs are 42 by 38 inches and are emblazoned with the state seal. Statewide, there are some 2,000 markers, about 700 of which concern the Civil War. The metro Atlanta area has about 600 historical markers.

The program was launched in 1951 and strongly emphasized Civil War history in the buildup to the 100th anniversary of the conflict. Artist and historian Wilbur Kurtz, who was a consultant on the movies *Gone With the Wind* and *Song of the South*, wrote the text for the markers between Tennessee and Atlanta. Another prominent historian, Col. Allen P. Julian, described Sherman's March to the Sea on the markers south of Atlanta to Savannah.

Historical markers are scattered across metro Atlanta. You can see some along DeKalb Avenue about two miles east of Five Points, the area that was at the center of the Battle of Atlanta. There are several markers around the Inman Park/Reynoldstown MARTA station; the fighting at this location is depicted in the Atlanta Cyclorama. There are also several in the Buckhead area near Peachtree Creek.

Georgia State Capitol
Intersection of Capitol Ave., M.L. King Jr. Dr. Washington Ave. and Mitchell St.
• **(404) 656-2844**

The Georgia Legislature first met in Atlanta in 1868, but the $1 million needed for construction of the capitol was not provided until 1883. Work got under way in October of 1884; when it was completed, the state treasury had spent all but $118.43. The building was dedicated on July 4, 1889.

The Chicago architectural firm Edbrooke and Burnham designed the Capitol, which was built of Indiana oolitic limestone by Miles and Horne of Toledo, Ohio. Georgia marble, judged impractically expensive for the exterior, was used for the floors, walls and steps. The open rotunda peaks at a height of more than 237 feet. The building's classical design pays homage to the U.S. Capitol in Washington, as if to avow post-Civil War Georgia's fealty to the Union.

Outside, atop the dome, stands a 15-foot-tall, 2,000-pound Greek-inspired statue of a female figure holding a torch in one hand and a sword in the other: It commemorates Georgia's war dead.

During a 1956 renovation program, 43 ounces of native gold, donated by the people of Dahlonega and Lumpkin County, site of America's first gold rush in 1828, were applied to the dome's exterior. Another application of gold in 1981 restored the dome's brilliance. The capitol was named a National Historic Landmark in 1977.

Inside and out, the capitol's memorials and mementos tell Georgia's diverse history. Statues of famous segregationists share the grounds with the touching modern sculpture "Expelled Because of Their Color," commissioned in 1976 by the General Assembly's black legislative caucus. It is "dedicated to the memory of the 33 black state legislators who were elected, yet expelled from the Georgia House because of their color in 1868" and is on the northeast side of the grounds.

The Georgia State Museum of Science and Industry on the first and fourth floors showcases Georgia's wildlife and minerals; other features include Native American artifacts and battle flags flown by Georgia regiments in various wars.

The capitol is open daily. Free guided tours of the capitol are offered year round, Monday through Friday, at 10 AM, 11 AM, 1 PM and 2 PM. The tour desk is on the main floor in the West Wing just outside the Governor's office. The capitol is also open on weekends, but no tours are given. Call for more information or to arrange a group tour or tour for hearing- or sight-impaired persons.

The Herndon Home
587 University Pl. N.W. • **(404) 581-9813**

This 1910 Beaux-Arts Classical mansion near Atlanta University is as amazing as the African-American family that built it. Alonzo Herndon began life as a slave in Social Circle, Georgia. As a young man possessing only one year of formal education, he learned the barbering trade and moved to Atlanta. Here Herndon's hard work was richly rewarded. His barber shop eventually employed some 40 men, and he founded the Atlanta Life Insurance Co. and became one of the city's wealthiest African Americans.

On a tall hill overlooking the city, Herndon

and his wife, the former Adrienne McNeil, built their dream home, designing it themselves without an architect. Constructed entirely by black craftsmen at a cost of $10,000, the mansion was completed in 1910 after two-and-a-half years of work and included such ultra-modern conveniences as electricity, central plumbing and steam heat. Tragically, the ailing Mrs. Herndon died just one week after moving into the home. The Herndons' only son, Norris, lived in the house until his death in 1977; since then, the Herndon Foundation has owned and operated the home.

The Herndon Home is opulent and magnificent with nine fireplaces, a lavish mahogany dining room and a recurring lion's-head motif. Other aspects, though, are charmingly personal. In the living room is a mural that tells the story of the elder Herndon's rise from slavery to riches. The flat roof was Adrienne's idea. A drama teacher and Shakespearean actress, she envisioned it as the ideal place for outdoor dramatic performances.

The Herndon Home is open to the public Tuesday through Saturday from 10 AM to 4 PM. Guided tours begin on the hour. Donations are accepted, but there is no admission charge.

The Martin Luther King Jr. Center for Nonviolent Social Change
449 Auburn Ave. N.E. • (404) 526-8900

The King Center is Atlanta's preeminent tourist attraction. All day, every day, visitors make their way past the eternal flame in the center's plaza and toward the tiered reflecting pool, in the center of which stands Dr. King's elevated marble tomb. West of the tomb is Ebenezer Baptist Church where Dr. King was co-pastor. East of the tomb is the King Center's main facility (see The Martin Luther King Jr. National Historic Site later in this chapter). Across the Boulevard is King's restored birth home, 526 Auburn Avenue.

King was assassinated on April 4, 1968, while in Memphis, Tennessee, lending his support to striking sanitation workers. Upon learning of the sudden tragedy, Atlanta Mayor Ivan Allen Jr. immediately began to prepare the city for the funeral that would become one of the largest events in its history. When Dr. King won the Nobel Peace Prize in 1964, Robert Woodruff led the movement to honor him with a gala banquet. In the hours after the tragedy, the Coca-Cola president called the mayor and insisted that no expense be spared in preparing the city to accommodate thousands of mourners and the international media. Woodruff himself guaranteed payment of any cost overruns.

During the grief-stricken days that followed the assassination, rioting in 126 U.S. cities claimed some 46 lives — but Atlanta remained calm. Mayor Allen and Police Chief Herbert Jenkins walked the streets of the city's black neighborhoods, expressing their sympathy and support. Hundreds of volunteers at the Southern Christian Leadership Conference offices worked around the clock to assist the thousands of mourners streaming into the city. Central Presbyterian Church downtown announced it was opening its doors to black visitors; hundreds of other white churches followed suit.

On April 9, more than 100,000 people crowded around Ebenezer Baptist Church for the funeral. Hundreds of dignitaries and celebrities attended, including Jacqueline and Bobby Kennedy, Wilt Chamberlain, James Brown, Nelson Rockefeller, Richard Nixon, Harry Belafonte and Vice President Hubert Humphrey. Georgia's Governor Lester Maddox, a pick-handle-waving segregationist who had complained about plans to fly flags at half-mast in the city, remained in his office under the protection of state troopers.

Some 200,000 mourners followed the humble mule-drawn wagon that carried Dr. King's body along Auburn Avenue and back to his alma mater Morehouse College, where he had been lain in state. There he was eulogized by Dr. Benjamin E. Mays, president emeritus of Morehouse.

Mrs. Coretta Scott King and 7-year-old son Dexter went to Memphis only four days after the murder to march with the striking sanitation workers. Within three months, the King Memorial Center had opened. Mrs. King and her children have continued working to keep Dr. King's dream alive. Following extensive lobbying and much controversy, Dr. King's birthday became a national holiday in 1986.

Many people today do not readily recall that Ebenezer Baptist Church was the scene of another unexpected tragedy in the life of the King family. During worship services on June 30, 1974, as she played "The Lord's Prayer" on the church organ, the 69-year-old Alberta King (affectionately known as "Mama King"), mother of Martin Luther King Jr., was shot dead by a young black man. Church deacon Edward Boykin was also slain, and another man was wounded. The gunman, Marcus Chennault of Dayton, Ohio, was a cult member who had come to Atlanta hoping to kill the Rev. Martin Luther King Sr. (known as "Daddy King"); Chennault believed black Christian ministers were deceiving African Americans. In the aftermath of the tragedy, Mayor Maynard Jackson said, "Never have I seen a family suffer so much for so long and yet give such brilliant leadership." Chennault was convicted of the murders; his death sentence was later commuted to life in prison. Following a stroke, Chennault died in August 1995. He was 44.

The King Center's exhibition hall contains a permanent display of photographs and memorabilia of Dr. King's public and private life. Freedom Hall is a space for meetings and other gatherings. The center's library and archives house the world's largest collection of primary information on the civil rights movement. There is no charge to visit Freedom Hall. It's open daily from 9 AM to 5 PM; during the summer, hours are extended to 6 PM. See the following entry for parking information.

The Martin Luther King Jr. National Historic Site
450 Auburn Ave. N.E. • (404) 331-5190

The 42-acre Martin Luther King Jr. National Historic Site encompasses the King Center and the King Birth Home on Auburn Avenue. The visitors center has exhibits about Dr. King and Atlanta as well as information on other National Parks in our area and the entire Southeast. Parking has always been lacking in the perpetually busy King district, but the center includes a large parking lot just north of Irwin Street that is one block north of Auburn Avenue.

The National Parks Service conducts guided tours of the King Birth Home daily every hour from 10 AM to 5 PM. The tour is free, but visitors must obtain a ticket at the National Parks Service office. The site is closed on Christmas and New Year's days. Call (404) 331-6922 for information.

Margaret Mitchell House
990 Peachtree St. • (404) 249-7012

Gone With the Wind was not the first novel about the Civil War, and few serious scholars place it at the pinnacle of Southern literature. But along the road to becoming the most popular novel of all time, Margaret Mitchell's compelling masterpiece created an indelible mark on history. As a book and as a movie, *Gone With the Wind* continues to influence the way Southerners, Northerners and people around the world view Atlanta, the South and the Civil War.

On May 16, 1997, after 10 years of renovations that included two fires, the Margaret Mitchell House opened as the city's tribute to its most famous author. It was listed on the National Register of Historic Places the year before it opened.

From 1925 to 1932, Mitchell and her husband, John Marsh, rented a modest apartment on the first floor of the building on the southwest corner of Peachtree and 10th streets. It was here, typing at a table she used as a desk, that Mitchell created her unforgettable characters. Abandoned for years and occupying coveted Peachtree Street real estate, the apartment house was slated for destruction in 1988 when a board of distinguished Atlantans rallied to preserve it.

Tourism officials report they annually receive more than one million inquiries about the novelist and her novel, and visitors were invariably astonished at the city's apparent lack of regard for the book's birthplace. In September 1994, while its roof was covered with thousands of inflated rubber gloves containing written messages urging world peace (a conceptual art piece created for the Arts Festival of Atlanta), the house was badly damaged in a mysterious fire. The long road to save the building Mitchell affectionately called "The Dump" seemed to have reached a brick wall.

But, as Scarlett taught us, "tomorrow is another day." Help arrived in the form of a $5 million donation from Daimler-Benz, the Germany-based maker of Mercedes Benz cars. In his announcement, chairman Edzard Reuter

Photo: The World of Coca-Cola Atlanta

Track the past, present and future endeavors of Coca-Cola
at The World of Coca-Cola Atlanta.

explained the South's growing importance to his company: "About 6,000 Americans will be part of the Daimler-Benz family by 1997 in just that one region of the United States. That, in itself, is reason enough for our social and cultural involvement in Atlanta, the growing business capital of the South."

In the project, Mitchell's apartment was restored and decorated with period furniture. Her original Remington portable typewriter is on loan from the Fulton County Public Library, as is her Pulitzer Prize. The remainder of the 10-unit building was gutted, remodeled and modernized for use as meeting and exhibit space. A separate visitors' center includes retail space, a video of Mitchell's story and photo galleries. There are two landscaped gardens designed to accommodate events.

Ironically, this section of Peachtree Street figured tragically in the final chapter of Mitchell's life. Three blocks north of her old apartment on August 11, 1949, Mitchell and Marsh (on their way to see the British art film *A Canterbury Tale*) were walking across Peachtree at the unmarked 13th Street crossing when a speeding car appeared. Mitchell panicked, screamed and bolted back across Peachtree toward her parked car. As he swerved left to miss the couple, the driver struck the retreating Mitchell directly; Marsh was unharmed.

Mitchell died on August 16th at Grady Memorial Hospital. Her funeral service was held at H.M. Patterson & Son's Spring Hill funeral home, Spring at 10th streets. The cortege followed the same route as the December 15, 1939, parade when 300,000 people packed Atlanta's streets to celebrate the world premiere of *Gone With the Wind* and get a glimpse of its stars. Mitchell and Marsh, who died in 1952, are buried at Oakland Cemetery.

The house is open daily from 9 AM to 4 PM. The last tour starts at 4 PM; allow 40 minutes. Admission is $6 for adults; $5 for seniors and youth ages 7 to 17; children 6 and younger are free. The museum shop is open an hour after the last tour. Group tours and special events rentals are available.

Oakland Cemetery
248 Oakland Ave. • (404) 688-2107

Almost in the shadows of downtown's skyscrapers lies one of Atlanta's most serene places: shaded, hilly Oakland Cemetery. In 1850 city leaders purchased six acres of land east of the city limits for a municipal burial ground. This was in keeping with the rural cemetery movement of the time that held a single large graveyard established on a city's outskirts was preferable to a plethora of church or private burial grounds scattered throughout the town.

Very nearly every person who died in Atlanta between 1850 and 1884 (when Westview Cemetery opened) was buried at Oakland, whose brick walls eventually came to enfold 88 acres. Majestic oaks and some of the oldest magnolias in Atlanta line its narrow lanes. Here are the unmarked graves of black and white paupers; here also are the stunning monuments and private mausoleums of the city's wealthiest families. In the years before Atlanta established public parks, families picnicked and relaxed here on weekend afternoons. Oakland's central road was once known as Old Hunter Street. Hunter Street is now Martin Luther King Jr. Drive, which begins at Oakland's front gate.

As you enter Oakland, the cemetery's oldest section lies just to your right and left. Above the door to his mausoleum, a life-size statue of businessman Jasper Newton Smith sits in a chair facing downtown. Even in death, Smith is without a tie; he hated ties and refused to wear one. Also in this section is the grave of Martha Lumpkin Compton, daughter of Gov. Wilson Lumpkin, in whose honor pre-Atlanta was briefly called Marthasville. Along the Memorial Drive wall lies the grave of golfing legend Bobby Jones. Here you may see the occasional golf tee and ball left by a fellow duffer in lieu of flowers.

In the two Jewish sections, most graves are closely spaced, and many monuments have Hebrew inscriptions. Rich's department store founders Emanuel and Morris Rich are buried here. Following Jewish tradition, some visitors bring small stones as tokens of respect and place them on the headstones.

"CSA" (Confederate States Army) is inscribed on the headstones of the 3,723 soldiers who lie buried in the Confederate section, which includes the remains of 20 Yankees who died in area hospitals. Of special interest in this section is the Monument to the Confederate Dead — an obelisk of Stone Mountain granite, it was once the tallest structure in Atlanta. Also, the Confederate Lion, an image of a mortally wounded lion, was carved from a single block of Georgia marble and is dedicated to the memory of the unknown Confederate dead. In the northeast corner of the cemetery along the railroad tracks are the graves of paupers and the marked and unmarked graves of thousands of people, both enslaved and free. The black section contains only a single mausoleum — that of real estate broker Antoine Graves.

Margaret Mitchell's grave is Oakland's most frequently visited site, but it's not easy to find since the famous author requested a plain headstone. To locate Mitchell's plot, go to the west side of the large white tower building (the cemetery office) at the center of Oakland and face the western wall (along Oakland Avenue). Nearby you'll see the large obelisk of another Mitchell family near the end of a lane. Follow this lane about halfway to the cemetery's western wall. Mitchell's plot will be on your left, marked by four cone-shaped shrubs. The headstone reads "Mitchell" on the eastern side and "Marsh" on the western side. The inscription above the author's grave reads simply "Margaret Mitchell Marsh."

Over the years, the elements and, most regrettably, vandals have taken their toll on Oakland, which is listed on the National Register of Historic Places. But happily the city of Atlanta, along with dedicated volunteers, is restoring this Victorian treasure plot by plot. In the "Adopt-a-Plot" program, individuals assume responsibility for abandoned grave sites, clearing away weeds and planting greenery and flowers that were typical of the era of burial.

A helpful $1 brochure from the cemetery

INSIDERS' TIP

The oldest buildings in downtown Atlanta are the Georgia Railroad Freight Depot at the eastern end of Underground Atlanta, built in 1869, and the Shrine of the Immaculate Conception at the corner of Martin Luther King Jr. Drive and Central Avenue, built in 1873.

office will assist you in locating graves and sections of interest. From March through October, a guide leads a tour of Oakland at 10 AM and 2 PM on Saturdays and at 2 PM on Sundays. The tour is $3 for adults, $2 for seniors and $1 for students and children. You are permitted to drive around Oakland, but proceed slowly and only on the asphalt-paved roads. Stone rubbings are prohibited; photography and sketching are encouraged. From the King Memorial MARTA station, walk south on Grant Street; go left on Martin Luther King Jr. Drive, which leads directly to the main gate.

Rhodes Hall

Georgia Trust for Historic Preservation, 1516 Peachtree St. N.W. • (404) 885-7800

Lavish Victorian-era mansions once lined parts of Peachtree Street, but very few remain today. One that has survived is Rhodes Hall, built in 1902-1904 by furniture tycoon Amos G. Rhodes. He asked architect Willis Denny to design the home in the style of the Rhineland castles Rhodes had seen in Europe. The result is a most unusual, eclectic, Romanesque mansion.

The house's most imposing feature, however, is not European at all, but distinctly Southern. As a boy growing up in Kentucky during the Civil War, Rhodes often saw both Yankee and Confederate troops. For his mansion, he commissioned a series of elaborate painted and stained-glass windows as a memorial to the Confederacy. In nine panels the windows show Jefferson Davis' inauguration, the firing on Fort Sumter, Stonewall Jackson at Manassas and Robert E. Lee at Appomattox. The windows curve around the massive carved mahogany staircase between the first and second floors.

Mr. Rhodes died in 1928; the following year, his family deeded the home to the state of Georgia. It was listed on the National Register of Historic Places in 1974. The Georgia department of Archives and History were housed in the mansion from 1931 to 1965. The original 150-acre estate has been reduced to a single acre. Since 1983 the mansion has been the headquarters for the Georgia Trust for Historic Preservation; it's also available as a rental reception facility. Rhodes Hall is open to the public Monday through Friday from 11 AM to 4 PM, Sunday noon to 3 PM. Admission is $3 per person.

SciTrek

395 Piedmont Ave. N.E. • (404) 522-5500

SciTrek, Atlanta's science and technology museum, is a hands-on interactive museum that allows visitors to explore science, math and technology in fun and interesting ways that relate these disciplines to everyday life. Lift a race car engine with one hand, whisper to a friend on the other side of the room or freeze your shadow on the wall. All this and more awaits you at SciTrek, a place that's entertaining and informative for both adults and kids.

Permanent displays at SciTrek include a 40-foot-tall lighted replica of the Eiffel Tower made of Erector set pieces that officially joined SciTrek's permanent exhibit collection on Bastille Day (July 14), 1993. The SciTrek Amateur Radio Station (STARS) lets users reach radio communicators worldwide. STARS is staffed by volunteer ham radio operators who help visitors use the station. SciTrek features an Information Petting Zoo, a series of exhibit stations that allow visitors to get hands-on experience with new multimedia, computer and Internet technologies. A section of Simple Machines is full of levers and pulleys as well as the people-by-the-pound scale.

Other permanent exhibit stations include Electric Magnetic Junction that lets you close a circuit with your own body, take a ride in an electric taxi and witness a 1,500-volt electrical discharge; Mind's Eye, a perception and illusion exhibit that lets you explore the range and limits of human senses; and The Color Factory where you can play with electrons and photons to produce an array of hues and split a beam of white light into a rainbow of colors.

Kidspace is a special play area where two-to seven-year-olds can make music, face paint, or build a foam house while learning science principals through play.

SciTrek is open Monday through Saturday, 10 AM to 5 PM, and Sunday, noon to 5 PM. Admission costs $7.50 for adults and $5 for kids 3 to 17, college students with ID, senior citizens and military personnel. Children younger than 3 and teachers with ID are admitted free. If you're coming with a group of 12 or more, make reservations two weeks in advance; special group rates apply.

Southern Christian Leadership Conference National Office
334 Auburn Ave. N.E. • (404) 522-1420

Founded in 1965 by Dr. Martin Luther King Jr. and others, the SCLC continues to fight for civil rights under the leadership of current president Dr. Joseph E. Lowery. The group's Auburn Avenue national headquarters is a working office (not a tourist attraction), but visitors are welcome to stop in, examine the historic photos from the civil rights movement and take photos of their own. The office is open from 9 AM to 5 PM Monday through Friday.

Underground Atlanta
Peachtree at Alabama Sts. S.W.
• (404) 523-2311

Want to hear a Dixieland band, buy a flag, quiz a fortune teller, feast your eyes on fossils or watch candy makers in action? All that and more awaits you at Underground Atlanta! In the heart of downtown, covering six city blocks, Underground is a must-see. The historic birthplace of downtown Atlanta, Underground resulted from our city's growth.

By the turn of the century, Railroad Gulch, a tangle of rail lines running through the center of town, had emerged as a major hazard, tying up traffic at busy intersections and endangering pedestrians' lives. Bridges over the tracks provided a temporary solution, but by the 1920s it was clear that Atlanta had to separate itself from its railroad tracks.

A viaduct project completed in 1929 placed most of Atlanta's original town-center streets underground. Businesses moved aboveground, many using their original first floors and basements as warehouses. Gradually, those lower floors were abandoned, and Old Atlanta decayed.

In 1969, the carefully restored Victorian-era buildings of old Atlanta once again bustled with activity. Underground Atlanta opened as an entertainment complex that would empha-size the area's historical aspects while providing a much-needed downtown party zone. A rousing success at first, that Underground Atlanta gradually succumbed to an economic recession, closing in the early '80s. In the true phoenix-rising spirit of Atlanta, community leaders vowed to rebuild.

The current complex, which opened in 1989, lets you touch Atlanta's history while enjoying its present. With retail and specialty shops, a food court, restaurants, a museum, colorful pushcart vendors, nightclubs, live concerts, street performers, galleries, murals and sculpture, Underground Atlanta offers an eclectic cornucopia of fun and excitement.

Underground Atlanta is easily accessible from I-75, I-85 and I-20. If you're riding MARTA, get off at the Five Points station, which has a pedestrian tunnel to the complex. Two parking decks adjacent to the project provide 1,250 parking spaces. The complex is open Monday through Saturday from 10 AM to 9:30 PM and Sunday from noon to 6 PM. Hours may be extended in the summer. Restaurants and clubs stay open until midnight and beyond. See our Shopping and Nightlife chapters for more on Underground Atlanta.

Westview Cemetery
1680 Westview Dr. S.W. • (404) 755-6611

In 1884 a private corporation purchased the land for Westview Cemetery. This enormous graveyard comprises some 600 acres, of which 300 are yet to be developed. Within Westview's walls are 22 miles of paved roads. During the Civil War, the city's western siege line passed through Westview's rolling hills; a fragment of Confederate breastwork remains.

Although other mausoleums have grown larger through additions, Westview Abbey is the largest mausoleum ever built from a single set of plans: It has spaces for 11,444 entombments. Its exotic design suggests a Medieval Italian monastery, and it is finished in 35 variet-

---

INSIDERS' TIP

The Candler Building (Peachtree Street at John Wesley Dobbs Avenue; built in 1906) is decorated with likenesses of Shakespeare, Raphael, Buffalo Bill Cody, Cyrus McCormick, Georgia writers Joel Chandler Harris and Sidney Lanier, and Asa Candler's parents carved in marble.

ies of marble. Twenty-seven stained-glass panels depict the life of Christ. The hushed and shadowy chapel, with its marble floors and stained-glass windows, is especially opulent.

Well-known persons buried at Westview include journalists Joel Chandler Harris, Henry Grady and Ralph McGill; Coca-Cola's leaders Asa G. Candler and Robert W. Woodruff; and Atlanta mayors I.N. Ragsdale and William B. Hartsfield. A free map of the cemetery is available in the office near the main gate.

To reach Westview from downtown, take I-20 W. to Ashby Street, turn left, then turn right at the second light onto Ralph David Abernathy Boulevard. Stay on Abernathy when it bears right and follow it a little more than .75 mile; you'll see Westview's entrance to your left. An alternate route is to take Westview Drive from the Atlanta University Center area directly to the cemetery's front gate.

The World of Coca-Cola Atlanta
55 Martin Luther King Jr. Dr. S.W.
• **(404) 676-5151**

Atlanta citizens have been swilling Coca-Cola since Dr. Pemberton first concocted the marvelous elixir in 1886. Legions of us went into mourning during the regrettable New Coke debacle of 1985. Since we're so loyal to Coke, it's fitting that our city boasts a museum dedicated to the world's favorite soft drink.

The World of Coca-Cola tells the story of Coke's past, present and future. You can view the largest collection of Coca-Cola memorabilia ever assembled, a nostalgic array of items dating from Coke's inception. A kinetic sculpture presents a whimsical facsimile of the early bottling process. Interactive video stations tell Coca-Cola history in five-year vignettes, and a film highlights Coke's international character, emphasizing that people the world over agree: Coke is the real thing.

The pavilion houses a replica of a 1930s soda fountain where an old-fashioned soda jerk demonstrates how Coke was prepared way back when. Time marches on as the ultramodern futuristic fountain shows. Here, sprays of Coke products shoot across the room into paper cups. It's really cool!

In the International Video Lounge, sample an array of international sodas the Coca-Cola company distributes — from the delicate apri-cot taste of Japan's Vegita Beta to the tangy Beverly from Italy. Watch international TV while you sip. Other fun features of The World of Coca-Cola include vintage TV ads, radio jingles, old vending machines and an array of Coke bottles from around the world.

At the end of your tour (for which you should allot at least an hour and a half) you exit through a shop jam-packed with Coca-Cola merchandise. Bring home an authentic Coca-Cola souvenir for a friend or family member. Choose from hats, T-shirts, sweatshirts, Coke trays, glasses, pencils and dancing Coke cans, to name a few.

The World of Coca-Cola averages a million visitors each year. Next to Underground Atlanta, it's hard to miss. A big red Coca-Cola globe dangles 18 feet above the entrance. When you call the previously listed number, a recorded message gives detailed directions, whether you're traveling by car or on MARTA.

The Coca-Cola pavilion opens for self-guided tours every day of the week. Monday through Saturday, The World of Coca-Cola opens at 10 AM; last admission is at 8:30 PM. Sunday hours run from noon to 6 PM (last admission at 5 PM). The pavilion closes 4th of July, Thanksgiving, Christmas Eve, Christmas Day, New Year's Day, the second Sunday in January (for maintenance) and Easter.

Admission is $6.00 for adults, $4 for seniors 55 and older and $3 for children 6 to 12. Kids younger than five enter free with an adult. If you just want to shop, tell them at the information desk and they'll let you enter the store without a ticket.

The Wren's Nest
1050 Ralph David Abernathy Blvd. S.W.
• **(404) 753-7735**

Joel Chandler Harris was a teenager during the Civil War. There is some evidence to suggest that his mother, a seamstress, may have cleverly altered his age to keep him from serving in the Confederate forces. At the Turnwold plantation near Harris' hometown of Eatonton, Georgia, about 70 miles east of Atlanta off I-20 (see our Getaways chapter), the young Harris learned the printing trade and spent many hours listening wide-eyed to an elderly slave, George Terrell, who amused the boy with folk tales and fables of African origin.

Harris' printing background led him into journalism. After a stint at *The Macon Telegraph*, he went to work at *The Atlanta Constitution*, where, in 1877, he was asked to write a story in dialect. (Such pieces were popular features and continued to appear in some Southern newspapers as late as the 1960s.) He called upon memories of his happy boyhood hours with Terrell and penned a story in which kindly Uncle Remus fascinates a young boy with a fable about plucky Br'er Rabbit. Harris' work instantly resonated with both black and white readers, many of whom recalled similar tales from their childhoods.

Not content to rely on his memory alone, Harris meticulously researched the folk tales, eventually collecting more than 200 of them. Although the dialect in the stories understandably makes some modern-day readers uncomfortable, many scholars credit Harris, a charter member of the American Folklore Society, with preserving a fragile literary heritage that otherwise might have been lost.

In 1881 Harris and family rented a five-room West End farmhouse that had been built shortly after the Civil War. He bought the house in 1883 and added several rooms. One day, when Harris discovered that tiny wrens had built a nest in his mailbox, the house got its nickname. The shy and gentle Harris wrote many of his stories in his "summer living room" (the broad front porch), and folks enjoyed riding by to glimpse the famous author at work. Harris died in 1908; the Uncle Remus Memorial Association operated the house from 1913 to 1984.

In 1984 the Joel Chandler Harris Association took over and began painstakingly restoring the house to its original condition. Today The Wren's Nest is again as it was when Harris lived there. On display are original and foreign editions of his works and some of the many gifts he was sent by admiring readers, including a stuffed great horned owl from President Theodore Roosevelt, whose mother was from Roswell, Georgia, and who entertained Harris at a White House dinner.

The Wren's Nest is open Tuesday through Saturday from 10 AM to 4 PM and Sunday from 1 to 4 PM. Tours last about an hour. The last tour begins at 4 PM. Admission is $6 for adults, $4 for seniors and teens and $3 for children 4 to 12. The tours last about one hour. Storytelling is often an added attraction; $4 is charged per person. Stories are told on Saturdays at 2 PM from September through May and at 11:30 AM, 12:30 PM and 1:30 PM from mid-June to mid-August. There's a small shop with lots of Uncle Remus books and gifts.

Zoo Atlanta
Grant Park, 800 Cherokee Ave. S.E.
• **(404) 624-5600**

Zoo Atlanta, in historic Grant Park, is one of the 10 oldest zoos in continuous operation in the United States. Founded in 1889 the zoo eventually fell into a state of disrepair. A multimillion dollar redevelopment project begun in 1985 has made profound changes, catapulting Zoo Atlanta into *Good Housekeeping* magazine's 1994 list of "10 Great Zoos" in the nation. The zoo's administration plays a preeminent role in nationwide zoo management and in worldwide efforts on behalf of endangered animals and the environment.

The zoo creates naturalistic environments that mimic the natural habitats of more than 250 species from all over the world. Many threatened and endangered animals call Zoo Atlanta home, including red pandas, high-climbing orangutans, Sumatran tigers, black rhinos, African elephants, Komodo monitors, big-mouthed African dwarf crocodiles, a Japanese giant salamander and western lowland gorillas, including Atlanta favorite Willie B. and his offspring, Kudzoo. (By the way, the big ape's name is a playful tribute to William B. Hartsfield, the forward-looking mayor who helped ready Atlanta for the jet age.)

Willie B. and his cronies hang out in the Ford African Rain Forest, a one-and-a-half-acre habitat that also houses the Monkeys of Makokou exhibit, where drill baboons and mona monkeys forage in tropical foliage and climb a man-made tree. Visitors can view the rain forest from a number of viewing stations, including the Sanaga Overlook, a walk-through aviary full of colorful African birds. Other species cavort in such areas as Flamingo Plaza, the Orangutans of Ketambe, the Sumatran Tiger Forest and the 5-acre Masai Mara, a savannah/grassland that simulates East African terrain. It's home to lions, rhinos, ostriches, giraffes, zebras, gazelles, impalas, white storks and crowned cranes. A moat separates Masai Mara's black rhino exhibit from the public, allowing close-up viewing.

To reach Zoo Atlanta from downtown, take I-20 E. to Exit 26. Turn right off Boulevard. You'll find Zoo Atlanta 1.5 miles away on the right. Park free at lots on Boulevard and Cherokee Avenue. On MARTA, take the 97-Cherokee Avenue bus from the Five Points Station. The zoo opens from 10 AM to 5:30 PM daily, but the last tickets are sold at 4:30 PM. Hours are extended during the summer and on weekends. The zoo closes on New Year's Day, Thanksgiving and Christmas. Admission costs $9 for adults, $6.50 for senior citizens and $5.50 for children 3 to 11. Kids younger than 3 and Zoo members get in free. Stroller rentals are $4 for a single and $7 for a double plus a $2 refundable deposit. Wheelchairs are available for free.

Be sure to get a schedule at the gate of the daily feeding schedule. Feeding times are when you get the best view of the animals. This is especially important in the summertime when the heat keeps the animals sitting far away in the shade. (See the Kidstuff chapter for more activities offered at the Zoo.)

Beyond Atlanta

Cobb County

Confederate Cemetery
Corner of N. 120 Loop and Cemetery St., Marietta • no phone

Established in 1863, this cemetery holds the remains of more than 3,000 Confederate soldiers buried in graves arranged by home state. Most of the soldiers fell in the fighting around Kennesaw and Marietta. The cemetery is always open.

Kennesaw Civil War Museum
2829 Cherokee St., Kennesaw
• (770) 427-2117

The bizarre Civil War railroad adventure that took place in this tiny town has been the subject of two famous motion pictures: Buster Keaton's *The General* and Walt Disney's *The Great Locomotive Chase*. On April 12, 1862, in

the town of Big Shanty, now called Kennesaw, a party of Union spies led by James J. Andrews stole the locomotive *General* while its conductor and crew were breakfasting nearby. They absconded northward on the Western & Atlantic line with the intention of burning bridges and cutting the rail line to Chattanooga.

Their plan might have succeeded but for the General's conductor, Capt. William Fuller, and his crew, who gave furious chase on foot, on a push car and on three different locomotives. Finally, running the locomotive *Texas* in reverse, Fuller and his men caught up to the General above Ringgold, Georgia, before the raiding party could burn the targeted bridges. Of the captured raiders, some escaped to Union lines; others were held as prisoners of war until the following year; seven were executed by hanging at the present intersection of Memorial Drive and Park Avenue in Atlanta; Andrews was hanged at the present intersection of Juniper and Third streets in Midtown.

In 1972, following a legal battle over its ownership that went all the way to the U.S. Supreme Court, the *General* steamed into an old cotton gin that had been newly renovated as its permanent home at the Kennesaw Civil War Museum, in the center of town off Exit 118 of I-75 N. The museum tour includes numerous descriptive exhibits and a narrated slide presentation. Open Monday through Saturday, 9:30 AM to 5:30 PM; Sunday, noon to 5:30 PM. Admission is $3 for adults, $2.50 for seniors and AAA members and $1.50 for kids 7 to 15; children 6 and younger are free.

The reverse-racing *Texas* is on permanent display in the lobby of the Atlanta Cyclorama.

Kennesaw Mountain National Battlefield Park
905 Kennesaw Mountain Dr., Kennesaw
• (770) 427-4686

In the spring and summer of 1864, the armies of U.S. Gen. William Sherman and Confederate Gen. Joseph Johnston played a deadly game of cat and mouse across north Georgia. Each time Sherman encountered strong Confederate lines, his troops would swing wide around them in a flanking maneuver, forcing the Confederates to drop back and retrench — a pattern that brought the fighting ever-closer to Atlanta.

When the Union troops reached Kennesaw Mountain, they found the Confederates strongly entrenched in superbly prepared fortifications. Sherman ordered an assault on these Confederate positions and was bloodily rebuffed. He then resumed his flanking strategy, and the Rebels, on July 2, were forced to abandon their fortifications and fall back yet again.

Today the Kennesaw battlefield is preserved as part of a 2,884-acre National Park with 16 miles of hiking trails featuring troop movement maps, historical markers, monuments, cannon emplacements and preserved trenchworks. In the visitors center you'll find a good selection of Civil War books for sale and a slide presentation that explains the Atlanta Campaign and the importance of the area's several battles.

On weekdays you can drive your own car to the top of the mountain. Due to the high volume of visitors, the mountain road is closed to private vehicles on weekends for much of the year, but there's a free shuttle bus to the top every 30 minutes beginning at 9:30 AM and ending at 6 PM. From the summit on a clear day, you can easily see downtown Atlanta, Decatur and Stone Mountain. To preserve the fragile mountain ecology, hikers must stay on trails or roadways. The possession or use of metal detectors on park grounds is illegal. The park is free and open daily to the public from 8 AM till 8:30 PM. From Atlanta, take I-75 N. to Exit 116 and follow the signs.

Marietta Museum of History
1 Depot St., Marietta • (770) 528-0431

Open less than three years, the city museum is housed in an elegant building that was once a hotel. Volunteers renovated the second level for exhibits and displays. A general exhibit of Marietta history features artifacts that were donated by residents, and it changes regularly as new donations arrive. View the displays and visit the small gift shop Tuesdays through Saturdays from 11 AM to 4 PM. Admission is $2 per person.

Marietta National Cemetery
500 Washington Ave., Marietta
• (770) 428-5631

More than 18,000 veterans, from the Civil War through Desert Storm, are buried in this 25.3-acre cemetery. Some 10,000 known and 3,000 unknown Civil War soldiers are interred here.

Six Flags Over Georgia
7561 Six Flags Rd. S.W. at I-20 W.
• (770) 948-9290

"A World of Fun, Not a World Away!" is a fitting motto for this sprawling family-oriented theme park 12 miles west of downtown Atlanta. Thrills, chills and excitement abound in more than 88 acres of attractions divided into eight themed areas that highlight the historical heritage of our region.

But to heck with history — the real fun at Six Flags lies in the delicious terror of some truly spectacular rides. Thrill to the whipsawing motion of monster roller-coasters — the Great American Scream Machine, the Mind Bender, the Dahlonega Mine Train, the Georgia Cyclone, the Ninja and the venomous Viper, which sends you from 0 to 60 miles in six seconds through a 360-degree elliptical loop, up a 70-degree incline, then does it all again, backwards. Yikes! Perhaps you favor that suspended-in-space feeling. If so, the Looping Starship, the Great Gasp parachute drop and the Free Fall, which simulates the feeling of falling from a 10-story building, are for you.

If water rides are your thing, you'll find plenty of fun on Ragin' River, where you can splash down contoured water channels in a two-person inflatable boat, and the Log Flume, a cool trip through chutes modeled after a feature of Georgia's early logging camps. Thunder River re-creates the thrill of whitewater rafting, and Splashwater Falls sends you racing down a roaring 50-foot waterfall. Be sure to wear something that can drip dry!

But Six Flags isn't just rides; it's show business, too. The Batman Stunt Spectacular takes place in a re-creation of Gotham City and features rockets, explosions and other daring exploits familiar to fans of the Caped Crusader. Other shows include the Wildwest Comedy Gunfight Show, sing-alongs on the Rabun Gap Stage and a nostalgia fest at the Remember When Drive-In. See a contemporary country music review at The Crystal Pistol Music Hall, or take in a concert at the Southern Star Amphitheater, which hosts a full season of concerts featuring top performers from country, rock and contemporary Christian music. There's usually an additional charge for ampitheater concerts.

You'll find plenty of food stands, restaurants and souvenir shops scattered throughout the park. A games area offers a variety of challenging games of skill.

Take I-20 W. to the Six Flags Exit. If you're riding MARTA, take the westbound line from the Five Points Station and get off at the Hightower Station. From there, MARTA bus No. 201 will take you to the park.

Six Flags is open Saturday and Sunday from early March through mid-May, except for spring break week in early April when the park opens every night to accommodate fun seekers on vacation from school. Daily operations go from mid-May to early September when the Saturday and Sunday schedule resumes until the end of the month. In October the park adds Friday nights to its schedule for the October Fright Fest. The park opens at 10 AM; closing times vary.

Admission costs $34 for adults, $23 for children 3 to 9 and seniors 55 and older. A two-day Best Buy pass costs $39 and entitles you to admission any two days during the operating season.

For information on group rates for 15 or more people, call (770) 739-3430. Admission prices include unlimited use of all rides, shows and attractions; you pay extra for parking, food, souvenirs and some games of skill. Parking is $6 per car.

DeKalb County

Georgia's Stone Mountain Park
U.S. Hwy. 78 east to Stone Mountain Village • (770) 498-5690

The world's largest exposed mass of granite, Stone Mountain, stands 825 feet high, rises 1,683 feet above sea level and covers 583 acres of rolling plateau. Formed when molten lava began pushing upward through the earth's surface, Stone Mountain took 300 million years to emerge in its present state.

Stone Mountain Park — encompassing 3,200 acres of lakes, woodlands and attractions — surrounds the mountain and hosts millions of visitors each year.

Stone Mountain boasts the world's largest bas-relief carving on the mountain's north face. The 90-foot-high by 190-foot-wide sculpture depicts Confederate war heroes Robert E. Lee, "Stonewall" Jackson and Jefferson Davis, all on horseback. The project, conceived in 1912, took more than 50 years to complete due to creative differences and technical problems.

In case you ever need them for a trivia game, here are a few colossal facts about the memorial carving:

• Its area is three acres, or more than a city block.

• At its deepest, the carving sinks 42 feet into the mountain's surface.

• Lee's horse Traveler is 147 feet long; a six-foot man can stand comfortably inside the mouth of Davis's horse Kentucky.

• To celebrate the memorial's completion, 20 people ate lunch on Lee's shoulder!

Although no major Civil War battles were fought on the soil of Stone Mountain, Sherman destroyed the Georgia Railroad Line between Stone Mountain and Decatur during his march to the sea. The Union army came within close range when it burned New Gibraltar, the small town at the base of the mountain. Today the rebuilt town is known as the Village of Stone Mountain.

Spend a day at Stone Mountain Park. Diverse recreational, leisure, historic and scenic attractions ensure something for everyone. Athletic types will enjoy the 15 miles of scenic sidewalks for walkers and joggers as well as the nature trails set aside for hiking. A 1.3-mile trail leads to the top of the mountain where you're rewarded with a panoramic view of the Atlanta metro area and a glimpse of the Appalachian Mountains. If you want the view without the work, ride the Mountaintop Skylift to the huge rock's summit.

On the skylift, you'll be whisked up and will pass right by the memorial carving on the quiet ride to the summit. There you'll enjoy a sweeping view that includes Atlanta and Kennesaw Mountain to the west and the Olympic Velodrome to the south.

Stone Mountain was designated the Olympic Sports Park for the 1996 Olympic Games. The park boasts a 36-hole championship golf course named one of the top-25 municipal courses in the United States by *Golf Digest* (read more about this in our Parks and Recreation chapter). The park's Sports Center offers 18 holes of minigolf, eight lighted tennis courts, batting cages, a game room and bicycle and stroller rental.

Fishing buffs can angle in the park's stocked lake from mid-March through October. The 363-acre Stone Mountain Lake offers swimming and sunning at the beach as well as canoe, rowboat, hydro-bike pedalboat and pontoon rentals. Those who prefer being piloted can traverse the lake aboard an authentic paddlewheel riverboat, the *Scarlett O'Hara*.

Train aficionados will enjoy the Stone Mountain Scenic Railroad. This attraction gives you a 25-minute ride around the base of the mountain in one of three Civil War-era steam trains.

Fans of Robert James Waller will delight in the century-old covered bridge on the site of Stone Mountain's Grist Mill, a rustic structure moved to the park from its original site in Ellijay, Georgia. For history buffs, Confederate Hall houses a 3-D look at the Civil War in Georgia. The Antebellum Plantation emulates a pre-Civil War agricultural establishment with 19 restored and authentically decorated buildings. The Road to Tara Museum, a name taken from one of the several titles Margaret Mitchell originally considered for her best-seller, is a collection of autographed and foreign editions of *GWTW*, movie posters, artists' renderings of key scenes and *GWTW* dolls. The Auto & Music Museum offers an intriguing array of antique automobiles and eclectic musical memorabilia.

On spring and fall weekends and every night from May through Labor Day, Atlantans and visitors enjoy Stone Mountain Park's spectacular Laser Show, a free extravaganza that begins after dark. As the audience relaxes on the park's Memorial Lawn, the mountain's north face lights up with laser-projected stories, special effects and graphic images. Rousing musical accompaniment adds to the drama (see our Festivals and Events chapter).

Special events scheduled throughout the year include Taste of the South food festival in May and the Scottish Highland Games in the fall (see our Festivals and Events chapter for details and other events at Stone Mountain).

Guests can find accommodations at the Colonial-style Stone Mountain Inn (see our Accommodations chapter) or pitch a tent or hook up an RV at the 441-site lakeside campground. The park's Evergreen Conference Center and Resort is a popular destination for meetings and other large indoor events.

Stone Mountain Park is approximately 15 miles east of downtown Atlanta, easily accessible from U.S. Highway 78, also called the Stone Mountain Freeway. The park opens at 6 AM and closes at midnight every day of the year. Attractions open at 10 AM and close at 8 PM during the summer; hours are 10 AM until 5 PM September through May. Attractions close on Christmas Day.

A $6 parking permit buys admission to the park; individual attraction prices are $3.50 for adults and $2.50 for children 3 to 11. Skylift tickets are $4 per adult; $3 per child. The multi-attraction pass (adults, $25; children, $20) buys admission to the Riverboat, the Antebellum Plantation, the Auto & Music Museum, the Wildlife Trails, the Skylift and the Railroad. The multi-attraction pass is nonrefundable and good for the entire year. The park also offers group rates for 25 people or more.

Old Courthouse on the Square
101 E. Court Sq., Decatur • (404) 373-1088

The lovely city of Decatur is 6 miles east of downtown Atlanta. Founded in 1823, it's more than a decade older than its big, noisy neighbor.

It's said that Decatur was considered the terminus point for the Western & Atlantic railroad in the 1830s, but local residents objected, fearing the smoke and general confusion. Instead the railroad line ended at what became Five Points, and the rest, as they say, is history. On July 22, 1864, a skirmish at Decatur's cemetery resulted in one of the few Confederate victories in the fighting around Atlanta.

Decatur, so near the center of the Atlanta metropolitan region, has been able to preserve its village-like atmosphere. The Old Courthouse (so named to distinguish it from the current modern DeKalb County Courthouse) presides over Decatur's central square, site of the first courthouse, a log cabin structure put up in 1823. Surrounding the square are numerous interesting structures from the early

Photo: Georgia's Stone Mountain Park

The world's largest bas-relief carving is at Georgia's Stone Mountain Park.

20th century and even some from before the Civil War.

The Old Courthouse is the home of the DeKalb Welcome Center, (404) 373-1088, and the DeKalb Historical Society, (404) 373-1088.

The Society's museum includes portraits of Baron DeKalb (the French mercenary and Revolutionary War hero for whom the county is named), Commodore Stephen Decatur (a naval hero in the War of 1812 for whom the city is named) and Mary Harris Gay (a Decaturite whose wartime diaries were published as *Life in Dixie During the War*). Two-thirds of what is called the Battle of Atlanta was fought in DeKalb County, and the museum has a Civil War collection that includes weapons, flags and medical equipment. The museum is open Monday through Friday from 9 AM to 4:30 PM.

Fulton County

Bulloch Hall
180 Bulloch Ave., Roswell
• (770) 992-1951, (770) 992-1731

One block west of the Roswell town square, Bulloch Hall is a Greek Revival mansion constructed of aged heart pine and completed in 1840. At the home in 1853, Maj. Bulloch's

daughter Mittie married Theodore Roosevelt Sr.; from their marriage came the future President Teddy Roosevelt, who visited his mother's childhood home in 1905. The senior Roosevelt's other son was the father of Eleanor Roosevelt, the wife of FDR. During her husband's therapeutic visits to Warm Springs, Georgia, Mrs. Roosevelt would sometimes drive to Roswell for a visit at the hall.

Bulloch Hall is open to the public daily. Tours are given on the hour from 10 AM to 2 PM Monday through Saturday and from 1 PM to 3 PM on Sundays. It is also home to guilds that keep alive such crafts as quilting and basketry. Periodic activities include the re-enactment of Mittie's 1853 wedding, Civil War encampments and cannon-firing demonstrations. Admission is $5 for adults and $3 for children 6 to 16.

Chattahoochee Nature Center
9135 Willeo Rd., Roswell • (770) 992-2055

On 127 acres along the banks of the Chattahoochee River, the Chattahoochee Nature Center is an environmental sanctuary with miles of fresh water ponds, wooded uplands and river marshes. The center offers a variety of classes and activities for children and adults. Weekly canoe floats in the summer let families learn basic boating skills while viewing native plants and wildlife. Special Sunday classes during the summer touch on everything from reptiles to how Native Americans used the marsh. You'll learn even more on weekend Naturalist Guided Walks through woodland or river marsh habitats.

Chattahoochee Nature Center stays open year round. Enjoy the gardens, pond studies and nature trails on a nice day any time of year; indoor exhibits entertain and edify when it's too hot or cold to be outdoors. Shop-a-holics will surely find something enticing at the Nature Store.

Chattahoochee Nature Center opens Monday through Saturday, 9 AM to 5 PM; Sundays, noon to 5 PM. Adults pay a $3 admission fee; the cost is $2 for kids and seniors.

Gwinnett County

Gwinnett Historic Courthouse
185 Crogan St., Lawrenceville
• (770) 822-5450

Designed by E.G. Lind in 1885, the Gwinnett County Courthouse evolved in an eclectic combination of Romanesque, Second Empire and WPA styles. It was last an active courthouse in 1988; an extensive renovation and restoration program was completed in 1992.

The courthouse stands on a full block at the center of the Lawrenceville town square and around it are monuments, picnic tables and a gazebo. In their upstairs headquarters, members of the Gwinnett County Historical Society, (770) 822-5174, will gladly give you information on other county attractions and historic sites. Society members staff the office from 9:30 AM to 1 PM Monday through Friday.

Visitors are welcome to explore the courthouse on a self-guided tour Tuesday through Friday from 10 AM to 4 PM. There is no admission charge. The courthouse is available as a rental facility for public and private gatherings both large and small.

Southeastern Railway Museum
3966 Buford Hwy., Duluth • (770) 476-2013

This popular 12-acre outdoor museum has been open since 1970. Train buffs will revel in the displays of more than 90 pieces of retired rolling stock including vintage steam locomotives, Pullmans and historic wooden cars. You can even take a train ride in a restored caboose that traverses the museum's half-mile loop track.

The museum, one block south of Pleasant Hill Road on U.S. Highway 23 (which we locals call Buford Highway), is open every Saturday from 9 AM to 5 PM and the third Sunday of every month from noon to 5 PM. Admission costs $5 for adults and $3 for senior citizens and children. Your admission price pays for train rides.

The Southeastern Railway Museum operates year round. Train rides on the restored cabooses are scheduled April through November. During other months, the trains don't run, and admission is free.

By the end of 1999, the railway will be moving to a new location, about a mile from where it is now. Thanks to a gift of 30 acres donated by a Maryland man, the museum will be expanding to almost three times its present size. The site includes plenty of space for indoor exhibits, as well as three sheds where restorations can be done.

Fun Freebies

Atlanta International Museum of Art and Design
Peachtree Center, Marquis Two, 285
Peachtree Center Ave. • (404) 688-2467

This museum celebrates the craftsmanship of the world's cultures through ethnographic, folk art and design exhibits. See The Arts chapter for more details.

The Atlanta Journal-Constitution
72 Marietta St. • (404) 526-5151

The lobby of the city's only daily newspaper is lined with famous front pages from the past. Check out how the Atlanta press covered the big breaking national news stories as well as local tragedies. Tours of the rest of the building are conducted Monday through Friday at 11:30 AM and 12:30 PM. Allow an hour to view the newsroom, advertising department, layout, composing, press and mail rooms. Tour reservations are required two weeks in advance.

Callanwolde Fine Arts Center
980 Briarcliff Rd. • (404) 872-5338

Originally the home of Howard Candler, the eldest son of Coca Cola's founder, Callanwolde now is a fine arts center. A non-profit foundation directs a variety of arts programs, including dance, drama, painting, photography, pottery, textiles, writing and more. In 1996, just prior to the Olympics, the center was renovated to house the Italian Delegation. New plantings and a restructuring of the greenhouse area were just a few of the changes made.

See The Arts chapter for a complete description of the center's offerings.

Crawford W. Long Museum
550 Peachtree St. N.E. • no phone

In the David Fischer Building of Crawford Long Hospital, a few blocks south of the Fox Theatre on Peachtree Street, this medical museum honors Atlanta legend Dr. Crawford W. Long, who died in 1878. Reputedly the first physician to use anesthesia during surgery, Long was one of the many forward-thinking Atlantans of his time. Tour the fine array of medical tools and accessories from the days of horse-and-buggy doctoring (back when doctors still made house calls)!

The museum is open Monday through Wednesday, 10 AM to 2 PM. There is no direct line to the museum; for more information, call the hospital at (404) 686-4411.

Federal Reserve Bank Monetary Museum
104 Marietta St. • (404) 521-8764

If, like us, you think the next best thing to spending money is looking at money, this museum is for you! Here you'll see the various forms our currency has taken over the decades — from beads to bars of gold — as well as learn about the history of the banking system. View samples of gold coins minted north of Atlanta at Dahlonega, and watch an enlightening 15-minute video, *Inside the Fed*, about how the Federal Reserve System works.

The museum welcomes individuals and small groups anytime, but groups of 10 or more need to call for an appointment. It's open Monday through Friday, 9 AM to 4 PM, except on bank holidays.

The High Museum of Art Folk Art and Photography Galleries
30 John Wesley Dobbs Ave. N.E.
• (404) 577-6940

This multilevel downtown branch of the High Museum showcases photography and folk art. It's open Monday through Friday from 9 AM to 5 PM. See The Arts chapter for a complete description.

Johnny Mercer Exhibit
103 Decatur St. S.E. • (404) 651-2477

Find this exhibit in Special Collections on the eighth floor of Georgia State University's Pullen Library South. Music lovers will enjoy seeing displays of awards, manuscripts, photos and letters from the life of this composer of enduring music. Savannah-born Mercer wrote such standards as "Blues in the Night," "Jeepers Creepers" and "Come Rain or Come Shine." Tour the Johnny Mercer Exhibit Monday through Friday, 8:30 AM to 5 PM, except on university holidays.

Margaret Mitchell Exhibit
Central Library, One Margaret Mitchell Sq.
• (404) 730-1700

This permanent display on the main floor of the library features reproductions of the author's pages from the *Gone With the Wind* manuscript, a movie script, the coat Mitchell wore while volunteering with the Red Cross, her library card and other rare memorabilia. View this exhibit during regular Central Library hours: Monday, Friday and Saturday, 9 AM to 6 PM; Tuesday, Wednesday and Thursday, 9 AM to 8 PM; and Sunday, 2 to 6 PM.

Telephone Museum
675 W. Peachtree St. N.E. • (404) 223-3661

This unusual attraction presents the social and political history of the communications systems we depend on so heavily. In the plaza level of the Southern Bell Center, it's open Monday through Friday from 11 AM to 1 PM.

Gather up your brood —
if you don't have kids,
borrow some — and
head for the fun!

Kidstuff

Just because we call it Kidstuff, don't think adults can't have loud, scary, splashy fun at many of the attractions listed in this chapter. Sports arcades, water parks, museums, wildlife shelters and more beckon youngsters to play, learn and explore. While many of the highlights touched upon here require an admission fee, don't forget that many of Atlanta's attractions are free and fun for folks of all ages.

Many of the activities we list here are staged at venues already mentioned in the more-extensive Attractions chapter. Here are some special highlights the kiddies will enjoy. So gather up your brood — if you don't have kids, borrow some — and head for the fun!

Abernathy Arts Center
254 Johnson Ferry Rd., Sandy Springs
- **(404) 303-6172**

This arts center, a program of the Fulton County Arts Council, offers year-round classes and workshops for kids as well as adults. Youth classes, which are taught in six- to 12-week sessions, cover such topics as oil painting, drawing, wheel pottery and multimedia. One- and two-day workshops include a holiday-themed program in which children learn to make a manger scene or menorah and a printing and stamping workshop that teaches kids how to create designs to print on paper for gift wrap and greeting cards. Similar programs are offered at Arts Council centers in College Park, 4645 Butner Road, (770) 306-3087, and Duluth, 9800 Medlock Bridge Road, (770) 442-0190. Children's workshops run about $25. (Adult sessions range from $80 to $110; seniors receive a 15 percent discount.)

Abracadabra! Children's Theatre at Onstage Atlanta
P.O. Box 54178, Atlanta GA 30308
- **(404) 897-1802**

In its sixth year of operation, Abracadabra! presents popular children's theater works aimed at 3- to 10-year-olds. The 1997-98 season includes performances of such classics as *The Little Mermaid* and *Peter Pan*. Saturday shows are at 10:30 AM and 1:30 PM, Sundays at 1:30 PM. Tickets are $7 for everyone.

Alpharetta Family Golf Center
1360 Upper Hembree Rd., Roswell
- **(770) 740-1674**

This family entertainment center features 70 lighted golf stations, two minigolf courses, driving ranges, softball and baseball batting cages. It's open from 8 AM to 10 PM Sunday through Thursday, 8 AM to 11 PM Friday and Saturday. Miniature golf costs $4.25 for 18 holes, $6 for 36 holes for kids younger than 19 and senior citizens. Adults pay $5.25 for 18 holes and $7 for 36 holes. Batting tokens are $20 for 18, $5 for 4 or $1.50 each (25 pitches per token).

American Adventures
250 N. Cobb Pkwy., Marietta
- **(770) 424-9283**

American Adventures is an eclectic amusement park with appeal to funsters of all ages. You can play outdoor miniature golf, speed around a race track, test your mettle in the arcade, ride the Super Slide or frolic in foam balls. When you're finished with that, there's still the carousel and a train ride. Kids are partial to the Foam Factory, a three-story, interactive arena where 50,000 foam balls are slung around the area.

In summer, the park's open Monday through Saturday from 10 AM to 9 PM and from 11 AM to 9 PM Sunday. Winter hours may vary but generally run from noon to 6 PM daily. Take Exit 113 off I-75 N. to reach American Adventures. Be prepared to pay a $2 parking fee. There's no admission charge, but each attraction costs money. You can pay as you go or opt for one of the economy packages available. All-day fun passes cost $13.99 for kids 4 through 17; parent fun passes are $2.99; toddlers are $4.99. There's no charge for parents of children who need assistance on rides and in the play area.

Atlanta Beach at Clayton County International Park
2300 Hwy. 138 S.E., Jonesboro
• (770) 473-5425

Clayton County operates this 200-acre family water and recreation park that hosted the beach volleyball competition during the 1996 Olympic Games. Frolic on the white sandy beach that circles an 8-acre spring-fed lake, or enjoy minigolf, two water slides, paddle boats, a 13-acre fishing lake and a kiddie pool with a small water slide. The park also features beach volleyball courts, softball fields, picnic tables and pavilions for parties, family reunions and other functions. Atlanta Beach allows no alcohol, no pets and no glass.

Admission is $6.95 for adults; $4.95 for seniors and kids 3 to 12. The beach is open on weekends in May and September from 10 AM to 6 PM; during the summer, the hours are extended — 10 AM to 6 PM Wednesday, Thursday and Friday and 10 AM to 8 PM on Saturday and Sunday. Inclement weather may force the beach to close, so it's best to call ahead.

Atlanta Botanical Garden
1345 Piedmont Ave. N.E., Piedmont Park at the Prado • (404) 876-5859

We described this delightful destination in our Attractions chapter. The Garden Adventure Pack makes a trip to the Atlanta Botanical Garden even more exciting for kids. Designed for children in preschool through 2nd grade or kids in 3rd through 5th grade, the Adventure Pack is a colorful backpack filled with informational materials for school groups and families visiting the Garden.

Kids can check out packs for one-hour periods, year round. They're designed to make exploring the Atlanta Botanical Garden a fun

FYI

Three area codes serve the metro Atlanta area: 404, 770 and 678. Whether you live on Peachtree Street or in New York City, you must dial the code to reach any number in the area. The difference? Outside the area, you must dial "1," then the area code and phone number; inside the area, you need only dial the area code followed by the phone number.

learning experience. The packs come equipped with instructions, a map and various activities to be carried out at 12 different sites around the grounds. Activities range from a scavenger hunt to touching and smelling herbs in the Herb Garden. Parents and teachers can choose the sites they want to visit on the map and plan their route accordingly. Call (404) 876-5859, extension 226, in the ABG Education Department to schedule a self-guided tour with a Garden Adventure Pack. Use of the Adventure Pack is included in garden admission and is best reserved in advance.

The garden is open Tuesday through Sunday, 9 AM to 6 PM, November through March; from April to October, the hours are extended to 7 PM. General admission is $6 for adults, $5 for seniors and $3 for children 6 through 12 and students. Children younger than 6 are admitted free.

Center for Puppetry Arts
1404 Spring St. N.W.
• (404) 873-3391

Kermit the Frog and the late Jim Henson cut the ribbon to officially open this center in 1978. The Center has a collection of more than 900 puppet figures from around the world. The Center's permanent museum exhibit, "Puppets: The Power Of Wonder," allows kids to experience the art of puppetry as it moves into a new age. Interactive discovery boxes let children explore various reactions that their touch can activate. They can also learn a little bit about new technologies via radio-controlled puppets. Children will delight in the re-creation of an Indonesian shadow puppet theater and marvel as a trash can at the entrance rises to form a 9-foot-tall Phoenix. The exhibit also contains a traditional display of puppets from the Center's collection, providing an historical, cross-cultural perspective of puppets as art objects.

Museum admission, purchased individually, costs $4 for kids 2 to 13, students and seniors, $5 for adults. Special exhibits are free with the purchase of any museum admission ticket for the same day. Admission is $2 when purchased in conjunction with any other event.

The Center for Puppetry Arts hosts a family series of performances presenting original adaptations of classic stories and new works in a variety of puppetry styles. These performances run September through May, Monday through Friday at 11 AM and 11:30 AM, Saturday at 11 AM, with an additional performance on Wednesday at 1 PM. Admission costs $6.50 for children ages 2 to 13, students and seniors; adults pay $7.50. (See The Arts chapter for more information.)

The Center also holds Create-A-Puppet workshops for children ages 4 and older; adults are welcome to tag along. Puppet designs are based on themes of the shows being presented in the theater. Puppet workshops run September through May, Monday through Friday at 10 AM and 11:30 AM; Saturday at noon and 2 PM. Workshops are $5 per person if purchased separately, $3 per person with the purchase of a performance or museum ticket for the same day. There is also a $5, preschooler and parents workshop on Saturdays at noon, for which reservations are recommended.

Chattahoochee Nature Center
9135 Willeo Rd., Roswell • (770) 992-2055
More than 55,000 school children visit this center annually. Kidstuff at the Chattahoochee Nature Center includes the chance to view small woodland creatures in the center's wildlife rehabilitation program. Night Owls overnight sleep-ins featuring wildlife workshops, live animal demonstrations and night hikes occur most Friday and Saturday nights from October through May. You must reserve a spot at least one month in advance.

The center also hosts birthday parties, which include nature walks and other activities, for kids ages 4 and older. Summer afternoon children's programs, on themes such as "Don't Bug Me" and "Wet and Slimy" continue the learning begun by the center's after-school programs during the school year. Monthly Young Naturalist's meetings benefit children aged 4 to 11. Those kids can also enjoy non-scary Halloween hikes in October, featuring an educational walk through the woods. Other outings include guided evening canoe floats.

A summer day-camp program, Camp Kingfisher, increases awareness and appreciation of nature and includes traditional outdoor recreation. Weekly sessions run from June through August. Kids from 5 to 12 are eligible for this popular camp, which attracted about 1,500 children in 1997. For more about Chattahoochee Nature Center, see our Attractions chapter.

The Center is open Monday through Saturday, 9 AM to 5 PM and Sunday, noon to 5 PM. Admission is $3 for adults, $2 for children and seniors.

Circus Pizza World
Outlets Mall, 3750 Venture Dr., Duluth
• (770) 622-9900
Kids love to visit Circus Pizza World, especially the two-level supervised play park where two- to ten-year-olds can wind through festively colored tunnels, scoot down spiral slides and pound their way through a punching bag forest. Admittance is $3.95 for children older than 3; $1.95 for one- and two-year-olds.

Circus World also has a midway with 10 minirides and 35 games. Each ride or game requires at least one 25¢ token. Shows in the Jamboree Showroom feature the wacky antics of mechanically animated characters. Hours are from 10 AM to 9 PM Monday through Thursday, 10 AM to 10 PM Friday and Saturday and noon to 7 PM Sunday.

Oh, yes — Circus World serves food, too. Hot dogs, chicken nuggets, sub sandwiches and pizzas are priced from $3.49 to $17.99.

Davidson-Arabia Mountain Nature Preserve
3787 Klondike Rd., Lithonia
• (770) 484-3060
This nature preserve is open to the public every day from 7 AM until dark. Admission is free. Featuring 535 acres of natural area, a gigantic rock outcropping (similar to Stone Mountain), an abandoned rock quarry and a lake, the preserve offers a variety of hiking and fishing opportunities. School and private groups can tour the area by appointment and learn about the endangered plant species that thrive there. Kids can also explore the life cycles of amphibians by observing the resident salamander population. A house on the grounds is

being converted as a nature center for live animals and should be open some time in 1998.

Discovery Zone

3701 Austell Rd., Marietta • (770) 801-9993
Ga. Hwy. 78, Stone Mountain
• (770) 413-5880
730 Holcomb Bridge Rd., Roswell
• (770) 640-8150
824 Barrett Pkwy., Kennesaw
• (770) 528-9399
1956 Mt. Zion Rd., Morrow
• (770) 603-1200

Discovery Zone is a colorful indoor play arena with slides, tubes and balls that kids can jump into and burrow under. A toddler area offers a scaled-down version for kids 3 and younger. Discovery Zone is open from 10 AM to 8 PM Monday through Thursday, 10 AM to 9 PM Friday and Saturday and 11 AM to 7 PM Sunday. Admission costs $6.29 for children 3 to 12; kids younger than 2 get in for $4.19. Parents must accompany children; everyone must keep their socks on at all times, and you can't bring in outside food.

Dixieland Fun Park

1675 Ga. Hwy. 85 N., Fayetteville
• (770) 460-5862

Dixieland Fun Park features go-cart tracks, bumper boats, miniature golf, batting cages and an outdoor sky coaster. The Pavilion has a video arcade, laser tag and a playmaze for little ones.

The park opens weekends after Labor Day through March 1, from 4 PM to midnight Friday, 11 AM to midnight Saturday and 1 PM to 10 PM Sunday. From March 1 through Labor Day, the park is opened every day: noon to 11 PM Monday through Thursday, noon to midnight Friday, 11 AM to midnight Saturday and 1 PM to 11 PM Sunday.

Tickets for rides are $4 each but may be bought in bulk: 10 tickets are $35.00 and 50 tickets are $125.00. It's $5 for laser tag. A full day in the playmaze, for children 9 and younger, costs $5 for the first child and $3 for additional siblings.

Dunwoody Nature Center

5343 Roberts Dr., Dunwoody
• (770) 394-3322

Dunwoody Nature Center, in Dunwoody Park, was founded to develop, improve and preserve Dunwoody Park as a wildlife habitat and outdoor learning center. The park includes hardwood and pine forests, a meadowland, a creek and wetlands. A 1.3-mile discovery path runs through the grounds.

The Center is open Mondays through Fridays from 9 AM to 5 PM. Dunwoody Park is open seven days a week, from sun up to sun down. Admission to both the Center and the park is free.

The Center offers outdoor discovery classes in six-week sessions for kids ages 2 to 10; prices range from $65 to $80, depending on the program, and registration is required. There are also field trips for grades K through 8. Holiday Earth Camp, held in December, teaches campers about worldwide holiday celebrations and allows them to observe nature in winter. The center also schedules special nature festivals, workshops and a Halloween celebration, Bats and Bones. These family programs generally cost about $6 for adults and $4 for children.

Families can join the Center for $35; individuals can join for $25, seniors for $15. Members enjoy discounted rates on classes and programs.

FAO Schwartz

Lenox Square, 3393 Peachtree Rd. N.E.
• (404) 814-1675

There are many fine toy stores and kids' specialty shops in the Atlanta area, but this

---

INSIDERS' TIP

Amusement parks aren't the only place to catch a ride on a carousel. You'll find the horses raring to go on a 30-foot-high merry-go-round inside the Northpoint Mall. Rides are $1 a piece.

one merits a mention simply because FAO Schwartz, which opened at Lenox Square in November 1995, is a mini-version of the store's famous Fifth Avenue location in New York. Features include a rain forest inhabited by a talking dinosaur, toucans, roaring lions and a bicycling Curious George; a book department kids enter by walking through a giant book monster's legs; and the World of Barbie boutique. Other Lenox Square stores of special interest to kids include Warner Bros Studio Store and The Disney Store.

The store is open during regular mall hours: Monday through Saturday from 10 AM to 9 PM, Sunday from noon to 6 PM. Hours are extended during the Christmas holiday season.

Fernbank Museum of Natural History
767 Clifton Rd. N.E. • (404) 378-0127

Fernbank, described more fully in our Attractions chapter, has many exhibits to fascinate both adults and children. Specifically for the small fry, Fernbank provides two bright, colorful environments in which kids can develop their natural curiosity. The Fantasy Forest, for kids 3 to 5, and the Coca-Cola Georgia Adventure, for the 6 to 10 set, teach youngsters about their natural environment through carefully designed quick experiments. Fantasy Forest gives children a chance to try on a bee glove and pick up "pollen balls" to "pollinate" large, brightly colored flowers. Georgia Adventure includes a colorful shrimp boat and simulations of the Chattahoochee River and the Okefenokee Swamp where children can play and pretend to fish. Admittance to both is included in a museum ticket. Note: Sometimes during the school year, the Forest and the Adventure exhibits are reserved for class trips, so it's best to call ahead to make sure they're open to the public.

The museum is open Monday through Saturday, 10 AM to 5 PM, and Sunday, noon to 5 PM. Admission is $8.95 for adults, $7.95 for students and seniors older than 62 and $6.95 for children 3 to 12.

Fernbank Science Center
156 Heaton Park Dr. N.E. • (404) 378-4311

Each weekend, the center offers special

Kids go crazy over Kudzoo, a baby gorilla at Zoo Atlanta.

planetarium shows with terminology and photos geared toward kids. Times are Saturday at 10 AM and 1:30 PM and Sunday at 1:30 PM. Admission is 50¢ per person, for all ages.

The center is open Monday, 8:30 AM to 5 PM; Tuesday through Friday, 8:30 AM to 10 PM; Saturday 10 AM to 5 PM; and Sunday, 1 PM to 5 PM. (See our Attractions chapter for information about the center.)

Georgia's Stone Mountain Park
Exit off U.S. Hwy. 78, Stone Mountain • (770) 498-5600

Stone Mountain offers a diverse array of entertainments for the whole family. Special kidstuff includes a petting zoo, minigolf, water slides at the beach, a playground, softball and baseball batting cages and a train ride around the base of the mountain. During the Christmas holidays, the youngsters will get a kick out of singing carols on the train as it winds its way around several wintry scenes of the North Pole.

The park opens at 6 AM and closes at midnight every day of the year, except Christmas. Attractions open at 10 AM and close at 8 PM during the summer and at 5 PM September through May.

A $6 parking permit buys admission to the park; individual attraction prices are $3.50 for adults and $2.50 for children 3 to 11. (See our Attractions chapter.)

Fun Art Inc.
3101 Roswell Rd., Ste. F-1, Marietta
• (770) 977-3998

You don't need an appointment to be creative here. Open studio hours give kids a chance to play with paints, pottery, pastels and stamp pads; older kids and adults can try their hands at printmaking and paper-mâché. Studio hours are Tuesday through Saturday, 10 AM to 8 PM. Prices per project range from $6 to $10 for unlimited supplies and time.

Fun Art also sponsors Saturday workshops and four-week sessions in drawing, sculpture and painting for kids and adults. Prices start around $60 for all ages.

Gymboree
Holcomb Center, 2880 Holcomb Bridge Rd., Alpharetta • (770) 641-0005
Gwinnett Prado Shopping Center, 2300 Pleasant Hill Rd., Duluth
Fountain Oaks Shopping Center, 4920 Roswell Rd., Sandy Springs
Merchants Walk, 1319 Johnson Ferry Rd., East Cobb County
Town Center Prado, 50 Barrett Pkwy., Kennesaw

For infants through children 5 years old, Gymboree provides once-a-week classes that stimulate kids to explore their abilities. Age-appropriate play programs help kids develop their coordination, improve their self-esteem and socialize with children their own age. Gymboree sessions run throughout the year. Classes are sold in sessions only, not singly, but Gymboree offers free trial classes. One year of Gymboree's weekly classes costs around $450; seven- to 10-week sessions offered only in the summer range from roughly $75 to $95, with a $15 lifetime registration fee for new families. The 45-minute classes are scheduled throughout the day, with the last class at 3:30 PM.

The main number above serves all locations.

The High Museum of Art
1280 Peachtree St. N.E. • (404) 733-4470

The High Museum sponsors family weekend workshops in which kids 6 to 12 and their parents can learn more about art and the creative process. Each Saturday, workshops are held from 10 AM to noon and 1 to 3 PM and include a gallery tour. Reservations are required for these two sessions. The Sunday Studio is a drop-in program that welcomes kids 6 though 12 between 1 and 4 PM for a variety of hands-on art activities.

The museum also hosts Toddler Thursdays from 1 to 4 PM, October through July. Children 2 to 5 years old are invited to drop in and make masks, fingerpaint and sculpt. All family programs are free with museum admission: $6 for adults, $4 for students with ID and $2 for kids 6 to 17. Youngsters 6 and younger are free.

(See The Arts chapter for more information about the High.)

Hobbit Hall
120 Bulloch Ave., Roswell
• (770) 587-0907

This bookstore in Roswell's historic district has a goldfish pond in front and a fenced garden and children's playhouse in back. Hobbit Hall carries approximately 25,000 titles and 100,000 volumes of quality children's books plus educational toys, games, puzzles and activity kits. Hobbit Hall events include interactive preschool story times on Mondays and Tuesdays at 10 AM. School-age kids are invited to special events (tea and cookies, beanie baby swaps) on Saturdays at 10 AM. Well-known children's authors and illustrators regularly visit the store and participate in Hobbit Hall's Meet the Authors/Illustrators in the Schools program. The cozy Victorian setting is also a favorite for birthday parties. All activities are free.

INSIDERS' TIP

Atlanta Parent and *Our Kids*, free publications you can pick up in bookstores and at other locations around town, are chock-full of helpful articles and suggestions about how to entertain the small fry.

Ice Forum
2300 Satellite Blvd., Duluth
• (770) 813-1010
Town Center, 3061 Busbee Pkwy.,
Kennesaw, (770) 218-1010

These enormous ice rinks offer skating sessions of various lengths every day of the week. The cost ranges from $5 to $7 per person, depending on how long you skate. Sessions are held Monday through Friday from 10 AM to noon; Monday, Wednesday and Friday, 4 to 5:30 PM; Tuesday and Thursday, 8 to 9:30 PM; Friday and Saturday, 8 to 11 PM; Saturday and Sunday, 1 to 3 PM, 2 to 4 PM and 3 to 5 PM. Skate rentals are $2.

Lake Lanier Islands
6950 Holiday Rd., Lake Lanier Islands
• (770) 932-7200

Kids will love Lake Lanier Islands' Beach and Water Park, with Wildwaves, Georgia's largest wave pool and spine-tingling water slides including the Intimidator, the Triple Threat, the Typhoon and the Twister. Splash Down and Racing Waters are twin-flume speed slides guaranteed to thrill, and Blackout sends riders down 160 feet of water in total darkness. Chattahoochee Rapids let you innertube through more than 725 feet of winding, shooting rapids. Smaller kids will enjoy Wiggle Waves, a kiddie wave pool featuring 6- to 12-inch waves, two 8-foot slides and colorful fountains of water bubbles.

For a family excursion, rent a paddleboat, sailboat or canoe. The cost of admission to the Water Park covers the rental. Take a swim off the 1.5-mile sandy beach, or play 18 holes of miniature golf. Lake Lanier Islands Stables offer trail rides, pony rides and lessons. Or rent a bike and explore more than 1,200 acres of beautiful woodlands.

At South Beach, try out surfwave (a simulated body-boarding experience), a rock climbing wall and video games. South Beach also has a DJ or some form of live entertainment on weekends; North Beach has a DJ from 11 AM to 4 PM all week. Wave-runners are available to those 18 or older for $10 an hour, $5 an hour for each extra rider.

Lake Lanier Islands' birthday club will host your child's birthday party, offering a complete package including lunch, ice cream and cake, tickets and admission to the Beach and Water Park.

Beach and Water Park admission is $16.95 for adults; senior citizens and children under 42 inches tall get in for $9.95; children 2 or younger are free. Season passes are also available. The Islands charge a $6 fee for each car entering the grounds. The Beach and Water Park is open daily from 10 AM to 7 PM Memorial Day through Labor Day.

Little General Playhouse
55 Atlanta St., Marietta • (770) 419-0088

This kids' arts center puts on about 12 children's plays during the year that feature local child actors in favorites such as *The Sound of Music*, *Alice in Wonderland* and *West Side Story*. At Halloween the playhouse hosts *The House of Little Horrors*, a stage show that includes an audience walk through a haunted house. Kids as young as 3 are welcome to join in the harmless fun and to have their faces painted or work on spooky arts and crafts projects. Tickets for all shows are priced between $5 and $8. Children younger than 3 are free with a paid adult; grandparents are free with a paid child.

Art and drama classes are offered after school from 3 to 6 PM. Registration is by the month; fees start at $40 a week for a once-a-week class. The playhouse also holds an art and drama summer day camp from 10 AM to 3 PM for children younger than 12. Prices are $125 for one week, $250 for two.

Malibu Grand Prix
5400 Brook Hollow Pkwy., Norcross
• (770) 416-7630

You can either speed up or slow down at Malibu Grand Prix, a sports and video arcade for the whole family. Bumper boats, batting cages, a video arcade, go-carts and Grand Prix race cars entertain the action-oriented. More laid-back family members can meander through a miniature golf course or settle back to watch races on a big-screen TV. Birthday parties and overnight lock-ins are popular here.

Malibu is open Monday through Thursday, 11 AM to 11 PM; Friday and Saturday, 11 AM to midnight; and Sunday, 11 AM to 11 PM. A round of miniature golf costs $5 per adult, $4.25 for kids younger than 12. Most of the attractions, such as bumper boats and go-carts, are $4 for each five-minute session. Arcade tokens are 25¢ each.

Malibu SpeedZone Kennesaw
3005 George Busbee Pkwy., Kennesaw
• (770) 514-8081
Malibu SpeedZone is a 12-acre racing park geared toward adults and teens who dream of being Mario Andretti. The park has four tracks for its 300-horsepower dragsters and an indoor arcade with more than 100 interactive video games described by the owners as being "so advanced even the government is nervous." There is one race-ride for kids at least 5-feet tall and one where kids shorter than 42 inches may ride, but otherwise, all drivers must have valid licenses to get on the track. Drivers purchase debit cards in any amount desired, and the cost of the races and games are deducted from that. Just to give racers a general idea, the cost can range from $5 for two laps around the race-track to $15 for two runs down the drag strip. SpeedZone also features a full-service, racing-themed restaurant serving pizza, burgers, salads and sandwiches from $4.95 to $14.

SpeedZone is open from 11 AM to midnight Sunday through Thursday and 11 AM to 2 AM Friday and Saturday.

Mountasia Family Fun Centers
8510 Holcomb Bridge Rd., Roswell
• (770) 993-7711
I-575 and Barrett Pkwy., Marietta
• (770) 422-3440
1099 Johnson Ferry Rd., Marietta
• (770) 977-1200
Mountasia fun centers stay open year round, offering miniature golf and video game

rooms. Golf costs adults $5.25 for 18 holes, $7.25 for 36 holes and $8.25 for 54 holes. Kids pay $4.50 for 18 holes, $5.50 for 36 holes and $6.50 for 54 holes. Arcade games generally use from one to three 25¢ tokens.

The Marietta location has go-carts and bumper boats, $3.50 for a five-minute ride.

Noah's Ark Rehabilitation Center Inc.
712 Locust Grove Rd., Locust Grove
• (770) 957-0888
This outdoor wildlife rehabilitation center has all kinds of exotic animals: cougars, tigers, bears, wolves, monkeys, baboons, iguanas and jungle birds. The Ark also accepts injured, orphaned and unwanted wildlife. Among the farm animals it has taken in are a pasture-full of horses as well as cows, sheep, goats and pigs.

The Ark is open Monday through Friday for guided tours only at noon, 1 PM, 2 PM and 3 PM. On Saturdays, visitors may enjoy the Ark on their own between noon and 3 PM. No tours are conducted when it rains or if the Ark is hosting a special event; it's best to call to confirm tour times.

Noah's Ark is a nonprofit organization supported entirely by donations. Admission is free, but donations are appreciated. The Ark is about 40 miles south of downtown Atlanta.

Outdoor Activity Center
1442 Richland Ave. S.W. • (404) 752-5385
Three miles southwest of downtown Atlanta, the Outdoor Activity Center is a 26-acre nature preserve with a hardwood urban forest, an interpretive center, a treehouse classroom, 650-gallon freshwater aquarium, picnic

---

INSIDERS' TIP

You have to work hard at being bored in Atlanta during the summer — especially if you're a kid. There are plenty of one-day workshops, weeklong camps and other short-term activities to help ward off the summertime blues. *Creative Loafing*, a free weekly newspaper, has a "Happenings" section that's a good source of information about children's activities — look under "Youth." In its Saturday "Leisure" section, *The Atlanta Journal-Constitution* runs a two-page spread devoted just to kids. A read-aloud story is paired with the latest listings of plays, movies, exhibits and classes for the young set.

Photo: S.E. Railway Museum

Take a ride on a restored caboose at the Southeastern
Railway Museum — watch out for the whistle!

tables and Naturescape, an ecological playscape. The center hosts tours and programs for grades K through 12, covering such topics as Tree Treasures, Urban Wildlife, Reptile Riches, Animals in Winter and Footprints of the Past, a program celebrating American Indian culture. The Center is open Monday through Saturday, 9 AM to 4 PM. Group tours for 15 or more cost $3 per student. Otherwise, the center is free and open to the public.

Parkaire Ice Arena
4880 Lower Roswell Rd., Marietta
• (770) 973-0753
Kids and adults skate daily at this regulation-size ice arena — as long as there's not a hockey tournament running. Sessions are held Monday through Friday, 10:30 AM to 12:30 PM; Tuesday and Thursday, 4 to 5:30 PM; Friday, 3:30 to 5:30 PM; Thursday and Friday, 8 to 10 PM; Saturday and Sunday, 1 to 3 PM and 3:30 to 5:30 PM; Saturday, 8 to 10 PM; and Sunday, 7:30 to 9:30 PM. Extra sessions are added during school holidays. Admission costs $5 for adults and children; if you don't have your own blades, skate rental is $2 per person.

Q-Zar
5920 Roswell Rd., Sandy Springs
• (404) 255-2326
800 Ernest W. Barrett Pkwy., Kennesaw
• (770) 428-9909
3750 Venture Dr., Duluth • (770) 497-1313
This high-tech spot seems like a video game come to life. Q-Zar's darkened mazes

pit teams against each other in a combative game of hide-and-seek laser tag. Teams zap opponents with safe laser beams until one side emerges victorious.

Admission costs $7.50 per person per game. Groups of eight or more get $1.50 per person off admission. Hours are Tuesday, Wednesday and Thursday, 3 to 9 PM; Friday, 3 PM to midnight; Saturday, 10 AM to midnight; and Sunday, 1 to 8 PM. Hours are extended during the summer months, but call before you go — private parties may book the entire place.

Six Flags Over Georgia
7561 Six Flags Rd. at I-20 W.
• (770) 948-9290

Although this family-oriented theme park is fun for all ages, children will delight in a special section designed just for them. Bugs Bunny World features scaled-down attractions and rides designed for little thrillseekers, including Convoy Grande, Swing Seville and The Little Aviator. The *What's Up, Rock?* show gives kids a chance to take part in the action, while Bugs Bunny's Playfort allows tots to explore soft play components and meet with the Looney Tunes characters. Monster Plantation takes kids on a boat ride through a flooded antebellum plantation, where lovable and not-so-frightening monsters come to life through computer electronics and animation technology. Small ones are thrilled to see Santa Maria, a fun-filled adventure on pirate ships that fly through the air and laugh at the antics of the Bullfrog Review, three wacky animated amphibians. The Riverview Carousel features 69 hand-carved wooden horses. The Carrot Club offers buffet-style family fare, a specially designed game room, Bugs Bunny cartoons and special appearances by the Looney Tunes clan.

Six Flags opens at 10 AM with closing times that vary by the week and month. The park is opened on weekends around March 1 until Memorial Day and from Labor Day until October; daily hours last from Memorial Day to Labor Day. Adult admission is $34; kids 3 to 9 and seniors older than 55 pay $23. Two-day passes are $39 for adults, $35 for kids.

SciTrek: The Science and Technology Museum of Atlanta
395 Piedmont Ave. • (404) 522-5500

Fun for all ages, SciTrek has some special exhibits just for kids. KidSpace is a special area exclusively for kids 2 to 7 and their parents or adult companions. Children can see themselves on TV, paint their faces, learn to turn a water wheel, create a dam and build a kid-size house.

The Holiday Express is an annual holiday exhibit that rolls in around Thanksgiving and stays until the New Year. The festive model railroad display features a collection of turn-of-the-century toy trains that run through miniature landscapes, animals and people on 400 feet of track.

SciTrek Overnights, held from September through June, treat campers and chaperons to an entire evening of hands-on science workshops, demonstrations and experiences. More than 150 interactive stations let kids explore; they also get to watch a movie. SciTrek provides breakfast and another science demonstration in the morning. Overnights serve groups of children between the ages of 8 and 12 on selected Thursdays, Fridays and Saturdays from 6 PM to 10 AM. You must have at least 10 paying campers ($30 per student) to book an Overnight. Admission is free for one adult per every five campers. Additional adults pay $10.

SciTrek Summer Day Camps program offers one-week summer sessions designed for children 5 through 12. Kids learn about a broad range of topics including light, color, chemistry, electricity, sound, outer space, earth science, biology, rocket science, architecture, ecology and more. Sessions include hands-on science, creative play and fun explorations. Half-day and week-long sessions prices range from $90 to $180.

SciTrek is open Monday through Saturday from 10 AM to 5 PM, Sunday, noon to 5 PM. General admission is $7.50 for adults and $5 for children 3 through 17.

Spruill Center
5339 Chamblee-Dunwoody Rd., Dunwoody • (770) 394-3447

The Spruill Center sponsors a summer series of morning performances for children that include storytelling and craft projects at its art gallery, 4681 Ashford-Dunwoody Road. Story sessions are free; craft classes run about $8 per child. Summer camps focusing on the performing and visual arts are held on the Center grounds each week from 9 AM to 2 PM and cost from $210 to $225 per child.

Sun Valley Beach
5350 Holloman Rd., Powder Springs
• (770) 943-5900

Fourteen miles west of Atlanta, Sun Valley has one of the Southeast's largest swimming pools, 1.5 acres, surrounded by a white sandy beach. The pool has 12 water slides, a Tarzan swing, a cascading umbrella and a log roll. Play volleyball on the beach, or enjoy softball, basketball and tennis on the fields and courts provided. Try your hand at minigolf, pitch some horseshoes, or play on the playgrounds and in the game room. Racers will enjoy the fast-paced go-cart track. Picnic spots and concession stands dot the 40-acre site, which is open weekends in May and daily from 10 AM to 8 PM, Memorial Day through Labor Day. Weekday admission is $10 for adults, $8 for children. On weekends, adults pay $12, kids $10. Seniors get in for $3.50. Seasonal memberships are also available.

White Water Park
250 N. Cobb Pkwy., I-75 at Exit 113, Marietta • (770) 424-WAVE

Forty scenic acres of water attractions, adjacent to American Adventures, make for a wild day of fun. You'll find more than 40 rides — body flumes, a wave pool, a lazy river and

more — from the relaxing to the shriek-provoking. Laze in the Little Hooch River, or enjoy thrills and spills sluicing down The Bermuda Triangle and Black River Falls. Tree House Island offers four stories of fun-filled activities, and Little Squirt's Island and Captain Kid's Cove let younger kids play safely with their peers.

With five restaurants on the premises, guests aren't allowed to bring their own food, but there are plenty of picnic tables just outside the main entrance. No thong or G-string bathing suits or street clothes are allowed either. Shower and locker facilities are available. The park is open from 10 AM to 8 PM, Memorial Day through the first weekend in September; hours are shorter on early spring and late fall weekends.

Admission is $11.99 for kids 3 years to 4 feet tall; guests taller than 4 feet pay $20.99. Season passes are $39.99 per person. Parking is $2. Discount coupons are available at various Blimpies sub shops and Publix grocery stores around the city.

W. H. Reynolds Memorial Nature Preserve
5665 Reynolds Rd., Morrow
• (770) 603-4188

About 3 miles of walking paths, ponds, springs, a wheelchair-accessible native plants trail, a compost demonstration site and a heritage garden count among the many pleasures this preserve has to offer. An indoor nature center teaches kids about various flora and fauna. The nature center is open Monday through Friday from 8:30 AM to 5:30 PM. The grounds open daily from 8:30 AM to dusk. Admission is free.

The Wren's Nest
1050 R.D. Abernathy Rd. S.W.
• (404) 753-7735

Joel Chandler Harris, author of the Uncle Remus tales, lived in this Victorian home. In keeping with his tradition of telling folk tales, the home hosts a Saturday storytelling at 2 PM, from September through May, and three sessions daily at 11:30 AM, 12:30 PM and 1:30 PM, from mid-June through mid-August. Story hours may vary depending on attendance; call to verify times. Storytimes require a $4-per-

person ticket for all ages. Local storytellers are featured. There's also a museum shop with Br'er Rabbit memorabilia.

The Wren's Nest is open Tuesday through Saturday from 10 AM to 4 PM and Sunday from 1 to 4 PM. Admission is $6 for adults, $4 for seniors and teens and $3 for children 4 to 12.

Yellow River Game Ranch
4525 Hwy. 78, Lilburn • (770) 972-6643

Six hundred animals and birds representing more than 25 indigenous Georgia species live here, including prairie dogs, goats, buffalo, white-tailed deer and Georgia black bears. General Beauregard Lee, the internationally renowned groundhog, resides in his own antebellum plantation house. Three Georgia governors have proclaimed General Lee the Official Weather Prognosticator for the state, and he's been recognized by the National Weather Service. He's the one who either sees or doesn't see his shadow on Groundhog Day, letting us know how much longer we can expect winter to last. General Lee has his own mailbox, and each child who writes to him gets a personal answer.

The game ranch sponsors a Sheep Shearing Saturday each year in mid-May. A professional shearer teaches kids about the shearing process, and a hand spinner spins the wool. Kids can take a sample of fleece to their schools' show-and-tell.

Every day is different at Yellow River Game Ranch, with various species having babies at different times of year. Kids can walk down a mile-long marked trail and pet the animals who come up to nuzzle. The ranch allows kids to feed the animals with food purchased at the ranch.

Yellow River opens every day of the year. Summer hours (Memorial Day through Labor Day) run from 9:30 AM to dusk; in other seasons, hours run from 9:30 AM to 6 PM. Adults pay $6 admission; kids 3 to 11 are $5. One child younger than 3 gets in free with a paying adult.

Zoo Atlanta
800 Cherokee Ave. S.E. • (404) 624-5600

Described more fully in our Attractions chapter, Zoo Atlanta offers a wide variety of kids' attractions and activities. The Egleston Ark Playground is open daily throughout the year, weather permitting. This smart playground features rocking elephants, turtles, bears, rabbits and lambs, as well as a telegraph station, climbing nets, steering wheels and compasses. The playground encourages kids to use their imaginations and helps educate parents about playground safety.

Photo: Center for Puppetry Arts

Kids enjoy learning and creating in the Center of Puppetry Arts' daily Create-A-Puppet workshops.

The Norfolk Southern Zoo Express is a handcrafted replica of an 1863 locomotive. The natural-gas-burning train features wide, comfortable seats and covered passenger coaches. Parents and kids wait in the Victorian-style train station for their turn on the train, which costs $1 per person and runs several times a day. Kids younger than 2 ride free.

Breakfast with a Keeper, scheduled on certain Saturdays throughout the summer, gives children 8 and older a chance to find out what it's like to care for zoo animals. Nightcrawlers Family Overnight, scheduled throughout the year, allows parents and kids 6 and older to enjoy a night hike, animal commissary tour and creature encounters. In October the Zoo hosts a Halloween event that includes a costume contest, trick-or-treat stations, face painting and more for little ghouls and goblins.

Zoo Atlanta's Summer Safari Day Camp and Junior Biologist Day Camp open doors to a world of animals, conservation and environmental discovery for students as young as 4 years old up through 8th graders. Sessions last a week, and campers can enjoy special events, arts and crafts, games and discovery activities. Rising 5th through 8th graders attend the Junior Biologist Day Camp, where they learn about zoo careers and conduct animal behavior research on their favorite animals. The zoo offers full-day, morning and afternoon programs as well as extended care from 7:30 AM to 6 PM, free for full-day students. Camp costs range from $65 to $155.

On most weekends,
there are festivals and
special events going on
somewhere in the area.

Festivals and Events

Atlantans love any excuse to throw a party. On most weekends throughout the year, there are festivals and special events going on somewhere in the metro area.

Some of these affairs are cozy block parties where nearly everyone knows everyone else. Many of the city's rejuvenated in-town neighborhoods hold festivals and tours of homes, inviting folks from all over to share in the community's life. Religious groups and international clubs parade their cultures and customs for others to experience and enjoy. And periodically there are truly massive events — drawing 100,000 and more — that organizers work throughout the year to stage.

In a city where nearly everyone came from somewhere else, these events may also help newcomers find their way by bringing people of similar interests or backgrounds together. And they can remind us all just how kaleidoscopically varied are the people making their lives here.

Many festivals are held in parks. For specific information on Atlanta's parks, see our Parks and Recreation chapter. Here's a quick location guide to parks that serve as venues to many events throughout the year.

• Piedmont Park is in Midtown; it's bordered primarily by 10th Street, Monroe Drive and Piedmont Avenue.

• Grant Park is in southeast Atlanta; its main entrances are on Cherokee Avenue and on Boulevard. Zoo Atlanta and the Cyclorama occupy the southern portion; festivals take place in the park's northern area.

• Chastain Park is in northwest Atlanta; take Roswell Road north through Buckhead; turn left on W. Wieuca Road and follow the signs.

• To reach Georgia's Stone Mountain Park, take U.S. 78 (Ponce de Leon Avenue — Scott Boulevard — Lawrenceville Highway — Stone Mountain Parkway) east of Atlanta to the Stone Mountain Park exit. A per-vehicle admission is always charged here: It's $6 per car. An annual pass is $25.

In this chapter, we'll tell you about some of the annual events that make life in Atlanta exciting.

January

King Week and the Martin Luther King Jr. National Holiday
Martin Luther King Jr. Center for Nonviolent Social Change, 449 Auburn Ave. N.E. (and other locations)
• **(404) 526-8900**

Dr. Martin Luther King Jr. was born in Atlanta on January 15, 1929. A national holiday was declared in his honor in 1986. Long before that, we Atlantans had been staging an annual celebration to laud our Nobel laureate. King Week, held the week preceding the Martin Luther King Jr. National Holiday, includes many free performances, concerts, special religious services and educational presentations. Check with the Center for specific times and places of events.

February

African-American History Month

Atlanta, the center of the Civil Rights movement for years, marks African-American History Month with numerous educational and entertainment events. The commemoration lasts the entire month. Big Bethel AME Church, 220 Auburn Avenue near the King Center, hosts an assortment of musical performances, lectures and programs that explore the African-American experience. The Atlanta-Fulton Public Library System sponsors special lectures on African-American authors. The Fernbank Science Museum takes a look at the skies over the Dark Continent with its program, African Astronomy. For specific dates and times, call (404) 730-1976.

Southeastern Flower Show

City Hall Exhibition Center, City Hall East, 640 Ponce de Leon Ave. N.E.
• **(404) 888-5638**

This show, held over a weekend late in the month, benefits the Atlanta Botanical Garden. It features a wide range of garden-related events including displays, demonstrations, workshops and children's activities. Adults pay $12 on the days of the show or $10 in advance. Admission for children 4 to 16 is $5.

March

Atlanta Passion Play

Atlanta Civic Center, 395 Piedmont Ave. N.E. • **(404) 347-8400**

Since 1976, the First Baptist Church of Atlanta has annually presented this pageant portraying Christ's life, death and resurrection. Its reputation is so widespread, it now draws people

from around the country. Each year's production varies slightly with different focuses on the story line and different music. The elaborately staged and costumed play is the work of more than 500 people, including a chorus and full orchestra. Due to the three-hour length, the sacred nature of the performance and the graphic portrayal of Christ's death, children younger than 6 are not admitted. The play is performed the final three weekends of Lent, not including Easter weekend. Admission is $14 per ticket.

Conyers Cherry Blossom Festival

International Horse Park, 1996 Centennial Olympic Pkwy., Conyers
• **(770) 918-2169**

In 1980 Hitachi Maxell's president donated 500 cherry trees to the city of Conyers, 30 minutes east of Atlanta on I-20, home to Maxell Corp. of America. The Conyers Cherry Blossom Festival has greeted spring here since 1982. The monthlong calendar of events includes art exhibits, a road race, other sporting tournaments, a beauty pageant, music and more. Most of the events are free, but there is a $5 parking fee. The Festival Day is usually held on the third or fourth Saturday at the Georgia International Horse Park on the edge of town.

St. Patrick's Day

Atlanta goes green with St. Patrick's Day celebrations. Sponsored by the Hibernian Society, the Atlanta St. Patrick's Day Parade is the highlight, having been held for more than 110 years. But the day usually begins with a 9:30 AM mass at the Cathedral of Christ the King in Buckhead, where proper dress and propriety are required. But the revelers let their hair down soon afterwards, starting at 11:30 AM with the parade through downtown. Across the city, Irish hangouts are packed with party-goers: check out the green beer and Irish stew at Fado's and McDuff's Irish Pub in Buckhead; Limerick Junction in Virginia-Highland; and Danny O'Shea's in Marietta. Even Reggie's British Pub at CNN Center gets into the swing, celebrating the Celtic roots of the

---

FYI

Three area codes serve the metro Atlanta area: 404, 770 and 678. Whether you live on Peachtree Street or in New York City, you must dial the code to reach any number in the area. The difference? Outside the area, you must dial "1," then the area code and phone number; inside the area, you need only dial the area code followed by the phone number.

Scots and Welsh. Depending on what day the feast falls, the celebration may extend for a day or two before and after the 17th.

Look for an array of concerts, readings and lectures at various locations around town. Theatre Gael, the Celtic-inspired dramatic group, and the W.B. Yeats Foundation at Emory University usually feature special programs. The city of Decatur, a few miles east of downtown Atlanta, holds its own parade near the day of green as well.

Baby & Kid Expo
Cobb Galleria Centre, 2 Galleria Pkwy. N.W. • (770) 395-7900

Families will enjoy this weekend exposition of products and services for the youngsters held in late March. Events include circus performers, a baby crawl-off, storytelling, a puppet theater, safety and product information and more. Admission is $5 for adults; children 12 and younger are admitted free.

April

Easter Sunrise Services
Georgia's Stone Mountain Park, U.S. Hwy. 78 east to Stone Mountain Park exit • (770) 498-5702

In the predawn darkness on Easter Sunday morning, the faithful gather atop Stone Mountain to await the sunrise on the holiest day of the Christian year. As morning breaks, local ministers lead an ecumenical worship service. This inspiring celebration is a longstanding Atlanta tradition. The weather is often windy and cold, so you might need to bring a blanket. The service is free, but you'll pay $6 per car to be admitted into the park.

Sheep to Shawl Day
Atlanta History Center, 130 W. Paces Ferry Rd. • (404) 814-4000

For city dwellers who don't get down to the farm too often, here's a day to experience nature — particularly sheep. Held the first Saturday of the month, the event features demonstrations of the art of sheep shearing, followed by the entire process required to turn it into something wearable. Spectators observe the fresh wool through the washing, spinning, dyeing and weaving

cycles. The completed process produces a new shawl. Displays are ongoing throughout the day. The center is open from 10 AM to 5:30 PM the day of the event. Admission is $7 for adults, $5 for students and seniors, $4 for kids 6 to 17 and free to children 5 and younger.

Atlanta Dogwood Festival
Piedmont Park, 10th St. and Piedmont Ave. • (404) 875-7275

For a few precious weeks each spring, Atlanta is bathed in a brilliant floral finery. The Dogwood Festival pays homage to the city's legendary botanical beauty; its highlights include a colorful hot-air balloon race, concerts, children's parades and the dog Frisbee championships. Most events are free. Note: Atlanta's dogwoods and azaleas bloom on a schedule all their own, and their peak does not always coincide with this festival that is held on a weekend in mid-April.

Druid Hills Home and Garden Tour
Various Druid Hills homes • (404) 524-TOUR

With an overall landscape plan by the world-renowned Olmsted firm and stunning homes designed by famous architects such as Neel Reid and Walter T. Downing, the elegant Druid Hills neighborhood is listed on the National Register of Historic Places. This weekend event in late April affords you a rare opportunity to tour selected homes and gardens in the $300,000 to million-dollar range. Tickets are available for the entire tour or for individual homes. You'll pay $12 in advance or $15 on the days of the tour. The homes are open all weekend; tickets are valid for both days.

Inman Park Festival
Edgewood and Euclid Aves. and other Inman Park streets • (770) 242-4895

Two miles east of Five Points, Inman Park was developed in the 1880s as Atlanta's first suburb, and along its broad, tree-lined streets are imposing Victorian mansions and charming bungalows. Coca-Cola founder Asa Candler lived here in the early 1900s; Mayor Bill Campbell lives here today. Inman Park declined precipitously after World War II until it was little better than a slum. Then, in the late 1960s, forward-looking citizens rediscovered the area, renovating once-grand homes and reclaiming the area as one of Atlanta's premier addresses. You'll find a parade, a tour of homes, antiques, food, crafts, music and more at this two-day street party held the last weekend of the month. The festival is free; home tour tickets are $12 per person and are good for the entire weekend. This is the oldest of Atlanta's many neighborhood festivals.

WalkAmerica
Various metro Atlanta streets
• (404) 352-WALK

Benefiting the March of Dimes, this walkathon annually attracts some 20,000 participants who sign up pledge donors and walk one of eight routes throughout the metro area. The minimum donation in 1997 was $10. The proceeds help fight birth defects and infant mortality. The event is held on a Saturday in late April.

www.insiders.com

See this and many other **Insiders' Guide®** destinations online — in their entirety.

Visit us today!

Georgia Renaissance Festival
I-85 at Exit 12, Fairburn • (770) 964-8575

Forsooth, this rollicking re-creation of the English Renaissance features more than 100 performances daily on 10 stages scattered across the 93-acre festival grounds. Strolling musicians, minstrels, magicians and other costumed characters are all part of the fun, along with knights in armor jousting on horseback. The festival is open seven consecutive weekends (Saturday and Sunday only) beginning in late April and lasting through the end of May or early June. Admission is $11.95 for adults, $5.95 for kids 6 to 15. There is no admission charge for children younger than 6. It's such a popular event that it's presented again (with some different attractions) in October.

May

Lasershow
Georgia's Stone Mountain Park, U.S. Hwy. 78 east to Stone Mountain Park exit
• (770) 498-5690

Seven nights a week from early May through Labor Day, the sky over Stone Mountain explodes with a rainbow of laser light. To stirring musical accompaniment, lasers are projected on the mountain's north face, which becomes a natural million-square-foot screen. Bring a blanket and relax under the stars. After Labor Day through late October, the show is presented on Friday and Saturday nights only. The show is free with admission to the park — $6 per car.

Springfest and the Corporate Garage Sale
Georgia's Stone Mountain Park, U.S. Hwy. 78 east to Stone Mountain Park exit
• (770) 498-5690

Cooks from around the South compete in a barbecue cookoff for thousands of dollars in cash and prizes. In addition to live music, the weekend in early May includes a huge garage sale that's a junk lover's dream come true. A registration fee is required for sellers. The event is free, but you'll pay $6 per car to get into the park. Bring your appetite! There's no charge for samples.

Bed and Breakfast Tour
Edgewood and Euclid Aves. and other Inman Park streets • (404) 876-2041

How many Mother's Days have you spent waiting in long lines at a restaurant to treat your mother to brunch? Looking for something different? The Atlanta Preservation Center came up with an alternative: tea and cakes at four charming Victorian bed and breakfast inns. In addition to the delectable desserts, tour-goers are escorted through the exquisitely decorated and restored mansions. Tickets are $12 per person.

National Historic Preservation Week
Various locations • (404) 876-2040

During a week in mid-May, the Atlanta Preservation Center offers its walking tours of historic Atlanta districts free of charge. The APC's tours are fun and highly informative; take advantage of this annual opportunity to enjoy them and save some money. (See our Attractions chapter for details on the tours offered.)

Photo: Georgia Renaissance Festival

Cheer your favorite knight on to victory at the Georgia Renaissance Festival.

Atlanta Celtic Festival
Oglethorpe University, 4484 Peachtree Rd. • (404) 261-1441

Don your kilts, laddies, and head for this two-day event, held the third weekend of the month, that celebrates the history and cultural heritage of Ireland, Scotland and Wales. International, national and local musicians, dancers and speakers are on-hand, along with Celtic crafts, foods and merchandise. There are free lessons in Scottish country dancing, children's games and sheepdog demonstrations. Members of Atlanta's Theatre Gael perform short works and entertain with storytelling. Hours are 10 AM to 10 PM Saturday and noon to 6 PM Sunday. Admission on Saturday is $8 for adults, $5 for seniors and students and $2 for children younger than 12. On Sunday, the adult charge is reduced to $5; all the other fees remain the same.

Midtown Music Festival
Peachtree and 10th Sts. • 404-872-1115

First held in 1994, this outdoor festival scored an immediate hit. In 1997, performers on the six stages included Better Than Ezra, Santana, ZZTop, Cake, Silverchair and the Steve Miller Band. Tickets are available through TicketMaster; call (404) 249-6400 (a $2.50 convenience charge applies). One-day admission is $19; tickets for the entire weekend (usually the first one in May) are $27.

Atlanta Jazz Festival
Grant Park, Georgia and Cherokee Aves. • (404) 817-6815

Started in 1977, this showcase of local and national jazz talent is one of the largest of its kind in the city. All events on the Saturday, Sunday and Monday of Memorial Day weekend are free and run from 1 to 10 PM. On the days before the event, various jazz artists give free, brown-bag lunchtime concerts in Woodruff Park, at Marietta and Peachtree streets downtown. The festival is sponsored by the City of Atlanta.

Atlanta Peach Caribbean Festival
Various locations • (404) 220-0158

Atlanta is home to many people who trace their roots to the Caribbean islands. This festival, held over Memorial Day weekend, celebrates Caribbean culture with a parade, a soccer tournament, parties, art shows and performances. Most events are free.

Decatur Arts Festival
Decatur town square and other locations • (404) 371-9583

The city of Decatur, 6 miles east of downtown, hosts this popular festival, which has grown substantially in recent years to a total of 40,000 in 1997. Among the many activities offered over Memorial Day weekend are art exhibits, a children's festival, storytellers, jugglers, magicians, pony rides, international music and dance and literary events.

Taste of the South
Georgia's Stone Mountain Park, U.S. Hwy. 78 east to Stone Mountain Park exit
• **(770) 498-5590**

If you've always been curious about okra (boiled or fried), grits (cheese or regular) and greens (collard or turnip), here's your chance to taste what you've been missing. Each Southern state shows off its best offerings in food, entertainment, travel and more over Memorial Day weekend. Admission to the park requires a $6 parking permit. The event itself is free, but be sure to bring a few bucks if you plan on doing a little taste-testing.

Georgia Renaissance Festival
I-85 at Exit 12, Fairburn • (770) 964-8575

Take a step, actually several steps, back in time to the era of knights and ladies fair at the Georgia Renaissance Festival. Music, munchies and a little harmless mayhem are offered on weekends throughout the month. See our April entry for more details.

June

Lasershow
Georgia's Stone Mountain Park, U.S. Hwy. 78 east to Stone Mountain Park exit
• **(770) 498-5690**

Enjoy the brilliance and colors of laser lights along with Robert E. Lee, Stonewall Jackson, Jefferson Davis and hundreds of Georgians nightly at Georgia's Stone Mountain Park. See our May entry for details.

Virginia-Highland Summerfest
John Howell Park, Virginia Ave. at Ponce de Leon Pl. • (404) 222-8244

Founded in 1916 and originally called North Boulevard Park, the Virginia-Highland neighborhood annually throws this popular, free party featuring bands, food from area res-

taurants and lots of fun for the kids. It's held the first full weekend in June.

Willie B's Birthday Party
Atlanta Zoo, 800 Cherokee Ave.
• **(404) 624-5600**

Willie B., the silverback Western lowland gorilla named after a former Atlanta mayor, has been one of the city's main attractions since he was a baby. In 1998 he hits midlife! His 40th birthday will be marked, as the day is each year on a weekend in early June, with an enormous cake, cupcakes, a huge card for visitors to sign, music, face painting and a rousing rendition of "Happy Birthday." Guests get the cake; Willie B. gets fresh fruit and vegetables. The celebration is free with a regular Zoo admission — $9 for adults, $6.50 for seniors, $5.50 for kids 3 to 11 and free for children younger than 3.

Georgia Shakespeare Festival
Oglethorpe University, 4484 Peachtree Rd. • (404) 264-0020

Shakespeare has come to Oglethorpe University every summer for more than a decade. Plans for the 1998 festival include three plays by the Bard and some light fare by Moliere, in the Conant Performing Arts Center on the campus of Oglethorpe University. The season opens in mid-June, with productions going on through October. About 90 minutes before each evening's performance or Sunday matinee, show goers are invited to picnic on the lawn around the Center.

Even if you're not a fan of Shakespeare, it's worth the price of admission to sit in the fabulous Conant Center. With only 509 seats, the feeling is intimate. And during the nice spring and fall weather, the walls of the Center are raised to the open air. But don't worry — it's also completely air-conditioned to handle hot, muggy July nights.

Tickets for the festival shows range from $18 to $24, and discounts are offered to seniors, students and groups.

National Black Family Reunion Celebration
Grant Park and Atlanta Marriott Marquis
• **(404) 524-6269**

This three-day event in mid-June, presented

by the National Council of Negro Women, begins with a leadership forum on Friday. On Saturday, there's a parade and a free expo in Grant Park with seminars, health screenings and merchandise vendors. An R&B show caps Saturday's activities. On Sunday, again in Grant Park, the expo continues with the event culminating in a gospel concert at 3 PM. Food and merchandise are available, and all activities and festivities except an ecumenical prayer breakfast that is held at the Atlanta Marriott Marquis (265 Peachtree Center Avenue, N.E.), are free. In 1997, the breakfast cost $20 per person.

Candler Park & Lake Claire Music & Arts Festival
Clifton at McLendon business district
• (404) 370-1003
The pleasant, laid-back neighborhoods of Candler Park and Lake Claire come together at their shared business district for a free street party with a 5K run and in-line skate race, refreshments and bands. It's $15 to register for the race. The Edgewood/Candler Park MARTA station serves this area. The event is held on a Saturday in mid-June.

Arts Festival of Atlanta
Centennial Park, Woodruff Park and other venues • (404) 589-8777
The largest annual event of its kind in the city, the Arts Festival draws an amazing 2 million visitors during its nine-day run. In September 1997 the Festival moved from Piedmont Park downtown to the site of Olympic Centennial Park now known simply as Centennial Park. Artists and planners were concerned that folks wouldn't make the journey downtown, but on opening weekend 180,000 people jammed the park. Hundreds of vendors come from throughout the United States to sell arts, jewelry and crafts.

There are concerts, dance performances and movie screenings that do have admission fees of $10 for children's tickets up to $70 for adult passes. Fine art exhibits in temporary gallery spaces along the Fairlie Poplar district were also an added attraction in '97. Woodruff Park on Peachtree Street, an uphill walk of about four blocks, is full of booths in what is called the Bazaar Bizzoso where the more funky, multimedia kinds of creations are located. *Creative Loafing*, and *The Atlanta Journal-Constitution* have inserts just prior to the festival that detail the extensive schedule and pertinent information. Opening and closing weekends are the most crowded; weekday afternoons are the least crowded.

Paid parking is available all around the park, and it's not hard to find spaces near the festivities during the week for $5 and more. On weekends, expect to park further away in lots under office buildings for the same or slightly higher rate. Public transportation is the best deal of all. Take MARTA and exit at Peachtree Center Station. Then walk just a few blocks downhill to Centennial Park where everything is free, but donations of $5 for a nine-day pin or $3 for a one-day sticker are much appreciated.

Note: The Arts Festival of Atlanta will not be held in 1998. In years past the festival was a September event, but beginning in 1999 it will be held in mid-June.

Atlanta Lesbian and Gay Pride Festival
Various locations • (770) 662-4533
Like similar celebrations across the United States, the Atlanta Lesbian and Gay Pride Festival commemorates the day, June 27, 1969, when patrons at New York's Stonewall Inn fought back against police oppression and ignited the modern gay liberation movement. The weekend in late June includes two days of entertainment and speeches and a massive Sunday afternoon parade along Peachtree Street to Piedmont Park. In 1997 the festival attracted an estimated 300,000 people. Fun-loving and supportive non-gays, lured by the carnival atmosphere of the weekend-long party, are more in evidence every year.

INSIDERS' TIP

For detailed festival information, check "Festivals & Celebrations" in the "Happenings" listing section of the weekly *Creative Loafing*, or pick up a copy of the weekend Leisure Guide of *The Atlanta-Journal Constitution*.

Atlanta Virtuosi's Hispanic Festival of the Arts
Atlanta Cuban Club, 5797 New Peachtree Rd., Doraville • (770) 938-8611

At the end of June and in early July, the Atlanta Virtuosi sponsors this festival of the arts from Hispanic-speaking people of Colombia, Peru, Dominican Republic, Brazil, Panama and many other nations. Lectures, displays of fine arts, storytelling, dance performances, photography exhibits as well as concerts and food complete the event. Admission is $15 for adults, $10 for students and seniors and free for children younger than 12.

July

Lasershow
Georgia's Stone Mountain Park, U.S. Hwy. 78 east to Stone Mountain Park exit • (770) 498-5690

What light through yonder window breaks? It's the Lasershow at Georgia's Stone Mountain Park. A rainbow of light and musical accompaniment showers the crowds that turn out nightly for this Georgia tradition. See our May entry for more information.

Fantastic Fourth Celebration
Georgia's Stone Mountain Park, U.S. Hwy. 78 east to Stone Mountain Park exit • (770) 498-5702

The park throws a four-day birthday party for America beginning on the 4th, with major concerts and other entertainment, plus nightly fireworks in addition to the Lasershow. Bring a blanket, picnic food, swim clothes, running shoes, bug spray and suntan lotion in case you want to spend the entire day and take advantage of all the offerings. The celebration is free with admission to the park, which is $6 per car, per day.

Independence Day
Various locations

There's almost too much fun to be had around Atlanta on the 4th. The action gets under way at the crack of dawn as 200,000 spectators line Peachtree Street to watch 50,000 runners compete in the annual Peachtree Road Race (see Spectator Sports). Midday there's WSB-TV's Salute 2 America parade with bands,

balloons and celebrities; it's the largest Independence Day parade in the nation. The parade starts at 1 PM at the Omni then continues on Marietta Street and up W. Peachtree Street. All in all the parade lasts about 90 minutes.

Marietta's historic town square welcomes visitors with Fourth in the Park. The Freedom Parade begins at 10 AM at the Roswell Street Baptist Church and ends at Cherokee Street and the North Loop. And, in historic Roswell Square, you'll enjoy carnival games, musical and theater performances, arts and crafts, food and evening fireworks. For information, call (770) 528-0615. It's all free.

Decatur throws a free party in the town square with bands and fireworks. It's sponsored by the Decatur Downtown Develop Authority. For details, call (404) 371-8386.

After dark, Atlanta skies explode in pyrotechnic glory. The Southeast's largest display is at Lenox Square, 3393 Peachtree Road, (404) 233-6767; it's always free. Live bands start playing at 6 PM, and the fireworks begin at 9 PM. Also enjoy a children's entertainment area and food and drink concessions. People park in the Square's enormous lot or across the street at the Phipps Plaza lot. You'll have to get there early if you hope to find a space.

Braves fans get a dandy display at Turner Field, 755 Hank Aaron Drive, following the ball game, call (404) 522-7630 (see Spectator Sports for more information).

Patrons at Lake Lanier Islands Beach and Waterpark, which is about an hour from Atlanta, can enjoy a variety of musical performances, capped by fireworks over the lake. Admission to the park is $17.95 per adult and $10.95 for children. After 5 PM it's half-price. For more information call (770) 932-7200.

National Black Arts Festival
236 Forsyth St. S.W. • (404) 730-7315

The National Black Arts Festival is presented biannually in early July. Events are held at various venues throughout the city. The celebration spotlights the work of artists of African descent in eight disciplines: music, dance, theater, film, folk art, visual arts, performance art and literature. Works by artists from the United States, Africa, the Caribbean, Europe and South America are featured. In 1996 events ranged in price from $5 to $25. The address and number

Photo: J.Sebo/Zoo Atlanta

Join Willie B. in celebrating his birthday in early June.

listed previously are for the office. Call for information or a catalog of merchandise, which includes posters, caps, mugs and more.

August

Lasershow
Georgia's Stone Mountain Park, U.S. Hwy. 78 east to Stone Mountain Park exit
• **(770) 498-5690**

August nights are bright in Georgia thanks to the Lasershow at Georgia's Stone Mountain Park. The mountain becomes a natural screen on which laser lights are projected. See our May entry for more information.

Hotlanta River Expo
Chattahoochee River and various venues
• **(404) 874-3976**

Thousands of gay men from around the nation arrive for this weekend in mid-August for intense partying and a raft trip down the Chattahoochee. It's an especially festive event that raises money for AIDS charities. The Mr. HotLanta contest and very large dance parties are big attractions. Individual admission fees to events range from $25 to $35, or you can enjoy all the festivities for $99. The weekend starts at The Westin Peachtree Plaza hotel, 210 Peachtree Street N.W., where the men gather and sign up for the upcoming events.

September

Lasershow
Georgia's Stone Mountain Park, U.S. Hwy. 78 east to Stone Mountain Park exit
• **(770) 498-5690**

After Labor Day, the Lasershow only lights up the Georgia sky on Friday and Saturday evenings. Come join the throng of Georgians who delight in the sights and sounds of this performance. See our May entry for details.

Montreaux Atlanta International Music Festival
Piedmont Park, 1085 Piedmont Ave.
• (404) 817-6815

Famous jazz acts perform at this free outdoor festival sponsored by the City of Atlanta. The event kicks off the week prior to Labor Day with local groups performing at afternoon concerts at either Woodruff Park or Centennial Park, both in downtown Atlanta. The three days of Montreaux concerts are held at Piedmont Park in Midtown and feature jazz, reggae, blues, rock and country music. Admission is free.

Tour D'Town
Bolling Wy. and E. Paces Ferry Rd.
• (404) 841-0700

This bicycle race, which raises money for the American Cancer Society, is an annual Labor Day event that attracts more than 3,000 bikers, in-line skaters and wheelchair racers. You can pick your poison, so to speak, and race 12, 24, 48 or 62 miles. Or you can just party after the race with the crowd. Registration is at Bolling Way and E. Paces Ferry Road in Buckhead at 7:30 AM. Your registration fee entitles you to a T-shirt. Races run from 8:30 AM until 1:45 PM. Donations are $20 for adults and $12 for children younger than 12. The 60K racers compete for a $5,000 prize.

U.S. 10K Classic and Family Sports Festival
The Cobb Galleria Centre, I-285 and Cobb Pkwy. • (770) 432-0100

While the sportspeople in your family bike, skate or run in this annual Labor Day event that begins at Cumberland Mall and ends at White Water Park, the rest of the family can party at the Galleria. Pony rides, exhibits and other activities keep the youngsters busy from 10 AM until 5 PM, and they're free. The racers pay a $20 registration fee and get to compete with about 10,000 others including wheelchair racers and walkers. There are $75,000 in prizes, which brings out the Olympians as well as other hopefuls. The 1998 festival adds a cycling competition and a longer route around Dobbins Air Force Base. The 1997 race raised $50,000 for children's charities.

Yellow Daisy Festival
Georgia's Stone Mountain Park, U.S. Hwy. 78 east to Stone Mountain Park exit
• (770) 498-5702

For more than 30 years in early September, Stone Mountain Park has staged this celebration of the Confederate Yellow Daisy, fields of which adorn the mountainside and bloom about this time. Arts and crafts booths line the wooded paved trails in the Special Events Meadow and Woodlands. Expect to see more than 400 vendors, live entertainment, a flower show, lots of food and more. The sale begins Saturday at 10 AM and closes at 7 PM and on Sunday runs from 10 AM to 6 PM. People show up to buy even earlier. The event is free with admission to the park — $6 per car, per day.

Olde English Festival
St. Bartholomew's Episcopal Church, 1790 LaVista Rd. • (404) 634-3336

Knights and knaves alike enjoy this pleasant festival on the wooded grounds of St. Bart's Church on a weekend in mid-September. The admission fee of $4 for adults and $2 for children is good for all three days; attractions include a flea market, a raffle, entertainment, wine, tea and more. There's no parking on-site; instead, park for free at Georgia Mental Health Institute, 1256 Briarcliff Road, and take the complimentary double-decker bus to the festival.

INSIDERS' TIP

MARTA's slogan, "MARTA is smarta!," is true. Atlanta's larger festivals routinely draw more than 100,000 people. Finding a parking spot near such big events can be a nightmare; you can save time and cut the hassle by taking MARTA for $1.50 per person.

Street of Dreams
Locations vary annually • (770) 614-7841

A popular September event, the Street of Dreams is always held at a new subdivision. A half-dozen expensive model homes are decorated by local designers and then opened for viewing. Each home is like a magazine page in 3D from the finest decor magazines where the au courant fabrics, colors and gizmos can be examined in depth. The homes are open for viewing every day except Mondays throughout the entire month. Tickets cost $8 for adults, $7 for seniors and children 4 through 12. Those younger than 4 can visit for free.

Alpenfest
Georgia's Stone Mountain Park, U.S. Hwy. 78 east to Stone Mountain Park exit
• (770) 498-5702

On a Saturday in late September, Stone Mountain Park welcomes visitors with "oom-pah-pah" bands that rock around the rock. Attractions at this two-day party include a German beer and wine garden serving wursts, kraut and strudel and a Festhalle with polka music and other entertainment. Admission to Alpenfest is $13 for adults and $6 for children younger than 11. Fee in addition to park admission of $6 per car, per day.

Ansley Park Home Tour
Various homes • (404) 872-TOUR

On a weekend in late September, owners of some of Atlanta's most distinctive older homes open their doors to visitors so that their neighborhood association can earn funds. Tickets are $12 in advance or $15 on tour days to view all the homes. Single home tours are $5. With your ticket you receive a walking map listing the homes you can see during the weekend. Visit one or many to get ideas on home renovation and decorating or to sneek a peek at how the other half lives. In 1997 the tour also included the headquarters of the Daughters of the American Revolution and the beautiful Christian Science Church.

Atlanta Greek Festival
Greek Orthodox Cathedral of the Annunciation, 2500 Clairmont Rd.
• (404) 633-5870

This annual fall tribute to Greek culture attracts more than 50,000 people over four days in late September. There's Greek music, dancing, wine, and Opa! what food: souvlaki, moussaka, gyros and honey-dripping baklava are made by members of the church. Admission is $3 for adults and $1 for children younger than 12.

The Atlanta Journal-Constitution Barbecue Fest
Gwinnett County Fairgrounds, 2405 Sugarloaf Pkwy., Lawrenceville
• (770) 963-6522

On a weekend in late September Atlanta's major daily hosts this annual event that features blues bands and barbecue. Participants get to vote on their favorite 'cue, stroll around and watch cooking demonstrations, enjoy children's activities and more. Children younger than 12 are free; everyone else pays $2 plus the cost of the food. Seventeen barbecue establishments participated in 1997.

Grant Park Tour of Homes
Various homes • (404) 522-7131

Grant Park is named for Col. Lemuel P. Grant, the transplanted Yankee civil engineer who designed the elaborate fortifications around Atlanta during the Civil War and who later donated 100 acres of wooded, hilly land near his home for a city park with no racial restrictions. The neighborhood around the park has many historic Victorian homes, both massive and modest. Fourteen homes were open to visitors in 1997, which was the 24th annual tour. You'll pay $10 to see the homes. No advance purchase is necessary. Tickets are distributed on the day of the tour in late September.

Sweet Auburn Heritage Festival
Auburn Ave. • (404) 525-0205

For nearly a century Auburn Avenue has been the backbone of black Atlanta. It picked up the "sweet" label at a time when it was functioning as the city's "other" main street, offering a full array of commercial, religious and entertainment institutions. Dr. Martin Luther King Jr.'s birth home, church and tomb are part of a National Historic Site on Auburn. The famous Royal Peacock Lounge once showcased soul music stars such as James Brown and Stevie Wonder; it continues to operate today. This festival in late September celebrates the street's rich heritage with three days of music, food, fun and shopping. No admission charged.

October

Lasershow

Georgia's Stone Mountain Park, U.S. Hwy. 78 east to Stone Mountain Park exit
• **(770) 498-5690**

October weekends are your last opportunities for the year to catch the Lasershow at Georgia's Stone Mountain Park. Grab a blanket for laying on top of or snuggling under during this performance that combines brilliant light with stirring musical refrains. See our May entry for more information.

Georgia Renaissance Festival

I-85 at Exit 12, Fairburn • **(770) 964-8575**

The Spring Renaissance Festival was so much fun they decided to have another one in the fall on each weekend in October. Lords and ladies, wenches, vassals and the occasional fool roam the 30-acre festival grounds, where more than 100 daily performances take place on 10 stages, and food concessions abound. A special attraction at the fall celebration is the Haunted Castle. The festival is open Saturdays and Sundays only. Admission fees are $11.95 for adults and $5.75 for children 6 to 15. Children younger than 6 are admitted free. Seniors pay $10.

AIDS Walk Atlanta

Piedmont Park and various streets
• **(404) 876-WALK**

Held on a Sunday in mid-October, this annual walkathon raises more than $1 million for AIDS service organizations. The event is organized by AID Atlanta. Stars appearing at the post-walk concert have included Atlanta's own Evander Holyfield and PC Carson and part-time Atlantan Elton John.

Tour of Southern Ghosts

Georgia's Stone Mountain Park, U.S. Hwy. 78 east to Stone Mountain Park exit
• **(770) 498-5702**

In mid-October something terrifying is happening out at the old plantation house. Seven nights a week, spooks, monsters and "haints"

take over the mansion at Stone Mountain. Storytellers spin webs of horror during evening candlelight tours of the antebellum plantation. Tours begin at 7 PM; the last tickets are sold at 9 PM. You'll pay $6 per adult and $3 per child (if you dare) in addition to the park's daily fee — $6 per car.

Japan Fest

Georgia's Stone Mountain Park, U.S. Hwy. 78 east to Stone Mountain Park exit
• **(770) 498-5702**

In late October this daylong celebration of Japanese culture offers a wide variety of demonstrations as well as performing arts workshops and exhibitions. It's sponsored by the Japanese Chamber of Commerce of Georgia, Japan American Society of Georgia and the consulate general of Japan in Georgia. The event is free with admission to the park — $6 per car, per day.

Oktoberfest

Helen • **(800) 858-8027**

Oompah pa! Hidden in the mountains just 70 miles northeast from Atlanta is an Alpine village look-alike. For more than 28 years during the last two weeks in October, Helen stages an Oktoberfest replete with lederhosen-clad bands, dancing ladies in dirndl skirts and beer, beer, beer. In 1997, 10 bands performed on their Festhalle. But if you prefer shopping to sitting, Alpine Helen, decorated like a Bavarian village, has lots of interesting shops along its cobblestone alleys that sell imported woolens and trinkets. Restaurants abound. Admission to the festival is $6 on weekdays, $7 on Saturdays, $3 for children 6 through 12 or free for those younger than 5. To get there from Atlanta, proceed north on I-85 to I-985; follow U.S. 129 to Cleveland, Georgia, until Ga. 75, which takes you directly to Helen. (See our Daytrips and Weekend Getaways chapter for more information about Helen.)

Scottish Festival and Highland Games

Georgia's Stone Mountain Park, U.S. Hwy. 78 east to Stone Mountain Park exit
• **(770) 498-5702**

Aye, 'tis the sons and daughters of Burns a-gathering for this annual celebration of Scottish heritage, also known as "Scots on the Rock." Kilted clans engage in athletic events, plus there are parades and pageantry galore with bagpiping, drumming and folk dancing. Daily admission is $11 for adults and $6 for kids. The military band starts up at 8 PM in the Coliseum. Tickets for band's concert are $17. There are also pipe and drum bands and brass bands, highland dancers and country dancers. All admission fees and ticket prices are in addition to the usual park admission of $6 per day, per car. Take MARTA — it's smarta and free.

Latin American Film Festival
Rich Auditorium of Woodruff Art Center, 1280 Peachtree Rd. • (404) 733-4570

Sponsored by the Latin American Art Circle of the High Museum of Art, this film festival is held at the end of October and extends through the beginning of November. Atlanta premieres of recent feature films from Latin America bring in film lovers and the cognoscenti. General admission is $5. Students and seniors pay $4.50, and museum members receive another discount. Frequently, talent from the films are present, and free receptions accompany the movies.

November

Lighting of Rich's Great Tree
Underground Atlanta, 50 Upper Alabama St. • (770) 913-5551

Even though Rich's once-proud downtown flagship store is gone, this holiday tradition begun in 1948 still continues. At 7 PM on Thanksgiving night, thousands of Atlantans gather to sing carols with mass choirs and await the lighting of Rich's Great Tree, an enormous evergreen decorated with basketball-size ornaments atop Underground Atlanta's parking garage. Even the scroogiest Scrooge is hard-pressed to produce a "bah, humbug!" when (during the highest note of "Oh, Holy Night") the switch is thrown, and the huge tree explodes with light. To share the fun but

in the privacy of your own home, tune in to the live broadcast on WSB-TV Channel 2.

Holiday Celebration
Georgia's Stone Mountain Park, U.S. Hwy. 78 east to Stone Mountain Park exit • (770) 498-5702

The park's holiday party goes on seven nights a week, with horse-drawn carriage rides, a decorated plantation home, Christmas music and a holiday laser show. The guest of honor, of course, is jolly ol' St. Nick, accompanied by his merry elves. More than two million lights are strung throughout the park, and you can go on a driving tour to see all the designs. Admission is $6 per car, per day. The lights are bright from the Friday after Thanksgiving through New Year's Eve.

December

The Atlanta Ballet-The Nutcracker
The Fox Theatre, 660 Peachtree St. N.E. • (404) 873-5811

The Atlanta Ballet's annual production of *The Nutcracker*, staged from early December through Christmas, has been a holiday tradition for more than 30 years. In 1994, for the first time in 10 years, the production returned to The Fox, which was the Atlanta Ballet's home for many years. (The ballet company and the movie palace share a common birth-year: 1929.) The production features an orchestra, a full company of dancers and more than 200 children. Tickets prices range from $20 to $45. Senior and children discounts are available. Tickets go on sale the beginning of October.

Atlanta Botanical Garden Country Christmas
1345 Piedmont Ave., at The Prado • (404) 876-5859

Since 1979, the Atlanta Botanical Garden has presented this one-day event, which attracts more than 2,000 visitors, as its gift to the city. The event is held the first Sunday afternoon in December. The garden and conservatory are bedecked in high holiday style, and there's fun for the whole family, with face painting, dancing, other entertainment and storytelling. Vendors sell a variety of foods, plus fresh greenery, and Santa himself pops in. There's very little parking on-site, so a free shuttle bus brings visitors from a nearby parking garage; call for the location of the garage. Admission is free.

Atlanta History Center Candlelight Tours
130 W. Paces Ferry Rd., N.W.
• (404) 814-4000

In early December, hundreds of candles illuminate acres of gardens and nature trails at the History Center in the heart of Buckhead. Traditional music and a bonfire enliven the Tullie Smith farm house; the grand 1928 Swan House mansion shimmers in holiday finery to the accompaniment of jazz music. Many of the center's paths are unpaved and not suitable for wheelchairs, but center personnel will gladly make arrangements for physically challenged persons. Phone ahead for assistance. Admission is $15 for adults, $12.50 for children younger than 12 and seniors. Members of the Atlanta History Center pay only $10.

Atlanta Symphony Orchestra Holiday Concerts
Symphony Hall, Woodruff Arts Center,
1280 Peachtree St. N.E. • (404) 733-5000

The Atlanta Symphony Orchestra's holiday performances are a great way to celebrate the season, and the lineup offers something for everyone. In 1997 the ASO again presented its very popular "Gospel Christmas" concerts, featuring the All-Atlanta Chorus under the direction of Sallie B. Parrish. Revered music director emeritus Robert Shaw conducted a program of holiday favorites as well as Handel's *Messiah*. There's also a children's holiday concert. "A Night in Old Vienna," New Year's Eve concert showcases favorite waltzes and

marches. Admission ranges from $18 to $47.50. Children's concerts are $13 and $15 for attending adults.

Christmas at Callanwolde
980 Briarcliff Rd. N.E. • (404) 872-5338

The first two weeks of December, you'll find Callanwolde bedecked in holiday finery. This elaborate, 27,000-square-foot mansion was once home to the eldest son of Coca-Cola's founder; now it's operated as a fine arts center. Some 20,000 people tour the lavishly decorated home during this two-week event. A special attraction is holiday music played on the gigantic 3,752-pipe, 20,000-pound Aeolian organ, the largest of its kind still in playable condition, around which the house was built. Admission is $10 for adults and $7 for seniors; it's $5 for children 4 through 12.

Egleston Children's Christmas Parade
Downtown Atlanta streets
• (404) 264-9348

Egleston Children's Hospital sponsors this annual Christmas parade through downtown Atlanta. The parade begins at 10:30 AM at Marietta Street and International Boulevard and continues up Peachtree Street where it concludes at the intersection of W. Peachtree and Peachtree streets at about 12:30 PM. Held the first Saturday morning in December, the parade features giant balloons, celebrities, bands, floats and Santa Claus. WSB-TV 2 telecasts the parade live; WFOX 97.1 FM broadcasts it on the radio.

Festival of Trees, Festival of Lights
Georgia World Congress Center, 285 International Blvd. • (404) 325-NOEL

For nine days in early December the Georgia World Congress Center (GWCC) sparkles with more than 200 trees and holiday vignettes created by noted interior designers as a fundraiser for Egleston Children's Hospital. The kiddies can get their kicks on an antique carou-

INSIDERS' TIP

Cirque de Soleil, the internationally acclaimed Montreal-based theatrical circus, sets up its big top in Atlanta every other year.

Conant Performing Arts Center at Oglethorpe University is
the venue for the Georgia Shakespeare Festival.

sel and a choo-choo train. Arts activities, shops
and entertainment complete the picture. Admission is $8 for adults, $5 for children 2 through
12 and for seniors. In 1997, a Festival of Lights
became part of this event. For the month of
December and into the first week of January
just across the boulevard from GWCC, Centennial Olympic Park is ablaze with holiday decorations including mega-light structures such as
a 50-foot "giving" tree. Each night, school and
church choirs perform. Viewing the park lights
and listening to the choirs are free.

Peach Bowl Parade
Downtown Atlanta streets
• (404) 586-8500

The Peach Bowl is played in the Georgia
Dome around New Year's Eve each year. A
big downtown parade preceding the game
honors the collegiate contenders. Usually 20
to 30 high school marching bands from across
the United States perform. Interspersed among
floats and baton groups and old-fashioned cars
are clowns and other street entertainment. The
parade begins at North Avenue and W.
Peachtree Street, continues up Peachtree
Street and terminates at Centennial Park. For

more information about the football game, see
our Spectator Sports chapter.

Firstnight Atlanta
Midtown streets • (404) 881-0400

Following a trend made popular in other
cities, Midtown businesses sponsor this alcohol-free, family-oriented New Year's Eve
celebration, which features music, art, theater and dance. Peachtree Street is closed
for several blocks in Midtown, and patrons
buy a button that entitles them to attend the
performances being offered continuously
throughout the evening. Admission is $7 in
advance or $12 at the gate.

Atlanta Rings in the New Year
**Underground Atlanta, 50 Upper Alabama
St. • (404) 523-2311**

A huge throng gathers every New Year's
Eve to ring out the old and ring in the new on
the plaza at Underground. Never to be outdone by the Big Apple, Atlanta drops its own
enormous piece of electrified fruit (a big peach,
of course!) down a tower to mark the beginning of the New Year. It's fun and free, but not
for the claustrophobic.

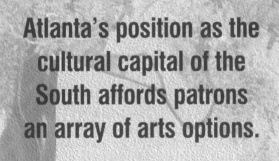

Atlanta's position as the cultural capital of the South affords patrons an array of arts options.

The Arts

From the early days, Atlantans have had a taste for big city entertainment. But it was to the northern meccas, primarily, that Atlantans trekked for their pleasures as Margaret Mitchell noted in *Gone With the Wind*, when she had her character Gerald O'Hara snipe about the Wilkeses — "Look at the way they go tearing up to New York and Boston to hear operas and see oil paintings." These days, it is no longer necessary to leave town to have the best cultural experiences. Within the last decade there has been tremendous growth in the Atlanta gallery and theater scene. In fact, an increasing number of Atlanta productions have made it successfully to off-Broadway and Broadway stages, and many of Atlanta's visual artists make fine livings right here, thank you very much.

With our ever-increasing population and our position as a rail hub, Atlanta has always been a natural stop for touring theater and opera companies, orchestras and lecturers. Our cultural interests were evident even during the tough years of Reconstruction when the arts were becoming big business: Two new opera houses opened in 1866, less than two years after Atlanta was put to the torch.

In 1882 Oscar Wilde, the Irish poet and apostle of Aestheticism, stopped in Atlanta near the end of a very successful U.S. lecture tour. (The long-haired, then 27-year-old, was so well-known here that a local man, Smith Clayton, had made a name for himself impersonating Wilde in a comedy act called "Wild Oscar.") During that visit to Atlanta, Wilde urged the audience to support the arts and encourage young artists.

As years passed and the city grew, Atlantans, wearied of importing their art from elsewhere, decided to heed Wilde's urgings and formed the city's first performance companies. The Atlanta Ballet danced its inaugural season in 1929; the Atlanta Symphony Orchestra first tuned up in 1945. In the 1970s and '80s, entrepreneurial directors and their supporters boldly launched theater groups in storefronts and attics. Some of these modest efforts survived to become leading Atlanta companies with widespread reputations for innovative theater.

Today, Atlanta's position as the cultural capital of the South affords patrons an array of arts options. The presence of both traditional and experimental arts organizations means that neither the classics nor avant-garde works are neglected: A typical year's offerings include traditional Shakespeare, symphony and grand opera as well as adult-oriented puppet theater, post-modern psychological drama and alternative productions of well-known works.

You can find varied offerings in the visual arts too. Besides such well-known venues as the architecturally renowned High Museum of Art, Emory University's Michael C. Carlos Museum and The High Museum of Art Folk Art and Photography Galleries, the city has myriad private and public galleries that show a variety of artists and styles. Traditional, primitive and modern painting, sculpture, studio crafts, drawing, photography and site specific pieces are part of the smorgasbord of artistic offerings on view at any given time in our city's vibrant gallery scene. We've listed a sampling of the many fine galleries in Atlanta. *The Atlanta Journal-Constitution* has a more complete listing of galleries and exhibits in its Saturday "Leisure" section. Also check *Creative Loafing's* "Happenings" section under "Visual Arts."

We've organized this chapter into the following categories: Performance Arts, including Music, Dance and Theater, in Atlanta and Beyond Atlanta; and Visual Arts, including Museums, Arts Centers and Galleries, in Atlanta and Beyond Atlanta. We cite recently produced or upcoming shows or events to give you an idea of an organization's areas of specialization. Call for performance dates and ticket information. Keep in mind that you save money by purchasing series or subscription tickets. We'll let you know when a group's performance venue is different than the address given after its name.

Performing Arts

Atlanta

Music and Dance

Atlanta Ballet
1400 W. Peachtree St. N.E.
• (404) 873-5811

The Atlanta Ballet has been a part of the city's life since dance visionary Dorothy Moses Alexander founded it in 1929. It's the oldest continually operating dance company in America and the official State Ballet Company of Georgia. Artistic Director John McFall is in his second season with the Atlanta Ballet, and Robert Chumbley is executive and music director.

The 1997-98 season began with *Peter Pan*, a ballet for all ages and wonderfully staged in the spectacular Fox Theatre where performers soared across the Fox's star studded ceiling. Also at the Fox is *Spring with Bouquet de Printemps* — an assortment of passionate premiers followed by *Swan Lake* Act II, an old favorite performed to Tchaikovsky's familiar music. *Coppelia*, a classic ballet in three acts based on a story by E.T.A. Hoffman (of *The Nutcracker* fame) charms The Fox audience in May 1998.

Aside from his activities with the Ballet, McFall leads the Atlanta Ballet Centre for Dance Education established in August 1996 that operates out of the Ballet's midtown studios and satellite facility in Buckhead. The Centre offers, among other things, classes for children in a preprofessional program of ballet, tap, jazz or modern movement techniques.

For dance lovers with busy schedules who can't commit to a date, the Atlanta Ballet of-

---

FYI

Three area codes serve the metro Atlanta area: 404, 770 and 678. Whether you live on Peachtree Street or in New York City, you must dial the code to reach any number in the area. The difference? Outside the area, you must dial "1," then the area code and phone number; inside the area, you need only dial the area code followed by the phone number.

---

fers a Flex Pass Option that allows for attendance at performances of choice, best seating available. The passbook contains four coupons that are redeemable two weeks prior to any performance.

The Atlanta Opera
1800 Peachtree St., Ste. 620
• (404) 355-3311

Opera has long held an important place in Atlanta's cultural life. From 1910 to 1987, the city was a regular stop on the Metropolitan Opera's tour, and Atlantans were treated to such legendary vocal talents as Enrico Caruso, Geraldine Farrar, Olive Fremstad and Birgit Nilsson. When the Met gave up touring for financial reasons in 1987, Atlanta was said to be the only city on the tour still meeting its financial obligation to the company.

Atlanta was the birthplace of the great diva Mattiwilda Dobbs. When she made her operatic debut in 1950 at age 25 at La Scala in Milan, Italy, the soprano was the first African-American to perform in that famous opera house. Dobbs, who graduated from Spelman College, went on to sing with the Metropolitan Opera. When her nephew, Maynard Jackson, was elected Atlanta's first black mayor, Dobbs returned to Atlanta to sing at his inauguration.

Several local companies produced a variety of operas through the years; then, in 1985 The Atlanta Opera was formed. The company produces fully staged operas with an excellent chorus of local singers and principal singers from around the nation and the world. Numerous veterans of the Metropolitan Opera have appeared in recent years, including Martile Rowland, Jan Grissom, Tatiana Troyanos, Hao Jiang Tian and Timothy Noble. Last fall, The Atlanta Opera received such widespread acclaim and exceptional attendance that it added a production as well as a subscription series and a matinee series to the '97-'98 season.

All performances are given in the original

language with English supertitles projected above the stage. A recent season included performances at the fabulous Fox Theatre and a benefit performance for the opera company held at the Piedmont Driving Club.

The 1998 Calendar of Events roster is Mozart's *Requiem*, *Andrea Chenier*, *Don Giovanni*, *Manon* and *La Traviata*. The benefit production is titled *Fantasies of the Opera*.

The company's Atlanta Opera Studio is an educational outreach program that brings fully staged and costumed operas into schools across Georgia. To charge season or individual tickets, call The Atlanta Opera at the number listed above or call (800) 35-OPERA.

Atlanta Symphony Orchestra
Symphony Hall, Woodruff Arts Center, 1280 Peachtree St. N.E. • (404) 733-5000

In only 50 years, the Atlanta Symphony Orchestra (ASO) grew from an inspired group of high school music students into a major orchestra with an international reputation. Since the 1976 release of its first commercial recording, the ASO's work has earned 14 Grammy Awards. The orchestra's renown grew steadily under the leadership of Robert Shaw, who passed the baton to Yoel Levi in 1988 after 21 years as music director. The ASO has commissioned and premiered works by Aaron Copland, Leonard Bernstein, Philip Glass and Gian Carlo Menotti. In 1994, the Pointer Sisters headlined the ASO's Gospel Christmas concerts, which were taped and broadcast nationally on PBS.

The regular ASO season runs from September to May. The festive summer series, inaugurated in 1972, takes place under the stars in the 6,000-seat amphitheater at Chastain Park, northwest of Buckhead. This very popular series, attracting more than 150,000 patrons, has grown to include 30 concerts headlined by famous pop and country stars. All shows feature reserved tables for picnicking in style. In 1998, the Atlanta Symphony celebrated its 25th season at Chastain.

Also during the summer, watch for the orchestra's free concerts in Piedmont and other city parks. Here you'll find tens of thousands of Atlantans lounging on blankets amid flickering candles, transported by the magic of music as the heat of the day breaks and the evening cool sweeps through the park.

A variety of full- and partial-season subscription packages is offered; call the Season Ticket Office (404) 733-4800. For tickets to orchestra concerts, call (404) 733-5000 or visit the High Museum Shop in Perimeter Mall, 4400 Ashford Dunwoody Road N.E. (a service charge applies). Ticket prices are reduced for family concerts and youth orchestra concerts. Public sneak preview rehearsals are held before the opening of six regular season concerts. These previews are given in Symphony Hall on the Thursday morning before the program's Thursday night premiere; general admission tickets for the previews are only $8.50.

Capitol City Opera Company
1266 W. Paces Ferry Rd. • (770) 592-4197

This local company produces traditional and modern operas at various performance venues during the year. In 1997 the troupe performed at the Michael C. Carlos Museum as well as 200 schools. Capitol City Opera offers a Chamber Players series and performs arias from various operas at special Tuesday night programs at San Gennaro Italian restaurant (see our Restaurants chapter for more information).

Dancers Collective
4279 Roswell Rd. N.E. Ste. 102-335 • (404) 233-7600

Organized in 1980 by Joanne McGhee and three other dancers formerly with the defunct Atlanta Contemporary Dance Company, the Dancers Collective provides Atlanta's only full-subscription season for contemporary dance. Since its inception, the Collective has brought to Atlanta more than 160 performances including the works of emerging artists Bebe Miller, David Dorfman and Susan Marshall and more established troupes including Pilobolus, Feld Ballet, Eiko & Koma, DanceBrazil and Urban Bush Women.

The Dancers Collective has no home to calls its own, but stages its season throughout the city at diverse venues including Agnes Scott College and The Rialto Center for Performing Arts.

The 1998 season includes Core Performance Company, a Decatur, Georgia-based group; David Dorfman Dance, a Manhattan company; and Garth Fagan Dance Company from Los Angeles.

From Great Tragedy, Great Hope

Atlanta's vibrant and thriving arts scene is a living and fitting memorial to the victims of one of the saddest events in the city's history. As part of a European tour organized by the Atlanta Art Association, 106 Atlantans boarded a chartered Air France 707 on June 3, 1962, at Orly airport in Paris. But as it taxied down the runway, the jet was unable to reach takeoff speed. The pilot tried unsuccessfully to abort, and the plane ran off the runway and exploded into flames. All 130 people on board, except three flight attendants in the tail section, were killed.

Close-up

In that awful moment, Atlanta lost many of its most ardent patrons of the arts. The arts movement in the city might have died with them but for the determination of Atlantans to continue the mission for which the 106 had lost their lives. In their memory, $13 million was raised through private donations to build the Atlanta Memorial Arts Center, 1280 Peachtree Street N.E., which opened in 1968.

The 10-acre arts complex was renamed the Robert W. Woodruff Arts Center in 1985 after its benefactor of the same name, an heir to the Coca-Cola fortune, but the structure that houses Symphony Hall, the Alliance Theatre and the Atlanta College of Art retains the name Memorial Arts Building.

The Richard Meier-designed High Museum of Art opened next-door in 1983

— continued on next page

Photo: High Museum of Art

The American Institute of Architects named The High Museum of Art one of the top-10 works of American architecture of the 1980s.

featuring a blazing white, marble facade. After a quarter-century as the physical and symbolic center of the Atlanta arts scene, the much-used Memorial Arts Building needed refurbishing. A $15 million renovation program was undertaken in mid-1994 and was completed in time for the '96 Olympics. During that time, the Memorial Arts Building reception area between Symphony Hall and the Alliance Theatre was dramatically redesigned and today features two stairways that flow like outstretched arms into the lobby where, at intermission, you can buy enormous raisin or chocolate chips cookies, alcohol, coffees or juice that must be consumed prior to returning to your seat. Displays of student art work frequently are showcased on moveable exhibit units in this area. The buildings facade was also modernized and is now more in sync, design-wise, with the look of the Meier structure next door.

On the lawn between the Memorial Arts Building and the High Museum stand two bronze sculptures, one is a striking, cigar-smoking Woodruff, the other is a casting of Rodin's *L'Ombre* (The Shade). It was donated by the French government in memory of the 106 Atlantans who died at Orly; their names are inscribed on black marble markers encircling the statue.

Georgia Tech's Robert Ferst Center for the Arts
349 Ferst Dr. N.W. • (404) 894-9600

On the campus of Georgia Tech, this center houses galleries, a student-run theater and the 1,200-seat Robert Ferst Theatre named for a benefactor who gave over 50 years of his time, talents and financial support to his alma mater. Between September and April, the Ferst Theatre hosts an eclectic arts series that typically includes leading artists in international and classical music, dance and opera. Series tickets are available.

Highlights of the 1998 schedule include soloist Ricardo Iznaola, the Paul Taylor Dance Company, the New York City Opera, Ying Quartet Strings, comedienne Paula Poundstone, vocal classicist Waverly Consort and violinist Itzhak Perlman.

Georgia Tech's student group DramaTech presents three major productions annually plus several one-acts in the Dean James E. Dull Theatre. The 1998 season marked 60 years of productions and includes *The Bacchae* and *Tommy*. Call (404) 894-2745 for ticket information.

Also performing at the Robert Ferst Center for the Arts at Georgia Tech is the Savoyards Musical Theatre Company. Established in 1980, the Savoyards perform Gilbert and Sullivan as well as other light opera favorites. Offerings in 1998 include *Kismet* and *Fiddler on the Roof*. Call (770) 565-9651 for tickets and information.

Look for more information about the Robert Ferst Center under "Arts Centers" later in this chapter.

Music at Emory
Glenn Memorial Auditorium, 1652 N. Decatur Rd.; Emory Performing Arts Studio, 1804 N. Decatur Rd.
• (404) 727-5050

Emory's Flora Glenn Candler International Artists series and Music à la Carte bring Atlanta audiences international stars. The 1998 program includes Academy of St. Martin in the Fields, Jeffrey Siegel's Keyboard Conversations, and a Renaissance vocal ensemble called The Tallis Scholars. "The Three Concertmasters" is a special program with the three renowned violinists: Cecylia Arzewski of the Atlanta Symphony Orchestra, Martin Chalifour of the Los Angeles Symphony and William Preucil of the Cleveland Orchestra.

The Rialto Center for the Performing Arts
80 Forsyth St. • (404) 651-4727

Having just opened in March 1996, this state-of-the-art hall is Atlanta's newest auditorium for the performing arts. It is housed in downtown Atlanta on the site of the old Rialto, a premiere movie palace complete with escalator. A declining downtown economy in the '80s closed the old theater's doors. Georgia State University, in 1991, purchased the site ultimately transforming it into a professionally managed, performing arts complex with 900 seats. Programming includes music, dance, theater and film to celebrate the cultural diversity and artistic excellence available in Atlanta. The Rialto season caters as much to the blue jean crowd as to the black-tie set. A sample of a recent season's offerings includes Brazil's *Bale Folclorico da Bahai*, Richard Goode and the Orpheus Chamber Orchestra, Suzy Boggus and the Rialto Symphony Orchestra, *Give 'em Hell, Harry!* with Tom Key (a local stage veteran) playing Harry Truman, Cecylia Arzewski, popular concertmaster of the Atlanta Symphony Orchestra and Jazz Jam Session with Dwight Andrews & Company.

Theater

7 Stages
1105 Euclid Ave. N.E. • (404) 523-7647

From its humble beginnings in a storefront in 1979, 7 Stages has grown into a major company operating two theaters in a former Little Five Points movie house. Risk-taking is a hallmark: An anti-Klan musical staged here in 1986 provoked the first Klu Klux Klan rally in the city in 30 years. Typical productions include experimental plays, dramas by local writers, international works and alternative stagings of classics. The complex has a 200-seat mainstage and a 90-seat black box space (entrance in the rear). A recent season features Brecht's *In the Jungle of Cities*, *The Burning Lake* by Celeste Miller, *The Bald Soprano* by Ionesco, The Freddie Hendricks Youth Ensemble of Atlanta in *PSALM 13* and *Dream Boy*, adapted and directed by Eric Rosen.

The Academy Theatre
501 Means St. N.W. • (404) 525-4111

The Academy produces all-original works and performs before school and community groups as well as at the playhouse. Through the spring, new plays are showcased through staged readings in the New Plays series. Offerings in the Academy's Theatre for Youth program include *Mixin' in the Mall*, a company-developed vehicle that explores conflict resolution and violence for grades 6 through 8, and *Fleas in the Cheese*, an introduction to theater for children in preschool through 2nd grade.

Actor's Express
King Plow Arts Center, 887 W. Marietta St. N.W., Ste. J-107 • (404) 875-1606

Founded in 1988 in a church basement, Actor's Express has grown into one of Atlanta's most respected theater companies led by artistic director/actor Chris Coleman. The group got its big break in 1991 when it produced the world premiere of *The Harvey Milk Show*, a musical based on the life of the assassinated San Francisco gay rights leader. It played to sold-out audiences and was later produced in other cities. In 1997 Actor's Express stepped on some toes when it modified *Oklahoma.* The publishers and copyright holders of the Rogers & Hammerstein work objected to the changes to the original *Oklahoma* script, so the director and cast had to make last-minute changes back to the original script or close the show.

A typical season includes classics, comedies and tough psychological dramas. For directions to the stage, read our King Plow Arts Center listing under "Arts Centers" in this chapter.

Agatha's — A Taste of Mystery
693 Peachtree St. N.E. • (404) 875-1610

Here's where you go when you can't decide whether to have dinner or solve a murder. Agatha's is a mystery dinner theatre where the audience is part of the show. When guests arrive, each is given a small assignment, such as making up goofy song lyrics or delivering a short line upon request. The plays are all originals with absurd names such as *An Affair to Dismember* and *Cat on a Hot Tin Streetcar*.

But while you're being entertained, you're also being wined and dined in high style: The evening includes a five-course meal, wine and beverages. (Cocktails, tax and tip are extra.) Admission is $39 per person Sunday through Thursday, $42 per person on Friday and $45 per person on Saturday. Monday through Saturday seatings are at 7:30 PM; on Sundays the fun starts at 7 PM. Agatha's is across from the Fox Theatre; call for reservations.

Alliance Theatre Company
Woodruff Arts Center, 1280 Peachtree St. N.E. • (404) 733-5000

The Alliance's status as a company of national importance was only enhanced when the Alfred Uhry (an Atlantan by birth) play, *Last Night at Ballyhoo*, won a Tony in 1996. Like his *Driving Ms. Daisy*, *Last Night* premiered in Atlanta at this Broadway-type theater in the heart of Midtown. The theater was also one of only three U.S. theaters chosen by playwright Tony Kushner to mount productions of his Tony Award- and Pulitzer Prize-winning play *Angels in America: Millennium Approaches*.

The Alliance Theatre Company is a nonprofit, professional company that produces mainstage, studio and children's productions. The company has historically been a vanguard for theatrical productions with world premieres including Tennessee Williams' *Tiger Tale* and Ed Gracyk's *Come Back to the Five and Dime, Jimmy Dean, Jimmy Dean*.

More recently Atlantan Pearl Cleage's *Flyin' West* as well as her latest play, *Bourbon at the Border*, were premiered in The Studio Theatre at Woodruff Arts Center. Seasons typically include contemporary plays, classic dramas and musicals. Plays scheduled for 1998 are *A Question of Mercy* by David Rabe, *The Colored Museum* by George C. Wolfe, *Medea* by Euripides, Richard Kalinoski's *Beast on the Moon* and Jon Marans' *Old Wicked Songs*.

Season ticket holders save 45 percent off the single-ticket price. A generous ticket exchange program exists that also means you might be able to pick up a last minute exchanged ticket. There isn't a bad seat in the house so take whatever is available. Call (404) 733-4600 for details.

Barking Dog Theatre
175 14th St. N.E. • (404) 885-1621

Now in its third season, Barking Dog Theatre was started by two 20-something Atlanta actors as a community of apprentices who speak about life with a collective voice that is raw, energetic and loud. The company presents an eclectic range of works each season and 1998 is no exception. The season begins with *10 x 10 Again!*, 10 plays each less than 10 minutes written by 10 authors and directed by 10 Atlanta directors. Barking Dog calls it a "Whitman's Sampler" of Atlanta theater and the ultimate in short attention-span entertainment. Christopher Kyle's play *The Monogamist* follows the sampler, and *Frankie and Johnny* at the Claire de Lune ends out the year. (First staged in Atlanta in 1989 by Horizon Theatre, *Frankie and Johnny* was a shocker since Horizon staged it with two actors getting out of bed with full frontal nudity for a brief segment at curtain rise. At the time, the city solicitor's office was run by a radical conservative who was responsible for having figurative paintings of undressed female models removed from public spaces as well as railing about other "public decency" issues. We often wondered how Horizon not only made it through that show's run without being raided but mounted the production a second time in 1990.)

Center for Puppetry Arts
1404 Spring St. N.W. • (404) 873-3391

Founded in 1978, this unusual theater and museum annually attracts more than 350,000 visitors. Housing three separate theaters and a museum featuring authentic Muppet characters plus puppets from around the world, the center is the largest facility of its kind in North America. Programs include family-oriented shows and puppet-making workshops and classes. (Read more about these programs in our Kidstuff chapter.) The center also has two adult-oriented series: the New Direction Series, which features innovative shows by the center's company as well as national and international artists, and the Xperimental Puppetry Theater, an annual showcase for works in progress for adult audiences. Shows for 1998 include *The Velveteen Rabbit*, *Peter Rabbit*, *The Body Detective* by Atlantan Jon Ludwig and Ludwig's *Aladdin*. The center is closed Sundays and holidays; museum admission is $5 for adults and $4 for children 13 and younger; performances cost extra, but the museum's special exhibits are $2 with the purchase of any other ticket for the same day. Call the above number for reservations and the ticket office, (404) 874-3089, or 24-hour hotline, (404) 874-0398, for schedules and performance prices.

Georgia Shakespeare Festival
Oglethorpe University, 4484 Peachtree Rd. N.E. • (404) 264-0020

This festival has seen its annual attendance more than double since its inaugural season in 1985. Performances are held on the campus of Oglethorpe University, whose Gothic architecture affords a fine setting for productions of Shakespeare. Originally staged in a tent, the Festival now has its own $5.7 million theater. The feel of the open-air tent has been retained through the use of roll-up walls for when the evenings are pleasant. But for those typical Georgia nights rich with humidity and the occasional thunderstorm, the walls will stay in place and air-conditioning will keep actors and audience blissfully comfortable.

An evening at the festival begins at 6:30 PM when the grounds open for picnicking. At 7 PM, there's cabaret-style entertainment. Performances begin at 8 PM. The rotating repertory schedule for 1998 begins in mid-June.

Horizon Theatre Company
1083 Austin Ave. N.E. • (404) 584-7450

Lisa and Jeff Adler have operated Horizon since 1983 out of an intimate, 185-seat theater in a rehabilitated school building at the intersection of Euclid and Austin avenues in Little Five Points. The professional, nonprofit company's productions range from satire to drama with a special emphasis on new plays and playwrights. In addition to four mainstage productions annually, Horizon develops new writers through its New Horizons readings and cultivates new theater-lovers through its Teen Ensemble and Senior Citizens Ensemble acting and playwriting programs.

In 1997 the season included *Abducting Hillary* by Dario Fo, Nicky Silver's *The Food Chain*, David Hare's *Racing Demon* and *The Screened-in Porch* by Marian X.

Jewish Theatre of the South
14th Street Playhouse, 173 14th St. • (770) 368-7469

Jewish Theatre of the South presents its first musical in 1998 with *Hello Muddah! Hello Faddah! The Allan Sherman Musical* as well as its first production of an American Jewish theater classic, Elmer Rice's *Counsellor-At-Law*. In the past, the Jewish community had attempted to create an audience for theater through the now defunct Habima, which was begun in the '70s under the direction of attorney/actor Howard Stopeck, but the Jewish Community Center auditorium was more like a high school stage than a professional theater. Audiences will love Jewish Theatre of the South's new home at the comfortable and centrally located 14th Street Playhouse in Midtown.

Jomandi Productions
1444 Mayson St. N.E. • (404) 876-6346

Founded in 1978, Jomandi is Georgia's oldest and largest African-American professional theater company. Jomandi has received numerous grants from prominent national arts organizations and tours more extensively than any other professional company in the Southeast. More than half its mainstage productions have been premieres; the remainder have been stage adaptations of works by established black writers. Performances are given at 14th Street Playhouse, 14th at Juniper streets. Jomandi also produces the annual Juneteenth emancipation celebration; see the entry in the June section of our Festivals and Events chapter.

MasterCard Broadway Series
659 Peachtree St. N.E., Ste. 900 • (404) 873-4300, (800) 278-4447 subscriber's hotline

The Fox Theatre is the setting for the American Express Atlanta Broadway Series, which presents national touring companies in top-notch productions of Broadway hits. A recent season included *Riverdance* at the Atlanta Civic Center and *Rent* at The Fox Theatre.

Tickets go on sale at the theater's box office six to eight weeks before a show opens. To charge by phone, call TicketMaster, (404) 817-8700; a convenience charge applies.

The Shakespeare Tavern
499 Peachtree St. N.E. • (404) 874-5299

Four blocks south of the Fox Theatre, this company produces the plays of Shakespeare and other classical authors. Although the setting is casual (chairs and tables for 175 people are arranged tavern-style), the productions are traditional — no need to worry that you'll find King Lear pushing a shopping cart through a post-nuclear slum. The company produces the trag-

Photo: High Museum of Art

The High Museum of Art's collection includes
more than 10,000 pieces.

edies as well as the comedies and tries hard to incorporate some of the lesser-known works.

Dine from a British pub-style menu provided by Chef for a Night catering before performances. You can buy beer, wine, coffee, tea and soft drinks before performances and at intermission.

Theater Emory
Mary Gray Munroe Theater at the Dobbs University Center, 600 Ashbury Cir.
• **(404) 727-5050**

Theater Emory has constructed a full-scale replica of an Elizabethan playhouse. Called "The Black Rose," both actors and studio audiences experience what it might have been like to go to a theater during the Elizabethan era. In 1998, a two-year Ibsen Project begins with *Pillars of Society* and two other Ibsen works. *The Lion and the Jewel* by Wole Soyinka, Nobel laureate and Emory professor, will end the 1998 season.

Theater of the Stars
P.O. Box 11748, Atlanta GA 30355
• **(404) 252-8960**

Since 1952, Theater of the Stars has brought national touring companies' shows to Atlanta. The regular season runs from June

to August, and performances are given at The Fox Theatre, 660 Peachtree Street. Past presentations have included *Stomp*, *A Chorus Line*, *Les Miserables*, *The Music Man*, *Phantom of the Opera* and *The King and I* with Hayley Mills. Having seen these same productions on Broadway, we can attest to the fact that the touring company shows are staged as glamorously and performed as diligently at ticket prices well below Big Apple fare.

Theatre Gael
14th Street Playhouse, 173 14th St.
• **(404) 876-1138**

Theatre Gael explores Celtic culture through the plays, poetry and music of Ireland, Scotland and Wales. Theatre Gael kicked off its 1997-98 season with Sean O'Casey's *The Shadow of a Gunman*, followed by Dylan Thomas' *Under Milkwood* and *Farewell The Fair Country* by Atlantan John Stephens, which toured the metro area. In 1998 Sebastian Barry's *The Steward of Christendom* is being staged followed by Brian Friel's *Molly Sweeney*.

Theatrical Outfit
14th Street Playhouse, 173 14th St.
• **(404) 872-0665**

Theatrical Outfit was founded in 1976 in a

space above an old laundromat in Virginia-Highland. In 1985 the company scored a big hit with a lavish production of *The Rocky Horror Show* that featured soon-to-be famous, cross-dressing Atlantan, RuPaul. Now the company stages four productions a year at the 14th Street Playhouse. The Outfit's annually updated *Appalachian Christmas*, a play written by local writer Tom Key, has become an Atlanta holiday tradition. The 1998 season consists of Flannery O'Connor's *Displaced Person* and *Cotton Patch Gospel*.

Beyond Atlanta

Music and Theater

Spivey Hall
Clayton State College, 5900 N. Lee St., Morrow • (770) 961-3683

Fifteen miles south of Atlanta (Exit 76 off I-75), Clayton State College is home to what many view as the finest performance venue in the entire metro area. Since it opened in 1991, the $4.5 million Spivey Hall has won raves from critics and performers alike. Overlooking a 12-acre lake, the 398-seat hall's centerpiece is its 79-rank, 4,413-pipe Ruffatti organ.

Spivey Hall presents some 175 concerts annually, covering a broad range of musical traditions. Subscription packages let patrons choose to attend all the concerts of a certain type, such as piano, organ or jazz, or custom-design their series with six or more concerts. In addition to guest-artist concerts, Clayton State College music students and faculty perform in the hall.

Theatre in the Square
11 Whitlock Ave., Marietta
• (770) 422-8369

This professional company, whose 225-seat facility is housed in a former cotton warehouse, attracts the second-largest audience of any Atlanta area theater (The Alliance Theatre takes the top spot). The company found itself at the center of an international controversy in 1995 when local politicians, outraged at a risqué comedy staged here, passed Cobb County's divisive resolution condemning "the gay lifestyle." The ensuing uproar caused the Atlanta Committee for the Olympic Games to move the preliminary Olympic volleyball events Cobb County had been scheduled to host.

The theater's 1998 offerings include *Moon Over Buffalo*, *Hedda Gabler*, *Appalachian Strings* and *Smoke on the Mountain*.

The Village Playhouses of Roswell
617 Holcomb Bridge Rd., Roswell
• (770) 998-3526

The Playhouses include Roswell Village Theater (RVT), Village Center Playhouse and Storybook Theater for children's fare. The 1998 season for Village Center includes *Steel Magnolias* by Robert Harling; *Mr. Hobbs Vacation* adapted by F. Andrew Leslie from the best-selling novel by Edward Streeter; *Fallen Angels* by Noel Coward; *You Can't Take it With You* by Moss Hart and George S. Kaufman; Neil Simon's *Plaza Suite*, *Nunsense* and the all-time holiday favorite, *A Christmas Carol*. RVT's season includes *Foxfire*, Susan Cooper and Hume Cronyn's tale about a Rabun County, Georgia, family and *Death on the Nile* by Agatha Christie. For the kiddies, Storybook Theater offers seven plays including *Winnie*

INSIDERS' TIP

The Atlanta Ballet makes sure the love of dance continues into the next generation by bringing dance to youngsters who might not otherwise attend a performance. Centre Force, a team of four professional dancers, performs at parks, schools, community centers and shopping malls. Kids-in-Step allows for more than 20,000 schoolchildren to see abridged productions of Atlanta Ballet classics by reducing admission costs to only $5 per student. And during the holiday season, the Atlanta Ballet visits schools to perform 50-minute exhibitions of *The Nutcracker* that encourage audience participation.

the Pooh, *Sleeping Beauty*, *Ali Baba* and the *Magic Cave*. Call the theaters for specific dates and times of performances.

Visual Arts

Atlanta

Museums

Atlanta International Museum of Art and Design
Peachtree Center, Marquis Two, 285 Peachtree Center Ave. N.E.
• (404) 688-2467

Established in 1989, this museum celebrates the craftsmanship of the world's cultures through ethnographic, folk art and design exhibits. It is a nonprofit educational organization supported by public and private funds. Admission is free; the museum is open Tuesday through Saturday, 11 AM to 5 PM.

Clark Atlanta University Art Galleries
Trevor Arnett Hall, Clark Atlanta University, 223 James P. Brawley Dr. S.W.
• (404) 880-6968

Open from 11 AM to 4 PM Tuesday through Friday and noon to 4 PM Saturday, this college art gallery has an extensive collection of African-American work. Included in the collection are examples from 20th-century masters Charles White, Jacob Lawrence, Elizabeth Catlett, Henry Ossawa Tanner and Romare Bearden. The galleries are on the second floor. Admission is free.

The Hammonds House Galleries and Resource Center of African-American Art
503 Peeples St. S.W. • (404) 752-8730

Housed in one of the oldest homes in historic West End, Hammonds House is the only Georgia museum dedicated to African-American fine art. What is believed to have been the first kindergarten in Atlanta once operated in one wing of this pre-Civil War home. Today the building houses a collection of more than 250 works of art, mainly by African Americans.

National and local artists are represented in the collection that also includes African and Haitian works. In addition to exhibitions, Hammonds House offers lectures, classes and a resource center for scholars (by appointment).

Admission is a $2 donation for adults and a $1 donation for children and seniors; the facility is closed to the public on Mondays. Hours are 10 AM to 6 PM Tuesday through Friday and 1 to 5 PM Saturday and Sunday. Hammonds House has free parking.

The High Museum of Art
Woodruff Arts Center, 1280 Peachtree St. N.E. • (404) 733-HIGH

When The High Museum of Art opened in its new building in October 1983, *The New York Times* called it "among the best museum structures any city has built in at least a generation." Richard Meier designed the gleaming white museum with its curved glass wall overlooking Peachtree Street. Its effect is at once both classical and ultramodern, rather like a wedding cake for the Jetsons. The $20 million High has won numerous design awards; in 1991 the American Institute of Architects named it one of the top-10 works of American architecture of the 1980s.

Inside the huge, skylit central atrium, sloping, half-circular ramps conform to the front wall's curve and climb to the top floor. You may wish to start at the top: It's fun to take the elevator all the way up, then walk through the galleries and down the ramps at your own pace. The museum's 10,000-piece permanent collection includes contemporary and classical paintings and sculpture by European and American artists plus African art, photography and folk art. Throughout the year, selections from the permanent collection share the space with major traveling exhibitions. The museum gift shop sells exhibition catalogs, posters and gifts.

The Visual Arts Learning Space on the main floor offers *See for Yourself* an interactive computer program designed to introduce visitors to the art disciplines including color, line, composition and light. The walls of the space are lined with art from the Museum's collection, and computers, strategically spaced, have a program which illustrates an artistic element.

Fräbel Glass: An Atlanta Tradition

Without a doubt, the artist whose work is most recognized and exported from Atlanta — through gifts to dignitaries — is the glass torchwork of Hans-Godo Fräbel, a native-born German who arrived in Atlanta in 1966. Queen Elizabeth II, Margaret Thatcher, Jimmy Carter, Julia Child, Anwar Sadat, even Billy Payne (who made the Centennial Olympic Games a reality for Atlanta) have received Fräbel crystal sculptures as gifts from the City of Atlanta, the State of Georgia or corporate entities who want something special as a commemoration of an event. In fact, you can pretty much count on sitting through a Fräbel-glass gift-giving speech whenever someone important leaves a post, visits the city or has achieved some importance in Atlanta.

Fräbel (pronounced like table) first learned his craft at the Jena Glaswerke in Mainz, West Germany. After immigrating to Atlanta, Fräbel worked initially at Georgia Tech in the scientific glass lab and later continued his studies of glass as an art form at Georgia State and Emory universities.

The Fräbel Studio was founded in 1968. In the European tradition, the master artist passes his talent on to apprentices who may work for years before they are considered accomplished enough to produce signature pieces.

What makes a Fräbel sculpture so popular is the fact that it is, after all, glass. Fragile, delicate glass. Secondly, his imagery is easily comprehended and offends no one: magnolia blooms, a peach (Georgia is known as "The Big Peach"), flamingos and dogwood blossoms are all popular motifs.

The Fräbel Studios design for any profession or sentiment (you can view President Jimmy Carter's glass donkey at the Carter Center), and not just for the rich and famous. Everyone is welcome to stop by the Buckhead gallery for a look-see and consultation. A self-guided tour of Fräbel's Buckhead atelier reveals a working studio and museum

— continued on next page

Photo: Fräbel Studio

The City of Atlanta has purchased Fräbel Studio glass gifts for visiting emperors, princesses and prime ministers.

where one can experience this unique art form Fräbel calls "sculptural flamework." Seated at stations in the hot glass area, apprentices and masters work the boron glass with gas-fed torches until the glass tubing has reached a temperature high enough to be fashioned into shapes and pieces. They are then joined together into elaborate branches of trees, arms and legs of dancers or even the semblance of reeds blowing in the wind. The next stop is the annealing ovens where the sculptures must slowly cool until the inside and outside of the glass is all of one temperature. It is here that poorly crafted pieces will explode if bubbles of air have been trapped in the glass. After six to eight hours the pieces are ready for further surface treatments. Some will be sand-blasted to render areas opaque. Many pieces are then exhibited in silhouette against dark velvet in lighted cubicles in the gallery area, which is part of the tour.

Fräbel Studio apprentices spend three months learning the craft and as many as five years as journeymen doing production work in the studio. They may also produce original designs for Mr. Fräbel's consideration. Once the journeymen have achieved a certain level of originality and competence of the art, they may be considered masters themselves. If you wonder how you can tell if a work is that of the master himself or of others from the studio, just look at the bottom of a sculpture: If it is signed "FS," it is probably a production piece. Those artworks that come directly from the hands of Mr. Fräbel are signed "GF." Each of the pieces has a completion date scratched into the surface of the glass.

You don't have to plan to purchase a Fräbel piece to visit the Fräbel Studio and Gallery at 695 Antone Street N.W., just off Northside Drive in Buckhead. Tour hours are from 9 AM to 6 PM, Monday through Friday, and from 9 AM to 3 PM on Saturday. Call for the tour (there's a six-person limit) at (404) 351-9794.

The goal is for participants to gain comprehension of art concepts through the computer as well as the viewing of actual artifacts.

The museum's exhibit, *Picasso: Masterworks from The Museum of Modern Art* that began in November 1997 and continued into early 1998 was made possible through contributions totalling $1.5 million from corporations, foundations and individuals. It was the most successful fund-raising effort in the Museum's history. Other exhibits in 1998 include *Henri de Toulouse-Lautrec: Prints from the Stein Collection*, *Walker Evans Simple Secrets: Photographs from the Collection of Marian and Benjamin A. Hill*, *Out of Bounds: 32 Self-Taught American Artists of the 20th Century*, and *Monet and Bazille and Ellsworth Kelly: The Early Drawings*.

The High Museum is open Tuesday through Thursday and Saturday, 10 AM to 5 PM; Sunday noon to 5 PM; and Friday, 10 AM to 9 PM. It's closed on Mondays and holidays. Admission is $6 for adults, $4 for students with ID and persons older than 64, and $2 for youth 6 to 17. Admission is free for museum members and children younger than 6. Occasionally a spe-

cial exhibition may have a surcharge but will be free to all on Thursday afternoons from 1 to 5 PM. Special admission prices and extended hours prevail during some exhibitions.

The 135,000-square-foot High Museum of Art is part of the Robert W. Woodruff Arts Center and is served by the Arts Center MARTA station. Paid parking is available in the Arts Center garage; there is limited on-street parking behind the Arts Center. You may also park on some streets in the Ansley Park neighborhood across Peachtree Street, but be sure to obey all posted regulations and cross busy Peachtree only at the pedestrian crosswalks. The least expensive and hassle-free transportation option is to take MARTA, exit at the Arts station, and simply walk across Lombardy Way to the museum. This is also the best way to get to the Atlanta Symphony, the Atlanta College of Art and the Atlanta Theatre.

The High Cafe with Alon's is a basement level eatery open at various hours throughout the museum's hours of operation. A chain of three, Alon's began in Virginia-Highlands, opened a branch across from The Fox Theatre. Alon's was asked to create a space at the museum. Visitors now get to take a break in this windowed-facility munching on Alon's signature sandwiches (delicious crusty bread), soups, croissants and muffins that look good and taste better.

The High Museum of Art Folk Art and Photography Galleries
30 John Wesley Dobbs Ave. N.E.
• **(404) 577-6940**

On the ground floor of the Georgia-Pacific Center at the corner of Peachtree Street and Dobbs Avenue, just north of Woodruff Park, the multilevel downtown branch of the High showcases photography and folk art. The museum is open Monday through Saturday, 10 AM to 5 PM, and admission is always free. Take MARTA to the Peachtree Center station; follow the signs to the station's south exit at Ellis Street; the 51-story Georgia-Pacific Center is across Peachtree Street; the museum's main entrance is on the Dobbs Avenue side; you may also enter through the building's lobby.

Exhibits during 1998 include *The Flag in American Indian Art*, *American Photographs: The First Century* and a retrospective of the works of Roy DeCarava an African-American photographer whose work includes a series on the daily life in Harlem.

Michael C. Carlos Museum
Emory University, 571 S. Kilgo St. N.E.
• **(404) 727-4282**

Internationally acclaimed architect Michael Graves designed this 45,000-square-foot building on the quadrangle at the heart of Emory University. Finished in rose and white marble, the museum's striking design suggests a temple. Dramatic twin staircases on the building's front rise to the third level, which is adorned by three levels of columns.

The design's interpretation of ancient and classical elements is strikingly appropriate to the museum's 12,000-piece collection that, although varied, is strongest in its selection of objects from antiquity. Art and objects of daily life from ancient Egypt, Greece, Rome, Africa and the Americas are displayed inside galleries whose proportions and features honor timeless design ideals.

Free parking is allowed on campus except where restricted or reserved; there's a small lot right behind the museum; paid parking is available in the Boisfeuillet Jones Building lot nearby. If you visit the Carlos on a weekend, you should have no trouble parking. On MARTA, take the 6 Emory bus (from Lindbergh or Edgewood/Candler Park stations) or the 36 North Decatur (from Arts Center or Avondale stations) and get off at the university's white front gate; follow the signs to the museum.

The museum is open seven days a week: Monday to Saturday, 10 AM to 5 PM (except Friday until 9 PM); Sunday noon to 5 PM; it's closed on major holidays. Admission is by donation — $3 is suggested. Exhibits at the museum in 1998 include *Tears of the Moon: Ancient American Precious Metals* from the permanent collection; *Sepphoris in Balilee: Crosscurrents of Culture*; and *The Buddha's Art of Healing*.

Robert C. Williams American Museum of Papermaking
Institute of Paper Science and Technology, 500 Tenth St. N.W.
• **(404) 894-7840**

On the outer limits of the Georgia Tech campus, this tiny museum is located on the main floor of the Institute of Paper Science and Technology. Each show lasts three months and features artifacts having to do with papermaking by hand or machine from B.C. to present times. Changing exhibitions bring in paper artists so that the entire spectrum of the paper arts from history to art to science are covered.

In 1998 the changing exhibition schedule

INSIDERS' TIP

Looking for an art or performance event? You can get free information on the Atlanta arts scene 24 hours a day by calling the Arts Hotline, (404) 853-3ART, a service of the City of Atlanta Bureau of Cultural Affairs.

began with Cynthia Alderice, followed by a Watermarks show, Maps, Maps, Maps, Zelda, and in the fall of 1999, the museum mounts a joint exhibition with the Corcoran Gallery in Washington, D.C.

Hours are 9 AM to 5 PM Monday through Friday. Admission is free.

William Breman Jewish Heritage Museum
1440 Spring St. N.W. • (404) 873-1661

The Southeast's largest Jewish museum, dedicated to collecting, preserving, studying and interpreting the history and culture of the Atlanta Jewish community, opened in June 1996. Rotating exhibits and educational programming and two core museums as well as archives and libraries distinguish the William Breman Jewish Heritage Museum.

Housed in the Atlanta Jewish Federation, the museum undertaking was made possible by a contribution from William Breman and the Atlanta Jewish Federation. A new building on Spring Street (the land itself a gift of the Selig family) was constructed just two blocks south of Interstate 75 in Midtown adjacent to the Center for Puppetry Arts.

The first core gallery documents the Holocaust years and the second profiles the Jews of Atlanta from 1845 to the present. Rotating exhibitions for 1998 include *French Children of the Holocaust/A Memorial Exhibition*; *Jews Germany Memory*, a photo exhibit chronicling the relationship between Germany and its Jews; *Masters of Ceremony*, the Second Annual Exhibition and Sale of Contemporary Handcrafted Judaica; and *Birth of Israel/Celebrating Fifty Years of Life*.

The museum also houses the Ida Pearle and Joseph Cuba Community Archives and Genealogy Center where individual and family papers, business and organizational records, oral histories and visual arts reveal Atlanta's Jewish history. A library with resource materials for genealogical research and archival materials including Holocaust-related books, videos and more is available for scholars and students, and a Discovery Center with hands-on activities related to the Museum's exhibitions keeps children involved.

The Lillian and A.J. Weinberg Center for Holocaust Education at the Museum sponsors summer courses for teachers, exhibitions, school programs, teacher guides and general public programs designed to heighten Holocaust awareness.

Security is tight at the William Breman Jewish Heritage Museum. Parking is free. Hours are Monday through Thursday 10 AM to 5 PM, Friday 10 AM to 3 PM and Sunday 1 to 5 PM. Admission is $5 for adults, $3 for students and seniors 62 and older. Children younger than 6 are admitted gratis if accompanied by an adult. Group rates are available.

Arts Centers

Callanwolde Fine Arts Center
980 Briarcliff Rd. N.E. • (404) 872-5338

Today operated as a fine arts center in a combined public/private effort, Callanwolde was originally the home of Howard Candler, the eldest son of Coca-Cola's founder. The dramatic Gothic-Tudor style mansion was designed by Henry Hornbostel, designer of Emory University, and completed in 1920. The 27,000-square-foot mansion's plan stresses openness: Almost all rooms adjoin great halls on each floor, and the entire building is centered around a large enclosed courtyard.

In addition to details such as walnut paneling, stained glass and delicate ceiling and fireplace reliefs, the house has an amazing feature: a 3,752-pipe, 20,000-pound Aeolian organ, the largest of its kind still in playable condition, that is audible in every room. In 1920, the new organ cost $48,200.

Callanwolde is in the elegant Druid Hills section (of *Driving Miss Daisy* fame) laid out by famed landscape architect Frederick Law Olmsted, designer of New York's Central Park. The original 27-acre estate has been reduced to 12 acres. With assistance from the federal Housing and Urban Development department and DeKalb County, a neighborhood association purchased the property in 1972 for $360,000 then turned it over to the county to maintain as an arts center.

A nonprofit foundation directs the arts programs, which include classes, performances and exhibitions. Dance, drama, painting, photography, pottery, textiles, writing and more are all part of Callanwolde's art offerings.

Christmas at Callanwolde is the center's most

popular event: Each year during the first two weeks of December more than 20,000 visitors tour the lavishly decorated mansion and enjoy holiday music on the grand organ. (See December in our Festivals and Events chapter.)

Except for special events, admission to Callanwolde and its formal garden is free. The art shop is open Monday through Saturday, 11 AM to 3:30 PM and has ever-changing art on the walls by local artisans. The conservatory has varied hours; call (404) 872-5730 for information.

Ichiyo Art Center
432 E. Paces Ferry Rd. N.E.
• (404) 233-1846, (800) 535-2263

This arts center focuses on Asian art with special emphasis on Japanese art and culture. The center offers classes for adults and children (see our entry in Kidstuff) in various subjects including Chinese brush painting, Japanese cooking, origami (the Japanese art of folded paper shapes) and ikebana, Japanese floral art. Ichiyo mounts exhibits of contemporary Japanese prints and other visual arts and offers a selection of Japanese papers, calligraphy supplies, gifts and home accessories including Noguchi lamps. Ichiyo has a mail-order catalog for paper, rubber stamps and ikebana supplies. The center is open Monday through Saturday 10 AM to 6 PM.

King Plow Arts Center
887 W. Marietta St. N.W. • (404) 885-9933

In an amazing transformation, an antiquated, 165,000-square-foot plow factory near the waterworks in northwest Atlanta became an exciting arts center. King Plow Arts Center, whose first phase opened in 1991, now houses more than 50 tenants. These include galleries representing both fine and commercial art, artists' residential and working space, architectural and graphic design firms, the Actor's Express theater and the Food Studio, a visually striking restaurant. King Plow's galleries host a variety of shows each year.

Throughout the Center, the original brick walls are exposed and dotted here and there with old brick molds and other industrial elements that blend well with the thoughtful renovations. Call for a current listing of art shows.

Use the free valet parking since many of the lot spaces are reserved for tenants.

Nexus Contemporary Art Center
535 Means St. N.W. • (404) 688-1970

Nexus has been a vibrant force on the Atlanta art scene since it was founded as a co-op storefront gallery in 1973. Later it occupied a former elementary school; then in 1989, it purchased a historic warehouse complex west of Five Points. The 40,000-square-foot center houses an art book press, studios, a large gallery that presents six major exhibitions annually and an 1,800-square-foot Performance Cafe. Shows at Nexus for 1998 include *Mouvement Quotidien: An Aspect of French Art in the Nineties*.

Admission is free to members. General admission is $3; students and seniors pay $1. The gallery is open Tuesday through Saturday, 11 AM to 5 PM.

Robert Ferst Center for the Arts Gallery at Georgia Tech
349 Ferst Dr. N.W. • (404) 894-2787

The Richards Gallery and the Westbrook Gallery, both housed at the Ferst Center, are side-by-side rooms and can be viewed easily together. The 1998 schedule includes Cynthia Alderdice paintings and woodcuts, Ellen Grobman paintings, a Georgia Tech student art show and the season ends with an Asian Artists group exhibition. The art shows are held in conjunction with performances at the center, and hours change accordingly.

Robert W. Woodruff Arts Center
1280 Peachtree St. N.E. • (404) 733-4200

This multi-building complex houses some of the city's premier arts institutions. Home to the High Museum, the Atlanta Symphony Orchestra, the Alliance Theatre Company and the Atlanta College of Art, the center occupies one large city block in the heart of midtown Atlanta. We detail the first three components of the center in other sections of this chapter. The Atlanta College of Art, founded in 1928, is one of the Southeast's outstanding independent art colleges. In addition to its four-year programs, the college offers community education classes.

Photo: Atlanta Symphony Orchestra

Yoel Levi has led the Atlanta Symphony Orchestra since 1988.

The college has its own gallery that hosts exhibitions of contemporary art and design.

TULA Arts Complex
75 Bennett St. N.W. • (404) 351-3551

TULA is at the end of the Bennett Street antique shopping district (left off Peachtree Road just north of Piedmont Hospital). A privately developed, multiuse arts center, it houses more than 45 galleries, artists' studios and arts-related businesses. TULA is home to IMAGE Film/Video Center, (404) 352-4225, which promotes the cinematic arts and exhibits lots of offbeat and experimental movies. Galleries at TULA include Ariel Gallery, (404) 352-5753; Kiang Gallery, (404) 351-5477; Opus One Gallery, (404) 352-9727; and Culture Room, (404) 355-9955. Hours for the complex are 10 AM to 6 PM Monday through Saturday and noon to 6 PM Sunday.

Galleries

Aliya/Ardavin Gallery
1402 N. Highland Ave. N.E.
• (404) 892-2835

Conveniently located near Indigo and Mambo, two of the most popular bistros in Atlanta (see our Restaurants chapter), Aliya/Ardavin is open late to accommodate the long waits the restaurants frequently demand. Works from Canadian artists, ceramics and glass art are featured.

Anthony Ardavin Gallery
309 E. Paces Ferry Rd. N.W., Ste. 110
• (404) 233-9686

This gallery specializes in young Georgia artists working in a variety of media and styles including narrative and abstract painting. Lee Bomhoff and Robert Sentz are two of the many up-and-coming artists Ardavin represents.

Abstein Gallery
558 14th St. N.W. • (404) 872-8020

This large gallery features a variety of artists and a broad range of work: abstract, figurative and landscape painting, sculpture, ceramics, drawings and collage. Sandi Tax and Eileen Tantillo are a few of the artists featured in the gallery.

Art With An Attitude
309 East Paces Ferry Rd. N.E., Ste. 140
• (404) 842-1913

Art With An Attitude devotes itself to national and international artists who make strong visual impact through either scale, color or unusual imagery. It's located in the Aaron Building which faces North Fulton Drive.

City Gallery East
675 Ponce de Leon Ave. N.E.
• (404) 817-7956

Operated by the city's Bureau of Cultural Affairs, the 6,000-square-foot City Gallery East is on the first floor of the City Hall East government building. Built by Sears, Roebuck & Co., the massive red brick structure opened in 1926 and was the retailer's Southeast catalog order center for decades. Directly across the street, the Atlanta Crackers baseball team used to play in a now-demolished stadium. (This was back in the days before Major League ball came to town.) The gallery presents five major exhibitions each year spotlighting contemporary visual art. Atlanta artists are a special focus, but the gallery does not exclude the works of other U.S. and international artists.

Connell Gallery
333 Buckhead Ave. N.E. • (404) 261-1712

Specializing in contemporary crafts, the Connell Gallery showcases craft media art incorporating fiber, wood, jewelry, furniture and ceramics. The gallery features well-known contemporary craft artists from all over the country including furniture artist Craig Nutt, ceramicist Tim Taunton, wood turner Rude Osolnik and jewelry designer Earl Pardon. Other artists include Bennett Bean, Michael Davis, Arline Fisch, John Garrett, Grady Kimsey, Sam Maloof, Dante Marioni on through the alphabet to Yvonne Porcella, Karyl Sisson and Pam Studstill.

C. Duncan Connelly Fine Art
309 East Paces Ferry Rd. N.E., Ste. 105
• (404) 816-1505

Antique prints and maps as well as 19th- and early 20th-century paintings are shown. Local Southern artists represented include Aiden Lassell Ripley, Walter Whitcomb Thomspon and Elisabeth Paxton Oliver.

Culture Room
75 Bennett St. N.W., Ste. B-1
• (404) 355-9955

Culture Room, formerly known as New.Vision.Space., showcases emerging and minority artists and cultural workers. It is a nonprofit gallery that has expanded its vision to include not only visual arts but the spoken word, panel discussions, music and theater.

Eclectic Electric
1393 N. Highland Ave. N.E.
• (404) 875-2840

This fun gallery features artists who work with light. With everything from sculptural lamps to bicycles-as-chandeliers, Eclectic Electric provides an illuminating (pardon the pun) artistic experience.

Fay Gold Gallery
247 Buckhead Ave. N.E. • (404) 233-3843

Fay Gold taught art privately prior to opening her gallery in 1980. She changed the gallery scene in Atlanta almost single-handedly by bringing in New York artists and others who could command top-dollar pricing for their goods. Now located in a 7,000-square-foot space designed by her architect son in the heart of Buckhead, she continues to house solo exhibitions and group shows of some of the biggest names in the art world — Radcliffe Bailey, Tony Herandez, John Okulick, Helmut Newton, Robert Mapplethorpe and Horst P. Horst, to name just a few. Periodically, the work of local artists are also exhibited.

Galerie Timothy Tew
309 E. Paces Ferry Rd. N.E.
• (404) 869-0511

Formerly housed in TULA, Galerie Timothy Tew is now on East Paces Ferry where so many other galleries are located. Artists represented include Sam Alterkruse, Marie-Cecile Aptel and Haidee Becker. Some of the highlights of the 1998 season include Jim Byrne, a painter with psychologically poignant works; Equisses by Foujio Takeya featuring pastel and crayon landscapes from the estate of the artist; geometric and organic forms by the New Mexican artist Jonathan Sobol and the flower paintings of Haidee Becker, a London-based artist.

Jackson Fine Art
3115 E. Shadowlawn Ave. N.E.
• (404) 233-3739

Specializing in 20th-century and contemporary photography, Jackson's client list includes the Metropolitan Museum of Art, the High Museum of Art, the Los Angeles County

Museum of Art, Coca Cola, Delta Airlines and the Woodruff Foundation. The gallery's inventory includes works by Ansel Adams, Walker Evans, Edward Steichen and Eudora Welty.

Lagerquist Gallery
3235 Paces Ferry Pl. N.W. • (404) 261-8273

Kind of hidden in a lovely, quiet pocket of exclusive shops, Lagerquist Gallery was established in 1970 and represents Henry Barnes, Beatriz Candioti, Dennis Campay, Marc Chatov and Teena Stern among others.

Lowe Gallery
75 Bennett St. N.W., Space A-2 at TULA
• (404) 352-8114

The Lowe Gallery showcases emerging and mid-career artists whose works honor classical traditions while reinterpreting them. Lowe represents artists who play a key role in today's international art marketplace, including Andrew Saftel, Gail Foster, Kathleen Morris, Steve Seinberg and Udo Noger.

Marcia Wood Gallery
1198 N. Highland Ave. N.E.
• (404) 885-1808

Marcia Wood Gallery showcases contemporary art, especially painting, although it also shows other media using narrative imagery. Important artists in 1998 include solo exhibitions of Anne Faber an Atlantan, Frances Barth of New York, Don Pollack from Chicago, Arron Sturgeon from Los Angeles and a group exhibit of four New Orleans artists.

The McIntosh Gallery
One Virginia Hill, 587 Virginia Ave. N.E.
• (404) 892-4023

Established in 1981, the McIntosh features works of emerging and established U.S. and European artists. Its primary focus is on Southeastern talents such as Bennie Andrews, Jim Bird, Beverly Buchanan, John Scott and Art Werger among others.

Modern Primitive Gallery
1393 N. Highland Ave. N.E.
• (404) 892-0556

Both serious collectors and curious browsers feel right at home at Modern Primitive, which offers folk, self-taught and local art. Famous folk artists represented here include the Rev. Howard Finster, Archie Byron and Minnie Evans.

Nancy Solomon Gallery
1037 Monroe Dr. N.E. • (404) 875-7100

International contemporary art is the focus of Nancy Solomon Gallery. Solomon, an art history graduate of Barnard College, grew up in France and Switzerland and has worked in galleries in London, Paris and New York. The gallery emphasizes conceptual painting, sculpture and video installation and experimental art.

Rolling Stone Press Fine Print Gallery
432 Calhoun St. N.W. • (404) 873-3322

A lithography atelier and fine print gallery, Rolling Stone Press is located on the border of the Georgia Tech campus. In 1998 the gallery houses The Printmaker's Renaissance Exhibition #4, a national juried print competition. Wayne Kline, director and master printer, works with artists to make original lithographs the traditional way using Bavarian limestone. The gallery usually has four exhibitions per year and focuses on working with important artists from the Southeast including William Christenberry, Beverly Buchanan, Benny Andrews and others. There are also prints on consignment in bins. Call first since Wayne is the only one in attendance.

Sandler Hudson Gallery
1831-A Peachtree Rd. N.E.
• (404) 350-8480

Sandler Hudson Gallery exhibits provocative imagery in a variety of media including painting, drawing, photography, sculpture and jewelry. Its primary focus is established contemporary artists from the Southeast. Larry Anderson, Tom Ferguson, Susan Loftin, Dana Cibulski and Gary Komarin are among the artists this gallery represents.

The Signature Shop & Gallery
3267 Roswell Rd. • (404) 237-4426

The Signature Shop & Gallery was the creation of Blanche Reeves, who was the first in Atlanta to give fine crafts (weavings, pottery, furniture and jewelry) a showcase. Because the Signature Shop educated patrons to the art of glass, galleries such as the Vesperman were more accepted into the local art scene. Many local artists got their starts in this modest space more than 35 years ago. Now in her mid-80s, Ms. Reeves has passed the baton to a new owner who appears to share Ms. Reeves' high standards in selecting which works will be displayed.

Trinity Arts Group
315 E. Paces Ferry Rd. N.E.
• (404) 237-0370

Trinity Arts Group carries a range of works from blue chip investment art — works on paper by such luminaries as Picasso, Chagall, Rembrandt and Toulouse Lautrec — to contemporary painting, sculpture and mixed media pieces. Southeastern talents Trinity represents include painter David Fraley, Lucite sculptor Frederick Hart and Jacob Colley, a painter.

Urban Nirvana
15 Waddell St. N.E. (corner of DeKalb Ave.) • (404) 688-3329

Housed in a former meat-packing plant, Urban Nirvana is easily one of the metro area's most unusual art galleries and manufacturing plants. The complex is home to goats, sheep, rabbits, turkeys, peacocks, ducks — and lots of art. Proprietor Christine Sibley is known for her garden sculptures, many of which are designed as fountains, and ornaments that are produced *en masse* at this facility and shipped to garden centers, designers who have custom orders produced for their clients and to catalog houses.

Urban Nirvana fronts DeKalb Avenue, but you must enter from the back at the Waddell Street gates that are easily distinguished by wall art. If you can walk past the gardens without being distracted by the profusion of interesting plants and weeds or the tinkling of fountains, or make it through the cave-like, labyrinthine anti-chambers lined with pots in various stages of completion, you'll find the gallery toward the front of the building and to the left. It's pastel, sponge-painted walls are covered

with cast *concrete puti*, and naif works by local artists in a variety of media. Frequently you can find true bargains since work priced here may differ from the sales prices by these very same artists at the more gentrified galleries around town.

Urban Nirvana, by the way, is a gallery children will love to visit with its menagerie and art work that is far less than fragile.

If you're riding the MARTA east rail line toward downtown, you can get a quick but intriguing glimpse of Urban Nirvana's fantastical facade shortly after you leave the Inman Park/Reynoldstown station; sit on the right side of the train and keep a lookout for metal dinosaurs, fountains and other objects bizarre.

V. Reed Gallery
780 N. Highland Ave. N.E. • (404) 897-1389

V. Reed Gallery showcases colorful, whimsical works by more than 400 artists. The gallery features an eclectic selection of handblown glass, metal and painted furniture, sculpture, ceramics, fine art, hand-crafted jewelry and book art. V. Reed represents more than 200 local artists including Susan Sisk, Daphne Covington, Robert Witherspoon, Laura Saville and John Carlos.

Vesperman Gallery
2140 Peachtree Rd. N.W. • (404) 350-9698

Artists themselves, the Vesperman family opened this gallery to feature glass art exclusively. You can also buy exquisite glass bracelets, earrings and pins at reasonable prices.

Beyond Atlanta

Museums

Marietta/Cobb Museum of Art
30 Atlanta St., Marietta • (770) 424-8142

This museum is housed in a 1909 Greek Revival-style post office building just off the square in Marietta. Typical offerings include mainstream exhibitions of American and European art from the 19th and 20th centuries and highlights from the museum's own collection of American art.

Admission is $2 for adults and $1 for seniors and students; the museum is open Tuesday through Saturday, 11 AM to 5 PM.

Arts Centers

Gwinnett Fine Arts Center
6400 Sugarloaf Pkwy., Duluth
• (770) 623-6002

The Gwinnett Council for the Arts is a non-profit organization that owns and operates the Fine Arts Center through contributions from private patrons, corporations and foundations. The '98 season will feature indoor sculpture by New York artist Nancy Azara, mixed media by Laurence Holden, photography and sculpture by Rafael Consuegra, indoor sculpture by Rachael Greene and the work of New Orleans artist Martin Laborde.

Admission is $3 for adults and $2 for students and seniors. Members and children younger than 6 are admitted for free.

Hambidge Center
Betty's Creek Rd., Dillard • (706) 746-5718

Experience the beauty of the Blue Ridge Mountains in north Georgia as you wend your way to Hambidge Center for the annual Jugtown Pottery Show in June and/or The Southern Folk Expressions exhibit in July. Throughout the year nature walks or any number of other delightful exhibitions of local arts and crafts are staged in Georgia's only residential center for creative arts. Founded by Mary Crovatt Hambidge in 1934, the Center offers artists' studios situated within the 600 acres of meadows, streams and woodlands. Approximately 90 fellowships are awarded each year and at anytime up to eight artists staying as long as two months will be in attendance at the Center. Artists pay $125 per week, for a private cottage with kitchen and five vegetarian meals per week.

Hambidge Center is located about 3 miles off Ga. Hwy. 441. Admission is free to the Gallery which is open year round. Hours are 10 AM to 4 PM, Monday through Saturday.

Galleries

Art & Frame Classics
4135 LaVista Rd., Ste. 220, Tucker
• (770) 270-0542

This shop specializes in military and aviation prints with a large selection of Civil War art. Prices range from less than $100 to $10,000. Custom framing is also offered.

Heaven Blue Rose
934 Canton St., Roswell • (770) 642-7380

Heaven Blue Rose, a contemporary cooperative gallery, takes its name from a group Marc Chagall belonged to in 1907. Run by five visual artists, the gallery features contemporary works in diverse media and subject areas. Since the gallery is artist-run, customers can meet at least one of the artists whenever they come in to shop.

Raiford Gallery
1169 Canton St., Roswell • (770) 645-2050

Judy Raiford, herself a jeweler, has for years offered her home just prior to Christmas to other artists wishing to reach the affluent residents of Roswell seeking unique holiday gifts. With the opening of a formal gallery, these very same artisans and others now have a much needed location in Roswell from which to vend on a daily basis. The Raiford Gallery, a two-story studio north of the city's historic square, was built out of timber frame and is quite unusual. In 9,000 square feet the gallery has room for delicate custom silver necklaces as well as enormous wood carvings, and the range in styles and media reflect the scale of the new exhibition space.

Studio 211
770 County Line-Auburn Rd., Winder
• (770) 867-1991

This gallery offers art, custom framing and art lessons. The art on display includes works by owners Jann Boxx and Kathy Walters as well as other regional and international artists. To reach Studio 211, take Exit 48 off I-85 N., then go south on Ga. Highway 211.

With our beautiful
landscape of rolling hills
and abundant greenery,
it's a shame to stay
indoors — and few
Atlantans do.

Parks and Recreation

Visitors are often amazed at how green Atlanta is. Our city boasts a lush tree canopy, a characteristic that distinguishes it from most urban areas. The city government is so protective of our tree canopy that a city ordinance requires a permit to cut down a tree, and all trees that are removed must be replaced by shade trees such as oak, maple, sycamore or cypress.

Trees Atlanta, a nonprofit volunteer advocacy organization, is dedicated to tree conservation and planting. Since it began in 1984, Trees Atlanta has planted more than 15,000 trees along Atlanta's streets and highways. The city has a tree replacement program, providing red maples, redbuds, dogwoods and crape myrtles to be planted along the right-of-way on city streets. The city plants these trees on request on a first-come, first-served basis. For more information, call the city forester's office, (404) 817-6752.

With our beautiful landscape of rolling hills and abundant greenery beckoning, it's a shame to stay indoors — and few Atlantans do. If you're into boardsailing, bicycling, tennis, soccer or even boccie ball, you'll find places to play and people to share your enthusiasm. We've presented a sampling of the leagues, clubs, networks and facilities available for various sports and hobbies. Not everybody loves being outside and — let's face it — sometimes it does rain, so we've included some indoor sports as well.

For more information on sports clubs and events, pick up a copy of *sports & fitness*, a free monthly magazine available at General Nutrition Center stores, various sports shoe stores, Australian Body Works fitness centers and Barnes & Noble bookstores. In addition to informative articles, the magazine runs an extensive listing of sports events and organizations and has an event hotline, (404) 843-2257. Another good source of information about sports groups and events is the free weekly newspaper, *Creative Loafing*, available at numerous bookstores and retail operations throughout the city. Look in *CL's* "Happenings" section under "Sports and Recreation."

Information about parks in the city of Atlanta can be obtained by calling the Bureau of Parks, 675 Ponce de Leon Avenue, at (404) 817-6744. City parks are open from sunrise to sunset.

You can hardly throw a stick in this town and not have it land in a park. (Not that we advocate wanton stick throwing; it could result in your mother's worst fear, putting somebody's eye out! — which could lead to a ruinous lawsuit.) In this chapter we mention some of the city's most popular parks that offer great spots to spread out a blanket and read or have a picnic. Some have walking and running trails or bike paths. But keep your eyes open; appealing green spaces pop up everywhere.

A word of warning to those from colder climes: Atlanta can get very hot, and besides lots of friendly residents, our city plays host to hordes of hungry bugs. Wise outdoor revelers will use sunscreen and insect repellent to ensure comfortable, itch- and pain-free good times in Atlanta's great outdoors.

Parks and Other Green Spaces

Agnes Scott College Tree Tour
141 E. College Ave., Decatur
• (404) 638-6484

This college, founded in 1859, has a lovely campus with many trees more than a century old. The college offers a booklet for self-guided tours of its unique tree heritage that includes protected old trees as well as new plantings. Southern magnolias, an incense cedar, sawtooth oaks and a white ash predating the Civil War are among the trees on this tour. With seven days notice, the college provides guided tree tours for groups of 10 to 30 people.

Chastain Memorial Park
235 W. Wieuca Rd.
• (404) 817-6744

About 8 miles north of downtown, the irregularly shaped Chastain is bounded by three main roads: W. Wieuca Road, Powers Ferry Road and Lake Forrest Drive. For more than 40 years, this multipurpose park has provided respite from city life.

Chastain has a 3.5-mile jogging trail, a gym and athletic fields for softball, soccer, football and baseball. The park also boasts picnic and playground areas plus a swimming pool. Chastain Arts Center and Gallery holds exhibits and classes regularly. The tennis facilities are the site of Atlanta Lawn Tennis Association tournaments, and the public golf course remains a popular draw.

The amphitheater seats more than 6,000 patrons. Here Atlantans revel in various entertainments, including symphony concerts, theater productions and performances by popular musical acts. On most balmy summer evenings, Atlantans pack an elegant picnic dinner and head for Chastain to enjoy an evening under the stars.

You'll find parking lots near the ball fields and the amphitheater. Some street parking is permitted along W. Wieuca Road. Or you can leave your car and take the No. 38 Chastain Park bus from the Lindbergh MARTA station.

Chattahoochee Nature Center
9135 Willeo Rd., Roswell
• (770) 992-2055

We've described this center in our Attractions and Kidstuff chapters. We mention it again here because the center has two trails that allow hikers to explore different environments. The woodland trail meanders through the forest near the river, which abounds with oak, hickory and evergreen trees and supports such wildlife as hawks, jays, woodpeckers and raccoons. The wetlands trail has a boardwalk that winds through Redwing marsh, a habitat for beavers, muskrats, ducks, geese, red-winged blackbirds and kingfishers. Hike the trails Monday through Saturday, 9 AM to 5 PM, and Sunday, noon to 5 PM. Admission is $3 for adults, $2 for children and seniors.

Chattahoochee River
National Recreation Area, 1978 Island Ford Pkwy., Dunwoody • (770) 399-8070

This recreation area offers more than 70 miles of trails divided into 10 land units that stretch along the Chattahoochee River's shoreline from Cobb Parkway on the west side of town to Buford Dam on Lake Lanier in the east. All the units offer scenic views of the river and surrounding forests; many also offer fishing and rafting opportunities. The area has a 3.1-mile fitness trail beginning at the Cochran Shoals unit off I-285 at Powers Ferry Road, complete with exercise stations. This trail is suitable for walking, jogging and biking. The trails vary in levels of difficulty; the park staff will advise you on which ones suit your needs and abilities. At Sope Creek off Paper Mill Road in East Cobb and Vickery Creek in Roswell,

---

FYI

Three area codes serve the metro Atlanta area: 404, 770 and 678. Whether you live on Peachtree Street or in New York City, you must dial the code to reach any number in the area. The difference? Outside the area, you must dial "1," then the area code and phone number; inside the area, you need only dial the area code followed by the phone number.

Photo: Chateau Elan

Golf courses abound in and around Atlanta.

you can explore the ruins of old mills. Throughout the recreation area, you will observe an array of plant life and wildlife and maybe even get in some people-watching at the more popular units. Parking permits at the various recreation sites are $2 per car. Trails are open daily, dawn to dusk.

Grant Park
Georgia and Cherokees Aves. S.E.
• (404) 817-6744

Historic Grant Park is about 2 miles southeast of downtown. Take I-20, get off at the Boulevard exit (Exit 26), go south to Sydney Street, west to Cherokee Avenue, then south to the park entrance.

Loaded with history, Grant Park was once home to Creek Indians. Confederate artillery troops lined the park's eastern perimeter during the Battle of Atlanta.

The park was named for Lemuel Grant, a 19th-century philanthropist and former Confederate engineer who designed Atlanta's defenses against Union troops. Col. Grant donated land for the park from his sizable estate. (All that remains today are the ruins of his house in the adjacent neighborhood.)

Grant Park's athletic fields and pavilions make it a popular relaxation spot. Various amateur leagues for football, softball and other

sports use the park's athletic facilities. Perhaps its prime attractions are the Atlanta Zoo and Cyclorama (see our Attractions chapter). Nearby you'll find Oakland Cemetery, a burial ground of famous figures such as Margaret Mitchell, author of *Gone With the Wind*, and golfing great Bobby Jones (read more about Oakland in our Attractions chapter). The area abounds in lovely old Victorian homes reflecting the neighborhood's heyday. Many have been fully restored; some are still in the process of restoration. Every September, the Grant Park Tour of Homes draws crowds to view these reminders of bygone days. Much of the area is on the National Register of Historic Places.

You can take MARTA here from several stations: Five Points, Peachtree Center and Lindbergh. Then connect with the No. 31 Grant Park/Lindbergh bus to the park.

Kennesaw Mountain National Battlefield Park
905 Kennesaw Mountain Dr., Marietta
• (770) 427-4686

Sixteen miles of hiking trails take you through a park in which a bloody Civil War battle was fought more than a century ago. See Confederate cannon, a monument to slain Union soldiers, preserved trenchworks and troop movement maps. If you don't care to study war, take in the beautiful mountain scenery instead. The visitors center has maps for self-guided walks. The park is free and open daily from 8 AM to sundown. See more about Kennesaw Mountain National Battlefield Park in our Attractions chapter.

Laurel Park
151 Manning Rd., Marietta
• (770) 528-0619

This public park on the west side of Marietta is popular with kids, who love to feed the ducks on the park's small lake. A 1-mile paved jogging trail winds alongside the water and through the woods, with exercise stations along the way. There are also 13 tennis courts; two covered picnic areas; basketball, volleyball and shuffleboard courts; and a playground. The park is open daily from 6 AM to 11 PM. To reserve a court or picnic pavilion, call the park office at the previously listed number.

Outdoor Activity Center
1442 Richland Rd. S.W. • (404) 752-5385

Three miles southwest of downtown Atlanta, the Outdoor Activity Center sits atop Bush Mountain. The center has a 26-acre hardwood urban forest that's a designated National Recreation Trail. Foot traffic only is allowed on the trail. The center also has an interpretive center, an ecological playscape, a tree house classroom and picnic tables. The Center is open Monday through Saturday, 9 AM to 4 PM. Admission is $3 per student for those in prekindergarten through high school who attend educational pro-

grams; otherwise, the center is free to the public. Find more about the Outdoor Activity Center in our Kidstuff chapter.

Panola Mountain State Conservation Park
2600 Ga. Hwy. 155, Stockbridge
• (770) 389-7801

Picture Stone Mountain without the development, but with 600 acres of a preserved natural environment surrounding a 100-acre granite outcropping. The park has 6 miles of trails. You can only hike the mountain trails on scheduled hikes led by park guides, but you can take self-guided hikes on the Watershed and Rock Outcrop trails (combined length, 2 miles) adjacent to the park's Interpretive Center. Panola Mountain State Conservation Park opens at 7 AM and closes at dark daily. The nature center is open from 9 AM until 5 PM Tuesday through Friday, noon to 5 PM Saturday and Sunday. Parking is $2 per car every day except Wednesday (when it's free).

PATH Foundation
(404) 875-PATH

Since 1991, the PATH Foundation has been building a network of greenway trails throughout the city for safe walking, bicycling and skating. This nonprofit organization relies on support from volunteers, businesses and government agencies. By July 1, 1996, PATH had completed construction of a 35-mile, multiuse system that includes greenways connected to on-street bicycle facilities with sidewalks. The trails run from

www.insiders.com
See this and many other **Insiders' Guide®** destinations online — in their entirety.
Visit us today!

INSIDERS' TIP

Thirsty from all the exertion? Virgin Pure Spring Water, taken from one of the few artesian springs in the world in Ball Ground, Georgia, is truly natural spring water. Virgin water comes from a protected spring in Cherokee County that has been filtered through a confining layer of marble/dolomite, rising naturally at a constant pressure and temperature, with consistent pH and mineral content. The water is collected in an all-natural marble reservoir and then stored in stainless steel tanks. To find out how to get some, call (770) 479-8488.

Greenbriar Mall in Southwest Atlanta to Stone Mountain in the east.

PATH trails are designed not only for riding, rolling and walking enthusiasts to use in their leisure time, but also to provide quick and easy walks or bike rides to MARTA stations for commuters. Trails intersect with rail stations at West Lake, Ashby and Vine City in the west, and East Lake, Decatur and Avondale in the east.

The City of Atlanta, the National Parks Service, the Chattahoochee River Keeper, DeKalb County, Cobb County and Fulton County are participating members of the PATH team. Eventually, PATH plans to construct and maintain a Greenway Trail Network of more than 100 miles. PATH membership entitles you to a quarterly newsletter, an invitation to all PATH activities and an opportunity to participate in trail building. Annual dues are $50 for families, $25 for singles; $10 for students.

Piedmont Park
Piedmont Ave. and 14th St. N.E.
• **(404) 817-6744**

Atlanta's largest park and home of the Atlanta Botanical Garden, Piedmont Park is the site of numerous fairs, festivals, Atlanta Symphony Orchestra concerts and much more.

In this 185-acre setting, you'll find a paved jogging trail plus other trails for walking, cycling and skating. Football and baseball games are commonplace, and softball leagues use the park's athletic fields for spring and summer competitions. Even the massive Peachtree Road Race, held each July 4, ends in Piedmont Park near the 10th Street entrance.

Piedmont's current happenings in no way outshine its colorful history. The land on which Piedmont Park stands was originally part of the Gentlemen's Driving Club (later the Piedmont Driving Club), a group whose members were the force behind Atlanta's progressive development at the end of the 1800s.

In 1895, the Cotton States and International Exposition took place in Piedmont Park. The Olmsted Brothers firm was hired to design the landscaping for the exposi-

tion; much of the park's current design dates from this period. The exposition drew close to a million visitors during its three-month duration. John Philip Sousa's band premiered "King Cotton," a march Sousa wrote especially for the event. Such luminaries as President Grover Cleveland, Booker T. Washington and William McKinley attended the event.

After the exposition, an 1898 reunion of Confederate veterans camped on the grounds. The park was home to the Atlanta Crackers baseball team until its move, following the 1904 season, to Ponce de Leon Park, which was opposite the present City Hall East. In their day, these players were heroes and won 17 pennants, more than any pro team except the Yankees.

Piedmont Park became a public park in 1904 when the city bought the land. A few years later, the solemn unveiling of the Peace Monument at the 14th Street entrance drew respectful crowds. This work of New York sculptor Allan Newman symbolized the growing spirit of peace and reconciliation between the North and the South. It is said to have been built from funds collected mostly from Northern states.

A citizens' support group called the Piedmont Park Conservancy was formed in 1989 to support and conserve the park's natural assets through citizen volunteer efforts. This nonprofit, membership group ($25 for individuals; $35 for couples) sponsors guided walking tours on weekends by appointment, starting at the 12th Street entrance to the park. The group schedules regular work parties to clean and repair features of the park. One of the main objectives is to raise money, and members are currently involved in a multiphase campaign to raise $25 million for a massive overhaul of the park. In 1996, with some of the $6.5 million already donated, the Conservancy refurbished the "ladies' comfort station" as the park's visitors center. Its showpiece is an 800-square-foot mural on the barrel ceiling, depicting the variety of activities that go on in the park. For more information on the Conservancy, write to P.O. Box 7795, Atlanta GA 30357, or call (404) 875-7275.

A favorite spot with strollers, the park provides slightly hilly terrain with lots of shade trees where you can stretch out to rest your weary bones. An approximately 4-mile loop trail through the park will give you a chance to take in all the scenery.

Parking around the park is limited, and during some events, it's completely prohibited. Make it easy on yourself and leave your car behind. MARTA's Midtown station is on 10th Street between Peachtree and W. Peachtree. The Arts Center station is on 15th Street behind the Arts Center. There's regular bus service along Piedmont Avenue on the No. 36 North Decatur bus that travels from the Arts Center station and the Decatur station.

Sweetwater Creek State Park
Mt. Vernon Rd., Lithia Springs
• **(770) 389-7275**

About 18 miles west of downtown, Sweetwater Creek State Park features a trail leading to the ruins of the New Manchester Manufacturing Company. During the Civil War, the New Manchester textile mill supplied goods to the Confederacy. Not surprisingly, the Yankees burned it down. The trail goes through a forest that contains the factory ruins and the ruins of some old homesteads from the abandoned mill village, then proceeds along the banks of Sweetwater Creek to Sweetwater Falls. The half-mile walk to the falls is not an easy trek. You have to climb over boulders and up steep hills. You'll walk about 3 miles if you hike to the ruins, the falls and back. It costs $2 per car to get into this park, which is open dawn to dusk daily.

Wills Park
332 Maddox St., Alpharetta
• **(770) 410-5780**

This recreational and equestrian center is maintained by the city of Alpharetta in north Fulton County. The public is permitted free use of the swimming pool, two playgrounds, baseball and football fields. The horse park has one covered and two open riding rings. Almost every weekend, horselovers will find a show or educational seminar going on there. (See "Horseback Riding" later in this chapter.)

Parks and Recreation Departments

Surely some of the metro area's greatest assets are the services offered by our fine parks and recreation departments. All four counties in the following listing present programs at various skill levels for youth, adults, seniors and the physically challenged. Complete written information, well-designed for easy reading, is yours with a call to the county of your residence.

What these departments offer would fill a book in itself. Safe to say, virtually no athletic interest is left out. Fitness, music instruction, after-school tutorials, arts and crafts and so much more are offered free or for small fees.

City of Atlanta Parks & Recreation, 675 Ponce de Leon Avenue N.E., Bureau of Recreation (information on city pools, tennis, junior golf and other programs), (404) 817-6785; Bureau of Parks (city park information), 817-6752; Bureau of Cultural Affairs (information on galleries, amphitheaters, music festivals), (404) 817-6815.

Cobb County Parks & Recreation, 1792 County Farm Road, Marietta, (770) 528-8800.

DeKalb County Parks & Recreation, 1300 Commerce Drive, Decatur, (404) 371-2631.

Fulton County Parks & Recreation, 1575 Northside Drive N.W., (404) 730-6200.

Gwinnett County Parks & Recreation, 75 Langley Drive, Lawrenceville, (770) 822-8840.

Recreation

Sports Clubs

Several clubs in the metro area offer organized league play and special events for members and nonmembers, including new-comers who might want to join. It's a good way to meet people and find congenial groups who share your passion for particular sports.

Atlanta Club Sport
120 W. Wieuca Rd. N.E., Ste. 102
• **(404) 257-3355**
This club offers its 1,500 members the chance to play in leagues devoted to ultimate Frisbee, softball, volleyball, soccer and flag football. The club offers coed and men's leagues and teams at various skill levels for certain sports. Members and nonmembers pay fees to play on teams. Members have the chance to join organized trips sponsored by the club. Annual dues are $35.

Atlanta Sport and Social Club
254 E. Paces Ferry Rd. N.E., Ste. No. 201
• **(404) 262-7665**
This organization brings people together through organized league sports participation and special events including parties, trips, tournaments and happy hours. Coed leagues include football, softball, soccer, billiards and volleyball. The club also sponsors a men's basketball league. All teams pay fees to cover such expenses as referees, equipment and prizes for winners. Membership costs $35; members get reduced rates on parties, team play and happy hours as well as discounts at local retailers.

Singles Outdoor Adventures Club
(770) 242-2338
Singles Outdoor Adventures (SOA) is an informal, nonprofit singles group with a focus on hiking. Activities include backpacking, bicycling, horseback riding, hiking, caving, rafting and canoeing. The annual membership fee of $25 covers summer and winter parties and mailing costs for the monthly calendar of events. Potential members may attend three SOA activities before joining. SOA meets in the Sandy Springs area once a month, except November and December. Meetings start at 7:30 PM and last about two hours; members generally get together for snacks and drinks afterward. SOA welcomes participants at all levels of expertise.

Auto Racing

Atlanta Motor Speedway
U.S. Hwys. 19 & 41, near Hampton
• **(770) 707-7970**
Race fans will delight in a visit to this premier facility for motor sports, which is about a 40-minute drive south of downtown Atlanta. Guided tours take you behind the scenes of the raceway, including visits to pit road, the NASCAR garage and the victory lane where such race-car greats as Bill Elliott, A.J. Foyt, Fireball Roberts and Dale Earnhardt have stood. A video in a luxurious VIP suite explains the speedway's past, present and future, and fans can visit a statue of Richard Petty in the Richard Petty Garden. For true thrills, ride a few laps around the track: Experience the 24-degree banking on the world's fastest 1.522-mile oval before swooping down onto the nine-turn nightmare racecourse. The fainthearted need not apply!

Tours cost $3 for adults; children younger than 12 are free. Groups gather on the half-hour from 9:30 AM to 4:30 PM Monday through Saturday, 1 to 4:30 PM Sunday. Groups of 15 or more need to make advance reservations. The gift shop is packed with Atlanta Motor Speedway apparel and Winston Cup racing souvenirs. Tour tickets are good for $3 off any purchase of $10 or more. Call the Speedway ticket office for information about racing schedules and reservations, (770) 946-4211.

Astronomy

Atlanta Astronomy Club
3595 Canton Rd. Ste. A9-305, Marietta
• **(770) 621-2661**
Established in 1947, the Atlanta Astronomy Club is a group of amateur and professional astronomers that meets the third Friday of every month at White Hall on the campus of Emory University, 1380 S. Oxford Road N.E. In addition to general meetings, the club sponsors at least one observing session per month at the club's observatory near Villa Rica. The observatory features a 20-inch reflector, the third largest telescope in Georgia. Members receive the club's monthly publication, *The Focal Point*, a

journal containing articles by noted astronomers and notices of astronomical activities sponsored by the club and other organizations. All meetings and observing sessions are free and open to the public. Call the hotline number listed above for up-to-the minute information. The hotline answers 24 hours a day.

Ballooning

Hot Air Balloon Company of Atlanta
Château Élan, 100 Tour de France, Braselton • (770) 389-8981

Based at Château Élan, about 45 minutes northeast of Atlanta, this company offers one-hour balloon tours that include a champagne picnic and a free T-shirt for each passenger. The flights run from sunrise to sunset, year round, and you should call well in advance (anywhere from two to six weeks, depending on the season) to book a flight for your special occasion, be it marriage proposal, anniversary, birthday, or just a yen to escape the bonds of gravity. Spring, summer and early fall are peak ballooning seasons. Sunrise trips include breakfast at Château Élan; evening flights are followed by hors d'oeuvres. A one-hour champagne balloon tour costs $175 per person.

Barefoot Sailing

Barefoot Sailing Club
(404) 256-6839

Call the hotline number for updates on monthly meetings and club activities. The club welcomes visitors to its meetings on the fourth Monday of each month in Buckhead.

Billiards

Fans of this sport, which is currently making a comeback, don't have to go to dark, smoky dives to enjoy a game. Several upscale billiards establishments in the Atlanta area offer pleasant surroundings and professional equipment.

Buckhead Billiards
200 Pharr Rd. • (404) 237-3705

This billiards club has been voted "Number One Place to Play Pool in Atlanta" three times

by *Creative Loafing's* annual Readers' Poll. With 10 billiards tables, a full bar and eight big-screen TVs, Buckhead Billiards draws a mixed crowd, from young people to business types in their 40s. Hours vary slightly each day, but generally the place is open from 3 PM until 1 or 2 AM during the week, 1 PM to 3 AM Saturday and 1 PM to 1 AM Sunday. Weekday daytime rates are $5.40 an hour; after 8 PM, it's $7.20 an hour. On weekends, it's $7.20 an hour to play; after 8 PM, you must be 21 or older to get in, and the price goes up to $9.60.

Dave and Buster's
2215 D&B Dr., Marietta • (770) 951-5554

This multimedia entertainment complex has 15 full-length billiards tables and one official snooker table crafted in Italian slate, mahogany and mother of pearl inlay, arranged around the square bar and dining room. You can rent billiards tables for $8 an hour during the day or $10 an hour after 5 PM. After 5 PM on Saturday and Sunday, tables are $12 an hour. Dave & Buster's is open Monday through Thursday from 11 AM to 1 AM; Friday, 11 AM to 2 AM; Saturday, 11:30 AM to 2 AM; and Sunday, 11:30 AM to midnight. On Friday and Saturday, there's a $3 per person cover charge after 10 PM. (See our Nightlife chapter for more information.)

Player's Billiards
2000 Powers Ferry Rd., Marietta
• (770) 859-9353

Thirty professional-size billiards tables surround a full-service bar in this billiards establishment. Player's has smoking and nonsmoking sections and a full line of cues and sticks. Play is $8.80 per hour at all times. Player's is open Monday through Thursday from 11:30 AM to 2 AM; Friday, 11:30 AM to 3 AM; Saturday, 2 PM to 3 AM; and Sunday, 2 PM to midnight.

Big Band Music

The Atlanta Blue Notes Orchestra
2366 N. Peachtree Wy., Dunwoody
• (770) 394-6879, (770) 448-8083

The Atlanta Blue Notes play Big Band music popularized by such greats as Glenn Miller, Tommy Dorsey, Count Basie and Duke Ellington. Some members of this 19-piece group actually toured with big bands before starting business careers that range from college professor to corporate executive. The Blue Notes play at special events all over town, some of which are open to the public. Call business manager Bob Bailey at the above numbers (home and office, respectively) to find out where you can catch the Blue Notes or how to book them. The Blue Notes also feature a 10-piece group and a five-piece combo for smaller occasions.

Sentimental Journey
1071 Piedmont Rd. • (770) 279-BAND

This 18-piece orchestra plays favorite standards from the '40s and '50s that will have even the most pigeon-toed twirling on the hardwood dance floor of the American Legion Post #1. The band's monthly dances are open to the public on the third Friday of every month, from 8:30 to 11:30 PM. It's $10 to get in and $8 if you want the steak, salad and potato dinner.

Bingo

Bingo boosters can find plenty of places to play in metro Atlanta. A free newspaper, the *Bingo Bugle*, publishes bingo-related articles and lists bingo games and groups in its Players Guide. Pick up this monthly bingo paper at Cub Foods locations or call the *Bugle's* office, (770) 578-8328, to find out how to obtain a copy of this informative bingo-phile gazette.

Bi-planing

Classic Bi-Plane Rides Inc.
DeKalb-Peachtree Airport, 2000 Airport Rd., Chamblee • (404) 315-9003

Bill Allison, owner of Classic Bi-Plane Rides Inc., will be glad to take you on a tour of Stone Mountain, downtown or the DeKalb-Peachtree Airport, where the firm is based. He offers flights year round, usually on a same-day or next-day basis. The two planes he uses date from 1943. Flights range from $50 to $150, depending on destination and length, and second passengers go for half price. For $200 an hour, Allison will map out a special destination flight. Classic Bi-Plane offers a fun, old-fashioned way to tour the city.

Boardsailing

Atlanta Boardsailing Club
(770) 908-0348

The Atlanta Boardsailing Club meets the second Tuesday of each month at 7:30 PM at Powers Court Sports Bar on the corner of Roswell and Wieuca roads in Buckhead. Meetings are a good source of information about instruction in this sport and where to find the best new and used equipment. The public is welcome at meetings.

Boccie Ball

Veni Vidi Vici
41 14th St. N.E. • (404) 875-8424

This elegant Midtown restaurant has a boccie ball court on the lawn next to the patio. Although there's no structured playing time, the court is available for anyone who wants to play. The equipment is provided, and there's no charge to play. Call to find out how you can get in the game.

Bowling

Brunswick Gwinnett Lanes
3835 Lawrenceville Hwy., Lawrenceville
• (770) 925-2000
2750 Austell Rd., Marietta
• (770) 435-2120
2749 Delk Rd., Marietta • (770) 988-8813
6345 Spalding Dr., Norcross
• (770) 840-8200
785 Old Roswell Rd., Roswell
• (770) 998-9437

The Atlanta area Brunswick Lanes are most crowded in the evenings (when leagues bowl) and on rainy days (when everyone wants to get out of the house). To check on lane availability and make a reservations, which are highly recommended on weekends but not necessary, call the alley of your choice before you head out. Before 6 PM, you pay $2.75 per game. After 6 PM, the price goes up to $3.50. Shoe rental costs $2.50. Hours are generally 9 AM to midnight, Sunday through Thursday; 9 AM to 3 PM, Friday through Saturday. But call ahead to confirm hours at the specific location near you.

Express Bowling Lanes
1936 Piedmont Cir. N.E. • (404) 874-5703

This bowling alley closes early only on Christmas Eve; the rest of the year, it's open 24 hours. Groups of 15 or more may call to make a reservation. From 9 AM to 6 PM, games cost $1.75 per person. After 6 PM, you'll pay $2.95 per game per person. On Friday, Saturday and Sunday after 6 PM, games are $3.25. Rent shoes for $2.25. You don't bowl but you crave the spotlight? No problem! Head for Express Lane's Sugar Daddy's lounge, where the laser karaoke machine may make you a star.

Camping

Georgia has 40 state park campgrounds that provide a variety of camping experiences including tent, RV or trailer camping, walk-in camping, pioneer camping and group camp facilities. All state campgrounds have modern comfort stations and dump sites, and many have laundries and camping supplies. Tent/RV campsites offer electrical and water hookups, cooking grills and picnic tables. Many state parks also offer fully equipped cottages and lodges. For more information about camping in the state park system, call or stop by **Georgia State Parks & Historic Sites**, 205 Butler Street S.E., Suite 1352, (404) 656-3530.

You can make reservations for campsites, cottages and lodges up to 11 months before your date of arrival. We've listed the phone numbers for the state parks described below (Cloudland Canyon, Red Top Mountain and Victoria Bryant), but you need to make reservations through the central reservation number: Locally, dial (770) 389-7275; from out of town, dial (800) 864-7275. In addition to a few state parks, we've included Georgia's Stone Mountain Park and Lake Lanier Islands, both of which offer close-in camping facilities.

Cloudland Canyon Park
122 Cloudland Canyon Park Rd., Rising Fawn • (706) 657-4050

Off Ga. Highway 136, 25 miles northwest of Lafayette, Cloudland is about a 1½-hour drive from Atlanta on the western edge of Look-out Mountain. The park has 75 tent and trailer sites, 30 campsites and 16 cottages. Although there's no lake, the park offers a swimming pool and tennis facilities. Wander the hiking trails and marvel at the scenery of this lovely park in the north Georgia mountains. The first night's deposit holds your reservation. Campsites cost $13 a night; $15 for RVs. Cabins have two or three bedrooms and cost $80 or $90 per night on Friday and Saturday; $70 or $80 Sunday through Thursday. Linens, towels and kitchen utensils are included in the cost.

Georgia's Stone Mountain Park Family Campground
Exit off U.S. Hwy. 78, Stone Mountain • (770) 498-5710

Just 16 miles east of Atlanta, this park's campground features more than 431 wooded lakeside camping sites as well as a supply store. You can make limited reservations subject to availability. The campground features complete RV hookups as well as rustic tent sites that rent from $16 to $19 per night. You must be 18 years or older to rent a campsite. Besides camping fees, you'll pay $6 per car to enter the park. Find out more about Georgia's Stone Mountain Park in our Attractions chapter and in this chapter's sections on golf and tennis.

Lake Lanier Islands
6950 Holiday Rd., Lake Lanier Islands • (770) 932-7270

Lake Lanier Islands has more than 300 lakeside campsites available year round. The campgrounds feature a fishing pier, an outdoor pavilion, laundry facilities, a store for supplies, a dump station and a boat launch ramp. All RV sites have water and electricity; some have sewer hookups. Primitive sites are $15.50 per night; RVs are $21 or $22.

Red Top Mountain Park
653 Red Top Mountain Rd. S.E., Cartersville • (770) 975-0055

One-and-a-half miles east of I-75 at Exit 123, Red Top, on a 1,950-acre peninsula along Lake Allatoona, offers 92 tent and trailer sites for $12 to $16 per night. A 33-room lodge costs $60 per room, double-occupancy, during the week; $65 on weekends. There are also 18 fully equipped cottages for $75 a night during the week, $80 on weekends. Cottages sleep up to eight people, and while they have no TV or phone, they do have fireplaces, decks and grills. Adding to the pleasures are 50 picnic sites, fishing, tennis facilities, nature trails, three marinas, boat ramps and five docks.

Victoria Bryant Park
1105 Bryant Park Rd., Royston
• **(706) 245-6270**

This park is 4 miles west of Royston off U.S. Highway 29. It offers 19 RV sites, six tent sites and one pioneer site for $12 or $14 per night. This well-maintained park has a lake for fishing and one fish pond reserved for campers only. You can swim in the pool, and kids can enjoy the several playgrounds scattered through the park. You also can play golf or roam the nature and hiking trails.

Photo: Chateau Elan

There are plenty of riding academies and stables in the area.

Canoeing

There are many venues for canoeing adventures close to the city. Georgia's Stone Mountain Park (listed previously under "Camping") rents canoes to boaters age 16 or older for $5 per hour, with a $5 refundable deposit.

Chattahoochee Outdoor Center
1990 Island Ford Pkwy. • (770) 395-6851

Chattahoochee Outdoor Center rents canoes by the day along with a convenient shuttle bus offering transportation between the put-in (Johnson Ferry and Powers Island) and take-out points (Powers Island and Paces Mill). Canoes rent for $35 a day with a $100 deposit. The shuttle costs $2.50 for adults and $1.25 for children 12 or younger. The Center opens for weekends in May, then daily after Memorial Day until the second weekend in September. See more about the Chattahoochee Outdoor Center in the "Whitewater Rafting and Tubing" section of this chapter.

Providence Outdoor Recreation Center
13440 Providence Park Dr., Alpharetta
• **(770) 740-2419**

At the Providence Outdoor Recreation Center qualified instructors will guide you through daylong classes on the basics of canoeing in both moving and flat water. Providence also

offers classes in map and compass reading, backpacking, rappelling and rock climbing. Backpacking excursions cost $100 per person for a weekend trip into the north Georgia Mountains. Providence supplies the equipment, transportation and cooking equipment. Basic canoeing instruction costs $30 per person per day. Rappelling classes cost $40 per person for a six-hour instruction period plus lunch. (See our entry in the "Climbing" section of this chapter.)

Climbing

Atlanta Climbing Club
(770) 621-5070

If climbing up tall structures turns you on, the folks in the Atlanta Climbing Club are your kind of people. They meet at 7:30 PM on the second Thursday of each month at the Garden Hills Community Center, 4058 E. Brookhaven Drive, in Buckhead. Call the hotline for directions and more information.

Challenge Rock Climbing School
1085 Capital Club Cir. N.E.
• **(404) 237-4021**

Challenge offers lessons, safety instruction and equipment as well as monthly free clinics to help you get started in rock climbing. The school teaches individuals, families and groups. Individual outdoor classes range from $50 to $90 for one day; two-day sessions run from $100 to $285.

Providence Outdoor Recreation Center
13440 Providence Park Dr., Alpharetta
• **(770) 740-2419**

As we mentioned in our "Canoeing" section, this outdoor center offers classes in rock climbing. Rock climbing costs $100 per person per session — sessions are three days of classes and a full day of climbing at Sand Rock in Alabama.

Cricket

Atlanta Georgia Cricket Association
(770) 416-6728

This group sponsors nine teams in league play. Teams play 16 games per year for the league championship. In between games, individual cricket clubs organize their own games with out-of-town teams. Most games are played in the College Park area and are free to spectators. Contact club president Dorrell Allen at the previously listed number for more information.

Cycling

When you're tired of walking, what better way to survey the scene than from the seat of a bike? You'll have lots of company. Cycling grows in popularity each year as Atlantans discover the pleasures and environmental benefits of the sport. Lots of informal groups schedule regular bike rides and welcome newcomers.

North Atlanta Road Club
2800 Canton Rd. N.E., Marietta
• **(770) 422-5237**

Call this club, headquartered in the Free Flite Bicycles Shop, for friendly cycling guidance. With a $30 annual membership, you get a host of goodies: a discount in the Free Flite shop in the northwest metro area of Marietta, a point system for ride participation earning more discounts, newsletters, information about practice rides and more. The club sponsors a Free Flite ride (with food) on the first and third Saturday morning of each month and weekly practice rides on Tuesday nights. Free Flite sells a full range of bikes as well as parts, clothing, shoes and triathlon equipment.

Southern Bicycle League
1285 Willeo Creek Dr., Roswell
• **(770) 594-8350**

This 25-year-old cycling group is one of the largest clubs in the country, with a membership of 2,200 adults. The league sponsors regularly scheduled bike rides throughout the metro area; nonmembers are welcome. Pick up a copy of the organization's monthly magazine *Freewheelin'* ($2) in local bike shops and bookstores. It's full of safety tips, ride calendars and directions to the best trails.

Southern Off-Road Bicycle Association
• **(770) 565-1719; (770) 565-1795, trail maintenance**

The Southern Off-Road Bicycle Association (SORBA) sponsors organized rides every weekend during warm weather, roughly late April through summer. The monthly newsletter, *Fat Tire Times*, gives a calendar of these

---

INSIDERS' TIP

Atlantans jog, bike, backpack, exercise and play golf and tennis more than the national average, according to an *Atlanta Journal-Constitution* survey. That's not surprising considering that our average temperature of 64.2 degrees means most of us can be outdoors almost year round. The Atlanta Lawn and Tennis Association (ALTA) has 80,000 members, for example. And although we are landlocked, 169,000 boats are registered in the 16-county metro area.

rides. Pick it up free at most metro area bike shops. SORBA is a nonprofit organization dedicated to off-road biking and trail maintenance.

Darts

The Metro Atlanta Darts Association
• **(770) 279-8537**

The association welcomes the public. To find out about tournament and league play, call Lewis Wells, president, at the number listed above.

Field Hockey

Georgia Field Hockey Association
2840 Peachtree Rd. N.E., No. 103
• **(404) 346-3982**

Some 25 teams are currently playing through the association, which has teams for male, female and children players. Games are held every Sunday morning. The above hotline number will give you current information on leagues and how to join.

Fishing

The placid art of angling requires a license. Nonresidents pay $24 for a license for the whole season. A seven-day license is $7; a one-day license is $3.50. Each of these except the one-day license also requires a $13 trout stamp for fishing in designated trout waters. Georgia fishing licenses are available in many convenient locations such as hardware stores, sports shops, bait and tackle shops and many discount stores. Popular fishing spots in and near Atlanta include the Chattahoochee River, Lake Lanier and Lake Allatoona.

The **Georgia Wildlife Resources Division**, (770) 918-6418, is located at 2123 U.S. Highway 278 in Social Circle. These are the people who operate public fishing areas around the state. The Division can provide you with information about public fishing areas, fishing regulations and river fishing predictions. Georgia waters hold a variety of game fish species, including many kinds of trout, bass,

bream, catfish, shad, pickerel and crappie. There is no closed season for fishing in most streams, reservoirs, lakes and ponds in Georgia except for trout streams, which are generally open from 30 minutes before sunrise to 30 minutes after sunset from the last Saturday in March to the last day in October. Different hours exist for specific managed areas; the Wildlife Resources Division will provide detailed information about this and the special rules on bait and tackle.

Anglers from 16 to 65 years of age must have a Wildlife Managed Area Stamp to fish, as well as a trout stamp attached to the Georgia fishing license when fishing in designated trout waters. The exception is the one-day license, which does not require a WMA stamp. Landowners fishing on their own property do not need a trout stamp.

Bass Pro Outdoor World
3825 Shackleford Rd., Duluth
• **(770) 931-1550**

This vast store is a one-stop resource for all your fishing, hunting, camping and other outdoor needs.

Charlie's Tradin' Post
648 McDonough Blvd. S.E.
• **(404) 627-4242**

Charlie's specializes in all types of fresh and saltwater fishing equipment, with everything you need for bridge and pier fishing as well.

The Classic Angler Fly Fishing Shop
2817 Peachtree Rd. • (404) 233-5110

Dealing exclusively with fly-fishing, this shop offers quality gear, private casting and fly-tying lessons and custom trips. Check out the collection of antique fishing gear.

The Fish Hawk
279 Buckhead Ave. N.E. • (404) 237-3473

At the venerable Fish Hawk, you can get a full line of tackle, gear and outdoor clothing as well as specialty fly-fishing items. What's more, you'll find advice and another source for fishing licenses. As fishing fanatics know, haunts like this will likely turn up information on where the fish are biting.

Golf

Public Courses

Several municipal golf courses offer convenient locations and excellent playing conditions. Most of these courses feature greens of bermudagrass on a rolling landscape, with rental clubs available. Unless otherwise noted, these are 18-hole courses. The following is a representative sampling; for complete lists, call the specific locality's parks and recreation departments listed in the gray box of this chapter.

Fees listed here are subject to change; please call before heading out. For municipally owned courses, resident and nonresident fees are quoted; otherwise, one fee applies to all. Weekdays on the golf course means Monday through Thursday.

Cobb County

Cobblestone
4200 Nance Rd., Acworth
• (770) 917-5151

This challenging, well-maintained course was designed by Ken Dye. It offers an athletic challenge as well as a tranquil setting of natural beauty. The facility has a golf shop and clubhouse. *Georgia Golf News* voted Cobblestone No. 1 among Atlanta public courses for 1994, 1995 and 1997. Nonresidents of Cobb County pay $52 with a cart during the week; $59 on weekends. It's $10 less without a cart. Residents pay $32 during the week; $39 on weekends. County residents may purchase a $19 discount card that entitles them to reduced rates for an entire year. Cobblestone is about 25 minutes north of I-285 off I-75 N.

Centennial
5225 Woodstock Rd., Acworth
• (770) 975-1000

Larry Nelson, PGA pro, designed this par 72 course. Considered one of the very best daily-fee facilities, its winding creeks gives golfers a challenge for their fees. These begin at $40 weekdays, $47 on Fridays; and $50 on weekends and holidays. Prices include a cart. Centennial is about a 30-minute drive from downtown in Cherokee County.

Legacy Golf Links
1825 Windy Hill Rd., Smyrna
• (770) 434-6331

A combination of beauty and challenge await you at this 18-hole course designed by Larry Nelson. Called a challenging executive course, it features sloping doglegs and rolling fairways that conceal fairway bunkers and traps. It has well-maintained Penn Links bentgrass greens. A driving and practice range, a clubhouse and a putting course are on the premises.

Weekday fees are $20, or $27 with a cart. Weekends are $25, or $32 to ride. Mondays and Wednesdays are ladies' days, when admission is $12, or $21 with a cart.

DeKalb County

Candler Park
585 Candler Park Dr. N.E.
• (404) 371-1260

This course has nine holes and a par of 32. Fees at Candler Park start at the low end with $4.50 for weekdays, $5 weekends, for residents. Nonresidents pay $5 on weekdays, $6.50 on weekends. Students and seniors get $1 off. Candler Park has a putting green, a chipping area and offers club repair. No carts are available; no tee times are required.

Mystery Valley
6094 Shadowrock Dr., Lithonia
• (770) 469-6913

This course has a championship caliber layout that makes for a challenging round of play. Designed by Dick Wilson, the 18-hole, par 72 course had bermudagrass fairways and greens until recently, when it was refurbished with bentgrass. Fees with a cart begin at $19 for weekdays and go up to $28.50 on weekends for county residents. Walkers get $10.50 off admission fees. Mystery Valley is approximately 18 miles from downtown Atlanta.

Fulton County

Alfred Tup Holmes
2300 Wilson Dr. S.W. • (404) 753-6158

This 18-hole course has a par score of 72. Bermudagrass greens cover the only slightly hilly terrain with wooded areas nearby. Intermediate golfers find the course a pleasure. Fees for weekday play for residents begin at $17 and rise to $20 on the weekends. For nonresidents, the weekday fee is $19; weekends cost $22. Carts are $10 for one person and twice that for two.

Bobby Jones
384 Woodward Wy. N.E. • (404) 355-1009
This is an 18-hole course with a par score of 71. The bermudagrass greens and fairways are popular with intermediate golfers. Weekday rates are $29 for residents who play during the week, or $35 on the weekends. Nonresidents pay $2 more. Prices include carts; walkers pay $10 less.

North Fulton Golf Course
216 W. Wieuca Rd. N.E. • (404) 255-0723
The Chastain course was built in the 1940s. Its low, rolling terrain is called a championship course. The stone clubhouse, perhaps in tribute to the country synonymous with golf, is modeled after venerable structures in Scotland. Here you will find a pro shop and snack bar. Resident weekday fees are $27, $30 on weekends. Nonresidents pay $2 extra. Walkers take $10 off fees.

Gwinnett County

Springbrook Golf Course
585 Camp Perrin Rd., Lawrenceville
• (770) 822-5400
Beautiful bermudagrass fairways with bentgrass greens make this course a pleasure to view as well as to play. The links feature a clubhouse, restaurant, driving range and putting green. Club and cart rentals are available. Other amenities in this county-operated complex include tennis courts and a pool. Weekday nonresident players pay $33.85; on weekends, the fee is $38, with a cart. Gwinnett residents pay $5 less.

Privately Owned Courses Open to the Public

Château Élan Golf Club
6060 Golf Club Dr., Braselton
• (770) 271-6050
At the Château Élan resort and winery

(about an hour from downtown, Exit 48 off I-85) you'll find a par 71, 18-hole course designed by Dennis Griffiths. Spread across 170 acres, the course includes three lakes and two creeks; water comes into play on 10 of the 18 holes. A practice facility simulates the course's challenges and prepares golfers to meet them. Rates are $60 per person Monday through Thursday, $70 per person Friday through Sunday. The rates include 18 holes of golf, cart rental and tax. (See our Accommodations and chapter for more information on Château Élan.)

Lake Lanier Islands Hilton Resort
7000 Holiday Rd., Lake Lanier Islands
• (770) 945-8787
Designed by Joe Lee, this 18-hole, par 72 course features 13 holes on the shores of Lake Lanier. Dubbed the "Pebblebeach of the South," this course has won accolades for its beauty and design.

Fees include the mandatory cart rental. In-season rates are in effect March 1 through October 31: $47 on Mondays, $57 Tuesday through Thursday and $67 on weekends. From November 1 through February 28, the rate is $37 per person, seven days a week. There's also a $6 per car fee to get into Lake Lanier Islands. (Read more about Lake Lanier our Accommodations and Attractions chapters.)

Metropolitan Club of Atlanta
3000 Fairington Pkwy., Lithonia
• (770) 981-5325
This 18-hole course, designed by Robert Trent Jones, is a scenic, par 72 challenge. The club also has a tennis facility. Monday through Friday you'll pay $37 for greens fee and cart; Saturday and Sunday, $47. Rental clubs are available.

Renaissance Pinelsle Resort
9000 Holiday Rd., Lake Lanier Islands
• (770) 945-8921
This resort's 18-hole championship course was designed by Gary Player and Ron Kirby & Associates. Eight holes skirt Lake Lanier. *Golfweek* magazine named the course on its list of America's best in 1992 and 1994. Greens fees and cart rental are $49 per person Monday through Thursday, $59 per person Friday through Sunday.

Stone Mountain Golf Course
U.S. Hwy. 78, Stone Mountain
• **(770) 498-5717**

The public is welcome at Stone Mountain Park's beautiful 36-hole course. Eighteen holes of the course were designed by expert Robert Trent Jones; the other 18, by John La Foy. Nine holes lie beside the park's lake.

There's a pro shop on the premises, with lessons and rental clubs available. The course also features a driving range, practice area and two large putting greens. Weekends and holidays require about a week's advance reservation. Otherwise, it's first-come, first-served. You'll pay a $6 fee for each car entering the park. Stone Mountain's course is open Monday through Friday from 8 AM to dark and from 7 AM to dark on weekends and holidays. Eighteen holes cost $42 on weekdays; $45 on the weekends. Prices include a mandatory cart fee. Stone Mountain Golf Course also offers a five-weekend golf school for $100. This includes five free rounds of nine holes, one golf lesson per week and unlimited range balls during the five weeks of the school. For more information, call the course number previously listed or the general information number, (770) 498-5690.

Horseback Riding

Riding enthusiasts of all ages can find plenty of riding academies and stables in the metro area. Lessons, trail rides, boarding and an assortment of equestrian services are all available. For a list of horseback riding and boarding facilities, call the Georgia Department of Agriculture Equine Division, (404) 656-3713. We've listed a few well-recommended facilities.

Hat Creek Stables
7940 Nesbitt Ferry Rd., Dunwoody
• **(770) 395-9200**

Hat Creek specializes in lessons, which are given by appointment. You can also sign up for Saturday afternoon trail rides. Hat Creek does not rent horses. Lessons are $30 for a 30-minute private session or $30 for a one-hour group session.

Lake Lanier Islands Stables
6950 Holiday Rd., Lake Lanier Islands
• **(770) 932-7233**

Enjoy horseback riding on miles of scenic trails along the shores of Lake Lanier. This stable offers guided walking trail rides, which are great for beginners as well as pony rides and riding lessons. A 45-minute trail ride costs $20 per person. Lessons cost $25 per hour.

Linda's Riding School Inc.
3475 Daniels Bridge Rd., Conyers
• **(770) 922-0184, (770) 918-1272**

This school and stable offers private and group horseback riding lessons for children and adults, trail riding rentals, Saturday camp for children and adults as well as special programs, hayrides, company parties, school carnivals and birthday parties.

Special overnight rides and moonlight rides can be arranged for groups of six or more. Rentals run $20 an hour, per person. Group lessons are $20 per person, per hour; individual instruction is $35 per hour.

Swan Center Monastery
3207 Amicalola Church Rd., Marble Hill
• **(770) 893-3525**

This monastery offers riding lessons and clinics for both kids and adults. About an hour north of downtown Atlanta, the center offers trails that wind through acres of beautiful

INSIDERS' TIP

If you were a betting person, would you put your money on Seattle or Atlanta as the wetter city? Although Seattle is certainly a grayer city, with approximately 95 days a year of drizzle, Atlanta wins umbrellas up with 50.8 inches of precipitation compared to Seattle's 38 inches per year. Atlanta usually gets its rain in massive doses rather than drizzles. And historically, July is the wettest month.

mountain scenery inhabited by abundant wild-life and dotted with natural springs. The Swan Center focuses on teaching people how to handle themselves with a horse, which includes developing a relationship with the animal. The Swan Center operates horse camps for children in spring, summer and fall. A 45-minute guided lesson costs $25 per person.

Wills Park
332 Maddox St., Alpharetta
• **(770) 410-5780**
Riders may put their own horses through the paces of the three public riding rings at Wills Park. Alpharetta residents pay $5; non-residents, $6, for use of the facility.

Ice Skating

Ice Forum
2300 Satellite Blvd., Duluth
• **(770) 813-1010**
3061 Busbee Pkwy., Kennesaw
• **(770) 218-1010**
These two rinks, one on the northeast, one on the northwest side of town are open Monday through Friday, 10 AM to noon; Monday, Wednesday and Friday, 4 to 5:30 PM; Tuesday and Thursday, 8 to 9:30 PM. On Saturday and Sunday, sessions overlap from 1 to 3, 2 to 4, and 3 to 5 PM. The rink is also open Friday and Saturday, 8 to 11 PM, and Sunday from 7 to 9:30 PM. A 1½-hour skate is $5; two hours are $6; three hours are $7 per person. Skate rental is $2, if needed.

Parkaire Ice Arena
4880 Lower Roswell Rd., Marietta
• **(770) 973-0753**
For ice skating, Parkaire has been a favorite with northwest area dwellers for more than 20 years. Youth hockey league play is a feature; for information call (404) 816-3033. Parkaire also offers lessons in seven-week series. Admission in two-hour increments is $5 for adults and kids 12 and younger, plus $2 skate rental if you need them. Hours are Monday through Friday, 10:30 AM to 12:30 PM; Tuesday and Thursday, 4 to 5:30 PM; Friday, 3:30 to 5:30 PM; Thursday and Friday, 8 to 10 PM; Saturday and Sunday, 1 to 3 PM and 3:30

to 5:30 PM; Saturday, 8 to 10 PM; and Sunday, 7:30 to 9:30 PM.

Martial Arts

Aikido Center of Atlanta
63 Valley Brook Rd., Decatur
• **(404) 297-7804**
Here you can study the defensive martial art in classes seven days a week. Aikido stresses channeling energy rather than brute strength for the purpose of self-defense. Increased strength and spiritual awareness are among the aims of devotees of aikido. Monthly fees are $75; new students must commit to three months for $195.

Atlanta Karate Club
2041 Carthage Rd., Tucker
• **(770) 938-9639**
This nonprofit organization offers instruction in traditional Shotokan karate in a non-commercial environment. Call for locations of classes. The club welcomes beginners; classes are held Monday through Wednesday from 7 to 9 PM.

Imperatori Family Karate Center
5290 Roswell Rd. N.E. • (404) 252-8200
This large 8,000-square-foot center houses training for men, women and children, plus a martial arts supplies store. Nationally ranked husband and wife team Joey and Sheldon Imperatori teach clients discipline and self-defense techniques while increasing confidence and fitness levels. The center also offers personal trainers and fitness equipment. Sessions cost approximately $60 per month.

Paintball

Arkenstone Paint Ball Games
7257 Cedarcrest Rd., Acworth
• **(770) 974-2535**
Arkenstone boasts a 1,750-foot clubhouse and paintball supply store where, if you choose not to rent equipment, you can buy the air guns and water-soluble paint pellets used in this sport. Arkenstone welcomes players at all levels, whether individuals or corporate groups.

The complex features 10 fields with forts, bunkers, foxholes, ravines and streams. Arkenstone opens year round on Saturday and Sunday from 10 AM to 5 PM. An all-day rental charge averages about $45 for a full day of paint-slinging.

Wildfire Paint Ball Games
1989 Tucker Industrial Blvd., Tucker
• **(770) 493-8978**

Wildfire has a 40,000-square-foot warehouse with two indoor playing fields. One is well-lighted with barrels and pallets, suitable for competition-style games such as capture the flag. The other 20,000-square-foot room has large boxes arranged in a kind of cityscape, with a Main Street that branches off into side streets and alleyways. Here, players can enjoy elimination games, capture the flag and other paintball variations.

Wildfire has three outdoor fields. South Fulton, Gwinnett and one in Madison, about 100 acres with four plywood townscapes, woods with both thick and thin brush, open fields and hills with 80-degree inclines. The outdoor facilities open only on certain weekends, as long as they aren't booked by a private group. The indoor paintball facility opens every day but Monday. Tuesday through Thursday hours are 1 to 8 PM; Friday and Saturday, 1 PM to 10 PM; and Sunday, 1 to 7 PM. Wildfire has a full retail store for supplies and accessories. Indoor players average five to six games per hour; outdoors, a day might be comprised of only five to eight games total. All sites charge $14 admission. Gun rental costs from $5 to $10, depending on whether you want a pump gun or a semiautomatic. Gun rental includes 50 paint balls plus everything you need to play: mask, vest and so on. Kids and adults from age 10 and older can play; children younger than 18 need a waiver signed by their parents.

Racquetball

Southern Athletic Club
754 Beaver Ruin Rd. N.W., Lilburn
• **(770) 923-5400**

For an $8 guest fee, you can play all day on one of seven courts, two of which are chal-

lenge courts. Call ahead to reserve a spot. All-inclusive membership fees run about $45 a month and include use of the outdoor pool, a volleyball court, tennis courts, basketball courts and sun deck. Among the full club amenities are a steam room, a sauna, a whirlpool, lockers and showers. Full workout equipment includes Body Master, free weights, Stairmasters, stationary bikes and treadmills.

Southlake Athletic Club
1792 Mt. Zion Rd., Morrow
• **(770) 968-1798**

Eight indoor racquetball courts await you for a guest fee of $10. Southlake is a family-oriented facility with child care available. Staff includes a pro racquetball instructor. Members and guests can engage in tournaments and league play. Southlake also offers aerobics, workout equipment, free weights, an indoor track, saunas and locker rooms. Memberships are available from $42 per month.

Tucker Racquet & Fitness Center
3281 Tucker Norcross Rd., Tucker
• **(770) 491-3100**

This facility has an open court for guests, who can play all day after paying a $5 guest fee and signing a liability waiver. In addition to eight racquetball courts, the club also has tennis courts and aerobics and weight exercise equipment. Memberships start at $40 per month, with a $35 initiation and administrative fee.

Rowing

The Atlanta Rowing Club
8341 Roswell Rd. • (770) 993-1879

This club's boathouse is across from the Chattahoochee River Park. The club holds novice clinics monthly from March to October.

Rugby

The Atlanta Rugby Football Club has a hotline to tell you about club activities, play and practices. Call (404) 303-5855. Another group called the Atlanta Renegades Rugby Football Club also maintains a hotline; call (770) 908-3999.

The Atlanta Botanical Garden is in the northwest corner of Piedmont Park.

Running and Walking

A strong case can be made that Atlanta's most popular recreation is human locomotion. When a city's track club has 10,000 members and when 50,000 participants show up on July 4th for the world's largest 10K race, you know the place is carrying on a love affair with running and walking.

The city's environment encourages exploration amidst the ivy-covered lawns, the towering tree canopy and the flower-bedecked walkways. From mall strollers to competitive athletes, Atlanta offers a trail for everyone. And besides, it's a great way to meet people while you become acquainted with the city.

Indoor walking programs, jogging with your dog, runners who prefer track running, walk/runs for kids, speed runners — a program for just about everyone is listed in Atlanta Track Club's *The Wingfoot*. (See the following Atlanta Track Club entry.) Many groups welcome newcomers and sometimes finish off their workout with a meal.

For guidance in walking the city neighborhoods, read a delightfully detailed book called *Atlanta Walks*, by Ren and Helen Davis. Published by Peachtree Publishers, the book sells for $9.95 in local bookstores. It will greatly enhance your walking experience, giving you a thorough grounding in the history and architecture of your favorite routes. You'll also want to try out the jogging and walking trails in some of our abundant parks; for more information see the "Parks and Other Green Spaces" section at the beginning of this chapter.

Atlanta Singles Running Club
• **(770) 977-9837**

Atlanta Singles holds runs on the second, third and fourth Sunday of every month. With about 200 members, the group welcomes single runners of any age and ability level.

Chattahoochee Road Runners
• **(770) 425-8184**

More than 400 members of this group get together every month at the Harvey Hotel off of New Powers Ferry Road on the third Thursday of each month at 8 PM. They've been organizing runs for club members almost every week since 1981. There are two major events each year: the New Year's Eve race and the Run by the River, a spring event held on the banks of the Chattahoochee. Individual, family and memberships are available; rates are $15 or $25.

Roswell Striders
• **(770) 641-3760**

On the third Monday evening of each month, Roswell Striders meet at the Community Activities Building in Roswell Park, 10495 Woodstock Road. Members participate in programs about walking and jogging fitness and take part in monthly walks around the town. A three-month membership is $4 for Roswell residents, $6 for nonresidents.

South Fulton Running Partners
• **(404) 762-0667**

Early every Saturday morning, about 30 members of the South Fulton Running Partners get together at a member's home, or a designated meeting place, for a run. Each year, the group participates in the Run for Sickle Cell in South Fulton County. Membership is $50 per year.

Walking Club of Georgia
• **(770) 593-5817**

This club sponsors weekly walks, monthly hikes, judged race walks and other events in various locations throughout Atlanta. It also publishes a newsletter.

Atlanta Track Club
3097 E. Shadowlawn Ave. N.E.
• **(404) 231-9065**

Have questions about running and walking in the metro area? Call the Atlanta Track Club, a top-notch source. To quote directly from the club's monthly magazine, *The Wingfoot*, the club "is a nonprofit, membership organization dedicated to the promotion of health and fitness for youth and adults through programs of amateur road racing, cross country, and track and field in the spirit of fun and competition." Individual memberships are $25.

Organized in 1964, ATC has grown to more than 10,000 members and has become one of the most active clubs of its type in the country. The club promotes some 25 events each year, such as the Thanksgiving morning Atlanta Marathon and Half Marathon.

King of them all is the gigantic Peachtree Road Race, a USA Track and Field-sanctioned event limited to 50,000 runners. Thousands of spectators, armed with water guns and shouting encouragement, create an exhilarating scene along the entire route. Hundreds of volunteers support the race by handling pre-race registration, staffing water stations, assisting runners in trouble and performing dozens of other unseen but necessary tasks behind this major event.

Besides the major races, ATC sponsors low-key biweekly road races and a summer series of informal track and field meets. To get information about each week's events, call the ATC-sponsored phone line, (404) 262-RACE. ATC also maintains a list of sports medicine specialists.

Sailing

Lanier Sailing Academy
6920 Holiday Rd., Buford
• **(770) 945-8810**

Beginners and more seasoned sailors benefit from instruction here, which encompasses every level from Basic Keelboat to Celestial Navigation. A daylong introduction to sailing course costs $99 for the class and one-day solar sailor boat rental. Other classes vary in price depending on number of sessions and where the sessions are held (some take place in the Caribbean). The academy also offers a sailing club, private instruction, charter cruises and boat rentals.

Windsong Sailing Academy
3966 Secluded Cir., Lilburn
• **(404) 256-6700**

With facilities on Lake Lanier and Lake Allatoona, Windsong Sailing Academy offers numerous sailing opportunities. Sponsored by the Parks & Recreation services, community adult education programs, marinas and sailing centers throughout Cobb, DeKalb and Gwinnett counties, Windsong offers affordable courses year round at a variety of locations. You may take courses in chartering, boat purchase and navigation, safety, weather, celestial navigation, on-board gourmet cooking and many other topics. The basic training course costs $99.

Scuba Diving

The Atlanta Reef Dweller Scuba Club
(770) 457-6008, Theresa Cohen; (770) 729-9350, Jim Clemmer

This club meets monthly to plan trips, listen to guest speakers who discuss various aspects of diving and view films on the sport. Dedicated to furthering diving safety and education, the club offers beginning classes as well as advanced training and practice sessions. Some sessions take place at Lake Lanier and in Panama City; seven-day diving trips can range as far as Cozumel. Nonmembers are welcome at all meetings. Call for more details or to receive the club's newsletter.

YMCA National Scuba Program
5825-2A Live Oak Pkwy., Norcross
• (770) 662-5172

The YMCA National Scuba Program, which certifies scuba divers, will help get you in touch with a scuba instructor.

Skating

For fast movers who still want to take in the scene, skating provides the solution for many Atlantans and visitors. Catch MARTA to the Midtown area and walk to prime skating territory in Piedmont Park. There are lots of other good skating areas in Atlanta. Skate store personnel can give you tips on fun, safe skating areas as well as let you know how to join organized skates.

You can also find places to skate indoors. We've listed some of Atlanta's skating rinks as well as a few of Atlanta's skating stores and schools.

Asphalt Flight School
1024 Monroe Dr. N.E. • (404) 853-5009

Asphalt Flight School (AFS) offers in-line skating lessons, apparel, equipment, accessories and rentals. The store is affiliated with Peachtree Road Rollers, which organizes skates Monday and Wednesday nights at Rio mall 8:30 PM, and on Sunday by the Flight School at 10:30 AM. Newcomers are welcome; all participants must wear helmets. As Georgia headquarters for the National Skate Patrol, AFS has certified Skate Patrol members who come on the group skates and offer advice on safety equipment, skating style and tips on improving your personal skill level.

AFS teaches an organized skating lesson Sunday at 2 PM for $15 per person. Individuals and groups can also schedule lessons at other times. Individual lessons cost anywhere from $30 to $60. Class prices include rental equipment. AFS also sells snowboards and skateboards.

The Golden Glide Roller Skating Rink
2750 Wesley Chapel Rd., Decatur
• (404) 288-7773

This rink designates specific nights for special age groups, with a basic rate of $1.50 skate rental plus admission price. Mondays through Wednesdays are reserved for private parties. On Thursdays from 8 PM to midnight the rink is reserved for skaters older than 18; admission is $5.

Family Night is Friday from 7:30 to 11 PM; admission is $4. Family skating is also offered on Saturday afternoons from 1 to 5 PM and Sundays from 3 to 7 PM; there's a $3.50 admission fee. Teen Night is Saturday from 7:30 to 11:30 PM with a $5.50 admission fee. On Adults Only Night, Sunday from 8 PM to midnight, the minimum age is 21; admission is $5.

Sparkles
4800 Davidson Rd., Mariettta
• (770) 973-2311

This popular roller rink schedules frequent fund-raising skates for area schools as well as birthday parties. Friday hours are 3 to 5:30 PM for $4 and 7 to 11 PM for Teen Night, $6. Saturday hours are 10 AM to 5 PM, $4, and 7 to 11 PM, $6. It's open on Sunday from 2 to 5 PM for $4. Skate rentals are $1.50. Other

Sparkles locations are in Canton, Smyrna, Kennesaw, Lawrenceville, Riverdale and Paulding County.

Skiing

Atlanta Ski Club
6303 Barfield Rd. N.E., Ste. No. 120
• **(404) 255-4800**

Atlanta Ski Club is one of the largest ski clubs in the world, with approximately 4,000 members. The club sponsors extensive snow skiing programs, year-round adventure trips and social events. Individual memberships cost $65 to join; $55 annually thereafter. Year-round activities include camping, hiking, whitewater rafting and canoeing, hot-air ballooning, horseback riding and windsurfing. The club hosts monthly socials at various restaurants or sports bars around the metro area.

College Park Recreation Department
3636 Main St., College Park
• **(404) 669-3773**

The College Park Recreation Department offers one annual ski trip to Black Mountain Ski Resort in North Carolina. The excursion is usually planned for February or March.

Skydiving

If jumping out of an airplane is the thing that blows your skirt up (not that they let you wear skirts to skydive, but you get the picture), metro Atlanta has some places where you can indulge your urge for free-falling thrills.

Peach State Skydiving Center
Covington Municipal Airport, 15200 Airport Rd., Covington • (770) 786-JUMP

About 23 minutes east of I-285, this skydiving outfit will train you and let you jump on your first day. Staffed by many skydiving world-record holders, Peach State bills itself as "Atlanta's professional drop zone." For prices ranging from $125 to $250, instructors will take you up in a plane then throw you out (with a parachute, of course.) Experienced jumpers also return regularly to Peach State to recapture that fabulous free-fall feeling.

Soccer

Soccer fans bow to no one in their enthusiasm, and Atlanta offers both kids and adults ample opportunity to indulge in the sport. Here are some examples of where to find information on league teams and other forms of play.

Georgia State Soccer Association
3684 B-1 Stewart Rd., Doraville
• **(770) 452-0505**

Metro Atlanta has a number of soccer leagues and two soccer seasons: fall and spring. The Georgia State Soccer Association is the place to call if you want to find a soccer league in your area for kids or adults. This is the governing body for the sport, and all soccer leagues are their affiliates. This office handles all registration, insurance and other administrative matters for organized league play. The association also offers coaching and referee courses. The office is open Monday through Friday from 8 AM to 4 PM. Registration costs vary from $9 to $13 per person.

Stone Mountain Youth Soccer Association
5585 Rockbridge Rd., Stone Mountain
• **(770) 879-1123**

Boys and girls from 4 to 19 enjoy the sport in this league in spring and fall. Two types of programs are offered, recreational and select, the select being the more competitive. Costs may vary with seasons but average between $60 and $70.

Tophat Soccer Club
1900 Emery St. N.W. • (404) 351-4466

This is an all-girls soccer club of about 700 players in the Buckhead area of Atlanta. It is one of the highest-ranked clubs in the Southeast and is very competitive on state and national levels.

Tucker Youth Soccer
2803 Henderson Rd., Tucker
• **(770) 414-0538**

Approximately 1,100 players make up this club of boys and girls. Both recreational and select programs are available for fall and spring seasons. Costs average $65.

Softball

Softball Country Club
3500 N. Decatur Rd., Scottdale
• (404) 299-3588

From about the second week of February through the first of December, the Softball Country Club swings with all-adult, slow-pitch play. The club has nine fields, a pro shop, batting cages, concession stands and an air-conditioned clubhouse for savoring those moments of glory after the big game. Most people come here as part of existing teams, but individuals are welcome to sign up for available slots; sometimes even spectators are pressed into service. Team members typically split the cost of play, which works out to around $40 to $60 per person for the season. Leagues play Sunday through Friday; tournaments are held on Saturday. There's a $2 parking fee per car that also gets visitors a $1 rebate off purchases in the pro shop or concession stands.

Swimming

We may be a distance from the ocean, but there's no lack of area pools for fun. For visitors, most hotels and motels have swimming facilities (see our Accommodations chapter). Residents journey down to their local municipal pool where, for a small fee, they can splash away a summer day. Some pools have seasonal membership cards available.

Atlanta

The City of Atlanta Bureau of Parks maintains 19 outdoor swimming pools and four indoor pools. For a complete listing or the pool nearest you, call the Department of Parks & Recreation, (404) 817-6766. Outdoor pools usually offer lessons in the mornings, then open to the public until 6 or 7 PM. Major municipal facilities include pools at:

Chastain Memorial Park, 235 W. Wieuca Road N.W., (404) 255-0863

Grant Park, 625 Park Avenue S.E., (404) 622-3041

Piedmont Park, 1085 Piedmont Avenue, (404) 892-0117

Cobb County

The **Cobb County Aquatics Center**, near the Cobb County Civic Center, (770) 528-8465, houses two heated pools, a diving well, a fitness room and locker facilities. The center offers instruction, a year-round competitive swim program, public swim times and a diving program. Two more pools in Cobb County are **Sewell Park** in east Cobb and **Powder Springs** in West Cobb. Call (770) 528-8800 for more information.

DeKalb County

The county operates 11 pools open daily during the summer months, closing each year around Labor Day. The pools are staffed by certified lifeguards. Annual passes and family discounts are offered. For information on DeKalb's pools, call (404) 371-2631.

Fulton County

Fulton County operates one pool, the **Clarence Duncan Park Natatorium**, outside I-285. (Other pools within the boundaries of Fulton County are operated by the City of Atlanta.) The natatorium has open swim hours every day of the week, year round. The facility offers swim passes in three-month increments and more than a half-dozen different classes, from water safety to arthritis exercise. Hours and classes are subject to change, so call ahead to inquire. The natatorium is at 6000 Rivertown Road, Fairburn; call (770) 306-3137.

Gwinnett County

Gwinnett operates five aquatics centers, four of which are open from Memorial Day weekend to Labor Day weekend. The facility at Mountain Park in Lilburn is open year round. Each facility offers a variety of swim lessons and classes. Season passes are available. For year-round information on schedules, costs and hours of operation, call **Mountain Park Pool**, (770) 564-4650.

Tennis

Tennis is big in the metro area, as you'll see by the many city and county parks with courts. The City of Atlanta alone maintains 50 tennis court locations. With our temperate weather, the heartiest of aficionados can play pretty much year round. We'll begin with information on the organization credited with changing the tennis scene in the metro area.

Atlanta Lawn Tennis Association (ALTA)
6849 Peachtree Rd. N.E.
• (770) 399-5788

A solid boost to the popularity of the sport came in 1971 when ALTA began league play with 1,000 members. Today more than 77,000 individuals pay $15 a year in dues to belong to the organization.

League play is scheduled for women, men, juniors and wheelchair competitors. ALTA also has a senior league for players older than 45. Leagues are divided according to expertise. Call ALTA's office for more information.

Bitsy Grant Tennis Center
2125 Northside Dr. N.W.
• (404) 609-7193

The city's Parks and Recreation Department also operates the popular Bitsy Grant Tennis Center, named for the local player who became a champion. You can play on 13 outdoor clay courts (six lighted at night) and 10 outdoor hard courts (four lighted). The center also has showers, lockers and a pro shop. USPTA-certified instructors offer lessons and clinics. The clay courts are open daily from 9 AM to 8 PM; hard courts stay open until 11 PM. Hard courts cost $1.50 per person per hour, $2 lighted. Clay courts are $2.25 per person per hour, $2.75 lighted.

Piedmont Park Tennis Center
Piedmont Park, Piedmont Ave. and 14th St. N.E. • (404) 875-7727

This tennis center in Piedmont Park has 12 outdoor hard courts lighted for night play. The center includes a pro shop, stringing services and concessions. Tennis Management, Inc., operates the facility, which also offers tennis lessons and clinics by certified instructors. Piedmont Park Tennis Center is open Monday through Friday from 11 AM to 9 PM; Saturday, 9 AM to 6 PM; and Sunday, 9:30 AM to 7 PM. The fee is $1.50 per person per hour before 6 PM; $1.75 per hour afterwards.

Beyond Atlanta

Cobb County Parks & Recreation
(770) 528-8800

Cobb County offers several designated tennis centers with league play, partner matching, classes, tournaments and more. For the location of the center closest to you, call Cobb County Parks & Recreation at the number above. Phone numbers for the centers are: the **Harrison Center**, 2650 Shallowford Road, Marietta, (770) 591-3151; **Kennworth**, 4100 Highway 293, Acworth, (770) 917-5160; **Sweetwater**, 2447 Clay Road, Austell, (770) 819-3221; **Fair Oaks**, 1460 Brandon Drive, Marietta, (770) 528-8480; and **Terrell Mill**, 480 Terrell Mill Road, Marietta, (770) 644-2770.

DeKalb County Parks & Recreation
(404) 371-2631

Residents of DeKalb County, just east of downtown, enjoy playing on a number of recreational tennis courts in parks throughout the county.

Three of the centers offering tennis facilities in DeKalb are the **Sugar Creek Center**, 2706 Bouldercrest Road, (404) 243-7149; the **Blackburn Center**, 3501 Ashford Dunwoody Road, (770) 451-1061; and the **DeKalb Center**, 1400 McConnell Drive, (404) 325-2520. Call these centers for more information on programs.

Fulton County Parks & Recreation
(404) 730-6200

Fulton County operates several tennis facilities. The **North Fulton Tennis Center**, 500 Abernathy Road, (404) 303-6182, has 24 lighted courts (20 hard surface and four soft courts). The Tennis Center is complete with a pro shop, showers, lockers and a full-time teaching staff. Twice, *Tennis Digest* named North Fulton as one of the top-50 public tennis facilities in the United States. Other Fulton County tennis centers include the **South Fulton Tennis Center**, 5645 Mason Road, College Park, (770) 306-3059, and **Burdett Tennis Center**, 5975 Old Carriage Road, College Park, (770) 996-3502.

Georgia's Stone Mountain Park
Stone Mountain Sports Complex Tennis Center, U.S. Hwy. 78 • (770) 498-5728

The tennis center at Stone Mountain Park's

Photo: Georgia's Stone Mountain Park

Take a ride on Stone Mountain Park's skylift to get a closer look
at Robert E. Lee, Stonewall Jackson and Jefferson Davis.

Sports Complex lets you enjoy the game on eight lighted courts. Fees are $2.50 per person per hour. Call for hours, which vary seasonally. And don't forget: you'll also pay $6 per car to enter the park grounds.

Gwinnett County Parks & Recreation
(770) 822-8840

To the northeast of the city, Gwinnett County residents flock to a beautiful tennis/golf/aquatics complex called **Springbrook**, 585 Camp Perrin Road, Lawrenceville, (770) 822-5400. The park offers three hard courts. See more about Springbrook golf course in the Golf section of this chapter. Six other Gwinnett County tennis centers also offer league play, lessons and tournaments on lighted courts.

Ultimate Frisbee

The Atlanta Flying Disc Club
(404) 351-0914

The Atlanta Flying Disc Club (AFDC) focuses on perfecting the sport of ultimate Frisbee flying discs. The club has a summer league for beginners, but players at all levels find opportunities to play through AFDC. The club holds two annual tournaments. Play adheres to the "spirit of the game" philosophy, in which players respect their opponents more than they try to compete to win. Players call their own fouls — there are no referees or officials — and the emphasis is on having fun more than gaining victory. Contact AFDC in early spring for summer league information and registration forms.

Whitewater Rafting and Tubing

For thrills that last long after you've soaked your clothing, try your hand at whitewater river rafting. Within easy distance of Atlanta, you'll find adventures galore via raft, canoe and kayak. Closer in, you can also raft and canoe on the Chattahoochee. It's not exactly whitewater, but it's a fun way to spend the day.

The scenic **Chattooga River**, two to 2½ hours northeast of the city, was the setting for the movie *Deliverance*. It's one of the last undammed whitewater streams in the Southeast. You can choose your level of difficulty on a variety of rapids, but if you dare, you can tackle one of the five rapids that drops more than 70 feet. The challenge varies with the season of the year as water levels change.

You can also find watery adventure on the Ocoee, Nantahala, Nolichucky and French Broad Rivers. The Chestatee and Etowah rivers, like the Chattahoochee, are better suited to laid-back tubing and rafting.

The Appalachian Outfitters
24 Park St., Dahlonega • (706) 864-7117

The Appalachian Outfitters near Dahlonega, about 1½ hours north of Atlanta, offers a couple of hours of lazy tubing, canoeing and kayaking on the Chestatee and Etowah Rivers. Appalachian Outfitters is open April through September from 9 AM to 4 PM on weekends and from 10 AM to 3 PM on weekdays.

Atlanta Whitewater Club
(404) 299-3752

If you want to find like-minded folks to share whitewater experiences, call the Atlanta Whitewater Club. This group promotes whitewater canoeing, kayaking, rafting and protecting the river environment. It sponsors trips, clinics and races for all skill levels. The club meets the first Tuesday of every month; meetings are relaxed, social and good places to meet paddling buddies.

Chattahoochee Outdoor Center
1990 Island Ford Pkwy., Dunwoody • (770) 395-6851

We mentioned the Chattahoochee Outdoor Center in this chapter's "Canoeing" section. In addition to renting canoes, the center also rents rafts for "rollin' on the river." Rentals are by day, and raft prices vary by size, ranging from $40 to $80. You must also put down a $75 deposit. The four-, six- and eight-person rafts all carry life jackets and paddles. A shuttle bus transports rafters between the put-in and take-out points; bus fare is $2.50 for adults and $1.25 for children 12 and younger.

The center is open from 9 AM to 8 PM on weekends and from 10 AM to 8 PM on weekdays, May to September. Rentals close at

1:30 PM at the Johnson Ferry put-in location; 4:30 PM at Powers Island. It's best to start out early to beat the heat and the crowds. Even though the Chattahoochee is fairly calm, there are a few areas with mild rapids, so expect to get wet.

Nantahala Outdoor Center's Chattooga Outpost
851-A Chattooga Ridge Rd., Mountain Rest, S.C. • (800) 232-7238

Farther north, the Nantahala Outdoor Center's Chattooga Outpost is just across the river from Georgia's northeast corner. Twenty-five years' experience underlies this employee-owned company based in Bryson City, North Carolina. The company also has an Ocoee outpost in Ocoee, Tennessee, which hosted part of the 1996 Olympics whitewater competition. If you're writing for information on river trips, direct your letter to NOC's main office, 13077 Highway 19 West, Bryson City, NC 28713.

NOC offers outings on five rivers: the Nantahala, Ocoee, Chattooga, Nolichucky and French Broad. A division of NOC, the Great Smokies Rafting Company, specializes in the dam-controlled, icy Nantahala; call (800) 238-6302 for details.

Southeastern Expeditions
50 Executive Park Dr. S. • (404) 329-0433

This company has organized whitewater outings since 1973. Southeastern's services also include ropes challenges, overnight trips, personalized instruction and group outings. Call for trip information and directions to the company's Chattooga outpost.

Wildwater
550 Fortson Rd., Long Creek, S.C. • (800) 451-9972

This firm provides whitewater rafting outings, canoe and kayak instruction, raft rental and a number of other services for watery adventures on the Chattooga, Ocoee, Nantahala and Pigeon rivers. Wildwater schedules trips daily from March through mid-November and offers half-day to two-day trips at various skill levels ranging from easiest to most advanced. You can do the whole Chattooga or certain sections, or shoot down the five-mile Ocoee, the river that was the venue for the 1996 Olympic whitewater events.

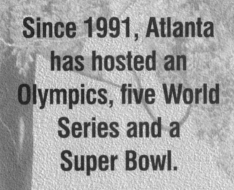

Since 1991, Atlanta
has hosted an
Olympics, five World
Series and a
Super Bowl.

Spectator Sports

We have hosted the 1996 Olympics, five World Series and the Super Bowl since 1991, and we can't wait for world-class hockey to come to Atlanta in 1999. Spectator or participatory, it hardly matters. You can see us jogging all over town, knocking balls about in our numerous neighborhood pocket-park tennis courts, cheering our kids on in everything from baby gymnastics to bowling. No doubt about it, Atlantans are passionate about sports!

With this kind of spirit, winning or losing is not necessarily an issue, but when it comes to pro sports, you gotta have a win now and then to keep ticket sales high. It wasn't until 1995, however, when the Braves bested the Cleveland Indians and brought home a world championship in the World Series, that an Atlanta professional team had a major win. Since then, things have been looking up.

Atlanta's long march to a pro sports championship began in 1966 when it became the first city ever to acquire franchises for both professional baseball and football teams in the same year. To meet franchise deadlines, the 58,000-seat Atlanta-Fulton County Stadium was designed and built in less than 12 months. Suddenly, Atlanta was in the big leagues. Win or lose, the new sports teams gave people across the nation reasons to think — and talk — about the perpetually building city in the South.

And for many years, Atlanta was the only city in the South with big league baseball, football and basketball teams. Our teams, therefore, became the "adopted" home team for millions of Southerners, many of whom seldom visit Atlanta and have never attended a game in person. These long-distance fans are fiercely loyal and follow the action as closely as folks in Atlanta; and they, too, shared in the delight of the Braves World Series victory.

Like any affair, Atlanta's love of sports has its ups and downs — and sometimes, even winning isn't enough. When the Hawks won the NBA Central Division in 1994, tickets to their playoff games were available right up to the last minute.

1995 proved an emotional roller coaster for Braves fans. The players' strike of 1994, which canceled the World Series for the first time in baseball's history, was followed by something akin to a fans' strike the next year. Some Tribe-trackers who gladly forgave the Braves their many long losing seasons bitterly washed their hands of the team after the players' strike, and their disappointment was evident: Game telecasts revealed plenty of empty seats in a stadium that was frequently sold out the year before.

Even after the Braves made baseball history by becoming the first National League team ever to clinch their division in four consecutive seasons, even after they swept the Cincinnati Reds in four games to take the National League championship and brought the World Series to Atlanta for a third time, fan enthusiasm was still lagging. On the eve of game six, the Braves' David Justice complained publicly that the fans weren't really behind the team. Justice was booed in his first at bat, but after he scored the only run in the decisive game, all was forgiven, and Atlanta celebrated all that Saturday night. Thousands filled the streets of Buckhead, where one TV reporter excitedly declared that people were "partying like wild ants." The following Monday, fans packed downtown for the Braves victory parade, and it's been sports mania ever since.

Mainly due to the enthusiasm generated by the Braves winning seasons, there's a scramble every spring for little league team slots in the rapidly growing suburbs. This bizarre ritual has become something of a late-winter tradition: TV news reports show shivering parents sitting in lawn chairs in line all night to get their kids signed up for a league close to home.

In 1994, Atlanta hosted Super Bowl XXVIII in the Georgia Dome. More than 800 million people worldwide, including 133 million in the United States, tuned in, making the game the most-watched event in TV history until the 1996 Olympics.

The 1996 Olympics, the largest staged in its history, was also the most viewed Olympics, thanks to cable and TV coverage worldwide. For Atlanta, the Olympics was like a three-week street festival highlighted by all the sports you could cram into 24 hours. And were we proud that Atlantans came out looking courteous and caring? You bet! We were proud that volunteerism was at an all time high for this Olympics that brought in guests and athletes from close to 200 countries, all requiring assistance from locals who worked almost around the clock doing everything from language translation to carrying water. We were proud that crime was kept to an all time low, and we handled the Centennial Olympic Park bombing (where over 100 people were injured and a young mother died) on the 10th day of the event without panic. The Olympic spirit did not flame out when the games were pronounced over: It is continually fanned by the Atlanta media with special features beginning each July 20th that bring back the highlights of The Games.

The world will not soon forget the image of Muhammad Ali carrying the Olympic torch. But Atlantans also recall torchbearer and Atlantan Olympic swimmer Janet Evans receiving the flame from fellow Atlantan Evander

Holyfield. And Olympic flag bearers Edwin Moses, Steve Lundquist, Geoff Gaberino, Dave Maggard, Benita Fitzgerald, Katrina McClain and Mary T. Meagher-Plant, Atlanta residents all, still show up at receptions and as honored guests at banquets and balls.

For Atlantans, 1997 wasn't a bad year in sports either. "How 'bout them Braves?" (this phrase ranks right up there with "Y'all come back, ya heah!") was again the refrain when they took their sixth consecutive division title. With that win, the Braves became the first team in 28 years of divisional play to win the division title consecutively so many times. Of course, there was lots of crying into beer mugs that '97 was also the first year in a child's age that the team did not make a run for the World Series.

We're already talking about the year 2002 when the Georgia Dome will host the NCAA Final Four and although the Omni, demolished in 1997, may be gone, it will not be forgotten as the place where the Hawks created magic.

In its stead will be another Turner property at this writing still unnamed. By 1999 the new venue will be "magnificent for basketball and historic for hockey" according to Stan Kasten, who is overseeing the development for Turner Broadcasting System Inc. The major reason for this undertaking is to create a new arena for the Hawks, but the National Hockey League franchise will also partake in the benefits of the facility. One hundred luxury suites and 20,000-fan seating will be part of what is being hyped as an entertainment complex with multimedia and interactive experiences combined with lots of amenities. The arena will be designed by HOK Sport and Arquitectonica (they designed downtown's Rio shopping mall years ago). It will have three roofs resembling a fanned set of cards and trusses that spell out "Atlanta" on one side of the structure and "CNN" on the other side. As a by-product of the arena, CNN Center will be renovated, and we can look forward to a new museum and a link between the Georgia World Congress Center, Underground Atlanta and Centennial Olympic Park.

FYI

Three area codes serve the metro Atlanta area: 404, 770 and 678. Whether you live on Peachtree Street or in New York City, you must dial the code to reach any number in the area. The difference? Outside the area, you must dial "1," then the area code and phone number; inside the area, you need only dial the area code followed by the phone number.

Since keeping downtown Atlanta attractive to conventioneers and suburbanites alike is vital to the city's financial well-being, any new construction receives careful scrutiny and then the tax blessing of the city. We can be sure the new complex will not make a fibber of Kasten.

(Note: Though correct at press time, ticket prices and policies for all sporting events are subject to change. Not all seats are available in all venues; many sections sell out to season ticket holders.)

Baseball

Atlanta Braves

Play Ball! Atlanta took its first step toward a World Series championship on April 12, 1966, when Major League baseball came to town. In their first game the newly relocated Milwaukee Braves played the Pittsburgh Pirates, losing 3-2 in 13 innings. Chief among the Braves' assets were future Hall of Famers Phil Niekro and Hank Aaron. In 1969, the Braves took the National League West title but lost the pennant in three games to the "Miracle" Mets.

In 1973 Hank Aaron, Dave Johnson and Darrell Evans made the record books by each hitting more than 40 homers. Then came the big moment: On April 8, 1974, millions watched as Hank Aaron smashed his 715th home run, besting Babe Ruth's long-standing record (a moment now immortalized in a large statue outside the stadium).

Back in the early 1980s, Braves games sometimes felt more like minor league contests. Attendance at games was often below 10,000; fans roamed the stadium freely and sat where they liked. But all that changed in 1982 when the Braves set a new record for the most games won (13) at the beginning of a season. Suddenly the Braves weren't a joke anymore, and Atlantans by the thousands spent their lunch hour standing in line for tickets.

In 1982 and 1983, Dale Murphy won back-to-back National League Most Valuable Player awards, helping the Braves capture the Western Division title in '82 and finish second in '83.

Then came the biggest shock. In 1990, the basement Braves chafed under the worst record in baseball. One year later, the amazing Braves brought the World Series to Atlanta for the first time, becoming the first team in baseball history to go from worst to first in a single season. New records were set for Atlanta wins (94) and for attendance (more than 2.1 million). After beating out the L.A. Dodgers for the Western title, the Braves fell behind the Pittsburgh Pirates three games to two in the playoffs then came back to win the pennant in the seventh game. In the first World Series ever played in Atlanta, the Braves held on 'til the end, losing to the Minnesota Twins 1-0 in the 10th inning of game seven.

Even though the Braves lost, the city was wild with excitement. Atlanta honored the Braves with a downtown parade that drew 750,000 people — far more fans than turned out in Minneapolis to cheer the victorious Twins.

In 1992 the Braves were back: They set a modern-day franchise record with 98 wins and topped 3 million in attendance. They took their second-straight division title, then beat the Pirates in a seven-game series to win the league championship, becoming the first National League team since the 1977-'78 Dodgers to win back-to-back pennants. Again, Atlanta hosted the World Series, but again the Braves came up just short, losing to the Toronto Blue Jays in six games.

More records were set in 1993 as the team won 104 games (53 on the road) and drew almost 3.9 million fans to the ballpark. Ten games behind at the All-Star break, the Braves battled back to grab the division title from the San Francisco Giants in the final game of the regular season. Atlantans were again talking World Series, but this time the honor went to the Philadelphia Phillies, who took the pennant in six games but lost the Series to Toronto Blue Jays.

When the players' strike ended the 1994 season, the Braves were in second-place in the National League East with a record of 68 wins and 46 losses.

In 1995, their 30th season in Atlanta, the Braves clinched the Eastern Division then beat the Colorado Rockies three games to one in the playoffs. The Braves humiliated the Cincinnati Reds, taking the National League championship four games to zero.

The Atlanta Braves' third World Series appearance got off to a good start when the team beat the American League champion Cleveland Indians in game one (3-2) and game two (4-3) in Atlanta. When the action moved to Cleveland, the Indians bounced back: They took game three (7-6), lost game four to Atlanta (5-2) and won game five (5-4). The Indians kept their dream alive until the end, but the Braves held on to win game six 1-0 and take the series four games to two.

Turner Field
755 Hank Aaron Dr. • (404) 577-9100

In 1997, the Braves said good-bye to Atlanta-Fulton County Stadium, their home of 31 years and at one time the pride of Atlanta and the South, the site of three World Series and the venue for a 1965 concert by the Beatles. Like the Omni Stadium that came down in just 11 seconds on the last weekend in July 1997, the Atlanta-Fulton County Stadium was demolished by implosion and fell like dominos at 8 AM on August 2, 1997. A total of about 8,700 much needed parking spaces now exist on the former Atlanta-Fulton County Stadium site adjacent to Turner Field, the new downtown home of the Braves just south of where I-20 and I-75/I-85 intersect. It was also the Olympic Stadium in 1996.

New to this field in 1997, fans and players alike adore everything about Turner Field with the exception of the cost of refreshments, which tends to be on the high side.

The 755 Club on the Club Level, a restaurant overlooking left field, is open only during games for lunch and dinner and only to members and guests of the club. It's also available for banquets and functions year round. Call (404) 614-2100 for reservations. Private luxury suites are also available for rental. Call (404) 577-9100 for information.

A Boston firm designed the entertainment complex that is meant to bring in the crowds much earlier than the start of the Braves' game — the goal being to not only get folks to spend money but to develop a new generation of baseball fans who can play interactive games, visit a museum about baseball, enjoy murals of some of the Braves heroes and party in the

huge plaza at the main gates. At Turner Field, which is called a "baseball theme park" rather than a ball park, you get to play as well as watch: There are batting games, electronic kiosks to check out the Braves Internet home page, TVs in the team store that show other major league games in action and an air-conditioned kids' corner financed by Coca-Cola called Tooner Field. You can select from a vast variety of foodstuffs vended by more counters than you'll find at the local mall.

The Braves Museum, which is run by the Atlanta History Center, features memorabilia and interesting tidbits about the team and players as well as the old railroad car used by the Boston and Milwaukee Braves during the '50s. Hank Aaron's bat and ball are there, too. The museum ticket costs $3. It's closed on game days but is open 9:30 AM to 4 PM when the Braves are playing nights or away games. Call (404) 614-2311 for specifics.

A behind-the-scenes tour of Turner Field includes the dugout, broadcast booths, press boxes, and suites, even the Atlanta Braves clubhouse. You can play some of the interactive games that line the breezeways and test your baseball skills. The tour is $7 for adults, $4 for children, and toddlers younger than 3 go free. When the team's in town, tours are given only in the mornings from 9:30 AM to noon. You can take a picnic lunch with you, by the way. It's best to call ahead, since hours depend on the team schedule. Dial (404) 614-2311 for specifics.

Tickets

Patrons may buy tickets to future games at the main plaza or by mail: Atlanta Braves Mail Order, P.O. Box 4064, Atlanta GA 30302; include a $5 handling charge and your daytime phone number. Allow seven days for delivery, or pick up tickets at Will Call. Tickets are $12, $10 and $5.

You may order by phone and charge tickets through the TicketMaster service. Call (404) 249-6400 in Atlanta; long distance, dial (800) 326-4000. Tickets are also sold at TicketMaster's 123 retail locations in Georgia, including Blockbuster Music and Tower

Photo: BellSouth Golf Classic

The BellSouth Golf Classic draws thousands of spectators each May.

Records. All TicketMaster retail centers require cash payment. TicketMaster adds a service charge ($5 per ticket) for both phone and in-person orders.

Season and group tickets are available directly from the Braves: Call (404) 577-9100.

If you don't have tickets, you can watch the Braves on SuperStation WTBS and the SportSouth cable network (selected games only). Every game is broadcast over the 150-station Braves Radio Network; Atlanta's flagship station is WSB-AM 750, whose clear-channel signal reaches 38 states at night.

Stadium Rules

Some Atlanta sports and concert venues have more rules than a religious order. In comparison, the Braves gate policies are positively liberal and getting more so by the moment. Severe public criticism over the cost of concession food may have been responsible for new allowances regarding fans bringing in their own chow. Upon entry, ticket-takers typically perform a cursory inspection of carry-in items looking for obvious violations of the following rules.

• Fans may bring in their own food and beverages in small coolers and plastic containers only if these are small enough to fit easily under the seat or in one's lap.

• No alcoholic beverages may be brought into the ballpark.

• Glass bottles and cans of any kind (except medicinal aerosol cans) are not allowed.

• Foam tomahawks are allowed and sold everywhere; real tomahawks (wooden or metal) are not.

• Smoking is not allowed in the stadium except in designated areas on each concourse. (Look for floor markings outlining a yellow box.)

• Fans may photograph or videotape the ball game, provided their equipment does not obstruct the view of other fans. However, no film or videotape may be reproduced or broadcast without the Braves' permission.

• Banners can only be hung off the upper deck, they must have no commercial references and, of course, they must be in good taste.

• Reselling tickets for more than their face value is a violation of Georgia law; both sellers and buyers are subject to prosecution.

• If it rains before the end of the fifth inning, your ticket stub is good for a rain check and can be exchanged at the ticket window.

• And if you catch a foul ball, go to Guest Relations in the plaza and pick up a "Grandstand Fielder" certificate.

Parking, MARTA and Getting Around at the Game

Although additional spaces were created near the field when Atlanta-Fulton County Stadium was demolished in 1997, parking is still at a premium, and many spaces are reserved for season ticket holders and VIPs. The lots and the main plaza open 3½ hours prior to game time (the rest of the ballpark opens two hours prior to the first pitch), and the team operates the lots and promises that flaggers will be on-site to provide security throughout the game and handle ins and outs in an orderly fashion. It costs $7 to park at these lots. There are also more than 10,000 private or illegal spaces in lots around the ballpark, but you "pays your money and takes your chances".

Your best bet is to park in one of MARTA's many free lots and take the train to the game ($1.50 for a token). Ninety minutes before each game, you can get a shuttle bus from MARTA's Five Points Station on the Forsyth Street side. Ask for a transfer at the MARTA station or else you will have to pay $1.50 for the shuttle itself. Shuttle service begins 90 minutes before each game and continues until the ballpark is empty. The shuttle bus drops you off at the corner of Ralph David Abernathy Drive and Central Avenue and then it's a two-block walk east to Turner Field. The streets are always cordoned off for pedestrians so walking is fun, especially since urban vendors line the streets hawking everything from boiled peanuts to water and kiddie T-shirts to tomahawks. We found the peanuts on the outside were sold in larger quantities and were subsequently less expensive if you needed to feed your own hungry hordes.

If you do decide to drive yourself to the stadium, we suggest that you call ahead and find out which gate is the closest to your seat — then try to park somewhere near that gate. Otherwise, be prepared to walk the entire stadium (not so awful considering all the fun things to see and do along the way). Odd aisle numbers are along the first-base line, even ones along the third-base line. Escalators flank the ballpark, and there are ramps and elevators too, but the stairs are easy to navigate and better than waiting for the elevators that take a lot longer to get to you than

they should considering we are only talking about three floors here.

For disabled fans, the Green Lot north of Ralph David Abernathy Drive, is a first-come, first-served parking lot for those with state-issued handicapped permits or plates. You can also drop off a disabled person at the stadium's East Gate on Hank Aaron Drive (the old Capitol Avenue). All levels have wheelchair seating and companion seating on raised areas so you won't have to worry about fans blocking your vision. Courtesy rides, restrooms, Braille signage, TTY and TDD services are all available here. There are even phone booths, drinking fountains and concession counters designed to enable fans who need out-of-the-ordinary services. Nevertheless, if you need more assistance, call (404) 614-1326.

At every game there are 110 guest relations personnel to help out. The main Guest Relations window is in the plaza, and there are others on each concourse. First aid stations are staffed by Emory University Hospital personnel and are located behind home plate on all three concourses.

Football

Atlanta Falcons

The Falcons played their first real game to a sold out stadium of 54,418 fans in the new Atlanta-Fulton County Stadium on September 11, 1966. Like the Braves, the Falcons hosted a California team; unfortunately, also like the Braves, they were defeated by the Rams, 19-14.

"Falcons" was a popular suggestion for the team name, for reasons best expressed by Griffin, Georgia, school teacher Julia Elliot: "The falcon is proud and dignified, with great courage and fight. It never drops its prey. It is deadly and has a great sporting tradition."

Following nine regular season losses and two wins on the road, the Falcons sealed their first home victory on December 11, 1966, beating St. Louis 16-10 before 57,169 fans. Linebacker Tommy Nobis became the first Falcon named to the all-pro team in December 1967. On November 30, 1970, 30 million viewers watched the first nationally telecast Falcons game on ABC's "Monday Night Football" (a 20-7 loss to Miami). Almost exactly one year later, the team got its first nationally televised victory (28-21 against Green Bay, in Atlanta). In November 1973, a national audience watched again as the Falcons racked up their sixth straight win (20-14) against the previously undefeated Minnesota Vikings.

The birds got a big name when they drafted California All-American quarterback Steve Bartkowski in January 1975.

After holding training camps in a variety of locations around the South, the Falcons built their current camp northeast of Atlanta off I-85 in Suwanee in April 1978. In December 1980, the team earned its first-ever NFC Western Division title. In the playoff, victory seemed certain as Atlanta led 24-10 going into the fourth quarter — then 60,022 fans (a record) watched in shock as the Cowboys rallied to score 20 points. The final: Dallas 30, Atlanta 27.

The Falcons changed their team colors in 1990, adopting the same black uniforms they wear today. In 1991, Falcon Deion Sanders signed to play with the Braves, becoming the first player in 30 years to play two pro sports in the same city.

The Falcons made the NFL Playoffs in both 1991 and 1995 and recently named a native Georgian, Dan Reeves, 53, as Head Coach. Reeves is the NFL's winningest active coach and 10th in all-time wins.

Tickets

Tickets for all home Falcons games are $33 or $30. Single-game tickets are sold at the Georgia Dome ticket office (between gates A and D). To order by mail, write: Atlanta Falcons Ticket Office, 1 Georgia Dome Drive, Atlanta GA 30313; include a $2 handling charge. Tickets may be purchased at any TicketMaster retail outlet or charged by phone, (404) 249-6400 or (800) 326-4000. (See ticket information under Baseball for more details.) TicketMaster adds a convenience charge to all orders. For season tickets, call the Falcons, (404) 223-8000.

Falcons games are broadcast over a 27-station radio network: The local flagship is WZGC-FM 92.9.

Note: The Falcons' training camp is in Suwanee, Georgia, about 40 minutes north-

Dan Reeves, the head coach of the Falcons, is a native Georgian.

east of Atlanta off I-85 at Exit 44. Camp begins about the middle of July and is completed near the end of August. Some training sessions are open to the public without charge. For information on attending a Falcons practice, call (770) 945-1111.

The Georgia Dome
One Georgia Dome Dr. • (404) 223-9200

The $214 million Georgia Dome is topped by the world's largest cable-supported dome. At its highest point, the roof is 275 feet — or 27 stories — above the playing field. The Teflon-coated Fiberglas roof weighs 68 tons and covers 8.6 acres. When configured as an arena, the Dome's capacity expands to 80,000.

Planning for the Dome began back in June 1984. After considerable negotiations, it was decided in October 1988 that the state would build the Dome with help from the city and county.

In May 1990, the still-unbuilt Dome was selected to host Super Bowl XXVIII in 1994. Construction began the very next month. In September 1990, Atlanta was awarded the 1996 Olympic Games, and the Dome was proposed as a venue for basketball and gymnastics.

By February 1992, the fabric roof was installed and made watertight. The 71,500 seats

Home of the Braves

New definitely means better if we are talking about the new home of the Atlanta Braves. Many baseball boosters complained bitterly about their old home, Atlanta-Fulton County Stadium, which converted to suit the needs of both baseball and football but put an unnatural distance between fans and the field. But Turner Field, formerly the

 1996 Olympics and the Paralympics Stadium, underwent sweeping renovations that transformed it to suit the needs of the Braves. Forty-one percent of the Olympic Stadium's 85,000 seats were eliminated (and sold at a post-Olympic auction to gung-ho fans), the Olympic track went to Clark Atlanta University where it still gets a good workout, and left over concrete is now supporting the bleachers at a local high school. And where once TV studios handled Olympic interviews, now there is the Braves' locker room. The remodeled stadium seats 49,831 fans in an environment designed exclusively for baseball.

The wonderful thing, for Atlantans taxpayers anyway, is that Turner Field, as a whopping $242.5 million project, was financed partly by money provided for the 1996 Olympics and partly by the Braves themselves. The team added $35.5 million to the reconstruction budget and got a few perks for doing so: The Braves locker room includes an artificial turf putting green so that ace pitchers, who love to golf, get in some below-the-knee swings when they are in the mood.

Turner Field, whose name is a nod to media mogul Ted Turner, combines revered

— continued on next page

Photo: Turner Field

Turner Field can seat close to 50,000 people.

baseball traditions with the latest in modern amenities. The stadium features steel trusses and an arched masonry facade of red brick with a precast stone base. Elevators, stairs, escalators and ramps throughout the park provide state-of-the-art vertical circulation among the ballpark's three levels. The stadium's color scheme features the Braves' team colors of red, white and blue, along with dark green accents, again evoking the appearance of an older, traditional ballpark.

The stadium's lower level seats 27,663, including 3,500 in a bleacher section. The second, or club, level holds 5,372 seats, in addition to 58 private suites and three party suites. The club level is an enclosed, climate-controlled concourse with four food courts and a stadium club restaurant and bar. The upper level seats 15,608.

The sky explodes with fireworks after each winning Braves game, so don't leave early to beat the traffic. Stay for the show. It's spectacular and kids of all ages will be thrilled with the colors, patterns — even the smell of blasting caps in the air. It's an experience that lingers and becomes part of the overall exhilaration of the event.

were in by June; the Astroturf rolled out in July; in August the Falcons kicked off the action in the brand new Georgia Dome. Total construction time was 31 months. On August 23, 1992, 66,834 fans watched the Falcons play and win (20-10 over Philadelphia) the first football game in the brand new Georgia Dome.

Enormous Sony TV monitors hang in each end zone; dozens of smaller Sonys are suspended from the ceiling throughout the complex. The four 1,250-ton air conditioners may work too well: Reports are that dome-goers complain more about being too cold than being too hot. The electricity used to power the Dome could light up a city of 13,000.

The Dome offers 183 executive suites and 5,600 executive club seats that are leased on a 10-year basis. Suite and club-seat members receive Falcons season tickets, one parking pass for every four seats and access to the private Executive Concourse and the private En-Zone restaurant. Club seats (extra-wide cushioned armchairs with high backs) may be leased for $1,050 to $1,890 a year; the club section includes waiter service. Executive suites are $20,000 to $120,000 a year and come complete with custom furnishings (although leasees may bring in a decorator of their choice), cable-ready TVs, a wet bar and a private rest room. A sliding glass door divides the interior of the suite from the open box, whose seats overlook the field. Suite and club-seat holders get first option to buy tickets to any public Dome event.

Dome Amenities

Eight Dome Service Centers are near the main entrance gates. These provide guests with various services, such as a check stand for items not allowed inside, lost child location and a designated-driver program. For the hearing impaired, amplification devices are offered with the deposit of a picture ID. (The Dome also features hearing-aid compatible phones with volume control, TDD phones, flashing exit signs and visual fire alarms.) A variety of food and drink is available at the Dome. There are two food courts on the upper and lower levels. Cocktails are also sold in the Dome, and you're allowed to take drinks to your seats. In fact, every seat comes with its own cup-holder.

Dome Rules

Here are some policies to keep in mind when planning your day at the Dome.

• Fans are not allowed to bring in the following: food, beverages (including alcoholic beverages), coolers, cans, bottles and mechanical or compressed air noise makers.

• Smoking is not allowed, except where designated.

• No audio or video recording is allowed at Falcons games.

• Fans may use portable TVs and radios (with earphones only) providing they fit on one's lap and do not annoy other guests.

• Tickets are required for all children except infants occupying the same seat as their parent.

Parking and MARTA

Mass transit is a key component in the Dome's downtown location. Unlike Atlanta-Fulton County Stadium, which was built in the middle of acres and acres of parking lots, the Dome is closely surrounded by business and residential areas and the Georgia World Congress Center.

There are only about 5,900 parking spaces at the Georgia Dome and the adjacent Georgia World Congress Center, and some of these are reserved for Executive members and media. These spaces go for about $4 to $6. Within walking distance are an additional 17,000 parking spaces in downtown lots, but all these together can only accommodate a fraction of the 71,500 fans at a sold-out Falcons game. Don't get any ideas about parking in the nearby Vine City neighborhood: Only residents with city-issued permits may park on Vine City streets during Dome events. Parking downtown can be a hassle at best; during Dome events it can be downright impossible.

Again, MARTA is the easy answer. The Dome is so huge that it's actually served by two MARTA stations on the east-west line: Vine City on the west side and Dome/Georgia World Congress Center on the east side. If you're returning to a station on the north-south line after the game, you can avoid changing trains at Five Points by taking the special express shuttle bus to the Garnett station. These buses board on the Dome's south side.

During Dome events, MARTA runs a shuttle on a downtown loop route; it picks up passengers at downtown parking lots and takes them to the Dome. This shuttle runs every five minutes before and after events and every 25 minutes during events. However, since you'll have to pay the full MARTA fare to ride the shuttle, it's clearly smarter to park for free at a MARTA rail station and take the train to the game.

Events

Peach Bowl
One Georgia Dome Dr. • (404) 586-8500
The Peach Bowl college football game has gained prestige since moving indoors to the Georgia Dome. The date varies slightly (between December 30 and January 2) to accommodate the TV schedule: It's cablecast on ESPN. The match-up pits the third pick from the ACC (Atlantic Coast Conference) against the fourth pick from the SEC (Southeastern Conference). For date and ticket information, call the Peach Bowl information line, (404) 586-8500, or TicketMaster at (404) 249-6400 or (800) 326-4000; a convenience charge applies.

Heritage Bowl
One Georgia Dome Dr. • (404) 223-8427
The Heritage Bowl is played annually at the Dome around New Year's. Football teams from two historically African-American colleges compete (one from the Southwest Athletic Conference, one from the Mid-Eastern Athletic Conference).

For date and ticket information, call the Dome ticket office, (404) 223-8427.

Basketball

Atlanta Hawks
One CNN Center at Marietta St., Ste. 405 • (404) 249-6400
The third jewel in Atlanta's pro sports crown was put into place in 1968 when the St. Louis Hawks basketball team relocated to Atlanta. On October 15, Cincinnati beat Atlanta 125-110, and NBA excitement became a part of Atlanta life.

The Hawks battled to first-place Central Division finishes in 1969-70, 1979-80, 1986-87. In 1993-94, the Hawks tied a franchise record with 57 wins against 25 losses, winning the Central Division and earning the No. 1 seed in the playoff after finishing the season with the best record in the Eastern Conference. After taking the first round three games to two, the Hawks were upset by Indiana, four games to two, in the second round.

For their first four seasons in Atlanta, the Hawks played in Georgia Tech's Alexander Memorial Coliseum before moving in 1972 to the then brand new 16,510-seat Omni Coliseum. In 1997, the Omni was demolished by implosion to make way for a spanking new entertainment complex to be built by Turner and scheduled for completion by 1999. In their final season at the Omni, Atlanta won a franchise-tying 36 home victories. One of the top teams in the Eastern Conference, Atlanta is coached by the NBA's all-time winningest coach, Lenny Wilkens.

Atlanta Hawks enshrined in the Basketball Hall of Fame include Walt Bellamy, Connie Hawkins and Pete Maravich.

Tickets

With the passing of the Omni, the Hawks play at either Georgia Tech Alexander Memorial Coliseum or the Georgia Dome and will continue to do so into 1999. After that season, they return to the site of the Omni and into a new, 20,000-seat arena that will rise from the rubble of the 25-year-old Omni. Until then, ticket pricing falls into two different price sets depending on which auditorium the Hawks play in. Tickets for games at the Georgia Dome range from $10 to $40; seats at the Coliseum run $25 to $35. Tickets are available at all TicketMaster retail locations and by phone: Call (404) 249-6400 in Atlanta; (800) 326-4000 long distance; a service charge applies. For season tickets, call the Hawks directly at (404) 827-DUNK.

You can watch the Hawks on WATL Channel 36 and the SportsSouth cable network. You can listen to the games on the Atlanta Hawks Radio Network, whose flagship station is WSB-AM 750.

Golf

BellSouth Golf Classic
2595 Sugarloaf Club Dr., Duluth
• **(770) 951-8777**

This $1.3 million-PGA golf tournament has traditionally been played in during a week in early May at Atlanta Country Club, but in 1997 the tournament moved to a new location: TPC (Tournament Players Club) at Sugarloaf in Duluth, Georgia. Key rounds are typically telecast on network and/or cable TV.

Tickets (for all seven days) are $30 and are available from the tournament headquarters, (770) 951-8777, or from TicketMaster,

(404) 249-6400 or (800) 326-4000; a service charge applies. Parking is about $5.

Tennis

AT&T Tennis Challenge
9185 Medlock Bridge Rd., Duluth
• **(770) 395-3500**

1998 marks the 14th year of this competition that has grown from an indoor exhibition at the Omni to a World Series event on the ATP tour. In 1997 it attracted more than 85,000 spectators who watched Marcelo Felippini win his first Challenge victory. The star-studded roster of tournament champions includes Andre Agassi, Michael Chang and Jim Courier. One of only 18 official U.S. stops on the ATP tour, it's now the nation's largest clay court tournament.

The tournament is typically held the last week in April or the first week in May at the Atlanta Athletic Club in Duluth. Single tickets range from $6 to $38; series tickets are $255 (reserved) and $195 (general admission). Call TicketMaster at (404) 249-6400; a convenience charge ($5) applies. To reserve box seats ($475 per seat; sold only in pairs) or a champagne table ($3,500 per table of four; four seats to all 15 sessions plus other amenities), call ProServ at (770) 395-3500. Parking is free.

Auto Racing

Atlanta Motor Speedway
1500 Hwys. 19 & 41 S., Hampton
• **(770) 946-4211**

Atlanta Motor Speedway is an 870-acre racing complex 30 miles south of downtown Atlanta in Hampton, Georgia; it features a 1.522-mile oval and a 2.5-mile road course. The short course is the world's fastest true oval track.

The track hosts NASCAR Winston Cup events in March and November. To book a tour, call (770) 707-7970.

INSIDERS' TIP

Need cash? There are seven ATMs at Turner Field, at least two on each level.

From Atlanta, take I-75 south to Exit 77, then take U.S. 19-41 south for 15 miles.

Tickets, which run from $30 to $80, are available from the track: To charge by phone, call (770) 946-4211. Tickets are also available from TicketMaster, (404) 249-6400 or (800) 326-4000; a service charge applies. Parking is free.

Dixie Speedway
150 Dixie Dr., Woodstock • (770) 926-5315

In Woodstock, about 45 minutes northwest of Atlanta, there's Saturday night racing weekly from early March through late November at Dixie Speedway. The regular program includes five auto events and one for trucks. Races are sometimes also held on Friday night, and there are special attractions throughout the season, such as monster trucks, demolition derby and outlaw sprint cars. The track is a .75-mile clay oval. Admission prices vary depending on whether you choose the pit area, the tailgate section or the alcohol-free grandstand. Adult tickets start at $10 and increase from there. Admission for kids 11 and younger is usually free; parking is also free. Tickets are sold at the gate. In September, the track hosts the finals in the Hav-a-Tampa Dirt Racing Series.

Take I-75 north to I-575; exit at GA-92 (Exit 4) and go west to the speedway.

Road Atlanta
5300 Winder Hwy., Braselton • (770) 967-6143

Road Atlanta is a 2.52-mile road racing track about 30 minutes northeast of the Perimeter. From March through November, Road Atlanta offers an array of sports car, vintage, motorcycle, moto-cross and go-cart races as well as entertainment events. Parking is free and so is in-field camping. Adult ticket prices vary with events; kids 12 and younger are always admitted for $5.

Purchase tickets from TicketMaster, (404)

249-6400 or (800) 326-4000; a service charge applies. Or call Road Atlanta, (770) 967-6143. From Atlanta, take I-85 north to Exit 49; turn left and follow the signs.

Running

Peachtree Road Race
3097 E. Shadowlawn Ave., Atlanta GA 30305 • no phone

This annual event is as much a part of an Atlanta 4th of July as is smuggling fireworks in from South Carolina, Tennessee and Alabama. The Peachtree is the world's largest 10K road race: It's more than 27 years old and annually draws 50,000 competitors with a few seeded runners racing for $50,000 in prize money.

The night before the race you'll find athletes and friends carbing up on spaghetti and bread at restaurants throughout the Peachtree corridor. The race starts at Lenox Square at 7:30 AM and runs down Peachtree Street, ending in Piedmont Park. Some 200,000 spectators (many fortified with eye-opening Bloody Marys) line the route to cheer the huffing and sweating throng. There are plenty of good places to watch the race; many bars and restaurants along the way open early for parties. Or, if you're really into watching others suffer, pick out a spot along the slope known as "Heartbreak Hill." It begins around Peachtree Battle Shopping Center and crests, conveniently, right in front of Piedmont Hospital.

To request information on how you can run in the Peachtree, write the Atlanta Track Club at the above address prior to March 1 and include a stamped, self-addressed envelope. Then, when you get your entry forms, fill them out immediately and drive right to the post office. The slots are filled in a strictly first-come first-served basis, and the 50,000 slots fill up almost immediately.

INSIDERS' TIP

Although the Atlanta-Fulton County Stadium has been demolished and replaced by a parking lot, relics of Hank Aaron's fabulous career in the stadium have been, shall we say, retained. The retaining wall over which Aaron sailed his record-breaking home run still stands and a spotlight illuminates an outline of the old baseball diamond.

Soccer

Atlanta Ruckus
1131 Alpharetta St., Roswell
- **(770) 645-6655**

1995 was the inaugural season for the Atlanta Ruckus professional soccer team. In 1997, the Ruckus merged with USISL to become a 24-team league. Soccer season is April through September. Home games are played at the 5,200-seat Roswell Stadium. Admission is $8 for adults and $4 for children younger than 14. To charge season or single tickets, call the Ruckus at the previously listed number. Parking is $3.

Equestrian

Atlanta Steeplechase
(404) 237-7436

Here's another Atlanta rite of spring: the annual Atlanta Steeplechase. The 'chase is run at a 435-acre site on U.S. Highway 411 west of Cartersville. The course accommodates up to 100,000 fans and in the best Southern tradition, this is as much a cocktail party as it is a race. Almost more important than the handsome horses are the elaborate hats, outrageous finery, antique cars and sumptuous buffets. Folks engage in tailgate parties (which is to say, they stand around their cars, trucks or station wagons) or set up elaborate tents from which they dispense the booze and/or take refuge from the sun or rain, whichever the gods deem appropriate for that year's event. The seven-race steeplechase benefits the Atlanta Speech School, which works with speech-hearing-impaired and learning-disabled students.

Tickets are $12.50 per person; a parking pass (you'll need one for tailgating) is $15. Important: tickets are sold only in advance — not at the gate. Tickets are limited; call well in advance of the big day.

Georgia International Horse Park
1996 Centennial Olympic Pkwy.
- **(770) 860-4190**

The 1,400-acre Georgia International Horse Park celebrated its grand opening on Labor

Greg Norman takes a shot at
the BellSouth Golf Classic.

Photo: BellSouth Golf Classic

Day weekend in 1995. During the Olympic Games, the park (about 30 minutes east of Atlanta off I-20) was the venue for equestrian events, mountain bike competitions and the two final events of the modern pentathlon.

The park includes a 165-acre Nature Center, an 18-hole Arnold Palmer golf course and driving range, a 200-room hotel, a 205-acre pedestrian-friendly traditional neighborhood, a steeplechase course and a covered arena with seating for 2,000 spectators.

The park's central feature is the open Grand Prix stadium. Permanent seating for 8,000 in an outdoor amphitheater offers excellent sight lines for competitions held on a sand floor. There are also 14 outdoor sand arenas for warm-up and other competitions, a 2,200-seat covered arena for rodeos, dressage, hunter/jumper shows and 12 miles of roads and tracks for cross-country events.

The Horse Park's mountain biking trails is the only Olympic course in the world for this sport and features 1,032 feet of elevation change over 8 miles of track. Additionally the park manages the new Cherokee Run Golf Course designed by Arnold Palmer. This 72 par, 7000 yard course traverses wetlands, granite outcroppings and rolling hills.

A 50-suite golf resort will open at the Georgia International Horse Park in the summer of 1998. The $4.5 million resort will include an 18-hole, 72 par course and a Hawthorne Suites hotel. It is anticipated that the '98-'99 season, along with the new golf resort, will be a boon to this growing suburban community of Conyers.

Information is available at the following numbers: for concert schedules, (770) 602-2606; for mountain biking, (770) 760-9002; for golf, (770) 785-7904; for trail riding, (770) 602-2606.

Polo Club of Atlanta
6300 Polo Club Dr., Cumming
• (770) 396-9109

The horsy set loves to gather at the Polo Golf and Country Club north of Atlanta. (Take Ga. Highway 400 north to Exit 12; turn left and follow the signs.) Except for the month of August (when the action is suspended due to the heat), exciting polo matches are held every Sunday from June through the end of October. Gates open at 1 PM, and the action gets under way at 2 PM; dress is casual. Admission is $5 per person or $15 per vehicle; a $25 fee admits your party and gets you a cabana to relax under (a very good idea on broiling Georgia afternoons). Bring a picnic, everyone does.

Professional Wrestling

World Championship Wrestling
(404) 827-2066

If gargantuan men in bizarre costumes threatening each other with grievous bodily harm is your idea of a big time, you've come to the right city. The sport known to Southerners as "rasslin" is perpetually popular with Atlanta fans of all ages.

World Championship Wrestling, a part of the Turner empire, is home to Hulk Hogan,

"Nature Boy" Ric Flair, "Macho Man" Randy Savage and many of the sport's other big names. Every week, the heroes and villains of the WCW burst into the homes of America through four hours of cable programming on the TBS SuperStation and three hours of syndicated shows that reach 94 percent of U.S. households. In 1995 Turner's TNT cable channel added a two-hour prime-time WCW show on Monday nights, appropriately entitled "Monday Nitro."

College Sports

If you're looking for high-powered college sports action, you'll find it in Atlanta. Call the number shown with each school's listing for information on schedules and tickets.

Georgia State University
1 Park Pl. S. • (404) 651-2772

GSU is best-known for its men's and women's basketball teams and its wrestling programs. The Panthers, whose colors are royal blue and white with crimson trim, compete in the NCAA's Division 1.

Georgia Tech
150 Bobby Dodd Wy. • (404) 894-5400

Tech teams compete in the ACC in many sports, but football and basketball are the major ones. Tech's colors are gold and white; the Yellow Jackets' arch-rivals are the Bulldogs of the University of Georgia in Athens.

Oglethorpe University
4484 Peachtree Rd. • (404) 364-8422

Oglethorpe University's Stormy Petrels take their name from a tough sea bird that flies right into storms. The birds compete in men's and women's soccer, cross-country, basketball and other sports in Division 3 of the Southern Collegiate Athletic Conference.

INSIDERS' TIP

Some people collected more than T-shirts and pins as memorabilia at the close of the 1996 Olympics: Stadium seats were hot sellers. And when the Omni was demolished, an auction house sold everything inside it from ladders to a 900-ton air-conditioner. Two goals with concrete bases, for example, went for $8,500 a piece.

Atlanta University Center

Three of the Atlanta University Center schools compete in football, basketball and other sports in the Southern Intercollegiate Athletic Conference. And although they are part of the same university system and historically African-American in population enrollment and philosophy, they are nonetheless rivals.

Clark Atlanta University
James P. Brawley Dr. at Fair St. S.W.
• (404) 880-8123

Elmer Mixon entered his second season of coaching Clark Atlanta University's Panthers in 1998. His team, in red, black and gray, battle it out in the Southern Intercollegiate Athletic Conference (SIAC).

Morehouse College
830 Westview Dr. • (404) 215-2669

Doug Williams, of the Morehouse College Tigers, is this school's fourth coach in the past five years. In 1996, the team, clad in maroon, came in 0-6 in SIAC. In 1997, the schedule ran 11 weeks without a break.

Morris Brown College
643 Martin Luther King Jr. Dr.
• (404) 220-3628

The Morris Brown fighting Wolverines football team, clothed in purple, black and white, made a better showing in '96 than it did in '95 finishing the season at 3-8 overall, a big im-provement over the 1995 record of 0-10. Coach Joe Crosby, entering his third year with the team in '98, is hoping for continued improvement.

Events

Georgia Games
3200 Downwood Cir. N.W. 4th fl.
• (404) 206-5420

In July of 1990 the first annual Georgia Games Championships with 3,000 amateur athletes competing in 18 Olympic-style sports took place. In 1997 more than 14,000 Georgians participated in 38 sports in a four-day event and the majority of the action took place on venues within which the Centennial Games were held such as The Georgia Tech Aquatic Center, Georgia Dome, Stone Mountain Tennis Center, Wolf Creek Shooting complex and others.

The Georgia Games, a legacy of the Centennial Olympic Games, will be an ongoing event for amateur athletes well into the millennium. Originally the vision of Billy Payne, whose dream it was to have the Olympics here in the first place, the Georgia Games gives local athletes a way of achieving recognition and preparing themselves for official sports for upcoming Olympics. In all, Georgia Games stages approximately 150 events annually, from running and biking challenges to tae kwon do, which has recently been added as an official sport in the 2000 Olympics.

When the hustle of city life hits home, residents head for the hills, the seashore or the nearby countryside.

Daytrips and Weekend Getaways

When the hustle of city life hits home, metro residents head for the hills, the seashore or the quiet charm of the nearby countryside. Georgia, the largest state east of the Mississippi River, has boundaries that extend from the Appalachian Mountains to the Atlantic coast. That means a plentiful variety of experiences awaits you. And thanks to a good road system, it doesn't take long to refresh yourself with a different perspective.

Here we just scratch the surface of scenic destinations throughout Georgia; for a broader perspective, contact the Georgia Department of Industry, Trade and Tourism, (800) VISIT GA. Whenever possible, we've listed street addresses , but some towns are so small that street addresses are sometimes irrelevant or unavailable. If we've left an address out, the restaurant, hotel or attraction is one you just can't miss once you've gotten into town. Subject to their availability, we've listed rates for the hotels, motels and bed and breakfasts we mention in this chapter. But rates can change; check with the places you want to stay to find out their current prices.

The North Georgia Mountains

For a natural tranquilizer, there's nothing like sparkling waterfalls, clear blue skies, silvery lakes and rising green vistas in the distance. You'll find all this and more in the north Georgia mountains, Atlanta's secret weapon against jangled nerves.

Georgia is home to 10 peaks rising 4,000 feet or more. The southernmost portions of the Blue Ridge Mountains extend into north central and northeastern Georgia. Springer Mountain, north of Atlanta in Amicalola Falls State Park, marks the southern end of the 2,150-mile Appalachian Trail that passes through 15 states. In the northwest section of the state near Tennessee, you'll find peaks and valleys covered with evergreens and wildflowers. Don't forget your camera!

Armed with a good map, you'll find many delightful mountain places within a few hours' drive of Atlanta. Charming shops in quaint villages offer handmade quilts, twig baskets, dulcimers and other traditional items. Carry home jars of mountain honey and apple butter. Browse the many galleries for sculpture, carvings, antiques, handwoven wall hangings and folk art. The profusion of inns and restaurants in the north Georgia mountains ensure you'll be well-fed and close to a bed, or you can camp at one of the many state parks in the area.

A number of the destinations we mention are within easy driving distance of each other. You could start your day shopping in an historic town square, have lunch at a family-style country restaurant, visit a state park in the afternoon, stop by a point of historic interest and end up at a bed and breakfast in a neighboring city.

Amicalola Falls

Amicalola Falls, the highest waterfall east of the Mississippi, takes its name from the Cherokee word for tumbling waters. The falls plunge 729 feet in seven cascades. Amicalola Falls State Park has campsites, cottages, scenic trails, a fishing stream, a lodge and picnic sites. Call the park (706) 265-8888 for directions, or dial the Dawsonville Chamber of Commerce (706) 265-6278. It takes about 1½ hours to reach Amicalola Falls from Atlanta, approximately a 65-mile drive. Ga. Highway 183 has signs that will lead you to the park. Amicalola Falls State Park is an easy drive from Dahlonega or Ellijay (see our sections below).

About 15 minutes from Amicalola Falls off Ga. Highway 53 on Amicalola Church Road, you'll find the Swan Center Monastery, a spiritual training center for the clergy of the Swanete (Swan-a-te) religion and a rehabilitation center for abused or neglected horses, dogs, cats and other animals. The Swan Center, on 123 scenic mountain acres, offers the public a place to retreat from the rigors of everyday living. Trail rides, riding lessons for children and adults, dog obedience classes, contemplative walks and educational workshops and clinics number among the center's many programs. The Swan Center also has a greenhouse and a custom framing shop. Money the center earns from its many outreach programs goes toward the care and feeding of the animals. Call (770) 893-3525 for more information.

Brasstown Bald

Brasstown Bald, a little more than two hours north of Atlanta, is the highest point in Georgia (4,784 feet.) Take Ga. Highway 400 to U.S. Highway 19, then take Ga. Highway 180 to the mountain. Deep in the heart of the Chattahoochee National Forest, the mountain offers a spectacular view of four states — Tennessee, North Carolina, South Carolina and Georgia — on clear days. The visitor information center, perched on the top of the mountain, offers interpretive programs, slide presentations and exhibits that trace the natural and cultural history of the area. (There's a shuttle to get you up the half-mile trail if you're not up for climbing.) You can take in wonderful wildflowers in the spring and bright autumn

FYI

Three area codes serve the metro Atlanta area: 404, 770 and 678. Whether you live on Peachtree Street or in New York City, you must dial the code to reach any number in the area. The difference? Outside the area, you must dial "1," then the area code and phone number; inside the area, you need only dial the area code followed by the phone number.

leaves in the fall. Hike one of the four hiking trails that range from .5 miles to 6 miles long. The Bald also has picnic tables and a log cabin bookstore. You can visit the mountain daily from Memorial Day through October, and on weekends in the early spring and late fall, depending on the weather. To find out more, call the visitor information center June through October, (706) 896-2556.

Brasstown Valley Resort, in nearby Young Harris, offers hunting lodge-style accommodations amid spectacular scenery. The resort features a 72-link golf course, tennis courts, an indoor/outdoor pool, a fitness center, interpretive hiking trails plus trout fishing and bird watching opportunities. Room rates range from $89 to $225. To find out more, call (800) 201-3205.

Nearby Blairsville hosts the annual Sorghum Festival and Indian Summer in October, a three-weekend event featuring arts and crafts, musical entertainment, clogging and games. Pick up a supply of sorghum syrup, cooked and jarred right in front of you by local Jaycees. To find out more, call the Blairsville/Union County Chamber of Commerce, (706) 745-5789.

The annual Georgia Mountain Fair, held in August, is a popular event with a long history — its been the high point of mountain summers since 1950. Just west of Hiawassee on the Georgia Mountain Fairgrounds, the 12-day fair offers music, craft exhibits and demonstrations. In Pioneer Village, visitors can examine a recreated mountain town and observe the arts of board-splitting, moonshining, quilting and soapmaking in progress. The fair also hosts a summer-long series of concerts featuring such country music names as Barbara Mandrell, Ronnie Milsap and Merle Haggard. In October a Fall Celebration takes place on the fairgrounds, featuring fiddling, gospel music and country music shows. For more information, contact Georgia Mountain Fair, (706) 896-4191.

Three miles west of Hiawassee on U.S. Highway 76 is the elegant Fieldstone Inn and Marina, winner of a coveted listing in the Great

Inns of America directory. Many of its 66 rooms overlook lovely Lake Chatuge. A restaurant, pool, and lighted tennis courts complete an inviting package. For information, call (800) 545-3408. Room rates are $89 to $150, from April 1st to the end of November; in winter, rooms cost $63. You can also find numerous cabins, bed and breakfasts and motels in the Blairsville area.

Other attractions include the Union County Courthouse in Blairsville, a restored 1899 building housing the County's Historical Society and its museum of local and regional history, (706) 745-5493. Trackrock Campground and Cabins also has a riding academy, (706) 745-2420, that offers horseback riding on scenic mountain trails. Trackrock Archaeological Area is a 52-acre area with ancient Indian carvings and historical markers to help you find your way. The Wasali-Yi Center, where the Appalachian Trail crosses U.S. Highway 19/129, is an outfitters' facility and rest stop for hikers in the Blood Mountain Archaeological Area. The Richard Russell Scenic Highway, Ga. Highway 348, offers 14.1 miles of dramatic mountain views and overlooks; this highway crosses the Appalachian Trail.

Vogel State Park, Woody Gap Recreation Area, DeSoto Falls Scenic Area and Dukes Creek Falls are among the many outdoor scenic and recreational venues in the region. You can camp at DeSoto Falls Scenic Area and Vogel State Park; Cooper's Creek Scenic and Recreation Area and Lake Nottely are two of the other camping venues in the area. For specifics, call the Blairsville/Union County Chamber of Commerce, (706) 745-5789.

Clarkesville

Clarkesville and its surrounding area have much to offer visitors. Historic Clarkesville, the Habersham County seat and scene of the annual Mountain Laurel Festival in May, is a charming little town off U.S. 441. Clarkesville has shopping, bed and breakfasts, fine food and opportunities for outdoor recreation from golf to camping. The town square, brightened by blooming seasonal flowers, is lined with quaint shops and restaurants. More than 40 structures in town have been listed on the National Register of Historic Places.

Ten miles from the town center on Ga. Highway 197, you'll find Mark of the Potter, a shop offering original handmade wooden crafts, metal and ceramic jewelry, pottery, hand-blown glass and weavings. Housed in a converted grist mill, the store, which opened in 1969, is the oldest craft shop in Georgia in its original location. Visitors can see mountain trout in their natural habitat from the shop's porch over the Soque (the Cherokee word for pig) River.

You say shopping's not your thing? You just want to relax? Escape to the woods at Clarkesville's Happy Valley Resort, (800) 354-4773, where you can stay in a fully equipped cabin (with a fireplace) for $80 to $90 per night and enjoy hiking trails, gardens, a swimming pool, a fishing pond, a collection of exotic birds and a variety of farm animals in barns and pastures throughout the grounds. (Note: the resort does not accept children.) You can also rent a cabin at LaPrade's on Lake Burton, (706) 947-3313, a rustic mountain retreat that offers fishing, swimming, hiking, boating and family-style dining. LaPrade's marina rents fishing boats, lake canoes, pontoon boats, pedal boats and rowboats. You can also get fishing guide service by appointment. Daily cabin rental rates of $38 per person include three family-style meals. But you don't have to be a guest to drop in for breakfast, lunch or dinner.

Sleep in a 100-year-old room at Glen-Ella Springs Inn, (706) 754-7295, listed on the National Register of Historic Places. This popular bed and breakfast, 8 miles north of Clarkesville in the Chattahoochee National Forest, has 16 guest rooms with private baths. Full breakfasts are included. The Inn is on 18 acres that include a meadow and herb, flower, and vegetable gardens, and a swimming pool. Even if you're not a guest, you can enjoy the Glen-Ella's varied cuisine in the dining room, open to the public for dinner, ranging from $16.50 to $22.50 per entree. Rooms at Glen-Ella range from $100 to $180. And if you like your weekends to be hair-raising, register for one of the inn's Murder Mystery weekends, where guests can test their detective skills.

You might also want to check out the Burns-Sutton Inn, (706) 754-5565, also on the National Register of Historic Places. Victorian antiques furnish the seven rooms in this 1901 house with wraparound veranda. The country inn has a restaurant, Jeffrey's, for guests as well for the public; entree prices range from $13 to $23 per person. Room rates are from $65 to $90. Some package deals are offered in conjunction with nearby golf, fishing and white-water rafting services.

Outdoor enthusiasts can camp at the Appalachian Camper Park, (706) 754-9319, which has 48 wooded sites, showers, restrooms and laundry facilities as well as a swimming pool, picnic tables, campfire pits and an ice machine. The park features a playground, shuffleboard court, fishing pond and nature and hiking trails. You can also camp at the Terrora Park and Campground adjacent to Tallulah Gorge State Park about 15 miles north of Clarkesville on old U.S. 441 in the town of Tallulah Falls.

Tallulah Gorge State Park, (706) 754-7970, created through a partnership between the Georgia Department of Natural Resources and Georgia Power Company, has a 500-yard walking trail along the rim of Tallulah Gorge. The gorge is 2 miles long and nearly 1,000 feet deep. It's one of the most spectacular gorges in the eastern United States; the breathtaking views make it a favorite stopping point along U.S. 441, the main route between Atlanta and the Great Smoky Mountains. The Terrora Visitors Center, (706) 754-3276, issues up to 100 permits per day, weather permitting, for hikers, mountain bikers, rock climbers and rappellers who want to descend to the bottom of the gorge. If you're found on the gorge floor without a permit, you could be fined. The center gives out free permits daily from 8 AM to 5 PM. No permit is required for the hiking trails, but there is a $2 parking fee.

As we mentioned above, you'll find plenty of spots to camp, picnic, hike, play tennis, fish and swim (during the summer only) at Terrora Park and Campground, operated by Georgia Power.

Dahlonega

The mountain town of Dahlonega, site of America's first gold rush, is about 90 minutes from Atlanta. Head north on Ga. 400 out of Atlanta to Dahlonega (Dah-LON-a-gah), named after the Cherokee word for precious yellow metal. Turn left off Ga. 400 at Ga. 60 and go 5 miles on a two-lane road that winds its way to this charming village.

Dahlonega's townspeople celebrate their past; many town buildings are listed on the National Register of Historic Places. More than three dozen gift, jewelry and specialty shops on the historic town square make for a pleasant afternoon of browsing. Find fine antiques, art, Appalachian crafts and more at shops such as Cranberry Corners gift shop. Mountain-made gifts featured at Cranberry Corners include birdhouses crafted from barnwood and tin, pottery and painted crocks. The Cranberry Christmas room is filled year round with holiday ornaments and gifts. Or browse through old-fashioned Dahlonega General Store, a typical country store on the square. Then stroll through Artist Avenue, a gallery showcasing handcrafted items from the North Georgia mountains.

The Gold Museum, in the 150-year-old former courthouse, tells the tale of the nation's first gold rush, (706) 864-2257. The discovery of gold near Dahlonega in 1828 encouraged the U.S. government to establish a branch mint here that operated from 1838 to 1861.

Looking southwest from the museum, you can see the steeple of Price Memorial Hall (part of North Georgia College) covered in Dahlonega gold. If you feel gold fever overtaking you, head for Consolidated Gold Mines, (706) 864-8473, inside the town's city limits. Consolidated was once the largest gold-mining operation east of the Mississippi. You'll see the mine as it was in the 1800s, go 250 feet into the miners' tunnel systems and have a chance to pan for gold. Or visit Crisson Gold Mine, (706) 864-6363, for gold panning and gemstone grubbing. Then, rest up from your labors with a trolley tour through historic Dahlonega.

You'll find plenty of places to eat in Dahlonega. The Smith House, (706) 867-7000, which has been serving food in Dahlonega for 70-plus years, is a family-style restaurant and

www.insiders.com

See this and many other **Insiders' Guide®** destinations online — in their entirety.

Visit us today!

inn where you sit down at a large table with about a dozen strangers and eat your fill of fried chicken, beef stew, ham, biscuits, corn, beans, candied yams, fried okra and more. The Smith House serves dinner guests on a first-come, first-served basis; many of their recipes are original. But if you don't want to chow down family style, you've got plenty of other choices, from pizza to gourmet dining. Papa's Pizza to Go, (706) 864-4444, offers pizza and subs, while Renee's Cafe, (706) 864-6829, features fine dining and a wine bar. You'll also find Mexican and Chinese cuisine, barbecue, ice cream shops and a coffeehouse.

Dahlonega offers plenty of scenic views, hiking trails, rafting, canoeing and fishing. Or rent a bike and ride around. Mountain Adventures Cyclery, Ga. Highways 400 and 60, Longbranch Station No. 11, (706) 864-8525, offers 24-hour bike rentals from $20 to $40, depending on how hi-tech you like your wheels. If you want to turn your daytrip into a weekend getaway, you'll find plenty of places where you can stay overnight: bed and breakfasts, cabins, cottages and motels. The area also offers a number of camping facilities.

Annual events in Dahlonega include the World Championship Gold Panning Competition, held the third weekend in April; the Wildflower Festival of the Arts, which takes place on the third weekend in May; and the Bluegrass Festival in June. Dahlonega also hosts Gold Rush Days in October and An Old-Fashioned Christmas in Dahlonega in December. For dates and times, call the Dahlonega-Lumpkin County Chamber of Commerce, (706) 864-3711.

Dalton

Known as Georgia's carpet capital, Dalton and environs also offer a number of historical sites. Eighty-seven miles from Atlanta (take I-75 north and follow the signs), Dalton is one of the gateways to the Chieftains Trail, designated a state historic trail by the Georgia General Assembly in 1988 as part of the 150th anniversary of the Cherokee Indian Nation's Trail of Tears. The Trail traces 150 miles of scenic highways throughout northwest Georgia, telling the story of the Cherokee Indians, whose culture preceded European settlement.

You can see homes, villages and mounds along the trail, as well as museums and ceremonial grounds. Chief Vann House, built in 1904, is a two-story classic brick mansion built by Cherokee Indian Chief James Vann. He contributed to his people's education by inviting Moravian missionaries to teach Cherokee children. Chief Vann House is about 10 miles east of Dalton at the intersection of Ga. Highways 225 and 52A, near the town of Chatsworth. Admission to this historic home costs $2.50 for adults and $1.50 for children older than 5. The house is open 9 AM to 5 PM Tuesday through Saturday, 2 to 5 PM Sunday. Call (706) 695-2598 for more information.

Dalton, a Confederate hospital and manufacturing town during the Civil War, is part of the Blue and Gray Trail, a series of monuments, plaques, parks, tablets and markers commemorating points of Civil War historic interest. Dalton's Blunt House, 506 S. Thornton Avenue, is on the National Register of Historic Places. Built in 1848, it was the home of Dalton's first mayor. The house opens by appointment; call (706) 278-0217. The Crown Gardens and Archives, 715 Chattanooga Avenue, (706) 278-0217, is headquarters of the Whitfield/Murray historical society which maintains a museum in this building that once served as offices for the Crown Cotton Mill. The c. 1890 structure, in a National Register Historic District, opens Tuesday through Friday 10 AM to 5 PM and Saturday 10 AM to 3 PM. Admission is a donation. Another National Historic Register site, the 1852 Dalton Depot, 110 Depot Street, has been transformed into an upscale restaurant/lounge. The lobby contains the original beginning point for surveying the city of Dalton. Dalton Depot's number is (706) 226-3160. Prater's Mill, a mile east of Ga. Highway 71 on Ga. Highway 2, is 10 miles northeast of Dalton. This historic grist mill was built with slave labor in 1855. The mill itself only opens twice a year, during the semiannual Country Fair in May and October. The grounds of this National Register of Historic Places site are open year round during daylight hours. Admission is free. Call the Dalton Convention and Visitors Bureau, (706) 272-7676, to find out more. The Ellis Collection Doll Museum, in The Pickity Place gift shop, (706) 278-9368, welcomes the public to look at a personal collection of more than 1,500 antique and modern dolls. You can view the dolls during store hours Monday through Friday, 10 AM to 5:30 PM, and Saturday, 10 AM to 3 PM.

You can find a number of interesting small shops scattered about in Dalton, as well as more than 100 carpet outlets offering savings from 30 to 70 percent off retail. If you're shopping for more than carpet, try Factory Stores Plaza, on Market Street adjacent to I-75, with 32 factory-direct stores.

Ellijay

Ellijay, approximately 20 miles northwest of Amicalola Falls on Ga. Highway 52, is about an hour's drive from Atlanta. The city was originally the site of a Cherokee Indian village. Ellijay boasts a number of shops selling mountain crafts, primitive art, antiques and more. Rivers Edge Antique Mall, at the intersection of Ga. highways 515 and 52, features 22 dealers offering a wide selection of antiques and collectibles. Other haunts for avid shoppers include Antiques & More and the Ellijay Antique Mall.

Outdoor enthusiasts can enjoy the many recreational venues in the area. You can canoe, fish, tube and kayak on the Cartecay River. The Cartecay's Class I, II and III rapids offer thrill-a-minute excitement. Contact Mountaintown Outdoor Expeditions, Ga. Highway 52 E., (706) 635-2524, or Beacon Sports Center, Ga. Highway 52 E., (706) 276-3600, to arrange expeditions on the Cartecay. Carters Lake, Ga. Highway 382, a flood control project of the U.S. Army Corps of Engineers, offers fishing, swimming, camping and boating. Hikers and mountain bikers will find trails in the nearby Cohutta Wilderness, (706) 695-6736, the Rich Mountain Wilderness and surrounding National Forest areas in Fannin and Gilmer counties, (706) 632-3031.

Ellijay is Georgia's apple capital, and throughout the fall, roadside stands abound with mountain apples, homemade apple butter, old-fashioned cider and other apple products. On the second and third weekends in October, Ellijay hosts the Georgia Apple Festival, an arts and crafts fair that's been attracting people from all over the nation for the past 24 years. Call (706) 635-7400 to find out more.

Cherry Log, just north of Ellijay, also hosts an annual apple festival, the Cherry Log Festival, on weekends in October; call (706) 635-7400 for details. From July 4 until Christmas, apple aficionados can take a self-guided tour through Hillcrest Orchards, (706) 273-3838, where picking your own is a popular sport on the second and third weekend of September. There are also wagon rides, a petting zoo, a cider mill and a market where you can find homemade jellies and jams, apple bread, apple butter, cider and other delicious items such as the Orchards' own apple cider doughnuts. The kitchen's open so you can watch Orchard cooks making pies, doughnuts and hot caramel or chocolate apples. Hillcrest is popular for school and church field trips. For $2 per person, groups can see an educational video, take a wagon ride, feed the animals in the petting zoo with feed provided by Hillcrest, get an apple, a cup of cider and a hat. Individuals pay $3 for the wagon ride as well as entrance to the petting zoo. Many families bring their own lunches and dine al fresco in the Orchards' picnic grounds.

History fans can explore parts of the Chieftain's Trail (which we mentioned in our section on Dalton) around Ellijay, and tour such historical sites as the Gilmer County Courthouse, on the square in Ellijay, an 1891 structure listed on the National Register of Historic Places; and The Perry House, 10 Broad Street, home of the Gilmers Arts & Heritage Association. Fort Mountain, about 20 miles from Ellijay, boasts prehistoric rock formations; Fort Mountain State Park, (706) 695-2621, offers camping, fishing, swimming and hiking trails.

Ellijay offers travelers much to eat besides apples. There's everything from pizza to authentic country fare. A few places you might want to try: Absolutely Country, 100 S. Main Plaza, (706) 276-7042, a down-home place featuring biscuits, fried ham, fried chicken and other cholesterol-laden country treats. Call Absolutely Country's menu line, (706) 635-7042 to find out the specials of the day. Or get some take-out barbecue at Mr. P's Take Out Food, 129 N. Main Street, (706) 635-4040. Mr. P's boasts that it has the best barbecue in the county, all freshly prepared, ranging from barbecue sandwiches to smoked chicken salad.

You can camp in and around Ellijay, (at Carter's Lake, Fort Mountain State Park,

Photo: The Creative Source, Okefenokee Swamp Park

Take a boat tour through the "land of the trembling earth" at Okefenokee Swamp Park.

Cohutta Wilderness and Rich Mountain Wilderness, to name a few) or stay in a motel, lodge, cabin or cottage. At Whitepath Lodge, (888) 271-7199, guests are ensconced in two-bedroom suites with full-equipped kitchens, laundry facilities, wraparound porches and panoramic views. The facility also offers tennis and swimming on the grounds; the property is on the 10th tee of the Whitepath Golf Club. Rates are $125 per night, or $700 a week, year round.

Gainesville

Gainesville, about an hour's drive northeast of Atlanta (take I-85 to I-985 and follow the signs), boasts the Green Street National Register historic district and a Smithsonian Museum, the Georgia Mountains Museum. Created in 1821, Gainesville became a trading center for the gold mining industry. In the late 1800s, after the railroad came, the town evolved into a prosperous cotton market. Green Street, the town's prime residential district, has a number of Victorian and Neoclassical Revival homes and businesses. To find out about walking and driving tours of the historic half-mile corridor, call the Greater Hall Chamber of Commerce, (770) 532-6206, or the Gainesville Hall County Convention and Visitors Bureau, (770) 536-5209.

The Georgia Mountains Museum, (770) 536-0889, features local history exhibits including the Ed Dodd/Mark Trail Memorabilia Exhibit and the General James A. Longstreet exhibit. Longstreet, a Confederate general, served as Robert E. Lee's right-hand man during the Civil War. Longstreet moved to Gainesville in 1875; he was a postmaster and opened a hotel where notables such as Henry Grady, Joel Chandler Harris and Woodrow Wilson stayed. The museum offers a self-guided tour. The Georgia Mountains Museum also operates a railroad museum in a renovated baggage car that houses railroad memorabilia and more than 300 cars on an HO gauge layout. The museum opens Tuesday through Friday, 10 AM to 5 PM, and Saturday, 10 AM to 3 PM. Admission is $2 for adults, $1 for students and seniors. If you'd rather have a piece of history in your home, stop by Antiques and Uniques, 2145 Cleveland Highway, which we mention in our Shopping chapter. Or stop by Stuff, 4760 Dawsonville Highway, another store offering antiques, collectibles and furniture.

There's more to do in Gainesville than ponder history — the area's rich in recreational venues. The rowing, spring canoe and kayak events for the 1996 Olympic Games took place in Gainesville's Clarks Bridge Park on Lake Lanier. Nearby Lake Lanier Islands, (800) 840-LAKE, which we describe in our Kidstuff and Parks and Recreation chapters, offers boating, swimming, sailing, golf and horseback riding, to name a few activities. Horse fans can find a nice selection of equestrian equipment and apparel at the Horse & Hound Tack Shop, 112 Main Street on the Square. Lanier Point Softball Complex, off Ga. Highway 53, at the end of Lanier Valley Drive, (770) 287-0208, is on the shores of Lake Lanier. The popular complex hosts league play and a number of major tournaments each year. Golfers will like the many challenging courses in the area with lovely scenery.

Every second weekend in October, Gainesville hosts the Mule Camp Market, an arts and crafts festival downtown on the square. Mule Camp features regional folk artists, musicians, cloggers, a children's carnival and more than 100 vendors selling artworks, pottery and food. Call the Gainesville Jaycees (770) 532-7714 for details. Kid and adults can learn about the environment at The Elachee Nature Science Center, 2125 Elachee Drive, (770) 535-1976, a 1,200-acre woodland nature preserve and science museum. The center has interactive exhibits, a natural history discovery center, live animal exhibits and a native plant garden designed to attract birds, butterflies and other wildlife. The museum opens from 10 AM to 5 PM Monday through Saturday; call for holiday schedules. Nonmem-

ber adults pay $3 admission; kids 2 to 12 pay $1.50. The center's hiking trails wind through the nature preserve. The trails open from 8 AM to dusk daily; admission is free.

Places to eat in Gainesville include Rafaello's, (770) 534-8668, 975 Dawsonville Highway, Suite 8. This southern Italian restaurant serves pasta, chicken, veal and seafood dishes. If you want some down-home cuisine, drop by the L&K Cafe, 839 Broad Street, (770) 531-0600, or if you yearn for authentic Mexican cuisine, try Chipicuaro, 711 Industrial Boulevard S.W., (770) 531-0290.

The Renaissance Pine Isle Resort, (770) 945-8921, and Lake Lanier Islands Hilton Resort, (770) 945-8787, are two excellent accommodations nearby that are described more fully in our Accommodations chapter

North of Gainesville on Ga. Highway 365 (285 Smithville Lane) in Alto, you'll find Smithville Village, a small shopping district that combines homespun charm and history. The Town Pavilion, a restored 1909 structure that moved to Alto from South Georgia, is a romantic setting for contemplation, private parties or weddings. The 1887 Country Store recreates the atmosphere of an old-fashioned mercantile emporium, and the Gift Gallery offers a variety of antiques, collectibles, gifts and accessories. Hungry? Have a snack at the Smithville Restaurant, the Hilltop Restaurant or the Country Grill. An authentic 1840 log smokehouse serves as a welcome center where you can find maps, brochures and information on area attractions. Want to get hitched? The Wedding & Vow Renewal Chapel can help you plan your intimate gathering. Smithville's general information number is (706) 778-5709.

Helen

Don't be fooled by the Alpine architecture in this charming town, approximately 90 minutes north from Atlanta on Ga. Highway 75. Helen isn't really a Swiss village transported to North Georgia, but it has taken on a new life as a year-round tourist attraction. Helen was a dying lumber mill town in the late '60s when local business leaders approached Clarkesville artist John Kollock for ideas. Having spent time in Bavaria, Kollock designed an Alpine village that melds perfectly with the mountains and river nearby. Funded entirely by local merchants, Helen's Alpine face-lift transformed the town into a Georgia landmark that annually draws hundreds of thousands of visitors from around the world.

The flowering window boxes, rooftop towers with steeples and beer halls with hearty German fare create a fairytale-like atmosphere. Annual celebrations include the Fasching Karnival (a kind of German Mardi Gras) in early February and Oktoberfest. Shopping ranges from inexpensive souvenirs to costly imported crystal in the 150 import and craft shops. You'll find bargains galore in Alpine Village Outlets' 30 national shops.

But there's lots more to do in Helen besides shop. Parts of the Appalachian trail cross highways near Helen, and you can find several other trails in the area. Many local stables offer horseback riding; call Sunburst Stables, (706) 947-7433; Chattahoochee Stables, (706) 878-7000; or Culpeppers Stables, (706) 865-9802 to reserve a ride.

You'll find tennis facilities at Unicoi State Park, (706) 878-2201 and White County Recreation Department, (706) 865-2756. Golf at Innsbruck Resort, (706) 878-2100 or Skitt Mountain Golf Course, (706) 865-2277. Canoe, raft or tube on the Chattahoochee river; to organize expeditions, call Cool River Tubing, (706) 878-2665, or Alpine Tubing, (706) 878-8823.

Take buggy rides around town (call Horne's Buggy Rides, (706) 878-3658, or Helen Carriage Works, (706) 878-3445). Pan for gold at Gold Mines of Helen, (706) 878-3052; or at Gold 'N Gem Grubbin', (706) 865-5454.

Nearby Yonah Mountain offers rappelling and hang-gliding opportunities. Historic attractions include Helen's Museum of the Hills, (706) 878-3140, with wax exhibits depicting life in the area at the turn of the century and a life-size storybook fantasy village for kids. The museum opens at 10 AM and closes at 6 PM from November to March; from April to November, it stays open until 10 PM. Adults pay $4 admission, students 13 and older pay $3, kids 5 to 12 cost $2. Children 4 and younger get in free. Seniors 62 and older pay $3.50.

The Nora Mills Granary, on the right going into Helen, (706) 878-2375, is a working water-powered mill open from 9 AM to 5 PM seven days a week. Watch them grind the grain they use for a variety of products including whole-grain white and yellow grits, cornmeal, many kinds of flours, pancake mixes, biscuit mixes, bread mixes and a special concoction called pioneer's porridge. Bridge fans will enjoy Stovall Mill Bridge, one of the few covered bridges still standing in Georgia.

Accommodations include cabins, cottages, motels, bed and breakfast inns and numerous campsites. The Hofbrauhaus Inn, 1 Main Street, (706) 878-2248, overlooks the Chattahoochee and features a dining room specializing in international cuisine. Georgia Mountain Madness, (706) 878-2851, rents one- and two-bedroom cabins on wooded lots; prices range from $70 to $165. Or try the Innsbruck Resort, (800) 204-3536, (706) 878-2400, on Bahn Road, a family resort offering individual rooms and three- and four-bedroom villas, ranging from $75 up to $279 for a large villa in the fall — peak leaf-changing season.

Dining is no problem, with numerous restaurants waiting to serve you. Alt Heidelberg Restaurant & Lounge, in White Horse Square, (706) 878-2986, is Helen's oldest German restaurant featuring a wide variety of home-style German food and a huge selection of imported beer. The Stovall House Country Inn, in nearby Sautee, 1526 Ga. Highway 255 N., (706) 878-3355, offers five guest rooms in a restored 1837 farmhouse that's on the National Register of Historic Places. Feast on creative regional cuisine in the inn's public dining room. Rooms at the Stovall House cost $50 for a single and $80 for a double, continental breakfast included. Dinners Thursday through Sunday are about $30 to $40 for two. You may bring your own wine with dinner if you have an extra bottle on hand; Sautee is a dry town. The inn's just a mile from the Sautee-Nacoochee Arts and Community Center, a highly regarded venue for arts and crafts shows and activities. Call (706) 878-3300 to find out what's up when you're planning to visit.

For more information, contact the Greater Helen Area Welcome Center, (800) 858-8027, on Chattahoochee Street in Helen.

Unicoi State Park, just 2 miles from Helen, offers cottages, campsites, swimming, fishing, boating plus a year-round schedule of activities including programs on mountain culture and the environment. To find out more about this scenic state park, call (706) 878-2201.

Nearby Anna Ruby Falls, in the heart of the Chattahoochee National Forest, is a spectacular double falls created by the junction of Curtis and York creeks. Curtis Falls drop 153 feet; York, about 50 feet. A .4-mile paved walking trail leads from the visitors center to the base of the falls. It takes about 30 minutes; walking is easy to moderate. The more challenging 4.6 mile Smith Creek trail leads from the base of Anna Ruby Falls to Unicoi State Park. Cars pay a $2 parking fee; RVs pay $10. To find out more, dial (706) 878-3574.

About 10 miles south of Helen, in the town of Cleveland, visit Babyland General Hospital, (706) 865-2171, original home of the once-wildly popular Cabbage Patch Dolls. Housed in a turn-of-the-century medical clinic, the "hospital" is open year round for families to discover how the cuddly toys are "born." Admission is free; hours are 9 AM to 5 PM, Monday through Saturday, and 10 AM to 5 PM Sunday.

Rosehips Gallery, 1611 Highway 129 S. in Cleveland, features the pottery of folk artist Lanier Meaders as well as contemporary Southern folk art by such recognized names as R.A. Miller, Mose Tolliver and Jake McCord. You can also find arts and crafts at Mountain Magic, 777 Helen Highway, which features a selection of one-of-a-kind works from local and regional artists and craftsmen. And while you're in Cleveland, be sure to drop by Afghans Galore on the square.

Eastward, Ho!

Head east from Atlanta and you'll find some charming towns that combine the elegance of the old world with the convenience of the new. Athens, Eatonton and Madison, along with several small towns in between, have undeniable charm and a coziness that's a welcome respite from the rigors of big-city life. They're all connected along U.S. 441, also known as Georgia's Antebellum Trail. Along this old stagecoach route, some of the state's oldest towns grew up on what was then the state's western frontier. Start at its northernmost point, Athens, and you can make it to the end of the

road in Macon in one long, leisurely day, with stops in Watkinsville, Madison, Eatonton and Milledgeville.

Athens

Athens, home of the University of Georgia (UGA), one of the oldest state-chartered universities in the United States, is also known for spawning rock groups the B-52's and R.E.M. A charming college town rich in history, Athens hosted the 1996 Olympic Games soccer finals, rhythmic gymnastics and volleyball. From north Atlanta, take I-85 N. to Ga. 316 to Athens. From east Atlanta and Gwinnett County, take U.S. 78 E. to Athens. It's a trip of approximately 90 minutes. For leisurely touring, avoid football weekends or you'll be surrounded by thousands of barking, howling UGA Bulldogs fans cheering on their team.

Begin your Athens visit at the symmetrical Church-Waddel-Brumby House, 280 E. Doughtery Street. Believed to be the city's oldest surviving house, it was built in 1920 for Alonzo Church, who later became president of the University. This fine example of Federal-style architecture is now home to the Athens Welcome Center, (706) 353-1820, which has information on guide services for group tours as well as all attractions.

Established in 1785, the University of Georgia campus, which covers many city blocks, offers various diversions to visitors as well as to its more than 28,000 students. You'll see the campus trademark, rounded-globe gaslights trimmed in black wrought iron, shining down on wide streets shaded by towering trees. The Arch, the entrance to the campus on Broad Street at the foot of College Avenue, was built in 1857 to represent the Great Seal of Georgia. The three cast iron columns signify wisdom, justice and moderation. The arch was gated when it first went up; it and the surrounding fence were designed to keep wandering livestock off the university campus. The Old North Campus Historic District, which you enter through the arch on Broad Street at the foot of College Avenue, is listed on the National Register of Historic Places and boasts a number of historic buildings, a double-barreled cannon from the Civil War and the Founder's Memorial Gardens, which surround an 1857 home that's headquarters for the Garden Club of Georgia. The Georgia Museum of Art, designated the State Museum of Art by the General Assembly in 1982, has a permanent collection of more than 7,000 works.

Off campus, follow the scenic tour signs through Athens' historic districts to view a diversity of architectural styles. Take note of the towering Doric columns of the Greek Revival-style Taylor-Grady House, 634 Prince Avenue, built in 1840. Or view the Victorian Gothic grandeur of Emmanuel Episcopal Church, 1899, on the corner of Prince and Pope streets, built of Georgia granite. Gothic Revival influences can be found in the style of the Sledge-Cobb-Spalding house, 749 Cobb Street, built c. 1860. Even if you're not into architecture, a leisurely drive through Athens' historic districts will impress you with the splendor of the city's historical structures. The city has four local and national historic districts: Boulevard, Cobbham, Bloomfield and Woodlawn. (You'll find signs throughout these districts, which include numerous streets in various sections of town.) For $2 at the Athens Welcome Center, you can buy a book with a map of these districts and descriptions of the historical sites.

Athens is home to the State Botanical Garden of Georgia. The University of Georgia uses this 313-acre horticultural preserve as a living laboratory for the study and enjoyment of plants and nature. Three miles from the UGA campus at 2450 S. Milledge Avenue, (706) 542-1244, the garden features 5 miles of nature trails through diverse ecosystems, 11 specialty gardens and a three-story conservatory with a permanent display of tropical and semitropical plants. The foyer of the visitors center offers changing exhibitions of original artwork. Admission is free, but the garden accepts donations. The grounds are open every day from 8 AM to 8 PM, April through September, and 8 AM to 6 PM, October through March. The visitors center is open 9 AM to 4:30 PM, Monday through Saturday, and 11:30 AM to 4:30 PM on Sunday.

Visit Morton Theatre, a living monument to Athens' African-American community, at 195 W. Washington Street, (706) 613-3770. Built by African Americans in 1910, the structure is listed on the National Register of Historic Places. Monroe Bowers "Pink" Morton's 554-seat performing arts center plus the adjoining shops and offices formed the heart of the community's business district. The offices housed professionals such as Dr. Ida Mae Johnson Hiram, the first female African American to be licensed to practice medicine in Georgia. Legendary performers, including Bessie Smith and Cab Calloway, played the Morton. Thanks to efforts of preservationists, the theater is once again thriving.

Athens' music/club scene is a diverse one that ranges from country to new wave, including the legendary 40 Watt Club, 285 W. Washington Street, (706) 549-7871, that launched many local rock bands who went on to national fame. Country fans can find live country music at Country Rock Cafe, 1720 Commerce Road, (706) 369-7625.

Diversity rules Athens' food scene too. You'll find fine dining and every ethnic cuisine represented. Feast on inexpensive Mexican dishes at the Mean Bean, 1675 S. Lumpkin Street, 549-4868, or sample homestyle Southern cooking at Weaver D's Delicious Fine Food, 1016 E. Broad Street, (706) 353-7797. Weaver D's motto is the source of the R.E.M. title, "Automatic for the People." Eat Italian or grab some wings in a friendly, casual atmosphere at Munchies, 131 E. Broad Street, (706) 543-1212.

There are plenty of motels in Athens, as well as picturesque bed and breakfasts. The Hutchens-Hardeman House, 5335 Lexington Road, (706) 353-1855, set on a 60-acre working horse and pony farm, is a restored antebellum plantation house c. 1855. Close to points of interest in Athens, the inn is decorated with antiques, family heirlooms and collectibles and serves a full Southern breakfast. Rooms here cost $55 per night. Oakwood Bed and Breakfast, 4959 Barnett Shoals Road, (800) 546-7886, is a Victorian-style house built more than 130 years ago. Oakwood, on five acres, offers three guest rooms in the main house and a two-bedroom private cottage. All rooms have private baths, telephones and TVs. Other features include a relaxing porch and a renovated barn with an exercise facility and conference room. Oakwood rents rooms by reservation or appointment only, accepts only credit cards and serves a full breakfast. Oakwood rooms cost between $75 and $100 per night.

About 10 minutes west of Athens, off Ga. Highway 211 in Statham, you can find an array of antiques and collectibles at the International Antique Gallery & Flea Market, 1946 E. Railroad Street. This market, housed in a converted textile mill, offers figurines, glassware, furniture, old vending machines, dolls and more. Although they're not antiques, the market also sells video games.

Madison

About 65 miles east of Atlanta, Madison is a showplace of antebellum homes that survived the Civil War. Incorporated in 1809, Madison was a prosperous cotton city and a stop on the stage coach route from Charleston to New Orleans. Madison politician Joshua Hill was friends with Senator John Sherman, Gen. William Sherman's brother. Hill was opposed to secession and resigned from the Senate when Georgia voted to leave the Union. Hill used his anti-secessionist stance and his influence to save Madison's houses from being burned down when Union soldiers under Gen. Slocum occupied the city.

Madison's Welcome Center, in the Chamber of Commerce building, 115 E. Jefferson Street on the picturesque town square, stays open seven days a week. You can find a wealth of information on attractions in the area including an informative book, *As It Was Told To Me*, by Hattie Mina Reid Hicky. This book contains capsule histories of Madison's historic homes as well as recipes, a map and information on Madison's historic churches and town square. Ms. Hickey's Regal Tours of Madison, Georgia, 651 Dixie Avenue, will arrange tours of the town that allow visitors a peek inside many of Madison's private homes — including her own. Call (706) 342-1612 to make a tour reservation. The Welcome Center offers a walking tour map and audio cassette for rent as well as information about private home tours, seasonal home tours, cultural events, nearby recreational facilities and accommodations. Call the Welcome Center at (706) 342-4454.

Madison's town square is loaded with antique shops, restaurants and gift shops. Utterly Yours, 182 S. Main Street, is a two-story store jam-packed with affordable, unusual gifts for house and garden. Wind chimes, prints, jewelry, silver, lamps and all manner of whimsical decorative items make this shop a browser's paradise.

Find Depression glass, coins, and American furniture from the 1840s to the 1940s at Old Madison Antiques, 184 S. Main Street; or drop in at The Creative Mark, 165 S. Main Street, a shop featuring pottery, glass, jewelry, paintings and limited-edition prints by regional artists and craftspeople. Stop for a sandwich and soda at Baldwin Pharmacy, 137 S. Main Street, an old-fashioned soda fountain/lunch counter and drugstore that's been on the square since the late 1800s. Or enjoy traditional Southern fare at Ye Olde Colonial Restaurant, 108 E. Washington Street, (706) 342-2211, housed in the 1800s Morgan County Bank Building. The main dining room still has the original bank vault, a patterned tile floor and pressed tin ceiling.

After you've explored the square, take a walking or driving tour through Madison's wide, tree-lined streets. Antebellum and Victorian homes, both opulent and modest, line the roads. Some have been converted to business usage; others are still family-owned. Homes such as the Gingerbread House, 5865 Main Street, a high Victorian; Boxwood, 357 Academy Street, a stately mansion that was the first home in Madison to have a hot water system; and the Carter-Newton Home, 53 Academy Street, a typical *Gone With the Wind* structure, are just a few of the impressive sights Madison offers.

With more than 32 different sites listed on the National Register of Historic Places, Madison is a history-lover's dream. It has several century-old churches, including St. Paul Methodist, 847 N. 5th Street, the oldest brick Methodist church built by an African-American congregation, and Madison Baptist, 328 S. Main Street. Union soldiers stabled their horses in the basement of Madison Baptist during their occupation. A Union soldier stole the silver communion service from Madison Presbyterian Church, 382 S. Main Street, but Gen. Slocum ordered him to return it.

Visit Heritage Hall, 277 S. Main Street, a Greek Revival home built in 1835 by Dr. Elijah Evans Jones, a Madison physician and Chairman of the Board of Trustees of the Georgia

Female College. Headquarters of the Madison County Historical Society, Heritage Hall has period furnishings, rich architectural detail, window etchings and a ghost silhouette on one of the upstairs hearths. When the girls in Dr. Jones' family got engaged, they followed the tradition of the day by inscribing some personal message ("I love Will," "Stewart and Jennie") on a window with their diamond rings. The ghost silhouette, which keeps returning after repeated paintings, is said to be the outline of a woman and her baby who died of typhoid fever in one of Heritage Hall's upstairs bedrooms. You can tour Heritage Hall for a $2.50 donation. It opens Monday through Saturday, 10 AM to 4:30 PM, and Sunday, 1:30 to 4:30 PM. Call (706) 342-9627 to find out more.

The Madison-Morgan Cultural Center, 434 S. Main Street, host to a history museum, art galleries and an auditorium for plays and concerts, was once the first graded public schoolhouse in Georgia. The center is in a restored Romanesque Revival brick building built in 1895. Historical exhibits include a completely restored turn-of-the-century classroom, portions of a reconstructed log cabin, 19th-century decorative arts, artifacts and interpretive information about Georgia's piedmont region. The center's art galleries offer varied exhibits by artists of regional, national and international renown. The center's apse-shaped playhouse, originally a school auditorium, boasts original woodwork, ceiling, seats and a chandelier; it's known for its excellent acoustics. The cultural center opens Tuesday through Saturday, 10 AM to 4:30 PM, and Sunday, 2 to 5 PM. For more information, dial (706) 342-4743.

The Morgan County African-American Museum, 156 Academy Street, highlights African-American heritage and contributions to Southern culture. The museum, in the historic Horace Moore House, has a reference library, period living room, a Morgan County room documenting the county's people and their history and an African room showcasing African art. The museum opens Tuesday through Saturday, 10 AM to 4 PM. To find out about group tours and annual events, call (706) 342-9191.

Bed and breakfasts in Madison include the Brady Inn, 250 N. Second Street, (706) 342-4400, and Burnett Place, 317 Old Post Road, (706) 342-4034. The Brady Inn is an 1800s Victorian cottage with pine floors and mantels, functioning fireplaces and period appointments. The inn has six rooms with private baths, a suite for larger parties and a dining room that serves full breakfast, and dinner by reservation. Rooms rent for $75 double and $60 single. Burnett Place, (706) 342-4034 is a two-story Federal-style house built around 1830. The present owners spent two years restoring the house and took great pains to retain its original features. A glass panel in an upstairs hall allows guests to view the original construction. Burnett Place has guest rooms with private baths and serves full breakfast, high tea and wine and cheese. Burnett's double rooms cost $85; singles are $75 per night.

To reach Madison from Atlanta, take I-20 East to Exit 51. While you're in the area, you might want to stop in nearby Social Circle (Exit 47 off I-20 E.) and eat at the Blue Willow Inn, 294 N. Cherokee Road, (770) 464-2131, which we also mention in our Restaurants chapter. The late *Atlanta Journal-Constitution* columnist and humor writer Lewis Grizzard lavishly praised the food at this authentic Southern restaurant housed in a Greek Revival mansion. In the heart of Social Circle's historic district, the restaurant has beautiful grounds, a wide front porch where guests can relax in rocking chairs, a gift shop and a fountain. After you've eaten, take a tour and do some tasting at Fox Vineyards & Winery, 225 Ga. Highway 11 S., (770) 787-5402.

Covington, a town near Madison, also warrants a visit. Take the Covington/Oxford Exit 45 off I-20 E. Covington, the Newton county seat, is most widely known for its role as Sparta, Mississippi, in the TV series *In the Heat of the Night*. Because this is another antebellum town Sherman didn't torch, Covington boasts a historic downtown square, manor homes, cottages, churches and parks. The city offers tours of its historic homes in the fall and winter. You can also tour nearby Oxford College of Emory University, where Emory University was born, and where most of the streets dead-end into the charming campus. To find out more, call the Covington/Newton County Convention & Visitors Bureau, (770) 787-3868; outside Atlanta, dial (800) 616-8626.

If you're en route to Madison from Athens

along U.S. 441, you'll pass through Watkinsville, the tiny seat of Oconee County. Clustered around Main Street are about 40 structures that are part of the town's historic district. Eagle Tavern, (706) 769-5197, is one of the oldest buildings in the county, dating back to the late 1700s when Watkinsville was a frontier town. Today, it is a museum and the Oconee County welcome center. It is open Tuesday through Friday from 9 AM to 5 PM, and Saturday from 2 to 5 PM.

Eatonton

Although author Joel Chandler Harris, creator of the Br'er Rabbit and Uncle Remus tales, is most closely identified with his Atlanta home, the Wren's Nest (see Attractions), the small town of Eatonton is where he was born and where the children's tales first took shape. About 18 miles east of Madison, Eatonton is the seat of Putnam County, The town is about 70 minutes from Atlanta, along I-20 E. and U.S. 441 S. You know you're in the right place when you see the statue of Br'er Rabbit gracing the courthouse lawn.

The Uncle Remus Museum, (706) 485-6856, was fashioned out of two log slave cabins. The rustic building is full of renderings, woodcarvings and paintings of the characters and scenes in the stories. There are also first editions of Harris' work and a collection of period memorabilia. The museum sits in Turner Park, once the grounds of the homeplace of Joseph Sidney Turner, the living person who provided the inspiration for the stories' "Little Boy" character. Hours are 10 AM to noon and 1 to 5 PM daily, Monday through Saturday, Sunday from 2 to 5 PM. From September to May, the museum is closed on Tuesday. Admission is 50¢ for adults, 25¢ for kids.

Eatonton is also the birthplace of Pulitzer-Prize winner Alice Walker, author of *The Color Purple*. The Eatonton-Putnam Chamber of Commerce, 105 Sumter Street, (706) 485-6856, has a driving map that takes riders past

some of Walker's childhood haunts. The town also boasts several streets of antebellum homes, including the Bronson House, the 1822 mansion that houses the local historical society. It is open by appointment; for information, call the Chamber.

Several gracious homes have been converted into bed and breakfast inns. Rosewood, (706) 485-9009, is an 1888 cottage where guests can retire to the Color Purple room or the Joel Chandler Harris bath. Make a reservation to enjoy afternoon tea on the porch. Rooms go for $72 or $82 per night. At the Crockett House, (706) 485-2248, guests are invited to roam the gardens on the four-acre grounds or relax on the wraparound porch of the 1895 Victorian home. If you love candlelight and romance, book one of the six rooms that has a claw-foot tub right next to the fireplace. Prices range from $65 to $95, and include a full breakfast. Dinner is served by reservation only, if made 10 days in advance.

U.S. Highway 441 south out of Eatonton leads to Milledgeville, Georgia's antebellum capital. The heart of Baldwin County, Milledgeville was the state capital for more than 60 years before it moved to Atlanta in 1868. The town's historic district includes more than 20 architectural landmarks, such as the Old Governor's Mansion and the Old State Capitol Building, which is now the administration building for Georgia Military College. Believed to be one of the oldest public buildings in the country, the capitol was built in a Gothic-style with dramatic arches and gates leading onto the grounds. St. Stephens Episcopal Church, c. 1841, survived being used as a stable for Union horses during the Civil War. As the home of Georgia College, Milledgeville bustles today with students as well as visitors. The college's library has the Flannery O'Connor Room, where writings of the late Georgia author are collected. For a free brochure highlighting the points of interest, stop by the Milledgeville-Baldwin County Visitors Bureau at 200 W. Hancock Street, or call (912) 452-4687 or (800) 653-1804.

INSIDERS' TIP

The tall, wispy plants growing on sand dunes at the beach are called sea oats. Picking sea oats is prohibited by law, because they are vital in preventing erosion.

Heading South

For a change of pace, come down out of the mountains and discover the charms of the regions south of Atlanta, such as Macon, Columbus, Warm Springs, Callaway Gardens and Pine Mountain. Each has special treasures to share with visitors.

Columbus

About two hours southwest of Atlanta you'll find Columbus, a Chattahoochee-riverbank city planned in the 1800s. Columbus, host of the 1996 Olympic softball competition, offers many attractions including a restored opera house and a riverwalk along the Chattahoochee where, in good weather, you can rent a bike and traverse the brick walk on wheels. Columbus is home to three museums that offer a nice twist with no admission fee. The Civil War Naval Museum, 202 4th Street, (706) 327-9798, is the only museum that focuses on the naval side of the conflict. The museum houses relics of the Confederate Navy, including hulls of the ironclad *Jackson* and the gunboat *Chattahoochee*. The National Infantry Museum, on Baltzell Avenue in nearby Fort Benning, (706) 545-2958, traces the evolution of the infantry from the 1750s to the present. The Columbus Museum, 1251 Wynnton Road, (706) 649-0713, has 86,000 square feet of exhibit space and classrooms. The museum focuses on regional history and American art and features a hands-on children's gallery called Transformations. Columbus State University is home to the Coca-Cola Space Science Center, (706) 649-1470, where visitors can enjoy laser shows, an observatory and the interactive Challenger Learning Center. Kids can sit in the a mock-up of the space shuttle cockpit and "fly" the Challenger or check out a replica of the Apollo capsule, which is on permanent display. The center is open Tuesday through Friday, 10 AM to 4 PM; Saturday, 1:30 to 9 PM; and Sunday, 1:30 to 4 PM. Admission is $5 for adults, $3 for children. Laser show tickets are $6, and children younger than 5 are not admitted.

Much of Columbus' historical architecture is showcased in a revitalized 26-block National Register Historic District, part of the original

Photo: Okefenokee Swamp Park

An alligator takes a break in the shade at Okefenokee Swamp Park.

1828 plan of the city. The Pemberton House, 11 Seventh Street, is part of Heritage Corner, a collection of five house museums. The cottage, once owned by Dr. John S. Pemberton, the pharmacist who invented Coca-Cola, is a cherished local landmark. (Some Columbus residents insist that the good doctor originated the magic formula in their city instead of in Atlanta.) Call The Historic Columbus Foundation, (706) 322-0756, for information on touring Pemberton House and other museums in this area.

The grandest structure in Columbus seemed doomed until determined citizens took action. The Springer Opera House, which opened in 1871 and played host to such stars as Lillie Langtry and Ethel Barrymore, now shines resplendent and restored with year-round entertainment for the whole family. In 1971, then-governor Jimmy Carter declared the Springer as the State Theatre of Georgia; it has been a National Historic Landmark since 1975.

There are numerous accommodations options in Columbus. A couple you might want to check out are the Rothschild-Pound House Bed & Breakfast, 201 Seventh Street, (800) 585-4075, and Southgate Suites Inn, 2339 Ft. Benning Road, (706) 687-2330. Rothschild-

Pound House is an 1870 Victorian structure decorated with antiques and original artwork. Each guest suite has a private bath including a tub and shower, fresh flowers and a mini-refrigerator stocked with cold drinks. Some suites have working fireplaces. Rates at Rothschild-Pound range from $85 to $140, including full breakfast and evening cocktails and hors d'oeuvres. Southgate Suites offers two-level town houses or single-level garden units that can accommodate two couples or a family for the same rates as a moderately priced motel. Each suite has a fully furnished kitchen. Southgate rates range from $50 to $79.

You'll find plenty of places to eat in Columbus, including Buckhead Grill, 5010 Armour Road, (706) 571-9995. Buckhead Grill offers indoor and outdoor dining in a casually upscale atmosphere and serves steaks, pasta dishes, seafood, sandwiches and salads. Crystal River Seafood, 2606 Manchester Expressway, (706) 324-0055, serves up treasures of the deep fried, broiled, grilled or steamed variety. Check out their daily specials. The Olive Branch Cafe, 1032 Broadway, (706) 322-7410, has been lauded by locals as the best fine dining establishment in town.

To reach Columbus, take I-85 S. from Atlanta to La Grange, then take I-185 to Columbus. For more information on the area, call the Columbus Convention and Visitors Bureau at (800) 999-1613.

Macon

Macon, the home of white columns and cherry blossoms, is in the heart of Georgia at the crossroads of two major interstates: I-75 (north-south) and I-16 (east-west). It's an easy trip from Atlanta, approximately 90 miles south on I-75. With the multitude of things to see and do, you may find yourself returning for a second chance to enjoy this hospitable setting.

It's a good thing Macon residents love their history because they're surrounded by it, from ancient Indian mounds to antebellum mansions. The Macon-Bibb County Convention & Visitors Bureau gives excellent assistance with information on Macon's pleasures. You'll find the Macon CVB in historic Terminal Station at the intersection of Mulberry Street and M. L. King Boulevard, (912) 743-3401 or (800) 768-3401.

When it comes to historic neighborhoods, Macon is unmatched, with more than 2,000 acres of neighborhoods listed on the National Register of Historic Places. Pick up the Macon CVB brochure that outlines three self-guided walking tours to acquaint you with bygone days of the South.

The Victorian Tour covers 17 sites of interest, including churches, Tuscan-Victorian homes and poet Sidney Lanier's Cottage. The White Columns Tour presents magnificently preserved mansions such as the Hay House, an example of Italian Renaissance Revival that had indoor plumbing, an intercom system, an elevator and 19 Carrara marble mantelpieces — fantastic luxuries when the house was completed in 1861. Other examples include the 1842 Inn, now a bed and breakfast with adjoining Victorian cottages, and the Cannonball House, an authentic example of Greek Revival architecture built in 1853 and struck by a Union cannonball, which crashed into the home's parlor and came to rest, intact, in the hall. The Downtown Walking Tour includes homes, churches, government buildings and the elegantly restored Grand Opera House, built in 1884 and still in use. This opera house once had the biggest stage south of the Mason Dixon line — large enough for a production of *Ben Hur*.

If you prefer to ride, Sidney's Old South Historic Tours (912) 743-3401, leave from the Welcome Center, Terminal Station, at 10 AM and 2 PM Monday through Saturday. Sidney's offers costumed tour guides who will escort you by bus through Macon's historic downtown. Or try Colonel Bond's Carriage Tours, (912) 749-7267, another costumed tour which lets you explore Macon's downtown business district in a horse-drawn surrey. Colonel Bond's tours leave from the Green Jacket restaurant, 325 Fifth Street, near the Terminal Station, Tuesday through Saturday from 7:30 to 10:30 PM. Practically all of Macon's downtown has been proclaimed a National Historic District, with 48 buildings and homes cited for architectural excellence.

Other Macon landmarks include Wesleyan College, founded in 1836. Wesleyan was the first college in the world chartered to grant degrees to women. Among its well-known graduates is Madame Chiang Kaishek. Brick and marble structures grace the lovely, 240-acre campus at 476 Forsyth Road.

To go farther back in time, visit an ancient Indian community at the Ocmulgee National Monument, 1207 Emery Highway, (912) 752-8257. You may explore a ceremonial earthlodge; its clay floor dates back 1,000 years. A museum, prehistoric trenches, a funeral mound and several temple mounds provide tantalizing clues to the sequence of cultures that lived on the Macon Plateau. Centuries later, in 1540, Spanish explorer Hernando DeSoto is said to have recorded the first Christian baptism here on the banks of the Ocmulgee River. Admission is free; the site is open from 9 AM to 5 PM every day, except Christmas and New Year's days. The park has a visitors center complete with exhibits, a short film and other information. From I-75, exit on I-16 E.; take either the first or second exit from I-16 and follow U.S. 80 east a mile to the park.

Millions of years ago, the ocean covered what is now Macon. Prehistoric fossils, sand dollars and shark teeth are frequent finds here. The Museum of Arts and Sciences and the Mark Smith Planetarium, 4182 Forsyth Road, presents nature trails and a 40-million-year-old whale fossil skeleton unearthed near Macon. Hours are 9 AM to 5 PM, Monday through Thursday and Saturday; 9 AM to 9 PM on Friday; 1 to 5 PM on Sunday. Call (912) 477-3232 for information on the planetarium shows, art galleries and rotating exhibits.

Macon's African-American history is rich with contributions to the arts, religion and education. The city's informative brochure, *Macon, Georgia: Black Heritage*, available from the Macon CVB, presents an African-American Heritage Tour and highlights such landmarks as the Harriet Tubman Historical and Cultural Museum, 340 Walnut Street, (912) 743-8544. Here, past meets present in the works of artists featured in the permanent collections as well as in visiting exhibits. Take note of local artist Wilfred Stroud's seven-panel mural *From Africa to America*, which visually traces a history filled with struggle and accomplishment.

While showing a deep respect for the past, the Macon of today marches to a modern tune. Its leaders guide the city to progress through several ventures. One is the renovation of the Douglass Theatre, where such greats as Cab Calloway, Bessie Smith, Little Richard and Otis Redding performed. Ground was broken in the summer of 1997 for a Sports Hall of Fame downtown. And the city hosts the Georgia Music Hall of Fame, (912) 750-8555, a $6 million investment in Georgia's cultural arts that memorializes musical greats from around the state. The hall opened in 1996, next to the historic Terminal Station in downtown Macon on Martin Luther King Jr. Boulevard. The three-story, 38,000-square-foot museum and more than 11,000-square-foot exhibition hall focuses on Georgia's rich and diverse musical heritage. The music and memorabilia of Georgia artists such as Lena Horne, Macon's own Otis Redding, the Allman Brothers and Little Richard are featured in a small village created in the exhibit hall. Visitors may enjoy music and memorabilia in a variety of venues including The Rhythm & Blues Revue, The Gospel Chapel and The 1950s Soda Fountain. The hall is open Monday through Saturday, 9 AM to 5 PM, and Sunday, 1 to 5 PM. Admission is $7.50 for adults; $5.50 for students and seniors; and $3.50 for children 6 to 16. Children younger than 6 are admitted free.

Another special showcase, The Museum of Aviation in Warner Robins, (912) 926-6870, is just 15 miles south of Macon and 7 miles from I-75. The Museum of Aviation presents more than 85 historic aircraft, from the Fairchild UC-119C Flying Boxcar to modern fighters such as the F-15 Eagle. Admission is free, though there's a small charge ($2 per adult, $1 per child younger than 12) for two 30-minute films (*To Fly* and *Flyers*) in a new 250-seat theater with surround sound and a 30-foot-by-40-foot screen. The attached Georgia Aviation Hall of Fame honors notable pilots such as early women aviators, the first African-American military aviator and the founder of Delta Air Lines. Hours are seven days a week, 10 AM to 5 PM.

If all that sightseeing makes you hungry, dine at The Green Jacket Restaurant, 325 Fifth Street, (912) 746-4680. This golf-themed restaurant is named after the green jacket awarded to winners of the Master's Tournament held each year in Augusta. The Green Jacket features a salad bar and a full menu offering steaks, seafood and sandwiches. Entrees run from $5.95 to $27.95 for lobster tails.

In addition to special events scheduled year round in Macon, a particular highlight occurs each spring. The blooming of Macon's 170,000 flowering Yoshino cherry trees heralds the annual Cherry Blossom Festival. Events, performances and exhibits topped with Southern hospitality fill the calendar. This event begins on the third weekend of March and lasts one week. The festival even has its own outlet, The Cherry Blossom Festival Gift Shop, 365 Third Street. The shop, open year round, sells an array of cherry blossom souvenirs and gifts.

The Georgia On My Plate festival celebrates Southern hospitality for three weeks in late July and early August at the Macon Centreplex, 200 Coliseum Drive. The fun features samplings of fresh Georgia produce and products, celebrity chef demonstrations, cooking contests and children's events. To find out more about the Cherry Blossom Festival and Georgia On My Plate, call the Macon CVB, (912) 743-3401.

While you're shopping, you might want to stop by Popper's, 1066 Magnolia Street, (912) 743-2234. This unique store is a resource for Maconites' home and garden decorating needs. Popper's carries a full line of unique, eclectic gifts including men's gifts, bath items, home fragrance, china, crystal, brass, collectibles and the Vera Bradley line of women's purses and luggage. The store also features antiques, books, home accessories and garden accents as well as a perennial nursery in the spring and fall and a seasonal Christmas shop. Popper's also offers interior and landscape design services. Founded in 1927, Popper's is in an 1850 building that was originally a pump house for the Macon Water Works.

The 1842 Historic Inn, 353 College Street, (912) 741-1842, (800) 336-1842 is a picturesque hostelry on a street of beautiful homes. The inn's guest rooms and public areas are in a Greek Revival antebellum mansion and an adjoining Victorian house that share a courtyard and garden. This award-winning inn offers in-room continental breakfast complete with newspaper and evening hors d'oeuvres in the library, among other amenities. Rooms range from $105 to $155.

Okefenokee Swamp

About 5 hours from Atlanta, the Okefenokee Swamp teems with abundant plant and animal life. The Okefenokee, a 483,000-acre National Wildlife Refuge and parkland, is 38 miles long and 25 miles wide. The swamp is a vast bog inside a saucer-shaped depression that was once part of the ocean floor.

Okefenokee is white man's version of the Native American words for "land of the trembling earth." Peat deposits in the swamp have spots so unstable that stomping the earth causes nearby bushes and trees to tremble. The swamp contains about 60,000 acres of marshland that harbors herons, egrets, ibises cranes and bitterns. Other wildlife in the swamp includes red-cockaded woodpeckers, American alligators, wood storks, sandhill cranes, deer, bears and otters.

You can reach the Okefenokee by three entrances, each of which charges admission. The east entrance, near Folkston, (912) 496-3331, gives access to the swamp via the manmade Suwanee Canal. The swamp's most extensive open areas branch off this canal. This entrance has a visitors center, a 4.5-mile wildlife observation drive, 4.5 miles of hiking trails, two observations towers and a 4,000 foot boardwalk into the swamp. The east entrance is 8 miles southwest of Folkston on Ga. Highway 121/23. Admission is $5 per vehicle. The west entrance lets you enter the park via Stephen C. Foster State Park, where you can camp at designated areas. The park is actually about 18 miles northeast of Fargo; it features cottages, campsites, a camp store, a museum, boating and boat rentals. Admission is $5 per vehicle. The north entrance to the Okefenokee, near Waycross, (912) 283-0583, takes you in through the Okefenokee Swamp Park, a private, nonprofit attraction operating under a leasing agreement with the U.S. Fish and Wildlife Service. The park, on U.S. 1 S., offers water trails, interpretive exhibits, boat tours and wilderness walkways. Northside admission is $8, ages 12 to 61, and $7, ages 5 to 11.

Capitalizing on its proximity to the Okefenokee, Waycross has other swamp-related attractions. Obediah's Okefenok, Swamp Road, (912) 287-0090, allows you to view the swamper's life in the mid-1800s through more than 50 exhibits, including an historic log home and living history demonstrations. Hours are 10 AM to 5 PM daily. Admission is $4.50 for adults; $3 for children ages 6 to 17; and $3.50 for seniors. The Okefenokee Heritage Center Museum on N. Augusta Avenue, (912) 285-4260, has an array of information on the history of the swamp and the early settlers of Waycross. The museum also hosts different art exhibits each month.

Pine Mountain

Pine Mountain, near Warm Springs, is home to the extraordinary resort complex Callaway Gardens.

Seventy miles south of Atlanta on I-85 and 30 miles north of Columbus on I-185, Callaway Gardens' 14,000 acres of natural beauty includes gardens, woodlands, lakes, wildlife and recreational areas. This floral wonderland was created in 1952 by the husband and wife team of Cason Callaway and Virginia Hand Callaway as a wholesome, family environment for relaxation and inspiration.

Visit Mr. Cason's Vegetable Garden, the Southern location of the PBS series *The Victory Garden* and the source of much of the good food served in the resort's restaurants. The Cecil B. Day Butterfly Center, billed as the largest free-flight butterfly conservatory in North America, houses approximately 1,000 free-flight butterflies from three continents. In the John A. Sibley Horticulture Center, a five-acre indoor/outdoor garden, you'll see unusual collections of native and exotic plants and flowers.

Callaway Gardens' most famous flora abound on the Azalea Trail, which has more than 700 varieties of this Southern charmer. Other flower trails include the Rhododendron and Holly trails. Take special note of cofounder Virginia Callaway's favorite, the Wildflower Trail. Rest awhile in the solitude of the Ida Cason Callaway Memorial Chapel. Dr. Norman Vincent Peale officiated at the chapel's dedication. In the summer, swim at Robin Lake Beach or watch Florida State University's "Flying High" Circus. Meander along the 7.5-mile bike trail through breathtaking scenery.

As a guest of Callaway Gardens Resorts, you can take advantage of tennis, fishing, sailing and golf on the Mountain View course. The resort offers 800 guest rooms and a considerable variety of packages. Prices vary according to length of stay, type of accommodations, meal plans and activities. For information on all Callaway Gardens attractions, call (800) CALLAWAY.

Visit the Pine Mountain Wild Animal Safari, 1300 Oak Grove Road, (800) 367-2751, near Callaway Gardens. Drive your car or ride a safari bus through a 500-acre preserve where llamas, antelopes, camel and nearly 300 different animal species roam freely. Then visit Old McDonald's Farm with a petting zoo, monkey house, snake house and alligator pit. Adults pay $11.95; kids 3 to 9 pay $8.95. The park is opened from 10 AM to 5:30 PM every day except Christmas. Hours extend to 7:30 PM in the summer.

A perfect spot for antique buffs awaits 2 miles north of Callaway Gardens at 230 S. Main Street in the Pine Mountain Antique Mall. More than 100 dealer booths and lobby showcases present period furnishings, clocks, books and jewelry. The Village of Pine Mountain offers a multitude of gift and antique shops, restaurants and motels.

Roosevelt Stables, 2970 Highway 190 in Pine Mountain, (706) 628-4533, offers guided trail rides lasting from one hour up to five days. The stables stay open seven days a week, 9 AM to 5 PM, year round. If you call and make an advance reservation, you can ride later than 5 PM.

Besides Callaway Gardens Resorts, Pine Mountain offers a number of accommodations including the Mountain Top Inn (which we describe in our Warm Springs section) and Pine Mountain Club Chalets, a cluster of Alpine chalets surrounding a fishing lake, tennis courts and swimming pool near Callaway Gardens, (800) 535-7622. Rooms rates are $95 per night.

The Storms House, in the heart of town, is a restored Victorian home with several large guest rooms from $99 to $115. Three small cottages with full kitchens were added on the grounds behind the house and rent for $140 to $300 per night. A few minutes from town, Magnolia Hall is an 1890s Victorian cottage filled with antiques and porch swings. Guest rooms are $85 or $95 and include a full breakfast.

To reach Pine Mountain from Atlanta, take I-85 S. to I-185 and continue south to Exit 14. Turn left on U.S. 27 and drive 11 miles to Callaway Gardens. For information about all the Pine Mountain attractions, call the Pine Mountain Tourism Office, (800) 441-3502.

Nature lovers will revel in Pine Mountain's 10,000-acre Franklin Delano Roosevelt State Park, approximately 12 miles from the Little White House (see our Warm Springs section) on Ga. Highway 190. This outstanding recreational facility offers camping, rental cabins and a mountain stone swimming pool. Beautiful woodlands surround lovely lakes for fishing and boating. For more information, call (706) 663-4858. The Pine Mountain Trail, a 23-mile blazed hiking trail, runs from the Callaway Country Store on U.S. 27 to the WJSP-TV tower on Ga. 85 W. Pick up a trail map at the FDR state park office. The park is open daily from 7 AM to 10 PM.

Warm Springs

From Atlanta, Warm Springs is about 80 miles south on I-85 and U.S. Alternate 27. Follow the signs to the peaceful place where Franklin Delano Roosevelt built the Little White House, Ga. Highway 85 W., (706) 655-5870. Serene and slow-paced, the setting moves visitors with its low-keyed spirit of tribute. Many of his administration's policies were formulated there. In the home, it is always April 12, 1945 — the day Roosevelt died there.

Roosevelt, who suffered from polio-induced paralysis, had heard of the restorative powers attributed to the natural springs in this resort area. He began visiting Warm Springs in 1924, finding solace not only in the water but in the countryside's whispering pines and wooded ravines.

It's a short walk from the Little White House to the adjacent and highly personal museum.

Stroll along an ornamental walkway flanked with state flags and native stones of the 50 states and the District of Columbia. In the museum you'll find a sense of history in a naturally beautiful environment. Peruse at your own pace Roosevelt's walking cane collection, gifts from heads of state and exhibits depicting the life of this world leader. Don't miss viewing the historic news reels, which featured never-seen footage of Roosevelt in leg braces and wheelchairs. The Little White House historic site is open from 9 AM to 5 PM daily, with the last tour beginning at 4 PM. It closes on Thanksgiving, Christmas and New Year's Day.

The nearby Warm Springs Village, which hit hard times after Roosevelt's death, revived in the 1980s with an infusion of craft and antique shops. A cluster of more than 65 boutiques, restaurants and accommodations include Spring Street's Bulloch House, (706) 655-9068. Built in 1892, it sits on a hilltop surrounded by bird houses. Described as "country with class," the restaurant offers home-cooked Southern food with hospitality to match.

You'll find 14 overnight guest rooms in the Hotel Warm Springs, built in 1907. It's at 17 Broad Street on U.S. 27-Alternate 41, the main thoroughfare of Warm Springs. Revived by owner Geraldine Thompson into a charming bed and breakfast, the hotel's history includes glory days when FDR's visits created much excitement. The style of bygone days remains alongside the welcome addition of modern conveniences such as individual heating/cooling units. The rooms feature period antiques as well as furniture made in a New York factory owned by Mrs. Roosevelt, which the owner calls Eleanor furniture. All the rooms have private baths, some with claw-foot tubs. One room has an iron bed more than 100 years old (it belonged to Geraldine's grandmother). Famous guests documented in the hotel's books include the King and Queen of Mexico and the King and Queen of Spain. You'll see a picture of FDR and Bette Davis at breakfast following her stint entertaining the troops at Fort Benning in Columbus. Rooms rent for $50 to $167. For reservations and information, call (800) 366-7616.

Another quality accommodation in the area is the Mountain Top Inn & Resort, on top of

Pine Mountain in the 14,000-acre Roosevelt State Park. The Inn's location, just a five-minute drive to Warm Springs or Callaway Gardens, is a special advantage. This facility offers house-size log cabins, Alpine-style chalets and world-theme guest rooms, a pool, tennis courts and hiking trails. Cabins rent for $145; chalets cost $85 to $125 a night. For information and reservations, call (800) 533-6376.

On the way to Warm Springs, you might want to take a detour at Newnan, about 45 minutes south of Atlanta off I-85. This town, dubbed the City of Homes, has a number of antebellum homes that were preserved due to Newnan's status as a neutral hospital zone during the Civil War. Courthouse Square and the downtown commercial district are on the National Register of Historic Places.

Make an appointment to stroll through the extensive gardens at Catalpa Plantation, 2295 Old Poplar Road, (800) 697-1835. Admission is $5 per person. Or take a driving tour of Newnan; pick up a brochure at the Male Academy Museum, 30 Temple Avenue, (770) 251-0207, which is also the home of the Newnan Historical Society. While you're there, check out the Civil War displays and an 1860s classroom. The museum is open Tuesday, Wednesday and Thursday from 10 AM to noon and 1 to 3 PM, 2 to 5 PM Saturday and Sunday. The Newnan-Coweta County Chamber of Commerce, 23 Bullshore Drive, (770) 253-2270, and Coweta County Convention & Visitors Bureau, (770) 254-2627, can give you more information; they, too, have brochures for the driving tour.

But Where's The Beach?

Atlanta, with all its boosterism and bravado, hasn't been able to attract the Atlantic Ocean to its city limits. But beach buffs need not despair. If nothing but the ocean will do, the interstates will get you to the beach in five or six hours.

You may head in either of two directions: due south to the Florida Panhandle and Alabama coast, or southeast to Georgia's Golden Isles. And although it doesn't have a beach of its own, the historic city of Savannah is a must-see destination of the Georgia coastal area. If Florida is your choice, the drive will take you to the Gulf of Mexico and Panama City's pow-

dery beach. For information, call (800) PC-BEACH. A slightly southwesterly direction from Atlanta takes you to Pensacola, in the northwest corner of Florida's Panhandle. Call the Pensacola Tourist Information Center, (800) 874-1234 for information. For detailed descriptions of all there is to see and do in Panama City and Pensacola read *The Insiders' Guide® to Florida's Great Northwest*.

Georgia's beaches offer an unbeatable combination: environmentally unique settings, traditional oceanfront pleasures and historic sights. You can reach four of the barrier islands protecting Georgia's coast by car: Jekyll Island, Tybee Island, St. Simons Island and Sea Island. These and a neighboring island, Little St. Simons, are collectively known as Georgia's Golden Isles. Besides the broad beaches, the landscape on these isles features 300-year-old oak trees draped in moss, towering pines and fragrant magnolias. The area of the barrier islands encompasses 165,000 acres divided between marsh and dry land. Nature's influence is evident in the constantly changing shoreline, reshaped by winds, tides and the serpentine river channels snaking through the inlets.

To the untrained eye, the barrier islands' marshes look like a sea of dead grass. In reality they are teeming with life, enormously productive and essential to Georgia's multimillion dollar seafood industry. Over the course of 25 years, one acre of marsh can produce a half-billion dollars worth of shellfish alone. Wildlife, including alligators, snakes, birds, raccoons, minks and otters, live, breed and feed in these ecosystems. On any causeway near the marshland and tidal creeks, you may see the graceful great blue herons or snow-white egrets. Nearly half of the 165,000 acres are protected, with approximately 87,700 acres now developed, a somewhat remarkable ratio compared with other seashore areas.

Cumberland Island

Cumberland Island, Georgia's southernmost barrier island, is a federally protected wilderness and seashore accessible by tour boat only. Cumberland has one small, privately operated inn, the Greyfield Inn, (904) 261-6408. You generally need to book three months in advance for this place, although they do take reservations with as little as 24 hours' notice if they're not fully booked. Rooms run from $275 to $350, double occupancy. Rates include breakfast, lunch and dinner, a three- to four-hour outing with a naturalist by Jeep, bicycles that can be taken out daily and round-trip boat fare on the inn's private ferry from Fernandina Beach on Amelia Island. Although the locals don't brag about it, the Greyfield Inn housed guests for the John Kennedy Jr. nuptials in 1996. (The wedding ceremony took place in a rustic church on the island.)

You can book a table at the Greyfield's dining room if you aren't staying at the inn; you can either come on your own boat or arrange for a special charter off the island after dinner. It costs about $45 per person for dinner, which includes hors d'oeuvres and a three-course meal. The dining room serves fresh seafood and produce from the inn's own garden.

Besides the inn, the only place to stay on Cumberland is in wilderness camp sites, for which you must make a reservation. Cumberland's appeal is that it's unspoiled. Wild horses and deer roam freely. The marshes are home to ducks and wading birds, while alligators thrive in freshwater lakes. Loggerhead turtles lay eggs by the dunes on Cumberland's pristine beach. You can also spot armadillos, wild turkeys, the occasional bottle-nosed dolphin and the ruins of two 18th- and 19th-century mansions. To find out more about traveling to Cumberland, call the Cumberland Island National Seashore office (912) 882-4335.

Jekyll Island

In 1886, 100 of America's wealthiest men — including members of the Pulitzer, Rockefeller, Morgan, McCormick and Gould families — bought Jekyll Island and formed the elite Jekyll Island Club. With their island virtually closed to the outside world, the club members began building vacation "cottages," actually elaborate mansions, in which to spend their winters. They also built an ornate Victorian-style clubhouse and spent the seasons hunting, horseback riding and playing golf and tennis in their secluded enclave.

At one time, the winter residents of Jekyll were said to control one-sixth of the world's wealth. You can see the telephone where the first interstate calls were made from the president of AT&T to President Woodrow Wilson in Washington, D.C., and to Alexander Graham Bell in New York.

After World War II, skyrocketing taxes and other financial changes made the luxury level on Jekyll impractical, even for barons. In 1947 the State of Georgia bought Jekyll and turned it into a getaway everyone could afford. Most of the 33 old cottages have been restored, and the renovated riverfront clubhouse is now the Jekyll Island Club Hotel, (912) 635-2600. A stay in one of the 134 guest rooms costs between $95 and $229 in the fall and winter; $115 to 250 in the summer. The hotel's elegant dining room serves three meals daily. The 240-acre area that the old Jekyll Island Club members inhabited is a National Historic Landmark District. You can tour the area daily; contact the Museum Orientation Center to find out more, (912) 635-2762.

Nowadays Jekyll attracts families, honeymooners, retirees, conferences and the entire gamut of pleasure seekers to its 10-mile beach and expansive assortment of fun activities. Jekyll offers accommodations to suit all budgets. Villas by the Sea, (800) 841-6262, is a seaside complex that rents guest rooms and condos. Rates vary from $114 to $154 in the fall and winter; summer prices are about $20 higher. The Clarion-Buccaneer Beach Resort, (800) 253-5955, is an oceanfront property offering rooms facing the beach and rooms facing the island mainland. Summer rates range from $119 to $159, depending on your choice of accommodation, which includes rooms with king-size or double beds and an efficiency unit with two double beds, a kitchen, dining room, sitting area and patio or balcony.

Cycle along 20 miles of paved trails around the island. You can bring your own bike or rent one at the Mini Golf Course, (912) 635-2648, most hotels or at the Jekyll Island campground, (912) 635-3021. Arrange fishing trips or sightseeing cruises through Jekyll Harbor Marina, (912) 635-3137. Golfers have four courses to choose from, three 18-hole courses and one nine-hole course that wind through deep woods, around lakes and along the

Savannah is notorious for seducing visitors with her beauty and Southern hospitality.

dunes. For rates and tee times, call Jekyll Island Golf Club, (912) 635-3464.

If you want a bird's-eye-view of the coastal life, take part in Jekyll's nature walks offered at 9:30 AM on Monday, Tuesday, Wednesday and Saturday. On Monday, the walk starts at the footbridge near Clam Creek; Tuesday's walk starts from the South Dunes picnic area, and Wednesday walkers meet at the St. Andrews picnic area. Visitors to the island can get a map at Jekyll's Collection Station (it costs $2 per vehicle to enter the island), which clearly delineates these spots. Tours cost $3 and last a couple of hours. Call the Jekyll Island Historic District office, (912) 635-2119, for more information.

Summer Waves, (912) 635-2074, a family aquatic theme park, opens daily from Memorial Day to Labor Day and on a few select weekends before Memorial Day and after Labor Day. In these 11 acres of planned frivolity, daring adventurers may brave the Hurricane Tornado and Pirate Passage, a five-story enclosed flume ride. Calmer spirits will gravitate toward the Kiddie Pool and the Slow Motion Ocean. Admission is $12.50 for anyone taller than 4 feet; $10.50 for munchkins.

Jekyll is midway between Savannah and Jacksonville, Florida. To get there from Atlanta, take I-75 S. then pick up I-16 near Macon. Follow I-16 S. to I-95 (about 80 miles). Take Exit 6 off I-95, and turn left on to U.S. 17. Travel 5 miles to Ga. 520, turn left and follow the Jekyll Island Causeway 6 miles. Contact the Jekyll Island Welcome Center, (800) 841-6586 for help in planning your trip.

Savannah

Between four and five hours southeast of Atlanta, the port city of Savannah is great for a weekend getaway. (Take I-75 S. to Macon, then I-16 to Savannah.) On the Savannah River, the city itself doesn't have a beach. Nearby

Tybee Island, described below, serves as Savannah's beach. In 1996 Savannah hosted the Summer Olympic yachting events in Wassaw Sound.

Savannah was the first city in the new colony of Georgia founded by English settlers led by Gen. James Edward Oglethorpe in 1733. Oglethorpe's planned grid pattern resulted in a city with two dozen picturesque squares shaded by live oaks and magnolias and blooming with oleander and azaleas. Many of these squares have historical markers and monuments honoring Savannah's rich history. A 2.2-square-mile area of downtown Savannah is one of the largest National Historic Landmark Districts in the United States. Here, you can see more than 1,400 restored 18th- and 19th-century structures. Other points of historical interest include Factor's Walk on Bay Street, the district that housed cotton merchant's offices when Savannah was the center of cotton commerce. Ornate iron bridgeways connect the buildings. The Old City Market, at Jefferson and St. Julian Streets, is a restored historic area featuring food, entertainment, shops and art galleries. The city's Riverfront Plaza on Old River Street comprises nine blocks along the Savannah River with fountains and benches. Old cotton warehouses now house shops, restaurants, pubs and museums. Old Fort Jackson, 1 Fort Jackson Road, (912) 232-3945, 3 miles from downtown, is the oldest standing fort in Georgia. On the south bank of the Savannah River, the fort has the largest cannon in the United States on display. The cannon was used in the War of 1812 and the Civil War. Other displays highlight the history of the city and the coast. The fort is open daily from 9 AM to 5 PM; admission is $2.50 for adults, $2 for students, seniors and children older than 5.

Savannah has long been a popular tourist destination, but recently its allure got a boost. John Berendt's bestselling book, *Midnight in the Garden of Good and Evil*, has caused even more people to flock to the city to see landmarks and people the author mentioned. Join a tour highlighting Berendt's landmarks, or take a self-guided tour following *The Savannah Map of Good & Evil*, from Backyard Publishing, (800) 880-0446. (The map is about $5.)

Fine restaurants, hotels to fit all budgets and charming bed and breakfasts abound in the city. We'll point you toward a few that stand out. The Ballastone Inn and Townhouse, 14 E. Oglethorpe Avenue, (800) 822-4553, has been recommended by *Condé Nast Traveler* and *The New York Times*. Built in 1838, the inn has 18 rooms; six more are in a townhouse four blocks away. Rooms run from $185 to $315. The Gastonian, 220 E. Gaston Street, (800) 322-6603, is an 1868 award-winning, luxury inn. Rooms at this inn range from $150 to $295. A quick way to find out prices and availability at the inns, hotels and condominiums in the historic district is to call Historic Reservations, (800) 792-9393.

The Pirate's House restaurant, a Savannah landmark at 20 E. Broad Street, (912) 233-5757, offers lunch, dinner and Sunday brunch in an authentic 1733 tavern. Pirates used an underground passage in this establishment to smuggle booty to and from nearby ships. Garibaldi's Cafe, 313 W. Congress Street, (912) 232-7118, is a highly praised cafe in the historic district serving nightly seafood specials. It gets crowded; call for reservations. To find out more about all Savannah has to offer, contact the Savannah Area Convention & Visitors Bureau, (912) 944-0456 or (800) 444-2427, or pick up a copy of *The Insiders' Guide® to Savannah*.

Sea Island

Sea Island is definitely not for beachgoers on a budget. The Cloister, one of Georgia's most highly rated resorts, is a favorite with the well-heeled. You can also rent private homes on the island, but these highly rated properties run more along the lines of the Jekyll Island Club "cottages," — that is, they're opulent. To give you an idea of how opulent: a two-week stay can run anywhere from $3,500 to $15,000. The Cloister, a truly elegant resort, offers a charming old section as well as new oceanfront rooms and suites that are $622, but in the off-season, December through Valentine's Day, all rooms are $314. Prices include three full meals. Guests can enjoy seafood in the renovated Beach Club restaurant, play golf or tennis, ride horses, stroll or swim on the beach and be pampered at the resort's spa. The Cloisters' executive chef offers a culinary tour, and the grounds supervisor will take guests on a tour of the grounds. For more information about The Cloister, call (800) SEA-ISLAND. To rent a cottage through the home rentals, dial (912) 638-5112.

St. Simons Island

Rich in history, natural beauty, recreational opportunities, sophisticated shopping, art galleries and nightlife, St. Simons is a popular beach destination. The novelist Eugenia Price has helped stimulate interest in the area with her historical novels set on the island. The Sea Island Singers, organized on St. Simons by Mrs. Maxfield Parrish, brought attention to St. Simons and Sea Islands through their performances and recordings. Although most of the original singers have passed away, a new generation carries on the tradition.

Sixteenth-century French explorers encountered the Guale Indians on St. Simons. Spanish Jesuit and then Franciscan missionaries tried to convert the native occupants to no avail. They finally gave up, leaving only their name for the place, "San Simon," which was later Anglicized to St. Simons. James Edward Oglethorpe, founder of the British colony of Georgia, brought settlers to St. Simons in 1736. They established the town of Frederica and built Fort Frederica, which was destroyed by fire in 1758. Today, the site is a National Monument. National Park Service interpretation helps you gain insight into the settlers' lives as you tour the tabby ruins, (912) 638-3639. Oglethorpe brought John and Charles Wesley with him, and they established Christ Church, on Frederica Road, before returning to England to found the Methodist church. The Bloody Marsh Battle Site on Demere Road, (912) 638-9014, is where British troops repelled Spanish invaders in 1742, which marked a turning point in the Spanish invasion of Georgia. Another point of historical interest is the 1872 Lighthouse and Museum of Coastal History, 101 12th Street, (912) 638-4666. Climb the 129 steps to the top of the lighthouse and enjoy a panoramic view.

Besides its historical attractions, St. Simons offers the usual range of island activities: swimming, golfing, fishing, biking and boating. Several companies offer tours of the area, including a cruise of the coastal waters; contact Golden Isles Jaunts Yachts, (912) 638-5678. Ocean Motion, (912) 638-5225, rents sailboats and kayaks in the summer, and bikes year round. Take a daytrip to Little St. Simons, a privately owned, unspoiled barrier island that, like Cumberland, is accessible only by boat. Little St. Simons offers more than 6 miles of undeveloped beach, swimming, shelling, fishing, canoeing, horseback riding and bird-watching. The island has one inn called The Lodge on Little St. Simon's Island, with 12 rooms that accommodate a maximum of 24 guests. Call (912) 638-7472 to make a reservation. Peak times are October through May; you should call to book a room at least one month in advance. If you want a specific date, call earlier. Rooms rent from $300 to $350 in the off-season; rates climb as high as $400 per night in the summer. Prices include three meals and use of all facilities.

Restaurants on St. Simons include Blanche's Courtyard and Seafood Restaurant, 440 Ocean Boulevard, (912) 638-3030, an island landmark serving low country cuisine in a Victorian atmosphere. Allegro's, 2465 Demere Road, (912) 638-7097, offers entrees in the $12-to-$22 range in a casually elegant atmosphere. Mullet Bay, 512 Ocean Boulevard, (912) 638-0703, serves lunch and dinner in a relaxed, Key-West type setting.

You can rent cottages and condos on St. Simons or stay at a variety of hotels and motels. The King and Prince Beach Resort, 201 Arnold Road, (800) 342-0212, is an island standard. Oceanfront rooms range from $170 to $365; two-bedroom villas cost $245 to $365 per weekday until November 30; add $15 for weekends. The Sea Gate Inn, 1014 Ocean Boulevard, (800) 562-8812, offers oceanfront rooms and suites from $125 to $280. Sports-minded vacationers enjoy the Sea Palms Golf & Tennis Resort, 5445 Frederica Road, (912) 638-3351, which offers rooms and suites for $129 to $368, with certain golf packages offering lower rates. To find out about renting cottages and condos, try Golden Isles Realty, (912) 638-8623; Parker-Kaufman Realtors, (912) 638-3368, or Trupp-Hodnett Enterprises, 520 Ocean Boulevard, (800) 627-6850. To find out more about St. Simons Island, call the St. Simons Island Chamber of Commerce, (912) 638-9014.

Tybee Island

Generations of Savannah families have escaped each summer to Tybee Island where the laid-back atmosphere encourages utter relaxation. Funky beachfront shops and cafes line the wide sandy beach of this closest-to-Atlanta of the barrier islands. Lack of pretension is Tybee's religion, coupled with a certain vagabond flavor that keeps visitors coming back year after year.

Visit the Tybee Island Lighthouse, which dates from 1773 and is one of the first public structures in Georgia. You can take a free guided tour of the lighthouse; for information, call (912) 786-5801. An adjacent museum has exhibits on the island's history.

Locals and tourists favor a bed and breakfast inn called Hunter House, 1701 Butler Avenue, (912) 786-7515. Built one block from the ocean in 1910, it's been given a snazzy renovation complete with tastefully decorated dining rooms. Relax with appetizers on the wide front porch before ordering from the full dinner menu. Rooms cost from $40 to $90. Tybee also offers several hotels and motels, beachfront homes and condos. Call Tybee Island Rentals, (912) 786-4034, to see what's available.

Popular restaurants on Tybee include the North Beach Grill, 141-A Meddin Drive, (912) 786-9003, a funky, reggae-filled place where you can eat crab cake sandwiches at an umbrella-covered outdoor table or dine at an inside table or barstool on the screened-in porch. Don't dress up. McElwee's Seafood House, 101 Lovell Avenue, (912) 786-4259, features crab stew, blackened seafood and steamed oysters on its bill of fare. Or go for the catch of the day at Goodfriends Galley, 8050 Old Tybee Road, (912) 897-0990.

To reach Tybee Island, take I-75 S. from Atlanta, follow it to Macon where you'll take I-16 into Savannah. Take the 37th Street Exit off I-16, and turn right onto Abercorn Street. Follow Abercorn to Victory Drive (which turns into Ga. 80). Turn left onto Victory Drive and follow

it for approximately 15 miles straight to the Atlantic and Tybee. To find out more about Tybee Island, call the Tybee Island Welcome Center, (912) 786-5444.

Nearby Major Destinations

One of Atlanta's happy advantages is its proximity and easy access to other major destinations. We'll take a quick look at four: Asheville, Black Mountain, Birmingham and Chattanooga.

Asheville, North Carolina

Asheville's motto, "The Sky's the Limit," is appropriate given the city's location, high up where the Great Smokies and the Blue Ridge Mountains meet. To enjoy this town of spectacular natural beauty, call the Asheville Travel and Tourism Office, (800) 257-1300. From Atlanta, take I-85 N. to I-26, and follow the signs to Asheville. If you're already in Asheville, stop by the visitors center, 151 Haywood Street, (704) 258-6100.

Asheville fires the imagination with a wondrous array of attractions and activities. For a complete guide to all that Asheville has to offer, read *The Insiders' Guide® to North Carolina's Mountains*. Here, we mention a few attractions to whet your appetite.

First, begin with a few attractions right in the city, such as the home of well-known author Thomas Wolfe. Entering from Woodfin Street beside the Radisson Hotel, you'll wander through the Dixie boardinghouse depicted in his novel, *Look Homeward, Angel*, and see furnishings, clothing and other memorabilia belonging to Wolfe. Call (704) 253-8304 for more information.

Asheville's downtown historic district is full of art deco architecture. You'll find crafts and antiques shops, restaurants and walking tours.

Visit the combined Antique Car Museum/ North Carolina Homespun Museum, which is

---

INSIDERS' TIP

Eighty-three percent of U.S. cities are within a two-hour flight of Atlanta.

open April through December. The museum has no phone, but is adjacent to the Grove Park Inn, (704) 252-2711, another must-see. Erected in 1913 and one of the South's oldest elegant resorts, the Inn, in a remarkable feat of engineering, was built of massive granite boulders. Room rates run from $180 to $325. On Macon Avenue off Charlotte Street, just a few blocks from downtown, the inn overlooks Asheville's skyline and the mountains beyond.

Don't miss the Botanical Gardens, (704) 252-5190. This 10-acre area of native plants, open during daylight hours, is just off Broadway on Weaver Boulevard.

Set aside an afternoon for Pack Place, (704) 257-4500, Asheville's arts and sciences center, 2 South Pack Square downtown. The $14 million complex includes the Asheville Art Museum, the Colburn Gem & Mineral Museum, a 520-seat performing arts theater and the historically rich African-American cultural center called YMI (Young Men's Institute). Hours are Tuesday through Saturday 10 AM to 5 PM, Sunday 1 to 5 PM.

The jewel in Asheville's crown has to be the 8,000-acre Biltmore Estate, billed as the largest private home in the United States. Designed by architect Richard Morris Hunt in the style of chateaux in France's Loire Valley, the mansion, completed in 1895, took five years to build. Its original 250 rooms were filled with treasures owner George Vanderbilt collected during his world travels. Works by John Singer Sargent and Pierre August Renoir grace the walls. Wedgewood china, Oriental rugs and the finest furnishings fill each room.

Guests of the Vanderbilts had a choice of 32 bedrooms. For entertainment, they chose from the billiard room, the winter garden, countless sitting rooms, an indoor pool, a bowling alley and a gymnasium. Vanderbilt equipped his home with luxuries unbelievable in that era — central heat, indoor bathrooms, mechanical refrigeration and electric lights and appliances. Presently, 60 rooms are open for your self-guided tour. A 75-acre-garden, filled with blooming flowers, offsets the manicured grounds and adjoining forest lands. Vanderbilt commissioned Frederick Law Olmsted, designer of New York's Central Park, to create this living work of art.

The Biltmore Estate Winery offers complimentary wine tastings in what were originally the estate's dairy barns. A 3,000-square-foot wine shop displays a wide assortment of gourmet foods, gifts and a sampling of Biltmore wines. Three restaurants provide dining for visitors who've gotten hungry from all the exploring. Browse through the half-dozen gift shops for candles, Victorian accessories and unique toys. The winery hours are 11 AM to 7 PM Monday through Saturday, noon to 7 PM Sunday.

The Biltmore Estate is on U.S. 25 just north of Exit 50 or 50B off I-40 in Asheville. The estate is open daily, except Thanksgiving, Christmas and New Year's Day, from 8:30 AM to 5 PM. Adult tickets cost $27.95; youngsters from 10 to 15 pay $21; children 9 and younger get in free with a paying parent. From November 12, through the holidays, tickets cost $1 more. For an additional charge, you can take a special behind-the-scenes tour. For more information, call (800) 543-2961, or write Biltmore Estate, One North Pack Square, Asheville, NC 28801. Allow the better part of a day to see it all.

Black Mountain

Take a short drive (approximately 17 miles from Asheville on I-40) to find Black Mountain, a nostalgic spot with a '50s feel that's a haven for artists. Find unusual pieces and keepsakes in the pottery, antique, jewelry and basketry shops in the quaint downtown area. Named for the Black Mountain range north of town, this spot, which was once Cherokee territory and then a railroad town, has a restored train depot, soda fountain drugstores and beautiful mountain scenery with sprays of waterfalls and countless wildflowers. For information, call the Asheville Travel and Tourism Office, (800) 257-1300.

Birmingham, Alabama

About a three-hour drive from Atlanta on I-20 W., Birmingham, nicknamed the "Magic City," attracts visitors with its friendly atmosphere and many historical, sports and recreational attractions. The drive takes visitors into the Central Time Zone, so don't forget that the hours for attractions and museums listed here are one hour behind Atlanta.

Named after its counterpart in England,

Birmingham was an iron and steel boom town in the late 19th century. The towering statue of Vulcan, the Roman god of the forge, looms over the city. The tallest cast-iron statue in the world, Vulcan has an observation deck that gives a commanding view of Birmingham and the surrounding area. The statue, at 20th Street S. and Valley Avenue, (205) 328-6198, opens seven days a week from 8 AM to 10:30 PM. Admission costs $1 per person for anyone older than 6. Sloss Furnaces National Historic Landmark pays homage to the city's industrial past. The Sloss, shut down in the 1970s, has an industrial museum and serves as a community gathering place for everything from music festivals to artistic metalworking. The Sloss Furnaces, 20 32nd Street, (205) 324-1911, open Tuesday through Saturday 10 AM to 4 PM, Sunday noon to 4 PM.

Although proud of its history, Birmingham keeps pace with the times. It's home to the Southern Research Institute, a nationally recognized innovator in the fields of medicine, electronics, metallurgy, engineering and environmental protection. You can tour the institute, at 2000 Ninth Avenue S., (205) 581-2317, Fridays at 2:30 PM for free. University Hospital, center of the urban campus of the University of Alabama at Birmingham, is a highly regarded medical care facility. The Birmingham Race Course, 1000 John Rogers Drive, (205) 838-7500, features seasonal thoroughbred racing and year-round greyhound racing. The track boasts one of the only parimutuel tracks in the United States to have both types of racing at the same facility. In 1996 Birmingham hosted part of the Summer Olympics soccer competition at Legion Field, where the University of Alabama Crimson Tide football team plays three times a year. Every other year, Legion Field hosts the annual Auburn/Alabama game, a fierce collegiate rivalry.

The Birmingham Museum of Art, 2000 Eighth Avenue N., (205) 254-2565, is the largest municipally owned art museum in the Southeast. With a sculpture garden and many examples of American, Renaissance, Oriental and African art, the museum is a must-see, especially since admission is free. The museum is open Tuesday through Saturday from 10 AM to 5 PM, Sunday from noon to 5 PM. Other points of interest include the Alabama Jazz Hall of Fame with its memorabilia exhibits in the art deco Carver Theatre, 1140 Fifth Avenue N., (205) 254-2731. Birmingham native Erskine Hawkins wrote "Tuxedo Junction" about a local street car crossing, and you'll find an exhibit dedicated to him. The Jazz Hall of Fame is open Tuesday through Saturday, 10 AM to 5 PM; Sunday, 1 to 5 PM.

The 67-acre Birmingham Botanical Gardens, 2612 Lane Park Road, (205) 879-1227, is open seven days a week, from sunup to sundown, with no admission. Stroll through gardens featuring rhododendrons, camellias, wildflowers, ferns and delicate bonsai plants.

Downtown Birmingham boasts a diversity of architecture as well as civic landmarks, parks and churches. The Second Avenue district is home to shops, galleries and offices. The Fourth Avenue district is the historic black business area. A statue of Dr. Martin Luther King Jr. stands in Kelly Ingram Park, within view of the 16th Street Baptist Church, site of the infamous bombing that killed four little girls during the days of the Civil Rights movement. The Birmingham Civil Rights Institute, 520 16th Street N., (205) 328-9696, chronicles some of the events of that tumultuous era. The institute opens Tuesday through Saturday, 10 AM to 5 PM; Sunday, 1 PM to 5 PM. Admission is free.

You can find places to stay in Birmingham from economy motels to the historic Tutwiler, Park Place at 21st Street N., (800) 845-1787. The Tutwiler, in downtown Birmingham is a refurbished old hotel with an excellent reputation. Rooms at the Tutwiler cost from $89 to $119. Or try the Mountain Brook Inn, 2800 U.S. Highway 280, (800) 523-7771. This midsize accommodation is convenient to the shops and restaurants of Mountain Brook Village and Brookwood Mall, the downtown area and the Birmingham Botanical Gardens. Locals like to gather at the inn's bar. Mountain Brook's room rates start at $69 and go as high as $189 for a suite. The Wynfrey Hotel, 1000 Riverchase Galleria, (205) 987-1600, is a 329-room facility adjoining U.S. Highway 31 and Ala. Highway 150 at I-459. Room prices range from $113 to $200.

Birmingham has a number of popular restaurants, including John's, 112 N. 21st Street, (205) 322-6014, for fine dining; Dreamland, a barbecue place, 1427 14th Avenue S., (205)

933-2133; and The Irondale Cafe, east of Birmingham in historic Irondale, the original inspiration for Fannie Flagg's *Fried Green Tomatoes at the Whistle Stop Cafe*, 1906 1st Avenue N., (205) 956-5258.

Birmingham hosts many annual festivals, including City Stages, a major downtown heritage and music festival held in June. The festival features local and nationally known musicians. For scheduling and information, call (205) 251-1272. The Birmingham Festival of Arts, held each spring, celebrates the culture, arts and society of a different nation each year. To find out more, call (205) 252-7652. The Greater Birmingham Convention and Visitors Bureau, (800) 458-8085, can send you information to help plan your trip.

Chattanooga, Tennessee

In the mountains, right over the Georgia-Tennessee state line, Chattanooga is a delightful town just an easy two-hour drive from Atlanta on I-75 N. Breathtaking scenery, a variety of attractions, a lovely art district and some excellent factory outlet stores add to Chattanooga's appeal. A convenient downtown shuttle service and helpful, friendly natives are additional positive factors.

The Chattanooga Choo-Choo Holiday Inn features a mall area with formal gardens and picturesque rail cars, many of which are rented out as guest rooms. (It's $125 a night to sleep in the train cars; $99 in the main hotel). Dinner in the Diner serves dinner in a Victorian-style dining car that harkens back to the golden era of railroad travel. Surrounding the rail cars you'll find about a dozen retail shops and The Station House restaurant, where singing servers bring your choice of steaks, ribs or seafood. Inside the Holiday Inn's main building, which was once Chattanooga's Terminal Station, try Cafe Espresso, a 1930s-style cafe serving gourmet espressos, cappuccino, desserts and deli selections. The Choo Choo also boasts the world's largest HO Gauge model railroad and offers an antique trolley you can ride on. Call the Choo-Choo Holiday Inn, (800) TRACK 29.

Across from the Choo-Choo in Shuttle Park South, hitch a ride on the electric shuttle that runs roughly every five minutes from 6 AM to 9:30 PM Monday through Friday, from 9 AM to 9:30 PM Saturday and from 9 AM until 8:30 PM Sunday. The shuttle runs from the Choo-Choo to the Tennessee Aquarium and the Chattanooga Visitors Center, stopping at every block in between to drop you off at a variety of attractions. Get off and shop 'til you drop at Warehouse Row, 1110 Market Street, a complex of factory shops including Ellen Tracy, Casual Corner, Villery & Boch and The J. Peterman Company, housed in buildings that were originally railroad warehouses. Let the shuttle drop you off to catch a concert or performance at the Tivoli Theatre, (423) 757-5050.

The Tennessee Aquarium, 1 Broad Street, is one of the largest in the world, featuring more than 6,000 species in a variety of freshwater habitats that include mountain forests, swamps, valleys and lakes. Surrounded by a park and plaza, the aquarium is a very popular attraction. Visit on weekdays, if possible, to avoid long lines. The aquarium is busiest from spring through Labor Day. If you can visit in the fall or winter, you'll avoid the crowds. The aquarium is open daily except Thanksgiving and Christmas. Tickets go on sale from 9 AM to 6 PM. The aquarium stays open extended hours from May 1 through Labor Day. Adults pay $10.25 admission; children 3 through 12 pay $5.50. Kids younger than 3 get in free. Combination tickets that include an IMAX 3-D movie cost $14 for adults, $8.50 for ages 3 to 12. Call the Tennessee Aquarium, (800) 262-0695.

Near the Tennessee Aquarium, kids enjoy the Creative Discovery Museum at the corner of Fourth and Chestnut streets. This hands-on educational facility includes a simulated dinosaur dig, an inventor's workshop, an artist's studio and a musician's workshop. Creative Discovery is open daily 10 AM to 6 PM, May through August. From September through April, the museum is open Tuesday through Saturday, 10 AM to 5 PM; Sunday, noon to 5 PM. It closes Thanksgiving and Christmas Day. The last tickets are sold an hour before closing. Admission is $7.75 for adults; $4.75 for children 2 to 12. For more information, call (423) 756-2738.

Points of interest for history buffs in Chattanooga include the Chattanooga African-

American Museum, 730 E. Martin Luther King Boulevard, (423) 267-1076, an educational institution that pays homage to African-American contributions to Chattanooga and the nation. Hours are 9:30 AM to 5 PM, Monday through Friday; noon to 4 PM Saturday. Admission is $5 for adults; $3 for students and seniors; and $1.50 for children 6 to 12. The Medal of Honor Museum of Military History, 400 Georgia Avenue, (423) 267-1737, highlights stories of Medal of Honor military history from the Revolutionary War to Desert Storm. The Chickamauga/Chattanooga National Military Park, (706) 866-9241, headquartered in nearby Fort Oglethorpe, Georgia, commemorates the bloody Civil War battle of Chickamauga and the battles for Chattanooga. The park is dedicated to soldiers from both the North and South. The Chickamauga Battlefield park has a visitors center, an audiovisual program, the Fuller Gun Collection, self-guided tours and hiking trails. At nearby Lookout Mountain, off I-24, the National Park Service maintains Point Park, site of the famous Battle Above the Clouds of 1863. Other park sites in the area include Missionary Ridge, Orchard Knob and Signal Point. There is no admission charged at any of these parks.

Near the park, Battlerama/Battle of Chickamauga, 759 Battlefield Parkway in Fort Oglethorpe, Georgia, offers a presentation of the battle as well as souvenirs, gifts and relics. Call Battlerama, (706) 866-5771. The Battles for Chattanooga Museum, at the foot of Lookout Mountain, features a three-dimensional electronic battle map with 5,000 miniature soldiers, 650 lights, sound effects and details of major battles fought in the area in November 1863. Call the museum, (423) 821-2812, for more information. Hours are 8:30 AM to 6 PM daily in the summer; 10 AM to 5 PM in the off-season. Adults pay $5; children 3 to 12 pay $3.

Lookout Mountain, near Chattanooga, off I-24, is the site of many popular attractions. The Incline Railway, 827 E. Brow Road, Lookout Mountain, Tennessee, is a National Historic Site and National Historic Mechanical Engineering Landmark, featuring trolley-style railcars that take you on a breathtaking ascent up the side of the mountain. With a 72.7 percent grade near the top, the Incline is the steepest passenger railway in the world. At the top, take in the panoramic view on an observation deck high in the clouds. If it's clear, you can see the Great Smoky Mountains in the distance. The Incline railway runs every day of the year except Christmas, making the trip uphill every 15 minutes from 9 AM to 5:20 PM. It costs $8 for adults, $4 for children. Call (423) 821-4224.

At the top of the Incline Railway, you'll find the popular Lookout Mountain attractions, Rock City and Ruby Falls. Atop Lookout Mountain, Rock City features lush gardens and spectacular rock formations. Fairyland Caverns and Mother Goose Garden delight the small fry, and families and couples enjoy the view of seven states from Lover's Leap. But don't jump! You're still having fun! Grab a bite at one of Rock City's many eateries, then see if you can wiggle your way through the Fat Man's Squeeze, a narrow rock formation. Or go view the white fallow deer at the Deer Park. Rock City Gardens open daily (except Christmas) from 8:30 AM to 6 PM. Closing times are later in the summer. Admission is $9.75 for adults, $5.50 for children 3 to 12. For more information, call (706) 820-2531.

Ruby Falls, in Lookout Mountain Caverns, is a 145-foot waterfall more than 1,100 feet deep inside Lookout Mountain. Enter through the Caverns Castle, modeled after 15th-century Irish architecture, and take a one-hour guided tour through the caverns, where you'll see the falls plus fascinating calcite formations. (If you're claustrophobic, you may not thrill at the low rock ceilings and the dimly lit passages.) Catch a great view of Chattanooga and the Tennessee Valley from the top of Lookout Mountain tower, and let kids work off steam in the Fun Forest. Ruby Falls is open from 8 AM to 9 PM Memorial Day through Labor Day; from 8 AM to 8 PM in September, October, April and May; and from 8 AM to 6 PM November through March. Tours leave every 15 minutes. Admission is $9 for adults, $4.50 for kids 6 to 12. To find out more, dial (423) 821-2544.

Chattanooga's Bluff View Art District is about a 10-minute walk from the Tennessee Aquarium at One Broad Street. Anyone at the aquarium or the adjacent Chattanooga Visitors Center can direct you to the district whose main streets are High Street, Bluff View and E. Second Street. This district offers breathtaking views of the Tennessee River and the restored pedestrian Walnut Street Bridge, sculpture gardens, a gallery, artists' studios, museums, restaurants and a delightful bed and breakfast called the Bluff View Inn. The Hunter Museum of Art, 10 Bluff View, (423) 267-0968, has an impressive collection of American art including paintings and sculpture. A modern annex adjoins the main building, a lovely old brick mansion restored to its original splendor. Stop by Tuesday through Saturday 10 AM to 4:30 PM, Sunday 1 to 4:30 PM. The Houston Museum, 201 High Street, (423) 267-7176, is paradise for fans of the decorative arts. It showcases a collection of decorative glass, antique furniture and textiles amassed by an eccentric antiques dealer, Anna Safley Houston. Hours are Monday through Saturday 9:30 AM to 4 PM, Sunday noon to 4 PM. Admission is $5 for everyone. River Street Gallery, High Street and Bluff View, (423) 265-5033, features an extensive collection of regional and national fine art and crafts including painting, ceramics, wood carvings, jewelry and basketry. The River Gallery Sculpture Garden, behind the Bluff View Inn, is a serene place to contemplate artistic shapes.

While you're wandering the district, grab a snack at Rembrandt's, a European-style coffeehouse, or the Back Inn Cafe, an Italian-style bistro. Both are part of the Bluff View Inn, 412 E. Second Street, (423) 265-5033. The Inn is a charming bed and breakfast housed in two beautifully restored buildings filled with antiques. The original building is a 1928 Colonial Revival mansion; this structure has three guest rooms, a sitting room and the inn's dining room, which is open to the public. The inn's second building, the T.C. Thompson House around the corner, is a sprawling gray frame structure with an old-fashioned front porch, complete with swing. Guests can stay in one of the two suites here, or rent one of the four downstairs rooms. Room rates range from $100 to $250 for a king-size suite. Each room has a private bath, cable TV, phone and individually controlled heating and air-conditioning.

Popular restaurants outside the Bluff View area include Southside Grill, a downtown neighborhood restaurant at the corner of 14th Street and Cowart, (423) 266-6511. Near the Chattanooga Choo Choo, the restaurant features an eclectic menu including creative takes on regional foods. The atmosphere is upscale casual; Southside serves lunch and dinner Monday through Saturday and only dinner on Sunday. The Loft, 328 Cherokee Boulevard, (423) 266-3061, is a popular seafood place that also serves beef and chicken dishes. Across from the Tennessee Aquarium, The Loft has been a local favorite for 20 years, serving lunch and dinner daily.

Besides the Bluff View Inn, the many inns in Chattanooga include The Milton House, 508 Fort Wood Place, (423) 265-2800, in the Fortwood Historic District adjacent to downtown. In a Greek Revival home built in the early 1900s, The Milton House offers stately home hospitality in a district that was the site of a Civil War redoubt. The Milton House has three bedrooms and one suite, each decorated in a specific style with antiques. Prices range from $65 to $125 per night. Adams Hilborne, 801 Vine Street, (423) 265-5000, is also in the Fortwood Historic District. This house, listed on the National Register of Historic Places, is an 1889 structure with 16-foot coffered ceilings. Room rates in this small European-style hotel range from $100 to $300, which includes breakfast. Guests and locals can enjoy brunch, lunch and dinner at Adams Hilborne's Repertoire Restaurant.

Neighborhoods and Real Estate

If you really want to understand Atlanta, get to know its neighborhoods.

From the mansions of millionaires to the more modest, working-class houses, Atlanta is a city of many different neighborhoods connected by a web of roads and rails. The various distinct communities, each with its own wealth of history and homes, is one of the features that make this city unique.

While the city neighborhoods have been the area's strength for decades, more recent housing history has been made in Atlanta's burgeoning suburbs. The building boom of the last 20 years has made what people once thought of as "Atlanta" an area that now spreads into several adjacent counties and beyond. The metro area has gotten so big that real estate experts have begun to make a distinction between "close-in" suburbs that border Atlanta's Fulton County and "exurbs" — those areas on the outer fringe where the one-way commute downtown may be 30 miles or more. No matter where they live, Atlantans love to discuss the relative advantages and disadvantages of life in various neighborhoods. You may hear diehard in-towners speak disparagingly of life beyond the I-285 Perimeter. You may also hear suburbanites discussing in-town Atlanta as if it were an outlaw zone or an exotic foreign land. And you'll find many Atlantans playfully but unabashedly chauvinistic about where they live. Perhaps you'll see a resident of laid-back Little Five Points sporting a T-shirt reading "30307: It's not just a ZIP code — it's a way of life;" or you may hear someone reciting the motto, "Gwinnett is great."

Wherever they call home, residents will find their neighborhood more than just a place to hang their hats and pick up their mail. It provides a refined sense of focus, bringing a manageable, human scale to urban life. To be one person among 3.4 million in a 20 county area or 6,150 square miles is overwhelming; to be one among a few thousand in a friendly neighborhood is to feel a sense of community.

Because so much of Atlanta life is organized around communities, and neighborhood names are widely used to identify locations, it's worthwhile for tourists as well as new residents to spend a few moments becoming familiar with the metro area's many distinct districts. In this chapter, we'll explain some of the parts of town you'll probably hear people talking about every day. Some of them have funny names — you can be forgiven if you snicker the first time you hear someone talking about Buckhead or Cabbagetown. Some, such as Inman Park, Grant Park and Ansley Park, have names that honor community leaders who helped make Atlanta a great city.

The happy truth is that whether you prefer to live in a high-rise condo or a gated country-club community, a downtown loft or a lofty mansion, you'll find what you're looking for in Atlanta if you're willing to be persistent and flexible.

As you begin to look for an Atlanta address, the first question to answer is a basic one: Do you prefer to live inside or outside I-285? Your answer to this question will be determined as much by your lifestyle and goals as where you work and play. Do you want to make your home far from the noise and hustle of the city, or right in the thick of everything? In this chapter, we'll talk about the city neighborhoods first, followed by a brief overview of the close-in metro counties. Space permits us to offer only an overview of Atlanta's neighborhoods, so we'll also suggest several ideas to aid you in further research.

Birth and Rebirth

Atlanta's city seal bears two dates: 1847, when the city was chartered, and 1865, when it began to rise from the ashes of the Civil War. In the same way, many Atlanta neighborhoods have a fascinating story of birth, decline and renewal.

In the 1960s and much of the '70s, Atlanta was widely perceived to be in big trouble. Once-proud areas, such as Inman Park, had badly declined. Peachtree Street in Midtown gained national attention as a bustling hippie hangout where drugs were sold openly. Adult bookstores and movie theaters were abundant. Shocked visitors returned from the city describing it as something akin to the Sodom of the South. Charging that the "sorry, no good, cowardly" city government was not able to control lawbreakers, segregationist Gov. Lester Maddox threatened in 1969 to call out state troopers to restore order.

Racial issues, which took on new importance in the 1960s and '70s, had always been important in Atlanta politics, and black people had long accounted for a very large minority of the city's residents. Atlanta's earliest black citizens were former slaves who, having been forced to build the city's fortifications during the Civil War, returned here to begin their new lives as free persons once peace was restored.

Then came the race riot of 1906, in which white mobs, enraged by inflammatory newspaper accounts of black "outrages" against white women, went on a rampage that lasted nearly a week, murdering blacks in the streets of downtown and burning black homes. Image-conscious Atlanta got some very bad publicity as the riot was reported around the globe. And in the wake of it, the progressive city

passed some very unprogressive legislation. In 1910, the city council passed a law requiring all restaurants to serve one race only. In 1913, Atlanta became the first Georgia city to legislate segregation in residential areas.

However, during the Civil Rights era, Atlanta integrated without much of the violence and rancor that tore apart many other Southern cities. Atlantans understood the importance of living up to Mayor William B. Hartsfield's famous remark, when he proudly dubbed Atlanta "the city too busy to hate." President Kennedy singled the city out for praise as its schools peacefully entered the era of integration. But beneath the veneer of cooperation, Atlanta was in turmoil. The end of residential segregation sent many affluent whites fleeing to the suburbs north of Atlanta and beyond. Newspaper articles warned of the creation of an all-black city surrounded by all-white suburbs. In 1975, *The Atlanta Journal-Constitution* published a mournful series of articles decrying Atlanta as a "City in Crisis." (Although this complete racial polarization did not come about, the white flight of the 1960s and '70s left Atlanta with a solid black majority.)

But even as many once-fashionable areas spiraled into seemingly endless decline, something remarkable happened. In the late 1970s and early '80s, Atlanta began to attract new residents who were eager to live in an integrated city. When these visionaries looked at the dusty old mansions and rundown bungalows along Atlanta's tree-lined streets, they saw not inevitable decay but dazzling opportunity. One by one, Atlanta's historic neighborhoods began to awaken as if from a dream. Freed from the backward and Draconian practices of segregation, Atlantans — whose city had always been multiracial — now began to integrate it, block by block and street by street.

This is not to say that Atlanta is entirely integrated: Segregated housing patterns are still quite evident today. The south side remains home to more blacks than whites; the north side, to more whites than blacks. But there are

FYI

Three area codes serve the metro Atlanta area: 404, 770 and 678. Whether you live on Peachtree Street or in New York City, you must dial the code to reach any number in the area. The difference? Outside the area, you must dial "1," then the area code and phone number; inside the area, you need only dial the area code followed by the phone number.

blacks who live on the north side just as there are whites who live on the south side. And in the in-town areas where the two halves of the city come together, black and white Atlantans, as well as those of other races and nationalities, live, learn, work, play and worship together with an ease that would have been thought impossible just a few decades ago.

In this chapter, we'll discuss neighborhoods in the northeast, northwest, southwest and southeast sections of town. On the north side, Peachtree Street and Roswell Road divide east and west; on the south side, Capitol Avenue divides east and west. On the east side, Edgewood Avenue and Boulevard Drive divide north and south; on the west side, Martin Luther King Jr. Drive divides north and south.

As you read about Atlanta's neighborhoods, keep the following points in mind. It's not uncommon for one street to be claimed informally by two different neighborhoods, which can be a little confusing. Also, the same name may be used for a neighborhood and for its primary park. For example, Candler Park is the name of a city park, the neighborhood around it and the area's MARTA station. Many neighborhoods are served by a nearby MARTA station; those without a rail station are served by MARTA buses.

Let's begin with a brief roundup of some of the interesting neighborhoods inside I-285. For more in-depth information, we recommend these excellent books: *Atlanta — A City of Neighborhoods*, by Joseph F. Thompson and Robert Isbell, and *Atlanta Walks*, by Ren and Helen Davis.

The prices shown for each Atlanta neighborhood reflects the average of the properties closed from January to October, 1997. The data was compiled with the assistance of RE/MAX agent Zac Pasmanick and his support team; Kim Boyd of RE/MAX Achievers; and Sheila Maddox of Coldwell Banker.

Neighborhoods

In the City

Downtown

There was a time, in the last five years, when Atlanta's downtown district was home to only banks, businesses, Rich's and Macy's main stores and a handful of decent places to eat. What a difference an Olympics can make!

The city's efforts to spruce up and restore an aging business district, anchored by the Five Points intersections of Marietta, Peachtree and Decatur streets, not only attracted new entrepreneurs, it captured the attention of a new wave of urban pioneers. Abandoned office buildings, stores, even old apartments took on new life as lofts whose main attraction was their location near Centennial Olympic Park, Underground and hundreds of employers. As residents returned, so did the restaurants, the corner coffee shops and, to a limited extent, the shopping conveniences usually found in residential neighborhoods. Areas once deserted after 6 PM now are places where residents jog, walk their dogs and stroll to dinner.

Most of downtown's restored living space is rented. Loft units, boasting high ceilings, oversized windows, hardwood floors and exposed pipes, go for anywhere from $495 to $1,600. Not far from Five Points, loft condominiums in the warehouse area of Castleberry Hill have sold for as much as $165,000.

West of Five Points, former industrial complexes have been revitalized as the Nexus and King Plow arts centers, which include studio and residential space for artists, a theater and an upscale restaurant. And the city council has formed a loft development task force to facilitate the renovation of old downtown properties into modern living and working spaces.

Neighborhoods in the city of Atlanta are organized into 26 Neighborhood Planning Units (NPUs) that invite residents to give input on zoning, public safety and quality-of-life issues affecting them on their blocks. The NPUs are an important link between the residents and City Hall.

Northeast Atlanta

Joel Hurt was a civil engineer, a developer and a visionary. In 1887 Hurt hired James Forsyth Johnson to design Atlanta's first garden suburb after the fashion of famed landscape architect Frederick Law Olmsted. Inman Park's name honors civic leader Samuel M. Inman. Since Inman Park was 2 miles east of Five Points, an important part of Hurt's plan was the building of the city's first electric trolley line, which ran from downtown to 963 Edgewood Avenue. The restored original Trolley Barn, (404) 521-2308, at that address is now a popular rental hall for weddings and other events. The trolley line went into service on August 22, 1889.

The plan for Inman Park's 189 acres included broad streets along which were planted coastal Georgia live oak trees. Though such trees had never been known to survive in Atlanta, many of these giants still tower over the neighborhood today. Many prominent Atlantans lived in Inman Park, including Coca-Cola founder Asa Candler, whose Callan Castle stands at the corner of Euclid Avenue and Elizabeth Street, and Hurt himself, who lived at 167 Elizabeth Street.

Inman Park peaked as a fashionable address around the turn of the century. Soon, the public's taste began to turn away from Victorian architecture, and the neighborhood began to lose its wealthy residents to other, more opulent developments such as Druid Hills and Ansley Park. The neighborhood declined in prestige and was considered little better than a slum by the 1960s, and its darkest hours occurred when some fine homes were knocked down to make way for two highways (though they were later halted before construction began). The amazing transformation symbolized by the neighborhood's logo (a butterfly) began in the late '60s when determined Atlantans began to revitalize the area; the process is ongoing.

Today, Inman Park is listed on the National Register of Historic Places and is home to Atlanta's Mayor Bill Campbell. Homes in Inman Park range from bungalows in need of work to fully restored Victorian mansions, and prices reflect this: Homes start at $110,00 and go up to $850,000. The district's annual springtime festival draws thousands of visitors and is one of the most popular of Atlanta's many neighborhood festivals. Lively Little Five Points, the eclectic shopping district between Inman Park and Candler Park, helps nearby areas attract new residents as well as visitors. The Inman Park/Reynoldstown MARTA station serves this area.

East of Little Five Points is Candler Park, which was once part of the independent town known as Edgewood. The neighborhood's centerpiece is Candler Park, a hilly green space with a public golf course; it's named for Asa Candler, who donated the land for recreation. In the early days of the automobile, the area gained popularity as a residence for Atlanta commuters. Though Candler Park lacks the grand Victorian mansions that grace Inman Park, the area has many pleasant homes both large and small. Homes here have been selling from $90,000 to $370,000.

Similar homes may be found in Lake Claire, which is just east of Candler Park and Clifton Road along McLendon Avenue. (And no, despite those whimsical "Ski Lake Claire" bumper stickers you may observe, there is not a lake here.) In general, the blocks north of McLendon are further along in their revitalization than those south of McLendon. If you're lucky enough to be here in the springtime, take a drive up steep, dogwood-lined Claire Drive, a much-photographed example of Atlanta's floral glory. Residents of the neighborhood host an annual "Tour of Funky Homes" and invite the public into some of their more unusual renovations and expansions. Candler Park and Lake Claire are served by the Edgewood/Candler Park MARTA station. Home prices start in the $80,000s and climb into the $400,000s.

Throughout much of the 1980s, neighbors in Lake Claire, Candler Park and Inman Park waged a fierce battle — in the courts, in the media and sometimes through bulldozer-blocking direct action — to prevent construction of the Presidential Parkway. The roadway was to have linked Ponce de Leon Avenue with the Downtown Connector via the Carter Presidential Center, but residents protested the big road's impact on the area's cherished parks and laid-back lifestyle. This was a case of "you can fight city hall"— even though the huge pylons that were to have held the big road were already built, residents prevailed. The renamed Freedom Parkway has a 35 mph speed limit and bike and jogging trails — and it stops at Moreland Avenue, instead of crossing the neighborhood to join Ponce.

Directly north of Candler Park along Ponce de Leon Avenue is one of Atlanta's most famous neighborhoods, 1,400-acre Druid Hills. Fresh from developing Inman Park, Joel Hurt hired renowned landscape architect Frederick Law Olmsted, designer of New York's Central Park, who was then in Asheville designing the grounds of the Vanderbilts' Biltmore Estate, to lay out the neighborhood. Olmsted worked on preliminary plans but died before he could finish them. He left it to his sons Frederick Jr. and John Charles to complete his work. Olmsted's plans placed six elegant linear parks like a string of pearls along winding Ponce de Leon. (These parks too would have been severely impacted by the original Presidential Parkway.)

Druid Hills' many beautiful homes preside over broad lawns that are ablaze with seasonal colors in the spring and fall. The present St. John's Melkite Catholic Church, 1428 Ponce de Leon Avenue N.E., was once the home of Asa Candler. Druid Hills' location beside Emory University helped preserve it even in the face of Atlanta's turbulent growth. The Druid Hills Historic District is listed on the National Register of Historic Places.

Druid Hills' most famous resident never actually existed — but her house does. Jessica Tandy won an Oscar for her portrayal of the feisty Druid Hills widow who is the title character in *Driving Miss Daisy*. The house that was the setting for the movie is at 822 Lullwater Road. Among the many other lovely homes here are architect Neel Reid's own residence at 1436 Fairview Road; the home of Walter T. Downing, another famous architect, at 893 Oakdale Road; and Boxwood, 794 Springdale Road, whose original owner, Charles Rainwater, designed the Coca-Cola bottle. Sales of Druid Hills homes have been between $130,000 and $765,000.

While we're on the east side of town, we'll touch on Decatur, 6 miles east of downtown Atlanta. Decatur is an independent city more than a decade older than Atlanta with its own fascinating history. It's home to Agnes Scott College and Columbia Theological Seminary. The Old DeKalb County Courthouse on the Decatur town square was built of Stone Mountain granite in 1917.

Ponce de Leon Avenue passes through the center of Decatur, becoming East Ponce de Leon. Another major east/west thoroughfare is College Avenue. Clairmont Road and Columbia Drive are big north/south routes. Decatur has areas of poverty and wealth as well as numerous transitional areas, and home values vary accordingly. In general, pricier housing is more likely to be found north of College Avenue than south of it. The south side, however, has many pleasant streets and areas, such as Winnona Park, that attract young homeowners looking for houses to improve. Homes prices in Decatur can be as low as $75,000 or as high as $615,000, for a renovated property in a historic district. Decatur is served by the East Lake, Decatur and Avondale MARTA stations.

One mile east of Decatur is another independent city, Avondale Estates. In the early 1920s, patent medicine millionaire George F. Willis' idea for a totally self-contained residential development attracted national attention. Willis bought an existing small community, Ingleside, and over a period of four years transformed it into a world of its own, with parks, clubhouses, a lake and a pool. Even so, the town as it stands today realizes about only one-third of Willis' elaborate original concept. While he worked on the giant carving at Stone Mountain, sculptor Gutzon Borglum, who was a friend of Willis, lived in a house at the corner of Berkeley and Kensington roads.

In 1926 the Georgia Legislature designated Avondale Estates an independent city with its own mayor, city council, police and sanitation departments. The district's commercial buildings are in a Tudor style that suggests an English village; its dwellings include English medieval, Craftsman bungalows, Dutch Colonial- and Spanish Mission-style homes. Home prices here fall between $110,000 and $350,000. Avondale Estates is listed on the National Register of Historic Places. MARTA's Avondale and Kensington Stations serve this area.

Now let's swing back west. As you travel north on Peachtree from Five Points downtown, the first substantial residential area you encounter is Midtown. Like Inman Park, it's about 2 miles from Five Points. And, like Inman Park, it was the brainchild of a streetcar builder. Developer Richard Peters bought up 405 acres in the early 1880s with the idea of building a neighborhood and operating a streetcar line to it. Peters' son Edward built the showy Queen Anne-style home at the corner of Piedmont and Ponce de Leon in 1883; the house has been a restaurant, appropriately named The Mansion, since 1973.

Building in Midtown continued for nearly 50 years, and there is a commensurate range in architecture, from simple bungalows to fine Victorian mansions. But after World War II Midtown lost many residents to the suburbs, and some homes were converted to apartments and boarding houses. In the late '60s and early '70s, Midtown went hippie in a big way; conservative people shunned the area and neighboring Piedmont Park, which was the site of numerous anti-Vietnam War protests.

By the mid-'70s, Midtown, like some other city neighborhoods, was turning a corner. Its solidly built homes, tree-lined streets and convenient location convinced adventurous buyers of the area's underlying value. Gays, singles and yuppie couples were drawn by Midtown's tolerance and urban charm and settled there by the thousands, many as homeowners who greatly improved their properties. Midtown property values and rents have climbed dramatically over the years, but some more moderate properties remain. As you drive across Midtown from the Ponce side (near Third Street) to the park side (bordering 10th Street), you'll generally notice the quality of the neighborhood going up along with the street numbers. Home prices in Midtown now run between $158,000 and $600,000. Midtown is served by the Midtown and North Avenue MARTA stations.

Between Midtown and Druid Hills, Virginia-Highland grew and took its name from its central intersection: Virginia and N. Highland avenues. When it was first developed in 1916 as North Boulevard Park, the subdivision was another "streetcar" community, with a line that ran down N. Highland to Ponce. Many of the houses are solid brick Craftsman structures with porches.

Virginia-Highland was damaged in the 1960s when the state tried to build an expressway, I-485, through the neighborhood. The road was eventually halted but not before homes were condemned and the community was disrupted. After that experience, Virginia-Highlanders took to jealously guarding their neighborhood against too much change. They keep a watchful eye, for example, on growth in the popular N. Highland Avenue commercial district, whose restaurants and bars attract visitors from all over town. Virginia-Highland home prices range from $150,000 to $450,000.

North of Virginia-Highland is the Morningside/Lenox Park section. Similar in many ways to Virginia-Highland, this area's residents also had to battle the state of Georgia over plans to build the I-485 Expressway. Morningside dates from the post-World War I years. A former farming community, it was purchased and developed by M.S. Rankin and James R. Smith. Lenox Park got under way in 1932, the product of the architectural firm Ivey and Crook.

Many Lenox Park homes are built of stone and brick in Tudor and English Country styles. Morningside's homes are in a variety of styles, reflecting the influence of neighboring districts Virginia-Highland and Ansley Park. Morningside Elementary is one of the city's most highly regarded public schools. Home prices in Morningside and Lenox Park start at about $180,000 and go into the high $400,000s.

North of Midtown is another of Atlanta's best-known neighborhoods: Ansley Park. Edwin Ansley launched this development in 1904. Unlike other early Atlanta neighborhoods, Ansley Park was designed as a community for automobile, not streetcar, commuters. The development was laid out by Solon Zachary Ruff, who had worked with the Olmsted firm in creating Druid Hills.

Ansley spent more than $500,000 to drain

Photo: Robert Thien

There are plenty of home styles to choose from in Atlanta and the suburbs.

swamps and otherwise whip the neighborhood's 350 acres into shape. Six hundred home lots of varying sizes and numerous small parks were planned in the district. Many Ansley Park homes sit atop hills with broad lawns descending to the street. In several sections, houses that might have sat directly across from each other are instead separated by parallel streets flanking a hilly park. As a result, Ansley Park — though it is bordered by two of Atlanta's busiest streets (Peachtree and Piedmont) — is a district of almost pastoral beauty. It's listed on the National Register of Historic Places.

You'll find homes of various sizes here, including many fashionable mansions by famous architects, such as Philip Shutze, Neel Reid, Walter Downing and Henry Hornbostel, whose signature designs made an indelible mark on Atlanta's architecture. From 1924 to 1967, the Georgia Governor's mansion was at 205 The Prado. Margaret Mitchell and John Marsh lived for a time in the apartments (now condos) at One South Prado and Piedmont Avenue. The Robert W. Woodruff Arts Center is nearby, as are the Colony Square complex and the Arts Center MARTA station. Before it was developed as Ansley Park, the entire district was part of the estate of George Washington Collier. Though it has been remodeled many times, the 1823 Collier House at 1649

Lady Marian Lane in the adjacent Sherwood Forest neighborhood is one of the oldest residential structures in Atlanta. Home prices in Ansley Park range from the mid-$300,000s to the $900,000s.

North of Ansley Park is another neighborhood that traces its origins to post-World War I enthusiasm and the growing popularity of the automobile: Brookwood Hills, developed by B.F. Burdette. The land (like Ansley Park) was owned by the Collier family; it was the site of the fierce Battle of Peachtree Creek during the Atlanta Campaign. Brookwood Hills has tennis courts, a community swimming pool and many shade trees. It's listed on the National Register of Historic Places. Brookwood Hills home prices start in the low $400,000s and go as high as $1 million.

Peachtree Hills is north of Brookwood Hills. It was established after the Depression; most houses are of brick and frame bungalow-style construction. The neighborhood has many apartments and a pleasant community commercial district at Peachtree Hills Avenue and Virginia Place. Peachtree Hills home prices average around $185,000.

North of Peachtree Hills is Garden Hills, another pleasant neighborhood of tree-lined streets and solid homes, most of which were

The Weed That Almost Ate Atlanta

After the daffodils dip their heads for the last time in spring, and the pinks, brilliant reds and unique orange blooms of the native azalea fade from sight, those of us more attuned to the sounds of nature might hear the first rustlings of the kudzu vine as it starts to creep into the Southern night.

 Close-up

Kudzu, a perennial vine which grows from tuberous roots and is a member of the pea family, has large attractive three-division lobed leaves that produce fragrant, purple blossoms in early fall. It cannot survive cold and cloudy weather so it forsakes the northern climates entirely and, with the first signs of fall, goes dormant in the South. But as the rays of the sun grow warmer, the kudzu begins to creep. It's vine is fibrous and difficult to cut and with time becomes thick and rope-like.

Kudzu is classified as a friend, foe or mixed blessing depending on whom you ask. Artisans in Atlanta use dried, old, wrist-thick and twisted kudzu vines to weave unusual baskets. Some cooks even prefer a powdered thickener ground from the kudzu leaf to cornstarch. But it is the fantastic growth properties of kudzu that truly astound all who witness them as homeowners struggle to keep new shoots from springing up in their lawns, and scientists continue to ponder this phenomenal plant.

To some Southerners, this crawling vine, which can consume entire pine timber forests within a few years, is a strong and diabolical opponent. It smothers all in its path with its beautiful, dense blanket of green, blocking the necessary rays of the sun from reaching anything under its cover. It resists chemical, disking and burning attempts at removal, inspiring frustration and ire in amateur and professional gardeners.

Photo: K.E. Wantuck

An urban myth says you can hear kudzu growing if you listen carefully enough.

During the early part of the 20th century, kudzu was brought to the states from Japan for its excellent anti-erosion qualities. Agricultural bulletins of the time credit Mr. C.E. Pleas of Chipley, Florida, with the introduction of kudzu as a forage crop. In 1902 three plants were allowed to flourish beside his summer home. Their luxuriant growth spread to a 40-by-60-foot area in three years.

Pleas sold cuttings to various organizations and independent farmers throughout the South. Within 27 years, kudzu had roamed over 3000 acres of land. It was planted in large, caving gullies and on steep, heavily eroded roads, cuts and slopes in the hope that it would hold down the loose soil. An agricultural journal notation in 1928 mentions that kudzu was used to mask the eroded "ugly spots and eye sores" found along Southern roadways.

In 1935, Dr. E.D. Alexander of the University of Georgia, recommended the use of

— continued on next page

kudzu as a porch shade plant and suggested it be further used as a grazing product and healthful hay. He wrote of its nutritious and palatable properties to all kinds of livestock. He stated that its advantages outweighed the disadvantages and that it should be advocated for greater use on farms in Georgia.

It wasn't until the 1940s that agronomists began to realize that although "rabbits are fond of kudzu and may damage the plants," a more effective method for stopping its phenomenal growth must be found if the pine forests and hardwoods endangered by its suffocating encroachment were to be protected.

Dow Chemical donated thousands of dollars to experiments at various Southern universities working to develop a herbicide that would stop the plant from devouring the Southern landscape. And in 1956 herbicides were successful in killing 80 to 100 percent of the leaves on test plots. However, the following spring brought vigorous regrowth. And that continues to be the pattern: spray growth, experience a dieback and with the next summer's heat — lo and behold! — the kudzu is back in the same old places. Regular mowing produces the same results without drenching the earth with pesticides. Of course, you can't mow in a pine forest.

But for all the annoyance and time spent trying to rid one's lawn of this determined weed, we almost have to admire it for its beauty. Fields and glens are made subtle and mysterious by its presence, appearing as if some celestial being has dropped a blanket of greenery from on high, covering trees, uninhabited cabins and old cars.

---

built in the 1920s and '30s. Developer Philip McDuffie laid out the area in accordance with the popular Frederick Law Olmsted aesthetics. To create more of a self-contained village, he called for two schools, a small commercial district and some multifamily housing. His vision is reflected in the International School, the Garden Hills Elementary school, a thriving business district along Peachtree Road, a community center with a clubhouse and a pool. Home styles in Garden Hills include American Colonial, Tudor, English Cottage, Georgian and more. The neighborhood is on the National Register; home prices start at about $220,000 and climb into the $800,000s.

South of Garden Hills is Peachtree Heights East, developed by Eurith Rivers (who became Georgia's Governor). Across Peachtree Road is its sister neighborhood, Peachtree Heights West, developed in the 1910s and '20s by Eurith Rivers and W.P. Andrews. Towering over many beautiful homes built by the city's leading architects is the high-rise Park Place condominium, Atlanta home of Elton John. Much of Peachtree Heights West is listed on the National Register of Historic Places. Home prices in the two neighborhoods run anywhere from $350,000 to $1 million.

Northwest Atlanta

Now let's talk about Buckhead, the city's famous district with both northeast and northwest addresses. This is an area where districts and neighborhoods overlap. As we just discussed, Brookwood Hills, Peachtree Hills and Garden Hills are each distinct neighborhoods, but they are all claimed by Buckhead, as are Peachtree Heights and Collier Hills, which we'll discuss in a moment. As defined by the Buckhead Coalition leadership group, Buckhead comprises all of Atlanta north of I-75, I-85 and Peachtree Creek to Cobb County in the west, the city limits in the north and DeKalb County in the east.

In the 1910s and '20s, Buckhead began to lure wealthy Atlantans who wanted more seclusion than was offered by such residential showplaces as Druid Hills and Ansley Park. Today Buckhead has a variety of home types and sizes, but when most people envision Buckhead real estate, they think of W. Paces Ferry Road and the Tuxedo Park neighborhood. Along W. Paces and the streets turning off it are homes of astonishing elegance and beauty, many that were built as summer retreats for Altanta's wealthy families. This area is home to the Georgia

Governor's Mansion and the Swan House, the opulent 1928 mansion that presides over the Atlanta History Center's grounds. Philip Shutze designed the Swan House and other area homes; Neel Reid also designed fabulous mansions in the area. Anne Cox Chambers of the Cox media empire, one of the world's wealthiest women, has a stately mansion here. Windcrofte, at 3640 Tuxedo Road, was the home of Coca-Cola president Robert Woodruff. Tuxedo Park prices start at $500,000 and can go as high as $5 million. However, a custom-designed architectural wonder can cost as much as $20 million.

Northwest of central Buckhead and about 8 miles north of downtown is Chastain Park, named for former Fulton County Commissioner Troy G. Chastain. The popular park has a golf course, athletic fields, a crafts center and an art gallery. Its best-known feature is its outdoor amphitheater, which holds nearly 6,000 people and presents some 60 popular and classical concerts between the spring and fall. The streets surrounding the park feature many fine homes. Chastain Park home prices run from $275,000 to $1 million.

Still on the west side, let's head back down Peachtree to Haynes Manor. Special attractions here are the Bobby Jones Golf Course, named for the famous Atlanta golfer and the Bitsy Grant Tennis Center, named in honor of the Atlantan tennis champion. Jeweler Eugene Haynes created it by selling parcels of his own estate. Today, its houses sell from $250,000 to just more than $1 million.

Immediately south of Haynes Manor is Collier Hills, which, along with Brookwood Hills on the other side of Peachtree, was the site of the bloody Battle of Peachtree Creek. Most of the houses here are in the traditional styles of the 1940s and '50s. Home prices range from $220,000 to $425,000. Homes here are extremely popular with young couples, singles and families.

West of Peachtree and south of 14th Street is Home Park, a working-class neighborhood whose modest homes and sleepy streets have been attracting new interest in recent years, particularly among the fixer-upper crowd. Rental properties here are popular with students at nearby Georgia Tech. Home prices run between $90,000 and $150,000.

Southwest Atlanta

Vine City is bisected by Martin Luther King Jr. Drive, where the addresses change from northwest to southwest. The district takes its name from Vine Street. It was home to African-American millionaire Alonzo Herndon, who built a stunning Beaux-Arts mansion at 587 University Place N.W. Until his assassination, Dr. Martin Luther King Jr. lived with his family in the house at 234 Sunset Street N.W. Vine City has middle-class and poor areas; the area underwent much upheaval with the construction of the Georgia Dome. The district is served by the Vine City and Ashby MARTA stations. Between Vine City and West End is Atlanta University Center, whose six historically black colleges form the nation's largest center of African-American higher education. Housing prices range from $30,000 to $50,000.

West of Vine City is Mozley Park, which was the site of the Battle of Ezra Church during the Atlanta Campaign. A former Rebel soldier, Hiram Mozley, settled in the area after the war, became a doctor and invented a

INSIDERS' TIP

A restored example of a shotgun house is on display at the Atlanta History Center, but architecture buffs may find a few examples of the three-room properties still standing around town. There are several in the Martin Luther King historic district and the Cabbagetown neighborhood. These one-level homes were named for the configuration of the main rooms, one behind each other, with connecting doors aligned from the front entrance to the rear. It was said a person aiming a shotgun through the front door could shoot clear into the backyard without touching a wall.

patent medicine. Following his death, his estate was divided into various home lots and sold. The neighborhood grew up around the city park named for Mozley. In 1949 a black clergyman and his family braved the color barrier, and by the late 1950s the area was home to more minority residents than whites. Mozley Park home prices run from $45,000 to $95,000.

Southwest of Mozley Park and bordering I-285 is Cascade Heights. This beautifully wooded area of rolling hills became a favored address with prominent black Atlantans after its desegregation in the 1960s. Home-run king (now TBS executive) Hank Aaron's five-acre spread includes a lake and a tennis court. Homes prices here start in the $130,000s and go up to $1 million.

South of Mozley Park is West End. It was here, on the corner of Lee and Gordon streets, that Charner Humphries opened his Whitehall Tavern alongside the Newnan-Decatur Road in 1835, two years before railroad surveyors drove in the "zero milepost" that marked the center of what became Atlanta. The area largely escaped destruction in the Civil War.

After the war, Col. George Washington Adair christened the area West End after the famous district in London. Adair ran a line of mule-drawn streetcars between West End and the present location of Midtown. Train service was also available to the central district, making the section a popular address for those employed downtown. West End's best-known resident was Joel Chandler Harris, the journalist who penned the Uncle Remus stories. His restored home, the Wren's Nest, is a National Landmark. West End is also home to Hammonds House, a pre-Civil War home that is now a museum of African-American fine art.

West End was adversely affected by the construction of I-20 and lost many residents to other neighborhoods, but it remains a vibrant community. The area's historic Queen Anne cottages and churches help provide stability. West End's annual neighborhood festival was established in 1975. The West End MARTA station serves the area. Home prices go from $70,000 to $225,000.

East of West End, Adair Park is named for Col. George Washington Adair. In addition to being a real estate developer and streetcar builder, Adair was a newspaper publisher, a train conductor and a wholesale grocer. Adair went bankrupt in 1873 and again in 1877; however, upon his death in 1899, he left his sons a vast real estate empire. Today this integrated residential district is served by the West End and Oakland City MARTA stations. Adair Park home prices start in the $50,000s and go into the mid-$80,000s.

Southeast Atlanta

Just east of Capitol Avenue, the Summerhill section is deriving a lasting benefit from having the Olympics in its front yard. Once a thriving neighborhood populated principally by African Americans and Jews, Summerhill was decimated by the construction of I-20 in the 1950s. The exodus from the neighborhood was only exacerbated when a big section of it was condemned to make way for Atlanta-Fulton County Stadium. Community activists worked closely with the city to make plans for the Olympic Stadium, now Turner Field, and to attract new homeowners to the area. The neighborhood's incredibly convenient location — near the Downtown Connector and downtown business district — have helped it attract a new wave of residents. Infill houses, as well as a new upscale town house community, have helped pull buyers into the area. Summerhill home prices start in the $30,000s and go into the mid-$60,000s.

Bordering Summerhill to the east is Grant Park. Col. Lemeul P. Grant was a civil engineer who moved to the South to help build the Western & Atlantic railroad and later designed the 10-mile system of fences and forts that encircled Civil War Atlanta, passing directly through the present-day Grant Park. Grant donated 100 acres of his land to the city in 1882 for use as a public park. Grant Park became a favorite playground for Atlantans, and a lovely Victorian neighborhood grew up around it. Grant Park faltered following World War II due to suburban migration and the construction of I-20 through the area. As in many other in-town neighborhoods, however, discounted property values and the area's charming homes began bringing people back. Today Grant Park residents continue to restore the district, which contains small, moderate-size and imposing homes, with prices ranging from $100,000 to the mid-$200,000s.

One Grant Park resident, Woodrow Mankin, is undertaking a truly massive project: the restoration of Col. Grant's own crumbling 20-room 1858 mansion at 327 St. Paul Avenue. Many years ago, Margaret Mitchell bought the house, determined to save one of the city's few surviving antebellum homes. In a court fight, however, she lost the house to its caretaker, an eccentric who lived there for decades until his death. Several owners later, Mankin plans to restore the mansion and use part of it as the headquarters for the Georgia Decorative Arts Society.

Directly east of Grant Park is Ormewood Park. It's one of the few remaining in-town areas with low-priced attractive housing for those who have been priced out of more established neighborhoods such as Midtown and Virginia-Highland. Small Craftsman cottages stand alongside more spacious infill housing. The Burns Club of Atlanta, a private social club, meets at 988 Alloway Place S.E. in a cottage that is a replica of poet Robert Burns' home in Scotland. Home prices in Ormewood range from $40,000 to the low $100,000s.

Directly north of Grant Park and across I-20, historic Oakland Cemetery stands serenely, a Victorian time capsule surrounded by a modern metropolis. Just east of Oakland on the other side of Boulevard is another reminder of days gone by: the Fulton Bag and Cotton Mill. The mill's 2,600 workers and their families, many of whom came to Atlanta from Appalachia, lived in the adjacent mill village. Developer George Adair originally named the development Pearl Park, in honor of his daughter, but over the years it gained, and retained, a less poetic name: Cabbagetown.

The mill closed in 1976, but many of its residents remained in their neighborhood and found other work in Atlanta. Winter Properties Inc. of Atlanta has an ambitious plan to renovate the giant mill structure into lofts, offices and retail space. Cabbagetown's streets are narrow, and its tiny houses are set close together. Here, as in other parts of town, good bargains on in-town homes have lured buyers. The King Memorial MARTA station serves this district. Cabbagetown home prices range from $50,000 to $75,000.

County by County

Whether you prefer to live in the center of everything or far from the maddening crowd, you'll find a wealth of options around Atlanta.

In the 1890s, the advent of streetcars made it possible for people to live some distance from where they worked. In the 1900s, the automobile accelerated that process, making more distant areas convenient to the downtown business district. After World War II, the interstate highway system created by President Dwight D. Eisenhower made it possible for Atlanta workers to commute from remote areas, some so remote they were a long day's buggy ride away in the previous century. This process, as we have seen, led to the virtual abandonment of some of Atlanta's original neighborhoods, which are now again attracting residents.

In this section, we'll briefly discuss the counties that make up the Atlanta metropolitan region. The real estate sales data evaluation was provided by Magellan Information Service Corporation and Steve Palm of Metro Brokers/Better Homes and Gardens. The information represents home closings from January through December 1996.

Close-in Counties

Clayton County

Principal cities/towns/communities: College Park, Forest Park, Jonesboro, Lake City, Lovejoy, Morrow, Riverdale.

Total number of re-sales in 1996: 2,469.
Total number of new homes sold is 1996: 872.
Average sale price for new homes: $109,442.

Clayton County is home to Hartsfield Atlanta International Airport; it's also the fictional site of the mythical plantations Tara and Twelve Oaks in *Gone With the Wind*. Houses in Clayton range from modest starters to elegant homes in planned communities and on the shores of Lake Spivey. Spivey Recital Hall on the campus of Clayton State College has been lauded as a world-class venue and hosts a performance series featuring many greats in the fields of classical music, opera and jazz. There are 27 elementary, 10 middle and seven high schools and eight private schools.

Cobb County

Principal cities/towns/communities: Acworth, Austell, Kennesaw, Marietta, Powder Springs, Smyrna.

Total number of re-sales in 1996: 8,079. Total number of new homes sold in 1996: 4,914. Average sale price for new homes: $175,635.

Cobb County, Atlanta's big, powerful neighbor to the northwest, saw its population increase by 50 percent in the 1980s. It's home to more than 500 manufacturing firms including Lockheed Aeronautical Systems Co., the state's largest industry, which employs 12,000, and to Dobbins Air Force base, where Air Force One lands whenever America's chief executive visits Atlanta. Cobb boasts an array of attractions, including Six Flags Over Georgia, White Water and the Kennesaw Mountain National Battlefield Park. An additional boost to business is the Cobb County Galleria Convention Centre. The Cobb County and Marietta public school systems, along with several private schools, educate the county's youth. Thanks to organizations such as the groundbreaking Theatre in the Square in Marietta, the arts are booming in Cobb.

DeKalb County

Principal cities/towns/communities: Avondale Estates, Chamblee, Clarkston, Decatur, Doraville, Lithonia, Stone Mountain, Pine Lake.

Total number of re-sales in 1996: 8,631. Total number of new homes sold in 1996: 1,798. Average sale price for new homes: $145,870.

The easternmost parts of Atlanta's city limits stretch into DeKalb County; it's named for Baron de Kalb, a German nobleman who fought alongside the Americans in the Revolution. DeKalb is home to the state's largest school system and claims the lowest dropout rate; it also pays teachers the highest starting and average salaries in the state. DeKalb is home to Emory University, the U.S. Centers for Disease Control and the American Cancer Society's national headquarters. DeKalb is part of the MARTA system, affording its citizens dependable transportation all around the county and Atlanta. DeKalb's housing opportunities range from inexpensive apartments to the luxury of Druid Hills estates to country living in the shadow of Stone Mountain.

Douglas County

Principal cities/towns/communities: Douglasville, Fairplay, Lithia Springs, Winston.

Total number of re-sales in 1996: 1,037. Total number of new homes sold in 1996: 524. Average sale price for new homes: $126,346.

Douglas County is bisected by I-20; its residents can make it to downtown in just 20 minutes. There are 166 acres of county parks, 50 acres of Douglasville city parks and the 2,000-acre Sweetwater Creek State Park. The county operates 12 elementary schools, five middle schools and three high schools. Two acute-care hospitals serve residents. Douglas was recently named one of the 50 fastest growing counties in the nation.

Fayette County

Principal cities/towns/communities: Brooks, Fayetteville, Peachtree City, Tyrone.

Total number of re-sales in 1996: 1,127. Total number of new homes sold in 1996: 936. Average sale price for new homes: $188,073.

Fayette County's per-capita income was the highest in Georgia from 1980 to 1990. Priding itself on a balance of progress and preservation, the county has developed a master plan to direct growth well into the next century. In much of the county, one-acre minimum zoning is still in place for residential properties. The planned community of Peachtree City, incorporated in 1959, is favored by retirees, airport employees and golf lovers — the town has 40 miles of pathways for golf carts (a favored local mode of transportation) and jogging. I-85 gets commuters to downtown Atlanta with ease.

Fulton County

North Fulton — Principal cities/towns/communities: Alpharetta, Mountain Park, Roswell, Sandy Springs.

Total number of re-sales in 1996: 6,694. Total number of new homes sold in 1996: 3,239. Average sale price for new homes: $259,736.

South Fulton — Principal cities/towns/communities: College Park, East Point, Fairburn, Hapeville, Palmetto, Union City.

Total number of re-sales in 1996: 3,460. Total number of new homes sold in 1996: 390. Average sale price for new homes: $136,652.

Fulton, which contains almost all of the City of Atlanta, is Georgia's most populous county. The city divides the county into northern and southern halves whose farthest reaches are 173 miles apart.

Major north Fulton businesses include Digital Equipment Corp., Equifax, American Honda and AT&T, which employs 2,500 workers in 1 million square feet of office space. Ninety percent of North Fulton students take the SAT, and almost that many continue their education after high school. Housing opportunities range from apartments and condos to private estates and golf/tennis communities such as the Country Club of the South. Ga. Highway 400 provides north Fulton with fast, easy access to downtown, the interstate highways and the airport.

South Fulton County's proximity to Hartsfield International Airport and its railroad infrastructure have made it a natural for commercial development: It has 12 industrial parks, the headquarters of Delta Air Lines and Chick-fil-A, a Ford plant and the facilities of many other major companies. It's also home to the internationally renowned private school Woodward Academy in College Park. The 40,000-square-foot Georgia Convention and Trade Center near the airport can accommodate groups of up to 5,000. The Southeast's only velodrome in East Point is every cyclist's dream. Homes available in this 109-square-mile district are in every category, including farmhouses, luxury condos, apartments and planned communities.

Gwinnett County

Principal cities/towns/communities: Buford, Grayson, Dacula, Duluth, Lawrenceville, Lilburn, Norcross, Suwanee, Snellville.

Total number of re-sales in 1996: 7,447. Total number of new homes sold in 1996: 6,111. Average sale price for new homes: $158,185.

This county's water towers beside I-85 have long crowed "Gwinnett is Great" — turns out they weren't joking. For some years, Gwinnett has been one of the fastest-growing counties in the United States. The giant Gwinnett Place

Mall has been hugely popular with shoppers northeast of Atlanta, who once faced a long drive to reach major malls in Atlanta. More than 94 percent of Gwinnett's kids achieve a high school diploma, and more than 70 percent go on to post-secondary education. The Gwinnett Civic and Cultural Center boasts a 1,200-seat performing arts theater.

Henry County

Principal cities/towns/communities: Hampton, Locust Grove, McDonough, Stockbridge.

Total number of re-sales in 1996: 1,063. Total number of new homes sold in 1996: 1,662. Average sale price for new homes: $119,393.

Henry County has seven interchanges on I-75. The county saw its population double in the 1980s; it has also attracted such businesses as NEC Technologies and BellSouth. Housing opportunities range from modest starter homes to lavish country club communities. Henry's school system is among the state's top five in terms of increased enrollment.

Outlying Counties

Cherokee County

Principal cities/towns/communities: Ball Ground, Canton, Holly Springs, Nelson, Woodstock, Waleska.

Total number of re-sales in 1996: 2,043. Total number of new homes sold in 1996: 1,651. Average sale price for new homes: $158,521.

Cherokee takes its name from the Native Americans who once called the area home. Sixty percent of county residents commute to work in metro Atlanta, most via I-575 and I-75. Homes are available at a wide range of prices. Canton is the site of a large marble finishing plant. The school district has 18 elementary, three middle and three high schools and a special education facility; there are also several private schools.

Coweta County

Principal cities/towns/communities: Corinth, Grantville, Haralson, Madras, Moreland, Newnan, Sargent, Senoia, Sharpsburg, Turin.

Total number of re-sales in 1996: 728. Total number of new homes sold in 1996: 761. Average sale price for new homes: $118,469.

Coweta is west of Fayette in the southwestern corner of the metro area. The county saw its population increase by 37 percent during the 1980s. Newnan has many antebellum homes that survived the Civil War and has often been used as the location for movies and TV shows. The 2,500-acre Shenandoah Industrial and Business Park is home to a Kmart distribution center and many other companies.

Forsyth County

Principal cities/towns/communities: Cumming

Total number of re-sales in 1996: 1,113. Total number of new homes sold in 1996: 2,517. Average sale price for new homes: $189,574.

North of Fulton and Gwinnett, Forsyth County lies along the western side of Lake Lanier. The county has six interchanges on Ga. 400, which gives it great access to the city and the interstate system to the south and to the mountains in the north. The educational system includes seven elementary schools, three middle schools, two high schools and one private school. Forsyth is home to 21 industrial parks. Housing opportunities range from apartments to lavish mansions on the hilly shores of Lake Lanier.

Paulding County

Principal cities/towns/communities: Dallas, Hiram.

Total number of re-sales in 1996: 732. Total number of new homes sold in 1996: 1,022. Average sale price for new homes: $103,754.

North of Douglas and west of Cobb is Paulding County, which is 20 miles from Atlanta on its east side and 40 miles away on its west side. Seventy percent of residents came here from elsewhere, and, though the county has more than 200 subdivisions, 70 percent of its land remains undeveloped. Paulding is home to the concrete manufacturer Metromont and to Shaw Industries, the world's largest carpet maker.

Newton County

Principal cities/towns/communities: Covington, Mansfield, Newbern, Oxford, Porterdale.

Total number of re-sales in 1996: 551. Total number of new homes sold in 1996: 761. Average sale price for new homes: $99,395.

South of Walton, Newton County is bisected by I-20, which helps it attract big corporate players such as Mobil Chemical, Stanley Tools and Bridgestone. Eight thousand students attend Newton's one high school, two middle schools and eight elementary schools; there are also three nearby private schools. Oxford is the town where Emory University was born; the two-year arm of that school still operates there. Newton was founded in 1821 and has 85 churches.

Rockdale County

Principal cities/towns/communities: Conyers, Milstead.

Total number of re-sales in 1996: 751. Total number of new homes sold in 1996: 1,257. Average sale price for new homes: $158,290.

Rockdale County is bisected by I-20, which makes it just a 30-minute commute to downtown Atlanta. The county's population mushroomed by 54 percent during the 1980s. Rockdale has four major industrial parks and has attracted many international, particularly Japanese, companies: It's home to Maxell, which donated the cherry trees whose annual springtime display sparks a large festival in Conyers. Major U.S. firms here include John

Looking for a million-dollar mansion? Head to North Fulton county. While most metro counties recorded no sales in that price range for 1996, the North Fulton area had 48 houses priced at a million or more. North Fulton includes Atlanta's Buckhead neighborhood as well as several exclusive country club communities north of the city.

Deere and AT&T. The Georgia International Horse Park in Conyers hosted equestrian events during the 1996 Olympics.

Walton County

Principal cities/towns/communities: Between, Good Hope, Jersey, Loganville, Monroe, Social Circle, Walnut Grove.

Total number of re-sales in 1996: 524. Total number of new homes sold in 1996: 333. Average sale price for new homes: $114,159.

Walton County, south of Barrow, traces its roots to 1818. Seven Walton County citizens served as Georgia's governor; two also served as U.S. senators. Alonzo Herndon, born a slave in Social Circle, went on to found Atlanta Life Insurance Co. and become Atlanta's first African-American millionaire. There are two public schools systems (Walton County and Social Circle City), plus the 21-acre private George Walton Academy. Walton County is about 45 minutes from downtown Atlanta.

Apartment Living

The metro area has thousands of apartments for rent at nearly every price level. Some areas, such as the Buford Highway in northeast Atlanta and the Chattahoochee River area in Cobb, have large concentrations of apartments. But you can also find apartments in areas such as Midtown and Garden Hills, which are best known for their single-family homes. The major sources of information on apartments for rent are *The Atlanta Journal-Constitution*, *The Marietta Daily Journal* and the free weekly *Creative Loafing*. Several free publications showcasing apartments for rent are available around town; they're listed with the real estate publications in our Media chapter.

Apartment Locators

If you'd like professional assistance in choosing your new Atlanta apartment home, call one of the following services.

Apartment Selector
3000 Windy Hill Rd., Marietta
• (770) 956-0177
In business since 1959, this national company has offices across the metro area. Offer-

ing properties of all sizes in all areas, the firm provides free transportation for your apartment search seven days a week. All services are paid for by the property owner. To prepare for your move to Atlanta, call (800) 543-0536.

Apartments Today
11285 Elkins Rd., Ste. D-1, Roswell
• (770) 664-4957
Call Apartments Today for free assistance in finding your new Atlanta address. This company can help you find a long- or short-term apartment to lease. Fees are paid by the owner.

Free Home Finder
3652 N. Peachtree Rd. • (770) 455-1781
This service will drive you to view the properties of your choice. A free roommate match service and a newcomer kit are available. Free Home Finder will even pick you up at MARTA stations. All prices and sizes of apartments, furnished and unfurnished, are available.

Promove
3620 Piedmont Rd. N.E. • (404) 842-0042
Promove will help you get settled in the city by narrowing your choices to focus on what's really important for you. It will loan you color photos of prospective properties and answer your questions about living in the metro area. The firm maintains three Atlanta offices; its services are free to renters.

Real Estate

Sometimes it seems as if there are no native Atlantans left in Atlanta. Although residents joke about it, it is true that the vast majority of Atlanta's population has arrived here from somewhere else. Couple the fair weather and job opportunities with the wide range of housing prices, and Atlanta is hard to beat.

Even though Atlanta real estate is priced more reasonably than that of many other cities, prices have risen steadily in the last 10 years. And as traffic becomes more and more of a concern, prices for those communities and counties closer to the heart of the city have climbed. As an example, home shoppers frequently note that real estate in East Cobb is usually $10,000 to $20,000 more than comparable homes on the west side, where the access to the interstate system is less convenient. But on the positive side, Atlanta does offer, within a reasonable distance of downtown, everything buyers could imagine in housing opportunities — from pastoral country estates to luxury high-rise condominiums.

Atlanta has a thriving real estate community with thousands of informed agents who are eager to assist you. Here's a small sample of metro area firms ready to help you in your relocation to Atlanta.

Buckhead Brokers
5395 Roswell Rd. • (404) 252-7030, (800) 989-7733

Despite the name, this firm covers the entire metro area with 10 offices. Its beginnings were in the Buckhead area. The firm offers all real estate services, including a home rental division. A call to the number listed previously will direct you to the regional office serving the area of your choice.

The Condo Store
2140 Peachtree Rd. • (404) 262-6636

Founded in 1993, this 45-agent-and-growing company is one of the few in the metro area that deals exclusively with condominiums, luxury high rises, town houses and cluster homes. A second office in Dunwoody opened in spring of '97.

Harry Norman Realtors
5229 Roswell Rd. N.E. • (404) 255-7505, (800) 241-6059

Twelve sales offices covering the entire northern metro area have grown from this firm's beginnings in 1930, when Harry Norman's mother started the company. Relocation is one of the firm's specialties. This service includes picking you up at the airport, making your hotel reservations and other helpful assistance. The company also operates an office in Highlands, North Carolina, (800) 233-8259.

Metro Brokers/Better Homes and Gardens
750 Hammond Dr. • (404) 843-2500

In 1997 this 15-office company joined forces with the real estate services of Better Homes and Gardens to offer more programs for agents, education, information networking — even sub-

scriptions to the magazine! The brokerage has about 700 agents who help buyers find homes across the metro area, from North Fulton to Peachtree City and Newnan on the south side.

Northside Realty
6065 Roswell Rd., Ste. 600
• (404) 252-3393, (800) 241-2540

With 800 sales associates in 22 residential branch offices, it's easy to see why many Atlantans think of Northside for their real estate needs. Georgia's largest independent real estate broker, Northside is among the top independent brokerages in the United States based on number of homes sold. In 1985 Northside was the first Atlanta real estate firm to sell more than $1 billion in residential real estate. That track record continues, with an estimated billion dollars in sales every year throughout the metro area and surrounding counties. Solid marketing information and devotion to service are Northside hallmarks. NR Hotline, (404) 843-1800, open round the clock every day of the week, allows you to enter a five-digit access number shown on a property's yard sign and get detailed information on the property being considered. Talk with a sales associate at any time by pressing the star (*) key. Northside's Relocation Division's services include group move assistance and personalized area tours. The corporate office listed above will direct you to the Northside office nearest you.

Jenny Pruitt & Associates Realtors
990 Hammond Dr. • (770) 394-5400

Another multilocation presence, this firm has three offices (in Buckhead, Cobb County and Sandy Springs) that serve the entire metro area. Special divisions for rental, relocation and new homes are provided. The corporate office, listed above, will put you in touch with the specific office you need.

RE/MAX
1100 Abernathy Rd. • (770) 393-1137

This company has about 55 individual franchises around the metro area. More than 2,600 agents handle new home sales, resales and relocation services. RE/MAX is the number one rated company in the city in sales volume; in 1996, their agents sold more than $5.7 billion dollars in sales in 43,000 transactions.

Education

Whether you've got small children who yearn to learn or older kids ready to go to college, Atlanta has a plethora of educational opportunities. Public and private schools educate students from ages 2 to 22 and older. In addition to a number of elementary and secondary schools, Atlanta boasts several top-notch colleges and universities.

This chapter provides an overview of five public school systems: City of Atlanta, Cobb County, DeKalb County, Fulton County and Gwinnett County. We also present a look at private elementary and secondary schools, schools for special students and institutions of higher education.

Experienced teachers and parents offer a few tips when checking out a school. Talk with the principal and inspect the school. Ask your neighbors or business associates if they have knowledge of a school's reputation. And ask to speak with a few parents of children in the school you're considering.

Another handy resource for finding just the right school is *The Ultimate Atlanta School Guide*, a comprehensive statistical look at more than 17 public school systems as well as the larger private schools in the greater metro area. The information was compiled by education writers from *The Atlanta-Journal Constitution*. This 400-plus page book tells you what schools service which ZIP codes, along with key information, such as enrollment, dropout rates and standardized test scores. It's available for $17.95. Call (404) 526-5696.

Public School Systems

The state's schools have seen significant improvement since Georgia established the Georgia Lottery for Education in 1992. Lottery revenues have helped fund instructional technology for Georgia's public schools, including 15 regional Technology Training Centers that provide teachers, principals and administrators the chance to learn about, use and experiment with new technologies. Lottery money has also funded the HOPE scholarship program and a very popular voluntary prekindergarten program for 4-year-olds.

If you are enrolling children in Georgia public schools, be aware that the law requires them to be 5 years old by September 1 for kindergarten and 6 years old by September 1 for 1st grade. Younger children moving into Georgia who have already attended a public or accredited private school may enroll in Georgia schools provided the kindergartners are 5 years old by December 31 or the 1st grader is 6 by that date.

Parents planning to enroll children in school should contact the school superintendent's office in the county or city where they'll be living. Each system decides what credits to accept from transfer students. Parents or guardians usually need to request that records or transcripts be forwarded to a student's new school or system.

Students enrolling in public school must provide a certificate of immunization for measles, rubella, tetanus, diphtheria, polio, mumps and whooping cough. Sixth graders must have at least one additional dose of MMR (measles, mumps, rubella) vaccine. The county health department may issue medical exemptions for children who cannot be immunized for medical reasons or whose parents or guardians present an affidavit stating that immunization is against their religious beliefs.

Students at all grade levels entering the public schools for the first time must provide certification of eye, ear and dental examinations. Students will also be asked to furnish a Social Security number. Parents who decline to provide the number may sign a statement to that effect, and their children will receive student identification numbers.

Atlanta Public Schools
210 Pryor St. S.W. • (404) 827-8000

The City of Atlanta system serves about 60,000 students in 97 schools (70 elementary, 16 middle and 11 high) where the student-teacher ratio is 16 to 1. It also has three adult education centers including Atlanta Area Technical School, a facility that provides post-secondary technical training in a variety of diploma programs including paralegal studies, dental assistant, computer programming and electronics. The system operates five alternative learning programs, a Parental Services Center and an Adult Learning Center focusing on literacy and preparing adults for the General Equivalency Development (GED) examination.

Atlanta city schools benefit from intense community support. Atlanta Partners for Education, a joint program of the metro Atlanta Chamber of Commerce and the Atlanta Public Schools, provides for the development and maintenance of partnerships in which businesses, community organizations, governmental institutions and other groups provide increased educational and enrichment opportunities for students in the Atlanta Public Schools. Partnerships help students increase self-esteem and achievement, as well as learn about the expectations and realities of the work world. Partnerships also boost school staff morale by providing educational opportunities and recognition. Other metro area school systems have instituted their own education partnership programs.

The Atlanta Magnet School Program offers 16 four-year programs for concentration in specific fields of study. Open to any Atlanta resident or tuition-paying non-city resident, the magnet programs encourage mature, self-motivated students to explore possibilities in the fields of their choice. Some magnets include on-the-job training and experience.

The magnet schools focus on a significant range of occupation areas, such as the performing arts, international studies, communications, science and mathematics, financial services, information processing and hospitality. Other subject areas include transportation, educational careers, engineering and applied technology, language studies, fashion retailing, entrepreneurship and healthcare professions.

Cobb County Public Schools
514 Glover St., Marietta • (770) 426-3300

This fast-growing suburban area across the Chattahoochee River from Atlanta has one of the largest school systems in Georgia. Cobb has more than 87,000 students in 61 elementary schools, 18 middle schools and 12 high schools. The system also has an Adult Education Center where adults 16 and older can take classes to improve their basic educational skills, work toward high school completion or earn a GED.

The pupil-teacher ratio varies by grade level and specific activity. In general, the ratio ranges from one teacher per 20 students to one teacher per 27 students. Almost 90 percent of Cobb's graduates go on to college.

The Cobb County system has 13 National Schools of Excellence and 26 Georgia Schools of Excellence. (Schools of excellence receive the designation based on their performances over three years in a number of areas including leadership, teaching environment, curriculum and instruction, student environment and parental and community support.) A magnet school for the performing arts is open to all high school students by audition.

Special Education programs, designed for all disabled students, include programs for students with special learning disabilities, health impairments and emotional/behavior disorders. Cobb County, along with the Marietta City Schools and the Cobb Chamber of Commerce, participates in Partners in Education, which matches businesses with schools to provide enrichment and incentives to students. Cobb also offers after-school programs in all elementary schools at a nominal cost. There

FYI

Three area codes serve the metro Atlanta area: 404, 770 and 678. Whether you live on Peachtree Street or in New York City, you must dial the code to reach any number in the area. The difference? Outside the area, you must dial "1," then the area code and phone number; inside the area, you need only dial the area code followed by the phone number.

Photo: Annemarie Poyo/Emory University

Thousands of students attend Atlanta's colleges and universities.

are programs for gifted students, and there is one open campus, Oakwood High in Smyrna, for nontraditional students who need to attend on a flexible schedule.

Cobb County schools garner a significant share of honors, including a National Secondary Counselor of the Year, National Invent America Outstanding Educator and several Georgia Teacher of the Year awards. Cobb County annually sends 60 students to the Governor's Honors program, a summer session for outstanding students held on a Georgia college campus.

DeKalb County School System
3770 N. Decatur Rd., Decatur
• (404) 297-1244

DeKalb's school district has an enrollment of approximately 92,000 students. DeKalb's 80 elementary schools, 19 high schools and 10 middle schools make it one of the largest school operations in Georgia. Statistics from

the school years 1987 to 1993 showed DeKalb's per-pupil expenditures as consistently higher than the state average; in the 1996-97 school year, $5,684 was spent on each student. Eighty-two percent of DeKalb students continue their education past high school.

In the DeKalb system, elementary schools for the most part extend through the 7th grade, with high schools serving grades 8 through 12. The county is moving to a middle school system, with 10 middle schools operating in 1997-'98. There is full-day kindergarten in every DeKalb elementary school and 77 prekindergarten programs.

Students in DeKalb enjoy a student-teacher ratio that ranges from 21 or 26 to 1, depending on enrollment and grade level. Sixty percent of teachers and administrators hold a master's degree or doctorate.

DeKalb's magnet school program for students with special interests and abilities offers bountiful opportunities. There are schools for high achievers, math, science and technology, computer education, the performing arts, writing and more than a half-dozen foreign languages, including Russian, Japanese and Chinese.

A special feature operated by the county school system is Fernbank Science Center. This museum, classroom and woodland complex is on 65 acres of old-growth forest. It houses the nation's third-largest planetarium. The telescope in its observatory is the largest in the world dedicated primarily to public education. Each year, the STT Program (Scientific Tools and Techniques) gives nearly 200 9th- and 10th-grade students the opportunity for independent study in science and math. (For more information on Fernbank, see our Kidstuff and Attractions chapters.)

Special education classes serve approximately 8,500 children with special needs in specific areas, including learning disabilities, hearing, vision, speech and emotional disorders. Unique in the Southeast, and one of only a handful in the country, is DeKalb's International Center. Established in 1985, the center acts as liaison between schools and minority language students and their families, who represent 160 countries and 66 language groups.

Fulton County Schools
786 Cleveland Ave. S.W.
• **(404) 763-6820**

Besides Atlanta, the county seat, nine other incorporated cities lie within Fulton's boundaries: Alpharetta, Roswell, Mountain Park, College Park, Hapeville, East Point, Fairburn, Palmetto and Union City. The Fulton County school system serves students in these cities as well as the unincorporated areas of the county.

More than 60,000 students from diverse backgrounds attend Fulton County's 38 elementary, 13 middle and 10 high schools. The communities represented are rural, suburban and urban; students have the opportunity to interact with and develop understanding of a variety of people.

Fulton County schools' curriculum stresses academic achievement and success. Local option sales taxes passed in 1997 have provided funds to ensure that every Fulton County school is either new or newly renovated. The income is also underwriting the construction of 17 new schools in the next five years. College Park Elementary School is the first in Georgia to offer a year-round schedule. Mimosa Elementary is a state pilot site for Japanese language instruction.

The system provides comprehensive programs for exceptional children including those with mental and behavioral disorders, high academic talent, physical limitations and learning disabilities. School counselors implement developmental guidance programs to help students maximize their potential.

Fulton's elementary schools offer afterschool child care, and half-day and full-day summer enrichment programs. Selected middle schools offer after-school enrichment programs as well as intramural physical education activities. Fulton County high schools offer a broad range of extracurricular activities including athletics, honor societies, career awareness opportunities and recreational programs. Four high schools offer magnet programs to help students interested in concentrating their studies in mathematics and science, international studies or visual and performing arts.

More than 80 percent of Fulton graduates continue their education. Fifteen Fulton County schools are Georgia Schools of Excellence; three are National Schools of Excellence.

www.insiders.com

See this and many other **Insiders' Guide®** destinations online — in their entirety.

Visit us today!

INSIDERS' TIP

The University System of Georgia includes 34 public institutions of higher learning: six universities, 13 senior colleges and 15 junior colleges. All of the schools receive some financial assistance from the state.

Fulton's honors include: Georgia Educator of the Year in numerous curricula and the Presidential Award Winner for Excellence in Science Teaching. In 1996, the system was recognized by *Money Magazine* as one of the top in the country. The College Board presented the system with an Award in Excellence for Advanced Placement Courses.

Gwinnett County Public Schools
52 Gwinnett Dr., Lawrenceville
• **(770) 822-6508**

In fast-growing Gwinnett, public school student enrollment is projected to reach 100,000 by the year 2000. Currently, 81 schools serve more than 93,500 students who enroll according to cluster attendance zones. (A cluster is a geographical area containing three to four elementary schools, one or two middle schools and a high school.)

Gwinnett provides educational opportunities through its vocational education center, special education center, community schools program and the Gwinnett Technical Institute, the state's largest vocational/technical school. With approximately 10,000 employees, the school district is one of the largest employers in the county. Each year, GCPS receives more than 3,000 teacher applications, eventually selecting more than 500 to meet its needs. The school system aims to match teachers with an increasingly diverse student population.

The student-teacher ratio averages 25 to 1. Currently, 60 percent of Gwinnett's teachers have postgraduate degrees. All grades and all schools offer gifted education programs; the system also offers enrichment opportunities in such areas as art, music, foreign language, drama and debate. Gwinnett students can benefit from extracurricular activities such as athletics, service and social clubs, Odyssey of the Mind and Invent America! Each elementary school offers a full-day kindergarten program.

Gwinnett's students and educators are recognized regularly for outstanding achievement. Eleven Gwinnett schools have been named National Schools of Excellence; 28 are Georgia Schools of Excellence. Nine GCPS educators have been honored at the national level since 1995. State-level recognitions include Teacher of the Year and Middle School Team of the Year.

About 80 percent of Gwinnett graduates continue education beyond high school. All high schools offer advanced placement courses, joint enrollment with area colleges and work/study programs.

Resources

Georgia Department of Education
Public Information/Publications Division, 2052 Twin Towers E. • **(404) 656-2476**

Call this office for general information on Georgia schools. This department can send you a guidebook with newcomer tips and helpful hints to help your child learn.

Private Schools

A sizeable number of educational facilities in the metro Atlanta area flourish apart from the public school system. Curricula range from traditional liberal arts programs to those designed for the gifted or the learning disabled.

We don't have the space to evaluate each of the metro area's many private schools, which number somewhere in the neighborhood of 100. As with the public schools, we offer an overview, presenting a sampling of schools by county.

The Atlanta Area School Directory, by Carla S. Rogg and Oskar H. Rogg, published by Care Solutions Inc., offers 270 pages of comprehensive information on metro area private schools. You can buy the book for $11.95, plus $3 shipping and handling, by calling the publishers at (770) 642-6722. Copies are also available at local Chapter 11 and Barnes & Noble bookstores. Be assured whatever your child's needs — academically gifted, learning disabled, developmentally delayed and all shades in between — the Atlanta area schools stand ready with an appropriate program.

Cobb County

Shreiner Academy
1340 Terrell Mill Rd., Marietta
• **(770) 953-1340**

This facility was founded in 1980 for preschool through grade 8. The accelerated curriculum focuses on traditional academics. With about 300 students, the school features foreign language and computer instruction, among many other offerings. Preschool for 2-year-olds and summer camps are also offered. The student-teacher ratio is about 18 to 1 in the elementary and middle grades; for the preschool classes, it's 10 to 1.

The Walker School
700 Cobb Pkwy. N., Marietta
• (770) 427-2689

Since its inception in 1957, this independent day school has focused on a college prep program for its students. The more than 800 students served are from 4-year-old kindergartners through 12th graders. The student-teacher ratio is about 14 to 1. Campus features include three libraries, two gyms, four computer centers, an auditorium and six science labs. After-school care is available. The school's student-produced literary magazine, *The Pegasus*, has received awards from the National Teachers of English and Columbia University. Thirty percent of the 1997 graduating class was commended or named a semifinalist in the National Merit Scholarship competition.

DeKalb County

The Friends School of Atlanta
121 Sams St., Decatur • (404) 373-8746

Approximately 170 students from 4-year-old kindergartners through 8th graders attend the Friends School. The focus is on each child's individual skills and needs. The school, with a student-teacher ratio of 13 to 1, also offers after-school care and summer programs.

Greenfield Hebrew Academy
5200 Northland Dr. N.W.
• (404) 843-9900

Founded in 1953, the Hebrew Academy offers a child-centered traditional approach in a curriculum specially designed for the school. About 600 students attend classes in prekindergarten through 8th grade. The first part of the day is spent doing traditional classwork; the afternoon is devoted exclusively to Judaic studies and the Hebrew language. Science and computer labs, music and art centers are part of the facilities. The student-teacher ratio is 19 to 1.

Marist School
3790 Ashford Dunwoody Rd. N.E.
• (770) 457-7201

This private Catholic college preparatory school educates boys and girls in grades 7 through 12. Founded in 1901, the school was originally in downtown Atlanta but relocated to its present 57-acre campus in 1962. Marist is owned and operated by the Society of Mary, a Roman Catholic religious order of priests and brothers. The Marists and their Board of Trustees have made a commitment to maintain an ecumenical diversity by limiting Catholic admissions to a maximum of 75 percent. The remaining 25 percent is open to students of other faiths. Marist accepts students of any race or national origin.

The staff includes 79 full-time classroom teachers plus administrators, librarians, guidance counselors and campus ministers. More than three-quarters of the staff hold advanced degrees. About 20 advanced placement classes are offered.

The Paideia School
1509 Ponce de Leon Ave.
• (404) 377-3491

Founded in 1971, Paideia (a Greek word for "community of learning") is an independent, nonsectarian school committed to having a racial, socioeconomic and intellectual cross-section of students. The school serves families with children ages 3 through 18. Paideia's philosophy is based on the belief that school can be informal and individualized yet still educate well. In addition to teaching basic skills and content areas, the school promotes development in art, music and physical education. About 750 students are enrolled, with a student-teacher ratio of 12 to 1.

St. Martin's Episcopal School
3110-A Ashford-Dunwoody Rd. N.E.
• (404) 237-4260

Academic excellence with a Christian orientation characterizes this school, founded in 1959, for more than 450 preschool to 8th-grade students. The student-teacher ratio is about 10 to 1 in the elementary and middle grades; early childhood classes have a ratio of 8 to 1. St. Martin's is part of an adopt-a-school program with Oglethorpe University, whose students work as teacher apprentices and aides in the after-school program. After-school care is offered until 6 PM.

St. Pius X Catholic High School
2674 Johnson Rd. N.E. • (404) 636-3023

As the Catholic high school of the Atlanta Archdiocese, this 40-year-old school offers three levels of instruction: accelerated, college prep I and college prep II. The philosophy, based on faith and religious belief, is to help students develop individual potential, to build the community and to foster service to others. A traditional class structure serves more than 1,000 students in grades 9 through 12; the student-teacher ratio is about 16 to 1.

Fulton County

The Galloway School
215 W. Wieuca Rd. N.E. • (404) 252-8389

Galloway was founded in 1969 by Elliott Galloway on the principle that children need to learn the values of common decency and dignity along with academics, the arts, physical fitness, problem solving and collaborative skills. Serving approximately 685 students from age 2 through grade 12, the school sits on a hill overlooking Chastain Park in north Atlanta. Galloway has more than 80 faculty members, more than half of whom have advanced degrees. Within the past several years, almost all the interior spaces in the original hand-hewn brick main building were extensively renovated. An attached classroom building contains 15 classrooms, a multipurpose room and school offices. A three-story, 16-classroom building and a gymnasium/fitness center were completed by the end of 1996.

The Heiskell School
3260 Northside Dr. N.W.
• (404) 262-2233

This nondenominational Christian school was founded in 1949 with a traditional class structure. The school is based on the belief that a child's home, church and school should complement each other. The approximately 400 students served are 2 years old through 8th grade. The student-teacher ratio is 12 to 1. Academic excellence is stressed as are learning responsibility and the history of the United States.

Holy Innocents' Episcopal School
805 Mount Vernon Hwy. • (404) 255-4026

The fourth largest independent school in the Atlanta area, Holy Innocents' has about 1,300 students for 3-year-olds through 12th graders. The school opened in 1959 with the mission of providing students with an enriching program guided by Judeo-Christian principals. The 33-acre campus includes a worship space, fine arts facility and sports fields. The student-teacher ratio averages 10 to 1.

The Lovett School
4075 Paces Ferry Rd. N.W.
• (404) 262-3032

On a picturesque 100-acre setting along the Chattahoochee River, Lovett aims to develop the whole child in all aspects of academic, arts and athletic programs by concentrating on the student's intellectual, physical, spiritual, social and emotional growth. This college-prep school was founded in 1926 and serves about 1,450 students from 4-year-old kindergartners through 12th graders. Afterschool care is available. The student-teacher ratio is approximately 8 to 1.

Pace Academy
966 W. Paces Ferry Rd. • (404) 262-1345

Pace Academy will celebrate its 40th anniversary in 1998. About 800 students in kindergarten through 12th grade study in an atmosphere of caring and personalized attention. The school's stated philosophy is "to have the courage to strive for excellence." The traditional college prep curriculum includes advanced placement classes and honors classes. One-hundred percent of Pace seniors go on to higher education. An extensive service program fosters good citizenship and community outreach. The school's 25-acre campus is anchored by a Tudor-style home built in 1931, dubbed "the Castle," that now houses administrative offices. The student-teacher ratio is 10 to 1.

Trinity School
3254 Northside Pkwy. N.W.
• (404) 231-8100

Founded in 1951, Trinity School is an elementary and preschool with 485 students, from 2-year-olds to 6th graders. In addition to a challenging academic program, Trinity emphasizes the ethical values of the Christian religion and its Jewish heritage as well as teaches respect for different backgrounds. Spanish, art, music, values education, physical education, and technology are key parts of the curriculum. Summer camp and after school programs are available. The student-teacher ratio is about 9 to 1.

The Westminster Schools
1424 W. Paces Ferry Rd. N.W.
- **(404) 355-8673**

Founded in 1951, Westminster educates students from pre-K through 12th grade with a rigorous academic program based on Christian philosophy. Westminster has a 171-acre campus with 16 tennis courts, a natatorium and an outdoor pool, four gyms and six playing fields. The traditional curriculum is college preparatory, while the school's mission statement conveys the schools' philosophy: Christian commitment, whole person development and excellent education. In grades 5 through 12, the average class size is 14. In classes with younger children, the average is nine.

Woodward Academy
1662 Rugby Ave., College Park
- **(404) 765-8262**

Woodward was founded in 1900 by Col. John Charles Woodward as Georgia Military Academy. In the mid-1960s, the school dropped the military focus, went coeducational and was renamed in honor of the founder. The curriculum is college prep with a traditional structure.

The diverse student population of 2,600 studies on three campuses. The Woodward-Busey campus in Riverdale hosts the prekindergarten through 6th-grade crowd; a third campus in north Fulton County is for grades prekindergarten through grade 6. The main campus, about 65 acres, has more than 30 buildings including a state-of-the-art science center and a library with approximately 200 Internet connections. Woodward also has an natatorium, five indoor basketball courts and football, track and practice fields.

Woodward has third generation students from some Atlanta families and about 33 alumni employed on campus. Woodward operates nearly 22 bus routes daily, transporting more than 900 students.

Approximately 80 percent of Woodward's faculty members have at least a master's degree. Small classroom settings encourage individual attention to each student's needs; the student-teacher ratio is approximately 18 to 1.

Yeshiva Atlanta
3130 Raymond Dr. • (770) 451-5299

Founded 25 years ago, Yeshiva enrolls about 170 students in grades 8 through 12. The traditional class structure is split, with students spending half-days in Judaic/Hebraic studies and half-days in general studies. The student-teacher ratio is about 12 to 1. The 50,000-square-foot facility sits on a 10-acre site.

Gwinnett County

Country Brook Montessori School
2175 Norcross-Tucker Rd., Norcross
- **(770) 446-2397**

An academic preschool and grade school founded in 1983, the facility serves children from age 1 through 12. One of many Montessori schools in the metro area, Country Brook has a staff trained in the Montessori curriculum, which supports full development of children in all aspects. The student-teacher ratio is 10 to 1 for students ages 6 to 9; it's 15 to 1 for students ages 9 to 12.

INSIDERS' TIP

The Council for School Performance at Georgia State University evaluates all lottery-funded educational programs as well as all schools in the state. For a copy of a free, two-page report on a specific elementary, middle, high school or school system that includes statistics on dropout rate, absenteeism and test scores, call (404) 651-3523.

Photo: Fulton County Schools

Atlanta area public schools offer more than reading, writing and arithmetic.

The variety of extracurricular activities available includes art, Spanish, gymnastics, music and computers. Country Brook has a hot lunch program and enrichment programs before and after school for enrolled children. Country Brook opens at 7 AM and closes at 6:30 PM.

Greater Atlanta Christian School
1575 Indian Tr., Norcross
• (770) 243-2000

After planning for seven years, this school opened in 1968 to offer a traditional class structure for children in kindergarten through grade 12. After-school care is available for kindergarten through 8th grade. More than 1,200 students attend the 74-acre campus of Greater Atlanta Christian School; average class size is 19. One hundred percent of the students pursue higher education.

Special Schools

Approximately 40 institutions exist for students with special needs beyond the public school system or private school programs. These needs encompass a wide range of physical, mental and emotional needs. For more information, call United Way of Metropolitan Atlanta at 211 or (404) 614-1000 for a listing of more than 2,000 community organizations, including many that deal with human service needs. County school boards also are a good source for referrals. A multitude of Atlanta agencies and organizations exist to lend assistance.

Atlanta Speech School
3160 Northside Pkwy. • (404) 233-5332

The Atlanta Speech School was founded in 1938 by the Junior League of Atlanta. It was based in a building the League bought with money raised at a ball to mark the opening of *Gone With the Wind*. The school housed the first audiology clinic in the area, which continues to provide evaluation of all kinds of communication disorders. Today, more than 330 students attend nursery, kindergarten classes, as well as grades 1 through 6. Speech pathologists and reading specialists work in each classroom. The student-teacher ratio is never more than 9 to 1.

Georgia Center for Students with Disabilities
542 Church St., Decatur • (404) 378-5433

This school offers comprehensive psychoeducational and medical evaluations and planning for children from birth to age 21. Admission is through review by a screening committee to determine eligibility, appropriateness and need. Educational evaluation is made through a fully equipped diagnostic classroom. Evaluations are made in the areas of occupational therapy, physical therapy, general medicine, psychology, speech therapy and others.

The Howard School
1246 Ponce de Leon Ave.
• (404) 377-0884

Founded in 1950, The Howard School specializes in programs for students with language and learning disabilities. More than 350 students, from age 4 to 18, attend classes at the Ponce de Leon campus in Druid Hills, or the north campus, 9415 Willeo Road, in Roswell. The focus in both locations is to provide students with a challenging and nurturing environment to help them understand their own learning styles. Classes usually have fewer than 10 students; the staff to student to teacher ratio is approximately 1 to 5.

Learning Disabilities Association of Georgia
2978 Canton Rd. • (770) 514-8088

This organization has 10 councils throughout the state that provide support group services to families of children and adults with learning disabilities.

Rehabilitation and Education for Adults and Children Inc. (REACH)
1815 Ponce de Leon Ave. N.E.
• (404) 377-3836

Services for children from birth to 3 years are designed for those who are moderate to severely developmentally delayed, those with multiple handicaps and those with neuromuscular and musculoskeletal disorders. The center also provides vocational and community living skills training for adults 18 and older. Supported employment for adults is also available. REACH serves Fulton and DeKalb counties.

Special Needs Resources

Atlanta Alliance on Developmental Disabilities (AADD)
828 W. Peachtree St., Ste. 304
• (404) 881-9777

AADD is a nonprofit United Way agency dedicated to improving the lives of Atlanta citizens with developmental disabilities. Staff and volunteers of AADD provide practical skill training, recreation and community participation for consumers as well as advocacy for their interests. AADD also promotes community education and greater acceptance of people with developmental disabilities.

Emory University Psychological Center
1462 Clifton Rd. N.E., Ste. 235 Dental Bldg. • (404) 727-7451

A component of Emory University's Department of Psychology, this center offers diagnostic and therapeutic services for educational, emotional and neuropsychological difficulties in children, adolescents and adults. The center offers psychotherapy with fees on a sliding scale as well as a broad range of testing services including IQ, achievement, neuropsychological, personality and learning disabilities assessments.

Colleges and Universities

Atlanta's richly varied colleges and universities make it a magnet for students and teachers from around the world. Here we have institutions specializing in a wide range of studies from engineering, law and medicine to religion, art and fashion design.

Beyond their own academic programs, Atlanta's colleges and universities give their students the broader benefits associated with life in a major city that is home to people from

INSIDERS' TIP

Gwinnett County enrolls more children in its public schools than any other in the metro area, with more than 93,500 pupils. Gwinnett is also the leader among districts attracting new students; in 1997 more than 4,600 children were added to the rosters. Fulton County followed, adding 2,845 new students to its rolls.

practically every culture. The Atlanta environment yields great possibilities for enhancing education through arts and cultural events, interaction with the business world, the resources of other area schools and daily exposure to people from all walks of life.

The following is a brief look at some of Atlanta's institutions of higher learning.

Agnes Scott College
141 E. College Ave., Decatur
• **(404) 638-6000**

Six miles east of downtown Atlanta, Agnes Scott College is a private, four-year liberal arts college for women. Founded in 1889 by Decatur Presbyterian Church, it was named for the mother of industrialist and developer Col. George Washington Scott whose $112,000 gift to the school was the largest contribution to education ever made in Georgia at that time. In 1907, Agnes Scott became the first of Georgia's colleges and universities to be accredited.

Today, Agnes Scott's 773 students come from 35 states and 16 countries. The college boasts an 8-to-1 student-faculty ratio; the average class size is 13; 100 of the 66 full-time faculty hold doctorates; 58 percent are women. About 16 percent of students are adult women returning to college to complete degree work. Approximately 85 percent of students life in campus dorms. The library maintains extensive collections relating to Robert Frost, who visited the college 20 times, and Catherine Marshall, alumna, class of '36.

The 100-acre campus is presently involved in a master renovation and expansion that will add parking, residences and administrative offices. ASC's many fine Gothic- and Victorian-style buildings are surrounded by broad lawns, old trees and winding brick walks. Portions of 20 movies, commercials and TV shows have been filmed here, including the *A Man Called Peter*, *Fried Green Tomatoes* and, most recently, *Scream II*.

The Art Institute of Atlanta
3376 Peachtree Rd. N.E.
• **(404) 266-2662**

The Art Institute of Atlanta was founded in 1972. It offers associate of arts degrees in culinary arts, fashion marketing, interior design, website administration, photographic imaging, graphic design, computer animation, multimedia and video production and a bachelor of fine arts degree in interior design and graphic design. Diploma programs are offered in advertising design, commercial photography and residential interiors. The school has programs for professionals in the above fields who want to update or acquire new skills.

The institute's facilities include IBM and Macintosh computer labs with two silicon graphic systems, a multicamera video studio, a computer animation lab, audio and video editing suites, photography studios, four teaching kitchens and labs. Some 1,200 students attend classes at the institute.

Atlanta College of Art
Woodruff Arts Center, 1280 Peachtree St. N.E. • **(404) 733-5001**

Founded in 1928, Atlanta College of Art offers a four-year program leading to a bachelor of fine arts degree. As a founding member of the Woodruff Arts Center, ACA is the only art college in the United States that shares a campus with three major arts organizations: the High Museum of Art, the Alliance Theatre and the Atlanta Symphony Orchestra. Woodruff Arts Center is in Midtown and is served by the Arts Center MARTA station.

Of ACA's 400 students, about 120 are housed on-campus in the six-story Lombardy Hall. The college has 23 full-time and 50 adjunct professors; the student-faculty ratio is 12 to 1. Each year, some 2,000 adults and children participate in the college's community education programs. ACA's facilities include studios, darkrooms, a sculpture building with a wood shop and foundry, a 400-seat auditorium and a 3,850-square-foot gallery that is open to the public free of charge.

Atlanta Metropolitan College
1630 Metropolitan Pkwy.
• **(404) 756-4000**

A coeducational, nonresidential institution, Atlanta Metropolitan College was founded in 1974 and today has more than 2,000 students. The college's 83-acre campus includes wooded areas and a lake.

AMC offers programs leading to associate's degrees in arts, science and applied science. The college offers extensive developmental studies programs for students requiring help with basic English, math and reading skills, and it has a cooperative program with Atlanta Area Technical School.

Bauder College
Phipps Plaza, 3500 Peachtree Rd. N.E.
• (404) 237-7573

A college in a mall? It sounds too good to be true, but Bauder's "campus" is also home to Saks Fifth Avenue, Lord & Taylor and Parisian. The college was founded in 1963 and offers associate of arts degrees in fashion merchandising, business administration, interior design and fashion design. Theoretical knowledge and applied skills are emphasized and provided through a variety of teaching techniques.

Atlanta itself is an important part of the students' education: The college is at one of the Southeast's leading fashion malls in a city that's a regional design and wholesale center — home to the Atlanta Apparel Mart, the Atlanta Merchandise Mart and the Atlanta Decorative Arts Center, the second-largest free-standing design center in the nation.

Bauder has dormitory apartments, for female students only, two blocks from the college. About 500 students are enrolled. The student-teacher ratio is about 18 to 1.

Columbia Theological Seminary
701 Columbia Dr., Decatur
• (404) 378-8821

Founded in South Carolina in 1828, Columbia Theological Seminary relocated in 1925 to a 57-acre campus in Decatur. Affiliated with the Presbyterian Church (USA), Columbia has about 600 students working toward master's (divinity, theological studies, theology) and doctoral (ministry, theology) degrees. The student-teacher ratio is about 12 to 1.

Centered in Biblical, historical and theological disciplines, Columbia's curriculum also includes innovative course work in international education, theology and media, clinical pastoral education, urban ministries, evangelism and spiritual formation. The school attracts clergy and lay persons from across the nation to its seminars, retreats and continuing education programs. Its center for Asian minis-

tries provides exchange programs and educational opportunities for Korean-American churches.

DeVry Institute of Technology
250 N. Arcadia Ave., Decatur
• (404) 292-7900

DeVry/Atlanta, established in 1969, moved to its own 22-acre campus in 1985 and now has more than 3,000 students. The average age of students is 26; 20 percent receive military benefits.

The institute confers bachelor's degrees in accounting, business administration, computer information systems, electronics engineering technology, technical management, telecommunications management and an associate's degree in applied science in electronics. DeVry's students are eligible for the state's Tuition Equalization Grant and HOPE scholarship program. The school boasts a student-to-computer ratio of 6 to 1 and reports that more than 97 percent of graduates who actively pursued employment find jobs in their chosen field within six months of graduation. The school also offers some of its programs at a branch campus in Alpharetta, where the average student age is 30.

Emory University
1380 S. Oxford Rd. N.E. • (404) 727-6123

Emory had just 15 students when it began back in 1836; today more than 11,000 (representing all 50 states, 98 nations) are enrolled there. In addition to the 631-acre Atlanta campus, Emory has a two-year division, Oxford College, in Oxford, Georgia, about 35 miles east of Atlanta.

Emory is made up of the 51-major undergraduate liberal arts Emory College; the graduate school of arts and sciences; Oxford College; schools of medicine, nursing, theology, law, business and public health. The undergraduate student-faculty ratio is 10 to 1. About 30 percent of students live on campus in residence halls and apartments. Emory's five libraries house more than 2 million volumes.

In 1980, Emory received the assets of the Emily and Ernest Woodruff Fund; the $105 million gift was the largest ever given to a philanthropically supported institution up to that time, and during the next dozen years its value more than quintupled. Since 1990 Emory has increased the size of its physical plant, building or acquiring more than 1.6 million square feet. Especially notable is the Michael C. Carlos Museum on campus (designed by famous architect Michael Graves). The Carter Center is an interdisciplinary arm of Emory. Emory University Hospital is a nationally known medical facility (and a favorite of ailing celebrities).

Georgia Institute of Technology
225 North Ave. N.W. • (404) 894-2000

Georgia Tech's reputation extends light years beyond its 330-acre campus west of the Downtown Connector near Midtown. In a 1997 ranking, *U.S. News and World Report* named Tech first in industrial and manufacturing engineering, 5th in aerospace engineering, 7th in mechanical engineering, 9th in civil engineering and 10th in environmental engineering.

During the 1996 Games, Tech was known to people around the world as the Olympic Village. Its 10,000-seat Alexander Memorial Coliseum hosted all 12 medal events in boxing. At the brand-new aquatic center, the water polo pool (seating capacity: 4,000) was the site of all aquatic events except the finals, which were held in the shaded, 15,000-seat aquatic stadium. The village's population included about 15,000 athletes and officials.

Immediately after the Olympics, Tech hosted the 1996 Paralympic Games for physically challenged athletes, using many of the same facilities the Olympics used.

Tech is gaining seven new residence halls as a result of Olympic construction. (Oddly enough, these are not the new buildings most visibly allied to the campus: the tall dorm buildings between Tech and the Downtown Connector will be occupied by Georgia State University students.)

Georgia Tech was established in 1885 and has fared especially well in the past 20 years. More than 13,000 students are enrolled in five colleges: architecture; computing; engineering,; sciences; and management, policy and international affairs. The student population is 74 percent male; 89 percent of freshmen rank in the top 10 percent of their high school class.

Tech's student radio station is WREK 91.1 FM; its mascot is the Yellow Jacket; its nemesis is the Bulldog of the University of Georgia, Athens; and its unofficial dining room is the Varsity, the world's largest drive-in, conveniently located just across the North Avenue bridge from campus.

Georgia Perimeter College
3251 Panthersville Rd., Decatur
• (404) 244-5090

Georgia Perimeter College, formerly DeKalb College, has approximately 16,000 students divided among four campuses: Decatur, Clarkston, Lawrenceville and Dunwoody. There is also a center with classrooms and a library in Conyers. Students work toward two-year associate's degrees in arts, science and applied science.

The average age of the students is late 20s; under the college's flexible schedule, classes are offered in the day, evening and on Saturdays, allowing students to earn their degree while fulfilling their responsibilities of work and family. A special College on TV program allows participating students to view classes and earn credits with a minimal number of visits to a campus.

Two-thirds of students work more than 20 hours a week and attend college part-time. Since Georgia Perimeter College, then DeKalb College, first held classes at its original Clarkston campus in 1964, more than a half-million students have passed through the system. Georgia Perimeter College is the third largest college in the University System of Georgia, which includes all of the state-assisted institutions.

Georgia State University
1 Park Pl. S. • (404) 651-2000

In downtown Atlanta just east of Five Points, GSU is the second-largest institution of higher learning in Georgia and the largest urban university in the Southeast. GSU has its own MARTA rail station, used daily by about 10,000 students, faculty and staff. The university has a total of 23,400 students.

There are 50 academic departments at GSU, divided among six colleges: arts and sciences, business administration, education, health sciences, law and public and urban affairs. There are 150 student organizations on campus, an award-winning student newspaper, *The Signal*, and a popular 100,000-watt student radio station (WRAS 88.5 FM).

Until the fall of 1997, GSU had no dormitories. But after the Olympics, the four dormitories adjacent to Georgia Tech (built at a cost of more than $85 million) were turned into GSU Village. The dorms now house 2,000 students as well as a post office, gym and fitness center and 24-hour security, parking and unlimited free access to MARTA. In addition GSU's physical education complex was remodeled to host the Olympic badminton competition. Work was completed in early 1996 on the renovation of the long-vacant Rialto movie theater (just south of the Central Library) into a concert hall for GSU's performing arts groups, as well as entertainers from around the country.

John Marshall Law School
1422 W. Peachtree St. • (404) 872-3593

John Marshall Law School, located in Midtown, was founded in 1933. The school has 10 full-time and 15 adjunct faculty members as well as a full-time librarian and assistant librarian. Morning, afternoon and evening classes are offered, full or part time. The number of John Marshall students who pass the Georgia Bar Exam the first time they take it has risen from an average of 20 percent to an average of 50 percent in the last four years. The school is accredited by the state of Georgia and is in the process of applying for accreditation by the American Bar Association. John Marshall has 350 students and confers the doctor of jurisprudence degree.

Keller Graduate School of Management
250 N. Arcadia Ave., Decatur
• (404) 298-9444

Founded in Chicago in 1973, Keller's MBA program has grown to become the seventh largest in the country. In 1987 Keller acquired the DeVry Institute system. Keller's Atlanta center opened in 1993; today the school operates 18 centers in eight states.

Telecommunications management is the newest of the eight concentrations offered in Keller's MBA program. Keller also offers master of human resource management and master of project management programs. The programs are geared toward working adults, who often find it easy to continue their studies at another Keller center if they are transferred out of Atlanta. In addition to the main campus, Keller has a north-side facility at Perimeter Center and an Alpharetta campus that opened in the fall of 1997.

Kennesaw State University
1000 Chastain Rd., Kennesaw
• (770) 423-6000

Some 13,000 students attend classes at Kennesaw State, which was founded in 1963 as part of the state's University system. Today, it's nationally recognized as an innovative, teaching-oriented university, offering a wide variety of undergraduate studies in the arts, sciences, education, nursing and business, as well as graduate degrees in business, education, accounting, professional

INSIDERS' TIP

HOPE, Helping Outstanding Pupils Educationally, is one of the three educational initiatives funded by the Georgia Lottery. The program provides recent high school graduates and other eligible residents with financial assistance for degree, diploma or certificate programs at Georgia public or private colleges, universities and technical institutes. Students with 3.0 cumulative grade averages can receive public college scholarships that include tuition, mandatory fees and a book allowance up to $100 per quarter. Students need to reapply for each academic year. In keeping with its name, HOPE offers a second chance for students whose grades slip after the first 45 credit hours. Sophomores may continue their education at their own expense, then reapply for HOPE assistance if they've earned a 3.0 cumulative average by the end of sophomore year.

writing, nursing and public administration. In addition, the school sponsors many free theater, dance and arts activities for the general public.

The campus is off I-75 at Exit 117, 10 miles north of Marietta. Enrollment includes many traditional and nontraditional students. The average student age is 27.

Life University
1269 Barclay Cir., Marietta
• (770) 424-0554

Founded with 22 students in 1974, Life College is now the single-largest chiropractic college in the world and has the world's largest chiropractic library. It has 15 buildings, almost 4,000 students and 265 faculty members. The campus also boasts a historic village of log structures dating from the 1790s that were moved to the school from around the Southeast; it's free and open to the public seven days a week during daylight hours.

Life confers the degrees doctor of chiropractic, bachelor of business administration, bachelor of science in nutrition for the chiropractic sciences, bachelor of science in nutrition for dietetics and master of sport health science. The college has more than 50 service, social and fraternal clubs and many sports teams, including nationally ranked basketball, track and rugby teams.

Mercer University
Cecil B. Day Campus, 3001 Mercer
University Dr. • (770) 986-3000

The second-largest Baptist-affiliated institution in the world, Mercer University was founded in 1833 and is based in Macon, Georgia. It has been rated one of the top 15 schools in the South by *U.S. News and World Report* for the last eight years. The 335-acre Cecil B. Day Campus in Atlanta is known as Mercer's Graduate and Professional Center, although it also offers undergraduate programs. Approximately 1,000 full-time and 700 part-time students at the Atlanta campus study programs including pharmacy, business and economics, education and engineering. The university offers off-campus centers in Douglas County and Covington, as well as at Grady Hospital and the Georgia Power Co.

Oglethorpe University
4484 Peachtree Rd. • (404) 261-1441

Named for the founder of Georgia, James Edward Oglethorpe, Oglethorpe University was founded in 1835 by Georgia Presbyterians to train ministers. It was originally located near Milledgeville, at that time the capital of Georgia. During the Civil War, the university's students became soldiers, its buildings became barracks and hospitals, and its endowment became worthless Confederate bonds. The college closed in 1862 and tried unsuccessfully to reorganize in Atlanta during Reconstruction.

Oglethorpe University was rechartered in 1913; two years later the cornerstone was laid for the present 118-acre campus, whose layout and Gothic Revival architecture were inspired by Corpus Christi College, Oxford, England, the honorary alma mater of James Oglethorpe.

The university's 1,230 students hail from 32 states and 31 nations; 50 percent are from Georgia. The student-faculty ratio is 13 to 1; 96 percent of faculty members hold terminal degrees. Internships are available in all of the school's 28 undergraduate and three graduate academic majors.

The International Time Capsule Society is headquartered at Oglethorpe, and there, behind a great steel door, lies the "Crypt of Civilization." This time capsule was considered finest ever developed when it was sealed in 1940. Its contents include a machine to teach English, a quart of Budweiser, a coffee maker and a Lionel train. It's not yet time to begin lining up for your place at the capsule's unsealing — check our Insiders' Guide for 8113 A.D.!

Southern Polytechnic State University
1100 South Marietta Pkwy., Marietta
• (770) 528-7281

Approximately 4,000 students are studying for their bachelor's and master's degrees at this school, founded in 1948 as the Southern College of Technology. The student population, from 33 states and 76 countries, attend day, evening and continuing education classes in 16 science programs. Master's programs include computer science, construction, engineering technology, management of technology, software engineering, technical and professional communication and quality assurance. The student-teacher ratio is 19 to 1.

Atlanta University Center

Atlanta University Center is a consortium of six historically black colleges in southwest Atlanta. Together, the six colleges form the largest predominantly African-American private institute of higher learning in the nation. Although the six institutions share a library and cooperate in many areas, they remain distinct from one another. The following is a look at Atlanta University Center's six member colleges.

Clark Atlanta University
223 James P. Brawley Dr.
• (404) 880-8000

Clark Atlanta University was formed in 1988 through the consolidation of Atlanta University, founded in 1865, and Clark College, founded in 1869. CAU is one of only two private, comprehensive, historically black universities in the nation offering programs of instruction and research from bachelor to doctorate degrees.

CAU's approximately 5,000-member student body is 69 percent female. The university provides on-campus housing for 1,800 students. The student-faculty ratio is 16 to 1. Several of CAU's dormitories provided the setting for Spike Lee's movie *School Daze*. CAU operates the popular jazz radio station WCLK 91.9 FM.

Clark Atlanta's new 5,000-seat stadium was one of two venues used for hockey competition during the Olympics. A new 470-bed dormitory, built for use by the Atlanta Committee for the Olympic Games, houses students. CAU was also the official institution for the Olympic Host Broadcast Training Program, which trained 1,200 college students to work with national and international professional journalists during the Games. More than $2 million of the program's state-of-the-art digital equipment was donated by Panasonic Broadcast Television Corp.

Interdenominational Theological Center
671 Beckwith St. S.W. • (404) 527-7700

Established in 1958, the Interdenominational Theological Center is made up of six separate seminaries: Gammon Theological Seminary, United Methodist, founded in 1872; Charles H. Mason Theological Seminary, Church of God in Christ, founded in 1970; Morehouse School of Religion, Baptist, founded in 1867; Phillips School of Theology, Christian Methodist Episcopal, founded in 1944; Johnson C. Smith Theological Seminary, Presbyterian Church USA, founded in 1867; and Turner Theological Seminary, African Methodist Episcopal, founded in 1894.

ITC's approximately 400 students come from 32 states and seven nations. ITC offers master's (divinity, Christian education and church music) and doctoral (ministry, theology and pastoral counseling) degrees.

Since its formation in 1958, ITC has graduated more than 25 percent of all trained black ministers in the world. ITC's James H. Costen Lifelong Education Center was used as Olympic housing during the 1996 Games.

Morehouse College
830 Westview Dr. S.W. • (404) 681-2800

Established as Augusta Institute in Augusta, Georgia, in 1867, this college relocated to Atlanta in 1879, where it was first known as Atlanta Baptist College and then, in 1913, as Morehouse College.

Today, Morehouse is the nation's only predominantly African-American, all-male liberal arts college. Its 3,000 students represent 40 states and 12 foreign countries; more than half graduate high school in the top 20 percent of their class. Of its 212 faculty members, almost 95 percent of assistant professors and above hold doctorate degrees. Morehouse confers bachelor of arts and bachelor of science degrees in 35 major areas of study.

Morehouse's most famous alumnus was Nobel laureate Dr. Martin Luther King Jr.; Morehouse is also where filmmaker Spike Lee spent his *School Daze*. Fourteen Morehouse men have gone on to serve as president of a college or university.

Morehouse's 6,000-seat arena was the site of early rounds of men's and women's basketball competition during the Olympics.

Morehouse School of Medicine
720 Westview Dr. S.W. • (404) 752-1500

Morehouse School of Medicine began with 24 students in 1975; today it has approximately 160 students. The 205-member faculty includes many off-site community physicians who work with interns and students. MSM confers the four-year doctor of medicine degree, the Ph.D. degree in biomedical sciences and a master's degree in public health.

Residency programs have been established in family medicine, internal medicine, preventive medicine, psychiatry, obstetrics, gynecology and surgery. In conjunction with testing services to be performed, the Atlanta Committee for the Olympic Games provided $1 million to help MSM establish a research laboratory to study sports performance-enhancing drugs.

Morris Brown College
643 Martin Luther King Jr. Dr. N.W.
• (404) 220-0270

In 1881, Morris Brown College first held classes for 107 students in a wooden building at the corner of Boulevard and Houston Street. Its name honors the memory of the second consecrated bishop in the African Methodist Episcopal Church; the college was founded through the generosity of the members of Big Bethel AME on Auburn Avenue.

For the past 47 years, Morris Brown College has been fully and continuously accredited by the Southern Association of Colleges and Schools. Its faculty members take pride in motivating not only average and better-than-average students but also those considered to be high risk. Today, more than 2,100 students are pursuing degrees in more than 40 areas of study. The student-teacher ratio is about 36 to 1.

Morris Brown's 15,000-seat Alonzo Herndon Stadium was the site of the finals in men's and women's hockey during the Olympics.

Spelman College
350 Spelman Ln. S.W. • (404) 681-3643

Founded in 1881, Spelman College is one of the oldest U.S. institutions dedicated to the education of African-American women. Recent years have brought new recognition to the long-respected school: Spelman has repeatedly made the top-10 list of U.S. women's colleges and the top-10 Southeast colleges in *Money* magazine's "Best Buys" issue. In 1997, the magazine ranked Spelman as the very best buy among historically black colleges. Highly acclaimed Dr. Johnetta B. Cole, who declined an offer to serve as U.S. secretary of education for the first Clinton administration, resigned in June 1997 after 10 years at the helm. During Dr. Cole's tenure Oprah Winfrey donated $1 million to Spelman's capital fund and praised "the extraordinary legacy of Spelman College and Dr. Johnetta Cole." Dr. Cole, who will take up an endowed professorship at Emory University in the fall of 1998, was followed by Dr. Audrey Forbes Manley, the school's eighth president and the first to come from its alumnae ranks (Class of '55).

Spelman has just more than 2,000 students and a student-faculty ratio of 14 to 1. More than 81 percent of full-time faculty have doctorate or other advanced degrees. Nearly half the students are engaged in some form of community service; 37 percent major in math or the natural sciences. Upon graduation, 45 percent of Spelman women continue their studies.

Resources

Southern Association of Colleges and Schools
1866 Southern Ln., Decatur
• (404) 679-4500

Call this association if you need help trying to decide which college to attend. It can provide information on schools throughout the region.

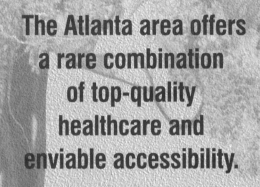

**The Atlanta area offers
a rare combination
of top-quality
healthcare and
enviable accessibility.**

Healthcare

We hope you'll be healthy and happy during your stay in Atlanta. But if you happen to get sick or injured, you've come to the right place. As a regional center for healthcare and research, the Atlanta area offers a rare combination of top-quality healthcare and enviable accessibility.

The Atlanta metropolitan area boasts a wealth of top-notch doctors and medical facilities, which says a lot about the desirability of the Atlanta area as a place to live. It also reflects the steady stream of new doctors, nurses and allied health professionals graduating from the many training centers in the metro and surrounding areas.

Medical students train at Emory University's School of Medicine and Morehouse School of Medicine, while future pharmacists study at Mercer University's Southern School of Pharmacy. Nursing programs are offered at Clayton State College, DeKalb College, Emory University, Georgia State University, Kennesaw State College, Morris Brown College and Oglethorpe University. The Medical College of Georgia Schools of Medicine and Nursing in Augusta and the Mercer College of Medicine in Macon are within two- to three-hour driving distance of the city.

Health-related research at these schools benefits Atlantans as well as thousands of healthcare seekers from all parts of the United States and the world. Because Atlanta is a national center in medical research, residents have the opportunity to participate in many clinical research trials that evaluate new treatments.

Numerous major medical organizations have headquarters in Atlanta. Foremost in this category is the **Centers for Disease Control and Prevention (CDC)**, an agency of the Public Health Service. A major research facility with programs taking place in the Atlanta headquarters and at field stations, health departments and other facilities throughout the world, CDC is an institution dedicated to promoting health and quality of life by preventing and controlling disease, injury and disability.

The **American Cancer Society's** national Atlanta headquarters coordinates and supports the state and county divisions of this, the largest voluntary health agency in the world. Although no research takes place at this office, the staff administers and supports the society's national research programs taking place at various venues throughout the country.

The **Arthritis Foundation** national headquarters coordinates research and offers nationwide community-based services including self-help courses, exercise classes, support groups and instructional video tapes. The foundation provides educational brochures and booklets for the public and publishes a national bimonthly consumer magazine, *Arthritis Today*.

Yerkes Regional Primate Research Center at Emory University is the oldest scientific institute dedicated to primate research. Yerkes Main Station facility specializes in biomedical research; the 117-acre Field Station studies primate social groups.

Georgia Institute of Technology Research Institute is one of the country's premier bioengineering programs producing advances in prosthetics and engineered assistance for the disabled. Tech's Medical Informatic Research Group, part of Georgia Tech's Graphics, Visualization and Usability Center, is exploring ways in which computer science methods and techniques can help solve problems in medicine and biomedicine.

The **Carter Center**, a separately chartered, independently governed part of Emory University, counts Global 2000 among its many other programs and initiatives. Global 2000 is a coalition of governments, corporations, individuals and organizations that addresses global environmental, agricultural, economic and public health concerns. Among its other accomplishments, Global 2000 has been instrumental in helping to eradicate Guinea worm disease and in building a modern center for the design and manufacture of artificial limbs in China. The Task Force for Child Survival and Development, headquartered at the Carter Center, addresses issues of immunization, malnutrition, disease control and child advocacy.

Since there are 50 or so medical facilities of varying sizes within the four-county area we focus on, and dozens more within close range, we can't do justice to their multispecialty programs in one chapter. We are, instead, providing an overview. Consider our thumbnail sketches the tip of the iceberg, and know that whatever your medical or mental health need, skilled and dedicated healthcare professionals in the Atlanta area are ready to serve you.

The major HMOs also have facilities throughout the metro-Atlanta area in ever increasing numbers: You'll find their main numbers listed in this chapter so that you may call to locate offices and/or affiliated physicians close by.

The metropolitan Atlanta area has a number of strategically located trauma centers. A rating of Level I trauma care indicates the hospital offers the most extensive, immediate and round-the-clock services for emergency, life-threatening needs. A Level II rating indicates 24-hour capability for surgery and specialty care. A Level III rating means these services, surgery and specialty care, are usually available within 30 minutes to an hour.

We present hospitals within the perimeter of I-285 as being in the city of Atlanta and list those outside the perimeter by county.

Hospitals

Atlanta

Columbia Metropolitan Hospital
3223 Howell Mill Rd. N.W.
• (404) 351-0500
Columbia Metropolitan Hospital, a specialty surgical facility, became part of Columbia West Paces Medical Center in 1994. The

hospital offers general surgery along with specialties such as laparoscopic surgery, oral and maxillofacial surgery and dentistry, plastic and reconstructive surgery, sports medicine and broncho-esophagealogy.

Columbia West Paces Medical Center
3200 Howell Mill Rd. N.W.
• (404) 351-0351
The 294-bed Columbia West Paces Medical Center is fully accredited by the Joint Commission on the Accreditation of Healthcare Organizations and utilizes the services of 600 trained physicians and an equal number of employees. Since 1972, an ever increasing variety of inpatient and outpatient programs, including general surgery, inpatient and outpatient psychiatric care, cardiology and cardiac catheterization, alcohol and substance abuse programs and endocrinology, have been made available.

The Cancer Center at West Paces offers comprehensive care for patients from diagnosis through all stages of treatment. The Center sponsors cancer support groups and has a cancer resource library.

The hospital's Behavioral Health Services offers many programs designed to reduce stress and alleviate anxiety. The Wound Care Center, Pain Management Center and Rehabilitation Services are additional areas of focus. The hospital's Greater Atlanta Sports Medicine program offers education and research, orthopedic evaluation, treatment and rehabilitation and The Birthing Center includes high-risk obstetrics, an eight-bed, Level III Neonatal Intensive Care Unity and certified nurse midwifery for deliveries in a private Labor, Delivery and Recovery (LDR) suite. Columbia West Paces Medical Center has a Level II trauma emergency department.

Columbia West Paces Medical Center and Columbia Metropolitan Hospital are part of the Columbia/HCA Healthcare Corporation.

Crawford Long Hospital of Emory University
550 Peachtree St. N.E. • (404) 686-4411
This hospital's name honors Dr. Crawford W. Long, the Atlanta surgeon who first used ether as anesthesia. Part of Emory Healthcare,

the 583-bed hospital offers a 24-hour emergency department and more than 600 board-certified or board-eligible physicians on staff.

Situated off the I-75/85 Downtown Connector (Exit 100), Crawford Long provides easy access for those in the central business district and Atlanta's downtown convention and tourism zone.

Crawford Long offers a wide spectrum of services: pulmonary medicine, thoracic and cardiovascular surgery, gastrointestinal medicine, gynecology and obstetrics, oncology, international travel medicine, plastic and reconstructive surgery and neonatology. Additional services include outpatient surgery and radiology, family-centered maternity care, a menopause center and in-vitro fertilization. The hospital's nationally recognized Carlyle Fraser Heart Center, now part of the Emory Heart Center, is dedicated to the prevention, diagnosis and treatment of heart and lung disorders.

Crawford Long was one of the first facilities in Georgia to have a cancer program approved by the American College of Surgeons. The hospital pioneered a treatment for prostate cancer called cryosurgery, which offers a shorter recovery period than traditional methods.

Volunteer international interpreters, who together speak more than 25 languages, assist patients and physicians. Crawford Long also provides speakers to business and civic organizations and offers many wellness, health information and screening programs.

DeKalb Medical Center
2701 N. Decatur Rd., Decatur
• (404) 501-1000

For more than 36 years, DeKalb Medical Center has provided the community with a variety of diagnostic, treatment and prevention services. The 523-bed, not-for-profit acute-care medical center has a medical staff of more than 800 physicians representing more than 40 specialty areas.

The medical center's programs and services include a 24-hour emergency department offering trauma triage and chest pain emergency center services, extensive wellness and health promotion programs and comprehensive cardiology and critical care services. Their surgery center was the first in Atlanta to

be fully equipped with fixed video surgery capabilities.

Other specialties include an extensive cancer program approved by the American College of Surgeons and family-centered maternity services featuring comfortable maternity suites, a Level III neonatal intensive care unit and specialized perinatology services for high-risk pregnancies. DeKalb Medical Center also offers a full array of rehabilitation and occupational health programs and a variety of behavioral health services.

Egleston Children's Hospital at Emory University
1405 Clifton Rd. N.E. • (404) 325-6000

Founded in 1916, Egleston Children's Hospital, a 235-bed facility, is the heart of Georgia's largest children's healthcare system, Egleston Children's Health Care System. Top pediatricians treat more than 100,000 children each year at the hospital and in 10 neighborhood centers. As a major referral center for the Southeast, the system has several nationally recognized programs, including the AFLAC Cancer Center at Egleston Hospital and the Emory Egleston Children's Heart Center.

The hospital provides comprehensive pediatric care ranging from the diagnosis and treatment of ear infections to complex diseases. Egleston physicians also perform heart surgery and organ transplants. As a clinical, teaching and research institution, the hospital offers all subspecialities in medical care. It enjoys a Level I rating for trauma care.

Egleston excels in several areas, including treatment of cystic fibrosis, care for brain tumors, orthopedics, medical-psychiatry patients and premature infants.

Egleston's Children's Advocacy Center disseminates injury prevention messages through billboards, newspapers, magazines, television and radio. Egleston is headquarters for SAFE KIDS of Georgia, a statewide coalition focusing on injury prevention. Each year, more than 500 heart surgeries are performed at Egleston Children's Hospital. It is the state's only pediatric facility to perform a full range of pediatric transplants and kidney dialysis.

The hospital's pediatric network includes outpatient services and treatment for minor injuries or illnesses. Satellite clinics in Gwinnett,

Cobb, Fulton and DeKalb counties put Egleston's services within easy range of many metro residents.

Emory University Hospital
1364 Clifton Rd. N.E. • (404) 712-7021

In March 1904, Wesley Memorial Hospital, Emory Hospital's predecessor, opened with 50 beds in a downtown Atlanta mansion that Sherman's Army spared during the Civil War. When the hospital needed bigger quarters in 1922, Coca-Cola founder and philanthropist Asa G. Candler donated a 275-bed facility on the hospital's current site on the Emory University campus. Today, the university-owned, not-for-profit institution has 587 beds, including 484 beds in the main facility, 56 in the Center for Rehabilitation Medicine, 47 beds for psychiatric treatment in the Uppergate Pavilion and 12 beds in an NIH-funded Clinical Research Center.

The hospital is one of the nation's largest centers for heart surgery and angioplasty and a referral center of choice for the most difficult cardiac cases. Emory's innovative Chest Pain Center provides 24-hour care to individuals experiencing symptoms of a heart attack. The Center offers immediate access to cardiology experts without a physician's referral.

Emory has a multiple organ and tissue transplantation program that includes heart, heart-lung, lung, heart-kidney, liver, kidney, kidney-pancreas, bone, bone marrow, cornea and sclera transplantation. The hospital also leads in the neurosciences, especially in the surgical treatment of aneurysms, brain tumors and movement disorders such as Parkinson's disease.

Although it's considered a general acute care facility, Emory Hospital doesn't provide maternity or pediatric services. The hospital is part of the Emory Healthcare, which is also comprised of Crawford Long Hospital of Emory University, the Emory Clinic and affiliates such as Egleston Children's Hospital and Wesley Woods Geriatric Center.

FYI

Three area codes serve the metro Atlanta area: 404, 770 and 678. Whether you live on Peachtree Street or in New York City, you must dial the code to reach any number in the area. The difference? Outside the area, you must dial "1," then the area code and phone number; inside the area, you need only dial the area code followed by the phone number.

Georgia Baptist Medical Center
303 Parkway Dr. N.E. • (404) 265-4000

From its 97-year heritage, Georgia Baptist has grown to more than 467 beds and approximately 2,500 employees. Part of the Georgia Baptist Health Care System, the facility offers the services of more than 500 physicians. Georgia Baptist's nursing school, established in 1902, now offers a four-year baccalaureate degree program that meets nurses' more demanding roles in today's healthcare field. The Medical Center is affiliated with the Medical College of Georgia and boasts a highly sought-after residency program.

The not-for-profit, general acute care institution has several centers of excellence, including heart, cancer, orthopedics, obstetrics and gynecology. The Medical Center has a 30-bed neonatal intensive care unit.

Georgia Baptist's Harris Cancer Center, in the Mary Thompson Way Building at 345 Boulevard, employs a multidisciplinary approach to cancer care. The Center supports cancer patients by providing treatment, education, counseling and research.

Georgia Baptist offers such highly technical services as laser angioplasty for the treatment of heart disease. The Center's nationally renowned cardiac rehabilitation program offers comprehensive physical, occupational and speech rehabilitation therapies.

Atlanta's first hospital-based aeromedical service is based at Georgia Baptist. The Life Flight program transports patients from accident sites and other medical facilities and is fully staffed for extreme emergencies. Georgia Baptist also offers the Transportation Express, a free ground transport system between the primary care locations and the main Medical Center campus. Equipped for handicapped patients in wheelchairs, the shuttle operates Monday through Saturday for stable patients who don't need medical care while in transit. Family members and friends may use the service to visit patients. Georgia Baptist Health

Care System has satellite facilities in the outlying areas of Morrow, Fayetteville, Palmetto, Stockbridge, Cumming and Peachtree City.

Grady Memorial Hospital
80 Butler St. S.E. • (404) 6l6-4307

This hospital, opened in 1892, is named for Henry W. Grady, a visionary Atlantan who promoted the progressive philosophy of the "New South." In the heart of downtown, Grady Memorial functions primarily to meet the healthcare needs of medically indigent residents of Fulton and DeKalb counties. Last year 4,315 women visited Grady for prenatal care, and 1,422 births took place in the maternity ward.

The hospital offers emergency care to anyone requiring it, as long as they can prove citizenship. Grady has four emergency centers, including a highly-rated Level I Trauma Center that provides round-the-clock care in surgery, anesthesia and specialized services such as neurosurgery and obstetrical surgery.

Grady's Georgia Poison Control Center stays open 24 hours a day, staffed by physicians, registered nurses, pharmacists and certified poison information specialists. The Rape Crisis Center provides a 24-hour hotline, examinations and medications as well as individual, family and group counseling.

Grady's Burn Center is one of the nation's largest. The National Institute of Health named Grady's Sickle Cell Center a National Center of Excellence. Grady has also been praised for its TB control and tracking program and for having the most comprehensive AIDS program in the nation. The hospital also operates a Regional Perinatal Center for high-risk mothers, a Diabetes Detection and Control Center and a Teen Center with programs to help teens postpone sexual involvement.

Grady is affiliated with the Emory University and Morehouse Schools of Medicine. It serves as a major training and research center and offers patients the latest advancements in various medical fields. The Grady Health System comprises many components, among them: Hughes Spalding Children's Hospital, five comprehensive Community Health Centers, two Women's and Children's Health Centers and a 400,000-square-foot Pavilion of Outpatient Care Centers, Operating Rooms,

Women's Health Services, Intensive Care Units and the Neonatal Intensive Care Nursery. The hospital also operates a 24-hour nurse advice line at (404) 616-0600.

Hughes Spalding Pediatric Hospital
35 Butler St. • (404) 616-6600

Founded in 1892 under the auspices of Grady Memorial Hospital, Hughes Spalding became a freestanding hospital in 1992. Hughes Spalding offers a full range of primary and acute care pediatric services for children from infancy to 18 years of age.

Specially trained pediatric physicians, nurses and staff members offer advanced pediatric expertise in areas such as respiratory care, physical therapy, diagnostic radiology, laboratory services and social services. Hughes Spalding's Emergency Care Center offers round-the-clock service in an urgent care center and in a walk-in clinic for patients with less urgent needs. Hughes Spalding uses nearby Grady Memorial for specialty pediatric care in a variety of fields including dermatology, ophthalmology, otolaryngology, genitourinary and pediatric surgery.

Northside Hospital
1000 Johnson Ferry Rd. N.E.
• (404) 851-8000

Northside Hospital is a 455-bed, not-for-profit, full-service community hospital serving the north Atlanta community. More than 1,425 physicians from a variety of fields staff the hospital, which cares for more than 100,000 patients annually.

With 12,000 babies born at Northside each year, the hospital ranks first in the nation among community hospitals in the baby delivery business. The hospital provides a Perinatal Diagnostic Unit as well as a High-Risk Perinatal Unit for women who must be hospitalized during high-risk pregnancies.

The hospital's Breast Care Center houses state-of-the art-equipment, and Northside's staff includes surgeons who are nationally known for treating complicated gynecological conditions. Staff surgeons helped pioneer videolaparoscopy, a technique that dramatically reduces recovery time for many operations. Northside opened Atlanta's first outpatient surgery center more than two decades ago.

Northside's Institute for Cancer Control features an American Cancer Society Information Center. Here patients find out about a program in which former cancer patients spend time with current patients and the "Look Good . . . Feel Better" program, which offers consultations on how to cope with the physical changes brought on by chemotherapy and radiation.

ScreenAtlanta, Northside Hospital's mobile health screening unit, fosters cancer's early detection by bringing education and low-cost screening procedures to the community. At the request of businesses and other organizations, the ScreenAtlanta van travels throughout metro Atlanta, offering tests for lung function, cholesterol and diabetes as well as computerized cancer risk assessment and information on breast, testicular, oral, skin and colorectal cancer. The mobile mammography van provides mammograms for $65.

Northside offers a variety of support groups and classes addressing such topics as parenting, children's issues, adolescence, divorce, assertiveness skills, stress reduction and communications skills. The hospital's Recovery Center focuses on programs and groups for adults and adolescents whose lives have been affected by alcohol and/or drug abuse.

Northside operates a 24-hour major emergency department. For minor emergencies, Northside's Health Express, open Monday through Friday from 11:30 AM to 8 PM, eliminates long waits.

Piedmont Hospital
1968 Peachtree Rd. N.W. • (404) 605-5000

On a ridge nicknamed "Heartbreak Hill" by the approximately 50,000 runners who pant up it during the annual Peachtree Road Race, Piedmont Hospital sits on historically significant land. It was at this Civil War site that troops from Confederate General Hardee's corps fought Union soldiers during the Battle of Peachtree Creek. A stone monument on the property commemorates that struggle.

Throughout most of this century, Piedmont Hospital has mirrored the growth of the Buckhead district it calls home. Founded as a 10-bed sanitarium in 1905, Piedmont now has 458 beds for acute care and a 42-bed extended care/skilled nursing care facility on its 26-acre site. More than 2,300 employees and a medical staff of more than 800 physicians offer care in every major category of medicine.

Piedmont Hospital offers obstetrics and women's services at the Maternity and Women's Center, a Breast Health Center and a Prostate Center. The Fuqua Heart Center of Atlanta at Piedmont provides cardiology and cardiovascular surgery services including open heart surgery. Piedmont also boasts The Sports Medicine Institute/Reconstructive Joint Center of Atlanta. Injured players from Atlanta's professional sports teams go to Piedmont for their sports-related medical procedures.

At Piedmont's Neuroscience Institute, neurosurgeons perform Gamma Knife surgery, a technique that uses sharply-focused gamma radiation to treat many brain tumors and vascular malformations without incision. Gamma Knife procedures take about half a day and patients can often resume normal activities the next day.

Among its other services, the hospital offers oncology, an inpatient rehabilitation unit and the Katherine Murphy Riley Outpatient Diagnostic Center. The T. Harvey Mathis Rehabilitation and Fitness Center includes The Piedmont Hospital Health and Fitness Club for employees and members of the community.

The hospital's Level III 24-hour emergency department features a fly-in helipad atop the building. Patients with minor illnesses and injuries can seek treatment at the Piedmont Medical Care Center in Brookhaven and Sandy Springs (see our section on Walk-in Clinics in this chapter).

In 1994 Piedmont Medical Center, Inc. became a founding partner of the PROMINA Health System. PROMINA is an alliance of 10 hospitals and numerous other primary and urgent care facilities operated by Piedmont Medical Center Inc., Gwinnett Hospital System, Inc. and Northwest Georgia Health System, Inc.

Saint Joseph's Hospital of Atlanta
5665 Peachtree Dunwoody Rd. N.E.
• **(404) 851-7001**

This is Atlanta's first hospital, established in 1880 by the Sisters of Mercy. A private, not-for-profit, 346-bed facility, it counts cardiac care, cancer care and orthopedic care as three specialty areas. Medical staff includes more than 700 physicians.

Well established as a regional referral hospital, Saint Joseph's provides outreach healthcare to the medically underserved and working poor through the Mercy Mobile Health Care Program.

Saint Joseph's has scored a number of firsts in cardiac care, among them, the first in the Southeast to perform open-heart surgery. Saint Joseph's features one of the busiest cardiac catheterization programs in the country; the hospital staff includes a heart transplantation team. Annually it performs more than 2,000 open-heart procedures.

The Specialty Center for Cancer Care & Research at Saint Joseph's houses the Community Clinical Oncology Program which coordinates nearly 100 clinical trials investigating various therapies for cancer and cancer prevention.

The hospital's orthopedic program provides joint replacement surgery and shoulder and knee reconstruction. Last year, the hospital opened the Specialty Center for Wellness & Rehabilitation Care. The center provides various rehabilitation services for conditions such as voice and swallowing problems and incontinence. Outpatient hospital services include a breast health center and surgery. Saint Joseph's coordinates vascular and gastrointestinal services and has a fully-staffed 24-hour emergency department.

Scottish Rite Children's Medical Center
1001 Johnson Ferry Rd. N.E.
• **(404) 256-5252**

This north Atlanta multispecialty pediatric center opened in 1915 as a small facility for indigent, disabled children. Since then, the facility has grown into a premier children's medical center, equipped to provide general pediatric care as well as advanced subspecialty care.

Scottish Rite Children's Medical Center is strongly committed to children's health, welfare and development. Pediatric advocacy programs include the Scottish Rite Child Care Fund, which offers financial aid; the Child Advocacy Center, the only hospital-based center in Georgia for child victims of sexual abuse; "Immunize Georgia's Little Guys," a coalition of businesses, organizations and individuals dedicated to raising the state's immunization rate for children aged 1-24 months; and various community education and parenting programs aimed toward keeping children healthy.

Scottish Rite's 24-hour pediatric emergency/trauma center is staffed with private-practice pediatricians. The center has 24 exam rooms including two pediatric trauma rooms and two X-ray suites. Two helicopter landing pads and two covered ambulance bays provide direct access for critically injured or ill children. Child-size equipment and an emergency staff trained to minimize pain and fear ensure an atmosphere of compassionate, competent care. The emergency center has a computerized diagnostic system for hard-to-diagnose cases.

Specialty areas at Scottish Rite include the Hematology/Oncology Center; the Asthma Education Center; the Pulmonology Function, Sleep Disorder and Bronchoscopy Laboratories; the Children's Epilepsy Center; and the Center for Craniofacial Disorders. Scottish Rite also has an extensive orthopedics program and comprehensive inpatient and outpatient rehabilitation units for children recovering from severe head and spinal cord trauma.

South Fulton Medical Center
1170 Cleveland Ave., East Point
• **(404) 305-3500**

South Fulton Medical Center (SFMC) is a 465-bed, not-for-profit hospital that provides a wide spectrum of medical services to the south metro Atlanta area. Conveniently located in East Point, the hospital is easily accessible from I-85 and I-75.

SFMC services include a Breast Health Center; a primary care center; a free physician referral and health information service; maternity care, complete with a Level II special care nursery; oncology; and cardiology. SFMC's rehabilitation center is the only facility of its kind south of I-20 for strokes, brain injuries and bone fractures. The hospital also provides wellness and community outreach programs, nuclear medicine and MRI, and inpatient and outpatient surgery.

SFMC's emergency room is the designated receiving center for Hartsfield-Atlanta International Airport. To meet the area's growing need for primary care physicians, South Fulton Medical Center has placed physicians specializing in internal medicine, family practice and OB/GYN in satellite offices throughout the south metro area.

Southwest Hospital and Medical Center
501 Fairburn Rd. S.W. • (404) 699-1111

Southwest dates back to 1943 when the Society of Catholic Medical Mission Sisters established the Catholic Colored Clinic in response to a lack of adequate medical care in south Atlanta. By 1974 governance of the hospital had passed to a Board of Trustees with an official name being bestowed in 1975. Southwest proudly proclaims its status as one of only six institutions of its kind in the nation that is owned, governed and managed by African Americans.

The 125-bed hospital's medical staff includes more than 200 physicians. In 1981, Southwest formed an affiliation with Morehouse School of Medicine for clinical training and services. The facility's Primary Care Center specializes in the treatment of children and adolescents.

Southwest offers cardiopulmonary services, a certified mammography program, maternity care, nuclear medicine, a gastroenterology lab, an intensive care unit, physical therapy, ultrasound and outpatient surgery. The radiology and laboratory departments perform diagnostic procedures. Southwest also has a 24-hour emergency

department. The Fulton County Department of Family and Children's Services (DFCS) operates on the hospital campus out of an $8.5 million complex.

V.A. Medical Center — Atlanta
1670 Clairmont Rd., Decatur
• (404) 321-6111

For our visitors and new residents who are veterans, this federally owned hospital provides general acute care in addition to a wide range of other services. With 455 beds in its general medical and surgical facility and 150 beds in the nursing home care unit, the VA Hospital, as it's locally known, is well-prepared to provide patients with quality medical care.

Affiliated with the Emory University School of Medicine, the VA Hospital carries on a broad-based research program with more than 73 investigators who participate in research projects focused on AIDS, Alzheimer's disease, cancer, infectious disease and many other health concerns. The hospital's Atlanta Rehabilitation Research and Development Center on Aging conducts research to identify the rehabilitative needs of older veterans, especially those with disabilities.

Special services include cardiac catheterization, open heart surgery and prosthetics programs for veterans with complex amputations. Clinical programs offer substance abuse and post traumatic stress disorder treatment, gynecology and gerontology, to name a few.

Wesley Woods Geriatric Center at Emory University
1821 Clifton Rd. N.E. • (404) 728-6200

Wesley Woods Geriatric Hospital, on the Emory University campus, is part of Emory Healthcare. The facility has four 25-bed units, each housing a different geriatric specialty service: acute and long-term acute medicine, psychiatry, neuropsychiatry and rehabilitation.

INSIDERS' TIP

Scottish Rite Hospital's RiteCall, (404) 250-KIDS, is a 24-hour information line offering such helpful hints as to how to get the little tike toilet trained, what to do if the baby won't sleep, how to handle the terrible twos and 4000+ other child-related topics. Just dial the number, punch in "4," then "1010," and pick from a category of topics to get prerecorded advice.

More than 100,000 children are treated at Egleston Children's Hospital each year.

Each specialty also sponsors outpatient assessment and treatment clinics.

Wesley Woods, Inc., the corporate umbrella of all the Wesley facilities in Georgia, has created a network of apartment and cottage residential retirement facilities throughout the state. In Atlanta, Asbury Harris Epworth Towers, Branan Towers and Wesley Woods Towers give senior citizens affordable housing options that feature a variety of floor plans, nutritious meals, planned activities, transportation and other services. Wesley Woods Towers also offers assisted living apartments. Budd Terrace offers long-term nursing care with 236 beds.

Wesley Woods' Cecil B. Day Alzheimer's Disease Pavilion is recognized as the preeminent center for Alzheimer's disease in the state. The hospital's geriatric neurologists and psychiatrists diagnose and treat patients with memory loss, movement disorders, sleep disorders, suspected dementia and other complex psychiatric and behavioral problems.

The Aging Helpline we mention in our "Numbers to Call" section is staffed by Wesley Woods personnel. They also have an Intake & Assessment Line. Dial (404) 728-6222 from 8 AM to 5 PM for expert advice and assistance from registered nurses and easy access to staff specialists.

Atlanta Specialty Hospitals

Charter Behavioral Health System of Atlanta at Laurel Heights
934 Briarcliff Rd. N.E. • (404) 888-7860

This licensed psychiatric hospital has more than 100 beds and approximately 150 employees on staff. Laurel Heights offers intensive residential care for children and adolescents, ages 5 to 17, and their families.

Charter Laurel Heights intensive residential treatment program provides long-term treatment for young people ages 4 to 17 and their families. In a highly structured environment, youth with emotional and behavioral problems learn to take responsibility for their choices in life. Year-round schooling by accredited teachers are also made available so that their general education will not be neglected.

Charter Midtown
811 Juniper St. N.E. • (404) 881-5800

Part of the Charter Behavioral Health System, Charter Midtown, the former site of Psychiatric Institute of Atlanta, is a 40-bed psychiatric and rehabilitation facility. This private specialty hospital provides both inpatient and outpatient care for adults experiencing acute or chronic disorders.

Charter Midtown is founded on the philosophy of combining the latest advances in treatment with a safe, caring and therapeutic setting. A staff of 70 employees supports the programs.

The facility offers free assessments 24 hours a day, seven days a week. Both day and evening outpatient programs ease coordination of patients' schedules. Charter Midtown's programs include those designed to assist with alcohol and substance abuse, anxiety and depression.

Hillside Psychiatric Hospital
690 Courtenay Dr. N.E. • (404) 875-4551

Founded in 1888, Hillside is Atlanta's oldest social service agency. Its various roles demonstrate great flexibility in responding to the changing needs of the community.

Originally founded as a home for needy children, today Hillside is a licensed psychiatric hospital serving children and adolescents from ages 10 to 18. The 61-bed facility offers individualized psychotherapy as well as group and family therapy.

Hillside's licensed special education program enables youngsters to continue their schooling. Diagnostic services for severely emotionally disturbed patients are available. With both open and closed facilities, Hillside provides the appropriate setting for a wide range of needs.

The hospital's excellent programs are designed to return the whole child to a well state. Activity therapy, art therapy, horticulture therapy and speech and language therapy, administered by members of Hillside's 120-employee staff, contribute to a child's progress. Twenty-four hour nursing and an extensive aftercare program are part of Hillside's comprehensive treatment.

The hospital has created a Therapeutic Foster Care program for children who are ready to leave Hillside but who do not have community or family resources available to them. These children can continue to receive a variety of Hillside services while living in the community with foster families.

Shepherd Center
2020 Peachtree Rd. N.W. • (404) 352-2020

Shepherd Center in Buckhead is a private, not-for-profit hospital specializing in catastrophic care. The hospital treats people with spinal cord injury and disease, acquired brain injury, multiple sclerosis and other neuromuscular disorders and urological problems.

Serving the Southeast since 1975, the 100-bed specialty hospital offers a continuum of healthcare services ranging from intensive care through acute rehabilitation and subacute care to outpatient services.

The Center houses the largest model spinal cord injury program in the country and a 20-bed Brain Injury Unit. The National Multiple Sclerosis Society designated Shepherd the official Southeastern Multiple Sclerosis Center. The hospital's MS Center treats 1,300 patients and participates in clinical research, including the Shepherd/Harvard Multiple Sclerosis Research Initiative.

Urology specialists at Shepherd diagnose and treat male potency and fertility disorders. They have unique expertise in treating continence-related problems.

Shepherd also has a fully-accessible fitness center with a 25-yard pool, weight room, track and gym. A variety of fitness programs as well as arts and crafts classes are open to people of all abilities.

Vencor Hospital Atlanta
705 Juniper St. • (404) 873-2871

Vencor Hospital is a licensed long-term acute care hospital specializing in extended care for the medically complex patient. Par-

INSIDERS' TIP

Canine Assistants provides dogs to physically challenged recipients for help with daily living tasks. The program's 1997 class "graduated" 21 dogs trained by 100 volunteers who work with the animals preparing them for their future owners. To donate funds or time, or for more information, call Canine Assistants at (770) 664-7178.

ticular focus is on pulmonary services for the ventilator-dependent patient. Most of Vencor's patients transfer from other acute-care hospitals' intensive care units.

A full range of medical services is available to Vencor patients, including renal dialysis, orthopedic care and diagnostic radiology. Psychiatric treatment and support groups address the psychological needs of patients.

Vencor is a regional referral center. Patients come from a five-state area. Three hundred employees staff this 72-bed hospital.

Fulton County

North Fulton Regional Hospital
3000 Hospital Blvd., Roswell
• **(770) 751-2500**

As a Level II Trauma Center, North Fulton Regional provides seven-day, 24-hour in-house anesthesia and operating room coverage. Since 1983, the 167-bed hospital has offered general acute care to the rapidly growing areas north of metro Atlanta, including Roswell, Alpharetta and Cumming.

Nearly 900 employees and a medical staff of some 400 physicians provide support to patients in this full-service medical/surgical community hospital. Treatment for major illnesses, such as cancer and heart problems, are part of North Fulton's programs. The hospital's Women's Health Center delivers some 1,100 babies annually, and a neonatal intensive care unit tends to the needs of infants born pre-term. The hospital also provides care in the areas of nuclear medicine, orthopedic services, diagnostic radiology and renal dialysis.

Individualized treatment in The Renaissance Rehabilitation Center focuses on progressive care that enables patients to return to normal life quickly. North Fulton offers special sports medicine programs, a pain control center and a sleep disorder center.

North Fulton provides outpatient surgery procedures in addition to a fully staffed emergency room. The hospital's ongoing series of health education programs is designed to raise the level of health awareness in the community. These are augmented by periodic screening programs and support groups.

Cobb County

PROMINA Cobb Hospital
3950 Austell Rd., Austell • (770) 732-4000

Part of the PROMINA Northwest Health System, the 322-bed Cobb Hospital serves one of the fastest-growing areas in metro Atlanta. The hospital's Women's Center provides innovative single-room maternity care, neonatal intensive care and many other services. The hospital's 24-hour emergency department includes a fast-track area for minor illness and injury, a chest pain center and trauma triage. The Children's Emergency Center is a service of Cobb Hospital and Scottish Rite Children's Medical Center.

PROMINA Kennestone Hospital
677 Church St., Marietta • (770) 793-5000

Licensed for 539 beds, this is the largest PROMINA Northwest hospital. Kennestone's full range of services includes a 24-hour emergency/trauma center, advanced laparoscopic and orthopedic surgery and cardiology services. The hospital also has an oncology center, a diagnostic center and a sleep center.

Health Place is a wellness and fitness center on Kennestone's campus. It offers classes and ongoing health programs. Egleston Children's Health Center-Kennestone offers after-hours pediatric care for minor illnesses and injuries. Atherton Place is a senior living community for independent senior adults. Scheduled to open in spring 1998, the Kennestone Women's Center, is a 153,000-square-foot facility for the care of women and children including maternity care, a neonatal intensive care unit and a women's heart program.

PROMINA Windy Hill Hospital
2540 Windy Hill Rd., Marietta
• **(770) 644-1000**

Another member of PROMINA Northwest Health System, Windy Hill Hospital has recently transitioned to a long-term acute care hospital for patients needing institutionalized care for at least 25 days continuously. Windy Hill Hospital also offers a surgical and diagnostic center for outpatient procedures.

Ridgeview Institute
3995 S. Cobb Dr., Smyrna
• **(770) 434-4567, (800) 329-9775**

Established in Smyrna in 1976, Ridgeview Institute is a private nonprofit behavioral healthcare system that provides treatment for children, adolescents and adults with psychiatric and addictive problems. The facility's comprehensive continuum of care includes intensive inpatient, partial hospitalization and outpatient treatment options, designed to keep costs down and promote a prompt return to job, family and community.

Special services at Ridgeview include the Impaired Professionals Program and the Women's Center. RESPOND, Ridgeview's mobile assessment team, provides free psychiatric and addiction assessment and referral services. The RESPOND mobile assessment team offers telephone consultations within 10 minutes and on-site evaluations, when needed, within one hour, seven days a week, 24 hours a day.

One of a minority of hospitals in the country not owned or managed by a healthcare corporation, Ridgeview has treated more than 30,000 patients. Ridgeview is also committed to professional and community education and offers monthly services for clinicians, support groups, and a family learning series to the community.

ValueMark Brawner Behavioral Healthcare System North
3180 Atlanta St., Smyrna • (770) 436-0081

ValueMark Brawner Behavioral Healthcare System North is a comprehensive, integrated system of outpatient and inpatient behavioral healthcare services for adults, adolescents, children and their families. With locations throughout greater metropolitan Atlanta, Value Mark Brawner provides convenient access to quality, cost-effective care.

ValueMark Brawner North provides a variety of services including ambulatory detoxification, 23-hour stabilization services, short-term inpatient crisis stabilization, day and evening treatment programs, adult halfway house services and no-cost mobile assessments. ValueMark Brawner offers inpatient, outpatient and partial hospitalization services as well as family program services, for adults, adolescents and children.

ValueMark Brawner's North location in Smyrna and the South location at Stockbridge in Henry County are 50-bed facilities where adults, adolescents and children suffering from illnesses such as depression, addictive diseases, drug dependencies, post traumatic stress, dual diagnosis, bipolar disorders, sexual abuse trauma, schizophrenia, anxiety disorders, substance abuse, explosive rage disorders and adjustment disorders are treated.

Most insurance and managed-care plans cover the majority of program expenses. Additionally, ValueMark Brawner is an authorized provider for Medicare and CHAMPUS.

For a no-cost assessment at ValueMark Brawner, call (770) 436-0081 for the Smyrna location or (770) 474-8888 for the Stockbridge location.

DeKalb County

Columbia Dunwoody Medical Center
4575 N. Shallowford Rd. • (770) 454-2000

Dunwoody Medical Center is a fully accredited, 168-bed general medical-surgical hospital. It belongs to the Columbia/HCA hospital network.

Dunwoody Medical Center's new Women's Pavilion features 10 labor/delivery/recovery rooms, 28 postpartum rooms and a neonatal intensive care unit. The same nurse cares for the mother and her baby to assure continuity of care and provide maximum educational opportunities.

Other women's services include Working Woman's Mammography, with Saturday appointments and on-site interpretation. The Endometriosis Care Center focuses on the diagnosis and treatment of endometriosis. Routine procedures include ultrasound and advanced laparoscopic surgery.

Outpatient surgery, a new cardiac catheterization lab, an educational program for diabetics and sports medicine specialists are just a few of the many services the medical center provides. Dunwoody Medical Center's 24-hour emergency services department is a Level III trauma center.

Columbia Northlake Regional Medical Center
1455 Montreal Rd., Tucker
- **(770) 270-3000**

Columbia Northlake Regional offers general acute care in a broad range of medical services. The 120-bed facility's special services include maternity care, oncology, cardiology, orthopedics and podiatry.

Maternity care takes place in The Birthplace, which has private labor/delivery/recovery/postpartum suites. Columbia Northlake's childbirth education program helps prepare parents for their baby's arrival. A newborn intensive care unit stands ready to assist babies in need of special care.

The spectrum of surgical procedures available includes general surgery, neurosurgery, podiatric reconstructive surgery, plastic reconstructive surgery, vascular and orthopedic surgery. Columbia Northlake provides same-day outpatient surgery services.

Columbia Northlake's extensive inpatient and outpatient rehabilitative programs include physical therapy, respiratory therapy and occupational and speech therapy. For diagnoses of illnesses, the hospital uses the latest technology, such as nuclear medicine, magnetic resonance imaging, ultrasound, EKG and EEG. For women, the Womancare Breast Diagnostic Center provides comprehensive care.

The hospital is home to a sleep diagnostic center and an occupational medicine program. Columbia Northlake Regional's 24-hour emergency department is staffed with board-certified doctors.

Gwinnett County

Founded in 1959, the Gwinnett Hospital System (GHS) was established as a not-for-profit healthcare organization to provide high-quality medical care to its neighbors. In 1994 GHS became part of the PROMINA Health System operated by Gwinnett Hospital System, Inc., Piedmont Medical Center, Inc. and Northwest Georgia Health System Inc.

Gwinnett Medical Center
1000 Medical Center Blvd., Lawrenceville
- **(770) 995-4321**

Opened in 1984, Gwinnett Medical Center is a 190-bed acute care hospital offering all general medical, surgical and diagnostic services. The center also provides cardiac catheterization, lithotripsy and magnetic resonance imaging services.

Gwinnett DaySurgery, on the Gwinnett Medical Center campus, houses the GHS Laser Institute. This facility specializes in some of the most advanced outpatient laparoscopic and laser surgeries available regionally and is the site of national physician and nurse training.

Centrally located in the county, the center houses a Level III 24-hour emergency department that is the trauma triage center for Gwinnett County. The Scottish Rite Children's Emergency Center at Gwinnett Medical Center serves pediatric emergency cases.

Gwinnett Women's Pavilion
550 Medical Center Blvd., Lawrenceville
- **(770) 822-6055**

The 34-bed Gwinnett Women's Pavilion, on the 120-acre Gwinnett Medical Center campus, opened in 1991. It's metro Atlanta's first freestanding hospital for women.

Gwinnett Women's Pavilion offers maternity, diagnostic and educational services to women of all ages. The diagnostic center provides mammography, ultrasound and osteoporosis screenings. Experienced healthcare professionals staff a 30-bed neonatal intensive care unit.

Joan Glancy Memorial Hospital
3215 McClure Bridge Rd., Duluth
- **(770) 497-4800**

This 90-bed general hospital offers medical, surgical, diagnostic and 24-hour emergency services. Thirty of the hospital's beds are dedicated to the Glancy Rehabilitation Center, established in 1988.

At the Rehab Center, accident and stroke patients get the training and therapy they need for independence. The Glancy Rehabilitation and Sports Medicine center offers outpatient services.

A new facility, opened in 1995, expanded the hospital's services. At Joan Glancy's Howell Station campus on Pleasant Hill Road, the Glancy Outpatient Center provides full-service outpatient surgery, laboratory and imaging services with the latest in convenience amenities.

SummitRidge
250 Scenic Hwy., Lawrenceville
• **(770) 822-2200**

This 72-bed facility is part of the Gwinnett Hospital System. The hospital provides psychiatric and chemical dependency treatment for adults and adolescents.

Services include inpatient, partial hospitalization and outpatient care as well as aftercare programs. Supported by a free, confidential assessment and referral service, assistance is provided 24 hours a day. SummitRidge's community services include education programs for schools and other groups, seminars and support groups.

Fayette County

Fayette Community Hospital
1265 Hwy. 54 W., Fayetteville
• **(770) 719-7070**

A not-for-profit subsidiary of Piedmont Medical Care Center, the parent organization of Piedmont Hospital and a partner of PROMINA Health System, Fayette Community Hospital opened in late 1997. This 141,000-square-foot facility is the first new hospital to open in metro Atlanta within the last 14 years. With a 100-bed capacity, the hospital offers a full range of services including medical, surgical, critical care, diagnostic, laboratory and 24-hour emergency care. An FAA-approved helipad is also located at the hospital. Comprehensive outpatient services and outpatient surgery as well as respiratory care and physical therapy are also available.

An 80,000-square-foot professional building occupied by board certified/qualified physicians is adjacent to the hospital. The hospital and professional building are located on 28 acres on Highway 54, just west of Sandy Creek Road.

Special Needs and Services

AID Atlanta
1438 W. Peachtree St. N.W.
• **(404) 872-0600**

This is Atlanta's largest HIV/AIDS service agency. AID Atlanta offers complete health services, financial assistance, HIV testing, prevention and education.

AIDS Education/Services for Minorities
1432 Donnelly Ave. S.W. • (404) 753-2900

AESM is a community-based organization that provides financial assistance, transitional housing, pre- and post-test counseling and other services for HIV-positive African-American males. The organization also conducts educational seminars and has a community outreach program. They advise you to call first, rather than drop by, to find out about AESM's programs.

Atlanta Care Center
3115 Piedmont Rd. N.E. • (404) 262-2273

This abortion alternative facility is not a clinic, although they do provide pregnancy testing. In addition, Atlanta Care offers counseling, support and adoption referrals.

Feminist Women's Health Center
580 14th St. N.W. • (404) 874-7551

Offering "all choices for all women," this clinic provides a variety of women's health services including pap smears, donor inseminations, anonymous HIV testing, free pregnancy testing and counseling and abortions. Although most services require appointments, HIV and pregnancy testing services are available on a walk-in basis.

INSIDERS' TIP

Community support services are at your fingertips with United Way's new dial 211 help line. Begun during the summer of 1997, the service provides a free link to 1,000 programs and services such as soup kitchens, child care, paying rent or utility bills and other services catalogued by a computer database at United Way.

Planned Parenthood of Atlanta
100 Edgewood Ave. N.E., Ste. 1604
• (404) 688-9300
Cobb Center, 617 Roswell St., Marietta
• (770) 424-1477
Gwinnett Center, 950 Indian Trail Rd., Ste.
5D, Lilburn • (770) 381-2664

Planned Parenthood of Atlanta has three health centers in the metro area. They provide a full range of gynecological services; blood pressure checks and cholesterol screenings; birth control instruction and supplies; prenatal vitamins, health information and referrals; HIV/AIDS testing, information and counseling; screening and treatment for sexually transmitted diseases; and pregnancy tests, counseling and referrals. The Edgewood Avenue clinic provides service on a walk-in basis; other clinics can give you an appointment within one to two days.

Project Open Hand Atlanta
176 Ottley Dr. • (404) 872-2535

Project Open Hand prepares and delivers two meals a day, seven days a week to more than 550 Atlanta residents living with HIV/AIDS. This service is provided free of charge; donations and volunteers are welcome.

Titus Community Health Center, Inc.
2317 Snapfinger Rd., Decatur
• (404) 289-9900

This by-appointment facility offers HIV and AIDS testing, counseling, support groups, referrals and case management. It also has a day treatment program for substance abuse that includes Narcotics Anonymous and Alcoholics Anonymous 12-Step groups, recovery education and group and individual therapy.

Hospice Care

Atlanta is blessed with a number of facilities offering alternatives in cases of life-limiting illness. Counseling services for the patient and family in bereavement are helpful. The services offered vary from hospice to hospice.

Here are some points you may want to consider when selecting a hospice. Ask if the institution is Medicare/Medicaid certified and if it accepts private insurance. Many hospices have a 24-hour emergency service line. Inquire about a specific hospice's membership in national certifying organizations as well as the types of licenses it holds.

Haven House at Midtown
250 14th St. N.E. • (404) 874-8313

Located in an old, restored home, Haven House accepts any terminally ill patient inpatient hospice or home hospice care. There is also a day care program where folks can come and drop off their loved ones while they work. Haven House has 19 beds and offers full medical nursing services. Patients remain under the care of their own physicians who work with the hospice's medical director. Insurance coverage includes Medicaid and Medicare; Haven House also has a fund available to indigent patients. It's staffed 24 hours a day, seven days a week.

Health Field Hospice
2045 Peachtree Rd. N.E. • (404) 355-3134

Health Field primarily takes care of folks in their homes but does operate an inpatient unit with 10 beds in rented space at South Fulton Medical Center that is separate and fully staffed by Health Field personnel. For home-care patients, Health Field provides RN, social and certified nursing services, chaplain, pharmaceuticals and palliative care (control of pain and comfort in the patient's final days). Medicare, Medicaid and private insurance pays for these services in an 18-county area.

Hospice Atlanta
1244 Park Vista Dr. • (404) 527-0740

Patients, including children, with a six-month life expectancy or less are eligible for care at Hospice Atlanta. Operated by Visiting Nurses Association, the facility has a 36-bed two-story building and three cottages, each with 12 beds. In-house laundry service and three meals a day are provided to patients. There are also family rooms and kitchens as well as individual kitchenettes in each cottage for family members who wish to make and store food for family members. The kitchen staff is on call 16 hours a day. Medicare, Medicaid, indigent funding and all standard insurance companies are accepted.

Northside Hospice
5825 Glenridge Dr. N.E., Bldg. 4
• (404) 851-6300

Affiliated with Northside Hospital, the hospice is a Medicare certified offshoot that provides care to terminally ill patients in their homes. A multidiscipline team approach is utilized that combines nursing, social service, home-health aides, a chaplain and volunteers. Services include 24-hour nursing seven days a week, and a bereavement follow-up for the family within 13 months of a death. Medicare or commercial insurance is filed.

Numbers to Call

When an emergency arises or you need general information and direction to community resources, refer to this list for assistance.

For emergencies requiring ambulance,
police or fire departments • 911
AID Atlanta • (404) 872-0600
Georgia Dental Association
• (404) 636-7553
Georgia Hospital Association
• (770) 955-0324
Georgia Psychological Association
• (404) 351-9555
Georgia Poison Center
• (404) 616-9000
Georgia Registry for Interpreters
for the Deaf
• (404) 299-9500
Medical Association of Atlanta/
Academy of Medicine • (404) 881-1714
Medical Association of Georgia
• (404) 876-7535
CDC National AIDS Hotline
• English (800) 342-AIDS
• Spanish (800) 344-SIDA
• Hearing Impaired (800) AIDS-TTY
Mental Health Association of
Metropolitan Atlanta • (404) 527-7175

Walk-In Clinics

In the Atlanta metro area, some but not all urgent care centers are affiliated with hospitals. In such centers, if the situation requires, patients are quickly transported to the hospital's main facility. All urgent care centers offer immediate care for a wide variety of needs, often with extended hours.

Atlanta

FamilyCare Centers
6038 Covington Hwy., Decatur
• (404) 501-2270
5019 LaVista Rd., Tucker • (404) 501-3270
1045 Sycamore Dr., Decatur
• (404) 501-4270

All of the FamilyCare Centers treat minor illnesses and injuries and are affiliated with DeKalb Medical Center. Each is staffed by a physician, an RN, X-ray technologist and lab technicians. The centers are open from 8 AM to 11 PM Monday through Friday and 10 AM to 6 PM weekends and holidays. FamilyCare files most insurance claims as well as Medicare and accepts all credit cards.

Northside Health Express
1000 Johnson Ferry Rd. N.E.
• (404) 851-6763

Northside Health Express is in the emergency room at Northside Hospital. Minor emergency care from sore throats to minor lacerations to minor extremity injuries are treated here. A nurse practitioner sees patients first, and if they need further evaluation, the emergency physician sees them. Hours of operation are from 10 AM to 9:30 PM, seven days a week. Most insurance plans, including Medicare and Medicaid, are accepted as are credit cards.

Piedmont Health Center
1830 Piedmont Rd. N.E., Ste. C
• (404) 874-1111

Piedmont Health Center is an independent doctor-owned facility that, despite its name, is not affiliated with Piedmont Hospital. The center is open Monday through Friday from 9 AM to 5 PM and Saturdays from noon to 4 PM. The owner/physician on-site is a general practitioner who handles everything from minor emergencies to office gynecology. X-Ray services are available at the office; some lab work is sent out.

Piedmont Hospital Medical Care Center-Brookhaven
4062 Peachtree Rd. N.E. • (404) 231-4231

This is an urgent care center not an emergency center, which means it does not handle major emergencies such as heart attacks and car wrecks. A family practice physician as well as X-ray and laboratory services are available on site. The center, which is affiliated with Piedmont Hospital, accepts most insurance plans including Medicare. It's open from 8 AM to 8 PM Monday through Saturday and Sundays from 10 AM to 6 PM. Most major credit cards are accepted.

South Fulton Medical Center Primary Care Center
1100 Cleveland Ave., East Point
• (404) 765-1700

Affiliated with South Fulton Medical Center, this urgent care center is not an emergency center, meaning it does not handle major emergencies such as heart attacks and car wrecks. The center offers a family practice physician as well as X-ray and laboratory services. Most insurance plans, including Medicare, are accepted as are most major credit cards. The center is open from 9 AM to 9 PM seven days a week.

Toco Hills Med+Plus
3019 North Druid Hills Rd. N.E.
• (404) 325-2100

Toco Hills Med+Plus is a walk-in minor emergency clinic that also provides surrounding area businesses with workers compensation physical therapy during the week. X-ray facilities are on site. Hours are 8 AM to 8 PM Monday through Friday, 9 AM to 5 PM Saturday and 10 AM to 5 PM Sunday. A physician is on staff at all times. About 15 insurance plans are accepted as well as Medicare; all credit cards are accepted. It's affiliated with Dunwoody Medical Center.

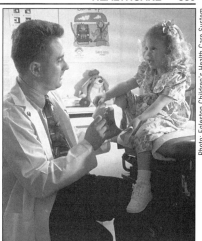

A young patient tells her doctor where it hurts.

Beyond Atlanta

Georgia Baptist Urgent Care Center — Fayetteville
105 Yorktown Dr., Fayetteville
• (770) 461-6666

Everything from colds to chest pains to broken bones are treated here seven days a week from 8 AM to 10 PM. The office does not accept ambulance patients. Although affiliated with Georgia Baptist Hospital, patients in need of hospital services will be referred to other facilities if needed. There is one doctor on staff full time, and if a specialist is needed, one will be called in. X-ray facilities and a lab are on-site. Numerous insurance plans, Medicare, Medicaid and workers compensation are honored. All credit cards are accepted.

KennMed Johnson Ferry
1211 Johnson Ferry Rd., Marietta
• (770) 479-7930
KennMed Kennesaw
3805 Cherokee St., Kennesaw
• (770) 426-5665
KennMed Marietta
700 Church St., Marietta • (770) 420-1630

These urgent care facilities, which are part

of the PROMINA Northwest Health System, do not accept ambulance patients. Each is staffed by in-house physicians who utilize on-site X-ray and laboratory facilities. The centers are open seven days a week from 8 AM to 8 PM. Most insurance plans are accepted as are all major credit cards.

Roswell Med+Plus
900 Holcomb Bridge Rd., Roswell
• **(770) 998-0605**

This walk-in minor emergency clinic also provides workers compensation physical therapy to surrounding area businesses during the week. X-ray and laboratory services are available on-site. Roswell is open every day from 8 AM to 8 PM. A physician is on staff at all times. All credit cards, Medicare and about 15 insurance plans are accepted.

Physician Referral Services

Virtually every hospital has a phone service, usually nurse-staffed, to provide physician referrals or to give general health information. You'll probably choose a physician based on your needs, your location and, in some cases, your health insurance policy requirements. We list a sample of the available help lines below.

Columbia Referral Service (covers six metro hospitals) • **(800) 265-8624**
Decatur Hospital Med-Match
• **(404) 501-4242**
DeKalb Medical Center • **(404) 501-9355**
Egleston Physician Referral
• **(404) 325-9700**
Emory Health Connection (services Emory Hospital and Crawford Long Hospital)
•**(404) 778-7744**
North Fulton Regional Hospital
• **(770) 751-2600**
Northside Hospital Doctor Matching
•**(404) 851-8817**
PROMINA Northeast Physician Finder
• **(404) 605-3556**
PROMINA Northwest Referral Service
• **(770) 793-7000**
St. Joseph's Hospital Physician Referral Service • **(404) 851-7312**

Scottish Rite Children's Resource Line (RiteCall) • **(404) 250-KIDS**
South Fulton Medical Center
• **(404) 305-3000**
Southwest Hospital and Medical Center
• **(404) 505-5295**
Vencor Hospital Atlanta (pulmonary services) • **(800) 634-2856**

Major HMOs in Atlanta

Aetna • **(404) 814-4300**
Affordable Medical Network
• **(770) 226-8300**
BlueChoice • **(404) 237-2429**
Cigna • **(800) 526-5481**
HealthStar-Georgia • **(770) 396-1009**
Kaiser Permanente • **(404) 261-2590**
Private Healthcare Systems
• **(770) 394-1084**
PruCare • **(770) 955-7735**
SouthCare • **(404) 231-9911**
United Health Care • **(800) 505-2273**
US Healthcare • **(800) 323-9930**

Alternative Medicine

Nontraditional medicine has been gaining followers throughout the nation at a remarkable rate and Atlanta is no exception. If one were to go by the number of health stores in a mile radius, it would seem that we are avid believers and with Atlanta's burgeoning Asian population, it is not at all surprising that acupuncture is particularly popular (although you'd be hard-pressed to locate a practitioner from the telephone directory).

For specific practitioners in alternative medicine, we suggest you call the referral numbers at the end of this chapter. And for your edification, we offer the following overview of some of the most popular alternatives to traditional medical doctors.

Acupuncture

Five thousand years ago, the principles of acupuncture evolved and became part of

Chinese culture. But it wasn't until 400 B.C. that the practice became a written treatise called the Nei Ching. Traditionally, acupuncture rebalances energy — Qi — life's energy, which travels through the body along meridians or channels. When the Qi is obstructed due to life's disturbances including climatic changes, diet, lifestyle and stress, blockages are formed in the body consisting of the buildup of lactic acid and carbon monoxide which manifest themselves by stiffness, pain and disease. Using sterile and disposable stainless steel needles as thin as a hair and heat producing materials along acupoints, the blocked meridians are unblocked.

In Georgia, chiropractors are licensed, massage therapists are certified, yet acupuncturists are neither. In fact, it's difficult to find an acupuncturist since they are not listed in the Yellow Pages. Within the two inches of Physician listings in the phone book, only one person has designated himself under the Acupuncture header, and that is a Doctor of Osteopathic Medicine. Not to suggest that Atlanta isn't brimming with practitioners. Most, however, are Asians who developed their clientele by word of mouth. The best way to find an acupuncturist is to ask a chiropractor for a referral.

Aromatherapy

Like Acupuncture, Aromatherapy has a history as old as the ages. In fact, Cleopatra used herbs as a birth control method and plant oils to seduce her legions of admirers. When she wanted a particular potion, she sent couriers throughout her lands to dig up the herbs she needed. We Atlantans have it a lot easier with health food stores in almost every strip shopping center carrying plant oils extracts in bottles of just a few ounces. And in case you have your doubts about the efficacy of aromatherapy, ask an employee at a health food store for excerpts from recent University of Cincinnati, Duke University and University of Arizona studies that seem to suggest Cleopatra knew more about such things than modern medicine. Some of the more popular herbal aromas include eucalyptus for colds, peppermint and ginger for upset stomachs and lavender for relaxation.

Homeopathy

Samuel Hahnemann, a doctor of medicine in the early 1790s, became frustrated with orthodox medical practices, in particular the bleeding and subsequent death of Emperor Leopold II of Austria. In place of standard, for the times, medicine, Hahnemann evolved a method for treating disease based on a doctrine for ascertaining the curative powers of drugs, and he called this method "homeopathy" in an essay published in 1796.

The Organon of Rational Therapeutics, his detailed exposition, instructions and philosophy of homeopathy, was first published in 1810. An edition of this monumental work appeared in 1921, almost a century after Hahnemann's death.

Homeopathy was practiced widely in Europe, particularly after French premier Guizot, when asked in the mid-1800s by the allopathist/apothecarian community to ban such treatment, instead noted that if homeopathy was "a valueless method" it would collapse on its own accord. But if it was truly an advance of traditional medicine, it would spread.

Referral Agencies

The following referral agencies are offered as a starting place for nontraditional healthcare services.
Georgia Chiropractic Association
• **(404) 688-3730**
Homeopathic Academy of Naturopathic Physicians • **(505) 761-3298**
National Center for Homeopathy
• **(703) 548-7790**
The Informed Choice • **(404) 812-7077**

Spas

Okay, so spas probably aren't what you think of immediately when you hear "healthcare." But with your busy life, destressing is essential and what better way to rid the body and soul of built up toxins, grease and grime, anger and anxiety than to lay back relax and receive a wide range of massages, facials, body treatments and aromatherapy at one of the many salons in and around Atlanta?

The office, the kids, the boss just disappear as muscles unwind while the massage therapists skillfully soothe away the stress. Try a therapeutic body wrap or body polish. Treat your feet to reflexology, a massage technique designed to de-stress your whole self by manipulating pressure points on your tootsies.

If you need these services to stay sane, start saving now because spa treatments are not inexpensive. Pricing is as diverse as the facilities, and many spas offer samplers and full- and half-day packages that combine several services. Holiday packages are especially bargains, and if you bring friends with you, ask for a discount. Expect to pay from $55 to $100 for a facial; full-day packages can cost anywhere from $175 to $270 and more; half-days fall in the $110 to $150 range, depending on the services offered. Spa Château Élan offers one night sleep-over packages from $459 on up and a luxury week can cost as much as a year's tuition at the local community college. But you'll feel like a million when you go home!

Atlanta

Amante Amour
Phipps Plaza, 3500 Peachtree Rd. N.E.
• **(404) 816-4836**

This shop provides aromatherapy for all ages from children to senior citizens. Shop here for bath oils, massage oils, aroma candles, body spray, soaps and skin and hair care products. At Amante Amour, you can enjoy soothing full body massages, chair massages and foot reflexology.

Dermess Skin Care Center
3726 Roswell Rd. N.E. • **(404) 261-5199**
Yin & Yang, 721 Miami Cir. N.E.
• **(404) 233-6241**

Therapeutic complexion and skin repair treatments are the speciality at Dermess. And you can also go bronze with their safe tan treatment. Peels, waxing and an extensive product line are also available.

Natural Body
1402-2 N. Highland Ave. N.E.
• **(404) 872-1039**
5975 Roswell Rd., Ste. 225
• **(404) 255-9699**
4200 Paces Ferry Rd., Ste. 257
• **(770) 319-9001**

Natural Body's diverse array of spa services includes glycolic, sea algae and aromatherapy rejuvenation facials; manicures, pedicures, and other hand and foot treatments; herbal wraps; body massages; steam therapy and Dead Sea mud treatments. Several spa treatment combinations are offered.

Aside from the standard spa treatments of massage and facials, Natural Body's Rejuvenation Bars offer Chinese elixirs served in small mixed-drink glasses which can fortify, enhance or relax you. Clients get the drinks gratis as part of their treatment; visitors can purchase them.

Natural Body also has a retail location across the parking lot from its spa on N. Highland Avenue where you can purchase 100 percent natural, chemical-free essential oils and other treatments to cleanse or refresh the body.

Noelle, The Day Spa
3619 Piedmont Rd. N.E. • **(404) 266-0060**

Noelle offers a selection of half- and full-day spa packages including a couple's day and a relaxation day for men and women. Choose from a variety of spa treatments including therapeutic and full body massages, aromatherapy mud wraps, seaweed cellulite treatments and repechage four-layer facials. In addition, Noelle provides hair design, scalp treatment, permanent waving, hair relaxing and hair coloring.

Spa Forever Young
4279 Roswell Rd. N.E., Ste. 602
• **(404) 250-9698**

This spa's European- and Oriental-trained staff help you repackage yourself to bring out your natural beauty. Forever Young offers a variety of facial treatments, body massages, body polishes and herbal wraps. They also provide nail care, hair removal, lash and brow tinting and makeovers.

Spa Sydell

Buckhead Plaza, 3060 Peachtree Rd. N.W.
• (404) 237-2505
Cumberland Mall, Cobb Pkwy. N.W., south
of I-285/75 in Cobb Co. • (770) 802-0804
Perimeter Square West, 1165 Perimeter
Center W. • (770) 551-8999
Pleasant Hill Square, 2255 Pleasant Hill
Rd., Duluth • (770) 622-5580

The most well known of Atlanta-originated spas, this four location company owned by the Harris family offers glamourous settings. Sydell Harris, respected for her charitable activities as well as her graciousness, is much in evidence. Specialties of the house include massage for two, a day at the spa which includes lunch from some of the best restaurants in the city, makeup consultations and hairdos, as well as gift certificates in handsome maroon packaging. Spa Sydell has rubbed, oiled, and otherwise pampered most of the glitterati in town as well as visiting Hollywood and sports stars.

The Buckhead location has recently been expanded to 6,500 square feet. Spa Sydell's other locations include Cumberland Mall, Perimeter Square West, and Pleasant Hill Square in Gwinnett. All offer the full range of treatments for body and face, wraps, hair removal, manicures, lash and brow tinting.

Beyond Atlanta

Repose

8610 Roswell Rd. N.E. • (770) 587-0480

Repose, in Loehmann's Plaza, offers a number of spa services including facials, exfoliation treatment, hand and foot therapy, waxing, herbal body wrap and sea salt body polish treatments. A day of pampering package is available.

The Spa at Château Élan

Haven Harbour Dr., Braselton
• (770) 271-6064

This spa, modeled after a European health spa, is part of the popular Château Élan complex, which is about an hour's drive northeast of downtown Atlanta. This is the only spa in the metro area where you can stay overnight, for several nights or for a whole week. The Spa at Château Élan offers a number of spa packages that entitle you to various spa services as well as meals and accommodations. Or just enjoy a day at the spa; choose one of their prepared packages or design your own.

Besides a full range of spa treatments and services, The Spa has a sauna, steam room, a whirlpool and exercise equipment. You can get an individual fitness assessment as well as a personalized exercise prescription. Outdoor types will enjoy the nature trails for hiking and biking. See more about Château Élan in our Accommodations and Daytrips and Weekend Getaways chapters.

In 1922 *The Atlanta Journal* launched the South's first commercial radio station, WSB-AM. (The call letters meant "Welcome South, Brother.")

Media

The same industry — transportation — that made Atlanta the business capital of the South also made it a regional media center. Along with bullets and beans, those early trains brought news from distant parts, news for which there was an eager and ever-growing audience.

Prior to the city's destruction after the Civil War, four regular newspapers were joined by three Tennessee papers whose staffs took refuge in Atlanta and continued publishing.

Atlanta struggled hard to get on its feet throughout the days of Reconstruction. During those days, Northern newspaper reporters wired dispatches back home making it clear that the bold young city was doing much more than sulking and nursing its wounds. Here's how one newspaper writer described our furiously rebuilding city to his readers in the North:

"From all this ruin and devastation a new city is springing up with marvelous rapidity …. Men rush about the streets with but little regard for comfort or pleasure, and yet find the days all too short and too few for the work at hand …. Atlanta seems to be the center from which this new life radiates; it is the great Exchange, where you will find everybody if you only wait and watch."

Media coverage like this helped Atlanta build its reputation as a Southern city focused on the future, not the past. This image was reinforced by national and international media reports from the great cotton expositions of 1881, 1887 and 1895.

To some degree, postwar Atlanta had the media to thank for setting the city on a course toward modernism. The visionary young newspaperman Henry Grady used his editorship of The Atlanta Constitution as the pulpit from which he preached the doctrine of a "New South" building its economy on industry, not just agriculture.

In 1922 The Atlanta Journal launched the South's first commercial radio station, WSB-AM. (The call letters meant "Welcome South, Brother.") The 100-watt station's studio was on the newspaper building's fifth floor; it's antenna was on the roof. Auto tycoon Henry Ford and movie star Rudolph Valentino were among early visitors to the tiny station. In 1948, WSB-TV, the first television station in the South, went on the air.

As technology improved, so did Atlanta's presence on the national and international media scenes. Now programming that originates here is beamed 24 hours a day to every part of our nation and all over the world.

Atlantans and visitors to the city can take advantage of a dizzying range of media possibilities, including the morning and afternoon daily newspapers, 11 television stations broadcast over the air (including four with extensive daily local news coverage), plus dozens of radio stations and scores of magazines, weekly and monthly newspapers and small newsletters.

Atlanta can be a boon town for those interested in becoming part of the media: Writers can get a jump start on their careers by offering their skills to any number of free press outlets; on-air talents can hone their skills on public access stations; and screen performers will find numerous opportunities to do ad agency work. In fact, the economic impact of the film and video industry in Georgia is substantial with revenues in 1996 of $158.1 million. Since the Georgia Office of Film and Videotape was created in 1973, more than 360 theatrical and made-for-TV movies have been filmed in our state. Of these, 173 were filmed, entirely or in-part, on-location around Atlanta. *Smokey and the Bandit I & II*, *Wise Blood*, *The Bear*, *The Slugger's Wife*, *Sharky's Machine*, *Tanner '88*, *Consenting Adults*, *Free Jack*, *Basket Case III*, *The Oldest Living Confederate Widow Tells All* and, most recently, *Scream II* used Atlanta or the environs as a backdrop. Two of the best-known made-in-Atlanta movies are Spike Lee's *School Daze*, which was filmed on the campus of Atlanta University Center, and the 1989 Oscar-winner for best picture *Driving Miss Daisy*, which includes scenes of Druid Hills, Little Five Points, The Temple on Peachtree Street and other recognizable locations.

In Atlanta, you'll never lack for something to read, watch or listen to. Following is a roundup of the city's best-known media outlets as well as lots of smaller ones. Whether you're visiting Atlanta or relocating here, you'll find our media to be a nonstop resource of information on the city's life.

Television

Turner Broadcasting System Inc.
One CNN Center, Marietta St. at Techwood Dr. N.W. • (404) 827-1700

Turner Broadcasting System, the mega company that owned *The Wizard of Oz*, the Atlanta Braves, Teenage Mutant Ninja Turtles, the Atlanta Hawks, Space Ghost Coast-to-Coast, World Championship Wrestling, *Gone With the Wind*, The Jetsons, CNN and Headline News, SportSouth, the Goodwill Games, Yogi Bear, *Dumb and Dumber*, *The Shawshank Redemption*, Johnny Quest, Huckleberry Hound, … (This list could fill the whole book!) remains a major media player even after the merger of the company with Time Warner.

Turner Broadcasting System Inc., prior to the sale, employed 8,200 people worldwide.

FYI

Three area codes serve the metro Atlanta area: 404, 770 and 678. Whether you live on Peachtree Street or in New York City, you must dial the code to reach any number in the area. The difference? Outside the area, you must dial "1," then the area code and phone number; inside the area, you need only dial the area code followed by the phone number.

The company entered the television business with the purchase of a single Atlanta UHF television station in 1970. Turner had moved to Atlanta in 1963 and quickly turned around his family's failing billboard company. In 1976, Channel 17 became the first cable superstation when its signal began beaming from a satellite 23,000 miles out in space. WTBS SuperStation had fewer than 700,000 subscribers then, who were treated to a mixed bag that included old movies and TV shows, Atlanta Braves baseball (TBS bought "America's Team" in 1976) and commercials for odd products such as the costume jewelry "Party Ring," Slim Whitman records and a kitchen-full of peelers, slicers and dicers. Today, with more than 71 million subscribers, it's America's top-rated 24-hour basic cable service.

When Turner launched CNN in 1980, detractors scoffed at the world's first 24-hour, all-news network. In the years since, its U.S. subscriber base has grown from 1.7 million to more than 71 million, and CNN has shown the world everything from the Gulf War to O.J. Simpson's car chase and trial. CNN and CNN International are broadcast to more than 160 million homes in 210 nations and territories worldwide, and those numbers keep growing.

Through the years, TBS continued to launch networks (Cartoon Network, Headline News, Turner Network Television, Turner Classic Movies) and acquire subsidiaries (Castle Rock Entertainment, Hanna-Barbera Cartoons Inc., New Line Cinema). Turner Entertainment Company also owned more than 3,300 film and TV titles, including *Gone With the Wind*, *The Wizard of Oz*, *King Kong*, *Casablanca*, *Ben Hur* (1926 and 1959 versions) and *Citizen Kane*.

TBS founder Ted Turner was hailed as "prince of the global village," by Time Magazine when it named him Man of the Year in 1991. In September 1995, after lengthy negotiations, Time Warner bought TBS for $7.5 billion. The resulting mega-corporation is the world's largest entertainment company;

Photo: The Weather Channel

Forecasters with The Weather Channel work around the clock
to broadcast up-to-the-minute weather coverage.

Turner is its vice-chairman and Time Warner's largest single individual shareholder.

Ted Turner has kept Atlanta as the capital of the Turner empire. Although some jobs were lost with the merger, others were created as the divisions grew. The transition, it is said, has been smooth. At this writing the company employs 9,000 worldwide, and Time Warner was able to boast second-quarter earnings of $30 million in 1997, a vast improvement over the $40 million loss reported just a year prior to its buying Turner's assets.

A leaner TBS has resulted from the elimination of publishing divisions, home video, merchandising and syndications such as Turner Pictures. Castle Rock Entertainment and Hanna-Barbera were merged into other Time Warner divisions.

See our Attractions chapter for information about the guided tour offered at CNN Center.

The Weather Channel
300 Interstate North Pkwy.
• **(770) 226-0000**

When they want to get the latest on hurricanes, floods or earthquakes — and when they just want to know what to wear to work — more than 90 percent of U.S. cable households can check The Weather Channel. The world's only 24-hour, continuous-coverage network devoted exclusively to the weather is headquartered in northwest Atlanta.

The Weather Channel reports local, regional, national and international weather conditions and runs a forecast specific to the viewer's local area every six to eight minutes around the clock. There are also regular reports such as Five-Day Business Planner (:20 past the hour) and International Weather (:45 past the hour). The channel's "weathertainment" shows focus on phenomena such as tornados and flooding.

As conditions warrant, the channel adds regular reports on fall foliage, heat or cold waves, holiday weather and beach forecasts.

The Weather Channel really shines when the weather acts up. Its forecasters meticulously track the path of big storms, often giving far more detailed information about their progress than other news sources. Frequently the channel has a crew beachside bravely beaming live video as a hurricane makes landfall.

The Weather Channel was launched in 1982, the brainchild of John Coleman. The weather forecaster on ABC's *Good Morning, America*, he served as the network's first president. The Weather Channel has generated an operating profit since 1985. Starting with an audience of only 2.5 million viewers, the channel now reaches 61.7 million households. It's owned by Landmark Communications Inc. in Norfolk, Virginia.

People TV
190 14th St. N.W. • (404) 873-6712

Radicals railing against the government; drag queens twirling batons or lip-syncing to Connie Francis; teens discussing the challenges facing youth today: You may find all this and more on People TV (Atlanta cable channel 12).

The 1980 franchise agreement between the City of Atlanta and its cable supplier provided for the creation of a public access cable TV channel, on which ordinary citizens can have their own programs shown free of charge. Atlanta's channel is a leader in the field of urban public access channels. Originally part of the cable company, public access is now a separate, private, nonprofit organization, called People TV, founded in 1986.

Through the facilities of People TV, Atlanta residents can take low-cost classes in video production, television directing and editing. Once certified, they can use the channel's professional equipment to produce their own shows, which are cablecast on Atlanta cable channel 12. Persons may also produce shows on home equipment and submit them for cablecast.

There are few rules as to the content of the shows; freedom of speech applies. Pop star RuPaul began his show biz career on People TV on *The American Music Show*, one of the longest-running public access shows in the United States.

Major Local TV Stations and Their Network Affiliates

Atlanta's WSB-TV gave the South its chance to marvel at the newfangled "radio with pictures" on September 29, 1948. A string of "firsts" followed: WSB-TV provided the South's first telecasts of professional football, local election results and church services (Christmas at First Presbyterian Church, 1948). The station was also the first in the South to broadcast a network show in full color, on February 16, 1954.

Television caught on with Atlantans, and more stations followed quickly. WAGA-TV began broadcasting in March 1949; WXIA-TV switched on in 1951.

In 1980, a shake-up occurred when WSB-TV switched its affiliation from NBC to ABC; WXIA-TV switched from ABC to NBC. There was even more moving and shaking in 1994 when WAGA-TV, the CBS affiliate, shocked many observers by switching to the up-and-coming FOX network. WAGA-TV is now one of the top three Fox affiliates in the United States and home to the nation's highest rated 10 PM newscast. WATL-TV is now the nation's No. 1 affiliate of WB, the Warner Bros. Network (it still carries Fox's kids' programming). Tribune Broadcasting's UHF station WGNX is the home of CBS in Atlanta. WVEU signed on with UPN in 1995 and changed its call letters to WUPA.

Naturally, all this channel-hopping left lots of Atlantans confused and led to many a malprogrammed VCR. But now everyone seems adjusted to the networks' new electronic addresses.

With more than 1.62 million TV households, Atlanta is the nation's 10th largest TV market.

Following is a listing of the television stations whose broadcast signals reach most of the metro area.

WAGA Channel 5 (FOX)
WATL Channel 36 (WB)
WGNX Channel 46 (CBS)
WGTV Channel 8 (Georgia Public TV/PBS)
WHSG Channel 63 (Trinity Broadcasting Network)
WPBA Channel 30 (PBS/Atlanta Board of Education)
WSB Channel 2 (ABC)
WTBS Channel 17 (Time Warner/Turner Broadcasting System)
WTLK Channel 14 (Independent/Paxson Communications Corp.)
WUPA Channel 69 (UPN)
WXIA Channel 11 (NBC)

Radio

You can tune in to any kind of music in Atlanta and have commentary in almost as many languages including Spanish, Greek and country (well, it is like another language to some of us). And if talk radio is your addiction, mid-days on WGST you can get your fix or have a fit over Rush Limbaugh. Flip the dial to WSB and get moralized by Dr. Laura. Before or after these two, check out Atlanta's own homespun demagogues like Neal Boortz (WSB), or fall in love with consumer maven Clark Howard (WSB) who not only helps resolve all your purchasing snafus, but announces the best airfare deals before they are published in the local tabloids. Prior to becoming a radio celeb, Howard owned a travel agency and his know-how in this area is astounding. But don't look to him for cushy, high-end vacation tips: He's a nut for a bargain. He suggests driving to Birmingham, Alabama (two hours away) to save $50 on airfare if Hartsfield and Delta aren't cooperating with his budget. All of our talkers, by the way, accept call-ins and have special numbers for that purpose. It

works best if you have auto dial 'cause these guys sure are popular.

Several "alternative" stations are clustered at the left, public portion of the FM band: These include college radio (WRAS, WCLK, WREK), the local National Public Radio affiliate and classical station (WABE) and a community-operated station with diversified programming from reggae to bluegrass (WRFG "Radio Free Georgia").

One station (WSTR "Star 94") is dedicated to playing the Top 40; several stations play recent releases in specific musical areas. Numerous stations program oldies or easy listening rock and jazz.

The following listing will guide you through the dials. You'll find that some of these stations come in loud and clear throughout Atlanta at all times; at night, some even reach distant states. Others, however, are so weak they're receivable on one side of town but not the other. Switch around, pick your favorites and set the dial for hours of enjoyment.

Adult Contemporary
WALR 104.7 FM/WALR 1340 AM (Light R&B/Soul oldies)
WPCH 94.9 FM (Light Rock)
WMKJ 96.7 FM
WSB 98.5 FM

Christian
WAEC 860 AM (Contemporary Christian)
WAFS 920 AM
WAOK 1380 AM (Gospel/Talk)
WDCY 1520 AM
WFOM 1230 AM
WFTD 1080 AM
WGUN 1010 AM
WJJC 1270AM (Gospel/Americana)
WNIV 970 AM/1400 AM (Contemporary Christian/Talk)
WPBS 1050 AM (Gospel)
WSSA 1570 AM (Christian Country)
WTJH 1260 AM (Gospel)
WWEV 91.5 FM (Contemporary Christian)
WXLL 1310 AM (Gospel)
WYZE 1480 AM (Gospel)

Classical
WABE 90.1 FM (NPR/Classical/Atlanta Board of Education)
WGKA 1190 AM

College Radio
WCLK 91.9 FM (Jazz/Soul; Clark Atlanta University)
WRAS 88.5 FM (New rock; Georgia State University)
WREK 91.1 FM (Diversified; Georgia Tech)

Community
WRFG 89.3 FM (Eclectic)

Country
WHNE/WMLB 1170AM (Americana/Country)
WKHX 590 AM/101.5 FM
WPLO 610 AM
WYAY 106.7 FM

Jazz
WJZF 104.1 FM

Latin
WAOS 1600 AM/WXEM 1460 AM
WAZX 1550 AM

News/Talk
WCNN 680 AM (News/Talk)
WDUN 550 AM (News/Talk/Sports)
WGGA 1240 AM (News/Talk)
WGST 640 AM/105.7 FM (News/Talk)
WSB 750 AM (News/Talk/Braves Baseball/Hawks Basketball)
WQXI 790 AM (Sports talk)

Oldies
WFOX 97.1 FM
WLKQ 102.3 FM

Rock
WKLS 96.1 FM (Album-oriented rock)
WNNX 99.7 FM (New rock)
WGZC 92.9 FM (Classic rock/Falcons Football)

Top 40
WSTR 94.1 FM (Contemporary hits)

Urban
WHTA 97.5 FM (Rap)
WVEE 103.3 FM (Urban pop/rap)

Publications

Daily Newspapers

Atlanta Daily World
145 Auburn Ave. N.E. • (404) 659-1110
Founded in 1928, *Atlanta Daily World* is the oldest African-American newspaper in Atlanta; in fact, it's the oldest African-American daily in the United States. With a daily circulation of 16,000 to 18,000, it covers local, national and international news.

The Atlanta Journal
The Atlanta Constitution
72 Marietta St. N.W.• (404) 526-5151
The Atlanta Constitution is the city's weekday morning daily; *The Atlanta Journal* is published each weekday afternoon. They are united in combined editions on Saturday and Sunday. The two papers differ significantly only in their editorial opinions; otherwise, they are two editions of the same paper.

The Atlanta Constitution was established in 1868. In its early years, *Constitution* staffers of note included editor Henry Grady (whose forward-looking "New South" philosophy helped energize and inspire the ruined region after the Civil War), Joel Chandler Harris (author of the "Uncle Remus" stories) and poet Frank Stanton (who became poet laureate of Georgia).

The afternoon paper, *The Atlanta Journal*,

INSIDERS' TIP

With the opening of a new $80 million facility at 260 14th Street N.W. in August 1997, Georgia Public TV became the first fully digitized public TV station in the United States. It houses not only makeup and green rooms, but also $17 million in digital equipment. And surprise, surprise, no tax dollars were used to fund the place. It's been debt-free from the get-go since funds raised from the lottery were used to make the place a reality.

was founded in 1883. In 1912, *The Journal* became the first Southern newspaper to publish its own Sunday magazine. As a staffer, Margaret Mitchell wrote 129 articles (under the byline "Peggy Mitchell") during her four-year tenure at the magazine. Other well-known writers whose work appeared in the magazine included New Yorker founder Harold Ross, golfing legend Bobby Jones, humorist Will Rogers and novelist Erskine Caldwell.

In 1939, *The Journal* and its radio station WSB were bought by James M. Cox, former three-time governor of Ohio and the Democrats' 1920 presidential nominee against Warren G. Harding. His granddaughter, Anne Cox Chambers, succeeded her father, James M. Cox Jr., in 1974 as chair of the combined Atlanta Newspapers (the business entity publishing the two papers, which merged in 1950).

The two papers moved into their present nine-story downtown headquarters in 1972. A single, combined edition is published each Saturday and Sunday. The Saturday paper is published as *Weekend* and includes a tabloid leisure guide. The Sunday paper hits the stands on Saturday afternoon; it carries extensive real estate listings and classified ads (job-seekers take note) and includes valuable grocery coupons. On Thursdays, both papers include city and county editions that target readers in various parts of metro Atlanta.

Fulton County Daily Report
190 Pryor St. S.W. • (404) 521-1227

Daily Report is Georgia's only daily newspaper of law and business; it was established in 1890. The official legal newspaper for Fulton County, it runs lots of legal and public notices and trial court calendars. The decisions of the Georgia Appellate Court are reported in full text in daily editions and in a weekly Friday supplement. *Daily Report* is of interest primarily to lawyers but is sometimes fun to surf; it's matter-of-fact reportage on the often shocking details of criminal, divorce and civil court cases can be compelling.

Gwinnett Daily Post
166 Buford Dr., Lawrenceville
• (770) 963-9205

Not yet one year old, *Gwinnett Daily Post*, owned by Gray Communications Systems, has a circulation of 48,000 thanks primarily to Northeast Cablevision who purchased a subscription for each of its viewers. In exchange, the paper develops a news and entertainment channel, G-Net, for the cable company. Both the *Gwinnett Daily Post* and G-Net cable are devoted primarily to features of interest to local residents. G-Net's programming includes a "Newsmakers" series as well as a "Hospital/Healthcare" segment which are cablecast repeatedly throughout a week.

Marietta Daily Journal and Neighbor Newspapers Inc.
580 Fairground St., Marietta
• (770) 428-9411

Founded in 1865, *Marietta Daily Journal* is published every morning of the year. Its coverage favors local Cobb County news, but it also reports on state, national and international events. The same company publishes the twice-weekly *Cherokee Tribune* and the 11 Neighbor editions, which are delivered free of charge to homes in targeted districts of the metro area. Publisher Otis A. Brumby Jr. is the grandson of Thomas M. Brumby, whose chair company, founded in 1875 and still in existence, made the classic Brumby rocker a fixture on Southern verandas.

General-Interest Periodicals

Unless otherwise noted, most free papers in Atlanta are found in front of or in stores and clubs that cater to the kind of people the publication wishes to reach. For example, sports bars and health clubs have sports-oriented publications and health and environment tabloids. Other publications, such as *Creative Loafing* and the apartment and real estate magazines, have their own boxes or racks. Still others are simply piled high in front of shops. Call the publication to find out where and when it's distributed.

Atlanta Magazine
1330 W. Peachtree St., Ste. 450
• (404) 872-3100

In its 37th year and with a readership of 68,000, *Atlanta* still has plenty of competition in the market but retains its status as the monthly most closely associated with our city. It was initially an organ of the Atlanta Chamber of Commerce. Through the years, *Atlanta* has had many manifestations including a stint as an investigatory and literary outlet for our finest writers. The magazine has won 115 awards from city, regional and national groups. Although coverage of where and what to eat seems to dominate issues, you'll also find articles profiling local political, social and business leaders and an occasional feature on Georgia-grown celebrities such as Amy Carter and Braves pitcher John Smoltz, to newly single, but very rich, mom Marla Maples Trump.

At this writing, a new publisher, Susie Love, has taken over the helm of *Atlanta Magazine*. Perhaps the magazine's editorial direction will change with her tenure.

Atlanta Now
233 Peachtree St. N.W., Ste. 2000
• (404) 249-1756

This slick bimonthly is published by the Atlanta Convention and Visitors Bureau and is the city's official tourists' guide. Features include a two-month calendar of upcoming happenings and in-depth information on selected events. You'll also find maps and restaurant listings. It's available for free in various locations around the downtown convention district.

Creative Loafing
750 Willoughby Wy. N.E.• (404) 688-5623

Begun in 1972 by Deborah Eason and produced in her living room on the proverbial shoestring, CL is Atlanta's best-known free paper. It also provided the jump start for many a local writer. So successful has been its concept, the publishers have successfully brought the *Creative Loafing* name, concept and format to readers in Charlotte, North Carolina, and Savannah, Georgia. In Raleigh, North Carolina, the paper is called *Spectator*, but it's still the same old *Loaf*, just under another banner. Each issue of CL is chock-full of political opinion from local media celebs of all persuasions, reviews of restaurants, gallery openings and theatrical productions. The classifieds are where you'll look for an apartment or house rental. The"Telly" keeps you up-to-date with

the daily scheduling on the tube, the "Cuisine" department gets you 'two-fer' restaurant coupons and discounts. "Soundboard," the paper's centerfold, tracks live music in the clubs. "Voice Personals" is a pullout section crammed full of classified ads of people seeking like minded 'friends.' Distributed every Wednesday on store racks and from green street boxes, this weighty tabloid newspaper has a circulation of 180,000.

Dossier
1428 Defoors Dr. • (404) 351-5433

Published eight times a year, businesses and lifestyles are featured with plentiful photos. A recent issue spotlighted Atlanta attorneys, sports passions and great camping sites. Look for *Dossier* at area newsstands.

Guide to Georgia
1655 Peachtree St. N.E., Ste. 1004
• 892-0961

The free monthly *Guide to Georgia* is available from state Welcome Centers, convention and visitors bureaus and in many hotels. Its chapters report on upcoming events of interest in Atlanta and throughout Georgia from the mountains to the sea, including exhibits, performances, festivals and more. A sports calendar details the month's pro and major college schedules.

Gwinnett Loaf
6659-E. Peachtree Industrial Blvd.,
Norcross • (770) 368-1880

Gwinnett Loaf is similar to its sister publication *Creative Loafing* (see previous listing), but it focuses on fast-growing Gwinnett County. The free tabloid paper is distributed every Wednesday.

The Hudspeth Report
5180 Roswell Rd. N.W., Ste. 1, Courtyard
South • (404) 255-3220

Focusing primarily on Buckhead and northside pubs and sport bars, this free monthly paper is aimed at the partying younger set rather than those seeking fine dining advice. But with a rapidly changing nightlife scene you need a scorecard to keep up with what's what — and *The Hudspeth Report* gives you one every month. You'll find lists of openings, closings and long-term survivors as well as restaurant menus from some establishments, so you can decide what you want before you get there. The paper also includes movie briefs, reports on galleries and exhibits and a night-by-night calendar of entertainment and sports happenings.

InSite
1 Corporate Sq., Ste. 210 • (404) 315-8485

Free on college campuses and select boxes around town, *InSite* is a monthly entertainment guide. Reviews of records, interviews with celebs, advice to grads, a sports section and various schedules for upcoming events will be useful for those of us who can plan a month ahead.

Style
1575 Northside Dr. Ste. 470
• (404) 352-2400

Style, a bimonthly glossy magazine, is available on newsstands as well as to a mailing list of families with similar demographic information as the *Jewish Times* (whose subscribers also receive *Style*). Fabulous photos depict the home architecture, interior design, arts, fashion and food which appeal to upscale nonsectarian metro-Atlantans. Articles run the gamut from electric train hobbyists to local builders who are making a mark on the city.

Topside Loaf
6659-E Peachtree Industrial Blvd., Norcross • (770) 368-1880

Topside Loaf is similar to its sister publication *Creative Loafing* (see previous listing), and the *Gwinnett Loaf* but focuses on north Fulton County and other parts of northern metro Atlanta. The free tabloid paper is distributed through street boxes every Wednesday.

Special-Interest Periodicals

African-American

Atlanta Tribune
875 Old Roswell Rd., Ste. C-100, Roswell
• (770) 587-0501

Established in 1987, this twice-monthly newsmagazine is marketed toward affluent African-American professionals and entrepreneurs. Its metro area coverage includes corporate and professional news, plus reports on cultural and entertainment events of interest. The magazine has some 32,000 subscribers.

The Atlanta Voice
633 Pryor St. S.W. • (404) 524-6426

J. Lowell Ware founded *The Atlanta Inquirer* in 1960 as a response to the lack of black voices in Atlanta media; it became *The Atlanta Voice* in 1966. Today the late Ware's daughter Janis is publisher of this free weekly paper, which includes editorials, news stories and reports on the activities of black religious and social groups. *The Voice* often covers local politics and news with a candor uncharacteristic of many Atlanta media outlets. Circulation is 133,000.

Arts/Creative

Art Papers
P.O. Box 77348, Atlanta GA 30357
• (404) 588-1837

Now the Southeast's primary critical art journal, *Art Papers,* by the Atlanta Art Worker's Coalition, was founded in 1976 as a four-page, typewritten newsletter. These days the bimonthly tabloid-size magazine provides a forum for the exchange of ideas among artists, art organizations and others in the arts community. Each issue carries in-depth articles on a topic of interest (such as art in an era of diminishing government funding), artist interviews, news briefs, commentary and an extensive section reviewing exhibits of note throughout the Southeast and beyond. Art Papers has received numerous awards for excellence from public and private agencies, including the Andy Warhol Foundation for the Visual Arts; Georgia Governor's Award for the Arts; and the Mary Ellen LoPresti Award for Excellence in Publishing.

Art Papers is available at museums, bookstores, galleries and cafes around town.

Oz
3100 Briarcliff Rd. N.E., Ste. 524
• (404) 633-1779

Self-described as "the journal of creative disciplines," *Oz* tracks trends in advertising, marketing and media. A free, bimonthly magazine, it includes an associations listing and calendar of events of interest to those in creative fields.

Poets, Artists & Madmen
175 W. Wieuca Rd. N.E., Ste. B-1
• (404) 705-9969

PA&M digs up the latest on the Atlanta arts scene. The local listings section includes auditions, galleries, poetry readings, writers' groups and more; there's also a monthly calendar of upcoming live music shows. The free monthly also runs poetry and profiles of artists. You'll find it at bookstores and shops around town.

Business and Enterprises

Atlanta Business Chronicle
1801 Peachtree St. N.E., Ste. 150
• (404) 249-1000

The *Chronicle* was established in 1978. Since then it has kept track of who's winning and losing and what's coming next in Atlanta's turbulent business world. More than 28,000 readers each week turn to *Atlanta Business Chronicle*. It has been recognized both regionally and nationally, winning recently both the Green Eyeshade Award from the Society of Professional Journalists and the Gerald Loeb Award for Excellence in Business Writing.

Issued weekly on Friday, the *Chronicle* may have a pullout section on real estate, or banking, or hospitality. Throughout the year everything from retail to healthcare will have a section. The paper also produces special supplementary publications, such as *Who's Who in Atlanta*, *The Book of Lists*, and *Metro Market Reports*, which gives an economic overview of each major county or business corridor. It also provides focus reports on golf, catering and other topics — all helpful info for marketing. In fact, these lists are also available on computer disks.

The *Chronicle* is highly pro-business (no surprise there), but occasionally bucks the boosterish attitude that sometimes seems like a city-wide religion. The mayor, city council and other government officials have felt the *Chronicle's* scrutiny; investigatory articles have won *Chronicle* writers awards. Not even sacred cows are safe: editorially, the *Chronicle*

opposed efforts to salvage "The Dump," the Peachtree Street apartment house, now a museum, where Margaret Mitchell wrote *Gone With the Wind* (see our Attractions chapter).

Atlanta International Magazine
119 Pharr Rd. N.W., Ste. A-4
• (404) 239-9225

Each month, *Atlanta International Magazine* is mailed to 11,000 senior-level Southeast executives involved in international trade. Regular departments are devoted to Latin America, the Pacific Rim and Europe; monthly special focus articles examine opportunities in various geographic markets and specific industries, such as banking, shipping and technology. With 75 percent of its readership comprised of top executives, AIM claims "the most senior-level international business audience in the Southeast."

Atlanta Small Business Monthly
6129 Oakbrook Pkwy., Norcross
• (770) 446-5434

Atlanta Small Business Monthly caters to the needs of small business owners and managers. Articles profile Atlanta business leaders and cover issues such as successful meetings, strategic career moves, and purchasing equipment, insurance and desktop software. *Atlanta Small Business Monthly* is sent free to your office or is available by subscription, a practice the publishers hope will catch on.

Georgia Trend
1770 Indian Trail Rd. Ste. 350, Norcross
• (770) 931-9410

Founded in 1985, this monthly details business activities throughout the state rather than concentrating on metro-Atlanta activities and people. A circulation of 50,000 includes copies sent free of charge to area business execs. Look for reports on real estate, politics and Southern stocks, plus features on money makers, media and sports moguls. Call to be added to the mailing list.

South.
P.O. Box 879221, Stone Mountain GA
30087 • (770) 879-3700

South. is published by Virgil R. Williams, a self-made millionaire who began his magazine experience with *Georgia Trend*. This new endeavor reads even better with fascinating articles on people and politics written by local wordsmiths who keep an edge and some humor to their writing. South. is sent free to business people and interested readers. Call to be added to the mailing list.

Home Decor

Atlanta Homes & Lifestyle
1100 Johnson Ferry Rd., Ste. 595
• (404) 252-6670

Beautiful Atlanta homes large and small fill the pages of Atlanta Homes & Lifestyle.

Nine times a year, the magazine takes its readers through fabulous metro homes and gardens. Article topics include home restoration, shopping for decor, art and vacation getaways. A biyearly publication from these same offices premiered last year. Called *Second Home*, it looks much like *Atlanta Homes & Lifestyles* with its profusion of luscious photographs and well designed pages. Second Home showcases Southern vacation getaways and must-have items to outfit them richly. Look for *Atlanta Homes & Lifestyle* at local newsstands. It's also available by subscription.

Veranda
455 E. Paces Ferry Rd. N.E., Ste. 216
• (404) 261-3603

Remember those high-toned Sugarbakers, the fictional Atlanta sisters who ran their own decorating firm in the hit TV sitcom *Designing Women*? Well, if they actually existed, you can be sure they'd subscribe to *Veranda*, "the gallery of Southern style." This 300-page color quarterly practically drips elegance from every page. Extensive photo layouts showcase the lovely homes of the affluent, while the many ads proffer an array of items and services for the well-heeled. Each issue reaches more than 200,000

readers. A copy of *Veranda*, available at area newsstands, will make your coffee table proud.

Environment and Health/Sexuality

The Adult Scene
750 Willoughby Wy. • (404) 688-5623

Articles on sexuality, advice columns and features on local dancers and club owners fill this free weekly tabloid. Written and published by the same folks who bring you *Creative Loafing*, Atlanta's largest and most frequently read free weekly, *The Adult Scene* is designed for the heterosexual community. A recent feature was titled "Swingers." Oh, yes, there are classifieds, too.

Aquarius
1028 Alpharetta St., Roswell
• (770) 641-9055

Published monthly, this free tabloid has a mission statement which states its purpose of expanding awareness and supporting personal growth. Articles deal with astrology, transformational bodywork, the psychic self, hypnotherapy and healing, review new age records and books and feature local practitioners of the healing arts as well as history and myth relative to the topics noted above.

The Environmental Times
P.O. Box 566723, Atlanta GA 30356
• (404) 303-1873

The Environmental Times reports on environmental, health and social issues; most of its articles are Associated Press stories datelined from locations around the nation and the world. Most articles relate to the environment ("South Carolina considered for nuclear waste site") or peace issues ("Japan considers the possibility of developing a nuclear weapons program"). The publication is free.

INSIDERS' TIP

When you ride MARTA pick up a copy of the *Rider's Digest*. This 8½ x 11 sheet of paper, folded down to a handy pocket size, lists the latest info on schedule changes, new routes and even dates of art exhibits, films and other public events and how to get there. MARTA also has a Speaker's Bureau. Call (404) 848-5167 for more information.

World Health News

P.O. Box 660153, Atlanta GA 30366
• (770) 451-8424

This free tabloid offers articles on physical, mental, spiritual and emotional well-being. Recent issues within its 40 pages featured the benefits of fasting, internal detoxification, how we are being poisoned by plastic, beef, fluorides and many stories on various detoxing methods. Ads in the paper are helpful in locating local shops and practitioners of your favorite new age treatments.

Gay and Lesbian

Atlanta Community Yellow Pages

(602) 350-6720

Sixty thousand copies of this book are available free from bookstores and outdoor racks throughout metro-Atlanta. Paid listings of businesses, professional service providers and shops who share the publishers vision of "ending discrimination and homophobia" advertise here. A helpful Resource Guide listing support networks, clubs, organizations and student and youth groups is located at the back of book. The Yellow Pages is published in Phoenix, Arizona.

Etcetera

151 Renaissance Pkwy • (404) 888-0063

Atlanta's *Etcetera* magazine, founded in 1985, was recently selected to represent gay publications from the South in a site on the World Wide Web computer network. The free, four-color magazine reaches a weekly circulation of 23,000 in six states, though Atlanta is its primary market. Its editorial focuses almost exclusively on gay and lesbian citizens and issues, while its multitude of ads keep tabs on gay entertainment and nightlife. Regular features include advice and gossip columns and show business news. It's available in businesses and street boxes each Thursday.

Southern Voice

1095 Zonolite Rd. • (404) 876-1819

Southern Voice was founded in 1988. A free weekly tabloid newspaper, it offers staff-written and news service coverage of political and social issues affecting gays and lesbians, plus articles on movies, the arts and more. *SoVo's* distribution takes it across the South; it's available in businesses and street boxes each Wednesday.

International

The Atlanta Bulletin

1655 Peachtree St., Ste. 1003
• (404) 874-1968

Established in 1974, this free weekly paper covers Atlanta from a multicultural slant. Issues include news of local businesses, newly introduced products, financial planning, the arts, travel, education, sports, movies, church news and health matters. There are even lucky numbers for all you Ca$h 3 and Lotto players! Look for the *Bulletin* at government buildings and libraries

Chinese

World Journal

5150 Buford Hwy., Ste. A-170, Doraville
• (770) 451-4509

World Journal is a Chinese-language daily headquartered in Taiwan; the southeastern edition covers international, national, regional and local news. The paper has more than 10,000 readers in the Southeast. Pick up a copy at bookstores, grocery stores, restaurants and boxes throughout the Asian community.

Latin

Mundo Hispánico

1929 Piedmont Cir. • (404) 881-0441

Since it was founded in 1979, *Mundo Hispánico* has won 18 national awards. With articles in Spanish and English, the paper is published twice monthly and is free. With an average of 3.6 readers per copy, *Mundo Hispánico* reaches more than 75,000 readers with each edition. A typical issue includes local Hispanic news, an extensive calendar of events, and news of Latin America, business, entertainment and sports. The publication is available through select grocery stores and malls that cater to the Hispanic community.

Neighborhood

There are dozens of newsletters and papers that cater to the residents of Atlanta's neighborhoods. We cannot possibly list them all here. What we have included is a sample of these publications to give you an idea of the kind of information they provide.

Atlanta 30306
1329 Berwick Ave. N.E. • (404) 586-0002
This free paper aimed at residents of Virginia-Highland, Druid Hills, Morningside and Lenox Park is a lively monthly report on the people and businesses of these popular northeast in-town neighborhoods, where interesting restaurants and shops abound. Articles spotlight interesting residents and profile area shops and services; issues such as crime and development are discussed. Similar editions are printed for folks who live in Buckhead (*Atlanta 30305*) and downtown (*Atlanta Downtown*). Be on the lookout for valuable restaurant coupons.

The Bond Community Star
P.O. Box 5499, Atlanta GA 30307
• **no phone**
Run from a volunteer's home, this little paper covers news and events for the close-in northeast neighborhoods of Little Five Points, Poncey-Highland, Candler Park, Inman Park and Lake Claire in 10 issues per year. It's free and available for pick up in area businesses; neighborhood volunteers also distribute it to homes and apartments. Activities at local schools and churches are covered along with updates on crime and development issues in the neighborhoods.

The Brookhaven Buzz
P.O. Box 942118, Atlanta GA 31141
• **(770) 938-8506**
This free magazine generally ties editorial to advertising and covers activities within the neighborhoods of Brookhaven, Buckhead, Chamblee and Doraville. Lightweight pieces on kids and pets with articles on home repair and neighborhood zoning predominate. Recipes and randomly dispersed humor items give this monthly a homey appeal. The editors also publish the *Decatur Dispatch* and *Tucker Times*. These publications are good places to find local home service providers such as plumbers, painters, people to do the housework and yards.

The Inman Park Advocator
P.O. Box 5358, Atlanta GA 31107
• **(404) 880-9400**
In the 1880s Inman Park became Atlanta's first suburb; in the 1960s, it became the first in a series of formerly elegant in-town neighborhoods to be restored by forward-looking urban pioneers. The neighborhood association publishes this free monthly newsletter, which covers area schools, churches, social activities and security issues. In 1997, the paper featured a series on cleaning up Little Five Points (loitering and sleeping on the streets were particularly at issue) and on ways to bring more productive clientele to the area. A result of these articles was Family Fridays: Families are encouraged to spend the day and evening at this popular in-town neighborhood with entertainment and specials directed to this segment of the population.

The Piedmont Review
3530 Piedmont Rd., Ste. 2H
• **(404) 560-3677**
Some 10,000 copies of this paper are distributed free every month in Buckhead, Midtown and Sandy Springs. Interviews with political and civic leaders are often featured along with news of the arts, vacation getaways and home upkeep. Each month, a casual restaurant and an upscale eatery are profiled. Check the back pages for valuable restaurant coupons.

Virginia-Highland Voice
1142 St. Charles Pl. N.E. • (404) 222-8244
The Virginia-Highland Civic Association publishes this free quarterly about its neighborhood. Typical article topics include recycling and conservation issues, home repair, school news, gardening and restaurants.

Society

Peachtree's Symbol of the South
120 Interstate North Pkwy., Ste. 445
• **(770) 956-1207**
Self-described as "the guide to the civilized South," *Peachtree's Symbol* is a slick look at Atlanta life from a decidedly northside perspective. Seventy-two percent of its readers are female; 91 percent are older than

30. The monthly favors women's fashions, social and charitable events and interior design. Special focus features look at matters such as weddings, getaways, antiques and home remodeling. *Peachtree's Symbol* is available by subscription or can be found at B. Dalton Bookseller at Lenox Square, Harry's Farmers Market and Kroger supermarkets and drugstores.

Presenting the Season
7 Piedmont Centre, Ste. 500
• **(770) 565-1499**
Opulent charity balls, getaways to Europe and the Caribbean, the luxurious weddings of the wealthy and more fill the shiny pages of *Presenting the Season*. The quarterly calls itself "the guide to Atlanta and the Southeast's finest people and events." It previews upcoming high-society happenings and gives reports on recent goings-on. Antiques, fashion and the latest advancements in plastic surgery are frequent article topics. The calendar of events lists lots of things for society folks to enjoy around Atlanta. You can find *Presenting the Season* at hotels, bookstores and Krogers. It's also available by subscription.

Southern Flair
403 W. Ponce de Leon Ave., Ste. 110
• **(404) 377-9998**
You'll find out all you need to know about the social and charitable events happening in our town in this monthly: The calendar is particularly helpful. Lots of photos of belles and beaus in fabulous attire and ads telling where to purchase the latest in fashion fill the pages of each issue. Look for *Southern Flair* at major supermarkets, bookstores and The Ritz-Carlton Buckhead.

Parenting
Look for these publications at libraries, child-care centers, bookstores and select children's shops around Atlanta.

Atlanta Baby
4330 Georgetown Sq. N.E., Ste. 506
• **(770) 454-7599**
Published six times a year, expectant mothers and the parents of babies will find

helpful info in these pages. Where to deliver the baby, newborn health concerns and other practical tips are given in this mag, produced by the publishers of *Atlanta Parent*.

Atlanta Parent
4330 Georgetown Sq. N.E., Ste. 506
• **(770) 454-7599**
Kids from birth through 14 years are the subject of this free monthly. Articles in the tabloid discuss a variety of topics important to parents, and special features examine topics such as summer camps, birthday parties and the holidays.

Real Estate and Apartments

The Atlanta Apartment Book, A Renter's Guide
3098 Piedmont Rd., Ste. 150
• **(404) 816-4242**
Atlanta has long been a hot destination for people who are relocating, and this digest-size free magazine seeks to help newcomers in their quest for an apartment home. A map divides the Greater Atlanta area into eight sections: You just pick the area where you'd like to live, then flip to that section of the magazine. There's very little in the way of articles, but the many apartment complex ads make this helpful for renters.

Atlanta Apartment Guide
3139 Campus Dr., Ste. 700
• **(770) 417-1717**
This nicely organized, 400-plus-page free magazine uses a color-coded map to help you locate ads for apartments in specific metro areas. The ads all have color photos or drawings of the complexes, and the consistent layout makes it easy to compare and contrast the different properties, as does the handy "features at a glance" chart, which lists standard amenities for hundreds of apartments.

KNOW Atlanta
7840 Roswell Rd., Ste. 328, Dunwoody
• **(770) 512-0016**
Published quarterly, *KNOW Atlanta* is primarily a relocation guide. It profiles more than a dozen metro area counties and gives the

basics on some of Atlanta's attractions, schools, medical facilities and cultural offerings. The real estate data is geared more toward home buyers than to apartment renters, but the general information will be useful to all new residents. Though sold on newsstands, the magazine is available for free from many real estate agents; you can request a free copy by calling the number above.

The Real Estate Guides
267 Langley Dr. N.W., Lawrenceville
• (770) 513-4600
This company publishes several househunting guides filled with ads for homes in various parts of metro Atlanta. The photos of homes, though small, are generally in color.

Religion

Catholic

The Georgia Bulletin
680 W. Peachtree St. N.W.
• (404) 888-7832
Catholics in the archdiocese of Atlanta are served by this weekly newspaper. The Georgia Bulletin features parish news, reports of recent ordinations, morality rankings of current movies and reports on national and international Catholic leaders.

Episcopalian

DioLog
2744 Peachtree Rd. N.W. • (404) 365-1026
The Episcopal Diocese of Atlanta includes some 52,000 members who worship in 89 parishes, three college centers and one camp. *DioLog*, founded in 1921, is the official newspaper of the diocese. The bimonthly paper reports on Episcopal charities at home and abroad, church politics, clergy and laity news and social activities.

Georgia Baptist Convention

The Christian Index
2930 Flowers Rd. S. • (770) 936-5312
Founded in 1822 by missionary Luther Rice, *The Christian Index* is the oldest religious periodical in America and the official

newspaper of the Georgia Baptist Convention. It's published 44 times a year, informing the faithful of Baptist news from around the state and the world. Inspirational stories, commentary and Sunday School resources are featured as well.

Jewish

Atlanta Jewish Times
1575 Northside Dr. N.W., Ste. 470
• (404) 352-2400
This weekly traces its roots to 1925, when it was founded as *The Southern Israelite*. The paper focuses on national and international news of special interest to Jews; it also covers social and religious observances in the Atlanta Jewish community.

The Atlanta Maccabiah Press
2290 Carousel Ct., Marietta
• (770) 973-6049
Published monthly, this free paper covers Atlanta's Jewish community. It tends to emphasize local happenings and focuses more on the social and religious (as opposed to political) aspects of Jewish life. Celebrations, promotions and business news, theater and literature of interest to Jews, activities of various community service organizations and travel are all featured in the paper, which was founded in 1992.

The Jewish Georgian
7252 Roswell Rd. • (770) 393-2790
Published bimonthly, this free paper is loaded with news of special interest to Jews. There are restaurant and book reviews, humor pieces, society and health reports and wise words from a rabbi.

Methodist

Wesleyan Christian Advocate
P.O. Box 54455, Atlanta GA 30308
• (404) 659-8809
Methodism has long been strong in Georgia; its symbolic father, John Wesley, traveled here himself to minister to the rough-and-ready young colony. The more than 432,000 Methodists in Georgia are served by this weekly newspaper, which includes inspi-

rational messages, movie and book reviews and news of goings-on in the state's many Methodist churches.

Religious Society of Friends

Atlanta Friends Meeting Newsletter
701 W. Howard Ave., Decatur
• **(404) 377-2474**

The Atlanta Friends Meeting is the local congregation affiliated with the Religious Society of Friends, commonly known as the Quakers. The congregation's monthly newsletter includes updates of recent and upcoming religious, social and political activities. The Atlanta congregation is heavily involved in the fight against racism and for civil rights for everyone.

Senior Citizens

Senior News
P.O. Box 941611, Atlanta GA 30341
• **(770) 921-6756**

The Macon-based free monthly *Senior News* reports a circulation of 50,000 for its metro-Atlanta edition. Financial issues of interest to seniors are covered in-depth, but there are also personality-centered articles: One recent issue introduced us to all five finalists in the Miss Georgia Nursing Home Pageant. Pick up a copy at senior citizen centers, libraries, supermarkets and drugstores.

Southern Lifestyles
6205 Barfield Rd. N.E., Ste. 280
• **(404) 255-5603**

Billing itself as "Georgia's premier retire-ment and relocation magazine," this color quarterly is distributed free in some visitors centers; it's also sold by subscription. Current happenings at Georgia attractions, health news, recipes and financial planning advice are all typical topics; retirement communities and services for seniors make up the majority of ads.

Singles

Atlanta Singles
180 Allen Rd., Ste. 304N • (404) 256-9411

Atlanta enjoys a reputation as a good town for singles: Lots of single young adults come to Atlanta looking for love, and many newly single people come here looking to start over. The upbeat bimonthly *Atlanta Singles* keeps its readers up on "People to meet — Places to go — Things to do." You'll find listings of social organizations, a calendar of fun happenings around Atlanta and pages and pages of personal ads. Look for *Atlanta Singles* at area newsstands.

Sports

Atlanta Sports and Fitness
359 E. Paces Ferry Rd. N.E., Ste. 101
• **(404) 842-0359**

Atlanta's amateur sporting and fitness scene takes center stage in this free monthly tabloid magazine, which has a circulation of about 75,000 and was founded in 1990. *Atlanta Sports and Fitness* also publishes *Georgia Athlete*, which is directed to the competitive athlete who is looking for race applications info. The publication is available at gyms, health food stores and some bookstores.

INSIDERS' TIP

More than 40 years ago, WJCC-AM radio out of Commerce, Georgia, offered country music fare hosted by a college kid named Bill Anderson. It was therefore fitting that for the station's 40th anniversary Bill Anderson, now a country singer, was brought back to honor the occasion. The Grand Ole Opry star performed at the local high school football field that was just a hog holler away from the building where he used to spin records. The town of Commerce also changed the name of the street where the station sat from Little Street to Bill Anderson Boulevard. WJCC now plays gospel and Americana tunes.

Braves Express
P.O. Box 2264, Lilburn GA 30226
• (770) 279-0382

You can get all the latest buzz on the Braves in this paper, which is free around town. You'll find the feature "Keeping Track of Former Braves" and articles on other ball clubs inside. There are also reports from the Braves' minor league teams in Richmond, Virginia, Greenville, South Carolina, and Macon, Georgia. Because it's published every month, you'll even be able to read about the Braves while they're playing golf in Florida all winter! *Braves Express* also publishes *Tech Express,* a biweekly about the sports scene at Georgia Tech.

Net News
7840 Roswell Rd., Ste. 328
• (770) 512-0016

This bimonthly magazine is the official publication of the Atlanta Lawn Tennis Association Inc. (ALTA). An often-told joke is that when sporting folks relocate to Atlanta, they join ALTA first — then start looking for a home. *Net News* carries the standings of ALTA's many teams and schedules of upcoming tennis events as well as articles on improving your game and looking good (fashion-wise) on the court. You have to join ALTA to receive the magazine — but if you're into tennis, you'll probably be doing that anyway.

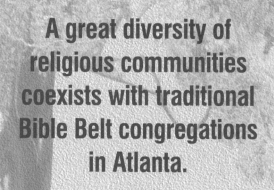

A great diversity of religious communities coexists with traditional Bible Belt congregations in Atlanta.

Worship and Spirituality

You'd be hard-pressed to leave Atlanta unfulfilled no matter what kind of religious service or experience you seek. In a powerful demonstration of the city's growing internationalism, a great diversity of religious communities coexists with traditional Bible Belt congregations.

Atlanta congregations include all those denominations conventionally represented in most cities and then some. The city's proclivity for the graceful melding of cultures displays itself in churches for Vietnamese Catholics, Spanish Seventh-day Adventists, Chinese Baptists and Korean Presbyterians. The city is home to a number of mosques and Buddhist and Hindu temples. A cluster of Russian Orthodox, Eastern Orthodox and Coptic churches give their members an opportunity to practice traditions and rituals common to their forebears in other lands. Other congregations include Baha'i, Eckankar, Jehovah's Witness, Moravian, Nazarene, Latter-Day Saints and Swedenborgian.

Community efforts toward interfaith action are commonplace. Three downtown churches jointly celebrate Palm Sunday with a procession of members bearing colorful banners and palms, accompanied by hymns and music from all three liturgies. The original buildings of these churches — Trinity Methodist, Central Presbyterian and The Shrine of the Immaculate Conception —

shared salvation from Gen. Sherman's torches due to the persuasive powers of Father Thomas O'Reilly, the shrine's pastor. Ecumenical efforts among Atlanta's synagogues, temples and churches include building community centers, operating homeless shelters and working to promote harmony among Atlanta's citizens.

From a visual standpoint, many of Atlanta's churches offer magnificent architecture and special features such as the cobblestone floors of St. Luke's Episcopal Church and the priceless Tiffany stained-glass windows in All Saints Episcopal Church. The area's best-known synagogue, The Temple, designed by Philip Shutze, plays an established role in local Jewish life. The Temple, which has a Reform congregation, was featured in the movie *Driving Miss Daisy* and is also the subject of *The Temple Bombing*, a compelling book by Melissa Fay Greene. Her book outlines, in narrative form, the 1958 bombing of this synagogue. Other prominent synagogues in the Atlanta area include Ahavath Achim (Conservative), Or VeShalom (Sephardic, traditional) and Beth Jacob (Orthodox). There is also the Chabad Outreach Center for Hasidic studies.

In Buckhead, the Episcopal Cathedral of St. Philip stands on a majestic rise above Peachtree Road. This congregation dates back to 1847, when five people met to organize Atlanta's first Episcopal church. The church

---

INSIDERS' TIP

Avoid the far right lane of traffic on Peachtree Road during Sunday morning hours as it officially becomes a parking lane for the overflow crowds from the clusters of churches on this main thoroughfare.

originated downtown but moved to north Atlanta in 1933. The current cathedral was built in 1962. In St. Mary's Chapel, beneath the cathedral apse, some items from the original church downtown are still in use today.

Across the street, you'll find the Catholic Cathedral of Christ the King. Bishop Gerald P. O'Hara blessed and laid the cornerstone of the cathedral in 1937. The Philadelphia firm of Henry D. Dagit designed the structure and Fratelli Ruffati of Padua, Italy, built the cathedral's 3,000-pipe organ. In 1939 *Architectural Record* chose the cathedral as the most beautiful building in Atlanta.

Besides the renowned Ebenezer Baptist Church, where the Rev. Dr. Martin Luther King Jr. preached, you'll find other influential predominately African-American churches near world-famous Auburn Avenue, the historical setting of thriving entrepreneurship among African Americans. Churches in this area include the Wheat Street Baptist Church, Big Bethel AME Church, which was founded in 1847 by slaves, and many others. Big Bethel is the oldest predominantly African-American congregation in the metro area. In 1870, church members formed the Daughters of Bethel Benevolent Society. Cited by W.E.B. Dubois as one of the first examples of economic cooperation among blacks, the Daughters cared for sick and aging ex-slaves. In 1880 the first public school classes for black children were held in "Old Bethel," the church the congregation used before building Big Bethel.

Atlanta's gay community supports several congregations whose primary ministry is to lesbian and gay Christians. These congregations include First Metropolitan Community Church of Atlanta and All Saints Metropolitan Community Church. There is also Bet Haverim, synagogue, a predominantly gay congregation currently led by a female rabbi.

Churches are an integral part of Southern culture, but Atlanta's diverse population seeks spiritual comfort in a variety of ways. At Atlanta Eckankar Center, "the religion of the light and sound of God," spiritual exercises assist members in having personal experiences with the ECK, or Holy Spirit. The Religious Society of Friends, more commonly known as the Quakers, meets in Decatur. This faith, which dates from the 1640s, has had a long involvement in civil rights, housing and racial issues, and during the height of the integration movement in the '60s, provided a meeting place for Martin Luther King, Jr., Andrew Young and high school students who were later to peacefully integrate the schools in Atlanta.

Greek Orthodox followers meet at Cathedral of The Annunciation. The church is renowned for the mosaic artwork on its dome, which is said to be one of the largest dome mosaics in the world. Each fall, the church stages an elaborate Greek festival (see Annual Events and Festivals) to raise money to support church activities.

Atlanta Masjid of Al-Islam, an Islamic congregation, is one of several in the metro area. Baha'i followers meet in Stone Mountain. Christian Scientists meet in the magnificent First Church of Christ, which was designed by Nashville architects Edward Dougherty and Arthur Neal Robinson and was completed in 1914. Restored in 1985, the building, which has a copper dome and elegant entrance facade, sits across Peachtree Street from the Robert W. Woodruff Arts Center.

And if the Eastern religions beckon, visitors are welcome at the Siddha Yoga Meditation Center, the Soto Zen Center and The Atlanta Shambhala Centre, which offers daylong meditation programs and classes in Tibetan Buddhism.

We've tried to give you a sampling of the options available. For a more complete list of Atlanta's worship opportunities, check *The Atlanta Journal-Constitution.* The newspaper publishes a "Faith and Values" section on Saturday where you can find articles and advertisements for services.

Index of Advertisers

Index

Going Somewhere?

Insiders' Publishing Inc. presents 48 current and upcoming titles to popular destinations all over the country (including the titles below) — and we're planning on adding many more. To order a title, go to your local bookstore or call (800) 582-2665 and we'll direct you to one.

Adirondacks	Minneapolis/St. Paul, MN
Atlanta, GA	Mississippi
Bermuda	Myrtle Beach, SC
Boca Raton and the Palm Beaches, FL	Nashville, TN
Boulder, CO, and Rocky Mountain National Park	New Hampshire
Bradenton/Sarasota, FL	North Carolina's Central Coast and New Bern
Branson, MO, and the Ozark Mountains	North Carolina's Mountains
California's Wine Country	Outer Banks of North Carolina
Cape Cod, Nantucket and Martha's Vineyard, MA	The Pocono Mountains
Charleston, SC	Relocation
Cincinnati, OH	Richmond, VA
Civil War Sites in the Eastern Theater	Salt Lake City
Colorado's Mountains	Santa Fe
Denver, CO	Savannah
Florida Keys and Key West	Southwestern Utah
Florida's Great Northwest	Tampa/St. Petersburg, FL
Golf in the Carolinas	Tucson
Indianapolis, IN	Virginia's Blue Ridge
The Lake Superior Region	Virginia's Chesapeake Bay
Las Vegas	Washington, D.C.
Lexington, KY	Wichita, KS
Louisville, KY	Williamsburg, VA
Madison, WI	Wilmington, NC
Maine's Mid-Coast	Yellowstone

THE INSIDERS' GUIDE ®

Insiders' Publishing Inc. • P.O. Box 2057 • Manteo, NC 27954
Phone (919) 473-6100 • Fax (919) 473-5869 • *www.insiders.com*